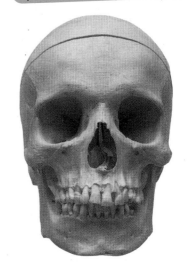

THE
TOP
10
OF EVERYTHING
1996

COCO
PARFUM
CHANEL
PARIS

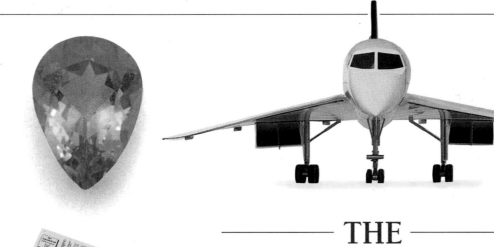

THE
TOP
10
OF EVERYTHING
1996

RUSSELL ASH

DORLING KINDERSLEY
London • New York • Stuttgart • Moscow

A DORLING KINDERSLEY BOOK

Designer Philip Ormerod

Project Editor Antonia Cunningham

Managing Art Editor Nigel Duffield

Senior Editor Stephanie Jackson

Senior Managing Art Editor Lynne Brown

Senior Managing Editor Josephine Buchanan

DTP Designer Raúl López Cabello

Production Hilary Stephens

US Editor Jill Hamilton

First American Edition, 1995
2 4 6 8 10 9 7 5 3 1

Published in the United States by
Dorling Kindersley Publishing, Inc.
95 Madison Avenue
New York, New York 10016

Library of Congress Cataloging-in-Publication Data
Ash, Russell.
The top 10 of everything 1996 / by Russell Ash. -- 1st
American ed.
p. cm.
Includes index.
ISBN 0-7894-0196-7
1. Curiosities and wonders. 2. Questions and answers. I. Title.
AG243.A713 1995
031.02--dc20
95-11541
CIP

Reproduction by HBM Print Ltd., Singapore.
Printed and bound in the United States by
R.R. Donnelley & Sons Company.

CONTENTS

INTRODUCTION

Welcome to this, the second annual edition of *The Top Ten of Everything* published in the United States. In the course of compiling the book I am often asked why so many of us are fascinated by lists. We all make lists, from Christmas card lists to lists of things to do, and we are constantly bombarded with lists in the press: the results of market surveys and polls, lists of bestselling books and CDs, Oscar-winners and annual crime figures. In an age when we are being assailed with information of all kinds, lists provide a way of presenting what might otherwise be an impenetrable mass of data and simplify everyday activities in a form that we can absorb and remember.

BEST AND WORST

"The human animal differs from the lesser primates in his passion for lists of Ten Best," wrote American humorist H. Allen Smith, the author of such curious books as *My Life in a Putty-Knife Factory*. I agree but the "bests" in *The Top Ten of Everything* are all things that can be measured – and so are the "worsts." None of the lists are simply a matter of personal opinion. "Most successful" in the world of the Top 10 usually means that large numbers of people have voted with their wallets by buying, renting, visiting, or watching the subjects of the list. Our Top 10s therefore represent the majority verdict.

Lists reflect daily life in many ways, and like our activities they can be serious, trivial, important, fascinating, revealing, entertaining, or bizarre. The wealthiest people, most rented videos, bestselling books or toys serve as a mirror of public taste. Lists also provide a measure of change: the breakup of the USSR and Yugoslavia, the rise of united Germany, and the aftermath of the global recession (we are starting to drink as much champagne as we used to, and new record prices are again being paid for paintings) are all reflected in certain lists.

INFORMATION RETRIEVAL

I am also asked how I compile Top 10s. The starting-off point is frequently my own library of often-obscure reference books. I also use other specialized library collections and, increasingly, information that is published on CD-ROM and the Internet. I make a lot of use of "official" sources, from the United Nations and sports governing bodies, as well as commercial organizations and research groups for information such as world food production, bestselling books, and auction records. Many official and commercial reports are published as expensive documents and read only by specialists, so one of the things *Top Ten* attempts to do is to present these figures in a form that non-specialists can access and understand.

The most rewarding source of all is that body of private individuals who have made special studies of such topics as the longest pub names, the highest-scoring words in Scrabble, or the world's tallest buildings. Without the cooperation of such people, there is no way that lists on many of these subjects could be compiled or updated.

WHAT'S NEW

The *Top Ten of Everything* changes a lot from year to year. Some "fixed" lists (tallest mountains, longest rivers, etc.) remain much the same, but a much larger number of Top 10s are completely revised and updated with the latest figures and new descriptive text. Even where the list title is the same as in a previous year it often contains totally different entries; this is especially evident in the broad field of "popular culture," where the bestsellers, chart-busters, or box-office smashes of one year are superseded by those of the following year. It is equally true with many "all time" lists, as exemplified by the number of movie lists in which relatively new releases such as *The Lion King*, *Forrest Gump*, and *Four Weddings and a Funeral* feature prominently.

CORRECTIONS AND SUGGESTIONS

There are many lists that remain elusive, among them the 10 People with the Longest Names, the 10 Biggest Robberies, and the 10 Most Produced Cars of All Time (does anyone know precisely how many Model-T Fords or VW Beetles were made?). Your amendments to existing lists and ideas for new ones – especially if you are a specialist who can supply the data – are always welcomed. You can write to me c/o the publishers (see page 4 for the address) or e-mail me at ash@pavilion.co.uk.

Russell Ash

THE 20TH CENTURY

A s we approach the end of the 20th century, it is revealing to look back at some of the immense changes that have taken place in the past 100 years. The opening pages present a retrospective view in the form of progressive lists showing record-holders at each decennial year (the first year of each decade) and Top 10 lists on a wide variety of topics. We look, for example, at how humans have traveled ever faster and deeper, built successively higher skyscrapers and larger ships, and transformed the nature of work. We note how the population has increased since 1900, and how increasingly higher prices have been paid for paintings over the decades. Finally, in anticipation of the 1996 Olympics, we consider some of the achievements of past Games.

THE PROGRESSION OF MECHANICALLY AIDED HUMAN SPEED, IN THE 20TH CENTURY*

Year	Pilot/ location/date	Vehicle	Speed km/h	mph
1900	Unnamed driver UK (1897)	Midland Railway 4-2-2 locomotive	144.84	90.00
1910	Alfred Léblanc US (1910)	Blériot monoplane	109.73	68.18
1920	Sadi Lecointe France (1920)	Nieuport-Delage 29 biplane	313.00	194.49
1930	A.H. Orlebar UK (1929)	Supermarine S.6 seaplane	575.62	357.67
1940	Unknown pilot Germany (1939)	Heinkel 176 jet	c.845.00	c.525.00
1950	Charles Elwood US (1948)	Bell XS-1 rocket aircraft	1,540.14	957.00
1960	Joseph A. Walker US (1960)	North American X-15 rocket aircraft	3,534.00	2,196.00
1970	Eugene Cernan, Thomas Stafford, John Young Reentry after lunar orbit (1969)	Apollo X space capsule (US)	39,897.00	24,790.80

* Record-holder as of December 31 of each decennial year

THE PROGRESSION OF DEEPEST UNDERWATER DESCENTS, IN THE 20TH CENTURY*

Year	Person/ date	Vessel/location	Depth m	ft
1900	Ernest Bazin 1865	Steel sphere Belle Ile, France	75	245
1910	Pino, 1903	Bathysphere Genoa, Italy	130	427
1920	Victor Campos 1919	Armored bell Mexico	185	608
1930	William Beebe and Otis Barton, 1930	Bathysphere Bermuda	244	800
1940	William Beebe and Otis Barton 1934	Bathysphere Bermuda	923	3,028
1950	Otis Barton 1949	Benthoscope Santa Cruz, California	1,372	4,500
1960	Jacques Piccard and Donald Walsh 1960	Bathyscaphe *Trieste 2* Marianas Trench, Pacific	10,916	35,814

* Record-holder as of December 31 of each decennial year

Since Piccard (Switzerland) and Walsh (US) descended to the deepest known point in the world's oceans, their record cannot be beaten. Jacques Piccard (1922–) is the son of Auguste Piccard (1884–1962), who made a 10,335-ft/ 3,150-m bathyscaphe descent in 1953.

FASTEST MEN ON EARTH

	Athlete/nationality	Date	Time (sec)
1	Leroy Burrell (US)	Jul 6, 1994	9.85
2	Carl Lewis (US)	Aug 25, 1991	9.86
3	Leroy Burrell (US)	Aug 25, 1991	9.88
4=	Dennis Mitchell (US)	Aug 25, 1991	9.91
4=	Davidson Ezinwa (Nig)	Apr 11, 1992	9.91
6	Linford Christie (UK)	Aug 25, 1991	9.92
7=	Calvin Smith (US)	Jul 3, 1983	9.93
7=	Mike Marsh (US)	Apr 18, 1992	9.93
9	Jim Hines (US)	Oct 14, 1968	9.95
9=	Frankie Fredericks (Nam)	Aug 25, 1991	9.95

The fastest-ever 100 meters with wind assistance was at Indianapolis, Indiana, on July 16, 1988, when Carl Lewis was timed at 9.78 seconds – but he had the benefit of winds measuring 17 ft/5.2 m per second.

GIANT LEAP *At the 1991 Tokyo World Championships Mike Powell finally broke the long-jump record.*

LONGEST LONG JUMPS

	Athlete/nationality	Date	Distance (m)
1	Mike Powell (US)	Aug 30, 1991	8.95
2	Bob Beamon (US)	Oct 18, 1968	8.90
3	Robert Emmiyan (USSR)	May 22, 1987	8.86
4=	Carl Lewis (US)	Jun 19, 1983	8.79
4=	Carl Lewis (US)	Jan 27, 1984	8.79*
6=	Carl Lewis (US)	Jul 24, 1982	8.76
6=	Carl Lewis (US)	Jul 18, 1988	8.76
8	Carl Lewis (US)	Aug 16, 1987	8.75
9	Larry Myricks (US)	Jul 18, 1988	8.74
10	Carl Lewis (US)	Sep 26, 1988	8.72

* Indoors

THE PROGRESSION OF THE LAND SPEED RECORD IN THE 20TH CENTURY*

Year	Driver/ location/date	Vehicle	Speed km/h	mph
1900	Camille Jenatzy Belgium (1899)	*Le Jamais Contente*	105.879	65.790
1910	Barney Oldfield US (1910)	*Blitzen*	211.267	131.275
1920	Tommy Milton US (1920)	*Duesenberg*	251.106	156.030
1930	Henry Segrave UK (1929)	*Golden Arrow*	372.476	231.446
1940	John Cobb UK (1939)	*Railton*	595.039	369.740
1950	John Cobb UK (1947)	*Railton-Mobil Special*	634.396	394.196
1960	As 1950			
1970	Gary Gabelich US (1970)	*The Blue Flame*	1,014.511	630.388
1980	As 1970			
1990	Richard Noble UK (1983)	*Thrust 2*	1,019.468	633.468

* Record-holder as of December 31 of each decennial year

FIRST ATHLETES TO RUN A MILE IN UNDER FOUR MINUTES

	Athlete/nationality	Location	Time min:sec	Date
1	Roger Bannister (UK)	Oxford, UK	3:59.4	May 6, 1954
2	John Landy (Aus)	Turku, Finland	3:57.9	Jun 21, 1954
3	Laszlo Tabori (Hun)	London, UK	3:59.0	May 28, 1955
4=	Chris Chataway (UK)	London, UK	3:59.8	May 28, 1955
4=	Brian Hewson (UK)	London, UK	3:59.8	May 28, 1955
6	Jim Bailey (Aus)	Los Angeles, US	3:58.6	May 5, 1956
7	Gunnar Nielsen (Den)	Compton, US	3:59.1	Jun 1, 1956
8	Ron Delany (Ire)	Compton, US	3:59.4	Jun 1, 1956
9	Derek Ibbotson (UK)	London, UK	3:59.4	Aug 6, 1956
10	István Rózsavölgyi (Hun)	Budapest, Hungary	3:59.0	Aug 26, 1956

Steve Cram holds the current world record for a mile (3:46.32 at Oslo, Norway, on July 27, 1985).

THRUST 2

SKYSCRAPERS, CITIES, & SHIPS

SKY HIGH
The Chrysler Building, with its distinctive stainless steel spire, held the record as the world's tallest building for only a matter of months before being overtaken by the Empire State Building.

100 YEARS OF THE "WORLD'S TALLEST" HABITABLE BUILDINGS

Year	Building	Stories	m	ft
1895	American Surety Building New York, US (remodeled 1975 as Bank of Tokyo)	21	90	300
1899	Saint Paul Building New York, US	16	94	310
1899	Park Row Building New York, US	29	118	386
1901	City Hall, Philadelphia, US	7	155	511
1907	Citibank, New York, US	57	226	741
1913	Woolworth Building, New York, US	59	241	792
1929	40 Wall Street, New York, US *with spire*	71	260 *282*	854 *927*
1930	Chrysler Building, New York, US	77	319	1,046
1931	Empire State Building New York, US *with spire*	102	381 *449*	1,250 *1,472*
1973	World Trade Center New York, US *with spire*	110	415 *521*	1,362 *1,710*
1974	Sears Tower, Chicago, US *with spires*	110	443 *521*	1,454 *1,709*
1996*	Petronas Tower, Kuala Lumpur, Malaysia	95	450	1,475
1997*	Chonging Tower Chonging, China	114	457	1,500
1998*	Nina Tower, Hong Kong *with spire*	100	468 *520*	1,535 *1,705*

* Under construction/expected completion year

In the decade before the construction of the American Surety Building, the world's tallest habitable building (cathedrals and structures such as the Eiffel Tower excluded) was the 20-story Auditorium Building, Chicago, US, completed in 1889 and measuring 270 ft/82 m. The Masonic Temple Building, also in Chicago and with the same number of stories, completed in 1891, just beat it at 274 ft/84 m. Since then, each successive world record holder was a New York City skyscraper, until the Sears Tower regained the crown for Chicago. However, as the table shows, a succession of tall buildings scheduled for completion before the end of the century will take the title of "world's tallest" from the US and establish it firmly in the Far East.

T O P 1 0

TALLEST HABITABLE BUILDINGS IN THE WORLD IN 2000

	Building	Year*	Stories	m	ft
1	Nina Tower, Hong Kong *with spire*	1998	100	468 *520*	1,535 *1,705*
2	Chonging Tower Chonging, China *with spire*	1997	114	457 *503*	1,500 *1,650*
3	Petronas Towers Kuala Lumpur, Malaysia	1996	95	450	1,475
4	Sears Tower, Chicago, US *with spires*	1974	110	443 *521*	1,454 *1,709*
5	Tour Sans Fin, Paris, France	1998	90	419	1,377
6	World Trade Center New York, US *with spire*	1973	110	415 *521*	1,362 *1,710*
7	Jin Mao Building Shanghai, China *with spire*	1997	93	382 *420*	1,255 *1,378*
8	Empire State Building New York, US *with spire*	1931	102	381 *449*	1,250 *1,472*
9	Amoco Building Chicago, US	1973	80	346	1,136
10	John Hancock Center Chicago, US *with spire*	1969	100	343 *450*	1,127 *1,476*

* Opened or expected completion year

T O P 1 0

LARGEST CITIES IN THE US 1900–90

	1900	Population	1950	Population	1990	Population
1	New York	3,437,202	New York	7,891,957	New York	7,322,564
2	Chicago	1,698,575	Chicago	3,620,962	Los Angeles	3,485,398
3	Philadelphia	1,293,697	Philadelphia	2,071,605	Chicago	2,783,726
4	St. Louis	575,238	Los Angeles	1,970,358	Houston	1,630,553
5	Boston	560,892	Detroit	1,849,568	Philadelphia	1,585,577
6	Baltimore	508,957	Baltimore	949,708	San Diego	1,110,549
7	Cleveland	381,768	Cleveland	914,808	Detroit	1,027,974
8	Buffalo	352,387	St. Louis	856,796	Dallas	1,006,877
9	San Francisco	342,782	Washington, D.C.	802,178	Phoenix	983,499
10	Cincinnati	325,902	Boston	801,444	San Jose	782,248

T O P 1 0

MOST HIGHLY POPULATED COUNTRIES IN THE WORLD 1900–90

	1900	1950	1990
1	China	China	China
2	India	India	India
3	Russia	USSR	USSR
4	US	US	US
5	Germany	Japan	Indonesia
6	Austria	Indonesia	Brazil
7	Japan	Germany	Japan
8	UK	UK	Nigeria
9	Turkey	Brazil	Pakistan
10	France	Italy	Bangladesh

T O P 1 0

MOST HIGHLY POPULATED CITIES IN THE WORLD 1894–1994

	1894	1944	1994
1	London	London	Mexico City
2	Paris	New York	Cairo
3	Peking	Tokyo	Shanghai
4	Canton	Berlin	Bombay
5	Berlin	Moscow	Tokyo
6	Tokyo	Shanghai	Calcutta
7	New York	Chicago	Beijing
8	Vienna	Leningrad	São Paulo
9	Chicago	Osaka	Seoul
10	Philadelphia	Paris	Paris

BIGGEST SHIP
The Royal Viking Line's 76,049-ton cruise ship Norway *is the largest liner afloat.*

100 YEARS OF THE WORLD'S LARGEST LINERS IN SERVICE

Ship	Gross tonnage	Years in service
Oceanic	17,274	1899–1914
Baltic	23,884	1904–33
*Lusitania**	31,550	1907–15
Mauretania	31,938	1907–35
Olympic	45,300	1911–35
*Titanic**	46,232	1912
Imperator/ Berengaria#	52,022	1913–38
Vaterland/ Leviathan#	54,282	1914–38
Bismarck/Majestic/ Caledonia#	56,621	1922–39
*Normandie/ Lafayette#**	79,301/ 83,102**	1935–42
Queen Mary	80,774/ 81,237**	1936–67
Queen Elizabeth	83,673/ 82,998**	1938–72
France/ Norway#	66,348/ 76,049**	1961–
Sovereign of the Seas	73,192	1987–

* *Sunk*
\# *Renamed*
** *Tonnage altered during refitting*

CITY CENTER
The identity of the world's largest cities has changed during the 20th century. Although Tokyo is still an important business center, it is slipping down as populations of other major cities overtake it.

PEOPLE & PRICES

DA VINCI MASTERPIECE
*Almost 500 years after he painted it,
Leonardo da Vinci's portrait* Ginevra de' Benci
*broke all world art records when it was sold in
1967 for more than $5,000,000.*

COCA-COLA PRODUCTION –
THE FIRST 100 YEARS

Year	Production (gallons)	Cumulative total (gallons)
1886	25	25
1890	8,855	14,033
1896	118,000	376,228*
1900	371,000	1,405,228
1910	4,190,000	21,338,228
1920	18,656,000	122,707,228
1930	27,730,000	331,330,228
1940	62,798,000	705,477,228
1950	130,245,000	1,685,507,228
1960	223,304,000	3,384,850,228
1970	514,942,000	6,963,903,228
1980	1,259,595,000	21,867,662,228
1985	1,584,847,000	25,444,901,228

* Totals have been rounded since 1896; therefore, the cumulative totals always ends in "228."

MOST EXPENSIVE PAINTINGS
THROUGH THE DECADES

Decade	Painting	Price ($)
1900	*Portrait of Marchesa Elena Grimaldi-Cattaneo* by Van Dyck Bought by US businessman Peter Widener, 1906	500,000

Until 1906 the world's most expensive painting had been Raphael's Ansidei Madonna, *sold by the Duke of Marlborough to the National Gallery in London for $340,000. The* Portrait of Marchesa Elena *is now in the National Gallery, Washington, D.C.*

Decade	Painting	Price ($)
1910	The *Benois Madonna* by Leonardo da Vinci Bought by Czar Nicholas II of Russia, 1914	1,500,000

This painting held the world record until November 15, 1961, when Rembrandt's Aristotle Contemplating the Bust of Homer *was bought by the Metropolitan Museum of Art, New York, for $2,300,000.*

Decade	Painting	Price ($)
1920	As above	

Thomas Gainsborough became increasingly fashionable among American collectors, and his Blue Boy *was sold in 1921 for $620,000. In 1929 Raphael's* Madonna *from Panshanger brought $840,000.*

Decade	Painting	Price ($)
1930	As above	

In 1931 American philanthropist Andrew Mellon bought several pictures from the Hermitage, Leningrad (St. Petersburg), for the National Gallery, Washington, D.C., including Raphael's Alba Madonna, *for which he is believed to have paid $1,170,000.*

Decade	Painting	Price ($)
1940	As above	

The effects of World War II depressed art prices generally, although in 1940 Dutch collector Baron von Beuningen paid $906,750 for Van Eyck's Three Marys at the Sepulchre.

Decade	Painting	Price ($)
1950	*Girl's Head* by Vermeer Sold to Charles Wrightsman, 1959	1,120,000

The Impressionists became increasingly appreciated in the 1950s. In 1958 Cézanne's Garçon au Gilet Rouge *sold for $616,000 and Van Gogh's* Public Garden in Arles *sold for $370,000.*

Decade	Painting	Price ($)
1960	*Ginevra de' Benci* by Leonardo da Vinci Bought by the National Gallery of Art, Washington, D.C., 1967	5,000,000

The actual price paid for da Vinci's Ginevra de' Benci *remained undisclosed, but it surpassed that paid in 1961 for Rembrandt's* Aristotle Contemplating the Bust of Homer.

Decade	Painting	Price ($)
1970	*Portrait of Juan de Pareja* by Velazquez Bought by the Wildenstein Gallery, New York, 1970	5,500,000
1980	*Les Noces de Pierrette* by Pablo Picasso	671,920

Juliet and Her Nurse by Turner briefly held the world record both for a British painting and for any work of art when it was sold at auction in 1980 to a private collector for $7,040,000.

Decade	Painting	Price ($)
1990	*Portrait of Dr. Gachet* by Vincent van Gogh Bought by Japanese businessman Ryoei Saito in New York, 1990	75,000,000

This is the equivalent of 220 times the price of the Raphael's Ansidei Madonna, *sold in 1885 for $340,200.*

HM THE QUEEN
HM Queen Elizabeth II receives almost £8,000,000 a year from the Civil List. The Queen Mother receives £643,000 – the second highest amount in the Royal Family.

US POPULATION BY DECADE

Year	Population
1900	75,994,575
1910	91,972,266
1920	105,710,620
1930	122,775,046
1940	131,669,275
1950	150,697,361
1960	179,323,175*
1970	203,302,031
1980	226,542,199
1990	248,709,873

* Includes Alaska and Hawaii from 1960 onward

The greatest rate of increase in one decade occurred not in this century but in the first decade of the nineteenth, when it expanded by 36.4 percent. The lowest growth rate, in the 1930s, was just 7.2 percent.

HIGHEST EARNING MOVIES OF EACH DECADE

Year	Film	Rental ($)
1900	*The Great Train Robbery* (1903)	*
1910	*The Birth of a Nation* (1915)	10,000,000
1920s	*The Big Parade* (1925)	5,120,791
1930s	*Gone With the Wind* (1939)	79,375,077
1940s	*Bambi* (1942)	47,265,000
1950s	*The Ten Commandments* (1956)	43,000,000
1960s	*The Sound of Music* (1965)	79,975,000
1970s	*Star Wars* (1977)	193,777,000
1980s	*E.T.: The Extra-Terrestrial* (1982)	228,618,939
1990s	*Jurassic Park* (1993)	208,000,000

* Unrecorded, but movie generally considered the highest-earning of the pioneer era

THE MONARCH'S INCOME

Year	Monarch	Annual Civil List payment(£)
1900	Victoria	60,000*
1909	Edward VII	470,000
1910	George V	470,000
1920	George V	470,000
1930	Edward VIII/George VI	410,000
1939	George VI	410,000
1950	Queen Elizabeth II	475,000
1960	Queen Elizabeth II	475,000
1970	Queen Elizabeth II	1,950,000
1980	Queen Elizabeth II	5,090,000
1990	Queen Elizabeth II	7,900,000

* Paid by the Duchy of Lancaster

The Civil List is the Government allowance made to the Royals for their staff and the costs incurred while doing public duties. The yearly payments are £10,237,000 until 2000.

IMMIGRATION IN THE US, 1901–1993

Decade	Immigrants
1901–10	8,795,386
1911–20	5,735,811
1921–30	4,107,209
1931–40	528,431
1941–50	1,035,039
1951–60	2,515,479
1961–70	3,321,677
1971–80	4,493,314
1981–90	7,338,062
1991–93	3,705,436
Total 1820–1993	*60,699,450*

The first 10 years of the 20th century was the peak decade of all time for immigration into the United States, and 1907 the record year with a total of 1,285,349 arrivals.

JURASSIC PARK, 1993

100 YEARS OF THE OLYMPIC GAMES

TOP 10

MEDAL-WINNING NATIONS

	Country	gold	Medals silver	bronze	Total
1	US	789	603	518	1,910
2	USSR/CIS	442	361	333	1,136
3	West Germany/Germany	186	227	236	649
4	UK	177	224	218	619
5	France	161	175	191	527
6	Sweden	133	149	171	453
7	East Germany	154	131	126	411
8	Italy	153	126	131	410
9	Hungary	136	124	144	404
10	Finland	98	77	112	287

THE 10

LAST NATIONS TO WIN THEIR FIRST OLYMPIC GOLD MEDAL

	Country	Year
1=	Algeria	1992
1=	Indonesia	1992
1=	Lithuania	1992
4	Suriname	1988
5=	China	1984
5=	Morocco	1984
5=	Portugal	1984
8	Zimbabwe	1980
9=	South Korea	1976
9=	Trinidad	1976

TOP 10

LONGEST-STANDING CURRENT OLYMPIC TRACK & FIELD RECORDS

	Event	Winning time/distance	Competitor/ nationality	Date
1	Men's long jump	8.90 m	Bob Beamon (US)	Oct 18, 1968
2	Men's javelin	94.58 m	Miklos Nemeth (Hungary)	Jul 25, 1976
3	Women's shot	22.41 m	Ilona Slupianek (GDR)	Jul 24, 1980
4	Women's 800 meters	1 min 53.43 sec	Nadezhda Olizarenko (USSR)	Jul 27, 1980
5	Women's 4 x 100 meters	41.60 sec	GDR	Aug 1, 1980
6	Men's 1500 meters	3 min 32.53 sec	Sebastian Coe (UK)	Aug 1, 1980
7	Women's marathon	2 hr 24 min 52 sec	Joan Benoit (US)	Aug 5, 1984
8	Men's 800 meters	1 min 43.00 sec	Joaquim Cruz (Brazil)	Aug 6, 1984
9	Decathlon	8,847 points	Daley Thompson (UK)	Aug 9, 1984
10	Men's 5,000 meters	13 min 05.59 sec	Said Aouita (Morocco)	Aug 11, 1984

Bob Beamon's record-breaking jump in 1968 is regarded as one of the greatest achievements in athletics history. He was aided by Mexico City's rarefied atmosphere, but to add a staggering 21¾ in/55.25 cm to the old record and win the competition by 28½ in/72.39 cm was no mean feat. Beamon's jump of 29 ft 2½ in /8.90 m was the first beyond both 28 and 29 feet (8.53 m and 8.84 m). The first 28-ft/8.53-m jump in the Olympics did not occur until 1980, 12 years after Beamon's leap, which came just 10 minutes before Lee Evans' record.

GOLDEN OPPORTUNITY
The opening ceremony of the 1992 Olympics at Barcelona. Three nations won their first-ever gold medals at the Games.

T O P 1 0
OLYMPIC SWIMMING COUNTRIES

	Country	gold	silver	bronze	Total
1	US	215	164	134	513
2	Australia	39	34	41	114
3	East Germany	40	34	25	99
4	Germany/West Germany	22	31	42	95
5	USSR/CIS	24	32	37	93
6	UK	18	22	29	69
7	Hungary	26	22	17	65
8	Sweden	13	20	21	54
9	Japan	15	18	17	50
10	Canada	10	15	17	42

(Medals: gold, silver, bronze)

The medal table includes medals for the diving and water polo events.

T O P 1 0
OLYMPIC TRACK & FIELD COUNTRIES

	Country	gold	silver	bronze	Total
1	US	288	213	175	676
2	USSR/CIS	71	67	77	215
3	UK	46	74	55	175
4	East Germany	39	47	39	125
5	Germany/West Germany	25	38	50	113
6	Finland	47	35	29	111
7	Sweden	16	25	44	85
8	Australia	18	17	24	59
9	France	11	21	20	52
10	Italy	16	11	21	48

(Medals: gold, silver, bronze)

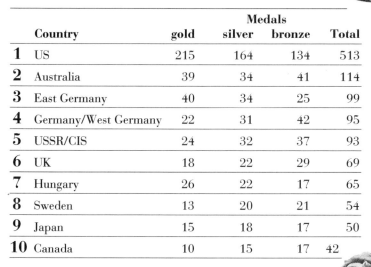

LARISSA LATYNINA

T O P 1 0
INDIVIDUAL GOLD MEDAL WINNERS AT THE SUMMER OLYMPICS

	Medallist/nationality	Sport	Years	Gold medals
1	Ray Ewry (US)	Athletics	1900–08	10
2=	Paavo Nurmi (Fin)	Athletics	1920–28	9
2=	Larissa Latynina (USSR)	Gymnastics	1956–64	9
2=	Mark Spitz (US)	Swimming	1968–72	9
5=	Sawao Kato (Jap)	Gymnastics	1968–76	8
5=	Carl Lewis (US)	Athletics	1984–92	8
5=	Matt Biondi (US)	Swimming	1984–92	8
8=	Aladár Gerevich (Hun)	Fencing	1932–60	7
8=	Viktor Chukarin (USSR)	Gymnastics	1952–56	7
8=	Boris Shakhlin (USSR)	Gymnastics	1956–64	7
8=	Vera Cáslavská (Cze)	Gymnastics	1964–68	7
8=	Nikolay Andrianov (USSR)	Gymnastics	1972–80	7

T O P 1 0
OLYMPIC GOLD MEDAL-WINNING HOST NATIONS

	Country	Venue	Year	Gold medals
1	US	Los Angeles	1984	83
2=	US	St Louis	1904	80
2=	USSR	Moscow	1980	80
4	UK	London	1908	56
5	US	Los Angeles	1932	41
6	Germany	Berlin	1936	33
7	France	Paris	1900	29
8	Sweden	Stockholm	1912	24
9	Japan	Tokyo	1964	16
10	Belgium	Antwerp	1920	14

The only host nation not to win a gold medal at the Summer Olympics is Canada, at the 1976 Montreal Games. At the most recent Games, the 1992 Barcelona Olympics, Spain won 13 gold medals, while South Korea, hosts of the 1988 Games at Seoul, won 12.

All Ewry's golds were in the standing jumps – long jump, high jump, and triple jump – that once formed part of the track and field events. Born in 1873, Ewry contracted polio as a boy, and it seemed that he would be in a wheelchair for life. However, by exercising and developing his legs to an amazing degree, he became one of the world's greatest athletes. Spitz's seven gold medals in 1972 is a record for medals won at a single celebration. Latynina is the all-time top Olympic medallist with 18 to her credit (9 gold, 5 silver, 4 bronze).

SPORTS

FIRST 10 PLAYERS TO HIT FOUR HOME RUNS IN ONE GAME

	Player/club	Date
1	Bobby Lowe, Boston	May 30, 1884
2	Ed Delahanty Philadelphia	July 13, 1896
3	Lou Gehrig New York	June 3, 1932
4	Chuck Klein Philadelphia	July 10, 1936
5	Pat Seerey, Chicago	July 18, 1948
6	Gil Hodges Brooklyn	August 31, 1950
7	Joe Adcock Milwaukee	July 31, 1954
8	Rocky Colavito Cleveland	June 10, 1959
9	Willie Mays San Francisco	April 30, 1961
10	Mike Schmidt Philadelphia	April 17, 1976

The only other players to score four homers in one game are Bob Horner, who did so for Atlanta on July 6, 1986, and Mark Whitten, for St. Louis on September 7, 1993.

TOP 10

PLAYERS WHO ACHIEVED THE MOST RUNS IN A CAREER

(*Regular season only, excluding World Series*)

	Player	Runs		Player	Runs
1	Ty Cobb	2,245	6	Stan Musial	1,949
2=	Babe Ruth	2,174	7	Lou Gehrig	1,888
2=	Hank Aaron	2,174	8	Tris Speaker	1,881
4	Pete Rose	2,165	9	Mel Ott	1,859
5	Willie Mays	2,062	10	Frank Robinson	1,829

"CHARLIE HUSTLE"
So-called for his aggressive play, Pete Rose holds the record for the most hits (4,256) in a Major League baseball career. He was banned from baseball for life in 1989 for betting on games, and convicted of tax offences in 1990.

TOP 10

PLAYERS WHO PLAYED THE MOST GAMES IN A CAREER

	Player	Games
1	Pete Rose	3,562
2	Carl Yastrzemski	3,308
3	Hank Aaron	3,298
4	Ty Cobb	3,034
5	Stan Musial	3,026
6	Willie Mays	2,992
7	Rusty Staub	2,951
8	Dave Winfield	2,927
9	Brooks Robinson	2,896
10	Robin Yount	2,856

T O P   1 0

PLAYERS WITH THE HIGHEST CAREER BATTING AVERAGES

	Player	At bat	Hits	Average*
1	Ty Cobb	11,429	4,191	.367
2	Rogers Hornsby	8,137	2,930	.360
3	Joe Jackson	4,981	1,774	.356
4	Ed Delahanty	7,502	2,591	.345
5=	Billy Hamilton	6,284	2,163	.344
5=	Tris Speaker	10,208	3,515	.344
5=	Ted Williams	7,706	2,654	.344
8	Willie Keeler	8,585	2,947	.343
9=	Dan Brouthers	6,711	2,296	.342
9=	Harry Heilmann	7,787	2,660	.342
9=	Babe Ruth	8,399	2,873	.342

* *Calculated by dividing the number of hits by the number of times a batter was "at bat."*

TEAMS WITH THE MOST WORLD SERIES WINS

	Team*	Wins		Team*	Wins
1	New York Yankees	22	5=	Pittsburgh Pirates	5
2=	Philadelphia/Kansas City/ Oakland Athletics	9	9	Detroit Tigers	4
2=	St. Louis Cardinals	9	10=	St. Louis/ Baltimore Orioles	3
4	Brooklyn/Los Angeles Dodgers	6	10=	Washington Senators/ Minnesota Twins	3
5=	Boston Red Sox	5			
5=	Cincinnati Reds	5			
5=	New York/San Francisco Giants	5			

* *Teams separated by / indicate changes of franchise and are regarded as the same team for Major League record purposes.*

Major League baseball started in the US with the forming of the National League in 1876. The rival American League was started in 1901, and two years later Pittsburgh, champions of the National League, invited American League champions Boston to take part in a best-of-nine games series to establish the "real" champions. Boston won 5–3. The next year the National League champions, New York, refused to play Boston and there was no World Series. It was resumed in 1905 and has been held every year since, except 1994. It has been a best-of-seven games series since 1905, with the exception of 1919–21, when it reverted to a nine-game series.

OLDEST STADIUMS IN MAJOR LEAGUE BASEBALL

	Stadium	Home club	Year built
1=	Tiger Stadium	Detroit Tigers	1912
1=	Fenway Park	Boston Red Sox	1912
3	Wrigley Field	Chicago Cubs	1914
4	Yankee Stadium	New York Yankees	1923
5	Mile High Stadium	Colorado Rockies	1948
6	County Stadium	Milwaukee Brewers	1953
7	Candlestick Park	San Francisco Giants	1960
8	Dodger Stadium	Los Angeles Dodgers	1962
9	Shea Stadium	New York Mets	1964
10	Astrodome	Houston Astros	1965

Each stadium has a unique history, but the Yankee Stadium is particularly notable for its association with Babe Ruth, the best-known name in baseball. The Stadium was built during the early 1920s to hold the huge crowds that he attracted, and was known as "The House Babe Built" because the revenue he brought in financed its construction.

SALARIES IN MAJOR LEAGUE BASEBALL IN 1995

	Player	Team	Salary($)*
1	Cecil Fielder	Detroit Tigers	9,237,000
2	Barry Bonds	San Francisco Giants	8,000,183
3	David Cone	Toronto Blue Jays	8,000,000
4=	Joe Carter	Toronto Blue Jays	7,500,000
4=	Ken Griffey, Jr.	Seattle Mariners	7,500,000
6	Frank Thomas	Chicago White Sox	7,150,000
7	Mark McGwire	Oakland Athletics	6,900,000
8	Jeff Bagwell	Houston Astros	7,875,000
9	Carl Ripken, Jr.	Baltimore Orioles	6,871,671
10=	Lenny Dykstra	Philadelphia Phillies	6,200,000
10=	Kirby Puckett	Minnesota Twins	6,200,000
10=	Ruben Sierra	Oakland Athletics	6,200,000

* *Figures include base salary and prorated signing bonuses as of opening day, but do not reflect the 11.1% reduction in base salary due to the players' strike.*

BASKETBALL

T O P 1 0

BIGGEST ARENAS IN THE NBA

	Arena/location	Home team	Capacity
1	Charlotte Coliseum, Charlotte, North Carolina	Charlotte Hornets	23,698
2	United Center, Chicago Illinois	Chicago Bulls	21,500
3	The Palace of Auburn Hills, Auburn Hills, Michigan	Detroit Pistons	21,454
4	The Coliseum, Richfield, Ohio	Cleveland Cavaliers	20,273
5	Meadowlands Arena, East Rutherford, New Jersey	New Jersey Nets	20,029
6	The Alamodome, San Antonio, Texas	San Antonio Spurs	20,500
7	Delta Center Arena, Salt Lake City, Utah	Utah Jazz	19,911
8	Madison Square Garden, New York	New York Knicks	19,763
9	America West Arena, Phoenix, Arizona	Phoenix Suns	19,023
10	Target Center, Minneapolis Minnesota	Minnesota Timberwolves	19,006

The smallest arena is the 12,888-capacity Memorial Coliseum, home of the Portland Trail Blazers. The largest-ever NBA stadium was the Louisiana Superdome, which was capable of holding crowds of 47,284 and was used by Utah Jazz from 1975 to 1979.

IT'S MAGIC
A member of the five-time World Championship-winning Los Angeles Lakers during the 1980s and Most Valuable Player three times, Magic Johnson retired after announcing that he was infected with HIV.

T O P 1 0

POINTS AVERAGES IN AN NBA SEASON

	Player	Club	Season	Average
1	Wilt Chamberlain	Philadelphia	1961–62	50.4
2	Wilt Chamberlain	San Francisco	1962–63	44.8
3	Wilt Chamberlain	Philadelphia	1960–61	38.4
4	Elgin Baylor	Los Angeles	1961–62	38.3
5	Wilt Chamberlain	Philadelphia	1959–60	37.6
6	Michael Jordan	Chicago	1986–87	37.1
7	Wilt Chamberlain	San Francisco	1963–64	36.9
8	Rick Barry	San Francisco	1966–67	35.6
9	Michael Jordan	Chicago	1987–88	35.0
10=	Elgin Baylor	Los Angeles	1960–61	34.8
10=	Kareem Abdul-Jabbar	Milwaukee	1971–72	34.8

T O P 1 0

HIGHEST-EARNING PLAYERS IN THE NBA, 1993–94

	Player	Team	Earnings ($)
1	David Robinson	San Antonio Spurs	5,740,000
2	John Williams	Cleveland Cavaliers	4,570,000
3	Vlade Divac	Los Angeles Lakers	4,133,000
4=	Robert Parish	Boston Celtics	4,000,000
4=	Ron Harper	Los Angeles Clippers	4,000,000
6	Sam Perkins	Seattle Supersonics	3,587,000
7	Benoit Benjamin	New Jeresey Nets	3,575,000
8	Patrick Ewing	New York Knicks	3,525,000
9	Danny Ferry	Cleveland Cavaliers	3,543,000
10	Brad Daugherty	Cleveland Cavaliers	3,541,000

TOP 10

TEAMS WITH THE MOST NBA TITLES

	Team*	Titles
1	Boston Celtics	16
2	Minnesota/Los Angeles Lakers	11
3=	Chicago Bulls	3
3=	Philadelphia/ Golden State Warriors	3
3=	Syracuse Nationals/ Philadelphia 76ers	3
6=	Detroit Pistons	2
6=	New York Knicks	2
8=	Baltimore Bullets	1
8=	Houston Rockets	1
8=	Milwaukee Bucks	1
8=	Rochester Royals#	1
8=	St. Louis Hawks**	1
8=	Seattle Supersonics	1
8=	Portland Trail Blazers	1
8=	Washington Bullets	1

Basketball is one of the few sports that can trace its exact origins. It was invented by Dr. James Naismith at Springfield, Massachusetts, in 1891. Professional basketball in the US dates to 1898, but the National Basketball Association (NBA) was not formed until 1949, when the National Basketball League and Basketball Association of America merged. The NBA consists of 27 teams split into Eastern and Western Conferences. At the end of an 82-game regular season, the top eight teams in each Conference play off and the two Conference champions meet in a best-of-seven final for the NBA Championship.

* Teams separated by / indicate change of franchise: they have won the championship under both names.
# Now the Sacramento Kings
** Now the Atlanta Hawks

TOP 10

PLAYERS TO HAVE PLAYED MOST GAMES IN THE NBA AND ABA

	Player	Games played
1	Kareem Abdul-Jabbar	1,560
2	Moses Malone*	1,438
3	Robert Parish*	1,413
4	Artis Gilmore	1,329
5	Elvin Hayes	1,303
6	Caldwell Jones	1,299
7	John Havlicek	1,270
8	Paul Silas	1,254
9	Julius Erving	1,243
10	Dan Issel	1,218

* Still active

The ABA (American Basketball Association) was established as a rival to the NBA in 1968 and survived until 1976. Because many of the sport's top players "defected," their figures are still included in this list.

TOP 10

POINTS-SCORERS IN AN NBA CAREER

(*Regular season games only*)

	Player	Total points		Player	Total points
1	Kareem Abdul-Jabbar	38,387	6	John Havlicek	26,395
2	Wilt Chamberlain	31,419	7	Alex English	25,613
3	Moses Malone*	27,360	8	Jerry West	25,192
4	Elvin Hayes	27,313	9	Dominique Wilkins*	24,019
5	Oscar Robertson	26,710	10	Adrian Dantley	23,177

* Still active

If points from the ABA were also considered, then Abdul-Jabbar would still be number one, with the same total. The greatest points-scorer in NBA history, he was born as Lew Alcindor but adopted a new name when he converted to the Islamic faith in 1969. The following year he turned professional, playing for Milwaukee. His career spanned 20 seasons before he retired at the end of the 1989 season. Despite scoring an NBA record 38,387 points, he could not emulate the great Wilt Chamberlain by scoring 100 points in a game, which Chamberlain achieved for Philadelphia against New York at Hershey, Pennsylvania, on March 2, 1962. Chamberlain also scored 70 points in a game six times, a feat Abdul-Jabbar never succeeded in rivaling.

TOP 10

MOST SUCCESSFUL NBA COACHES

	Coach	Games won*
1	Red Auerbach	938
2	Lenny Wilkens#**	926
3	Jack Ramsay	864
4	Dick Motta	856
5	Bill Fitch	845
6	Cotton Fitzsimmons	805
7	Don Nelson#	803
8	Gene Shue	784
9	John Macleod	707
10	Pat Riley#	701

* Regular season games only. #Still active
** Wilkens surpassed Auerbacj's total on January 6, 1995, when the Atlanta Hawks beat the Washington Bullets 112–90.

Pat Riley, coach of the LA Lakers from 1981 to 1990, has the best percentage record with 701 wins from 973 games (73.3 percent).

FOOTBALL

LOS ANGELES MEMORIAL COLISEUM
Host of the 1984 Summer Olympics, it may lose the LA Raiders if owner Al Davis moves his franchise back to Oakland.

T O P 1 0

MOST SUCCESSFUL RUSHERS
IN AN NFL CAREER

	Player	Total yards gained rushing
1	Walter Payton	16,726
2	Eric Dickerson	13,259
3	Tony Dorsett	12,739
4	Jim Brown	12,312
5	Franco Harris	12,120
6	John Riggins	11,352
7	O.J. Simpson	11,236
8	Ottis Anderson	10,273
9	Marcus Allen*	10,018
10	Earl Campbell	9,407

* *Still active at end of 1994–95 season*

T O P 1 0

LARGEST NFL STADIUMS

	Stadium	Home team	Capacity
1	Pontiac Silverdrome	Detroit Lions	80,500
2	Rich Stadium	Buffalo Bills	80,290
3	Cleveland Stadium	Cleveland Browns	78,512
4	Arrowhead Stadium	Kansas City Chiefs	78,067
5	Giants Stadium	New York Giants/Jets	77,311
6	Mile High Stadium	Denver Broncos	76,273
7	Tampa Stadium	Tampa Bay Buccaneers	74,292
8	Sun Devil Stadium	Phoenix Cardinals	73,473
9	Joe Robbie Stadium	Miami Dolphins	73,000
10	Georgia Dome	Atlanta Falcons	70,500

The smallest NFL stadium is the Robert F. Kennedy Stadium, home of the Washington Redskins, with a capacity of 55,677. Between 1946 and 1979 the capacity of the Los Angeles Memorial Coliseum was 92,488 – the largest-ever capacity of any stadium in the NFL.

T O P 1 0

MOST SUCCESSFUL TEAMS

(Based on two points for a Super Bowl win, and one for runner-up)

	Team	Wins	Runners-up	Points
1	Dallas Cowboys	4	3	11
2	San Francisco 49ers	5	0	10
3=	Pittsburgh Steelers	4	0	8
3=	Washington Redskins	3	2	8
5=	Miami Dolphins	2	3	7
5=	Oakland/Los Angeles Raiders	3	1	7
7=	Buffalo Bills	0	4	4
7=	Denver Broncos	0	4	4
7=	Green Bay Packers	2	0	4
7=	Minnesota Vikings	0	4	4
7=	New York Giants	2	0	4

The Dallas Cowboys, known as "America's Team," have played in seven and won four of the 29 Super Bowls, but the San Francisco 49ers, powerhouse team of the last decade, have won on all five visits.

JIM BROWN
Star running back for the Cleveland Browns from 1957 to 1966, Brown rushed 12,312 yards, scored 125 touchdowns, and never missed a start in his 118-game career.

TOP 10

BIGGEST WINNING MARGINS IN THE SUPER BOWL

	Winners	Runners-up	Year	Score	Margin
1	San Francisco	Denver	1990	55–10	45
2	Chicago	New England	1986	46–10	36
3	Dallas	Buffalo	1993	52–17	35
4	Washington	Denver	1988	42–10	32
5	LA Raiders	Washington	1984	38–9	29
6	Green Bay	Kansas City	1967	35–10	25
7	San Francisco	Miami	1985	38–16	22
8	San Francisco	San Diego	1995	49–26	23
9	Dallas	Miami	1972	24–3	21
10=	Green Bay	Oakland	1968	33–14	19
10=	New York Giants	Denver	1987	39–20	19

The closest Super Bowl was in 1991 when the New York Giants beat the Buffalo Bills 20–19. Scott Norwood missed a 47-yard field goal only 8 seconds from the end of time to deprive the Bills of their first-ever Super Bowl win.

TOP 10

POINTS-SCORERS IN AN NFL SEASON

	Player	Team	Year	Points
1	Paul Hornung	Green Bay	1960	176
2	Mark Moseley	Washington	1983	161
3	Gino Cappelletti*	Boston	1964	155
4	Chip Lohmiller	Washington	1991	149
5	Gino Cappelletti	Boston	1961	147
6	Paul Hornung	Green Bay	1961	146
7	Jim Turner	New York Jets	1968	145
8=	John Riggins	Washington	1983	144
8=	Kevin Butler#	Chicago	1985	144
10	Tony Franklin	New England	1986	140

Including a two-point conversion   # The only rookie in the Top 10

TOP 10

PLAYERS WITH THE MOST TOUCHDOWNS IN AN NFL CAREER*

	Player	Touchdowns		Player	Touchdowns
1	Jerry Rice	139	6	Lenny Moore	113
2	Jim Brown	126	7	Don Hutson	105
3	Walter Payton	125	8	Steve Largent	101
4	Marcus Allen	120	9	Franco Harris	100
5	John Riggins	116	10	Eric Dickerson	96

To end of 1994–95 season

TOP 10

COLLEGES WITH THE MOST BOWL WINS

	College	Wins
1	Alabama	27
2	University of Southern California (USC)	24
3	Oklahoma	20
4=	Penn State	19
4=	Tennessee	19
6=	Georgia Tech	17
6=	Texas	17
8=	Georgia	15
8=	Nebraska	15
10=	Mississippi	14
10=	Florida State	14

Bowl games are annual end-of-season college championship games, played at the end of December or beginning of January.

TOP 10

MOST SUCCESSFUL COACHES IN AN NFL CAREER

	Coach	Games won
1	Don Shula	337
2	George Halas	325
3	Tom Landry	270
4	Curly Lambeau	229
5	Chuck Noll	209
6	Chuck Knox	189
7	Paul Brown	170
8	Bud Grant	168
9=	Steve Owen	153
9=	Joe Gibbs	153

GOLF – THE MAJORS

PROGRESSION OF LOWEST FOUR-ROUND TOTALS IN THE BRITISH OPEN

Golfer	Venue	Year	Total
Harold Hilton	Muirfield	1892	305
Harry Vardon	Prestwick	1903	300
Jackie White	Sandwich	1904	296
James Braid	Prestwick	1908	291
Bobby Jones	St. Andrews	1927	285
Gene Sarazen	Prince's	1932	283
Bobby Locke	Troon	1950	279
Peter Thomson	Royal Lytham	1958	278
Arnold Palmer	Troon	1962	276
Tom Watson	Turnberry	1977	268
Greg Norman	Sandwich	1993	267

THE 10
LOWEST FOUR-ROUND TOTALS IN THE BRITISH OPEN

	Player/nationality	Venue	Year	Total
1	Greg Norman (Australia)	Sandwich	1993	267
2=	Tom Watson (US)	Turnberry	1977	268
2=	Nick Price (Zimbabwe)	Turnberry	1994	268
4=	Jack Nicklaus (US)	Turnberry	1977	269
4=	Nick Faldo (UK)	Sandwich	1993	269
4=	Jesper Parnevik (Sweden)	Turnberry	1994	269
7=	Nick Faldo (UK)	St. Andrews	1990	270
7=	Bernhard Langer (Germany)	Sandwich	1993	270
9=	Tom Watson (US)	Muirfield	1980	271
9=	Fuzzy Zoeller (US)	Turnberry	1994	271

The lowest individual round is 63, which has been achieved by seven golfers: Mark Hayes (US), Turnberry 1977; Isao Aoki (Jap), Muirfield 1980; Greg Norman (Aus), Turnberry 1986; Paul Broadhurst (UK), St. Andrews 1990; Jodie Mudd (US), Royal Birkdale 1991; Nick Faldo (UK), Sandwich 1993; and Payne Stewart (US), Sandwich 1993. Hubert Green (1980), Tom Watson (1980), Craig Stadler (1983), Christy O'Connor, Jr. (1985), Seve Ballesteros (1986), Rodger Davis (1987), Ian Baker-Finch (1990 and 1991), Fred Couples (1991), Nick Faldo (1992 and 1994), Raymond Floyd (1992), Steve Pate (1992), Wayne Grady (1993), Greg Norman (1993), Fuzzy Zoeller (1994), Anders Forsbrand (1994), Larry Mize (1994), and Mark Brooks (1994) have all recorded rounds of 64. A further 30 men have registered rounds of 65; the first to do so was Henry Cotton at Sandwich in 1934, whose second round 65 is regarded as one of the finest of Championship golf between the wars. Having already opened with a 67, he became the first man to shoot two sub-70 rounds in the Open. His 65 lowered the record of 67 set by Walter Hagen at Muirfield in 1929. he became the first British winner of the Open for 11 years when he beat South Africa's Sid Brews by five strokes with a then-record total of 283, which was not surpassed until 1977.

TOP 10
MOST FREQUENTLY USED COURSES FOR THE BRITISH OPEN

	Course	First used	Last used	Times used
1	St. Andrews	1873	1995	24
2	Prestwick	1860	1925	24
3	Muirfield	1892	1992	14
4	Royal St. George's Sandwich	1894	1993	12
5	Hoylake	1897	1967	10
6	Royal Lytham	1926	1988	8
7	Royal Birkdale	1954	1991	7
8=	Musselburgh	1874	1889	6
8=	Royal Troon	1923	1989	6
10	Carnoustie	1931	1975	5

The Open, begun in 1860, has also been staged at Turnberry (three times), Deal (twice), and once each at Sandwich, Prince's, and Royal Portrush (the only Irish course to stage it). In 1968, the Carnoustie course became the longest course ever used for the Open, measuring 7,252 yd/6,592 m.

TOP 10
HIGHEST-EARNING GOLFERS ON THE PGA TOUR

	Player	Country	Winnings ($)
1	Tom Kite	US	9,159,418
2	Greg Norman	Australia	7,937,869
3	Fred Couples	US	6,889,149
4	Paul Azinger	US	6,774,728
5	Tom Watson	US	6,751,328
6	Nick Price	South Africa	6,726,418
7	Payne Stewart	US	6,523,260
8	Curtis Strange	US	6,433,442
9	Ben Crenshaw	US	6,107,759
10	Lanny Wadkins	US	5,931,370

LOWEST WINNING TOTALS IN THE US OPEN

	Player	Year	Venue	Score
1=	Jack Nicklaus (US)	1980	Baltusrol	272
1=	Lee Janzen (US)	1993	Baltusrol	272
3	David Graham (Australia)	1981	Merion	273
4=	Jack Nicklaus (US)	1967	Baltusrol	275
4=	Lee Trevino (US)	1968	Oak Hill	275
6=	Ben Hogan (US)	1948	Riviera	276
6=	Fuzzy Zoeller (US)	1984	Winged Foot	276
8=	Jerry Pate (US)	1976	Atlanta	277
8=	Scott Simpson (US)	1987	Olympic Club	277
10=	Ken Venturi (US)	1964	Congressional	278
10=	Billy Casper (US)	1966	Olympic Club	278
10=	Hubert Green (US)	1977	Southern Hills	278
10=	Curtis Strange (US)	1988	Brookline	278
10=	Curtis Strange (US)	1989	Oak Hill	278

PLAYERS TO WIN THE MOST MAJORS IN A CAREER

	Player/ nationality	British Open	US Open	Masters	PGA	Total
1	Jack Nicklaus (US)	3	4	6	5	18
2	Walter Hagen (US)	4	2	0	5	11
3=	Ben Hogan (US)	1	4	2	2	9
3=	Gary Player (South Africa)	3	1	3	2	9
5	Tom Watson (US)	5	1	2	0	8
6=	Harry Vardon (UK)	6	1	0	0	7
6=	Gene Sarazen (US)	1	2	1	3	7
6=	Bobby Jones (US)	3	4	0	0	7
6=	Sam Snead (US)	1	0	3	3	7
6=	Arnold Palmer (US)	2	1	4	0	7

The four Majors are the British Open, US Open, US Masters, and US PGA. The oldest is the British Open, first played at Prestwick in 1860 and won by Willie Park. The first US Open was at the Newport Club, Rhode Island, in 1895 and was won by Horace Rawlins, playing over his home course. The US PGA Championship, probably the least prestigious of the four Majors, was first held at the Siwanoy Club, New York. Jim Barnes beat Jock Hutchison by one hole in the match-play final. It did not become a stroke-play event until 1958. The youngest of the four Majors is the Masters, played over the beautiful Augusta National course in Georgia. Entry is by invitation only, and the first winner was Horton Smith. The Masters and the Augusta course were the idea of Robert Tyre "Bobby" Jones, the greatest amateur player the world of golf has ever seen. No player has won all four Majors in one year.

LOWEST WINNING SCORES IN THE US MASTERS

	Player*	Year	Score
1=	Jack Nicklaus	1965	271
1=	Raymond Floyd	1976	271
3=	Ben Hogan	1953	274
3=	Ben Crenshaw	1995	274
5=	Severiano Ballesteros (Spain)	1980	275
5=	Fred Couples	1992	275
7=	Arnold Palmer	1964	276
7=	Jack Nicklaus	1975	276
7=	Tom Watson	1977	276
10=	Bob Goalby	1968	277
10=	Johnny Miller	1975	277
10=	Gary Player (SA)	1978	277
10=	Ian Woosnam (UK)	1991	277
10=	Raymond Floyd	1992	277
10=	Bernhard Langer (Germany)	1993	277

* All players from the US unless otherwise stated

GOLDEN OPPORTUNITY
The winner of 18 professional Majors, the record of Jack Nicklaus, known as "The Golden Bear," seems unlikely to be challenged in the foreseeable future.

HORSE RACING

TOP 10

MONEY-WINNING JOCKEYS IN A CAREER

	Jockey	1st places	Total Winnings
1	Laffit Pincay, Jr.	8,261	183,910,301
2	Chris McCarron	6,075	177,751,276
3	Angel Cordero Jr.	7,057	164,526,217
4	Pat Day	6,306	149,697,293
5	Ed Delahoussaye	5,375	138,119,051
6	Bill Shoemaker	8,833	123,375,524
7	Jorge Velasquez	6,611	123,231,105
8	Gary Stevens	3,684	118,316,558
9	Jerry Bailey	3,315	99,568,597
10	Pat Valenzuela	2,810	89,327,536

TOP 10

MONEY-WINNING HORSES IN A HARNESS-RACING CAREER

	Trotters			Pacers	
	Horse	Winnings ($)		Horse	Winnings ($)
1	Peace Corps	4,907,307		Nihilator	3,225,653
2	Ourasi	4,010,105		Artsplace	3,085,083
3	Mack Lobell	3,917,594		Presidential Ball	3,021,363
4	Reve d'Udon	3,611,351		Matt's Scooter	2,944,591
5	Ideal du Gazeau	2,744,777		On The Road Again	2,819,102
6	Vrai Lutin	2,612,429		Beach Towel	2,570,357
7	Grades Singing	2,607,552		Western Hanover	2,541,647
8	Embassy Lobell	2,566,370		Cam's Card Shark	2,498,204
9	Napoletano	2,467,878		Precious Bunny	2,281,142
10	Sea Cove	2,505,047		Jake and Elwood	2,273,187

Harness racing is one of the oldest sports in the US, its origins going back to the Colonial period when many races were held along the turnpikes of New York and the New England colonies. After growing in popularity in the nineteenth century, the exotically titled governing body, the National Association for the Promotion of the Interests of the Trotting Turf (now the National Trotting Association) was founded in 1870. While widespread in the United States, harness racing is also popular in Australia and New Zealand, and, increasingly, elsewhere in the world. It has enjoyed a following in Britain since the 1960s with the opening of the trotting track at Prestatyn, North Wales. Harness racing horses pull a jockey on a two-wheeled "sulky" (introduced in 1829) around an oval track. Unlike thoroughbred racehorses, standardbred harness racing horses are trained to trot and pace, but do not gallop. A trotter is a horse whose diagonally opposite legs move forward together, while a pacer's legs are extended laterally and with a "swinging motion." Pacers usually travel faster than trotters.

TOP 10

JOCKEYS IN THE BREEDERS CUP

	Jockey	Years	Wins
1	Pat Day	1984–94	8
2=	Eddie Delahoussaye	1984–93	7
2=	Laffit Pincay, Jr.	1985–93	7
4	Pat Valenzuela	1986–92	6
5=	Chris McCarron	1985–92	5
5=	José Santos	1986–90	5
7=	Angel Cordero, Jr.	1985–89	4
7=	Mike Smith	1992–94	4
9=	Craig Perret	1984–90	3
9=	Randy Romero	1987–89	3
9=	Gary Stevens	1990–94	3
9=	Jerry Bailey	1991–94	3

Held at a different venue each year, the Breeders Cup is an end-of-season gathering. Seven races are run during the day, with the season's best throughbreds competing in each category. Staged in October or November, there is $10,000,000 prize money on offer with $3,000,000 going to the winner of the day's senior race, the Classic.

TOP 10

JOCKEYS IN THE EPSOM DERBY

	Jockey	Years	Wins
1	Lester Piggott	1954–83	9
2=	Jem Robinson	1817–36	6
2=	Steve Donahue	1915–25	6
4=	John Arnull	1784–99	5
4=	Bill Clift	1793–1819	5
4=	Frank Buckle	1792–1823	5
4=	Fred Archer	1877-86	5
8=	Sam Arnull	1780–98	4
8=	Tom Goodison	1809–22	4
8=	Bill Scott	1832–43	4
8=	Jack Watts	1887–96	4
8=	Charlie Smirke	1934–58	4
8=	Willie Carson	1979–94	4

FASTEST WINNING TIMES OF THE KENTUCKY DERBY

	Horse	Year	Time min	sec
1	Secretariat*	1973	1	59.4
2	Northern Dancer	1964	2	00.0
3	Spend a Buck	1985	2	00.2
4	Decidedly	1962	2	00.4
5	Proud Clarion	1967	2	00.6
6=	Lucky Debonair	1965	2	01.2
6=	Affirmed*	1978	2	01.2
6=	Thunder Gulch	1995	2	01.2
9	Whirlaway*	1941	2	01.4
10=	Middleground	1950	2	01.6
10=	Hill Gail	1952	2	01.6
10=	Bold Forbes	1976	2	01.6

* Triple Crown winner

America's best-known race, the Kentucky Derby, is run over 1¼ miles of the Churchill Downs track in Louisville, Kentucky, on the first Saturday each May. It was begun in 1875 and between then and 1895 the race was run over 1½ miles. Eddie Arcaro and Bill Hartack, each with five wins, have been the most successful jockeys, and the top trainer, with six wins, is Ben A. Jones. The slowest time for the current 1¼-mile distance was in 1908, when Stone Street won in 2 mins 15.2 secs.

HARNESS-RACING DRIVERS OF ALL TIME

Most wins				Money won	
Driver	**Wins**		**Driver**	**Winnings ($)**
Herve Filion	14,525	**1**	John Campbell	128,787,234
Carmine Abbatiello	7,132	**2**	Herve Filion	83,485,489
Michel Lachance	7,041	**3**	Bill O'Donnell	81,551,891
John Campbell	6,687	**4**	Michael Lachance	76,330,321
Dave Magee	6,519	**5**	Ron Waples	59,366,938
Walter Case, Jr.	6,481	**6**	Jack Moiseyev	50,784,611
"Cat" Manzi	6,284	**7**	"Cat" Manzi	50,767,140
Jack Moiseyev	5,969	**8**	Doug Brown	50,164,511
Ron Waples	5,959	**9**	Carmine Abbatiello	49,705,424
Eddie Davis	5,844	**10**	Dave Magee	44,998,965

JOCKEYS IN THE US TRIPLE CROWN RACES

	Jockey	K	P	B	Total
1	Eddie Arcaro	5	6	6	17
2	Bill Shoemaker	4	2	5	11
3=	Bill Hartack	5	3	1	9
3=	Earle Sande	3	1	5	9
5	Jimmy McLaughlin	1	1	6	8
6=	Angel Cordero, Jr.	3	2	1	6
6=	Pat Day	1	3	2	6
6=	Chas Kurtsinger	2	2	2	6
6=	Ron Turcotte	2	2	2	6
9=	Eddie Delahoussaye	2	1	2	5
9=	Lloyd Hughes	0	3	2	5

	Jockey	K	P	B	Total
9=	Johnny Loftus	2	2	1	5
9=	Chris McCarron	2	2	1	5
9=	Willie Simms	2	1	2	5

K – *Kentucky Derby*
P – *Preakness Stakes*
B – *Belmont Stakes*

The US Triple Crown consists of the Kentucky Derby, Preakness Stakes, and Belmont Stakes. Since 1875 only 11 horses have won all three races in one season. The only jockey to complete the Triple Crown twice is Eddie Arcaro, on Whirlaway in 1941 and on Citation in 1948.

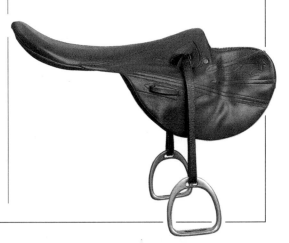

TENNIS

TOP 10
WINNERS OF MEN'S GRAND SLAM SINGLES TITLES

	Player/nationality	A	F	W	US	Total
1	Roy Emerson (Australia)	6	2	2	2	12
2=	Bjorn Borg (Sweden)	0	6	5	0	11
2=	Rod Laver (Australia)	3	2	4	2	11
4=	Jimmy Connors (US)	1	0	2	5	8
4=	Ivan Lendl (Czechoslovakia)	2	3	0	3	8
4=	Fred Perry (UK)	1	1	3	3	8
4=	Ken Rosewall (Australia)	4	2	0	2	8
8=	René Lacoste (France)	0	3	2	2	7
8=	William Larned (US)	0	0	0	7	7
8=	John McEnroe (US)	0	0	3	4	7
8=	John Newcombe (Australia)	2	0	3	2	7
8=	William Renshaw (UK)	0	0	7	0	7
8=	Richard Sears (US)	0	0	0	7	7
8=	Mats Wilander (Sweden)	3	3	0	1	7

A = *Australian Open*; F = *French Open*; W = *Wimbledon*;
US = *US Open*

TOP 10
WINNERS OF WOMEN'S GRAND SLAM SINGLES TITLES

	Player/nationality	A	F	W	US	Total
1	Margaret Court (*née* Smith) (Australia)	11	5	3	5	24
2	Helen Wills-Moody (US)	0	4	8	7	19
3=	Chris Evert-Lloyd (US)	2	7	3	6	18
3=	Martina Navratilova (Czechoslovakia/US)	3	2	9	4	18
5	Steffi Graf (Germany)	4	3	5	3	15
6	Billie Jean King (*née* Moffitt) (US)	1	1	6	4	12
7	Maureen Connolly (US)	1	2	3	3	9
8=	Suzanne Lenglen (France)	0	2	6	0	8
8=	Molla Mallory (*née* Bjurstedt) (US)	0	0	0	8	8
8=	Monica Seles (Yugoslavia)	3	3	0	2	8

A = *Australian Open*; F = *French Open*; W = *Wimbledon*;
US = *US Open*

TOP 10
PLAYERS WITH THE MOST WIMBLEDON TITLES

	Player/nationality	Years	Singles	Doubles	Mixed	Total
1	Billie Jean King (*née* Moffitt) (US)	1961–79	6	10	4	20
2	Elizabeth Ryan (US)	1914–34	0	12	7	19
3	Martina Navratilova (Cze/US)	1976–93	9	7	2	18
4	Suzanne Lenglen (Fra)	1919–25	6	6	3	15
5	William Renshaw (UK)	1880–89	7	7	0	14
6=	Louise Brough (US)	1946–55	4	5	4	13
6=	Lawrence Doherty (UK)	1897–1905	5	8	0	13
8=	Helen Wills-Moody (US)	1927–38	8	3	1	12
8=	Reginald Doherty (UK)	1897–1905	4	8	0	12
10=	Margaret Court (*née* Smith) (Aus)	1953–75	3	2	5	10
10=	Doris Hart (US)	1947–55	1	4	5	10

Billie Jean King's first and last Wimbledon titles were in the ladies' doubles. In the first, in 1961, she and Karen Hantze beat Jan Lehane and Margaret Smith 6–3, 6–4. King won her record-breaking 20th title in 1979, with Martina Navratilova when they beat Betty Stove and Wendy Turnbull. William Renshaw also won two of his titles in the doubles, then known as the Oxford University Doubles Championship, now regarded as having full championship status, in 1880 and 1881. William and his twin brother Ernest won 22 titles between them.

ROY EMERSON
During the 1960s Roy Emerson and fellow Australian Rod Laver were the world's two best players. Both remain the only men to win all four Grand Slam titles, Emerson winning a record 12.

T O P 1 0

PLAYERS WITH MOST US SINGLES TITLES

	Player	Years	Titles
1	Molla Mallory (*née* Bjurstedt)	1915–26	8
2=	Richard Sears	1881–87	7
2=	William Larned	1901–11	7
2=	Bill Tilden	1920–29	7
2=	Helen Wills-Moody	1923–31	7
2=	Margaret Court (Aus)	1962–70	7*
7	Chris Evert-Lloyd	1975–82	6
8	Jimmy Connors	1974–83	5
9	Robert Wrenn	1893–97	4
9=	Elisabeth Moore	1896–1905	4
9=	Hazel Wightman (*née* Hotchkiss)	1909–19	4
9=	Helen Jacobs	1932–35	4
9=	Alice Marble	1936–40	4
9=	Pauline Betz	1942–46	4
9=	Maria Bueno (Bra)	1959–66	4
9=	Billie Jean King	1967–74	4
9=	John McEnroe	1979–84	4
9=	Martina Navratilova	1983–87	4

* *Includes two wins in Amateur Championships of 1968 and 1969, which were held alongside the Open Championship*

Players are from the US unless otherwise stated

Organized tennis started in the US following the formation of the USLTA in 1881. On August 31 of that year the first national championships began at the Casino at Newport, Rhode Island. There were no stands – the courts were simply roped off. Men's singles and doubles were the only events contested, with competitors playing in a wide variety of attire, including colored blazers and cravats. The first winner of the singles titles was Richard Sears, who won the first seven titles until deposed by Henry Slocum in 1888.

T O P 1 0

GRAND SLAM TITLES BY AMERICANS SINCE WORLD WAR II

	Name	Singles	Doubles	Mixed doubles	Total
1	Martina Navratilova*	18	31	5	54
2	Billie Jean King (*née* Moffitt)	12	17	11	40
3	Doris Hart	6	14	15	35
4	Louise Brough	6	9	15	30
5	Margaret Osborne du Pont	6	16	7	29
6=	Chris Evert-Lloyd	18	3	–	21
6=	Darlene Hard	3	13	5	21
8=	Shirley Fry	4	12	1	17
8=	John McEnroe	7	9	1	17
10	Vic Seixas	2	5	8	15

* *Navratilova won two of her titles before becoming a US citizen. She defected to the US on September 6, 1975.*

T O P 1 0

PLAYERS WITH MOST AUSTRALIAN CHAMPIONSHIP SINGLES TITLES

	Player	Years	Titles
1	Margaret Court (*née* Smith)	1960–73	11
2=	Nancy Bolton (*née* Wynne)	1937–51	6
2=	Roy Emerson	1961–67	6
4	Daphne Akhurst	1925–30	5
5=	Pat Wood*	1914–23	4
5=	Jack Crawford	1931–35	4
5=	Ken Rosewall	1953–72	4
5=	Evonne Cawley (*née* Goolagong)	1974–77	4
5=	Steffi Graf (Ger)	1988–94	4
10=	Joan Hartigan	1933–36	3
10=	Adrian Quist	1936–48	3
10=	Rod Laver	1960–69	3
10=	Martina Navratilova (US)	1981–85	3
10=	Mats Wilander (Swe)	1983–88	3
10=	Monica Seles (Yug)	1991–93	3

* *Men's singles*

Players are Australian unless otherwise stated

T O P 1 0

PLAYERS WITH MOST FRENCH CHAMPIONSHIP SINGLES TITLES

	Player	Years	Titles
1	Chris Evert-Lloyd (US)	1974–86	7
2	Bjorn Borg (Swe)	1974–81	6
3	Margaret Court (*née* Smith) (Aus)	1962–73	5
4=	Henri Cochet (Fra)	1926–32	4
4=	Helen Wills-Moody (US)	1928–32	4
6=	René Lacoste (Fra)	1925–29	3
6=	Hilde Sperling (Ger)	1935–37	3
6=	Yvon Petra (Fra)	1943–45	3
6=	Ivan Lendl (Cze)	1984–7	3
6=	Mats Wilander (Swe)	1982–88	3
6=	Monica Seles (Yug)	1990–92	3
6=	Steffi Graf (Ger)	1987–93	3

The French Championship, founded in 1891, was a "closed" tournament for French Nationals until 1925, when it opened to players from other countries. The list covers winners since then. Before 1925, Max Decugis won 8 titles. Since 1928, all championships have been held at the Stade Roland Garros at Auteil, built in 1927 to celebrate France's winning the Davis Cup.

MOTOR RACING

TOP 10

FASTEST WINNING SPEEDS OF THE INDIANAPOLIS 500

	Driver*	Car	Year	Speed km/h	mph
1	Arie Luyendyk (Netherlands)	Lola-Chevrolet	1990	299.307	185.984
2	Rick Mears	Chevrolet-Lumina	1991	283.980	176.457
3	Bobby Rahal	March-Cosworth	1986	274.750	170.722
4	Emerson Fittipaldi (Brazil)	Penske-Chevrolet	1989	269.695	167.581
5	Rick Mears	March-Cosworth	1984	263.308	163.612
6	Mark Donohue	McLaren-Offenhauser	1972	262.619	162.962
7	Al Unser, Jr.	March-Cosworth	1987	260.995	162.175#
8	Tom Sneva	March-Cosworth	1983	260.902	162.117
9	Gordon Johncock	Wildcat-Cosworth	1982	260.760	162.029
10	Al Unser	Lola-Cosworth	1978	259.689	161.363

* *From the US unless otherwise stated*

The current track record, set by Emerson Fittipaldi in the 1990 qualifying competition, is 225.301 mph/362.587 km/h.

TOP 10

WINNERS OF THE INDIANAPOLIS 500 WITH THE HIGHEST STARTING POSITIONS

	Driver	Year	Starting position
1=	Ray Harroun	1911	28
1=	Louis Meyer	1936	28
3	Fred Frame	1932	27
4	Johnny Rutherford	1974	25
5=	Kelly Petillo	1935	22
5=	George Souders	1927	22
7	L.L. Corum and Joe Boyer	1924	21
8=	Frank Lockart	1926	20
8=	Tommy Milton	1921	20
8=	Al Unser, Jr.	1987	20

Of the 75 winners of the Indianapolis 500, 44 have started from a position between 1 and 5 on the starting grid. The Top 10 is of those winners who have started from farthest back in the starting lineup.

RACING INTO HISTORY
Ray Harroun, in his Marmon Wasp, speeds down the home straight to win the very first Indianapolis 500, in 1911.

TOP 10

DRIVERS WITH THE MOST WINSTON CUP TITLES

	Driver	Years	Titles		Driver	Years	Titles
1	Richard Petty	1964–79	7	7=	Herb Thomas	1951–53	2
2	Dale Earnhardt	1980–93	6	7=	Tim Flock	1952–55	2
3=	Lee Petty	1954–59	3	7=	Buck Baker	1956–57	2
3=	David Pearson	1966–69	3	7=	Ned Jarrett	1961–65	2
3=	Cale Yarborough	1976–78	3	7=	Joe Weatherly	1962–63	2
3=	Darrell Waltrip	1981–85	3				

The Winston Cup is a season-long series of races organized by the National Association of Stock Car Auto Racing, Inc. (NASCAR). Races take place over enclosed circuits and are among the most popular motor races in the US. The series started in 1949 as the Grand National series but changed its name to the Winston Cup in 1970 when the R.J. Reynolds tobacco company, manufacturers of Winston cigarettes, started to sponsor it.

TOP 10

MONEY-WINNERS AT THE INDIANAPOLIS 500, 1994

	Driver	Chassis	Prize money ($)
1	Al Unser, Jr.	Mercedes	1,373,813
2	Jacques Villeneuve	Ford Cosworth	622,713
3	Bobby Rahal	Ilmor VB-D	411,163
4	Jimmy Vasser	Ford Cosworth	295,163
5	Michael Andretti	Ford Cosworth	245,563
6	Eddie Cheever	Mercedes	238,563
7	Bobby Gordon	Ford Cosworth	227,563
8	Teo Fabi	Ilmor VB-D	216,563
9	Brian Herta	Ford Cosworth	212,213
10	John Andretti	Ford Cosworth	191,750

The first Indianapolis 500, known affectionately as the "Indy," was held on May 30, 1911 and won by Ray Harroun. Then, as today, the race, over 200 laps of the 2¼-mile Indianapolis Raceway, formed part of the Memorial Day celebrations. Prize money in 1994 totaled $7,864,800. Roberto Guerrero, who finished in 33rd (last) position, having completed only 20 of the 200 laps, still earned $143,912.

INDY 500 CUP
The winner of the Indy 500 is awarded this highly decorated cup, which is adorned with portraits of past champions.

TOP 10

NASCAR MONEY-WINNERS OF ALL TIME

	Driver*	Total prizes ($)		Driver*	Total prizes ($)
1	Dale Earnhardt	20,362,376	6	Harry Gant	8,184,519
2	Bill Elliott	13,918,144	7	Rickey Rudd	8,030,985
3	Darrell Waltrip	13,110,818	8	Geoff Bodine	7,887,153
4	Rusty Wallace	10,167,556	9	Richard Petty	7,757,964
5	Terry Labonet	8,300,950	10	Bobby Allison	7,102,233

TOP 10

CART* DRIVERS WITH MOST RACE WINS

	Driver	Wins
1	A.J. Foyt	67
2	Mario Andretti	52
3	Al Unser	39
4	Bobby Unser	34
5=	Michael Andretti	29
5=	Rick Mears	29
7	Johnny Rutherford	27
8	Roger Ward	26
9	Gordon Johncock	25
10=	Ralph DePalma	24
10=	Bobby Rahal	24
10=	Al Unser, Jr.	24

* Championship Auto Racing Teams

TOP 10

FASTEST WINNING SPEEDS OF THE DAYTONA 500

	Driver*	Car	Year	Speed km/h	mph
1	Buddy Baker	Oldsmobile	1980	285.823	177.602
2	Bill Elliott	Ford	1987	283.668	176.263
3	Bill Elliott	Ford	1985	277.234	172.265
4	Richard Petty	Buick	1981	273.027	169.651
5	Derrike Cope	Chevrolet	1990	266.766	165.761
6	A.J. Foyt	Mercury	1972	259.990	161.550
7	Richard Pett	Plymouth	1966	258.504	160.627#
8	Davey Allison	Ford	1992	257.913	160.260
9	Bobby Allison	Ford	1978	257.060	159.730
10	LeeRoy Yarborough	Ford	1967	254.196	157.950

* All winners from the US   *# Race reduced to 495 miles/797 km*

First held in 1959, the Daytona 500 is raced every February at the Daytona International Speedway. One of the most prestigious races of the NASCAR season, it covers 200 laps.

ICE HOCKEY

TOP 10

GOALSCORERS IN AN NHL SEASON

	Player	Team	Season	Goals
1	Wayne Gretzky	Edmonton Oilers	1981–82	92
2	Wayne Gretzky	Edmonton Oilers	1983–84	87
3	Brett Hull	St. Louis Blues	1990–91	86
4	Mario Lemieux	Pittsburgh Penguins	1988–89	85
5=	Phil Esposito	Boston Bruins	1970–71	76
5=	Alexander Mogilny	Buffalo Sabres	1992–93	76
5=	Teemu Selanne	Winnipeg Jets	1992–93	76
8	Wayne Gretzky	Edmonton Oilers	1984–85	73
9	Brett Hull	St. Louis Blues	1989–90	72
10=	Wayne Gretzky	Edmonton Oilers	1982–83	71
10=	Jari Kurri	Edmonton Oilers	1984–85	71

TOP 10

BEST-PAID PLAYERS IN THE NHL, 1994–95

	Player	Team	Salary* ($)
1	Wayne Gretzky	Los Angeles Kings	6,540,028
2	Mark Messier	New York Rangers	6,293,103
3	Scott Stevens	New Jersey Devils	5,800,000
4	Pavel Bure	Vancouver Canucks	4,500,000
5	Mario Lemieux	Pittsburgh Penguins	4,071,429
6	Eric Lindros	Philadelphia Flyers	3,640,000
7	Pat Lafontaine	Buffalo Sabres	3,563,795
8=	Al MacInnis	St. Louis Blues	3,500,000
8=	Brendan Shanahan	St. Louis Blues	3,500,000
10	Patrick Roy	Montreal Canadiens	3,485,276

Signing bonuses are not included

TOP 10

WINNERS OF THE HART TROPHY

	Player	Years	Wins
1	Wayne Gretzky	1980–89	9
2	Gordie Howe	1952–63	6
3	Eddie Shore	1933–38	4
4=	Bobby Clarke	1973–76	3
4=	Howie Morenz	1928–32	3
4=	Bobby Orr	1970–72	3
7=	Jean Beliveau	1956–64	2
7=	Bill Cowley	1941–43	2
7=	Phil Esposito	1969–74	2
7=	Bobby Hull	1965–66	2
7=	Mario Lemieux	1988–93	2
7=	Guy Lafleur	1977–78	2
7=	Mark Messier	1990–92	2
7=	Stan Mikita	1967–68	2
7=	Nels Stewart	1926–30	2

The Hart Trophy has been awarded every year since 1924 and is presented to the player "adjudged to be the most valuable to his team during the season." The winner is chosen by the Professional Hockey Writers' Association, and the trophy is named after Cecil Hart, the former manager/coach of the Montreal Canadiens. The first winner of the trophy was Frank Nighbor of Ottawa.

TOP 10

BIGGEST NHL ARENAS

	Stadium	Home team	Capacity
1	Thunderdome, Tampa	Tampa Bay Lightning	28,000
2	United Center, Chicago	Chicago Blackhawks	20,500
3	Olympic Saddledrome, Calgary	Calgary Flames	20,230
4	Joe Louis Sports Arena, Detroit	Detroit Red Wings	19,875
5	Kiel Center, St. Louis	St. Louis Blues	19,260
6	Meadowlands Arena, East Rutherford	New Jersey Devils	19,040
7	Madison Square Garden, New York	New York Rangers	18,200
8	USAir Arena, Landover	Washington Capitals	18,130
9	Northlands Coliseum, Edmonton	Edmonton Oilers	17,503
10	The Spectrum, Philadelphia	Philadelphia Flyers	17,380

The 10th position on this list was formerly occupied by the Chicago Stadium, home of the Chicago Black Hawks (capacity 17,317), but this stadium was demolished at the end of the 1993–94 season. The smallest arena is the Ottawa Civic Centre, home of the Ottawa Senators, which has a capacity of 10,585. The Quebec Nordiques are reportedly moving to Denver, and the New Jersey Devils may relocate to Nashville at the end of the 1994–95 season, while the Boston Bruins will begin playing in the new Fleet Center – all of which developments may change this Top 10 radically in the future.

TOP 10
TEAMS WITH THE MOST STANLEY CUP WINS

	Team	Wins
1	Montreal Canadiens	24
2	Toronto Maple Leafs	11
3	Detroit Red Wings	7
4	Ottawa Senators	6
5=	Boston Bruins	5
5=	Edmonton Oilers	5
7=	Montreal Victorias	4
7=	Montreal Wanderers	4
7=	New York Islanders	4
7=	New York Rangers	4
10=	Chicago Black Hawks	3
10=	Ottawa Silver Seven	3

The Stanley Cup trophy was first presented in 1893 by Sir Frederick Arthur Stanley, then Governor General of Canada. It was won by the Montreal Amateur Athletic Association. In 1914 the Cup was contested by the champions of the National Hockey Association (formed 1910; became the National Hockey League, [NHL] in 1917) and the Pacific Coast Hockey Association (formed 1912). The two groups continued to play each other until the PCHA disbanded in 1926. Since then the NHL play-offs have decided the Cup finalists.

TOP 10
GOALSCORERS IN AN NHL CAREER
(*Regular season only*)

	Player	Seasons	Goals
1	Wayne Gretzky	16	814
2	Geordie Howe	26	801
3	Marcel Dionne	18	731
4	Phil Esposito	18	717
5	Mike Gartner	16	619
6	Bobby Hull	16	610
7	Mike Bossy	10	573
8	Jari Kurri	14	565
9	Guy Lafleur	16	560
10	John Bucyk	23	556

TOP 10
GOALTENDERS IN AN NHL CAREER
(*Regular season only*)

	Goaltender	Seasons	Games won
1	Terry Sawchuk	21	435
2	Jacques Plante	18	434
3	Tony Esposito	16	423
4	Glenn Hall	18	407
5	Rogie Vachon	16	355
6	Gump Worsley	21	335
7	Harry Lumley	16	332
8	Andy Moog	15	313
9	Billy Smith	18	305
10	Turk Broda	12	302

TOP 10
ASSISTS IN AN NHL CAREER
(*Regular season only*)

	Player	Seasons	Assists		Player	Seasons	Assists
1	Wayne Gretzky	17	1,692	6	Ray Bourque	15	908
2	Gordie Howe	26	1,049	7	Bryan Trottier	18	901
3	Marcel Dionne	18	1,040	8	Mark Messier	16	877
4	Paul Coffey	15	978	9	Phil Esposito	18	873
5	Stan Mikita	22	926	10	Bobby Clarke	15	852

TOP 10
POINTS-SCORERS IN AN NHL CAREER
(*Regular season only*)

	Player	Seasons	Goals	Assists	Total points
1	Wayne Gretzky	16	814	1,692	2,506
2	Gordie Howe	26	801	1,049	1,850
3	Marcel Dionne	18	731	1,040	1,771
4	Phil Esposito	18	717	873	1,590
5	Stan Mikita	22	541	926	1,467
6	Bryan Trottier	18	524	901	1,425
7=	John Bucyk	23	556	813	1,369
7=	Mark Messier	16	492	877	1,369
9	Guy Lafleur	17	560	793	1,353
10	Gilbert Perreault	17	512	814	1,326

TOP 10
POINTS-SCORERS IN STANLEY CUP PLAY-OFF MATCHES

	Player	Total points
1	Wayne Gretzky	346
2	Mark Messier	259
3	Jari Kurri	222
4	Glenn Anderson	207
5	Bryan Trottier	184
6	Jean Beliveau	176
7	Denis Potvin	164
8=	Mike Bossy	160
8=	Gordie Howe	160
10	Bobby Smith	155

WATER SPORTS

FASTEST WINNING TIMES IN THE OXFORD VS. CAMBRIDGE BOAT RACE

	Winner	Year	Distance (lengths)	Time min	sec
1	Oxford	1984	3¾	16	45
2	Oxford	1976	6½	16	58
3	Oxford	1991	4¼	16	59
4	Cambridge	1993	3½	17	0
5	Oxford	1985	4¾	17	11
6	Oxford	1990	2¼	17	15
7=	Oxford	1974	5½	17	35
7=	Oxford	1988	5½	17	35
9	Oxford	1992	1½	17	48
10	Cambridge	1948	5	17	50

LARGEST SPECIES OF FRESHWATER FISH CAUGHT IN THE US

	Species	Angler/location/year	Weight kg	g	lb	oz
1	White sturgeon	Joey Pallotta III, Benicia, California, 1983	212	28	468	0
2	Alligator gar	Bill Valverde, Rio Grande, Texas, 1951	126	55	279	0
3	Blue catfish	George A. Lijewski, Cooper River, South Carolina, 1991	49	62	109	4
4	Chinook salmon	Les Anderson, Kenai River, Arkansas, 1985	44	18	97	4
5	Lake sturgeon	James M.DeOtis, Kettle River, Montana, 1986	41	91	92	4
6	Flathead catfish	Mike Rogers, Lake Lewisville, Texas, 1982	41	46	91	4
7	Big skate	Scotty A. Krick, Humboldt Bay, Eureka, California, 1993	41	28	91	0
8	Bigmouth buffalo	Delbert Sisk, Bussey Brake, Bastrop, Louisiana, 1980	31	98	70	5
9	Smallmouth buffalo	Jerry L. Dolezal, Lake Hamilton, Arkansas, 1984	31	20	68	8
10=	Striped landlocked bass	Hank Ferguson, O'Neull Forebay, San Luis, California, 1992	30	75	67	8
10=	Muskellunge	Cal Johnson, Hayward, Wisconsin, 1949	30	75	67	8

LARGEST SPECIES OF SALTWATER FISH CAUGHT IN THE US

	Species	Angler/location/date	Weight kg	g	lb	oz
1	Tiger shark	Walter Maxwell, Cherry Grove, South Carolina, 1964	807	41	1,780	0
2	Pacific blue marlin	Jay W. Debeaubien, Kaaiwi Point, Kona, Hawaii, 1982	624	15	1,376	0
3	Great hammerhead shark	Allen Ogle, Sarasota, Florida, 1982	449	52	991	0
4	Dusky shark	Warren Girle, Longboat Key, Florida, 1982	346	55	764	0
5	Jewfish	Lynn Joyner, Ferdinanda Beach, Florida, 1961	308	45	680	0
6	Giant sea bass	James D. McAdam Jr., Anacapa Island, California, 1968	255	74	563	8
7	Bull shark	Phillip Wilson, Dauphin Island, Alabama, 1986	222	26	490	0
8	Warsaw grouper	Steve Haeusler, Gulf of Mexico, Destin, Florida, 1985	197	92	436	12
9	Lemon shark	Colleen D. Harlow, Buxton, North Carolina, 1988	183	71	405	0
10	Bigeye Atlantic tuna	Cecil Browne, Ocean City, Maryland, 1977	170	46	375	8

ROWER'S ROYAL REVENGE

In 1920 Philadelphia bricklayer John B. Kelly was barred from competing in the British Henley Royal Regatta because, according to Queen Victoria's husband Prince Albert, he was ineligible as a lower class "mechanic, artisan or laborer". At the Antwerp Olympics in that year, however, Kelly triumphed by winning the gold medal in both the single scull and the double scull rowing events. In 1949 Kelly's son, John Jr., not only entered but won the prestigious Diamond Sculls at Henley, while his daughter, the film actress Grace Kelly achieved royal status by marrying Prince Ranier of Monaco.

WOMEN'S WORLD WATER-SKIING TITLE WINNERS

	Skier/nationality	Overall	Slalom	Tricks	Jump	Total
1	Liz Shetter (*née* Allen) (US)	3	3	1	4	11
2	Willa McGuire (*née* Worthington) (US)	3	2	1	2	8
3	Cindy Todd (US)	2	3	0	2	7
4	Deena Mapple (*née* Brush) (US)	2	0	0	4	6
5=	Marina Doria (Swi)	1	1	2	0	4
5=	Natalya Ponomaryeva (*née* Rumyantseva) (USSR)	1	0	3	0	4
7	Maria Victoria Carrasco (Ven)	0	0	3	0	3
8=	Leah Marie Rawls (US)	1	0	1	0	2
8=	Vickie Van Hook (US)	1	1	0	0	2
8=	Sylvie Hulseman (Lux)	1	0	1	0	2
8=	Jeanette Brown (US)	1	1	0	0	2
8=	Jeanette Stewart-Wood (UK)	1	0	0	1	2
8=	Christy Weir (US)	1	0	0	1	2
8=	Evie Wolford (US)	0	2	0	0	2
8=	Kim Laskoff (US)	0	2	0	0	2
8=	Dany Duflot (Fra)	0	0	2	0	2
8=	Ana Marie Carrasco (Ven)	1	0	1	0	2
8=	Nancie Rideout (US)	0	0	0	2	2
8=	Renate Hansluvka (Aut)	0	0	0	2	2
8=	Karen Neville (Aus)	2	0	0	0	2
8=	Tawn Larsen (US)	0	0	2	0	2
8=	Helen Kjellander (Swe)	0	2	0	0	2

MOST RECENT WINNING BOATS AND SKIPPERS IN THE AMERICA'S CUP

	Winning Boat	Winning Skipper	Score	Year
1	*Black Magic*	Russell Coutts	5–0	1995
2	*America 3*	Bill Koch	4–1	1992
3	*Stars & Stripes*	Dennis Conner	2–0	1988
4	*Stars & Stripes*	Dennis Conner	4–0	1987
5	*Australia II*	John Bertrand	4–3	1983
6	*Freedom*	Dennis Conner	4–1	1980
7	*Courageous*	Ted Turner	4–0	1977
8	*Courageous*	Ted Hood	4–0	1974
9	*Intrepid*	Bill Ficker	4–1	1970
10	*Intrepid*	Emil Mosbacher, Jr.	4–0	1967

MEN'S WORLD WATER-SKIING TITLE WINNERS

	Skier/nationality	Overall	Slalom	Tricks	Jump	Total
1	Patrice Martin (France)	3	0	4	0	7
2	Sammy Duvall (US)	4	0	0	2	6
3=	Alfredo Mendoza (US)	2	1	0	2	5
3=	Mike Suyderhoud (US)	2	1	0	2	5
3=	Bob La Point (US)	0	4	1	0	5
6=	George Athans (Canada)	2	1	0	0	3
6=	Guy de Clercq (Belgium)	1	0	0	2	3
6=	Wayne Grimditch (US)	0	0	2	1	3
6=	Mike Hazelwood (UK)	1	0	0	2	3
6=	Ricky McCormick (US)	0	0	1	2	3
6=	Billy Spencer (US)	1	1	1	0	3

The first world championships were held in 1949 at Juan Les Pins, France, three years after the formation of the international governing body, the World Water Ski Union. America's Willa Worthington was the first women's champion, while the men's titles were shared between Christian Jourdan (France) and Guy de Clerq (Belgium).

WORLD CHAMPION
Sammy Duvall, seen here in 1987, the year of his record-breaking fourth overall world title, took his first world crown in 1981. He retained it in 1983 and 1985, also winning two jumping world titles.

SPORTING MISCELLANY

HIGHEST-EARNING SPORTSMEN IN THE WORLD IN 1994

	Name*	Sport	Income ($) Salary/ winnings	Other#	Total
1	Michael Jordan	Basketball	100,000	30,000,000	30,100,000
2	Shaquille O'Neal	Basketball	4,200,000	12,500,000	16,700,000
3	Jack Nicklaus	Golf	300,000	14,500,000	14,800,000
4	Arnold Palmer	Golf	100,000	13,500,000	13,600,000
5	Gerhard Berger (Aut)	Motor racing	12,000,000	1,500,000	13,500,000
6	Wayne Gretzky	Ice hockey	9,000,000	4,500,000	13,500,000
7	Michael Moorer	Boxing	12,000,000	100,000	12,100,000
8	Evander Holyfield	Boxing	10,000,000	2,000,000	12,000,000
9	Andre Agassi	Tennis	1,900,000	9,500,000	11,400,000
10	Nigel Mansell (UK)	Motor racing	9,300,000	2,000,000	11,300,000

* *All sportsmen are from the US, unless otherwise stated*
\# *Sponsorship and royalty income from endorsed sporting products*

Used by permission of Forbes Magazine

Thanks to endorsements, Michael Jordan remains at the top of the list for a third year despite earning very little from basketball after his retirement to pursue a baseball career in 1994. He returned to basketball in March 1995 and may well top the list for a fourth year when his 1995 earnings are published. *Forbes Magazine* lists 40 athletes with total incomes of over $4,800,000. Motor racing is best represented, with eight people in the chart, followed by boxing and tennis, both with seven, football six, basketball five, golf three, and baseball, ice hockey, and soccer with one each. Tennis players Steffi Graf and Gabriela Sabatini, with incomes of $8,000,000 and $4,900,000 respectively, are the only women featuring in the extended list. Nancy Kerrigan, with $4,000,000, came just outside the Top 40.

NIELSEN'S TV AUDIENCES OF ALL TIME FOR SPORTS EVENTS IN THE US

	Program	Date	Households viewing total	%
1	Super Bowl XVI (San Francisco v Cincinnati)	Jan 24, 1982	40,020,000	49.1
2	Super Bowl XVII (Washington v Miami)	Jan 30, 1983	40,500,000	48.6
3	XVII Winter Olympics	Feb 23, 1994	45,690,000	48.5
4	Super Bowl XX (Chicago v New England)	Jan 26, 1986	41,490,000	48.3
5	Super Bowl XII (Dallas v Denver)	Jan 15, 1978	34,410,000	47.2
6	Super Bowl XIII (Dallas v Pittsburgh)	Jan 21, 1979	35,090,000	47.1
7=	Super Bowl XVIII (LA Raiders v Washington)	Jan 22, 1984	38,800,000	46.4
7=	Super Bowl XIX (San Francisco v Miami)	Jan 20, 1985	39,390,000	46.4
9	Super Bowl XIV (LA Rams v Pittsburgh)	Jan 20, 1980	35,330,000	46.3
10	Super Bowl XXI (Giants v Denver)	Jan 25, 1987	40,030,000	45.8

Copyright © 1994 Nielsen Media Research

"TV households" indicates the number of households with TV sets: population growth and the acquisition of sets steadily increase this figure (it now stands at 94,000,000), so recent events attract higher audiences. Thus, the percentage of households with access to a TV who watch a particular sport event provides a more accurate picture of the overall audience.

HIGHEST-EARNING FILMS WITH SPORTING THEMES

	Film	Sport
1	*Rocky IV* (1985)	Boxing
2	*Rocky III* (1982)	Boxing
3	*Rocky* (1976)	Boxing
4	*A League of Their Own* (1992)	Women's baseball
5	*Rocky II* (1979)	Boxing
6=	*Days of Thunder* (1990)	Stock car racing
6=	*White Men Can't Jump* (1992)	Basketball
8	*Chariots of Fire* (1973)	Track
9	*Field of Dreams* (1989)	Baseball
10	*The Main Event* (1979)	Boxing

Boxing dominates Hollywood's biggest sporting successes, followed by baseball, which is also represented by films just outside the Top 10 such as *The Natural* (1984), *Bull Durham* (1988), and *Major League* (1989). Stock car racing, women's baseball, and basketball are unique as sporting themes of successful films.

PARTICIPATION SPORTS, GAMES, AND PHYSICAL ACTIVITIES IN THE US

	Activity	No. participating
1	Walking	70,800,000
2	Swimming	60,300,000
3	Bicycle riding	49,800,000
4	Fishing	45,700,000
5	Exercising with equipment	43,800,000
6	Camping	42,900,000
7	Bowling	37,400,000
8	Billiards/pool	34,000,000
9	Basketball	28,200,000
10	Motor/power boating	26,400,000

A survey by the National Sporting Goods Association showed that in the US, baseball as a participation – rather than a spectator – sport scored relatively low (15,100,000), below softball (18,100,000). Soccer (12,500,000) was up by 21.8 percent on the previous year.

MOST COMMON SPORTING INJURIES

	Common name	Medical term
1	Bruise	A soft tissue contusion
2	Sprained ankle	Sprain of the lateral ligament
3	Sprained knee	Sprain of the medial collateral ligament
4	Low back strain	Lumbar joint dysfunction
5	Hamstring tear	Muscle tear of the hamstrings
6	Jumper's knee	Patella tendinitis
7	Achilles' tendinitis	Tendinitis of the Achilles' tendon
8	Shin splints	Medial periostitis of the tibia
9	Tennis elbow	Lateral epicondylitis
10	Shoulder strain	Rotator cuff tendinitis

WORST DISASTERS AT SPORTS VENUES

(20th century only)

	Location/disaster	Date	No. killed
1	Hong Kong Jockey Club (stand collapse and fire)	Feb 26, 1918	604
2	Lenin Stadium, Moscow, Russia (crush in soccer stadium)	Oct 20, 1982	340
3	Lima, Peru (soccer stadium riot)	May 24, 1964	320
4	Sinceljo, Colombia (bullring stand collapse)	Jan 20, 1980	222
5	Hillsborough, Sheffield, UK (crush in soccer stadium)	Apr 15, 1989	96
6	Le Mans, France (racing car crash)	Jun 11, 1955	82
7	Katmandu, Nepal (stampede in soccer stadium)	Mar 12, 1988	80
8	Buenos Aires, Argentina (riot in soccer stadium)	May 23, 1968	73
9	Ibrox Park, Glasgow, UK (barrier collapse in soccer stadium)	Jan 2, 1971	66
10	Bradford Stadium, UK (fire in soccer stadium)	May 11, 1985	56

The US has been mercifully free of the disasters that have occurred elsewhere at open-air sport venues. However, if gambling is included within the parameters of "sport," the worst incident on record would be that at the MGM Grand Hotel, Las Vegas, NV, on November 21, 1980, when a fire in a kitchen caused a fireball that engulfed the hotel's enormous casino and filled the building with deadly fumes, leaving 84 dead and over 500 injured.

FASTEST WINNING TIMES OF THE IDITAROD DOG SLED RACE

	Winner	Year	day	hr	min	sec
1	Doug Swingley	1995	9	2	42	19
2	Martin Buser	1994	10	13	02	39
3	Jeff King	1993	10	15	38	15
4	Martin Buser	1992	10	19	17	15
5	Susan Butcher	1990	11	01	53	28
6	Susan Butcher	1987	11	02	05	13
7	Joe Runyan	1989	11	05	24	34
8	Susan Butcher	1988	11	11	41	40
9	Susan Butcher	1986	11	15	06	00
10	Rick Swenson	1981	12	08	45	02

The race, which has been held annually since 1973, stretches from Anchorage to Nome, Alaska, the course following an old river mail route covering 1,158 miles/1,864 km. Iditarod is a deserted mining village on the way. The race commemorates an emergency expedition in 1925 to get medical supplies to Nome following a diphtheria epidemic. Men and women compete together on equal terms. Rick Swenson has won the race a record five times. Susan Butcher has won it four times.

THE HUMAN WORLD

THE 10
LONGEST BONES IN THE HUMAN BODY

	Bone	Average length cm	in
1	Femur (thighbone – upper leg)	50.50	19.88
2	Tibia (shinbone – inner lower leg)	43.03	16.94
3	Fibula (outer lower leg)	40.50	15.94
4	Humerus (upper arm)	36.46	14.35
5	Ulna (inner lower arm)	28.20	11.10
6	Radius (outer lower arm)	26.42	10.40
7	Seventh rib	24.00	9.45
8	Eighth rib	23.00	9.06
9	Innominate bone (hipbone – half pelvis)	18.50	7.28
10	Sternum (breastbone)	17.00	6.69

These are average dimensions of the bones of an adult male measured from their extremities (ribs are curved, and the pelvis measurement is taken diagonally). The same bones in the female skeleton are usually 6 to 13 percent smaller, with the exception of the sternum, which is virtually identical.

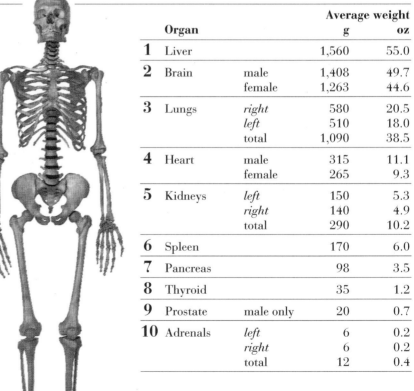

THE 10
LARGEST HUMAN ORGANS

	Organ		Average weight g	oz
1	Liver		1,560	55.0
2	Brain	male	1,408	49.7
		female	1,263	44.6
3	Lungs	*right*	580	20.5
		left	510	18.0
		total	1,090	38.5
4	Heart	male	315	11.1
		female	265	9.3
5	Kidneys	*left*	150	5.3
		right	140	4.9
		total	290	10.2
6	Spleen		170	6.0
7	Pancreas		98	3.5
8	Thyroid		35	1.2
9	Prostate	male only	20	0.7
10	Adrenals	*left*	6	0.2
		right	6	0.2
		total	12	0.4

This list is based on average immediate post-mortem weights, recorded at several hospitals over a 10-year period. If the skin were considered an organ, and since it can comprise 16 percent of a body's total weight (384 oz/10,886 g in a person weighing 150 lb/68 kg), it would head the Top 10.

T O P 1 0

MOST COMMON PHOBIAS

	Object of phobia	Medical term
1	Spiders	Arachnephobia or arachnophobia
2	People and social situations	Anthropophobia or sociophobia
3	Flying	Aerophobia or aviatophobia
4	Open spaces	Agoraphobia, cenophobia, or kenophobia
5	Confined spaces	Claustrophobia, cleisiophobia, cleithrophobia, or clithrophobia
6	Heights	Acrophobia, altophobia, hypsophobia, or hypsiphobia
7	Cancer	Carcinomaphobia, carcinophobia, carcinomatophobia, cancerphobia, or cancerophobia
8	Thunderstorms	Brontophobia or keraunophobia; related phobias are those associated with lightning (astraphobia), cyclones (anemophobia), and hurricanes and tornadoes (lilapsophobia)
9	Death	Necrophobia or thanatophobia
10	Heart disease	Cardiophobia

A phobia is a morbid fear that is out of all proportion to the object of the fear. Many people would admit to being uncomfortable about these principal phobias, as well as others, such as snakes (ophiophobia), injections (trypanophobia), or ghosts (phasmophobia), but most do not become obsessive about them nor allow such fears to rule their lives. True phobias often arise from some incident in childhood when a person has been afraid of some object and has developed an irrational fear that persists into adulthood. Nowadays, as a result of the valuable work done by the Phobics Society and other organizations, phobias can be cured by taking special desensitization courses, for example, to learn how conquer one's fear of flying, or how to face social situations.

T O P 1 0

MOST COMMON ALLERGENS

(Substances that cause allergies)

Food		Environmental
Nuts	**1**	House dust mite (*Dermatophagoides pteronyssinus*)
Shellfish/seafood	**2**	Grass pollens
Milk	**3**	Tree pollens
Wheat	**4**	Cats
Eggs	**5**	Dogs
Fresh fruit (apples, oranges, strawberries, etc.)	**6**	Horses
Fresh vegetables (potatoes, cucumber, etc.)	**7**	Molds (*Aspergillus fumigatus, Alternaria, Cladosporium*, etc.)
Cheese	**8**	Birch pollen
Yeast	**9**	Weed pollen
Soya protein	**10**	Wasp/bee venom

An allergy has been defined as "an unpleasant reaction to foreign matter, specific to that substance, which is altered from the normal response and peculiar to the individual concerned." Allergens are usually foods but may also be environmental agents, such as pollen, which causes hay fever. Reactions can result in symptoms ranging from severe mental or physical disability to minor irritations suchas a mild headache in the presence of fresh paint. "Elimination dieting" to pinpoint and avoid food allergens and identifying and avoiding environmental allergens can result in the complete cure of many allergies.

HOUSE DUST MITE

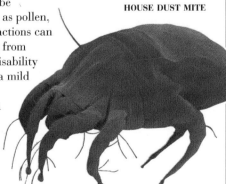

T O P 1 0

MOST COMMON BLOOD GROUPS IN THE UK

(Data provided by the National Blood Transfusion Service)

	Group	Percentage*		Group	Percentage*
1	O+	37.44	**6**	A_1–	5.04
2	A_1+	28.56	**7**	AB_1+	2.72
3	B+	8.00	**8**	B–	2.00
4	A_2+	7.14	**9**	A_2–	1.26
5	O–	6.60	**10**	AB_1–	0.48

This list presents a breakdown for blood groups in 10 categories. A US equivalent is unavailable, since US methods divide blood into eight groups, but the proportions are very similar (the percentage of O+ and O– are in fact identical), emphasizing the common racial stock of the two countries.

* Total is less than 100 percent as a result of rounding-off and the existence of rare subgroups.

MATTERS OF LIFE & DEATH

TOP 10

COUNTRIES WITH THE MOST HOSPITALS

	Country	Beds per 10,000	Hospitals
1	China	23	63,101
2	Brazil	37	28,972
3	India	8	25,452
4	Russia	135	12,711
5	Nigeria	9	11,588
6	Vietnam	25	10,768
7	Pakistan	6	10,673
8	Japan	136	10,096
9	North Korea	135	7,924
10	US	47	6,738

TOP 10

COUNTRIES WITH THE MOST DOCTORS

	Country	Patients per doctor	Doctors
1	China	648	1,808,000
2	Russia	226	657,800
3	US	416	614,000
4	India	2,337	365,000
5	Germany	313	251,877
6	Italy	228	249,704
7	Ukraine	226	228,900
8	Japan	583	211,797
9	Brazil	848	169,500
10	Spain	257	153,306

Comparing doctor numbers and patient-doctor ratios between countries is tricky: the figures for Russia and the Ukraine include dentists, and those for China include practioners of traditional medicine.

TOP 10

COUNTRIES WITH THE MOST NURSES

	Country	Nurses*
1	US	1,853,000
2	Russia	1,691,000
3	China	1,040,000
4	Japan	721,403
5	Germany	708,000
6	Ukraine	618,000
7	India	340,208
8	France	308,141
9	UK	300,698
10	Canada	262,288

* Totals include midwives

TOP 10

COUNTRIES WITH THE HIGHEST MALE LIFE EXPECTANCY

	Country	Life expectancy at birth (years)
1	Japan	75.9
2=	Iceland	75.1
2=	Macau	75.1
4	Hong Kong	75.0
5	Israel	74.9
6	Sweden	74.6
7	Spain	74.4
8	Switzerland	74.1
9=	Andorra	74.0
9=	Netherlands	74.0
9=	Norway	74.0
	US	72.0

The generally increasing life expectancy for males in the Top 10 countries contrasts sharply with that in many underdeveloped countries, particularly the majority of African countries, where it rarely exceeds 45 years. Sierra Leone at the bottom of the league with 41.4 years.

TOP 10

COUNTRIES WITH THE MOST DENTISTS

	Country	Dentists
1	US	179,000
2	Brazil	97,675
3	Japan	74,208
4	Germany	56,342
5	France	38,146
6	Argentina	21,900
7	UK	17,456
8	Poland	16,615
9	Canada	14,621
10	Colombia	14,050

TOP 10

COUNTRIES WITH THE HIGHEST FEMALE LIFE EXPECTANCY

	Country	Life expectancy at birth (years)
1	Japan	81.8
2=	France	81.0
2=	Andorra	81.0
4	Switzerland	80.9
5	Iceland	80.8
6=	Hong Kong	80.3
6=	Macau	80.3
8=	Sweden	80.2
8=	Netherlands	80.2
10	Norway	80.0
	US	78.9

Female life expectancy in all of the Top 10 countries exceeds 80 years. This represents the average: as many women are now living beyond this age as die before attaining it. The comparative figure for such Third World countries as Sierra Leone, where it is 44.6 years for women, makes for less encouraging reading.

TOP 10

MOST COMMON CAUSES OF DEATH IN THE US

	Cause	1992	1993
1	Diseases of the heart	717,706	739,580
2	Cancer	520,576	530,870
3	Cerebrovascular diseases	143,769	149,740
4	Chronic obstructive pulmonary diseases and allied conditions	91,938	101,090
5	Accidents and adverse effects	86,777	88,630 *
6	Pneumonia and influenza	76,120	81,730
7	Diabetes	50,067	55,110
8	Human Immune deficiency Virus infection	33,566	38,500
9	Suicide	30,464	31,230
10	Homicide and legal intervention	25,488	25,470

Comprises: motor vehicle accidents (40,982) and all other accidents and adverse affects (45,795)

Source: National Center for Health Statistics

The principal causes of death in the United States remain broadly similar from year to year, though with an observable downward trend for heart disease and an increase in the incidence of cancer. Suicides, similarly, have risen inexorably during the 20th century from a 1900 total of 2,036. Deaths resulting from once significant diseases such as tuberculosis are now relatively rare. In the "Accidents and adverse effects" category, almost half the deaths result from motor vehicle accidents.

TOP 10

COUNTRIES WITH THE MOST DEATHS CAUSED BY CANCER

	Country	Deaths per 100,000 population
1	Isle of Man	337.8
2	Guernsey	314.3
3	Hungary	313.0
4	Denmark	292.2
5	UK	280.8
6	Belgium	274.6
7	Czech Republic	270.0
8	Germany	263.2
9	Luxembourg	255.4
10	Italy	251.5

TOP 10

COUNTRIES WITH THE MOST DEATHS CAUSED BY DISEASES OF THE CIRCULATORY SYSTEM

	Country	Deaths per 100,000 population
1	Bulgaria	768.1
2	Latvia	759.9
3	Estonia	746.7
4	Hungary	738.6
5	Romania	707.7
6	Isle of Man	701.6
7	Ukraine	671.0
8	Czech Republic	649.8
9	Russia	625.8
10	Lithuania	620.1
	US	364.7

TOP 10

OVER-THE-COUNTER* HEALTH CARE PRODUCTS IN THE US

	Product	Annual sales ($)
1	Cough, cold, allergy, and sinus remedies	1,590,000,000
2	Internal analgesics (painkillers)	1,097,000,000
3	Oral care products	1,071,000,000
4	Feminine products	990,000,000
5	Vitamins	880,000,000
6	First aid	823,000,000
7	Laxatives	752,000,000
8	Eye and contact lens care	575,000,000
9	Foot care products	241,000,000
10	Diet needs	228,000,000

* Nonprescription, drugstore sales only

Total sales through drugstores of just the Top 10 nonprescription or "over-the-counter" health care products exceeds $8,000,000,000 a year, an ever-escalating figure that reflects such factors as increasing public interest in health self-help and the growing availability of medicines that were previously obtainable only from a pharmicist by prescription. Sales of many such items follow trends, both those related to health (influenza epidemics, for example, naturally mean an increase in the sales of flu remedies), and fashions that may be prompted by advertising or other factors: in the UK there was a well-documented surge in the sales of vitamins following a much-publicized TV program that had linked their consumption with intelligence in children. As a result vitamins briefly became the No.1 bestselling nonprescription item. They remain the drugstore item with most different types available, a total approaching 2,000 varieties.

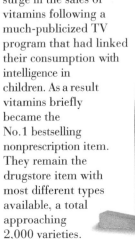

FOR BETTER OR FOR WORSE

In 1946, immediately after the end of World War II, the number of marriages in the United States hit a new high of 2,291,000, a figure that was not exceeded until 1979. The all-time peak was reached in 1984, when there were 2,477,000 marriages and, despite population increases, has since declined to levels that were reached during the 1970s. Although high divorce rates are a relatively modern phenomenon, the national censuses taken around the turn of the century show that the US was already the world leader with 199,500 people (114,930 women and 84,570 men) recorded as divorced. As with the postwar marriage boom, a postwar divorce boom was registered in 1946, when 610,000 divorces were granted. The number first topped 1,000,000 in 1975 and by 1992 had escalated to 1,215,000.

TOP 10

MOST COMMON CAUSES OF MARITAL DISCORD AND BREAKDOWN

1	Lack of communication
2	Continual arguments
3	Infidelity
4	Sexual problems
5	Physical or verbal abuse
6	Financial problems, recession, and unemployment fears
7	Work (usually one partner devoting excessive time to work)
8	Children (whether to have them; attitudes toward their upbringing)
9	Addiction (to drinking, gambling, spending, etc.)
10	Step-parenting

Although this list is based on research by the British marriage counseling organization Relate, its findings are similar to those encountered in the US and throughout Western industrialized society. In recent years financial problems have featured increasingly prominently among the difficulties facing many married couples.

TOP 10

COUNTRIES WITH THE HIGHEST DIVORCE RATE

	Country	Divorces per 1,000 p.a.
1	Maldives	7.9
2	US	4.7
3	Latvia	4.2
4	Cuba	4.1
5	Russia	4.0
6=	Puerto Rico	3.9
6=	Ukraine	3.9
8	Estonia	3.7
9	Belarus	3.4
10	Moldavia	3.0
	UK	2.9

TOP 10

COUNTRIES WITH THE HIGHEST MARRIAGE RATE

	Country	Marriages per 1,000 p.a.*
1	Northern Mariana Islands	31.2
2	US Virgin Islands	18.0
3	Bermuda	15.2
4	Benin	12.8
5	Guam	12.0
6	Bangladesh	11.6
7	Mauritius	10.7
8	Azerbaijan	10.4
9=	Kazakhstan	10.0
9=	Cayman Islands	10.0
9=	Uzbekistan	10.0
	US	9.4
	UK	6.0

During latest period for which figures available

The apparent world record marriage rate in the US territory of the Northern Mariana Islands, which has a total population of under 44,000, may be something of a statistical "blip" resulting from marriages of those visiting the islands, which has the effect of distorting the national pattern.

DID YOU KNOW

"I DO, I DO, I DO . . . "

Polygyny, the custom of a man taking more than one wife, has been practiced since ancient times: according to the Bible, King Solomon had 700 wives. In the nineteenth century, Joseph Smith, who was the American founder of Mormonism, had 49 wives, and his successor, Brigham Young, had 27 (17 of whom, along with 56 children, outlived him). Polygyny is now illegal in the West, but serial marriages, especially among the rich and famous, have taken over: US millionaire Tommy Manville (1894–1967) married 13 times, while movie stars Zsa Zsa Gabor, Mickey Rooney, and Elizabeth Taylor have all married eight times. Ms. Taylor married and divorced Richard Burton twice.

TOP 10

MONTHS FOR MARRIAGES IN THE US

	Month	Marriages
1	August	254,000
2	June	252,000
3	July	235,000
4	May	221,000
5	September	218,000
6	October	216,000
7	December	185,000
8	April	174,000
9	November	162,000
10	March	157,000

The figures are for 1993, when 2,334,000 weddings took place in the US, a decrease of 28,000 from 1992. February is in 11th place with 154,000 weddings, and January in 12th with 103,000. Overall, marriages in the US topped 1,000,000 a year early this century and exceeded 2,000,000 per year for the first time in 1946, a figure that was not reached again until 1968. The peak year on record was 1982, with 2,456,000 marriages.

FIRST WEDDING ANNIVERSARY GIFTS

1	Cotton
2	Paper
3	Leather
4	Fruit and flowers
5	Wood
6	Sugar (or iron)
7	Wool or copper
8	Bronze (or electrical appliances)
9	Pottery (or willow)
10	Tin (or aluminum)

The custom of celebrating each wedding anniversary with a specific type of gift has a long tradition but has changed much over the years – for example, in the association of electrical appliances with the 8th anniversary. It varies considerably from country to country: in the US and UK many of the earlier themes are often disregarded in favor of the "milestone" anniversaries: the 25th (silver), 40th (ruby), 50th (gold), and 60th (diamond). Actually, it is the 75th anniversary that is the "diamond" one, but few married couples live long enough to celebrate it, so it is usually commemorated as the 60th.

US STATES WITH THE MOST WEDDINGS

	State	Weddings (1993)
1	California	203,897
2	Texas	185,642
3	New York	151,477
4	Florida	142,937
5	Nevada	123,184
6	Illinois	91,579
7	Ohio	88,864
8	Pennsylvania	76,679
9	Tennessee	73,052
10	Michigan	71,222

US STATES WITH THE MOST DIVORCES

	State*	Divorces (1993)
1	Texas	98,650
2	Florida	83,581
3	New York	56,729
4	Ohio	51,243
5	Illinois	43,228
6	Pennsylvania	39,639
7	Michigan	39,183
8	Georgia	38,349
9	North Carolina	34,927
10	Tennessee	33,199

* *Figures not available for California, Indiana, Louisiana, and Nevada*

WHAT'S IN A NAME?

TOP 10

GIRLS' AND BOYS' NAMES IN THE US

Girls		Boys
Brittany	**1**	Michael
Ashley	**2**	Christopher
Jessica	**3**	Matthew
Amanda	**4**	Joshua
Sarah	**5**	Andrew
Megan	**6**	James
Caitlin	**7**	John
Samantha	**8**	Nicholas
Stephanie	**9**	Justin
Katherine	**10**	David

American name fashions are highly volatile and vary considerably according to the child's ethnic background and the influences of popular culture. Jennifer, for example, rose to No. 2 position because the heroine of the book and 1970 movie *Love Story* had this name, and Tiffany entered the Top 10 in 1980 in the wake of the TV series *Charlie's Angels* and its character Tiffany Welles. Ashley rose to prominence only in the 1980s: by 1984 it was already being noted as the girl's name of the year, (just as Angela had been 10 years earlier), and by 1990 it had reached No. 1. This pattern has been mirrored in the 1990s with Brittany, a name that does not even make an appearance among the Top 100 of British girls' names; only Jessica and Katherine (or, rather, Catherine with a "C") appear in the Top 10s of both countries. In contrast, six of the Top 10 US boys' names (Michael, Christopher, Matthew, Joshua, Andrew, and James) also appear in the British Top 10. Michael has topped every US list for 30 years, while Joshua appeared in the Top 10 for the first time in 1983. Richard plummeted from the ranking after Richard Nixon's disgrace in the Watergate scandal and has not regained its former popularity.

TOP 10

MOST COMMON SURNAMES IN THE US

	Surname	Number
1	Smith	2,382,509
2	Johnson	1,807,263
3	Williams/Williamson	1,568,939
4	Brown	1,362,910
5	Jones	1,331,205
6	Miller	1,131,205
7	Davis	1,047,848
8	Martin/Martinez/ Martinson	1,046,297
9	Anderson/Andersen	825,648
10	Wilson	787,825

The United States Social Security Administration last published its survey of the most common surnames 20 years ago, based on the number of people for whom it had more than 10,000 files, which covered a total of 3,169 names. The SSA has not repeated the exercise, but it is probable that the ranking order has remained very similar.

TOP 10

MOST COMMON NAMES OF MOVIE CHARACTERS

	Name	Characters
1	Jack	126
2	John	104
3	Frank	87
4	Harry	72
5	David	63
6	George	62
7=	Michael	59
7=	Tom	59
9	Mary	54
10	Paul	53

Based on Simon Rose's *One FM Essential Film Guide* (1993) survey of feature films released in the period 1983–93.

TOP 10

MOST COMMON US SURNAMES DERIVED FROM OCCUPATIONS

1	Smith
2	Miller
3	Taylor
4	Clark (cleric)
5	Walker (cloth worker)
6	Wright (workman)
7	Baker
8	Carter (driver or maker of carts)
9	Stewart (steward)
10	Turner (woodworker)

It is reckoned that about one in six US surnames – especially among families of European origin – recalls the occupation of the holder's ancestors. Several US Presidents have borne such surnames, including Zachary Taylor and Jimmy Carter, both of which feature in the Top 10. Less obvious is that of 19th President Rutherford Hayes, since Hayes was the name once given to a person in charge of hedges.

TOP 10

INITIAL LETTERS OF SURNAMES IN THE US

%	Rarest letter		Most common letter	%
0.1	X	**1**	S	9.8
0.3	Q	**2**	B	7.0
0.9	U	**3**	M	6.5
1.2	I	**4**	K	6.4
1.3	Y	**5**	D	5.9
2.0	J	**6**	C, P	5.5
2.2	Z	**7**	G	5.2
2.5	E	**8**	L	5.0
2.6	0	**9**	A	4.8
2.7	N, V	**10**	T	4.6

The frequency of the in-between initial letters is: H and R – 4.4%, F – 3.3%, and W – 3.1%.

TOP 10

MOST COMMON SURNAMES OF EUROPEAN ORIGIN IN THE US

(As recorded by the US Social Security Administration, 1974)

	German*	Irish	Italian	Scottish	Welsh#
1	Myers	Murphy	Russo	Morrison	Williams
2	Schmidt	Kelly #**	Lombardo/Lombardi	Scott	Jones
3	Hoffman(n)	Sullivan	Romano	Campbell	Davis
4	Wagner#	Kennedy**	Marino	Stewart	Thomas
5	Meyer	Bryant	Lorenzo ##	Ross	Lewis
6	Schwarz	Kelley #**	Costa ##	Graham	Evans
7	Schneider	Burke	Luna	Hamilton	Rogers
8	Zimmerman(n)	Riley	Rossi/Rossini	Murray	Morgan
9	Keller	O'Brien	Esposito	Kennedy‡	Hughes
10	Klein	McCoy	Gallo	Gordon	Price

* *Excluding those that have been anglicized, such as Schmidt/Smith*

\# *Sometimes of English origin*

***Sometimes of Scottish origin*

\#\#*Sometimes of Spanish/Portuguese origin*

‡ *May also be of Irish origin*

The SSA's method of enumerating names was based on the first six letters, so that the count of some names may be distorted – the Morrisons by those with the surname Morris, for instance. The highest number recorded for a Mc or Mac surname is that of Mackinnon (98,162 examples).

TOP 10

MOST COMMON PATRONYMS IN THE US

1	Johnson ("son of John")	7	Wilson ("son of Will")
2	Williams/Williamson ("son of William")	8	Harris/Harrison ("son of Harry")
3	Jones ("son of John")	9	Thomas ("son of Thomas")
4	Davis ("son of Davie/David")	10	Thomson/Thompson ("son of Thomas")
5	Martin/Martinez/Martinson ("son of Martin")		
6	Anderson/Andersen ("son of Andrew")		

Patronyms are names recalling a father or other ancestor. Up to one-third of all US surnames may be patronymic in origin.

THE 10

LAST NAMES IN THE SAN FRANCISCO PHONE BOOK

1	Zytron First Image Management Co.
2	Zyzinski, John
3	Zyzzyva
4	Zzcor, W.
5	Zzoble, N.
6	Zzyzx Group
7	Zzzzonzo, Z.
8	Zzzzyux
9	Zzzzzz, Bob
10	Zzzzzz, Otto

TOP 10

MOST COMMON SURNAMES IN THE MANHATTAN TELEPHONE DIRECTORY

1	Smith
2	Brown/Browne
3	Williams/Williamson
4	Cohen (and variant spellings)
5	Lee
6	Johnson
7	Rodriguez
8	Green/Greene
9	Davis
10	Jones

TOP 10

MOST COMMON SURNAMES OF HISPANIC ORIGIN IN THE US

1	Rodriguez
2	Gonzalez
3	Garcia
4	Lopez
5	Rivera
6	Martinez
7	Hernandez
8	Perez
9	Sanchez
10	Torres

ORGANIZATIONS

TOP 10

MOST COMMON TYPES OF MEMBERSHIP ORGANIZATION IN THE US

	Organization*	Number
1	Commercial	3,837
2	Health, medical	2,235
3	Public affairs	2,209
4	Cultural	1,897
5	Social welfare	1,833
6	Hobby, avocational	1,516
7	Scientific, technological	1,360
8	Educational	1,301
9	Religious	1,230
10	Agriculture	1,130

* Nonprofit organizations as assessed by the Encyclopedia of Associations

TOP 10

MEMBERSHIP ORGANIZATIONS IN THE US

	Organization	Approx. membership
1	American Automobile Association	35,000,000
2	American Association of Retired Persons	33,000,000
3	National Right to Life Committee	7,500,000
4	National Parents and Teachers Association	7,000,000
5	National Committee to Preserve Social Security and Medicare	6,000,000
6	Boy Scouts of America National Council	5,355,397
7	National Council of Senior Citizens	5,000,000
8	American Farm Bureau Federation	4,200,000
9	National Wildlife Federation	4,000,000
10	American Heart Association	3,510,313

TOP 10

LABOR UNIONS IN THE US

	Union	Members
1	National Education Association	2,000,000
2=	International Brotherhood of Teamsters, Chauffeurs, Warehousemen and Helpers of America	1,400,000
2=	United Food and Commercial Workers' International Union	1,400,000
4	American Federation of State, County and Municipal Employees	1,300,000
5	International Union of Service Employees	1,030,000
6	American Federation of Teachers	850,000
7	International Brotherhood of Electrical Workers	800,000
8	International Union of Automobile, Aerospace and Agricultural Implement Workers of America	796,729
9	Laborers' International Union of North America	700,000
10	Communications Workers of America	650,000

The declining membership of labor unions in the US corresponds to that of other countries, reflecting the reduction in the labor forces of many industries. Fifty years ago 35.5 percent of all US workers belonged to unions: by 1993 this figure had fallen to 15.8 percent.

TOP 10

ENVIRONMENTAL ORGANIZATIONS IN THE US

	Organization	Year founded	Annual Budget ($)	Membership
1	National Wildlife Federation	1936	82,816,324	4,000,000
2	Greenpeace	1971	48,777,308	1,700,000
3	World Wildfire Fund	1961	60,791,945	1,000,000
4	The Nature Conservancy	1951	278,497,634	708,000
5	Sierra Club	1892	41,716,044	550,000
6	National Audubon Society	1905	40,081,591	542,000
7	National Parks and Conservation Association	1919	11,285,639	400,000
8	The Wilderness Society	1935	16,093,764	293,000
9	Environmental Defense Fund	1967	17,394,230	250,000
10	Natural Resources Defense Council	1970	20,496,829	170,000

While some of the organizations in this list are relatively modern foundations, their growing membership mirroring international concerns with the environment, the National Audubon Society has celebrated its 90th anniversary and the venerable Sierra Club, founded by Scottish-born naturalist John Muir, has passed its centenary.

US STATES WITH THE MOST GIRL SCOUTS

	State	Girl Scouts
1	California	217,441
2	New York	176,092
3	Illinois	150,737
4	Texas	150,561
5	Pennsylvania	149,987
6	Ohio	143,597
7	Michigan	116,872
8	New Jersey	94,901
9	Florida	93,200
10	Missouri	87,642

The Girl Guides, founded by Juliet Gordon Low in Savannah, Georgia, on March 12, 1912, took the British Girl Guides as its model. It changed its name to Girl Scouts in 1913. Total membership declined in the mid-1980s, but has increased since then to levels approaching those of the early 1970s. There are now 2,561,378 girl members.

COUNTRIES WITH THE HIGHEST GIRL GUIDE AND GIRL SCOUT MEMBERSHIP

	Country	Membership
1	US	3,510,313
2	Philippines	1,250,928
3	India	758,575
4	UK	707,651
5	South Korea	184,993
6	Pakistan	101,634
7	Indonesia	98,656
8	Malaysia	92,539
9	Japan	88,331
10	Australia	87,331

The Girl Guide Movement was started in 1910 by Sir Robert Baden-Powell and his sister, Agnes (1858–1945). Today the World Association of Girl Guides and Girl Scouts has 128 national member organizations with a total membership of 8,500,000.

COUNTRIES WITH THE HIGHEST BOY SCOUT MEMBERSHIP

	Country	Membership
1	US	4,625,800
2	Philippines	2,350,710
3	India	2,272,700
4	Indonesia	2,134,368
5	UK	657,466
6	Bangladesh	368,063
7	Pakistan	326,753
8	South Korea	309,460
9	Thailand	274,123
10	Canada	269,425

Following an experimental camp held from July 29 to August 9, 1907 on Brownsea Island, Dorset, England, Sir Robert Baden-Powell (1857–1941), a former general in the British army, launched the Scouting Movement. There are now more than 25,000,000 Scouts in 211 countries and territories. There are just 13 countries where Scouting does not exist or is forbidden for political reasons, such as China.

BOY SCOUTS
The Boy Scouts organization, founded in 1908, accepts boys between 11 and 15 years of age. It combines an emphasis on moral values with enjoyable and challenging physical activities.

US WOMEN'S ORGANIZATIONS

	Organization	Membership
1	National Organization for Women	280,000
2	National Organization for Female Executives	250,000
3	Daughters of the American Revolution	204,000
4	Association of Junior Leagues International	190,000
5	International Ladies Garment Workers Union	173,000
6	American Association of University Women	135,000
7	National Federation of Business and Professional Women's Clubs	125,000
8	National Women's Political Caucus	75,000
9	National Council of Negro Women	40,000
10	Women's Campaign Fund	23,000

BOYS SCOUTS' MERIT BADGES

	Badge	Badge No.	Total awarded
1	Swimming	21	83,131
2	First Aid	0	82,790
3	Camping	1	62,146
4	Environmental Science	4	59,870
5	Leatherwork	1	57,353
6	Canoeing	2	52,054
7	Citizenship in Nation	5	52,000
8	Citizenship in Community	4	51,014
9	Safety	06	48,667
10	Citizenship in World	6	48,556

PEOPLE IN POWER

TOP 10

LONGEST-SERVING PRESIDENTS IN THE WORLD TODAY

	President	Country	Took office
1	Marshal Mobutu Sésé Séko	Zaïre	November 24, 1965
2	General Suharto	Indonesia	March 28, 1967
3	General Gnassingbé Eyadéma	Togo	April 14, 1967
4	El Hadj Omar Bongo	Gabon	December 2, 1967
5	Colonel Mu'ammar Gadhafi	Libya	September 1, 1969
6	Lt.-General Hafiz al-Asad	Syria	February 22, 1971
7	Fidel Castro	Cuba	December 2, 1976
8	France Albert René	Seychelles	June 5, 1977
9	Hassan Gouled Aptidon	Djibouti	September 30, 1977
10	Daniel Teroitich arap Moi	Kenya	October 14, 1978

Félix Houphouët-Boigny, President of the Côte d'Ivoire, died on December 7, 1993 after serving as leader of his country since November 27, 1960. Having been born on October 18, 1905, he was, at 88, the oldest President in the world. President Kim Il-song of North Korea was President from December 28, 1972 until his death on July 8, 1994. Alhaji Sir Dawda Kairaba Jawara, President of The Gambia from April 24, 1970, was ousted by a military coup on July 23, 1994.

DID YOU KNOW

FIFTY YEARS ON

The United Nations was set up in 1945 to maintain international peace and security and to solve economic, social, cultural, and humanitarian problems and disputes through international cooperation. It has no right of intervention but acts as negotiator in the event of a dispute, with or between states. It depends entirely on the goodwill of its members for its effectiveness. UN troops can defend only themselves and may never act as aggressors. The UN initially had 51 member states that signed the original charter in 1945. Today, only a few countries do not belong, usually because they have extremely small populations and limited financial resources, although there are two notable exceptions: Switzerland and the Vatican City are not members, although they have permanent observer status, so they are able to maintain absolute neutrality.

THE 10

FIRST NATIONS TO RATIFY THE UN CHARTER

	Country	Date
1	Nicaragua	Jul 6, 1945
2	US	Aug 8, 1945
3	France	Aug 31, 1945
4	Dominican Republic	Sep 4, 1945
5	New Zealand	Sep 19, 1945
6	Brazil	Sep 21, 1945
7	Argentina	Sep 24, 1945
8	China	Sep 28, 1945
9	Denmark	Oct 9, 1945
10	Chile	Oct 11, 1945

In New York on June 26, 1945, only weeks after the end of World War II in Europe, 50 nations signed the World Security Charter. Each of the individual signatories ratified the Charter within their own countries over the ensuing months, and the United Nations came into effect on October 24. It now has 184 members.

TOP 10

US PRESIDENTS WITH THE MOST POPULAR VOTES

	President	Year	Votes
1	Ronald Reagan	1984	54,455,075
2	George Bush	1988	48,886,097
3	Richard Nixon	1972	47,169,911
4	Bill Clinton	1992	44,909,889
5	Ronald Reagan	1980	43,899,248
6	Lyndon Johnson	1964	43,129,484
7	Jimmy Carter	1976	40,830,763
8	Dwight Eisenhower	1956	35,590,472
9	John F. Kennedy	1960	34,226,731
10	Dwight Eisenhower	1952	33,936,234

Despite population increases and the enfranchisement of 18- to 21-year-olds in 1972, the Top 10 ranking shows that it is not the most recent Presidential elections that have attracted the greatest number of popular votes for the winning candidate. Also, many Presidents have won with less than 50 percent of the total popular vote: in 1824, John Quincy Adams achieved only 108,740 votes, or 30.5 percent of the total, and in 1860 Abraham Lincoln had just 1,865,593 – 39.8 percent.

TOP 10

US PRESIDENTS WITH THE MOST ELECTORAL VOTES

	President	Year	Votes
1	Ronald Reagan	1984	525
2	Franklin Roosevelt	1936	523
3	Richard Nixon	1972	520
4	Ronald Reagan	1980	489
5	Lyndon Johnson	1964	486
6	Franklin Roosevelt	1932	472
7	Dwight Eisenhower	1956	457
8	Franklin Roosevelt	1940	449
9	Herbert Hoover	1928	444
10	Dwight Eisenhower	1952	442

T H E 1 0

FIRST COUNTRIES TO GIVE WOMEN THE VOTE

	Country	Year
1	New Zealand	1893
2	Australia (South Australia 1894; Western Australia 1898; Australia united 1901)	1901
3	Finland (then a Grand Duchy under the Russian Crown)	1906
4	Norway (restricted franchise; all women over 25 1913)	1907
5	Denmark and Iceland (a Danish dependency until 1918)	1915
6	Canada	1917
7	Great Britain and Ireland (Ireland part of the United Kingdom until 1921; women over 30 only – lowered to 21 in 1928)	Feb 6, 1918
8	USSR	Jun 1918
9	Germany	Nov 12, 1918
10	Latvia	Nov 18, 1918

Although not a country, the Isle of Man was the first place to give women the vote, in 1880. Until 1920 the only other European countries to enfranchise women were Sweden in 1919 and Czechoslovakia in 1920. Certain states of the US gave women the vote at earlier dates (Wyoming in 1869, Colorado in 1894, Utah in 1895, and Idaho in 1896), but it was not granted nationally until 1920. A number of countries, such as France and Italy, did not give women the vote until 1945. Switzerland did not allow women to vote in elections to the Federal Council until 1971, and Liechtenstein was one of the last to relent, in 1984. In certain countries, such as Saudi Arabia, women are not allowed to vote at all – nor are men.

MRS. INDIRA GANDHI
Unrelated to Mahatma Gandhi, but daughter of India's first Prime Minister, Jawaharlal Nehru, Indira Gandhi died in office, shot by Sikh extremists. She was succeeded by her son Rajiv, who was himself later assassinated by Tamil Tigers.

T O P 1 0

WORLD PARLIAMENTS WITH MOST WOMEN MEMBERS

	Country	Women MPs	Total MPs	% women
1	Sweden	141	349	40.40
2	Norway	65	165	39.39
3	Denmark	60	179	33.52
4	Finland	67	200	33.50
5	Netherlands	47	150	31.33
6	Seychelles	9	33	27.27
7	Germany	177	672	26.34
8	Mozambique	63	250	25.20
9	South Africa	100	400	25.00
10	Iceland	15	63	23.81

Based on up-to-date general election results for all democratic countries, this list is based on the lower chamber if the parliament has two chambers. Just 18 countries have more than 20 percent of women MPs. With 62 women MPs out of 651, the UK has 9.5 percent, its highest ever proportion.

T H E 1 0

FIRST FEMALE PRIME MINISTERS AND PRESIDENTS

	Name	Country	Period in office
1	Sirimavo Bandaranaike (PM)	Ceylon (Sri Lanka)	1960–64/1970–77
2	Indira Gandhi (PM)	India	1966–84
3	Golda Meir (PM)	Israel	1969–74
4	Maria Estela Perón (President)	Argentina	1974–75
5	Elisabeth Domitien (PM)	Central African Republic	1975
6	Margaret Thatcher (PM)	UK	May 1979–Nov 1990
7	Dr. Maria Lurdes Pintasilgo (PM)	Portugal	Aug–Nov 1979
8	Vigdís Finnbogadóttir (President)	Iceland	Jun 1980–
9	Mary Eugenia Charles (PM)	Dominica	Jul 1980–
10	Gro Harlem Brundtland (PM)	Norway	Feb–Oct 1981/ May 1986–Oct 1989

The first 10 have been followed by Corazón Aquino, who became President of the Philippines in 1986, Benazir Bhutto, Prime Minister of Pakistan (1988–90; 1993–), Violeta Barrios de Chamorro, President of Nicaragua (1990–), Ertha Pascal-Trouillot, President of Haiti (1990–), and Mary Robinson, President of the Irish Republic (1990–). Since 1990, several more countries have appointed female Prime Ministers, including France (Edith Cresson), Canada (Kim Campbell), Burundi (Sylvie Kinigi), and Turkey (Tansu Çiller).

ALL THE PRESIDENTS

48

FIRST PRESIDENTS OF THE US

President (dates)	Period of office
1 George Washington (1732–99)	1789–97
2 John Adams (1735–1826)	1797–1801
3 Thomas Jefferson (1743–1826)	1801–09
4 James Madison (1751–1836)	1809–17
5 James Monroe (1758–1831)	1817–25
6 John Quincy Adams (1767–1848)	1825–29
7 Andrew Jackson (1767–1845)	1829–37
8 Martin Van Buren (1782–1862)	1837–41
9 William H. Harrison (1773–1841)	1841
10 John Tyler (1790–1862)	1841–45

TALLEST US PRESIDENTS

President	Height m	ft	in
1 Abraham Lincoln	1.93	6	4
2 Lyndon B. Johnson	1.91	6	3
3= William Clinton	1.89	6	2½
3= Thomas Jefferson	1.89	6	2½
5= Chester A. Arthur	1.88	6	2
5= George H.W. Bush	1.88	6	2
5= Franklin D. Roosevelt	1.88	6	2
5= George Washington	1.88	6	2
9= Andrew Jackson	1.85	6	1
9= Ronald W. Reagan	1.85	6	1

HIGH OFFICE
It has been suggested that Abraham Lincoln, the tallest US President, suffered from an hereditary disease known as Marfan syndrome. Those affected tend to be lanky, have hands with extremely long fingers, and large feet.

LONGEST-SERVING US PRESIDENTS

President	Period in office years	days
1 Franklin D. Roosevelt	12	39
2= Grover Cleveland	8*	
2= Dwight Eisenhower	8*	
2= Ulysses S. Grant	8*	
2= Andrew Jackson	8*	
2= Thomas Jefferson	8*	
2= James Madison	8*	
2= James Monroe	8*	
2= Ronald W. Reagan	8*	
2= Woodrow Wilson	8*	

* Two four-year terms – now the maximum any US President may remain in office

SHORTEST-SERVING US PRESIDENTS

President	Period in office years	days
1 William H. Harrison		32
2 James A. Garfield		199
3 Zachary Taylor	1	128
4 Gerald R. Ford	2	150
5 Warren G. Harding	2	151
6 Millard Fillmore	2	236
7 John F. Kennedy	2	306
8 Chester A. Arthur	3	166
9 Andrew Johnson	3	323
10 John Tyler	3	332

SHORTEST US PRESIDENTS

President	Height m	ft	in
1 James Madison	1.63	5	4
2= Benjamin Harrison	1.68	5	6
2= Martin Van Buren	1.68	5	6
4= John Adams	1.70	5	7
4= John Quincy Adams	1.70	5	7
4= William McKinley	1.70	5	7
7= William H. Harrison	1.73	5	8
7= James K. Polk	1.73	5	8
7= Zachary Taylor	1.73	5	8
10= Ulysses S. Grant	1.74	5	8½
10= Rutherford B. Hayes	1.74	5	8½

THE 10

LAST US PRESIDENTS AND VICE-PRESIDENTS TO DIE IN OFFICE

	Name/date	Office
1	John F. Kennedy* November 22, 1963	P
2	Franklin D. Roosevelt April 12, 1945	P
3	Warren G. Harding August 2, 1923	P
4	James S. Sherman October 30, 1912	VP
5	William McKinley* September 14, 1901	P
6	Garret A. Hobart November 21, 1899	VP
7	Thomas A. Hendricks November 25, 1885	VP
8	James A. Garfield* September 19, 1881	P
9	Henry Wilson November 10, 1875	VP
10	Abraham Lincoln* April 15, 1865	P

* *Assassinated*

PRESIDENT FOR A DAY

David Rice Atchison served as US President for a single day – March 4, 1849. Newly elected President Zachary Taylor's predecessor James Knox Polk's term of office ended at noon on March 4, 1849 but that was a Sunday. Taylor, a strict Episcopalian, refused to take the oath until Monday. According to the US Constitution, since there was technically no President or Vice President in office, Atchison, as President of the US Senate, technically became President of the United States until Taylor swore his oath. Exhausted from Senate business, Atchison is reported to have spent most of his presidency asleep.

THE 10

LONGEST-LIVED US PRESIDENTS

	President	Age at death years	months
1	John Adams	90	8
2	Herbert Hoover	90	2
3	Harry S Truman	88	7
4	James Madison	85	3
5	Thomas Jefferson	83	2
6	Richard M. Nixon	81	3
7	John Quincy Adams	80	7
8	Martin Van Buren	79	7
9	Dwight D. Eisenhower	78	5
10	Andrew Jackson	78	2

THE 10

OLDEST US PRESIDENTS

	President	Age at inauguration years	days
1	Ronald W. Reagan	69	349
2	William H. Harrison	68	23
3	James Buchanan	65	315
4	George H.W. Bush	64	223
5	Zachary Taylor	64	100
6	Dwight D. Eisenhower	62	98
7	Andrew Jackson	61	354
8	John Adams	61	125
9	Gerald R. Ford	61	26
10	Harry S Truman	60	339

THE 10

YOUNGEST US PRESIDENTS

	President	Age at inauguration years	days
1	Theodore Roosevelt	42	322
2	John F. Kennedy	43	236
3	Bill Clinton	46	154
4	Ulysses S. Grant	46	236
5	Grover Cleveland	47	351
6	Franklin Pierce	48	101
7	James A. Garfield	49	105
8	James K. Polk	49	122
9	Millard Fillmore	50	184
10	John Tyler	51	8

PRESIDENT OF THE UNITED STATES, BILL CLINTON

ROYAL HIGHNESSES

T H E 1 0
FIRST ROMAN EMPERORS

	Caesar	Born	Acceded	Died	Fate
1	Julius Caesar*	Jul 12, 100 BC	48 BC	Mar 15, 44 BC	Assassinated
2	Augustus	Sep 23, 63 BC	27 BC	Aug 19, AD 14	Died
3	Tiberius	Nov 16, 42 BC	14 BC	Mar 16, AD 37	Died
4	Caligula	Aug 31, AD 12	AD 37	Jan 24, AD 41	Assassinated
5	Claudius	Aug 1, AD 10	AD 41	Oct 13, AD 54	Assassinated
6	Nero	Dec 15, AD 37	AD 54	Jun 9, AD 68	Suicide
7	Galba	Dec 24, AD 3	AD 68	Jan 15, AD 69	Assassinated
8	Otho	Apr 28, AD 32	AD 69	Apr 16, AD 69	Suicide
9	Vitellius	Sep 24, AD 15	AD 69	Dec 22, AD 69	Assassinated
10	Vespasian	Nov 18, AD 9	AD 69	Jun 23, AD 79	Died

* Did not rule under the title of Emperor, but included among the "Twelve Caesars"

T H E 1 0
SHORTEST-REIGNING BRITISH MONARCHS

	Monarch	Reign	Duration
1	Jane	1553	14 days
2	Edward V	1483	75 days
3	Edward VIII	1936	325 days
4	Richard III	1483–85	2 years
5	James II	1685–88	3 years
6	Mary I	1553–58	5 years
7	Mary II	1689–94	5 years
8	Edward VI	1547–53	6 years
9	William IV	1830–37	7 years
10	Edward VII	1901–10	9 years

T H E 1 0
LONGEST-REIGNING MONARCHS IN THE WORLD

	Monarch	Country	Reign	Age at accession	Reign years
1	Louis XIV	France	1643–1715	5	72
2	John II	Liechtenstein	1858–1929	18	71
3	Franz-Josef	Austria–Hungary	1848–1916	18	67
4	Victoria	UK	1837–1901	18	63
5	Hirohito	Japan	1926–89	25	62
6	George III	UK	1760–1820	22	59
7	Louis XV	France	1715–74	5	59
8	Pedro II	Brazil	1831–89	6	58
9	Wilhelmina	Netherlands	1890–1948	10	58
10	Henry III	England	1216–72	9	56

T H E 1 0
LONGEST-REIGNING QUEENS IN THE WORLD*

	Queen	Country	Reign	Reign years
1	Victoria	UK	1837–1901	63
2	Wilhelmina	Netherlands	1890–1948	58
3	Wu Chao	China	655–705	50
4	Salote Tubou	Tonga	1918–65	47
5	Elizabeth I	England	1558–1603	44
6	Elizabeth II	UK	1952–	43
7	Maria Theresa	Hungary	1740–80	40
8	Maria I	Portugal	1777–1816	39
9	Joanna I	Italy	1343–81	38
10=	Suiko Tenno	Japan	593–628	35
10=	Isabella II	Spain	1833–68	35

Some authorities have claimed a 73-year reign for Alfonso I of Portugal, but his father, Henry of Burgundy, who conquered Portugal, ruled as Count, and it was this title that Alfonso inherited on April 30, 1112, at the age of two. His mother, Theresa of Castile, ruled until he took power in 1128, but he did not assume the title of king until July 25, 1139, during the Battle of Ourique at which he vanquished the Moors. He thus ruled as king for 46 years until his death on December 6, 1185. More extravagant claims are sometimes made for long-reigning monarchs in the ancient world. One example is the alleged 94 years of Phiops II, a Sixth Dynasty Egyptian pharaoh, but since his dates of birth and death are uncertain, he has not been included.

* Queens and empresses who ruled in their own right, not as consorts of kings or emperors

As well as being the longest-reigning queen, Victoria is among the longest-reigning monarchs in the world. She also holds first place as the British monarch who occupied the throne for the longest time, beating her nearest rival, George III, by some four years.

LE ROI SOLEIL
Nicknamed the "Sun King" because of the splendor of his court, Louis XIV began his reign at five years of age, but he was not crowned until he was 16 years old.

THE 10
YOUNGEST BRITISH MONARCHS
(Since the Norman Conquest)

	Monarch	Reign	Age at accession years	months
1	Henry VI	1422–61	0	8
2	Henry III	1216–72	9	1
3	Edward VI	1547–53	9	3
4	Richard II	1377–99	10	5
5	Edward V	1483	12	5
6	Edward III	1327–77	14	2
7	Jane	1553	15	8
8	Henry VIII	1509–47	17	10
9	Victoria	1837–1901	18	1
10	Charles II	1660–85	18	8

Born on December 6, 1421, Henry VI became King of England on September 1, 1422, the day after the death of his father, Henry V. At the age of 10 months (following the death of his grandfather, Charles VI, on October 21, 1422), he also became King of France. Before the Norman Conquest, Edward the Martyr became king in 975 when aged about 12, and Ethelred II ("the Unready") in 978 at the age of about 10.

THE 10
LONGEST-REIGNING BRITISH MONARCHS

	Monarch	Reign	Age at accession	Age at death	Reign years
1	Victoria	1837–1901	18	81	63
2	George III	1760–1820	22	81	59
3	Henry III	1216–72	9	64	56
4	Edward III	1327–77	14	64	50
5	Elizabeth I	1558–1603	25	69	44
6	Elizabeth II	1952–	25	–	43
7	Henry VI	1422–61 (deposed, d.1471)	8 months	49	38
8	Henry VIII	1509–47	17	55	37
9	Charles II	1660–85	19	54	36
10	Henry I	1100–35	31–32*	66–67*	35

* Henry I's birthdate is unknown, so his age at accession and death are uncertain

This list excludes the reigns of monarchs before 1066, so omits such rulers as Ethelred II who reigned for 37 years. Queen Elizabeth II overtook Henry VI's reign (38 years and 185 days) in August 1990 and is on target to pass that of her namesake Queen Elizabeth I in June 1996. If she is still on the throne on September 11, 2015, she will have beaten Queen Victoria's record by one day. She will then be 89 years old, and will be the UK's oldest ruler.

QUEEN VICTORIA
After the deaths of her father's brothers, George IV and William IV, Princess Alexandrina Victoria became Queen of Great Britain and Ireland and Empress of India.

THE 10
OLDEST MONARCHS TO ASCEND THE BRITISH THRONE

	Monarch	Reign	Age at accession
1	William IV	1830–37	64
2	Edward VII	1901–10	59
3	George IV	1820–30	57
4	George I	1714–27	54
5	James II	1685–88	51
6	George V	1910–36	44
7	George II	1727–60	43
8	Edward VIII	1936	41
9	George VI	1936–52	40
10	William I	1066–87	39

THE 10
LONGEST-REIGNING LIVING MONARCHS IN THE WORLD
(Including hereditary rulers of principalities, dukedoms, etc.)

	Monarch	Country	Date of birth	Accession
1	Bhumibol Adulyadej	Thailand	Dec 5, 1927	Jun 9, 1946
2	Rainier III	Monaco	May 31, 1923	May 9, 1949
3	Elizabeth II	UK	Apr 21, 1926	Feb 6, 1952
4	Hussein	Jordan	Nov 14, 1935	Aug 11, 1952
5	Hassan II	Morocco	Jul 9, 1929	Feb 26, 1961
6	Isa bin Sulman al-Khalifa	Bahrain	Jul 3, 1933	Nov 2, 1961
7	Malietoa Tanumafili II	Western Samoa	Jan 4, 1913	Jan 1, 1962
8	Jean	Luxembourg	Jan 5, 1921	Nov 12, 1964
9	Taufa'ahau Tupou IV	Tonga	Jul 4, 1918	Dec 16, 1965
10	Qaboos bin Said	Oman	Nov 18, 1942	Jul 23, 1970

There are 25 countries that have emperors, kings, queens, princes, dukes, sultans, or other hereditary rulers as their heads of state. Malaysia, uniquely, has an elected monarchy.

52

EXPLORATION & ENDEAVOR

FIRST PEOPLE TO REACH
THE SOUTH POLE

	Name	Nationality	Date
1=	Roald Amundsen*	Norwegian	Dec 14, 1911
1=	Olav Olavsen Bjaaland	Norwegian	Dec 14, 1911
1=	Helmer Julius Hanssen	Norwegian	Dec 14, 1911
1=	Helge Sverre Hassel	Norwegian	Dec 14, 1911
1=	Oscar Wisting	Norwegian	Dec 14, 1911
6=	Robert Falcon Scott*	British	Jan 17, 1912
6=	Henry Robertson Bowers	British	Jan 17, 1912
6=	Edgar Evans	British	Jan 17, 1912
6=	Lawrence Edward Grace Oates	British	Jan 17, 1912
6=	Edward Adrian Wilson	British	Jan 17, 1912

* Expedition leader

SCOTT'S TELESCOPE

Just 33 days separated the first two expeditions that reached the South Pole. Although several voyages had sailed close to Antarctica, no one set foot on the mainland until the 19th century. The first to do so was Robert Falcon Scott, a young naval lieutenant, in 1902. In 1909 Ernest Shackleton marched to within 113 miles/182 km of the Pole, and a multinational race for its conquest began. A British Antarctic Expedition, led by Scott, was organized in 1910 "to reach the South Pole and to secure for the British Empire the honour of this achievement," but on arrival in Australia, Scott learned that the Norwegian Roald Amundsen was also leading an expedition to the Pole. Scott's party left after Amundsen's. The weather was severe and, after problems with motor sleds, ponies, and dogs, they relied on man-hauled sleds. Amundsen relied on just dogs, and even used them as part of his food supply. On arrival at the Pole, Scott found that the Norwegians had gotten there first. His team journeyed back in bad weather, hungry, tired, and ill. The whole expedition died: Evans died after injuring himself; Oates sacrificed himself in a blizzard after realizing that they had insufficient rations; and while Amundsen's achievement was being reported to the world, the remaining three died in their tent.

FIRST CROSS-CHANNEL SWIMMERS

	Swimmer	Nationality	Time hr:min	Date
1	Matthew Webb	British	21:45	Aug 24–25, 1875
2	Thomas Burgess	British	22:35	Sep 5–6, 1911
3	Henry Sullivan	American	26:50	Aug 5–6, 1923
4	Enrico Tiraboschi	Italian	16:33	Aug 12, 1923
5	Charles Toth	American	16:58	Sep 8–9, 1923
6	Gertrude Ederle	American	14:39	Aug 6, 1926
7	Millie Corson	American	15:29	Aug 27–28, 1926
8	Arnst Wierkotter	German	12:40	Aug 30, 1926
9	Edward Temme	British	14:29	Aug 5, 1927
10	Mercedes Gleitze	British	15:15	Oct 7, 1927

The first three crossings were from England to France, the rest from France to England. Gertrude Ederle was the first woman to swim the Channel, and on September 11, 1951 American Florence Chadwick became the first woman to swim from England to France. In 1934 Edward Temme also swam from England to France, becoming the first person to cross successfully in both directions. The Channel has been swum underwater (by Fred Baldasare in 1962), and by an 11-year-old girl. The record for the fastest crossing was held at one time by a 16-year-old American girl, Lynne Cox. It is now held by another American, Chad Hundeby, who crossed in 7 hr 17 min on September 27, 1994.

FASTEST CROSS-CHANNEL SWIMMERS

	Swimmer	Nationality	Year	Time hr:min
1	Chad Hundeby	American	1994	7:17
2	Penny Lee Dean	American	1978	7:40
3	Tamara Bruce	Australian	1994	7:53
4	Philip Rush	New Zealand	1987	7:55
5	Richard Davey	British	1988	8:05
6	Irene van der Laan	Dutch	1982	8:06
7	Paul Asmuth	American	1985	8:12
8	Anita Sood	Indian	1987	8:15
9	John Van Wisse	Australian	1994	8:17
10=	Monique Wildschut	Dutch	1984	8:19
10=	Susie Maroney	Australian	1991	8:19

CAPTAIN WEBB AND THE FIRST CROSS-CHANNEL SWIM

Captain Matthew Webb (1848–83) was hailed as a national hero when he swam the English Channel, a feat thought to be impossible at the time. Webb created his record on August 24, 1875, greased with porpoise oil as protection against the cold and followed by a small flotilla of boats. He was sustained by beef-tea, beer, coffee, and an omelette, and after being stung by a starfish he also had some brandy. During the last hours, within sight of the French coast, he had to battle with a strong sea and tide, but as a contemporary report put it, ". . . unflinching bulldog pluck kept the man going." He landed at Calais after 21 hours 44 minutes 55 seconds. After this, Webb went on to new challenges, attempting to swim the rapids and whirlpool below Niagara Falls in 1883. But, sadly, he was drowned.

FIRST EXPLORERS TO LAND IN THE AMERICAS

	Explorer	Nationality	Discovery/ exploration	Year
1	Christopher Columbus	Italian	West Indies	1492
2	John Cabot	Italian/ English	Nova Scotia/ Newfoundland	1497
3	Alonso de Hojeda	Spanish	Brazil	1499
4	Vicente Yañez Pinzón	Spanish	Amazon	1500
5	Pedro Alvarez Cabral	Portuguese	Brazil	1500
6	Gaspar Corte Real	Portuguese	Labrador	1500
7	Rodrigo de Bastidas	Spanish	Central America	1501
8	Vasco Nuñez de Balboa	Spanish	Panama	1513
9	Juan Ponce de León	Spanish	Florida	1513
10	Juan Díaz de Solís	Spanish	Río de la Plata	1515

After his pioneering voyage of 1492, Columbus made three more journeys to the West Indies and South America. Following him, several later expeditions landed on the same West Indian islands (which have not been included as new explorations). Of the three voyages that arrived in 1500, that of Pinzón (who had been with Columbus in 1492) landed on January 26, and therefore is listed first. Cabral followed in April, while Corte Real, who is thought to have landed late in 1500, disappeared on the voyage. America was named after Amerigo Vespucci, who was on the 1499 expedition.

FIRST MOUNTAINEERS TO CLIMB EVEREST

	Mountaineer	Nationality	Date
1	Edmund Hillary	New Zealander	May 29, 1953
2	Tenzing Norgay	Nepalese	May 29, 1953
3	Jürg Marmet	Swiss	May 23, 1956
4	Ernst Schmied	Swiss	May 23, 1956
5	Hans-Rudolf von Gunten	Swiss	May 24, 1956
6	Adolf Reist	Swiss	May 24, 1956
7	Wang Fu-chou	Chinese	May 25, 1960
8	Chu Ying-hua	Chinese	May 25, 1960
9	Konbu	Tibetan	May 25, 1960
10=	Nawang Gombu	Indian	May 1, 1963
10=	James Whittaker	American	May 1, 1963

Nawang Gombu and James Whittaker climbed the last few feet side by side since neither man wished to deny the other the privilege of being the first to reach the summit.

NOBEL PRIZES

NOBEL PRIZE-WINNING COUNTRIES

	Country	Phy	Che	Ph/Med	Lit	Pce	Eco	Total
1	US	57	38	70	10	17	21	213
2	UK	20	23	23	8	10	6	90
3	Germany	19	27	14	6	4	–	70
4	France	11	7	7	12	9	1	47
5	Sweden	4	4	7	7	5	2	29
6	Switzerland	2	5	5	2	3	–	17
7	USSR	7	1	2	3	2	1	16
8	Stateless institutions	–	–	–	–	14	–	14
9	Italy	3	1	3	5	1	–	13
10=	Denmark	3	–	5	3	1	–	12
10=	Netherlands	6	2	2	–	1	1	12

Phy – Physics; Che – Chemistry; Ph/Med – Physiology or Medicine; Lit – Literature;
Pce – Peace; Eco – Economic Sciences

A century ago, on November 27, 1895, the Swedish scientist Alfred Nobel signed his will in which he left the major part of his fortune of 31,600,000 Swedish kroner, amassed through his invention of dynamite, to establish a trust fund, now estimated to be worth over $225,000,000. Nobel died the following year, but interest earned from this money has enabled annual prizes to be awarded since 1901 to those who have achieved the greatest common good in the fields of Physics, Chemistry, Physiology or Medicine, Literature, Peace, and, since 1969, Economic Sciences. All the award ceremonies take place in Stockholm, Sweden, with the exception of the Peace Prize, which is awarded in Oslo, Norway.

FIRST US WINNERS OF THE NOBEL PRIZE FOR PHYSIOLOGY OR MEDICINE

	Winner	Prize year
1	Thomas Hunt Morgan (1866–1945)	1933
2=	George Hoyt Whipple (1879–1976)	1934
2=	George Richards Minot (1885–1950)	1934
2=	William Parry Murphy (1892–1987)	1934
5	Edward Adelbert Doisy* (1893–1986)	1943
6=	Joseph Erlanger (1874–1965)	1944
6=	Herbert Spencer Gasser (1888–1963)	1944
8	Hermann Joseph Muller (1890–1967)	1946
9=	Carl Ferdinand Cori*# (1896–1984)	1947
9=	Gerty Theresa Cori, née Radnitz*# (1896–1957)	1947

* Prize shared with other nationalities
 # Joint award to husband and wife; both born in Prague, then part of Austria

FIRST US WINNERS OF THE NOBEL PEACE PRIZE

	Winner	Prize year
1	Theodore Roosevelt (1858–1919)	1906
2	Elihu Root (1845–1937)	1912
3	Thomas Woodrow Wilson (1856–1924)	1919
4	Charles Gates Dawes* (1865–1951)	1925
5	Frank Billings Kellogg (1856–1937)	1929
6=	Jane Addams (1860–1935)	1931
6=	Nicholas Murray Butler (1862–1947)	1931
8	Cordell Hull (1871–1955)	1945
9=	John Raleigh Mott (1865–1955)	1946
9=	Emily Greene Balch (1867–1961)	1946

* Prize shared with other nationalities

In 1962 the American Linus Carl Pauling (1901–94), winner of the 1954 Chemistry Prize, became the only person to win two unshared Prizes in separate categories. Martin Luther King, Jr. (1929–68) won in 1964, and Henry Kissinger (b. 1923) was joint prize-winner in 1973 with Vietnamese statesman Le Duc Tho (1911–90).

FIRST US WINNERS OF THE NOBEL PRIZE FOR PHYSICS

	Winner	Prize year
1	Albert Abraham Michelson (1852–1931)	1907
2	Robert Andrews Millikan (1868–1953)	1923
3	Carl David Anderson* (1905–91)	1936
4	Clinton Joseph Davisson* (1881–1958)	1937
5	Ernest Orlando Lawrence (1901–58)	1939
6	Otto Stern# (1888–1969)	1943
7	Isidor Isaac Rabi** (1898–1988)	1944
8	Percy Williams Bridgman (1882–1961)	1946
9=	Felix Bloch (1905–1983)‡	1952
9=	Edward Mills Purcell (1912–)	1952

* Prize shared with other nationalities
 # German-born
** Austrian-born
‡ Swiss-born

THE 10

FIRST WOMEN TO WIN A NOBEL PRIZE

	Winner	Nationality	Prize	Year
1	Marie Curie* (1867–1934)	Polish	Physics	1903
2	Bertha von Suttner (1843–1914)	Austrian	Peace	1905
3	Selma Lagerlöf (1858–1940)	Swedish	Literature	1909
4	Marie Curie (1867–1934)	Polish	Chemistry	1911
5	Grazia Deledda (1875–1936)	Italian	Literature	1926#
6	Sigrid Undset (1882–1949)	Norwegian	Literature	1928
7	Jane Addams** (1860–1935)	American	Peace	1931
8	Irène Joliot-Curie## (1897–1956)	French	Chemistry	1935
9	Pearl Buck (1892–1973)	American	Literature	1938
10	Gabriela Mistral (1899–1957)	Chilean	Literature	1945

The American writer Pearl Buck (1892–1973) won the Nobel Prize for Literature in 1938. Until 1924 she spent most of her life in China, from which she drew the inspiration for many of her novels and plays. Her most famous works include *East Wind: West Wind* (1930), *The Good Earth* (1931; Pulitzer Prize), *Dragon Seed* (1942), *Imperial Woman* (1956), and *Mandala* (1976).

* *Shared half with husband Pierre Curie; other half to Henri Becquerel*
\# *Awarded 1927*
** *Shared with Nicholas Murray Butler*
\#\# *Shared with husband Frédéric Joliot-Curie*

THE 10

FIRST US WINNERS OF THE NOBEL PRIZE FOR CHEMISTRY

	Winner	Prize year
1	Theodore William Richards (1868–1928)	1914
2	Irving Langmuir (1881–1957)	1932
3	Harold Clayton Urey (1893–1981)	1934
4=	James Batcheller Sumner (1887–1955)	1946
4=	John Howard Northrop (1891–1987)	1946
4=	Wendell Meredith Stanley (1904–1971)	1946
7	William Francis Giauque (1895–1982)	1949
8=	Edwin Mattison McMillan (1907–1991)	1951
8=	Glenn Theodore Seaborg (1912–)	1951
10	Linus Carl Pauling (1901–94)	1954

The scientific bias of the Nobel Prizes reflects the fact that Alfred Nobel was himself a chemist and inventor of note, with a total of 355 patents in his name, and the founder of the first multinational chemicals companies.

THE 10

FIRST US WINNERS OF THE NOBEL PRIZE FOR ECONOMIC SCIENCES

	Winner	Prize year
1	Paul Anthony Samuelson (1915–)	1970
2	Simon S. Kuznets (1901–1985)	1971
3	Kenneth Joseph Arrow* (1921–)	1972
4	Wassily Leontief# (1906–)	1973
5	Tjalling Charles Koopmans* (1910–1985)**	1975
6	Milton Friedman (1912–)	1976
7	Herbert Alexander Simon (1916–)	1978
8	Theodore William Schultz* (1902–)	1979
9	Lawrence R. Klein (1920–)	1980
10	James Tobin (1918–)	1981

* *Prize shared with other nationalities*
\# *Russian-born*
** *Dutch-born*

This award – officially designated the Prize in Economic Sciences in Memory of Alfred Nobel – was instituted by the Bank of Sweden at the time of its tercentenary in 1968 and first awarded the following year.

THE 10

FIRST US WINNERS OF THE NOBEL PRIZE FOR LITERATURE

	Winner	Prize year
1	Sinclair Lewis (1885–1951)	1930
2	Eugene O'Neill (1888–1953)	1936
3	Pearl Buck (1892–1973)	1938
4	William Faulkner (1897–1962)	1949
5	Ernest Hemingway (1899–1961)	1954
6	John Steinbeck (1902–1968)	1962
7	Saul Bellow (1915–)	1976
8	Isaac Bashevis Singer (1904–1991)	1978
9	Czeslaw Milosz* (1911–)	1980
10	Joseph Brodsky# (1940–)	1987

* *Polish-born*
\# *Russian-born*

The most recent US recipient of the Nobel Prize for Literature is Toni Morrison (b. 1931), awarded the prize in 1993.

THE GOOD & THE BAD

TOP 10

ORGANIZED RELIGIONS IN THE WORLD

	Religion	Followers
1	Christianity	1,900,174,000
2	Islam	1,033,453,000
3	Hinduism	764,000,000
4	Buddhism	338,621,000
5	Sikhism	20,204,000
6	Judaism	13,451,000
7	Confucianism	6,334,000
8	Baha'ism	5,835,000
9	Jainism	3,987,000
10	Shintoism	3,387,800

This list excludes the followers of various tribal and folk religions, new religions, and shamanism. Since reforms in the former USSR, many who practiced Christianity in secret while following the Communist anti-religion line in public have now declared their faith openly. The list is based on the work of David B. Barrett, who has been monitoring world religions for many years.

TOP 10

LARGEST MUSLIM POPULATIONS IN THE WORLD

	Country	Total Muslim population
1	Indonesia	169,840,000
2	Pakistan	127,230,000
3	Bangladesh	101,730,000
4	India	100,000,000
5	Turkey	60,690,000
6	Iran	59,140,000
7	Egypt	52,600,000
8	Nigeria	42,060,000
9	Algeria	27,790,000
10	Morocco	26,240,000

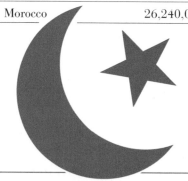

TOP 10

LARGEST BUDDHIST POPULATIONS IN THE WORLD

	Country	Total Buddhist population
1	China	101,000,000
2	Japan	97,320,000*
3	Thailand	54,340,000
4	Vietnam	48,220,000
5	Myanmar (Burma)	40,760,000
6	South Korea	16,130,000
7	Sri Lanka	12,360,000
8	Taiwan	9,060,000
9	Cambodia	9,050,000
10	India	6,000,000

Including many who also practice Shintoism

India now features 10th among countries with high Buddhist populations, but the religion originated there in the 6th century BC. Its espousal of peace and tolerant coexistence ensured its appeal and encouraged the spread of Buddhism through Asia and beyond.

LARGEST CHRISTIAN POPULATIONS IN THE WORLD

	Country	Total Christian population
1	US	222,580,000
2	Brazil	138,300,000
3	Mexico	87,860,000
4	Germany	61,930,000
5	Philippines	61,450,000
6	UK	50,910,000
7	Italy	47,580,000
8	Nigeria	45,800,000
9	France	42,850,000
10	Russia	37,400,000

Christian communities are found all over the world, yet it is difficult to put a precise figure on nominal membership (a declared religious persuasion) rather than active participation (regular attendance at a place of worship). It is claimed, for example, that 62.86 percent of the US population (156,336,384 people out of 248,709,873) are active members in a religious organization, whereas the survey on which this Top 10 is based asserts a nominal figure for Christians alone that equals almost 90 percent of the total population.

RELIGIOUS AFFILIATIONS IN THE US

	Religion/ organization	Membership
1	Roman Catholic Church	59,220,723
2	Southern Baptist Convention	15,358,866
3	United Methodist Church	8,789,101
4	National Baptist Convention, USA, Inc.	8,200,000
5	Islam	8,000,000*
6	Judaism#	5,981,000
7	Church of God in Christ	5,499,875
8	Evangelical Lutheran Church in America	5,234,568
9	Church of Jesus Christ of Latter-day Saints (Mormons)	4,330,000
10	Presbyterian Church	3,788,358

* Estimate
# Combined membership of several groups

If this listed only Christian affiliations, the African Methodist Episcopal Church and the National Baptist Convention of America would be equal 9th after the Presbyterians, with 3,500,000 members.

LARGEST HINDU POPULATIONS IN THE WORLD

	Country	Total Hindu population
1	India	734,000,000
2	Nepal	16,820,000
3	Bangladesh	14,240,000
4	Sri Lanka	2,760,000
5	Pakistan	1,980,000
6	Malaysia	1,370,000
7	US	900,000
8	Mauritius	570,000
9	South Africa	440,000
10	UK	410,000

LARGEST JEWISH POPULATIONS IN THE WORLD

	Country	Total Jewish population
1	US	5,981,000
2	Israel	3,755,000
3	Russia	1,449,117
4	France	600,000
5	Canada	350,000
6	UK	300,000
7	Argentina	250,000
8	Brazil	150,000
9	South Africa	114,000
10	Australia	92,000

There are Jewish communities in almost every country. In 1939 it was estimated that the world population was 17,000,000. Some 6,000,000 fell victim to Nazi persecution, reducing the figure to about 11,000,000, but by 1994 it was estimated to have grown to 13,451,000.

CHRISTIAN DENOMINATIONS IN THE WORLD

	Denomination	Adherents
1	Roman Catholic	872,104,646
2	Slavonic Orthodox	92,523,987
3	United (including Lutheran/ Reformed)	65,402,685
4	Pentecostal	58,999,862
5	Anglican	52,499,051
6	Baptist	50,321,923
7	Lutheran (excluding United)	44,899,837
8	Reformed (Presbyterian)	43,445,520
9	Methodist	31,718,508
10	Disciples (Restorationists)	8,783,192

The Top 10 is based on mid-1980s estimates that have not been subsequently updated. The difficulty at arriving at figures for religious adherence is illustrated by a later report by the Vatican that increased the figure for Roman Catholics to 911,000,000, while independent sources put the number at over 1,000,000,000, and that of Anglicans at a 50 percent higher figure, notwithstanding the global decline of church membership.

THE CHRISTIAN FAITH

THE 10
SHORTEST-SERVING POPES

	Pope	Year in office	Duration (days)
1	Urban VII	1590	12
2	Valentine	827	c.14
3	Boniface VI	896	15
4	Celestine IV	1241	16
5	Sisinnius	708	20
6	Sylvester III	1045	21
7	Theodore II	897	c.21
8	Marcellus II	1555	22
9	Damasus II	1048	23
10=	Pius III	1503	26
10=	Leo XI	1605	26

Many in this list were elderly and in poor health when they were elected. Boniface VI and Sylvester III were deposed, and Damasus II possibly poisoned. Pope Johns have not fared well: John XXI died in 1277 after nine month when a ceiling fell on him, John XII was beaten to death by his lover's husband, while more recently, John Paul I was pontiff for just 33 days in 1978.

YOUNG CHRISTIAN
A girl in traditional white kneels to receive Holy Communion for the first time.

THE 10
FIRST POPES

1	Saint Peter
2	Saint Linus
3	Saint Anacletus
4	Saint Clement I
5	Saint Evaristus
6	Saint Alexander I
7	Saint Sixtus I
8	Saint Telesphorus
9	Saint Hyginus
10	Saint Pius I

The first 10 popes all lived during the first 150 years of the Christian Church. As well as all being revered as martyrs, they have one other feature in common: virtually nothing is known about any of them.

THE 10
LONGEST-SERVING POPES

	Pope	Period in office	Years
1	Pius IX	Jun 16, 1846– Feb 7, 1878	31
2	Leo XIII	Feb 20, 1878– Jul 20, 1903	25
3	Peter	c.42–67	c.25
4	Pius VI	Feb 15, 1775– Aug 29, 1799	24
5	Adrian I	Feb 1, 772– Dec 25, 795	23
6	Pius VII	Mar 14, 1800– Aug 20, 1823	23
7	Alexander III	Sep 7, 1159– Aug 30, 1181	21
8	Sylvester	Jan 31, 314– Dec 31, 335	21
9	Leo I	Sep 29, 440– Nov 10, 461	21
10	Urban VIII	Aug 6, 1623– Jul 29, 1644	20

If he is still in office, the present pope, John Paul II, will enter the Top 10 in 1999 and could top it in 2010, when he will be 90 years old.

TOP 10
NATIONALITIES OF POPES

	Nationality	No.
1	Roman/Italian	208–209*
2	French	15–17#
3	Greek	15–16**
4	Syrian	6
5	German	4–6#
6	Spanish	5
7	African	2–3
8	Galilean	2
9=	Dutch	1
9=	English	1
9=	Polish	1
9=	Portuguese	1

* *Gelasius I was Roman, but of African descent; it is unknown whether Miltiades was African or Roman.*
# *The Franco-German frontier was variable at the births of two popes, hence their nationalities are uncertain.*
** *Theodore I was of Greek descent, but born in Jerusalem.*

Before John Paul II (the only Polish pope to date) took office, the last non-Italian pope was Hadrian VI, a Dutchman, who held office from 1522 to 1523. The only English pope to date was Nicholas Breakspear, who took the name Hadrian IV in 1154.

TOP 10
MOST COMMON NAMES OF POPES

	Name	No.
1	John	23
2	Gregory	16
3	Benedict	15
4	Clement	14
5=	Innocent	13
5=	Leo	13
7	Pius	12
8	Boniface	9
9=	Alexander	8
9=	Urban	8

T O P 1 0

WORDS MOST MENTIONED IN THE BIBLE

	Word	OT*	NT*	Total
1	the	52,948	10,976	63,924
2	and	40,975	10,721	51,696
3	of	28,518	6,099	34,617
4	to	10,207	3,355	13,562
5	that	9,152	3,761	12,913
6	in	9,767	2,900	12,667
7	he	7,348	3,072	10,420
8	for	6,690	2,281	8,971
9	I	6,669	2,185	8,854
10	his	7,036	1,437	8,473

* Occurrences in verses in the King James Bible

THE GOOD BOOK
This is a copy of the rare Gutenberg Bible, produced in Mainz, Germany, in 1455. It was the first Bible printed using movable type.

T O P 1 0

ANIMALS MOST MENTIONED IN THE BIBLE

	Animal	OT*	NT*	Total
1	Sheep	155	45	200
2	Lamb	153	35	188
3	Lion	167	9	176
4	Ox	156	10	166
5	Ram	165	0	165
6	Horse	137	27	164
7	Bullock	152	0	152
8	Ass	142	8	150
9	Goat	131	7	138
10	Camel	56	6	62

* Occurrences in verses in the King James Bible (Old and New Testaments), including plurals

The sheep are sorted from the goats (itself a biblical expression – "a shepherd divideth his sheep from the goats," in Matthew 25:32) in this Top 10, in a list of the animals regarded as most significant in biblical times, either economically or symbolically. A number of generic terms are also found: beast (337 references), cattle (153), fowl (90), fish (56), and bird (41). Leviticus 11 contains a list of animals that are considered "unclean" (such as the weasel, chameleon, and tortoise). There are 40 references to the dog, but the cat is not mentioned anywhere in the Bible.

T O P 1 0

NAMES MOST MENTIONED IN THE BIBLE

	Name	OT*	NT*	Total
1	Jesus (984) Christ (576)	0	1,560	1,560
2	David	1,005	59	1,064
3	Moses	767	80	847
4	Jacob	350	27	377
5	Aaron	347	5	352
6	Solomon	293	12	305
7=	Joseph	215	35	250
7=	Abraham	176	74	250
9	Ephraim	182	1	183
10	Benjamin	162	2	164

* Occurrences in verses in the King James Bible (Old and New Testaments), including possessive uses, such as "John's"

The name Judah also appears 816 times, but the total includes references to the land as well as the man with that name. "God" is mentioned 4,105 times (2,749 Old Testament, 1,356 New Testament). The most mentioned place names produce few surprises: Israel (2,600 references) heads the list, followed by Jerusalem (814), Egypt (736), Babylon (298), and Assyria (141).

T H E 1 0

LONGEST NAMES OF PEOPLE AND PLACES IN THE BIBLE

1	Mahershalalhashbaz (Isaiah's son)	18
2=	Kibrothhattaavah (desert encampment of the Israelites)	16
2=	Chepharhaamonai (Ammonite settlement)	16
2=	Chusharishathaim (king of Mesopotamia)	16
2=	Selahammahlekoth (stronghold in Maon)	16
6=	Abelbethmaachah (town near Damascus)	15
6=	Almondiblathaim (stopping-place of Israelites)	15
6=	Apharsathchites (Assyrian nomads)	15
6=	Bashabavothjair (alternative name of Argob)	15
6=	Berodachbaladan/Merodachbalodan (king of Babylon)	15
6=	Helkathhazzurim (battlefield)	15
6=	Ramathaimzophin (town)	15
6=	Tilgathpilneser (king of Assyria)	15
6=	Zaphnathpaaneah (name given to Joseph by Pharoah)	15

CRIME

COUNTRIES WITH THE HIGHEST CRIME RATES

	Country	Reported crime rate per 100,000 population
1	Dominica	22,432
2	Suriname	17,819
3	St. Kitts and Nevis	15,468
4	Sweden	14,188
5	New Zealand	13,247
6	Canada	11,443
7	US Virgin Islands	10,441
8	Denmark	10,270
9	Guam	10,080
10	Gibraltar	10,039
	England and Wales	*8,986*
	US	*5,652*

These figures are based on reported crimes: the reporting of crimes is not solely a response to lawlessness but also relates to the public confidence in the ability of the police. There are many countries in which crime is so commonplace and law enforcement so inefficient or corrupt that many incidents go unreported, since victims know that doing so would achieve no result.

COUNTRIES WITH MOST BURGLARIES

	Country	Annual burglaries per 100,000 population
1	US Virgin Islands	3,183.7
2	The Netherlands	2,621.8
3	Israel	2,483.0
4	New Zealand	2,447.6
5	Denmark	2,382.9
6	Bermuda	2,092.3
7	England and Wales	1,991.2
8	Australia	1,962.8
9	Malta	1,907.1
10	Greenland	1,883.5
	US	*1,168.2*

COUNTRIES WITH THE LOWEST CRIME RATES

	Country	Reported crime rate per 100,000 population		Country	Reported crime rate per 100,000 population
1	Togo	11.0	6	Guinea	32.4
2	Bangladesh	16.8	7	Mali	33.0
3	Nepal	29.1	8	Burkina Faso	41.0
4=	Congo	32.0	9	Syria	73.0
4=	Niger	32.0	10	Burundi	87.0

COUNTRIES WITH MOST CAR THEFTS

	Country	Annual thefts per 100,000 population		Country	Annual thefts per 100,000 population
1	Switzerland	1,504.6 *	7	US	631.5
2	New Zealand	1,026.4	8	Denmark	575.9
3	US Virgin Islands	954.0	9	Italy	546.0
4	Sweden	879.0	10	Puerto Rico	526.9
5	England and Wales	858.2			
6	Australia	770.6			

* Including motorcycles and bicycles

US STATES WITH THE HIGHEST CRIME RATES

	State	Crimes per 100,000 population		State	Crimes per 100,000 population
1	District of Columbia	11,761.1	6	Texas	6,439.1
2	Florida	8,351.0	7	Hawaii	6,277.0
3	Arizona	7,431.7	8	New Mexico	6,266.1
4	Louisiana	6,846.6	9	Georgia	6,193.1
5	California	6,456.9	10	Nevada	6,180.0

US STATES WITH THE LOWEST CRIME RATES

	State	Crimes per 100,000 population		State	Crimes per 100,000 population
1	West Virginia	2,532.6	6	Kentucky	3,259.7
2	North Dakota	2,820.3	7	Pennsylvania	3,271.4
3	New Hampshire	2,905.0	8	Idaho	3,845.1
4	South Dakota	2,958.2	9	Iowa	3,846.4
5	Maine	3,153.9	10	Vermont	3,972.4

THE 10
WORST YEARS FOR CRIME IN THE US

	Year	Crimes per 100,000 of population
1	1980	5,950.0
2	1991	5,897.8
3	1981	5,858.2
4	1990	5,820.3
5	1989	5,741.0
6	1988	5,664.2
7	1992	5,660.2
8	1982	5,603.6
9	1979	5,565.4
10	1987	5,550.0

This list tends to refute the notion that the United States crime rate increases inexorably from year to year. It indicates that 1980 was the worst year on record, with 13,408,300 crimes reported in a population of 225,349,264, while 1993, with a crime rate of 5,482.9 per 100,000, does not even make the Top 10. However, the general postwar trend is up, and we may look back with nostalgia to the 1960–62 period, when the US population was 179,323,175 and there were 1,946,500 crimes reported nationwide – a rate of just 1,085.5 per 100,000.

TOP 10
CARS MOST VULNERABLE TO THEFT IN THE US*

1	Mercedes SL Convertible
2	Volkswagen Cabriolet
3	Ford Mustang Convertible
4	Ford Mustang
5	Chevrolet Corvette Convertible
6	BMW 318i/325i Convertible
7	Nissan 300ZX
8	Nissan 300ZX 2 + 2
9	BMW 525i/535i
10	BMW 318i/325i

* Figures cover 1991–1993 and refer to the relative average theft loss payments for each insured vehicle, for vehicles and contents.

TOP 10
TYPES OF PROPERTY THEFT IN THE US

	Property	Total value ($)
1	Motor vehicles	6,682,729,000
2	Jewelry and precious metals	1,145,813,000
3	TVs, radio, stereos, etc.	1,017,950,000
4	Currency, notes, etc.	886,242,000
5	Clothing and furs	328,787,000
6	Office equipment	327,563,000
7	Household goods	223,149,000
8	Firearms	113,969,000
9	Consumable goods	103,112,000
10	Livestock	36,549,000

In 1993, in addition to a category that was listed as "Miscellaneous" and worth an estimated $2,438,705,000, property worth a total of $13,304,578,000 was stolen in the United States – more than the entire Gross Domestic Product of some developing countries. Overall, some $4,578,141,000-worth, or 34.4 percent of the items stolen, was recovered. Motor vehicles were the most likely to be retrieved (a total value of $4,125,665,000, or 61.7 percent of those stolen), and TVs, radios, and stereos were the least likely ($45,095,000, or 4.4 percent).

TOP 10
COUNTRIES' EMBASSIES IN THE US WITH THE MOST UNPAID PARKING FINES

	Country	Unpaid fines ($)*
1	Russia	2,768,635
2	Former USSR	1,661,535
3	Nigeria	195,860
4	Cameroon	72,940
5	Egypt	65,935
6	South Korea	58,980
7	India	58,610
8	China	53,730
9	Spain	53,100
10	Ukraine	49,135

* As of April 1994

The use of diplomatic immunity by embassy staff to evade both serious criminal offences and misdemeanors, including parking fines, is an international problem, with some embassies appearing prominently in such lists in different parts of the world: the Soviet Union consistently headed the comparative list in the UK, for example, although its place has now been taken by Nigeria. (The US Embassy in London has not always had an unblemished record; in 1994 it failed to pay 22 parking fines.)

TOP 10
LARGEST FEDERAL CORRECTIONAL INSTITUTIONS IN THE US
(By population)

	Institution	Location	Rated capacity
1	Federal Correctional Institution	Fort Dix, New Jersey	3,140
2	US Penitentiary	Atlanta, Georgia	2,148
3	US Penitentiary	Leavenworth, Kansas	1,620
4	Federal Correctional Institution	El Reno, Oklahoma	1,597
5	Federal Correctional Institution	Tallahassee, Florida	1,474
6	Federal Correctional Institution	Milan, Michigan	1,434
7	Federal Medical Center	Fort Worth, Texas	1,417
8	US Penitentiary	Lompoc, California	1,412
9	US Penitentiary	Lewisburg, Pennsylvania	1,375
10	Federal Correctional Institution	Marianna, Florida	1,327

MURDER FACTS

MOST COMMON MURDER WEAPONS/METHODS IN ENGLAND AND WALES

	Weapon/method	Victims 1983	1993
1	Sharp instrument	98	190
2	Hitting and kicking	47	109
3	Strangulation and asphyxiation	30	90
4	Shooting	22	72
5	Blunt instrument	32	69
6	Burning	9	16
7	Motor vehicle	3	13
8	Poison and drugs	3	10
9	Drowning	9	5
10	Explosives	4	3

According to statistics, there were 606 homicides in England and Wales (375 male and 231 female) in 1993. In addition to the methods listed, the methods in 20 incidents are described as "other" and nine of "cause unknown." This is a slight increase over 1991, although some offenses first recorded as murder were later reclassified. Murder victims first exceeded 400 in 1952, 500 in 1974, and 600 in 1979. Gun killings have fallen from a peak of 78 in 1987, while blunt weapons rose to 31 percent of all murders in 1993. Even so, England and Wales are relatively safe: the chances of being murdered is one in 79,090. The US is more than six times more dangerous.

TO BE OR NOT TO BE...

Menelik II, Emperor of Ethiopia (1889–1913), ordered an electric chair before being told that an electricity supply was a significant requirement – something Ethiopia unfortunately lacked. Undaunted, he had it converted into an elegant throne. Had they been in Ethiopia, two murderers executed in Florida on October 6, 1941 would have welcomed this news; aptly, their names were Willburn and Frizzel.

RELATIONSHIPS OF MURDER VICTIMS TO PRINCIPAL SUSPECTS IN THE US

	Relationship	Victims
1	Acquaintance	6,217
2	Stranger	3,259
3	Wife	928
4	Friend	859
5	Girlfriend	603
6	Husband	335
7	Son	334
8	Boyfriend	256
9	Daughter	248
10	Neighbor	207

These offenses – which, remarkably, remain in identical order from year to year – accounted for 23,271 murders in 1993. FBI statistics also recorded 9,145 murders where the victim's relationship to the suspect was unknown, 361 "other family members," 175 brothers, 173 fathers, 133 mothers and 38 sisters.

WORST CITIES FOR MURDER IN THE US

	City	Murders
1	New York	1,946
2	Los Angeles	1,076
3	Chicago	845
4	Detroit	579
5	Washington, D.C.	454
6	Houston	446
7	Philadelphia	439
8	New Orleans	395
9	Seattle	356
10	Baltimore	353

The identity of America's 10 murder capitals remains fairly consistent from year to year, although in 1993 Seattle ousted Dallas, which had 317 murders. In that year, the Top 10 accounted for 6,889, or 30 percent of the total 23,271 murders in the US.

WORST YEARS FOR MURDER IN THE US

	Year	Victims
1	1993	23,271
2	1992	22,540
3	1980	21,860
4	1991	21,505
5	1981	20,053
6	1990	20,045
7	1982	19,485
8	1986	19,257
9	1989	18,954
10	1983	18,673

MOST COMMON MURDER WEAPONS/METHODS IN THE US

	Weapon/method	Victims
1	Handguns	13,252
2	Knives or cutting instruments	2,957
3	"Personal weapons" (hands, feet, fists, etc.)	1,164
4	Firearms (type not stated)	1,086
5	Shotguns	1,059
6	Blunt objects (hammers, clubs, etc.)	1,024
7	Rifles	754
8	Strangulation	329
9	Fire	217
10	Asphyxiation	113

"Other weapons or weapons not stated" were used in the 1,198 murders committed in 1993. Less common methods included explosives (26 cases), drowning (23), and poison (9). Murders for the year totaled 23,271 – equivalent to one person in every 11,083 in the US. The list order has not varied much recently, but the numbers have risen dramatically: in 1965, for example, there were 8,773 murders in the US, with firearms used in 5,015 cases. By 1993 the total had risen by 323 percent, with 16,189, or 70 percent, committed using firearms.

TOP 10
COUNTRIES WITH THE HIGHEST MURDER RATES

	Country	Murders p.a. per 100,000 population
1	Swaziland	87.8
2	Lesotho	51.1
3	Colombia	40.5
4	Sudan	30.5
5	Philippines	30.1
6	Guatemala	27.4
7	French Guiana	27.2
8	Nauru	25.0
9	Aruba	24.9
10	Puerto Rico	24.1
	US	9.3

The incidence of murder is affected by intertribal conflicts and by the prevalence of drug-related killings in Colombia.

THE 10
WORST STATES FOR MURDER IN THE US

	State	Firearms used	Total murders
1	California	3,007	4,094
2	New York	1,739	2,415
3	Texas	1,535	2,142
4	Florida	753	1,223
5	Illinois*	832	1,217
6	Michigan	681	922
7	Pennsylvania	573	804
8	North Carolina	493	771
9	Georgia	506	750
10	Louisiana	586	721

* 1992 figures

Of the 15,059 murders in these states in 1993, firearms were used in 10,705, or 71 percent of them. In Pennsylvania, ranked 7th, there were 129 more murders than in England and Wales, which has a population over four times greater. The top four states all had murder rates of 10 to 14 per 100,000 of the population, while of those in the Top 10, Louisiana had the highest murder rate (24 per 100,000) and Pennsylvania had the lowest (9 per 100,000). Maine had just seven murders in 1993, a rate of 0.6 per 100,000.

THE 10
WORST YEARS FOR GUN MURDERS IN THE US

	Year	Victims
1	1993	16,189
2	1992	15,377
3	1991	14,265
4	1980	13,650
5	1990	12,847
6	1981	12,523
7	1974	12,474
8	1975	12,061
9	1989	11,832
10	1982	11,721

THE POINT OF THE MATTER
Although knives remain the second most common murder weapon in the US, their use has declined in recent years while that of firearms has steadily increased.

MURDER HISTORY

The grisly task of ranking murderers is highly problematic, particularly for murders up to the 20th century. Medical diagnoses and police and forensic methods were often poor, so poisoning (a particularly popular method) often went undetected. The 19th century was also an age of migrations, especially in the US, when people could simply disappear without trace without any authorities being aware of their whereabouts. Earlier still, charges of mass murder were often invented for political motives or as part of broader accusations of witchcraft. Often the only information that we have is that which emerged when people were caught and brought to trial, sometimes making dramatic (if not always believable) confessions. Therefore, the victim quota in these lists is based on such reliable evidence as may be available, but with the proviso that some may be underestimates, and also that there are probably other similarly active murderers who have never been discovered and brought to trial.

MASS MURDERER
Gilles de Rais, nicknamed "Bluebeard," was charged with witchcraft and the murder of six of his seven wives and perhaps 200 children.

TOP 10

MOST PROLIFIC POISONERS IN THE WORLD*

Poisoner	Victims
1 Susannah Olah	up to 100

Susi Olah, a Hungarian nurse and midwife, was believed to have prophetic powers after she "predicted" the deaths of up to 100 people, who then died from poisoning. Her victims ranged from the old, handicapped, and newborn to local husbands – in most cases with the help of their relatives. She committed suicide when the law caught up with her in 1929.

Poisoner	Victims
2 Gesina Margaretha Gottfried	at least 30

Having poisoned her first husband and two children with arsenic in 1815, German Gesina Mittenberg killed her parents and her next husband, Gottfried, whom she married on his deathbed, in the same way. Although she had inherited his fortune, her income dwindled, and she embarked on a series of murders, including those of her brother, a creditor, and the entire family of a Bremen wheelwright called Rumf, who became suspicious, and in 1828 Gottfried was arrested. She admitted to over 30 murders and was executed.

Poisoner	Victims
3 Hélène Jegado	23

Jegado was a French housemaid believed to have poisoned 23 people with arsenic. She was tried in 1851, and guillotined in 1852.

Poisoner	Victims
4 Mary Ann Cotton	20

Probably the UK's worst murderer, Cotton killed her husband, children, step-children and other victims, by arsenic poisoning. She was hanged on March 24, 1873.

Poisoner	Victims
5= Dr. William Palmer	14

A compulsive gambler, Palmer killed his wife, brother, children, and various men whom he robbed to pay off his gambling debts. He was hanged on June 14, 1856.

Poisoner	Victims
5= Sadamichi Hirasawa	14

On January 26, 1948 Hirasawa entered the Shiinamachi branch of the Imperial Bank of Tokyo. Posing as a doctor, he gave 16 members of staff what he claimed was a medicine but was, in fact, cyanide. 14 people died. He was caught and jailed for 40 years.

Poisoner	Victims
7 Johann Otto Hoch	at least 12

In 1895 German-born Hoch (1862–1906), who used a variety of aliases, moved to the US where he preyed on widows, many of whom he married before murdering them, usually with poison. He certainly killed 12, probably 24, and possibly 50 before being hanged in Chicago on February 23, 1906.

Poisoner	Victims
8 Marie Becker	12

In the 1930s Marie Becker, the 53-year-old wife of a cabinetmaker in Liège, France, carried out a series of poisonings that left at least 12 dead, and possibly as many as 20. In the autumn of 1932 she poisoned her husband Charles with digitalis, followed by her lover Lambert Bayer. In order to finance her own extravagant lifestyle, she then embarked on murdering a series of elderly women whom she nursed, using the same drug, traces of which were detected in their bodies. She was sentenced to life imprisonment, and died in jail.

Poisoner	Victims
9 Lydia Sherman	at least 11

Known as the "Queen Poisoner," American killer Lydia Sherman murdered her husband, a policeman called Edward Struck, and her six children during the 1860s. After this she married and murdered New Haven farmer Dennis Hurlbrut, followed by Nelson Sherman and his two children, all with arsenic, bringing her total to 11 – although it has been suggested that she may have killed at least twice as many (a total of 42 has been claimed by some authorities). Sentenced to life imprisonment, she died in jail on May 16, 1878.

Poisoner	Victims
10= Dr. Thomas Neill Cream	5

In 1881 Cream, a Scottish-born doctor, was sentenced in the US to 10 years in prison for a murder using strychnine. Released in 1891, he moved to London where he soon poisoned four more people and became known as the "Lambeth Poisoner." He was caught and executed on November 15, 1892. It is said that as he died he blurted out, "I am Jack. . .," which some have taken to mean that he was Jack the Ripper. The flaw in this is that the Ripper's crimes were carried out in 1888, when Cream was still behind bars in the US.

Poisoner	Victims
10= Herman Billik	5

In the period 1905 to 1906, Herman Billik, a Chicago eccentric who offered his services as a sorcerer, murdered his creditor Martin Vzral and four members of his family, using arsenic – although it seems likely that Vzral's widow was an accomplice. At his trial in 1907, Billik was sentenced to death, but this was later commuted to life imprisonment.

Poisoner	Victims
10= Amy Archer-Gilligan	at least 5

While under the care of Amy Archer-Gilligan, a nursing home owner in Hartford, Connecticut, at least five residents died after being poisoned with arsenic. She was tried in 1917, sentenced to life imprisonment, and died in jail in 1923.

* *Prior to 1950; excluding poisoners where evidence is so confused with legend (such as that surrounding the Borgia family) as to be unreliable*

TOP 10

MOST PROLIFIC MURDERESSES

	Murderess	Victims
1	Countess Erszébet Báthory	650

(See Serial Killers Before the 20th Century, below)

	Murderess	Victims
2	Susannah Olah	up to 100

(See Most Prolific Poisoners, p.64)

	Murderess	Victims
3	Delfina and Maria de Jesús Gonzales	80

(See Serial Killers in the 20th Century, p.66)

	Murderess	Victims
4	Bella Poulsdatter Sorensen Gunness	42

Bella, or Belle Gunness (1859–1908?), a Norwegian-born immigrant to the US, is believed to have killed her husband Peter Gunness for his life insurance (she claimed that an ax had fallen off a shelf and onto his head). After this she lured between 16 and 28 suitors through "lonely hearts" advertisements, as well as many others – totaling 42 – to her Indiana farm where she murdered them. Her farm burned down on April 28, 1908, and a headless corpse was found and identified as Gunness. It seemed that she had been murdered – with her three children – by her accomplice Ray Lamphere. However, she may have faked her own death and disappeared.

	Murderess	Victims
5	Gesina Margaretha Gottfried	at least 30

(See Most Prolific Poisoners, p.64)

	Murderess	Victims
6	Jane Toppan	30

Boston-born Nora Kelley, also known as Jane Toppan (1854–1938), was almost certainly insane. She trained as a nurse, and within a few years, after numerous patients in her care had died, their bodies were exhumed revealing traces of morphine and atropine poisoning. It seems probable from the evidence and her own confession that she killed 30 people. She died on August 17, 1938 in an asylum, aged 84.

	Murderess	Victims
7	Hélène Jegado	23

(See Most Prolific Poisoners, p.64)

	Murderess	Victims
8	Genene Jones	21

In 1984 Jones, a nurse, was found guilty of killing a baby, Chelsea McClellan, at the San Antonio Hospital in Texas by adminstering the drug succinylcholine. She was sentenced to 99 years. Jones had been dismissed from the previous hospital where she had worked after 20 babies in her care had died of suspicious but uncertain causes. Some authorities link her with as many as 42 deaths.

	Murderess	Victims
9	Mary Ann Cotton	20

(See Most Prolific Poisoners, p.64)

	Murderess	Victims
10	Waltraud Wagner	15

Wagner was the ringleader of a group of four nurses found guilty of causing numerous deaths through deliberate drug overdoses and other means at the Lainz hospital, Vienna, Austria, in the late 1980s. Between 42 and possibly up to several hundred patients were murdered, for which she was sentenced to life imprisonment on charges that included 15 counts of murder and 17 of attempted murder.

TOP 10

MOST PROLIFIC SERIAL KILLERS BEFORE THE 20TH CENTURY

	Murderer	Victims
1	Behram	931

Behram (or Buhram) was the leader of the Thugee cult in India, which was reckoned to be responsible for the deaths of up to 2,000 people. At his trial Behram was found guilty of personally committing 931 murders between 1790 and 1830, mostly by ritual strangulation with the cult's traditional cloth known as a ruhmal. From the end of his reign of terror onward, the British in India mounted a campaign against Thugee, and the cult was eventually suppressed.

	Murderer	Victims
2	Countess Erszébet Báthory	up to 650

In the period up to 1610 in Hungary, Báthory (1560–1614), known as "Countess Dracula" – the title of a 1970 Hammer horror movie about her life and crimes – was alleged to have murdered between 300 and 650 girls (her personal list of 610 victims was described at her trial) in the belief that drinking their blood would prevent her from aging. She was eventually arrested in 1611. Tried and found guilty, she died on August 21, 1614 walled up in her own castle at Csejthe.

	Murderer	Victims
3	Gilles de Rais	up to 200

Baron de Rais, one-time supporter of Joan of Arc, dabbled in the occult and committed murders as sacrifices in black magic rituals. He was accused of kidnapping and killing between 60 and 200 children. Found guilty, he was tortured, strangled, and burned on October 25, 1440.

	Murderer	Victims
4	Herman Webster Mudgett	up to 150

Also known as "H. H. Holmes," Mudgett was believed to have lured over 150 women to his Chicago "castle," which was fully equipped for torturing and murdering them and disposing of the bodies. Arrested in 1894 and found guilty of murder, he confessed to killing 27. Regarded as America's first mass murderer, he was hanged in Philadelphia on May 7, 1896.

	Murderer	Victims
5	Gesina Margareth Gottfried	at least 30

(See Most Prolific Poisoners, p.64)

	Murderer	Victims
6	Hélène Jegado	23

(See Most Prolific Poisoners, p.64)

	Murderer	Victims
7	Mary Ann Cotton	20

(See Most Prolific Poisoners, p.64)

	Murderer	Victims
8	William Burke and William Hare	at least 15

Irishmen Burke and Hare murdered at least 15 people to sell their bodies to anatomists before human dissection was legal. Burke was hanged on January 28, 1829, while Hare died in London, a blind beggar, in the 1860s.

	Murderer	Victims
9	Dr. William Palmer	14

(See Most Prolific Poisoners, p.64)

	Murderer	Victims
10	Johann Otto Hoch	at least 12

(See Most Prolific Poisoners, p.64)

* Includes only individual murderers; excludes murders by bandits, those carried out by groups, such as political and military atrocities, and gangland slayings

MURDER MOST FOUL

MOST PROLIFIC SERIAL KILLERS OF THE 20TH CENTURY

Serial killers are mass murderers who kill repeatedly, often over long periods, in contrast to the so-called "spree killers" who have been responsible for massacres on single occasions, usually with guns, and other perpetrators of single outrages, often by means of bombs, resulting in multiple deaths. Because of the secrecy surrounding their horrific crimes, and the time spans involved, it is almost impossible to calculate the precise numbers of serial killers' victims. The numbers of murders attributed to these criminals should be taken as "best estimates" based on the most reliable evidence available. Such is the magnitude of the crimes of some of them, however, that some of the figures may be underestimates.

ANDREI CHIKATILO
Chikatilo successfully led a double life as a married father and schoolteacher and Communist party member for the 12 years he preyed on the citizens of Rostov-on-Don.

1   Pedro Alonzo (or Armando) López

After he was captured in 1980, López, known as the "Monster of the Andes," led police to 53 graves, but he had probably murdered a total of more than 300 young girls in Colombia, Ecuador, and Peru. He was sentenced to life imprisonment.

2   Henry Lee Lucas

The subject of the film, Henry, Portrait of a Serial Killer, Lucas (b.1937) may have committed up to 200 murders. In 1983 he admitted to 360 and was convicted of 11, and is now on Death Row in Huntsville, Texas. His full toll of victims will probably never be known.

3   Bruno Lüdke

Lüdke (b.1909) was a German who confessed to murdering 86 women between 1928 and January 29, 1943. Declared insane, he was incarcerated in a Vienna hospital where he was subjected to medical experiments, apparently dying on April 8, 1944 after a lethal injection.

4   Delfina and Maria de Jesús Gonzales

After abducting girls to work in their Mexican brothel, Rancho El Angel, the Gonzales sisters murdered as many as 80 of them, and an unknown number of their customers, and buried them in the grounds. In 1964 the two were sentenced to 40 years' imprisonment.

5   Daniel Camargo Barbosa

Eight years after the arrest of Lopez (see No. 1) in Ecuador, Barbosa, another Ecuadorean, was captured after a similar series of horrific child murders – with a probable total of 71 victims. He was sentenced to just 16 years in prison.

6   Kampatimar Shankariya

Caught after a two-year spree during which he killed as many as 70 times, Shankariya was hanged in Jaipur, India, on May 16, 1979.

MOST PROLIFIC MURDERERS IN THE US

1   Henry Lee Lucas   up to 200

Lucas ranks as America's worst serial killer, with up to 200 victims (see No. 2 in The 10 Most Prolific Serial Killers of the 20th Century).

2   Herman Webster Mudgett   up to 150

See No. 4 in The 10 Most Prolific Pre-20th Century Serial Killers on page 65.

3   Julio Gonzalez   87

On the morning of Sunday March 25, 1990, following an argument with his girlfriend, Lydia Feliciano, Gonzalez, a 36-year-old Cuban refugee who had lived in the US for 10 years, firebombed her place of employment, Happy Land, an illegal discotheque in the Bronx, New York (ordered closed in 1988 because it lacked basic fire safety measures), killing 87 – although Ms Feliciano was one of six survivors.

4   Randolph Kraft   67

See No. 7 in The 10 Most Prolific Serial Killers of the 20th Century).

5   Donald Harvey   58

See No. 9 in The 10 Most Prolific Serial Killers of the 20th Century).

6   John Gilbert Graham   44

In order to claim on a total of six life insurance policies, Graham placed a time bomb in the luggage of his mother, Daisy King, as she boarded a DC-6B airliner in Denver, Colorado, on November 1, 1955. En route for San Francisco, it blew up killing all 44 on board. On January 11, 1957, Graham was found guilty – only on the charge of murdering his mother – and executed in the gas chamber of Colorado State Penitentiary.

7   Daniel Burke   43

On a flight from Los Angeles to San Francisco on December 7, 1987, a Pacific Southwest Airlines British Aerospace 146-200 commuter jet crashed near San Luis Obispo, killing 43 on board. Gunshots had been heard over the radio, and the FBI later found a note from a passenger, London-born Jamaican Daniel Burke, an aggrieved former airline employee, from which they concluded that he had shot the pilot with the .44 Magnum found in the wreckage of the plane.

8   Bella Poulsdatter Sorensen Gunness   42

See No. 4 in The 10 Most Prolific Murderesses in the World on page 65.

9   Ted Bundy   36

After spending nine years on death row, Bundy (b.1947) was executed by electrocution at Florida State Prison on January 24, 1989. During his last hours Bundy confessed to 23 murders. Police linked him conclusively to the murders of 36 girls, and he once admitted that he might have killed as many as 100 times.

10   John Wayne Gacy   34

On March 13, 1980 John Wayne Gacy (b.1942) was sentenced to death by electrocution for the Chicago murders of 34 men. He was executed on May 10, 1994.

7 Randolph Kraft

From 1972 until his arrest on May 14, 1983, Kraft is thought to have murdered 67 men. On November 29, 1989 he was found guilty on 16 counts and was sentenced to death in the San Quentin gas chamber.

8 Dr. Marcel André Henri Felix Petiot

Dr. Marcel Petiot (b.1897), once mayor of Villeneuve, is known to have killed at least 27 but admitted to 63 murders at his Paris house during World War II. He claimed that they were Nazi collaborators, but it is probable that they were wealthy Jews whom he robbed and killed after pretending to help them escape from occupied France. Petiot was guillotined on May 26, 1946.

9 Donald Harvey

Working as an orderly in hospitals in Kentucky and Ohio, Harvey is believed to have murdered some 58 patients up to the time of his arrest in March 1987. He pleaded guilty to 24 murders for which he received multiple life sentences, later confessing to further charges and receiving additional sentences.

10 Andrei Chikatilo

Russia's worst serial killer was convicted in Rostov-on-Don in 1992 of killing 52 women and children between 1978 and 1990. He was executed by a firing squad at Novocherkassk prison on February 14, 1994.

---

* Includes only individual murderers; excludes murders by bandits, those carried out by groups, such as terrorist atrocities, and gangland slayings.

On July 17, 1961, William Estel Brown claimed that on March 18, 1937, he had deliberately loosened the gas pipes in his school basement in New London, Texas, resulting in an explosion that killed 297 children and teachers, and injured 437. If true, he would qualify for the No. 1 position in this grim list. The claims that Johann Otto Hoch, executed in 1906, had killed as many as 50 women, and modern serial killer Randall Brent Woodfield (known as the "I-5 Killer") up to 44, are – along with those for various other candidates – unlikely to be confirmed. In California in 1968–74 the "Zodiac Killer," so called because he used zodiacal signs both at the murder scenes and to sign letters to the press, may have murdered 37, but was never identified.

WORST GUN MASSACRES OF ALL TIME

(By individuals, excluding terrorist and military actions; totals exclude perpetrator)

Perpetrator/location/date circumstances	Killed
1 Woo Bum Kong Sang-Namdo, South Korea, April 28, 1982	57

Off-duty policeman Woo Bum Kong (or Wou Bom-Kon), 27, went on a drunken rampage with rifles and hand grenades, killing 57 and injuring 38 before blowing himself up.

Perpetrator/location/date circumstances	Killed
2 Baruch Goldstein Hebron, Occupied West Bank, Israel, February 25, 1994	29

Goldstein, a 42-year-old US immigrant doctor, carried out a gun massacre of Palestinians at prayer at the Tomb of the Patriarchs before being beaten to death by the crowd.

	Killed
3= James Oliver Huberty San Ysidro, California, July 18, 1984	22

Huberty, aged 41, opened fire in a McDonald's restaurant, killing 21 before being shot dead by a SWAT marksman. A further 19 were wounded, one of whom died the following day.

	Killed
3= George Hennard Killeen, Texas, October 16, 1991	22

Hennard drove his pickup truck through the window of Luby's Cafeteria and, in 11 minutes, killed 22 with semiautomatic pistols before shooting himself.

	Killed
5= Charles Joseph Whitman, Austin, Texas, July 31–August 1, 1966	16

25-year-old ex-Marine marksman Whitman killed his mother and wife. The following day he took the elevator to the 27th floor of the campus tower and ascended to the observation deck at the University of Texas at Austin, from where he killed 14 and wounded 34 before being shot dead by police officer Romero Martinez.

	Killed
5= Michael Ryan, Hungerford, Berkshire, UK, August 19, 1987	16

Ryan, 26, shot 14 dead and wounded 16 others (two of whom died later) before shooting himself.

	Killed
5= Ronald Gene Simmons Russellville, Arkansas, December 28, 1987	16

47-year-old Simmons killed 16, including 14 members of his own family, by shooting or strangling. He was caught and on February 10, 1989 was sentenced to death.

Perpetrator/location/date circumstances	Killed
8= Wagner von Degerloch Muehlhausen, Germany, September 3–4, 1913	14

Wagner von Degerloch, a 39-year-old school-teacher, murdered his wife and four children before embarking on a random shooting spree, as a result of which nine more were killed and 12 injured. Regarded as one of the first "spree killers," von Degerloch was committed to a mental asylum where he died in 1938.

	Killed
8= Patrick Henry Sherrill Edmond, Oklahoma, August 20, 1986	14

Sherrill, aged 44, shot 14 dead and wounded six others at the post office where he worked before killing himself.

	Killed
8= Christian Dornier Luxiol, Doubs, France, July 12, 1989	14

Dornier, a 31-year-old farmer, went on a rampage leaving 14 dead and nine injured, including several children, before being wounded and caught by police.

	Killed
8= Marc Lépine Montreal University, Canada, December 6, 1989	14

In Canada's worst gun massacre, Lépine, a 25-year-old student, went on an armed rampage, firing only at women, then shot himself.

GEORGE HENNARD
Police found over 100 spent cartridges in the carnage that spree-killer Hennard left behind.

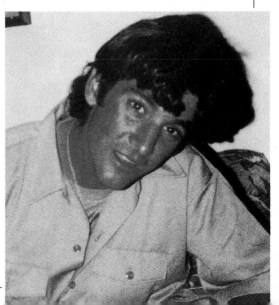

CAPITAL PUNISHMENT

TOP 10

COUNTRIES TO ABOLISH CAPITAL PUNISHMENT

	Country	Abolished
1	Russia	1826
2	Venezuela	1863
3	Portugal	1867
4=	Brazil	1882
4=	Costa Rica	1882
6	Ecuador	1897
7	Panama	1903
8	Norway	1905
9	Uruguay	1907
10	Colombia	1910

Russia was first to abolish the death penalty but later reinstated it. Capital punishment is retained in some countries for treason or during wartime only. In others, like Mexico, it has been abolished in practice: the last execution there was in 1946.

THE HOT SEAT
This form of capital punishment was first adopted by New York State, and the first person to be executed in this way was William Kemmler, on August 6, 1890, in Auburn Prison.

THE 10

FIRST EXECUTIONS BY LETHAL INJECTION IN THE US

	Name	Date
1	Charles Brooks	December 7, 1982
2	James Autry	March 14, 1984
3	Ronald O'Bryan	March 31, 1984
4	Thomas Barefoot	October 30, 1984
5	Doyle Skillern	January 16, 1985
6	Stephen Morin	March 13, 1985
7	Jesse De La Rosa	May 15, 1985
8	Charles Milton	June 25, 1985
9	Henry Porter	July 9, 1985
10	Charles Rumbaugh	September 11, 1985

Although Oklahoma was the first state to legalize execution by lethal injection, the option was not taken there until 1990. All of the above were executed in Texas (where, curiously, death row inmates with the first name of Charles figure prominently). Over the past ten years, this option has become the most common form of execution in states that allow its use.

Source: Death Penalty Information Center

TOP 10

STATES WITH THE MOST EXECUTIONS, 1930–1993

	State	Executions
1	Georgia	383
2	Texas	368
3	New York	329
4	California	294
5	North Carolina	268
6	Florida	202
7	Ohio	172
8	South Carolina	166
9	Mississippi	158
10	Louisiana	154

Eight states (Wisconsin, Rhode Island, North Dakota, Minnesota, Michigan, Maine, Hawaii, and Alaska) had no executions during this period; several had abolished the death penalty at an earlier date. Michigan was the first in 1847, followed by Wisconsin in 1853, Maine in 1887 and Minnesota in 1911. In 1977, the US Supreme Court permitted the reinstitution of the death penalty, and 21 states have carried out executions since then, led by Texas with 71.

THE 10

NAZI WAR CRIMINALS HANGED AT NUREMBERG

(Following the International Military Tribunal trials, November 20, 1945 to August 31, 1946)

	Name	Age
1	Joachim Von Ribbentrop	53

Former Ambassador to Great Britain and Hitler's last Foreign Minister (the first to be hanged, at 1:02 am)

	Name	Age
2	Field Marshal Wilhelm Von Keitel	64

Keitel had ordered the killing of 50 Allied air force officers after the Great Escape

	Name	Age
3	General Ernst Kaltenbrunner	44

SS and Gestapo leader

	Name	Age
4	Reichminister Alfred Rosenburg	53

Ex-Minister for Occupied Eastern territories

	Name	Age
5	Reichminister Hans Frank	46

Ex-Governor of Poland

	Name	Age
6	Reichminister Wilhelm Frick	69

Former Minister of the Interior

	Name	Age
7	Gauleiter Julius Streicher	61

Editor of anti-Semitic magazine Die Stürmer

	Name	Age
8	Reichminister Fritz Sauckel	52

Ex-General Plenipotentiary for the Utilization of Labor (the slave-labor program)

	Name	Age
9	Colonel-General Alfred Jodl	56

Former Chief of the General Staff

	Name	Age
10	Gauleiter Artur Von Seyss-Inquart	?

Governor of Austria and later Commissioner for Occupied Holland (the last to be hanged)

TOP 10
DECADES FOR EXECUTIONS IN THE US

	Decade	Executions		Decade	Executions
1	1930–39	1,670	**6**	1910–19	1,042
2	1940–49	1,287	**7**	1950–59	719
3	1890–99	1,215	**8**	1960–69	192
4	1900–09	1,190	**9**	1980–89	117
5	1920–29	1,169	**10**	1970–79	3

THE 10
CAPITAL PUNISHMENT STATES IN THE US

	State	Death penalty now in use	No. of people executed 1930–93
1	Georgia	Electrocution	383
2	Texas	Lethal injection	368
3	New York	Lethal injection	329
4	California	Lethal gas	294
5	North Carolina	Lethal gas or injection	268
6	Florida	Electrocution	202
7	Ohio	Electrocution	172
8	South Carolina	Electrocution	166
9	Mississippi	Lethal injection or gas	158
10	Pennsylvania	Lethal injection	154

TOP 10
STATES WITH THE MOST PRISONERS ON DEATH ROW

	State	No. under death sentence
1	California	363
2	Texas	357
3	Florida	324
4	Pennsylvania	169
5	Illinois	152
6	Ohio	129
7	Oklahoma	122
8	Alabama	120
9	Arizona	112
10	North Carolina	99

There are 34 states in the Federal Prison System which still operate death penalty laws. As of December 31, 1993, there were 2,716 inmates on death row.

Source: Department of Justice

THE 10
US EXECUTION FIRSTS

1 First to be hanged

John Billington, for the shooting murder of John Newcomin, Plymouth, Massachusetts, September 30, 1630

2 First to be hanged for witchcraft

Achsah Young, in Massachusetts, May 27, 1647

3 First to be hanged for treason

Jacob Leisler, for insurrection, City Hall Park, New York, May 16, 1691

4 First to be hanged for slave trading

Captain Nathaniel Gordon, Tombs Prison, New York, February 21, 1862

5 First US civilian to be hanged for treason

William Bruce Mumford, for tearing down the American flag in New Orleans, June 7, 1862

6 First man to be electrocuted

William Kemmler, alias John Hart, for the ax murder of Matilda Ziegler, Auburn Prison, New York, August 6, 1890

7 First woman to be electrocuted

Martha M. Place, for murdering her step-daughter Ida, Sing Sing Prison, New York, March 20, 1899

8 First to be executed in the gas chamber

Gee Jon, for murder, Carson City, Nevada, February 8, 1924

9 First to be electrocuted for treason

Julius and Ethel Rosenberg, Sing Sing Prison, New York, June 19, 1953

10 First to be executed by lethal injection

Charles Brooks, for murder, Department of Corrections, Huntsville, Texas, December 6, 1982

WAR CRIMES
Nazi leaders in the dock at the Nuremberg Trials. The four central figures are Hermann Goering, who committed suicide, Rudolf Hess, who was imprisoned, and Joachim Von Ribbentrop and Wilhelm Von Keitel, both of whom were hanged on October 16, 1946.

THE WORLD AT WAR

ALLIES
This World War I badge shows the united flags of France, Britain, and Belgium.

TOP 10

COUNTRIES WITH THE MOST PRISONERS OF WAR, 1914–18

	Country	Personnel
1	Russia	2,500,000
2	Austria–Hungary	2,200,000
3	Germany	1,152,800
4	Italy	600,000
5	France	537,000
6	Turkey	250,000
7	British Empire	191,652
8	Serbia	152,958
9	Romania	80,000
10	Belgium	34,659

DID YOU KNOW

THE STATISTICS OF WAR

Although World War II (1939–1945, with American involvement from 1941) resulted in the greatest number of military deaths that the US has ever experienced when considered in relation to the size of the population existing at that time, a greater number died in the Civil War (1861–65) – some 140,414 killed in battle, and a further 224,097 dying from wounds or disease, many of them while prisoners of war. In the 20th century, in addition to the two World Wars, an estimated 54,246 Americans were killed in the Korean War, 58,151 in the Vietnam War, and 293 in the Gulf War. In modern conflicts the US has lost more than 600,000 personnel with a further 1,000,000 wounded.

TOP 10

COUNTRIES SUFFERING THE GREATEST MILITARY LOSSES IN WORLD WAR I

	Country	Killed
1	Germany	1,773,700
2	Russia	1,700,000
3	France	1,357,800
4	Austria–Hungary	1,200,000
5	British Empire*	908,371
6	Italy	650,000
7	Romania	335,706
8	Turkey	325,000
9	US	116,516
10	Bulgaria	87,500

* Including Australia, Canada, India, New Zealand, South Africa, etc.

TOP 10

LARGEST ARMED FORCES OF WORLD WAR I

	Country	Personnel*
1	Russia	12,000,000
2	Germany	11,000,000
3	British Empire	8,904,467
4	France	8,410,000
5	Austria–Hungary	7,800,000
6	Italy	5,615,000
7	US	4,355,000
8	Turkey	2,850,000
9	Bulgaria	1,200,000
10	Japan	800,000

* Total at peak strength

As well as the ten principal military powers engaged in World War I, several other European nations had forces that were similarly substantial in relation to their populations: Romania had an army of 750,000, Serbia 707,343, Belgium 267,000, Greece 230,000, Portugal 100,000, and Montenegro 50,000.

The number of battle fatalities and deaths from other causes, such as malnutrition, illness, and poor conditions, among military personnel varied enormously from country to country: Romania's death rate was highest at 45 percent of its total mobilized forces; Germany's was 16 percent, Austria-Hungary's and Russia's 15 percent, and the British Empire's 10 percent, with the US's 2 percent and Japan's 0.04 percent among the lowest.

WORLD WAR I SOLDIER
This German's equipment includes a gas mask – gas was first used by Germany in 1915.

TOP 10

LARGEST ARMED FORCES OF WORLD WAR II

	Country	Personnel*
1	USSR	12,500,000
2	US	12,364,000
3	Germany	10,000,000
4	Japan	6,095,000
5	France	5,700,000
6	UK	4,683,000
7	Italy	4,500,000
8	China	3,800,000
9	India	2,150,000
10	Poland	1,000,000

* Total at peak strength

TOP 10

SMALLEST ARMED FORCES OF WORLD WAR II

	Country	Personnel*
1	Costa Rica	400
2	Liberia	1,000
3=	El Salvador	3,000
3=	Honduras	3,000
3=	Nicaragua	3,000
6	Haiti	3,500
7	Dominican Republic	4,000
8	Guatemala	5,000
9=	Bolivia	8,000
9=	Paraguay	8,000
9=	Uruguay	8,000

* Total at peak strength

Several of the South American countries entered World War II at a very late stage: Argentina, for example, did not declare war on Germany and Japan until March 27, 1945. Denmark, whose maximum strength was 15,000, had the smallest armed force in Europe. Just 13 of the Danish soldiers were killed during the one-day German invasion of April 9, 1940, when Denmark became the second country after Poland to be occupied.

TOP 10

TANKS OF WORLD WAR II

	Tank/country/(introduced)	Weight (tons)	No. produced
1	Sherman, US (1942)	31.0	41,530
2	T34 Model 42, USSR (1940)	28.5	35,120
3	T34/85, USSR (1944)	32.0	29,430
4	M3 General Stuart, US (1941)	12.2	14,000
5	Valentine II, UK (1941)	17.5	8,280
6	M3A1 Lee/Grant, US (1941)	26.8	7,400
7	Churchill VII, UK (1942)	40.0	5,640
8=	Panzer IVD, Germany (prewar)	20,0	5,500
8=	Panzer VG, Germany (1943)	44.8	5,500
10	Crusader I, UK (1941)	19.0	4,750

The tank named after US Civil War General William Tecumseh Sherman was used in large numbers by US and British troops during World War II. It carried a crew of five and could cruise at up to 25 mph/40 km/h. Its weaponry was comprised of two maching guns and, originally, a 75-mm cannon. After 1944 about half the Shermans had their cannons replaced by ones capable of firing a powerful 17-lb shell or a 12-lb armor-piercing shell.

TOP 10

COUNTRIES SUFFERING THE GREATEST MILITARY LOSSES IN WORLD WAR II

	Country	Killed
1	USSR	13,600,000
2	Germany	3,300,000
3	China	1,324,516
4	Japan	1,140,429
5	British Empire* (of which UK	357,116 264,000)
6	Romania	350,000
7	Poland	320,000
8	Yugoslavia	305,000
9	US	292,131
10	Italy	279,800

* Including Australia, Canada, India, New Zealand, etc.

The actual numbers killed in World War II have been the subject of intense argument for nearly 50 years. The immense level of the military casualty rate of the USSR in particular is hard to comprehend. It is included here at its likely lowest level, but most authorities now reckon that, of the 30,000,000 Soviets who bore arms, as many as 8,500,000 died in action and up to 2,500,000 of wounds received in battle and disease. Some 5,800,000 were taken prisoner, of which perhaps 3,300,000 may have died in captivity. It should also be kept in mind that these were military losses: to these should be added many untold millions of civilian war deaths.

ACES HIGH

The term "ace" was first used during World War I for a pilot who had brought down at least five enemy aircraft; the British regarded the tally for an "ace" as varying from three to ten aircraft. The first reference in print to an air "ace" appeared in an article in *The Times* (September 14, 1917). The names of French pilots who achieved this feat were recorded in official communiqués, but while US and other pilots followed the same system, the British definition of an "ace" was never officially approved, remaining an informal concept during both world wars. The German equivalent of the air "ace" was *Oberkanone*, which may be translated as "top gun."

LVG CVI, 1917
This German aircraft, fitted with guns and able to carry bombs, was one of the most versatile of the World War I airplanes.

T O P   1 0

BRITISH AND COMMONWEALTH AIR ACES OF WORLD WAR I

	Pilot	Nationality	Kills claimed
1	Edward Mannock	British	73
2	William Avery Bishop	Canadian	72
3	Raymond Collishaw	Canadian	60
4	James Thomas Byford McCudden	British	57
5=	Anthony Wetherby Beauchamp-Proctor	British	54
5=	Donald Roderick MacLaren	British	54
7	William George Barker	Canadian	53
8	Robert Alexander Little	Australian	47
9=	Philip Fletcher Fullard	British	46
9=	George Edward Henry McElroy	Irish	46

This Top 10 takes account of British Empire pilots belonging to the Royal Flying Corps, the Royal Naval Air Service, and (after April 1, 1918) the Royal Air Force. The total of Edward "Mick" Mannock (1887–1918) may actually be greater than those definitely credited to him. Similarly, British pilot Albert Ball is generally credited with 44 kills (and hence not in the Top 10), but with the qualification that his total may have been greater. If this list were extended to include French pilots it would include René Paul Fonck (1894–1953) at No. 1 with 75 kills and Georges-Marie Ludovic Jules Guynemer (1894–1917) with 54.

T O P   1 0

GERMAN AIR ACES OF WORLD WAR I

	Pilot	Kills claimed
1	Manfred von Richthofen*	80
2	Ernst Udet	62
3	Erich Loewenhardt	53
4	Werner Voss	48
5	Fritz Rumey	45
6	Rudolph Berthold	44
7	Paul Bäumer	43
8=	Josef Jacobs	41
8=	Bruno Loerzer	41
10=	Oswald Boelcke	40
10=	Franz Büchner	40
10=	Lothar Freiherr von Richthofen*	40

* *Brothers*

Top World War I "ace" Rittmeister Manfred, Baron von Richthofen's claim of 80 kills has been disputed, since only 60 of them have been completely confirmed. Richthofen, known as the "Red Baron" and leader of the so-called "Flying Circus" (because the aircraft of his squadron were painted in distinctive bright colors), shot down 21 Allied fighters in the single month of April 1917. His own end a year later, on April 21, 1918, has been the subject of controversy ever since, and it remains uncertain whether his Fokker tri-plane was shot down in aerial combat with British pilot Captain A. Roy Brown (who was credited with the kill) or by shots from Australian machine gunners on the ground.

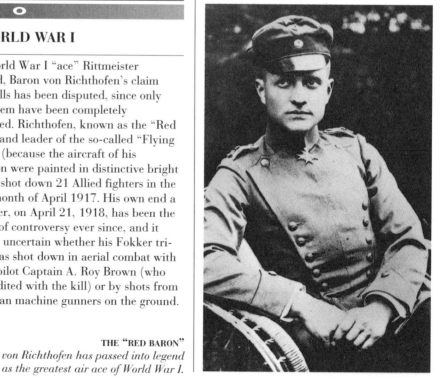

THE "RED BARON"
Baron von Richthofen has passed into legend as the greatest air ace of World War I.

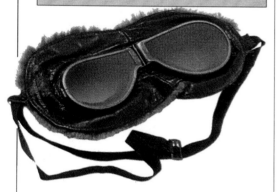

TOP 10

US AIR ACES OF WORLD WAR I

	Pilot	Kills claimed
1	Edward Vernon Rickenbacker	26
2	Frank Luke, Jr.	21
3	Gervais Raoul Lufbery	17
4	George Augustus Vaughn, Jr.	13
5=	Field E. Kindley	12
5=	David Endicott Putnam	12
5=	Elliot White Springs	12
8=	Reed Gresham Landis	10
8=	Jacques Michael Swaab	10
10=	Lloyd Andrews Hamilton	9
10=	Chester Ellis Wright	9

Edward ("Eddie") Rickenbacker (1890–1973) first achieved fame in the US as a champion racing-car driver. A visit to England in 1917 encouraged his interest in flying and when the US entered World War I (April 6, 1917) he enlisted, serving initially as chauffeur to General Pershing before transferring to active service as a pilot. On March 19, 1918 Rickenbacker took part in the first-ever US patrol over enemy lines and on April 29 shot down his first airplane. A month later, with five kills to his credit, he became an acknowledged "ace," eventually achieving a total of 26 kills (22 aircraft and four balloons) and winning the US Congressional Medal of Honor, the country's highest award. Rickenbacker also served in World War II and later became CEO of Eastern Airlines. He died in 1973. As well as the 151 kills credited to the pilots in the Top 10, a further 76 US pilots each shot down five to nine enemy aircraft. Frank Leaman Baylies had 12 kills but served solely with the French air force and hence is not included in the US list.

TOP 10

BRITISH AND COMMONWEALTH AIR ACES OF WORLD WAR II

	Pilot	Nationality	Kills claimed
1	Marmaduke Thomas St. John Pattle	South African	41
2	James Edgar "Johnny" Johnson	British	38
3	Adolf Gysbert "Sailor" Malan	South African	35
4	Brendan "Paddy" Finucane	Irish	32
5	George Frederick Beurling	Canadian	31⅓
6=	John Robert Daniel Braham	British	29
6=	Robert Roland Stanford Tuck	British	29
8	Neville Frederick Duke	British	28⅚
9	Clive Robert Caldwell	Australian	28½
10	Frank Reginald Carey	British	28⅓

Kills that are expressed as fractions refer to those that were shared with others, the number of fighters involved and the extent of each pilot's participation determining the proportion allocated to him. As a result of this precise reckoning, British pilot James Harry "Ginger" Lacey, with 28 kills, just misses sharing 10th place with Frank Reginald Carey by ⅓ of a kill.

TOP 10

LUFTWAFFE ACES OF WORLD WAR II

	Pilot	Kills claimed
1	Eric Hartmann	352
2	Gerhard Barkhorn	301
3	Günther Rall	275
4	Otto Kittel	267
5	Walther Nowotny	255
6	Wilhelm Batz	237
7	Erich Rudorffer	222
8	Heinrich Baer	220
9	Herman Graf	212
10	Heinrich Ehrler	209

Although these apparently high claims have been dismissed by some military historians as inflated for propaganda purposes, it is worth noting that many of them relate to kills on the Eastern Front, where the Luftwaffe was undoubtedly superior to its Soviet opponents. Few have questioned the so-called "Blond Knight" Eric Hartmann's achievement, however, and his victories over Soviet aircraft so outraged the USSR that after the war he was arrested and sentenced to 25 years in a Russian labor camp. He was released in 1955, returned to serve in the West German air force, and died on September 20, 1993.

MISSING
Most of "Pat" Pattle's kills were made flying an out-of-date Gladiator biplane. On April 22, 1941, after three kills, he was himself shot down over the Aegean and was never seen again.

TOP 10

US AIR ACES OF WORLD WAR II

	Pilot	Kills claimed
1	Richard I. Bong	40
2	Thomas B. McGuire	38
3	David McCampbell	34
4	Frances S. Gabreski	31
5=	Gregory Boynington	28
5=	Robert S. Johnson	28
7	Charles H. MacDonald	27
8=	George E. Preddy	26
8=	Joseph J. Foss	26
10	Robert M. Hanson	25

AIR WARFARE

Seldom has a weapon had as many different names as the V1. Originally called the Fi-103 (From Fiesler, its main manufacturer) or *Flakzeitlgerät 76* ("antiaircraft aiming device 76") or FZG 76, it was developed under the code name *Kirschkern*, "cherry stone." The weapon eventually became known to the Germans as the V1 (from *Vergeltungswaffe Eins* – "vengeance weapon 1"), and to its British victims as the "flying bomb," "buzz bomb," or "doodlebug." These pilotless jet-propelled aircraft, measuring 25 ft 4½ in/7.7 m, were made of sheet steel and plywood and carried 1,874 lb/850 kg of high explosive. Using 150 gallons/1,591 liters of gasoline oxidized by compressed air, they achieved an average speed of 350 mph/563 km/h and a range of about 130 miles/209 km, which they reached in 20–25 minutes. Their engines then cut out, and eyewitnesses tell of the "ominous silence" before the explosion some 12 seconds later.

The first ten V1 rockets were launched against England on June 13, 1944. Of these, five crash-landed near their launch site in Watten, France, one vanished (probably falling into the Channel), and four reached England. Only one reached its London target and caused casualties – six killed in Grove Road, Bethnal Green. The second wave, on the night of June 15, was more successful: 244 missiles were launched, of which 73 reached their goal of London, where 11 were shot down. In subsequent months more than 8,000 missiles were launched. Many were erratic and strayed off course or crashed, and of those that continued toward London, a large proportion were brought down by barrage balloons, antiaircraft fire, and particularly by fighter pilots either shooting them down or flying alongside and "tipping their wings" to send them away from their targets. Nonetheless, they managed to cause over 23,000 casualties.

The V1 was the precursor of the far deadlier V2. Masterminded by Werner von Braun (1912–77), who was later the leader of the US space program, the 46 ft/14 m V2 rocket (known to its German developers as the "A4") was more accurate and far more powerful than the V1. It produced a thrust of 56,000 lb/25,400 kg capable of carrying 1 ton of explosive up to 225 miles/362 km, while its speed of 3,600 mph/5,794 km/h made it virtually impossible to combat with antiaircraft fire or to intercept with fighter aircraft. V2 technology was used by the US to develop missiles suitable for carrying nuclear bombs.

TOP 10

AREAS OF EUROPE MOST BOMBED BY ALLIED AIRCRAFT*, 1939–45

	Area	Bombs dropped (tons)
1	Germany	1,205,644
2	France	520,820
3	Italy	327,254
4	Austria, Hungary, and the Balkans	161,454
5	Belgium and Netherlands	79,231
6	Southern Europe and Mediterranean	68,308
7	Czechoslovakia and Poland	19,124
8	Norway and Denmark	4,729
9	Sea targets	504
10	British Channel Islands	83

* *British and US*

Between August 1942 and May 1945 alone, Allied air forces (Bomber Command plus 8 and 15 US Air Forces) flew 731,969 night sorties (and Bomber Command a further 67,598 day sorties), dropping a total of 1,652,606 tons of bombs.

TOP 10

LUFTWAFFE AIRCRAFT OF WORLD WAR II

	Model	Type	No. produced
1	Messerschmitt Me 109	Fighter	30,480
2	Focke-Wulf Fw 190	Fighter	20,000
3	Junkers Ju 88	Bomber	15,000
4	Messerschmitt Me 110	Fighter-bomber	5,762
5	Heinkel He 111	Bomber	5,656
6	Junkers Ju 87	Dive bomber	4,881
7	Junkers Ju 52	Transport	2,804
8	Fiesler Fi 156	Communications	2,549
9	Dornier Do 217	Bomber	1,730
10	Heinkel He 177	Bomber	1,446

Over 60 years after its first flight, the Junkers Ju 52 is still in service as a transport airplane in South America.

TOP 10

FASTEST FIGHTER AIRCRAFT OF WORLD WAR II

	Aircraft	Country	Maximum speed mph	km/h
1	Messerschmitt Me 163	Germany	596	959
2	Messerschmitt Me 262	Germany	560	901
3	Heinkel He 162A	Germany	553	890
4	P-51-H Mustang	US	487	784
5	Lavochkin La11	USSR	460	740
6	Spitfire XIV	UK	448	721
7	Yakolev Yak-3	USSR	447	719
8	P-51-D Mustang	US	440	708
9	Tempest VI	UK	438	705
10	Focke-Wulf FW190D	Germany	435	700

Also known as the *Komet*, the Messerschmitt Me 163 was a short-range rocket-powered interceptor brought into service in 1944–45, when it scored a number of victories over its slower Allied rivals. The Messerschmitt Me 262 was the first jet in operational service.

T O P 1 0
MOST HEAVILY BLITZED CITIES IN THE UK

	City	Major raids	Tonnage of high explosive dropped
1	London	85	21,383
2	Liverpool/ Birkenhead	8	1,747
3	Birmingham	8	1,654
4	Glasgow/Clydeside	5	1,187
5	Plymouth/ Devonport	8	1,096
6	Bristol/ Avonmouth	6	821
7	Coventry	2	730
8	Portsmouth	3	613
9	Southampton	4	578
10	Hull	3	529

The list, which is derived from official German sources, is based on total tonnage of high explosives dropped in major night attacks during the "Blitz" period, from September 7, 1940 to May 16, 1941.

T O P 1 0
ALLIED AIRCRAFT OF WORLD WAR II

	Model	Type	No. produced
1	Illyushin Il-2m3 (USSR)	Ground-attack	36,200
2	Supermarine Spitfire (UK)	Fighter	20,350
3	Consolidated Liberator (US)	Bomber	18,500
4	Yakolev Yak-9D (USSR)	Fighter	16,800
5	Republic Thunderbolt (US)	Fighter	15,630
6	North American Mustang (US)	Fighter	15,470
7	Hawker Hurricane (UK)	Fighter	14,230
8	Curtis Kittyhawk (US)	Fighter-bomber	13,740
9	Vought Corsair (US)	Carrier-fighter	12,750
10	Boeing Flying Fortress (US)	Bomber	12,700

T O P 1 0
CITIES MOST BOMBED BY THE RAF AND USAAF, 1939–45

	City	Estimated civilian deaths
1	Dresden	100,000
2	Hamburg	55,000
3	Berlin	49,000
4	Cologne	20,000
5	Magdeburg	15,000
6	Kassel	13,000
7	Darmstadt	12,300
8=	Heilbronn	7,500
8=	Essen	7,500
10=	Dortmund	6,000
10=	Wuppertal	6,000

The high level of casualties in Dresden was primarily due to the saturation bombing and the firestorm that followed Allied raids.

V2 ROCKET
German V1s and V2s were the only long-range missiles successfully employed in World War II. The V2 was more precise than the notoriously inaccurate V1 – there was no effective defense against it.

T O P 1 0
MONTHS FOR AIR STRIKES AGAINST JAPAN*

	Month/ year	Bombs (tons) High-explosive	Incendiary	Total
1	Jul 1945	8,382	29,610	37,992
2	Jun 1945	8,887	20,168	29,055
3	May 1945	6,194	15,489	21,683
4	Aug 1945	7,534	11,242	18,776
5	Apr 1945	11,794	3,824	15,618
6	Mar 1945	3,665	9,945	13,610
7	Feb 1945	2,144	1,446	3,590
8	Dec 1944	2,724	545	3,269
9	Jan 1945	2,242	803	3,045
10	Nov 1944	1,570	399	1,969

* By US Twentieth Air Force, June 1944 to August 1945

The US Twentieth Air Force began attacks in June 1944, originally flying B-29 bombers from bases in India. After the capture of the Marianas islands, which were much closer, raids with 500 or more B-29s flew from there, attacking Japanese military and civilian targets with increasing frequency. Although only a fraction of the bombs dropped on Germany were used, casualties, especially from fires in densely populated areas, were much higher. The US Twentieth Air Force flew a total of 28,826 sorties (US Navy and other aircraft flew fewer), dropping 57,312 tons of high-explosive bombs and 94,148 tons of incendiary bombs. At the end of the war, the raids grew in intensity, culminating in the dropping of atomic bombs on the cities of Hiroshima on August 6 and Nagasaki on August 9, and resulting in the Japanese surrender on August 15, 1945.

WAR AT SEA

AN ENIGMATIC SECRET

The capture on May 8, 1941 of *U-110*, the first German submarine to be captured by the British in World War II, was a military secret until 1966, owing to the discovery on board of cipher books that enabled the cracking of the German code known as Enigma. Sadly, *U-110* sank as it was towed to Scapa Flow. All hands were lost, including Commander Julius Lemp – the officer responsible for the sinking earlier of the passenger liner *Athenia*.

T O P 1 0
LARGEST BATTLESHIPS OF WORLD WAR II

	Name	Country	Status	Length ft/m	Tonnage
1=	*Musashi*	Japan	Sunk Oct 25, 1944	862/263	72,809
1=	*Yamato*	Japan	Sunk Apr 7, 1945	862/263	72,809
3=	*Iowa*	US	Still in service with US Navy	887/270	55,710
3=	*Missouri*	US	Still in service with US Navy	887/270	55,710
3=	*New Jersey*	US	Still in service with US Navy	887/270	55,710
3=	*Wisconsin*	US	Still in service with US Navy	887/270	55,710
7=	*Bismarck*	Germany	Sunk May 27, 1941	823/251	50,153
7=	*Tirpitz*	Germany	Sunk Nov 12, 1944	823/251	50,153
9=	*Jean Bart*	France	Survived WWII, later scrapped	812/247	47,500
9=	*Richelieu*	France	Survived WWII, later scrapped	812/247	47,500

T O P 1 0
COUNTRIES SUFFERING THE GREATEST MERCHANT SHIPPING LOSSES IN WORLD WAR I

	Country	Vessels sunk Number	Tonnage
1	UK	2,038	6,797,802
2	Italy	228	720,064
3	France	213	651,583
4	US	93	372,892
5	Germany	188	319,552
6	Greece	115	304,992
7	Denmark	126	205,002
8	Netherlands	74	194,483
9	Sweden	124	192,807
10	Spain	70	160,383

T O P 1 0
COUNTRES SUFFERING THE GREATEST MERCHANT SHIPPING LOSSES IN WORLD WAR II

	Country	Vessels sunk Number	Tonnage
1	UK	4,786	21,194,000
2	Japan	2,346	8,618,109
3	Germany	1,595	7,064,600
4	US	578	3,524,983
5	Norway	427	1,728,531
6	Netherlands	286	1,195,204
7	Italy	467	1,155,080
8	Greece	262	883,200
9	Panama	107	542,772
10	Sweden	204	481,864

During 1939–45, Allied losses in the Atlantic alone totaled 3,843 ships (16,899,147 tonnes). June 1942 was the worst period of the war, with 131 vessels (652,487 tonnes) lost in the Atlantic and a further 42 (181,709 tonnes) lost elsewhere.

T O P 1 0

BIGGEST NAVIES 100 YEARS AGO

	Country	Guns*	Men	Ships*
1	UK	3,631	94,600	659
2	France	1,735	70,600	457
3	Russia	710	31,000	358
4	Italy	611	23,000	267
5	Germany	608	16,500	217
6	Austria	309	9,000	168
7	Netherlands	256	10,000	140
8	Spain	305	16,700	136
9	Turkey	382	23,000	124
10	US	284	10,000	95

* Battleships, cruisers, gunboats, and torpedo-boats

By the 18th century Britain was the world's leading naval nation, often at war with France and Spain, both central in international politics. France retained her large navy into the 19th century, but Spain's navy decreased as she became less powerful on the international scene.

T O P 1 0

US NAVY SUBMARINE COMMANDERS OF WORLD WAR II

	Commander	Submarines commanded	Ships sunk
1	Richard H. O'Kane	*Tang*	31
2	Eugene B. Fluckley	*Barb*	25
3	Slade D. Cutter	*Seahorse*	21
4	Samuel D. Dealey	*Harder*	20½ *
5	William S. Post Jr	*Gudgeon* and *Spot*	19
6	Reuben T. Whitaker	*S-44* and *Flasher*	18½*
7	Walter T. Grifith	*Bowfin* and *Bullhead*	17#
8	Dudley W. Morton	*R-5* and *Wahoo*	17#
9	John E. Lee	*S-12*, *Grayling* and *Croaker*	16
10	William B. Sieglaff	*Tautog* and *Tench*	15

* ½ refers to shared "kills"
# Gross tonnage used to determine ranking order

T O P 1 0

SUBMARINE FLEETS OF WORLD WAR II

	Country	Submarines
1	Japan*	163
2	US*	112
3	France	77
4	USSR	75
5	Germany	57
6	UK	38
7	Netherlands	21
8	Italy	15
9	Denmark	12
10	Greece	6

* Strength at December 1941

The list shows submarine strengths at the outbreak of the war. During hostilities, the belligerent nations increased their production prodigiously: from 1939 to 1945, the Axis powers (Germany, Italy, and Japan) commissioned a further 1,337 submarines (1,141 by Germany alone), and the Allies 422.

T O P 1 0

U-BOAT COMMANDERS OF WORLD WAR II

	Commander	U-boats commanded	Ships sunk
1	Otto Kretshchmer	U-23, U-99	45
2	Wolfgang Luth	U-9, U-138, U-43, U-181	44
3	Joachim Schepke	U-3, U-19, U-100	39
4	Erich Topp	U-57, U-552	35
5	Victor Schutze	U-25, U-103	34
6	Heinrich Leibe	U-38	30
7	Karl F. Merten	U-68	29*
8	Günther Prien	U-47	29*
9	Johann Mohr	U-124	29*
10	Georg Lassen	U-160	28

* Gross tonnage used to determine ranking order

Günther Prien (born January 16, 1908, killed in action March 7, 1941) performed the amazing feat of penetrating the British naval base at Scapa Flow on October 14, 1939 and sinking the Royal Navy battleship *Royal Oak* at anchor. For this exploit he was awarded the Knight's Cross, the first of 318 to be won by members of the German navy during World War II. Prien was killed when *U-47* was sunk.

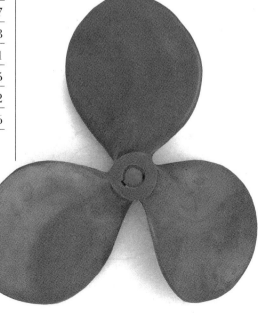

MODERN MILITARY

LONGEST-SERVING JOINT CHIEFS OF STAFF

	Name/Rank	Branch of Armed Forces	Length of time served Years	Months	Took office	Left office
1	General Earle G. Wheeler*	US Army	6	–	July 3, 1964	July 2, 1970
2	Admiral Arthur W. Radford*	US Navy	4	–	August 15, 1953	August 15, 1957
3=	General of the Army Omar N. Bradley	US Army	4	–	August 16, 1949	August 15, 1953
3=	Admiral William J. Crowe Jr.	US Navy	4	–	October 1, 1985	September 30, 1989
3=	Admiral Thomas H. Moorer	US Navy	4	–	July 2, 1970	July 1, 1974
3=	General Colin L. Powell	US Army	4	–	October 1, 1989	September 30,1993
7	General David C. Jones	US Air Force	4	–	June 21, 1978	June 18, 1982
8	General George S. Brown*	US Air Force	4	–	July 1, 1974	June 20, 1978
9	General John W. Vessey Jr.	US Army	3	3	June 18, 1982	September 30, 1985
10	General Nathan F. Twining	US Air Force	3	1	August 15, 1957	September 30, 1960

* Deceased

The office of Chairman, Joint Chiefs of Staff, was created in 1949. The incumbent is appointed by the President with the advice and consent of the US Senate. Originally, the Chairman served a two-year term with the possibility of a second term, but since October 1, 1986, he may be appointed for two additional terms, except in the time of war, when there is no limit on the number of reappointments.

COUNTRIES WITH THE LARGEST DEFENSE BUDGETS

	Country	Budget ($)
1	US	315,500,000,000
2	Russia	52,500,000,000
3	Japan	45,500,000,000
4	UK	42,000,000,000
5	Germany	37,300,000,000
6	France	33,000,000,000
7	Saudi Arabia	16,500,000,000
8	Italy	16,100,000,000
9	China	15,700,000,000
10	South Korea	13,000,000,000

RANKS OF THE US NAVY, ARMY, AND AIR FORCE

	Navy	Army	Air Force
1	Admiral	General	General
2	Vice-Admiral	Lieutenant-General	Lieutenant-General
3	Rear Admiral (Upper Half)	Major-General	Major-General
4	Rear-Admiral (Lower Half)	Brigadier-General	Brigadier-General
5	Captain	Colonel	Colonel
6	Commander	Lieutenant-Colonel	Lieutenant-Colonel
7	Lieutenant Commander	Major	Major
8	Lieutenant	Captain	Captain
9	Lieutenant (Junior Grade)	First Lieutenant	First Lieutenant
10	Ensign	Second Lieutenant	Second Lieutenant

SMALLEST ARMED FORCES IN THE WORLD*

	Country	Estimated total active forces		Country	Estimated total active forces
1=	The Gambia	800	6	Cape Verde	1,100
1=	Luxembourg	800	7	Equatorial Guinea	1,320
1=	The Seychelles	800	8	Guyana	1,700
4	The Bahamas	850	9	Switzerland	1,800
5	Belize	950	10	Malta	1,850

* Excluding those countries not declaring a defense budget

THE 10
20TH-CENTURY WARS WITH MOST MILITARY FATALITIES

	War	Years	Military fatalities
1	World War II	1939–45	15,843,000
2	World War I	1914–18	8,545,800
3	Korean War	1950–53	1,893,100
4=	Sino–Japanese War	1937–41	1,000,000
4=	Biafra–Nigeria Civil War	1967–70	1,000,000
6	Spanish Civil War	1936–39	611,000
7	Vietnam War	1961–73	546,000
8=	India–Pakistan War	1947	200,000
8=	USSR invasion of Afghanistan	1979–89	200,000
8=	Iran-Iraq War	1980–88	200,000

TOP 10
COUNTRIES WITH THE LARGEST UN PEACEKEEPING FORCES*

	Country	Total
1	France	5,149
2	Pakistan	3,982
3	UK	3,918
4	Jordan	3,716
5	US	3,317
6	Bangladesh	3,164
7	Canada	3,098
8	Poland	2,093
9	Nepal	2,074
10	Netherlands	1,916

As of March 31, 1995

COUNTRIES WITH THE LARGEST UN PEACEKEEPING MISSIONS*

	Country	Total
1	Bosnia	22,258
2	Croatia	14,482
3	Liberia	6,505
4	Rwanda	5,884
5	Lebanon	4,963
6	Cyprus	1,183
7	Iraq/Kuwait	1,142
8	F.Y.R. Macedonia	1,102
9	Angola	527
10	Arab/Israeli	220

As of March 31, 1995

TOP 10
LARGEST ARMED FORCES IN THE WORLD

	Country	Estimated active forces			
		Army	Navy	Air	Total
1	China	2,200,000	260,000	470,000	2,930,000
2	US	559,900	482,800*	433,800	1,476,700
3	India	1,100,000	55,000	110,000	1,265,000
4	Russia	780,000	295,000	170,000	1,245,000#
5	North Korea	1,000,000	46,000	82,000	1,128,000
6	South Korea	520,000	60,000	53,000	633,000
7	Pakistan	520,000	22,000	45,000	587,000
8	Vietnam	500,000	42,000	15,000	557,000
9	Turkey	393,000	54,000	56,800	503,800
10	Taiwan	289,000	68,000	68,000	425,000
	UK	*123,000*	*55,600*	*75,700*	*254,300*

Plus 174,000 Marines
 # Balance of total comprises Strategic Deterrent Forces, Paramilitary, National Guard, etc.

In addition to the active forces listed here, many of the world's foremost military powers have considerable reserves on standby; South Korea's is estimated at some 4,500,000, Vietnam's at 3,000,000–4,000,000, Russia's 3,000,000, the US's 1,784,050, China's 1,200,000 and Turkey's 1,107,000.

TOP 10
US MEDAL OF HONOR CAMPAIGNS

	Campaign	Years	Medals awarded
1	Civil War	1861–65	1,520
2	World War II	1941–45	433
3	Indian Wars	1861–98	428
4	Vietnam War	1965–73	238
5	Korean War	1950–53	131
6	World War I	1917–18	123
7	Spanish–American War	1898	109
8	Philippines/Samoa	1899–1913	91
9	Boxer Rebellion	1900	59
10	Mexico	1914	55

The Congressional Medal of Honor, the highest military award in the US, was first issued in 1863. In addition to the medal itself, recipients receive such benefits as a $200-per-month pension for life, free air travel, and the right to be buried in Arlington National Cemetery.

CULTURE & LEARNING

TOP 10

LARGEST UNIVERSITIES IN THE WORLD

	University	Students
1	University of Calcutta, India	300,000
2	University of Paris, France	295,036
3	University of Mexico, Mexico	271,358
4	University of Bombay, India	222,713
5	University of Guadalajara Mexico	214,986
6	University of Buenos Aires Argentina	206,658
7	University of Rome, Italy	184,000
8	University of Rajasthan, India	175,000
9	University of Wisconsin	154,620
10	State University of New York, US	146,873

Several other universities in the US, India, Egypt, and Italy have more than 100,000 students. For certain universities listed, such as the State University of New York and the University of Paris, which are divided into numerous separate centers, the figures are for the totals of all centers.

TOP 10

COUNTRIES WITH MOST UNIVERSITIES

	Country	Universities
1	India	7,513
2	US	3,559
3	Mexico	1,832
4	Argentina	1,540
5	Japan	1,114
6	China	1,053
7	France	1,062
8	Bangladesh	997
9	Brazil	918
10	Indonesia	900
	UK	86

This list compares the number of universities in countries around the world in 1990 (the latest data available). In that year, of the 3,559 universities in the US, 2,141 were four-year colleges and 1,418 two-year colleges. Of the total in the UK, 70 are in England, 12 are in Scotland, two are in Wales, and two are in Northern Ireland. The high figure for India reflects both the country's large population and the high value placed on education in Indian culture.

TOP 10

OLDEST UNIVERSITIES AND COLLEGES IN THE US

	University	Year chartered
1	Harvard University Massachusetts	1636
2	College of William and Mary Virginia	1693
3	Yale University, Connecticut	1701
4	University of Pennsylvania Pennsylvania	1740
5	Moravian College, Pennsylvania	1742
6	University of Delaware, Delaware	1743
7	Princeton University, New Jersey	1746
8	Washington and Lee University Virginia	1749
9	Columbia University, New York	1754
10	Brown University, Rhode Island	1764

When the London-born John Harvard (1607–38) died of consumption just a year after arriving in America, his estate of £779 17s 2d and 320 books became the first bequest to the Cambridge college that was subsequently named in his honor.

TOP 10

STATES WITH MOST SPENT PER GRADE SCHOOL PUPIL

	State	$
1	New Jersey	8,770
2	District of Columbia	8,286
3	Alaska	7,901
4	New York	7,770
5	Connecticut	7,652
6	Rhode Island	6,501
7	Pennsylvania	6,372
8	Vermont	6,342
9	Massachusetts	6,141
10	Maryland	6,060

TOP 10

STATES WITH LEAST SPENT PER GRADE SCHOOL PUPIL

	State	$
1	Utah	2,967
2	Mississippi	3,159
3	Idaho	3,471
4	Alabama	3,572
5	Tennessee	3,674
6	Arkansas	3,859
7	New Mexico	3,929
8	Louisiana	4,010
9	Arizona	4,088
10	Oklahoma	4,090

TOP 10

STATES WITH THE HIGHEST STUDENT/TEACHER RATIO

	State	%
1	Utah	24.7
2	California	24.0
3	Washington	20.1
4	Michigan	19.9
5	Idaho	19.7
6	Oregon	19.5
7	Arizona	18.9
8	Tennessee	18.8
9	Nevada	18.7
10	Colorado	18.6

TOP 10

HIGHEST HIGH SCHOOL GRADUATION RATES

	State	Rate %
1	Utah	90.0
2	Alaska	89.2
3	Wyoming	89.0
4=	Colorado	88.5
4=	Washington	88.5
6	Nebraska	87.5
7	Kansas	87.1
8	Hawaii	86.6
9	New Hampshire	86.3
10=	Minnesota	86.0
10=	Montana	86.0

TOP 10

LOWEST HIGH SCHOOL GRADUATION RATES

	State	Rate %
1	West Virginia	68.5
2	Mississippi	71.7
3	Tennessee	72.0
4	South Carolina	73.3
5	Louisiana	73.7
6	Kentucky	73.9
7	Rhode Island	74.1
8	Georgia	74.7
9	North Carolina	74.8
10	Arkansas	75.0

TOP 10

STATES WITH THE LOWEST STUDENT/TEACHER RATIO

	State	%
1	Vermont	12.7
2	District of Columbia	13.3
3	New Jersey	13.6
4	Maine	14.1
5	Connecticut	14.4
6	Nebraska	14.6
7	Rhode Island	14.8
8=	Massachusetts	14.9
8=	South Dakota	14.9
8=	West Virginia	14.9

TOP 10

BACHELOR'S DEGREE MAJORS IN THE US

	Degree	Degrees
1	Business	256,842
2	Social Sciences/History	135,703
3	Education	107,781
4	Health professions*	67,089
5	Psychology	66,728
6	Engineering	61,973
7	English Language, Literature, & Letters	56,133
8	Communications	53,874
9	Visual & Performing Arts	47,761
10	Biological & Life Sciences	47,038

*Excluding medical degrees

LIBRARIES

LARGEST LIBRARIES IN THE WORLD

	Library	Location	Founded	Books
1	Library of Congress	Washington, D.C.	1800	28,000,000
2	British Library	London, UK	1753*	18,000,000
3	Harvard University Library	Cambridge Massachusetts	1638	12,394,894
4	Russian State Library#	Moscow, Russia	1862	11,750,000
5	New York Public Library	New York, New York	1848	11,300,000**
6	Yale University Library	New Haven Connecticut	1701	9,937,751
7	Biblioteca Academiei Romane	Bucharest, Romania	1867	9,397,260
8	Bibliothèque Nationale	Paris, France	1480	9,000,000
9	University of Illinois	Urbana, Illinois	1867	8,096,040
10	National Library of Russia##	St. Petersburg, Russia	1795	8,000,000

LIBRARY OF CONGRESS
Founded in 1800 to make books available to senators and representatives, the Library of Congress in Washington, D.C. is, in effect, the national library of the US. The world's largest collection of books and pamphlets, manuscripts, photographs, maps, and music has been amassed through gifts, purchase, exchanges, and copyright deposits.

* *Founded as part of the British Museum 1753; became an independent body 1973*
\# *Founded as Rumyantsev Library; formerly State V.I. Lenin Library.*
** *Reference holdings only, excluding books in lending library branches*
\## *Formerly M.E. Saltykov-Shchedrin State Public Library*

T O P 1 0

LARGEST UNIVERSITY LIBRARIES IN THE US

	Library	Location	Founded	Books
1	Harvard University	Cambridge, Massachesetts	1638	12,877,360
2	Yale University	New Haven, Connecticut	1701	9,485,823
3	University of Illinois	Urbana, Illinois	1867	8,474,737
4	University of California	Berkeley, California	1868	8,078,685
5	University of Texas	Austin, Texas	1883	7,019,508
6	University of Michigan	Ann Arbor, Michigan	1817	6,664,081
7	Columbia University	New York, New York	1754	6,532,066
8	University of California	Los Angeles, California	1868	6,460,391
9	Stanford University	Stanford, California	1885	6,409,239
10	University of Chicago	Chicago, Illinois	1892	5,579,629

T O P 1 0

LARGEST PUBLIC LIBRARIES IN THE US

	Library	State	Founded	Books
1	New York Public Library (The Research Libraries)	New York	1895*	10,534,818#
2	Queen's Borough Public Library	New York	1896	9,271,960
3	Free Library of Philadelphia	Pennsylvania	1891	6,687,777
4	Carnegie Library of Pittsburgh	Pennsylvania	1895	6,409,300
5	Boston Public Library	Massachusetts	1852	6,319,206
6	Chicago Public Library	Illinois	1872	6,037,756
7	Brooklyn Public Library	New York	1896	5,859,444
8	Los Angeles Public Library	California	1872	5,000,000
9	Public Library of Cincinnati and Hamilton County	Ohio	1853	4,452,300
10	Houstion Public Library	Texas	1901	4,020,637

Peterboro Public Library, New Hampshire, founded on April 9, 1833 with 700 volumes, was the first public library (in that it was the first to be supported by public taxes) in the US. New York's Astor Library, founded in 1848 with a bequest of $400,000 from America's richest man, John Jacob Astor, opened to the public on February 1, 1854 – although it did not lend out books. In 1895 it merged with the Lenox Library (founded by philanthropist James Lenox) and the Tilden Trust (based on the fortune of Samuel Jones, who was a Presidential candidate) to form the New York Public Library.

* Astor Library founded 1848; consolidated with Lenox Library and Tilden Trust to form New York Public library in 1895

Lending Library holdings only; excluding reference collections, which are listed in The 10 Largest Libraries in the World.

BRITISH LIBRARY
This is now the second largest library in the world. Use of the library is restricted to people involved in research.

WORDS & LANGUAGE

TOP 10

LONGEST WORDS IN THE ENGLISH LANGUAGE

1 MethionylglutaminylarginyltyrosylglutamylserylleucylphenylalanylalanylglutaminylleucyllysylglutamylarginyllysylglutamylglycylalanylphenylalanylvalylprolylphenylalanylvalylthreonylleucylglycylaspartylprolylglycylisoleucylglutamylglutaminylserylleucyllysylisoleucylaspartylthreonylleucylisoleucylglutamylalanylglycylalanylaspartylalanylleucylglutamylleucylglycylisoleucylprolylphenylalanylserylaspartylprolylleucelalanylaspartylglycylprolylthreonylisoleucylglutamiylasparaginylalanylthreonylleucylarginylalanylphenylalanylalanylalanylglycylvalylthreonylprolylalanylglutaminylcysteinylphenylalanylglutamylmethionylleucyalanylleucylisoleucylarginylglutaminyllysylhistidylprolylthreonylisoleucylproIylisoleucylglycylleucylleucylmethionyltyrosylalanylaspartaginylleucylvalylphenylalanylasparaginyllysylglycylisoleucylaspartylglutamylphenylalanyltyrosylalanylglutaminylcysteinylglutamyllysylvalylglycylvalylaspartylserylvalyllleucylvalylalanylaspartylvalylprolylvalylglutaminylglutamylserylalanylprolylphenylalanylarginylglutaminylalanylalanylleucylarginylhistidylasparaginylvalylalanylprolylisoleucylphenylalanylisoleucylcysteinylprolylprolylaspartylalanylaspartylaspartylaspartylleucylleucylarginylglutaminylisoleucylalanylseryltyrosylglycylarginylglycyltyrosylthreonyltyrosylleucylleucylserylarginylalanylglycylvalylthreonylglycylalanylglutamylasparaginylarginylalanylalanylleucylprolylleucylaspaaginylhistidylleucylvalylalanyllysylleucyllysylglutamyltyrosylasparaginylalanylalanylprolylprolylleucylglutaminylglycylphenylalanylglycylisoleucylserylalanylprolylaspartylglutaminylvalyllysylalanylalanylisoleucylaspartylalanylglycylalanylalanylglycylalanylisoleucylserylglycylserylalanylisoleucylbalyllysylisoleucylisoleucylglutamylglutaminylhistidylasparaginylisoleucylglutamylprolylglutamyllysylmethionylleucylalanylalanylleucyllysylvalylphenylalanylvalylglutaminylprolylmethionyllysylalanylalanylthreonylarginylserine (1,909)

The scientific name for Tryptophan synthetase A protein, an enzyme with of 267 amino acids, has appeared in print several times. The systematic name of deoxyribonucleic acid, or DNA, has an alleged 207,000 letters but, although published in shortened form in Nature *on April 9, 1981, it has never been printed in full. Words for chemical compounds are the most likely to be long since they are created by linking the scientific names of their components. Words invented with the sole intention of being long words have been excluded.*

2 Acetylseryltyrosylserylisoleucylthreonylserylprolylserylglutaminylphenylalanylvalylphenylalanylleucylserylserylvalyltryptophylalanylaspartylprolylisoleucylglutamylleucylleucyllasparaginylvalylcysteinylthreonylserylserylleucylglycyllasparaginylglutaminylphenylalanylglutaminylthreonylglutaminylglutaminylalanylarginylthreonylthreonylglutaminylvalylglutaminylglutaminylphenylalanylserylglutaminylvalyltryptophyllysylrolylphenylalanylprolylglutaminylserylthreonylvalylarginylphenylalanylprolylglycylaspartylvalyltyrosyllsyslvalyltyrosylarginyltyrosylasparaginylalanylvalylleucylaspartylprolylleucylisoleucylthreonylalanylleucylleucylglycylthreonylphenylalanylaspartylthreonylarginylasparaginylarginylisoleucylisoleucylglutamylvalylglutamylasparaginylglutaminylglutaminylserylprolylthreonylthreonylalanylglutamylthreonylleucylaspartylalanylthreonylarginylarginylvalylaspartylaspartylalanylthreonylvalylalanylisoleucylarginylserylalanylasparaginylisoleucylasparaginylleucylvallasparaginylglutamylleucylvalylarginylglycylthreonylglycylleucyltyrosylasparaginylglutaminylasparaginylthreonylphenylalanylglutamylserylmethionylserylglycylleucylvalyltryptophylthreonylserylalanylprolylalanylserine (1,185)

The scientific name for the Tobacco Mosaic Virus, Dahlemense Strain, this has been printed in the American Chemical Society's Chemical Abstracts.

3 Ornicopytheobibliopsychocrystarroscioaerogenethliometeoroaustrohieroanthropoichthyopyrosiderochpnomyoalectryoophiobotanopegohydrorhabdocrithoaleuroalphitohalomolybdoclerobeloaxinocoscinodactyliogeolithopessopsephocatoptrotephraoneirochiroonychodactyloarithstichooxogeloscogastrogyrocerobletonooenoscapulinaniac (310)

Used by medieval scribes to mean: "A deluded human who practices divination or forecasting by means of phenomena, interpretation of acts or other manifestations related to the following animate or inanimate objects and appearances: birds, oracles, Bible, ghosts, crystal gazing, shadows, air appearances, birth stars, meteors, winds, sacrificial appearances, entrails of humans and fishes, fire, red-hot irons, altar smoke, mice, grain picking by rooster, snakes, herbs, fountains, water, wands, dough, meal, barley, salt, lead, dice, arrows, hatchet balance, sieve, ring suspension, random dots, precious stones, pebbles, pebble heaps, mirrors, ash writing, dreams, palmistry, nail rays, finger rings, numbers, book passages, name letterings, laughing manners, ventriloquism, circle walking, wax, susceptibility to hidden springs, wine, and shoulder blades."

4 Aopadotenachoselachogaleokranioleipsanodrimhipotrimmatosilphioparaomelitokatakechymenokichlepikossyphophattoperisteralektryonoptekephalliokigklopeleiolagoiosiraiobaphetraganopterygon (182)

The name of a 17-ingredient dish, transliterated from a 170-letter Greek word in a play by the playwright, Aristophanes (c.448–380BC).

5 Aequeosalinocalcinosetaceoaluminosocupreovitriolic (52)

Invented by Dr. Edward Strother (1675–1737) to describe the spa waters at Bath, England.

6 Asseocarnisanguineoviscericartilaginonervomedullary (51)

Coined by Thomas Love Peacock (1785–1866), who used it in his satire Headlong Hall *(1816) to describe the structure of the human body.*

7 Pneumonoultramicroscopicsilicovolcanoconiosis (45)

A lung disease caused by breathing fine dust, it was first printed (ending in "-koniosis") in F. Scully's Bedside Manna *[sic] (1936). It then appeared in* Webster's Dictionary *and is now in the* Oxford English Dictionary.

8 Hepaticocholangiocholecystenterostomies (39)

Surgical operations to create channels of communication between gall bladders and hepatic ducts or intestines.

9= Pseudoantidisestablishmentarianism (34)

Derived from antidisestablishmentarianism (28), this means "false opposition to the withdrawal of state support from a Church". Another composite (though usually hyphenated) is ultra-antidisestablishmentarianism, which means "extreme opposition to the withdrawal of state support from a Church" (33).

9= Supercalifragilisticexpialidocious (34)

An invented word, but eligible as it is in the Oxford English Dictionary. *Popularized by a song in the film* Mary Poppins *(1964) where it means "wonderful," it was first used in 1949 in an unpublished song by Parker and Young, spelled "supercalafajalistickespialadojus" (32 letters). In 1965–66, Parker and Young unsuccessfully sued the makers of* Mary Poppins, *claiming infringement of copyright. If compound chemical names or transliteration from the Greek are ineligible, the next longest words are* encephalomyeloradiculoneuritis; hippopotomonstrosesquipedalian; *and* pseudopseudohypoparathyroidism, *with 30 letters.*

MOST WIDELY SPOKEN LANGUAGES IN THE WORLD

	Country	Approx. no. of speakers
1	Chinese (Mandarin)	931,000,000
2	English	463,000,000
3	Hindustani	400,000,000
4	Spanish	371,000,000
5	Russian	290,000,000
6	Arabic	215,000,000
7	Bengali	193,000,000
8	Portuguese	180,000,000
9	Malay-Indonesian	153,000,000
10	Japanese	126,000,000

According to 1993 estimates by Sidney S. Culbert of the University of Washington, only French (122,000,000) and German (119,000,000) are spoken by more than 100,000,000 people. A further 12 languages are spoken by between 50,000,000 and 100,000,000 people. They range from Urdu with 99,000,000 to Turkish with 58,000,000. The rest in descending order are: Punjabi, Korean, Telugu, Tamil, Marathi, Cantonese, Wu, Italian, Javanese, and Vietnamese.

COUNTRIES WITH THE MOST ENGLISH LANGUAGE SPEAKERS

	Country	Approx. no. of speakers
1	US	215,000,000
2	UK	56,000,000
3	Canada	17,000,000
4	Australia	14,000,000
5	Ireland	3,300,000
6	New Zealand	3,000,000
7	Jamaica	2,300,000
8	South Africa	2,000,000
9	Trinidad and Tobago	1,200,000
10	Guyana	900,000

The Top 10 represents the countries with the greatest numbers of inhabitants who speak English as their mother tongue. After the 10th entry, the figures dive to around 250,000 for Barbados and the Bahamas, while Zimbabwe at No. 13 has 200,000 English speakers. In addition to these and others that make up a world total probably in excess of 463,000,000, there are perhaps as many as 1,000,000,000 who speak English as a second language.

MOST STUDIED LANGUAGES IN THE US

	Language	Registrations*
1	Spanish	533,944
2	French	272,472
3	German	133,348
4	Italian	49,699
5	Japanese	45,717
6	Russian	44,626
7	Latin	28,178
8	Chinese	19,490
9	Ancient Greek	16,401
10	Hebrew#	12,995

* In US Institutions of Higher Education
# Comprises 5,724 registrations in Biblical Hebrew and 7,271 in Modern Hebrew

These figures are from the most recent survey conducted by the Modern Language Association of America from colleges and universities in the fall of 1990, which indicated a total of 1,184,100 foreign language registrations, the highest enrollment ever recorded since the surveys began in 1958. Japanese showed the greatest gain since the previous poll (in 1986), with a 12.3 percent increase.

LANGUAGES MOST SPOKEN IN THE US

	Country	Speakers
1	English	198,601,000
2	Spanish	17,339,000
3	French	1,702,000
4	German	1,547,000
5	Italian	1,309,000
6	Chinese	1,249,000
7	Tagalog	843,000
8	Polish	723,000
9	Korean	626,000
10	Vietnamese	507,000

US STATES WITH MOST NON-ENGLISH SPEAKERS

	State	Total population*	English speakers	Non-English speakers	Non-English speakers (%)
1	New Mexico	1,390,048	896,049	493,999	35.5
2	California	27,383,547	18,764,213	8,619,334	31.5
3	Texas	15,605,822	11,635,518	3,970,304	25.4
4	Hawaii	1,026,209	771,485	254,724	24.8
5	New York	16,743,048	12,834,328	3,908,720	23.3
6	Arizona	3,374,806	2,674,519	700,287	20.8
7	New Jersey	7,200,696	5,794,548	1,406,148	19.5
8	Florida	12,095,284	9,996,969	2,098,315	17.3
9	Rhode Island	936,423	776,931	159,492	17.0
10	Connecticut	3,060,000	2,593,825	466,175	15.2

* 5+ years old, as per 1990 Census

THE OXFORD ENGLISH DICTIONARY

Although conceived earlier, work on the *Oxford English Dictionary* started in earnest in 1879 with James Murray as editor. He and his colleagues scoured thousands of English texts for quotations representing the changing usages of English words, frequently chopping up copies of rare books, pasting extracts onto slips of paper, and filing them. The first part, covering A–Ant, was published in 1884, and other sections followed at intervals. Murray died in 1915, but work continued until 1928 when the first edition was complete. Its 12 volumes defined 414,825 words and phrases, with about 2,000,000 quotations providing information on the first recorded use, continuing usage, and later variations in the use of each word. Supplements were added over the ensuing years until it was decided to computerize all the material, work on which commenced in 1984. The original *Dictionary*, *Supplements*, and new entries were incorporated into a gigantic, 540-megabyte database. Over 120 keyboard operators keyed in more than 350,000,000 characters, their work checked by over 50 proofreaders. The complete second edition, costing about $15,000,000 to produce, was published in 1989. Its 20 volumes, currently priced at $2,750, contain 21,728 pages with about 60,000,000 words of text defining some 557,889 words (over 34 percent more than the first edition), together with 2,435,671 quotations. The entire dictionary is now available on CD-ROM (a single compact disc) for $895.

THE 10
EARLIEST DATED WORDS IN THE *OXFORD ENGLISH DICTIONARY*

	Word	Source	Date
1=	town	Laws of Ethelbert	601–4
1=	priest	Laws of Ethelbert	601–4
3	earl	Laws of Ethelbert	616
4	this	Bewcastle Column	c.670
5	streale	Ruthwell Cross	c.680
6	ward	Cædmon, Hymn	680
7	thing	Laws of Hlothær and Eadric	685–6
8	theft	Laws of Ine	688–95
9	worth	Laws of Ine	695
10	then	Laws of King Wihtræd	695–6

The 10 earliest citations in the *OED* come from seventh century Anglo-Saxon documents and stone inscriptions. All have survived as commonly used English words, with the exception of "streale," which is another name for an arrow. A few other English words can be definitely dated to before 700, among them "church" which, like "then," appears in a law of King Wihtræd.

TOP 10
LONGEST WORDS IN THE *OXFORD ENGLISH DICTIONARY*

	Word	Letters
1	pneumonoultramicroscopicsilicovolcanoconiosis	45
2	supercalifragilisticexpialidocious	34
3	pseudopseudohypoparathyroidism	30
4=	floccinaucinihilipilification	29
4=	triethylsulphonemethylmethane	29
6=	antidisestablishmentarianism	28
6=	octamethylcyclotetrasiloxane	28
6=	tetrachlorodibenzoparadioxin	28
9	hepaticocholangiogastronomy	27
10=	radioimmunoelectrophoresis	26
10=	radioimmunoelectrophoretic	26

Words that are hyphenated, including such compound words as "transformational-generative" and "tristhio-dimethyl-benzaldehyde," have not been included. Only one unhyphenated word did not make it into the Top 10, the 25-letter "psychophysicotherapeutics." After this, there is a surprisingly large number of words containing 20–24 letters (radioimmunoprecipitation, spectrophotofluorometric, thyroparathyroidectomize, roentgenkymographically, and immunosympathectomized, for example) – few of which are ever used by anyone except scientists and crossword compilers.

A WORD IN EDGEWISE
All 20 volumes of the Oxford English Dictionary *have now been compressed onto a single CD-ROM.*

TOP 10

WORDS WITH MOST MEANINGS IN THE OXFORD ENGLISH DICTIONARY

	Word	Meanings
1	set	464
2	run	396
3	go	368
4	take	343
5	stand	334
6	get	289
7	turn	288
8	put	268
9	fall	264
10	strike	250

TOP 10

LETTERS OF THE ALPHABET WITH MOST ENTRIES IN THE OXFORD ENGLISH DICTIONARY

	Letter	Entries
1	S	34,556
2	C	26,239
3	P	24,980
4	M	17,495
5	A	15,880
6	T	15,497
7	R	15,483
8	B	14,633
9	D	14,519
10	U	12,943

This list of the 10 most common first letters does not correspond with the list of the 10 most frequently used letters in written English, which is generally held to be ETAINOSHRD. If the alphabet were restricted to just these letters, among the useful phrases that could be created – without repeating any letters – are "the inroads," "note radish," "date rhinos," and "hot sardine."

TOP 10

MOST-QUOTED AUTHORS IN THE OXFORD ENGLISH DICTIONARY

	Author	Approx. no. of references
1	William Shakespeare (1564–1616)	33,303
2	Sir Walter Scott (1771–1832)	16,659
3	John Milton (1608–74)	12,465
4	John Wyclif (c.1330–84)	11,972
5	Geoffrey Chaucer (c.1343–1400)	11,902
6	William Caxton (c.1422–91)	10,324
7	John Dryden (1631–1700)	9,139
8	Charles Dickens (1812–70)	8,557
9	Philemon Holland (1552–1637)	8,419
10	Alfred, Lord Tennyson (1809–92)	6,972

The figures given here may not be exact because of variations in the way in which sources are quoted, or in instances where more than one example is included from the same author. All those in the Top 10 are prolific "classic" British authors whose works were widely read in the late nineteenth century.

TOP 10

MOST-QUOTED SOURCES IN THE OXFORD ENGLISH DICTIONARY

	Source	Approx. no. of references*
1	*The Times*	19,098
2	*Cursor Mundi*#	11,035
3	*Encyclopedia Britannica*	10,102
4	*Daily News***	9,650
5	*Nature*	9,150
6	*Transactions of the Philological Society*	8,972
7	*Chronicle***	8,550
8	*Westminster Gazette*	7,478
9	*History of England***	7,180
10	*Listener*	7,139

* *These figures may not be precise because of the varied ways in which source books and journals are quoted, when there is more than one example from the same source, etc.*

\# *Cursor Mundi is a long 14th-century Northumbrian poem which is extensively cited for early uses of English words.*

**References may include several different works with similar titles.*

TOP 10

LETTERS OF THE ALPHABET WITH FEWEST ENTRIES IN THE OXFORD ENGLISH DICTIONARY

	Letter	Entries
1	X	152
2	Z	733
3	Q	1,824
4	Y	2,298
5	J	2,326
6	K	3,491
7	V	5,430
8	N	5,933
9	O	7,737
10	W	8,804

The number of entries beginning with "x" has increased in the past 100 years, with the introduction of such terms as "x-ray" in 1896, "X-certificate" or "X-rated" films (1950), "xerography" (the photocopying process, invented by Chester F. Carlson in 1948), and "Xerox," the proprietary name derived from it in 1952.

BOOKS & READERS

TOP 10

MOST EXPENSIVE BOOKS AND MANUSCRIPTS EVER SOLD AT AUCTION

Book/manuscript/sale	Price ($)*
1 The Codex Hammer Christie's, New York, November 11, 1994	30,800,000

This is one of Leonardo's notebooks, which includes many scientific drawings and diagrams. It was purchased by Bill Gates, the billionaire founder of Microsoft.

2 *The Gospels of Henry the Lion*, c.1173–75 Sotheby's, London, December 6, 1983	10,841,000

The most expensive manuscript, book, or work of art other than a painting ever sold.

3 *The Gutenberg Bible*, 1455 Christie's, New York, October 22, 1987	5,390,000

One of the first books ever printed, by Johann Gutenberg and Johann Fust in 1455, it holds the record for the most expensive printed book.

4 *The Northumberland Bestiary*, c.1250–60 Sotheby's, London, November 29, 1990	5,049,000

The highest price ever paid for an English manuscript.

5 Autographed manuscript of nine symphonies by Wolfgang Amadeus Mozart, c.1773–74 Sotheby's, London, May 22, 1987	3,854,000

The record for a music manuscript and for any postmedieval manuscript.

Book/manuscript/sale	Price ($)*
6 John James Audubon's *The Birds of America*, 1827–38 Sotheby's, New York, June 6, 1989	3,600,000

This collection of over 400 hand-colored engravings holds the record for a natural history book. A facsimile reprint published by Abbeville Press, New York (1985), listed at $30,000, is the most expensive book ever published.

7 The Bible in Hebrew Sotheby's, London, December 5, 1989	2,932,000

A manuscript written in Iraq, Syria, or Babylon in the ninth or tenth century, it holds the record for any Hebrew manuscript.

8 *The Monypenny Breviary*, illuminated manuscript, c. 1490–95, Sotheby's, London, June 19, 1989	2,639,000

The record for any French manuscript.

9 *The Hours and Psalter of Elizabeth de Bohun*, Countess of Northampton, c. 1340–45 Sotheby's, London, June 21, 1988	2,530,000

10 *Biblia Pauperum* Christie's, New York, October 22, 1987	2,200,000

This block-book bible was printed in the Netherlands in c.1460. (The pages of block-books, with text and illustrations, were printed from single carved woodblocks rather than movable type.)

* *Excluding premiums*

FIRST EDITIONS
This engraving by the Swiss artist Jost Amman from his series on arts and trades depicts a typical scene in the early days of the book printing industry.

TOP 10

BESTSELLING CHILDREN'S BOOKS OF ALL TIME IN THE US

	Author/title/first published	Total sales ($)
1	Beatrix Potter, *The Tale of Peter Rabbit* (1902)	9,000,000
2	Dr. Seuss, *Green Eggs and Ham* (1960)	6,500,000
3	Dr. Seuss, *One Fish, Two Fish, Red Fish, Blue Fish* (1960)	6,200,000
4	S.E. Hinton, *The Outsiders* (1967)	6,000,000
5	Dr. Seuss, *Hop on Pop* (1963)	5,900,000
6	Dr. Seuss, *Dr. Seuss's ABC* (1963)	5,800,000
7	Dr. Seuss, *The Cat in the Hat* (1957)	5,600,000
8	Judy Blume, *Are You There, God? It's Me, Margaret* (1970)	5,500,000
9	L. Frank Baum, *The Wonderful Wizard of Oz* (1900)	5,200,000
10	E.B. White, *Charlotte's Web* (1952)	4,900,000

Total sales are estimates for combined hardback and paperback domestic sales since first publication. Extending the list to a Top 20 would include other works by several featured authors, including S.E. Hinton and Judy Blume, as well as Laura Ingalls Wilder, the author of *Little House on the Prairie* (1953) and other bestsellers.

A number of earlier American children's classics, such as Louisa May Alcott's *Little Women* (1868–69), its sequels, and Mark Twain's *Tom Sawyer* (1876), have long been out of copyright and available in countless editions; cumulative sales over a century or more are impossible to calculate, but might qualify some for the Top 10.

THE 10

LAST PULITZER PRIZEWINNERS FOR GENERAL NONFICTION

Year	Author/book title
1995	Jonathan Weiner, *The Beak of the Finch: A Story of Evolution in Our Time*
1994	David Remnic, *Lenin's Tomb: The Last Days of the Soviet Empire*
1993	Garry Wills, *Lincoln at Gettysburg*
1992	Daniel Yergin *The Prize: The Epic Quest for Oil*
1991	Bert Holldobler and Edward O. Wilson, *The Ants*
1990	Dale Maharidge and Michael Williamson, *And Their Children After Them*
1989	Neil Sheehan *A Bright Shining Lie: John Paul Vann and America in Vietnam*
1988	Richard Rhodes *The Making of the Atomic Bomb*
1987	David K. Shipler, *Arab and Jew*
1986	Joseph Lelyveld, *Move Your Shadow*; J. Anthony Lukas, *Common Ground*

A STING IN THE TALE
Dorothy Parker was famous for her acid wit. She wrote short stories and a bestselling book of verse, Enough Rope, *and was also a tough reviewer of other children's books (such as* Winnie the Pooh*).*

THE 10

FIRST POCKET BOOKS

	Author/book title
1	James Hilton, *Lost Horizon*
2	Dorothea Brande, *Wake Up and Live!*
3	William Shakespeare *Five Great Tragedies*
4	Thorne Smith, *Topper*
5	Agatha Christie *The Murder of Roger Ackroyd*
6	Dorothy Parker, *Enough Rope*
7	Emily Brontë, *Wuthering Heights*
8	Samuel Butler, *The Way of All Flesh*
9	Thornton Wilder *The Bridge of San Luis Rey*
10	Felix Saltern, *Bambi*

All 10 Pocket Books were published in the US in 1939. All had pictorial covers, the first ten created by Isador N. Steinberg and Frank J. Lieberman. A sales survey in 1957 showed that of these 10, the volume of Shakespeare's tragedies was the bestselling title with over 2,000,000 copies in print, followed by *Lost Horizon* (1,750,000), *Topper* (1,500,000), and *Wuthering Heights* (over 1,000,000).

TOP 10

TRADE PUBLISHERS IN THE US

	Company	Sales ($)*
1	Random House	1,170,000,000
2	Bantam Doubleday Dell	655,000,000
3	Simon & Schuster	518,000,000
4	HarperCollins	355,000,000
5	Penguin USA	340,000,000
6	Time Warner Trade	260,000,000
7	Putnam Berkley	250,000,000
8	Hearst Trade Group	159,000,000
9	St. Martin's Press	145,000,000
10	Houghton Mifflin	92,000,000

* *1993 sales*

THE 10

LAST PULITZER PRIZEWINNERS FOR FICTION

Year	Author/book title
1995	Carol Shields, *The Stone Diaries*
1994	E. Annie Proulx, *The Shipping News*
1993	Robert Olen Butler, *A Good Scent from a Strange Mountain*
1992	Jane Smiley, *A Thousand Acres*
1991	John Updike, *Rabbit at Rest*
1990	Oscar Hijuelos, *The Mambo King Plays Songs of Love*
1989	Anne Tyler, *Breathing Lessons*
1988	Toni Morrison, *Beloved*
1987	Peter Taylor, *A Summons to Memphis*
1986	Larry McMurtry, *Lonesome Dove*

THE 10

LAST WINNERS OF THE NEWBERY MEDAL

Year	Author/book title
1995	Sharon Creech, *Walk Two Moons*
1994	Lois Lowry, *The Giver*
1993	Cynthia Rylant, *Missing May*
1992	Phyllis Reynolds Naylor, *Shiloh*
1991	Jerry Spinelli, *Maniac Magee*
1990	Lois Lowry, *Number the Stars*
1989	Paul Fleischman *Joyful Noise: Poems for Two Voices*
1988	Russell Freedman *Lincoln: A Photobiography*
1987	Sid Fleischman, *The Whipping Boy*
1986	Patricia MacLachlan *Sarah, Plain and Tall*

WORLD BESTSELLERS

T O P 1 0

BESTSELLING BOOKS OF ALL TIME

1 The Bible   6,000,000,000

No one really knows how many copies of the Bible have been printed, sold, or distributed. The Bible Society's attempt to calculate the number printed between 1816 and 1975 produced the figure of 2,458,000,000. A more recent survey up to 1992 put it closer to 6,000,000,000 in more than 2,000 languages and dialects. Whatever the precise figure, it is by far the bestselling book of all time.

2 *Quotations from the Works of Mao Tse-tung*   800,000,000

Chairman Mao's "Little Red Book" could scarcely fail to become a bestseller: between the years 1966 and 1971 it was compulsory for every Chinese adult to own a copy. It was both sold and distributed to the people of China – though what proportion voluntarily bought it must remain open to question. Some 100,000,000 copies of his Poems *were also disseminated.*

3 *American Spelling Book* by Noah Webster   100,000,000

First published in 1783, this reference book by American man of letters Noah Webster (1758–1843) – of Webster's Dictionary *fame – remained a bestseller in the US throughout the 19th century.*

4 *The Guinness Book of Records*   76,000,000+*

First published in 1955, The Guinness Book of Records *stands out as the greatest contemporary publishing achievement. There have now been 37 editions in the UK (it was not published annually until 1964), as well as numerous foreign language editions.*

5 *The McGuffey Readers*
   by William Holmes McGuffey   60,000,000

Published in numerous editions from 1853, some authorities have put the total sales of these educational textbooks, originally compiled by American anthologist William Holmes McGuffey (1800–73), as high as 122,000,000. It has also been claimed that 60,000,000 copies of the 1879 edition were printed, but since this is some 10,000,000 more than the entire population of the US at the time, the publishers must have been extremely optimistic about its success.

6 *A Message to Garcia* by Elbert Hubbard   40–50,000,000

Now forgotten, Hubbard's polemic on the subject of labor relations was published in 1899 and within a few years had achieved these phenomenal sales, largely because many American employers purchased bulk supplies to distribute to their employees. The literary career of Elbert Hubbard (1856–1915) was cut short in 1915 when he went down with the Lusitania, *but even in death he was a record-breaker: his posthumous* My Philosophy *(1916) was published in one of the largest-ever "limited editions" – a total of 9,983 copies.*

7 *The Common Sense Book of Baby and Child Care*
   by Dr. Benjamin Spock   39,200,000+

Dr. Spock's 1946 manual became the bible of infant care for subsequent generations of parents. Most of the sales have been of the paperback edition of the book.

8 *World Almanac*   38,000,000+*

Having been published annually since 1868 (with a break from 1876 to 1886), this wide-ranging reference book has remained a bestseller ever since.

9 *Valley of the Dolls* by Jacqueline Susann   28,712,000+

This racy tale of sex, violence, and drugs by Jacqueline Susann (1921–74), first published in 1966, is, perhaps surprisingly, the world's bestselling novel. Margaret Mitchell's Gone With the Wind, *which has achieved sales approaching 28,000,000, is its closest rival.*

10 *In His Steps: "What Would Jesus Do?"*
   by Rev. Charles Monroe Sheldon   28,500,000

Though virtually unknown today, Charles Sheldon (1857–1946) achieved fame and fortune with this 1896 religious treatise.

* Aggregate sales of annual publication

It is extremely difficult to establish precise sales even of contemporary books, and virtually impossible to do so with books published long ago. How many copies of the complete works of Shakespeare or Conan Doyle's Sherlock Holmes books have been sold in countless editions? The publication of variant editions, translations, and pirated copies all affect the global picture, and few publishers or authors are willing to expose their royalty statements to public scrutiny. As a result, this Top 10 list offers no more than the "best guess" at the great bestsellers of the past, and it may well be that there are other books with a valid claim to a place in it.

There are problems of definition: what, for example, is the status of a book that is revised and reissued annually, and what precisely is a "book"? A UNESCO conference in 1950 decided it was "a nonperiodical literary publication containing 49 or more pages, not counting the covers" (which is baffling in itself, since all publications have to contain an even number of pages, while, according to this criterion, a 32-page children's book would not be regarded as a book at all). If *Old Moore's Almanac* is classified as a book rather than a periodical or a pamphlet, it would appear high on the list. Having been published annually since 1697, its total sales to date are believed to be over 112,000,000. More than 107,000,000 copies of the Jehovah's Witness tract, *The Truth That Leads to Eternal Life*, first published in 1968, are believed to have been distributed in 117 languages, usually in return for a donation to the sect, but since they were not sold it does not rank as a "*bestseller.*"

TOP 10

WORLD'S BESTSELLING FICTION

As with the bestselling books of all time, it is virtually impossible to arrive at a definitive list of fiction bestsellers that encompasses all permutations including hardback and paperback editions, book club sales, and translations, and takes account of the innumerable editions of earlier classics such as *Robinson Crusoe* or the works of Jane Austen, Charles Dickens, or popular foreign authors such as Jules Verne. Although only Jacqueline Susann's *Valley of the Dolls* appears on the all-time list, and publishers' precise sales data remains tantalizingly elusive (it has been said that the most published fiction is publishers' own sales figures), there are many other novels that must be close contenders for the Top 10. It seems certain that all the following have sold in excess of 10,000,000 copies in hardback and paperback worldwide:

Richard Bach	*Jonathan Livingstone Seagull*
William Blatty	*The Exorcist*
Peter Benchley	*Jaws*
Erskine Caldwell	*God's Little Acre*
Joseph Heller	*Catch-22*
D.H. Lawrence	*Lady Chatterley's Lover*
Harper Lee	*To Kill a Mockingbird*
Colleen McCullough	*The Thorn Birds*
Grace Metalious	*Peyton Place*
Margaret Mitchell	*Gone With the Wind*
George Orwell	*Animal Farm*
George Orwell	*1984*
Mario Puzo	*The Godfather*
Harold Robbins	*The Carpetbaggers*
J.D. Salinger	*Catcher in the Rye*
Erich Segal	*Love Story*

There are also several prolific popular novelists whose books have achieved combined international sales of colossal proportions. The field is led by detective story authoress *extraordinaire* Agatha Christie, with total sales of more than 2,000,000,000 since 1920, followed by romantic novelist Barbara Cartland (650,000,000), Belgian detective novelist Georges Simenon (600,000,000), and American crime-writer Erle Stanley Gardner (320,000,000). If this list were extended to embrace other prolific bestselling novelists during the postwar period, it would probably include such writers as Jeffrey Archer, Catherine Cookson, Ian Fleming, Robert Ludlum, Alistair MacLean, and Mickey Spillane.

TOP 10

MOST PUBLISHED AUTHORS OF ALL TIME

	Author	Nationality
1	William Shakespeare (1564–1616)	British
2	Charles Dickens (1812–70)	British
3	Sir Walter Scott (1771–1832)	British
4	Johann Goethe (1749–1832)	German
5	Aristotle (384–322 BC)	Greek
6	Alexandre Dumas (*père*) (1802–70)	French
7	Robert Louis Stevenson (1850–94)	British
8	Mark Twain (1835–1910)	American
9	Marcus Cicero (106–43 BC)	Roman
10	Honoré de Balzac (1799–1850)	French

This Top 10 is based on a search of a major US library computer database. Shakespeare is cited over 15,000 times.

DID YOU KNOW

BESTSELLER OF 100 YEARS AGO?

The year 1896 was a vintage one for the publication of strange books, but none more so than *Premature Burial and How It May Be Prevented* by William Tebb and Colonel Edward Perry Vollum. The Victorians were obsessed with the idea of being accidentally buried alive – it was the theme of a horror story by Edgar Allan Poe – and this book, which was to run to many editions, explained how the risk might be avoided.

BESTSELLING CHILDREN'S AUTHORS IN THE WORLD

René Goscinny and Albert Uderzo

René Goscinny (1926-77) and Albert Uderzo (b. 1927) created the comic-strip character Astérix the Gaul in 1959. They produced 30 books with total sales of at least 220,000,000 copies.

Hergé

Georges Rémi (1907-83), the Belgian author-illustrator who wrote under the pen name Hergé, created the comic-strip character Tintin in 1929. Appearing in book form from 1948 onward, they achieved worldwide popularity and have been translated into about 45 languages and dialects. Total sales are believe to be at least 160,000,000.

Enid Blyton

With sales of her Noddy books exceeding 60,000,000 copies and more than 700 children's books to her name (UNESCO calculated that there were 974 translations of her works in the 1960s alone), total sales of her works are believed to be over 100,000,000, making her the bestselling English language author of the 20th century.

Dr. Seuss

His books in the US Top 10 alone total about 30,000,000 copies; to this must be added those titles that have sold fewer than 5,000,000 in the US and all foreign editions of all his books, suggesting totals of more than 100,000,000.

Beatrix Potter

The Tale of Peter Rabbit *(1902) was one of a series of books, the cumulative total sales of which probably exceed 50,000,000.*

Lewis Carroll

Total world sales of all editions of Carroll's two classic children's books, Alice's Adventures in Wonderland and Alice Through the Looking Glass, are incalculable, but just these two books probably place him among the 20 bestselling children's authors of all time.

It is impossible to make a definitive list of the bestselling children's books in the world, but based on total sales of their entire output, these authors have produced titles that have been bestsellers – especially those in numerous translations – over a long period.

US BESTSELLERS

T O P 1 0

NONFICTION BESTSELLERS OF 1994

	Author/title	Sales
1	Rosie Daley, *In the Kitchen with Rosie*	5,487,369
2	John Gray, *Men Are from Mars, Women Are from Venus*	1,853,000
3	John Paul II, *Crossing the Threshold of Hope*	1,625,883
4	Thomas Baccei of N.E.Thing Enterprises Inc., *Magic Eye I*	1,589,882
5	William J. Bennett, Ed., *The Book of Virtues*	1,550,000*
6	Thomas Baccei of N.E.Thing Enterprises Inc., *Magic Eye II*	1,383,339
7	Betty J. Eadie with Curtis Taylor *Embraced by the Light*	1,224,074
8	Tim Allen, *Don't Stand Too Close to a Naked Man*	1,125,283
9	Paul Reiser, *Couplehood*	1,000,003
10	Thomas Baccei of N.E.Thing Enterprises Inc., *Magic Eye III*	964,288

* Approximate – precise figures undisclosed

T O P 1 0

ALMANACS, ATLASES, AND ANNUALS OF 1994

	Title	Sales
1	*The World Almanac and Book of Facts 1995*	1,965,000
2	*The World Almanac and Book of Facts 1994*	1,830,000
3	*J.J. Lasser's Your Income Tax 1995*	595,000
4	*The 1994 Information Please Almanac*	302,463
5	*The Ernst & Young Tax Guide 1994*	265,692
6	*The Old Farmer's Almanac 1995 Edition*	207,533
7	*The 1994 Christmas Ideals*	152,135
8	*1995 Sports Almanac*	126,925
9	*The 1995 Official Price Guide to Baseball Cards, 14th Edition*	112,714
10	*The 1994 Information Please Sports Almanac*	104,421

Still the leader of the pack by a considerable margin, *The World Almanac and Book of Facts* was first published in 1868 by the New York World. It originally focused on political matters of the day, including Southern Reconstruction following the Civil War. It ceased publication in 1876, but was revived in 1886 by the newspaper's publisher, Joseph Pulitzer, as a "compendium of universal knowledge," and has been published annually ever since.

T H E 1 0

PUBLISHERS WITH MOST WEEKS ON THE BESTSELLER CHARTS, 1994

	Company	Hardback books	Hardback weeks	Paperback books	Paperback weeks	Total weeks
1	Random House, Inc.	37	331	36	276	607
2	Simon & Schuster	32	269	31	306	575
3	Bantam Doubleday Dell	27	190	35	239	429
4	HarperCollins	14	135	18	157	292
5	Time Warner	11	172	14	94	266
6	Putnam Berkley	19	136	·21	123	259
7	Penguin USA	5	37	13	79	116
8	Andrews & McMeel	3	67	6	31	98
9	Workman	-	-	4	63	63
10	Hearst	2	14	7	28	42

John Grisham and Danielle Steel have most contributed to Bantam Doubleday Dell's third place showing, and Robert James Waller has almost singlehandedly given Warner its fifth position. Knopf failed to make the Top 10, even with the No. 1 bestselling contribution of Rosie Daley's *In the Kitchen with Rosie*.

BESTSELLING PROFESSOR
Writing on one of the topics least likely to top the charts, British professor of physics Stephen Hawking, of Cambridge University, has brought theoretical physics to the widest possible audience. Although his book A Brief History of Time *is no longer among the Top 10 Nonfiction Bestsellers, it has sold over 5,000,000 copies worldwide since it was first published in 1985.*

TOP 10
FICTION BESTSELLERS OF 1994

	Author	Title	Sales
1	John Grisham	*The Chamber*	3,189,893
2	Tom Clancy	*Debt of Honor*	2,302,529
3	James Redfield	*The Celestine Prophecy*	2,092,526
4	Danielle Steel	*The Gift*	1,500,000
5	Stephen King	*Insomnia*	1,398,213
6	James Finn Garner	*Politically Correct Bedtime Stories*	1,300,000
7	Danielle Steel	*Wings*	1,225,000*
8	Danielle Steel	*Accident*	1,150,000*
9	Robert James Waller	*The Bridges of Madison County*	844,574*
10	Michael Crichton	*Disclosure*	764,599*

* Approximate – precise figures undisclosed

KING RULES
Stephen King's novels have been the bestselling hardback fiction titles in three out of the past 10 years, while films derived from his books include such smash hits as Carrie, The Shining, The Dead Zone, *and* Creepshow – *in which he makes a cameo appearance.*

THE 10
HARDBACK FICTION BESTSELLERS WITH MOST WEEKS ON THE CHARTS, 1994

	Author	Title	Weeks
1	Robert James Waller	*The Bridges of Madison County**	51
2	James Redfield	*The Celestine Prophecy**	43
3	Laura Esquivel	*Like Water for Chocolate*	26
4	Caleb Carr	*The Alienist*	25
5	James Finn Garner	*Politically Correct Bedtime Stories**	24
6	Robert James Waller	*Slow Waltz at Cedar Bend**	21
7	Michael Crichton	*Disclosure**	20
8	John Grisham	*The Chamber**	19
9	Tom Clancy	*Debt of Honor**	17
10	Danielle Steel	*Accident**	15

* Hit the No.1 spot during the year

Robert James Waller's *The Bridges of Madison County*, now with more than three years on the bestsellers list, has been reprinted over 65 times by Warner Books, and has 5,700,000 copies in print. Waller's other bestseller of the year, *Slow Waltz at Cedar Bend*, has fared less well, dropping out of the Top 10 after six months on the chart.

THE 10
HARDBACK NONFICTION BESTSELLERS WITH MOST WEEKS ON THE CHARTS, 1994

	Author	Title	Weeks
1	John Gray	*Men Are from Mars, Women Are from Venus*	51
2	William J. Bennett	*The Way Things Ought to Be*	48
3	Betty J. Eadie with Curtis Taylor	*Embraced by the Light**	39
4	John Berendt	*Midnight in the Garden of Good and Evil*	36
5	Rosie Daley	*In the Kitchen with Rosie**	35
6	Thomas Baccei of N.E. Thing Enterprises Inc.	*Magic Eye*	32
7	Thomas Baccei of N.E. Thing Enterprises Inc.	*Magic Eye II*	22
8	Thomas Moore	*Soul Mates*	21
9=	Deepak Chopra	*Ageless Body, Timeless Mind*	17
9=	Susan Powter	*Stop The Insanity*	17

* Hit the No1 spot during the year

READD ALL ABOUT IT

TOP 10

DAILY NEWSPAPERS IN THE WORLD

	Newspaper	Country	Average daily circulation
1	*Yomiuri Shimbun*	Japan	8,700,000
2	*Asahi Shimbun*	Japan	7,400,000
3	*People's Daily*	China	6,000,000
4	*Bild Zeitung*	Germany	5,900,000
5	*The Sun*	UK	4,064,905
6	*Daily Mirror*	UK	2,463,945
7	*Wall Street Journal*	US	1,857,131*
8	*Daily Mail*	UK	1,765,320
9	*USA Today*	US	1,557,171
10	*Daily Express*	UK	1,288,012

* National edition only

The official Soviet newspaper *Pravda*, which is no longer published, formerly topped this list with alleged daily sales peaking in May 1990 at 21,975,000 copies. If true, it would hold the world record for a daily newspaper. The *Wall Street Journal* and *USA Today* were founded almost a century apart on July 8, 1889, and September 15, 1982. The other English-language newspapers were founded as follows: *Daily Mail* – May 4, 1896; *Daily Express* – April 24, 1900; *Daily Mirror* – November 2, 1903; *The Sun* – September 15, 1964.

TOP 10

DAILY NEWSPAPERS IN THE US

	Newspaper	Average daily circulation*
1	*Wall Street Journal*	1,823,207
2	*USA Today*	1,570,624
3	*New York Times*	1,170,869
4	*Los Angeles Times*	1,058,498
5	*Detroit Free Press/News*	886,228
6	*Washington Post*	840,232
7	*New York Daily News*	725,599
8	*Chicago Tribune*	691,283
9	*Long Island Newsday*	669,739
10	*San Francisco Chronicle/ Examiner*	610,849

* Through March 1995

Apart from the *Wall Street Journal*, which focuses on financial news, *USA Today* is the United States' only true national daily.

THE 10

FIRST NATIONAL NEWSPAPERS IN THE UK

	Newspaper	First published
1	*The London Gazette*	Nov 16, 1665

First published as The Oxford Gazette, *while the royal court resided in Oxford during an outbreak of plague. After 23 issues it moved to London with the court and changed its name.*

	Newspaper	First published
2	*Lloyds List*	1726

Originally providing shipping news on a weekly basis, but since 1734 Britain's oldest daily.

	Newspaper	First published
3	*The Times*	January 1, 1785

Originally the Daily Universal Register, *it became* The Times *on March 1, 1788.*

	Newspaper	First published
4	*Observer*	December 4, 1791

Although Johnson's British Gazette and Sunday Monitor *(1780–1829) was the first Sunday paper,* The Observer *has run the longest.*

	Newspaper	First published
5	*The Licensee*	February 8, 1794

Britain's oldest trade newspaper (a daily established by the Licensed Victuallers Association to earn income for its charity), and the first national paper on Fleet Street, the Morning Advertiser *changed its name to* The Licensee *and became a twice-weekly news magazine in 1994, at the time of its 200th anniversary.*

	Newspaper	First published
6	*The Scotsman*	January 25, 1817
7	*Sunday Times*	February 1821

Issued as the New Observer *until March 1821 and the* Independent Observer *from April 1821 until October 22, 1822 when it changed its name to the* Sunday Times. *On February 4, 1962 it became the first British newspaper to issue a color supplement.*

	Newspaper	First published
8	*The Guardian*	May 5, 1821

A weekly until 1855 (and called the Manchester Guardian *until 1959).*

	Newspaper	First published
9	*News of the World*	October 1, 1843
10	*Illustrated London News*	May 14, 1842

T O P 1 0
SUNDAY NEWSPAPERS IN THE US

	Newspaper	Average Sunday circulation*
1	New York Times	1,724,708
2	Los Angeles Times	1,457,925
3	Washington Post	1,141,964
4	Detroit Free Press	1,136,440
5	Chicago Tribune	1,080,862
6	New York News	964,030
7	Philadelphia Enquirer	930,862
8	Boston Globe	811,100
9	Dallas News	797,206
10	Long Island Newsday	779,629

* Through September 30, 1994

T O P 1 0
COUNTRIES WITH MOST DAILY NEWSPAPERS

	Country	No. of daily newspapers
1	India	2,300
2	US	1,586
3	Turkey	399
4	Brazil	373
5	Germany	355
6	Russia	339
7	Mexico	292
8	Pakistan	274
9	Argentina	190
10	Spain	148
	UK	101

	Country	Sales per 1,000 inhabitants
1	Hong Kong	819
2	Liechtenstein	700
3	Norway	606
4	Japan	576
5	Iceland	519
6	Finland	515
7	Sweden	511
8	Macau	510
9	South Korea	407
10	Austria	400
	UK	383
	US	240

Certain countries have large numbers of newspapers each serving relatively small areas and hence with restricted circulations: the US is the most notable example, with 1,586 daily newspapers, but only four of them with average daily sales of more than 1,000,000, while the UK, with fewer individual newspapers, has five with circulations of over 1,000,000. If the table is arranged by total sales of daily newspapers per 1,000 inhabitants, the result is somewhat different (see following list).

One curious anomaly is that of the Vatican City's one newspaper, l'Osservatore Romano, of which an average of 70,000 are printed. Since the population of the Vatican is only about 738, it implies a daily sale of 94,850 per 1,000, or 95 copies per head. In fact, most of them are sent outside the Holy See.

T H E 1 0
FIRST PROVINCIAL NEWSPAPERS IN THE UK

	Newspaper	First published
1	Berrow's Worcester Journal	c.1709

Originally The Worcester Post-Man, Berrow's Worcester Journal, from 1808, is Britain's oldest surviving provincial newspaper. Claims that it started in 1690 have never been verified.

2	Lincoln, Rutland and Stamford Mercury	c.1710

Originally published as the Stamford Mercury c.1710 (allegedly 1695, and possibly 1712).

3	Northampton Mercury and Herald	1720
4	Norwich Mercury	1726
5	Salisbury Journal	1729
6	Western Gazette (Somerset)	1737
7	News Letter (Belfast)	1738
8	Yorkshire Post	1754
9	Essex Chronicle	1764
10	Kentish Gazette	1768

T O P 1 0
CONSUMERS OF NEWSPRINT

	Country	Consumption per inhabitant		
		kg	lb	oz
1	Sweden	54.32	119	12
2	US	47.633	105	0
3	Austria	46.271	102	0
4	Switzerland	46.235	101	15
5	Norway	42.654	94	1
6	Denmark	42.226	93	1
7	Australia	37.395	82	7
8	Hong Kong	36.500	80	8
9	Singapore	36.367	80	3
10	UK	32.243	71	1

National consumption of newsprint – the cheap wood-pulp paper used for printing newspapers – provides a measure of the extent of the newspaper sales in the Top 10 countries.

MAGAZINES & COMICS

FIRST COMIC BOOKS IN THE US

(First published commercially: earlier comic books were given away as promotional items)

	Comic	First published
1	*Famous Funnies: Series 1*	Feb 1934

35,000 copies of this 64-page comic book sold at 10 cents each mark the beginning of the comic book era.

	Comic	First published
2	*Famous Funnies No.1*	Jul 1934

The first monthly comic ("The Nation's Comic Monthly"), it ran for 21 years, an incredible total of 218 issues.

	Comic	First published
3	*New Fun*	Feb 1935

Became More Fun after the 6th issue.

	Comic	First published
4	*Micky Mouse Magazine*	Jun 1935

Became Walt Disney's Comics and Stories from October 1940.

	Comic	First published
5	*New Comics*	Dec 1935

Became New Adventure Comics after No.12.

	Comic	First published
6	*Popular Comics*	Feb 1936
7=	*King Comics*	Apr 1936
7=	*Tip Top Comics*	Apr 1936

One of the longest-running of the early comic books, it ceased publication in May 1961 with its 225th issue.

	Comic	First published
9	*The Funnies*	Oct 1936

Became The New Funnies from issue No.65.

	Comic	First published
10	*Detective Picture Stories*	Dec 1936

The first ever thematic comic book, in July 1938 its title was changed to Keen Detective Funnies.

WOMEN'S MAGAZINES IN THE US

	Magazine/ no. of issues a year	Circulation*
1	*Better Homes and Gardens* (12)	7,615,315
2	*Good Housekeeping* (12)	5,056,700
3	*Ladies Home Journal* (12)	5,036,495
4	*Family Circle* (17)	5,004,635
5	*McCall's* (12)	4,636,022
6	*Woman's Day* (17)	4,508,333
7	*Redbook* (12)	3,253,746
8	*Cosmopolitan* (12)	2,528,280
9	*Glamour* (12)	2,186,214
10	*New Woman* (12)	1,316,771

* Average for first six months of 1994.

MOST VALUABLE AMERICAN COMICS

	Comic	Value ($)*
1	*Action Comics* No.1	105,000

Published in June 1938, the first issue of Action Comics marked the original appearance of Superman.

	Comic	Value ($)*
2	*Detective Comics* No.27	96,000

Issued in May 1939, it is prized as the first comic to feature Batman.

	Comic	Value ($)*
3	*Marvel Comics* No.1	75,000

The Human Torch and other heroes were first introduced in the issue dated October 1939.

	Comic	Value ($)*
4	*Superman* No.1	72,000

The first comic devoted to Superman, it reprinted the original Action Comics story and was published in summer 1939.

	Comic	Value ($)*
5	*Detective Comics* No.1	51,000

Published in March 1937, it was the first in a long-running series.

	Comic	Value ($)*
6	*Whiz Comics* No.1	44,000

Published in February 1940 – and confusingly numbered "2" – it was the first comic book to feature Captain Marvel.

	Comic	Value ($)*
7	*All American Comics* No.16	39,000

The Green Lantern made his debut in this issue, dated July 1940.

	Comic	Value ($)*
8	*Batman* No.1	38,000

Published in Spring 1940, this was the first comic book devoted to Batman.

	Comic	Value ($)*
9	*Captain America Comics* No.1	38,000

Published in March 1941, this was the original comic book in which Captain America appeared.

	Comic	Value ($)*
10	*New Fun Comics* No.1	36,000

Its February 1935 publication was notable as the first-ever D.C. comic book.

* For example, in "Near Mint" condition Source: © Overstreet Publications, Inc.

The actual prices paid both at auction and in private transactions vary considerably, with even higher prices than these occasionally reported. All the most expensive comic books in the Top 10 come from the so-called "Golden Age" (1938–1945), and to command very high prices must be in "Very Fine" or "Near Mint" condition.

COMIC BOOK PUBLISHERS IN THE US

	Publisher	Market share %*
1	Marvell	33.51
2	D.C.	20.87
3	Image	16.58
4	Dark Horse	6.93
5	Valiant	4.73
6	Malibu	3.94
7	Wizard	1.65
8=	Difiant	1.11
8=	Topps	1.11
10	Viz	1.05
	Others total	8.52

* As of August 1994

Between August 1991 and August 1994 old established market leaders Marvell and D.C. have seen their combined market share fall from 80.0 percent to 54.38 percent as various new kids arrive on the block – most notably the publishers of the anarchic British comic book *Viz*, emulating its stratospheric rise to bestsellerdom on the other side of the Atlantic.

THE 10

EARLIEST-ESTABLISHED MAGAZINES IN THE US

	Magazine	Founded
1	*Saturday Evening Post*	1821

The often-stated claim that the Saturday Evening Post was started as early as 1728 is unfounded: it is suggested that it was a descendant of the Universal Instructor in All Arts and Sciences and Pennsylvania Gazette, founded by Samuel Keimer in 1728, and bought in 1729 by Benjamin Franklin, who published it as the Pennsylvania Gazette, but this journal had ceased publication by 1815, and the Saturday Evening Post was started in Philadelphia in 1821 by Samuel C. Atkinson and Charles Alexander, neither of whom had any connection with the earlier magazine.

	Magazine	Founded
2	*Scientific American*	1845

Began publication in New York on August 28 in a newspaper format.

	Magazine	Founded
3	*Town & Country*	1846
4	*Harper's Magazine*	1850

The magazine began its life in New York as Harper's Monthly.

	Magazine	Founded
5	*The Atlantic*	1857

Started in Boston (as the Atlantic Monthly) under editor James Russell Lowell.

	Magazine	Founded
6	*The Nation*	1865

Founded by Irish-born Edwin Lawrence Godkin, it commenced publication in New York.

	Magazine	Founded
7	*Harper's Bazaar*	1867

William Randolph Hearst bought the magazine in 1913 and subtly changed its name from Harper's Bazar with one "a."

	Magazine	Founded
8	*Popular Science*	1872

Founded in New York as Popular Science Monthly by Edward Livingston Youmans, an author and teacher who had been blind for most of his life. Its first issue, published in May and priced at 50 cents, contained articles on subjects ranging from "Science and Immortality" and "Women and Political Power" to "The Causes of Dyspepsia."

	Magazine	Founded
9	*American Field*	1874
10	*Thoroughbred Record*	1875

Appropriately, first published in the inaugural year of the Kentucky Derby.

In 1916 American bank clerk DeWitt Wallace published a booklet called *Getting the Most Out of Farming*, which consisted of extracts from various US Government agricultural publications. While recovering after being wounded in France during the war, he contemplated applying the same principle to a general interest magazine and in 1920 produced a sample copy of *Reader's Digest*. He and his wife, Lila Acheson, solicited sales by subscription and published 5,000 copies of the first issue in February 1922. It was an enormous success, rapidly becoming the bestselling monthly magazine in the US. Today 41 editions are published in 17 languages. DeWitt died in 1981 and Lila Wallace in 1984.

TOP 10

SPECIALIZED MAGAZINES IN THE US

	Magazine/ no. of issues a year	Circulation*
1	*TV Guide* (52)	14,266,000
2	*National Geographic* (12)	9,368,000
3	*Sports Illustrated* (52)	3,815,000
4	*Prevention* (12)	3,416,000
5	*Vegetarian Times* (12)	3,164,000
6	*Smithsonian* (12)	2,238,000
7	*Money* (13)	2,226,000
8	*Motorland* (12)	2,127,000
9	*Ebony* (12)	2,034,000
10	*Field and Stream* (12)	2,007,000

Source: Standard Rate & Data Service

TOP 10

MAGAZINES IN THE US

	Magazine/ no. of issues a year	Circulation*
1	*Modern Maturity* (36)	22,140,641
2	*NRTA/AARP Bulletin* (10)	22,045,194
3	*Reader's Digest* (12)	15,231,649
4	*TV Guide* (52)	14,266,020
5	*National Geographic Magazine* (12)	9,367,954
6	*Better Homes and Gardens* (12)	7,615,315
7	*Good Housekeeping* (12)	5,056,700
8	*Ladies Home Journal* (12)	5,036,495
9	*Family Circle* (17)	5,004,635
10	*McCall's* (12)	4,636,022

* Average for first six months of 1994

Reader's Digest held the No. 1 position for many years in the US. The syndicated color weekly *Parade*, distributed with more than 350 Sunday newspapers across the United States, has the largest circulation of any magazine, 36,730,000.

TOP 10

TRADE MAGAZINES IN THE US

	Title/ no. of issues per year	Circulation
1	*Independent Business* (6)	694,670
2	*Chief Financial Officer* (12)	365,311
3	*The Journal of the American Medical Association* (48)	328,412
4	*American Medical News* (48)	304,520
5	*Registered Nurse* (12)	296,945
6	*Industry Week* (24)	281,069
7	*Farm Industry News* (12)	257,779
8	*PC Week* (51)	235,302
9	*Soybean Digest* (11)	233,819
10	*Infoworld* (51)	225,047

Figures given are for the combined paid and nonpaid average circulations for the six months ended June 1994.

ART AT AUCTION

MOST EXPENSIVE PAINTINGS EVER SOLD

Artist/work/sale	Price ($)
1 Vincent van Gogh, *Portrait du Dr. Gachet* Christie's, New York, May 15, 1990	75,000,000

Sold to Ryoei Saito, head of Japanese Daishowa Paper Manufacturing.

2 Pierre-Auguste Renoir, *Au Moulin de la Galette* Sotheby's, New York, May 17, 1990	71,000,000

Also purchased by Ryoei Saito – two days later.

3 Pablo Picasso, *Les Noces de Pierrette* Binoche et Godeau, Paris November 30, 1989	51,671,920

Sold by Swedish financier Fredrik Roos and bought by Tomonori Tsurumaki, a property developer, bidding from Tokyo by phone.

4 Vincent van Gogh, *Irises* Sotheby's, New York, November 11, 1987	49,000,000

After much speculation, its mystery purchaser was eventually confirmed as Australian businessman Alan Bond. However, since he was unable to pay for it in full, its former status as the world's most expensive work of art has been disputed. In 1990 it was sold to the J. Paul Getty Museum, Malibu, for an undisclosed sum, with speculation ranging from $60,000,000 to as little as $35,000,000.

5 Pablo Picasso, Self Portrait: *Yo Picasso* Sotheby's, New York, May 9, 1989	43,500,000

The anonymous purchaser may have been Greek shipping magnate Stavros Niarchos.

6 Pablo Picasso, *Au Lapin Agile* Sotheby's, New York, November 15, 1989	37,000,000

The painting depicts Picasso as a harlequin at the bar of the café Lapin Agile. The owner of the café acquired the picture in exchange for food and drink at a time when Picasso was hard up. In 1989 it was bought by the Walter Annenberg Foundation.

7 Vincent van Gogh, *Sunflowers* Christie's, London, March 30, 1987	36,225,000

At the time, the most expensive picture ever sold (and still the most expensive sold in the UK), it was bought by the Yasuda Fire and Marine Insurance Company of Tokyo.

8 Pablo Picasso, *Acrobate et Jeune Arlequin* Christie's, London, November 28, 1988	35,500,000

Until the sale of Yo Picasso, this held the world record for a 20th-century painting. It was bought by Mitsukoshi, a Japanese department store. (In Japan, many major stores have important art galleries.)

9 Jacopo da Carucci (Pontormo) *Portrait of Duke Cosimo I de Medici* Christie's, New York, May 31, 1989	32,000,000

The world record price for an Old Master – and the only one in the Top 10 – it was bought by the J. Paul Getty Museum, Malibu.

10 Paul Cézanne, *Nature Morte – Les Grosses Pommes* Sotheby's, New York, May 11, 1993	26,000,000

Sold by one Greek shipowner, George Embiricos, and bought by another, Stavros Niarchos.

ARTISTS WITH MOST PAINTINGS SOLD FOR MORE THAN $1,000,000

DR GACHET BY VINCENT VAN GOGH

	Artist	Paintings sold for $1M+
1	Pablo Picasso	153
2	Auguste Renoir	142
3	Claude Monet	132
4	Edgar Degas	65
5	Marc Chagall	55
6	Camille Pissarro	50
7	Henri Matisse	45
8	Paul Cézanne	42
9=	Amedeo Modigliani	33
9=	Vincent van Gogh	33

FIRST PAINTINGS AUCTIONED FOR OVER $3M

Work/artist/sale	Sale date
1 *Portrait of Juan de Pareja*, Diego Rodriguez de Silva y Velasquez (Spanish; 1599–1660) Christie's, London ($5,524,000)	November 27, 1970
2 *The Death of Actaeon*, Titian (Italian; c.1488–1576), Christie's, London ($4,036,000)	June 25, 1971
3 *The Resurrection*, Dirk Bouts (Dutch; 1400–75) Sotheby's, London ($3,740,000)	April 16, 1980
4 *Saltimbanque Seated with Arms Crossed* Pablo Picasso (Spanish; 1881–1973), Sotheby's, New York ($3,000,000)	May 12, 1980
5 *Paysan en Blouse Bleu*, Paul Cézanne (French; 1839–1906), Christie's, New York ($3,900,000)	May 13, 1980
6 *Le Jardin du Poete, Arles*, Vincent van Gogh (Dutch; 1853–80), Christie's, New York ($5,200,000)	May 13, 1980
7 *Juliet and Her Nurse*, J.M.W. Turner (British; 1775–1851), Sotheby's, New York ($6,400,000)	May 29, 1980
8 *Samson and Delilah*, Sir Peter Paul Rubens (British; 1577–1640), Christie's, London ($5,474,000)	July 11, 1980
9 *The Holy Family with Saints and Putti* Nicolas Poussin (French; 1594–1665) Christie's, London ($3,564,000)	April 10, 1981
10 Self Portrait: *Yo Picasso*, Pablo Picasso Sotheby's, New York ($5,300,000)	May 21, 1981

TOP 10
MOST EXPENSIVE OLD MASTER PAINTINGS

Work/artist/sale	Price ($)
1 *Portrait of Duke Cosimo I de Medici*, Jacopo da Carucci (Pontormo) (1493–1558) Christie's, New York May 31, 1989	32,000,000
2 *The Old Horse Guards, London, from St James's Park* Canaletto (1697–1768) Christie's, London April 15, 1992	16,008,000
3 *Venus and Adonis*, Titian (1488–1576), Christie's, London December 13, 1991	12,376,000
4 *View of the Giudecca and the Zattere, Venice* Francesco Guardi (1712–93) Sotheby's, Monaco December 1, 1989	11,316,457
5 *View of Molo from Bacino di San Marco, Venice,* and *View of the Grand Canal Facing East from Campo di Santi, Venice* (pair), Canaletto Sotheby's, New York June 1, 1990	10,000,000
6 *Adoration of the Magi* Andrea Mantegna (1431–1506) Christie's, London April 18, 1985	9,525,000
7 *Portrait of a Girl Wearing a Gold-trimmed Cloak* Rembrandt (1606–69) Sotheby's, London December 10, 1986	9,372,000
8 *Portraits of Kurfurst Herzog Johann von Sachsen and his son Johann Friedrich* (pair) Lucas Cranach the Elder (1472–1553), Christie's, London, July 6, 1990	7,920,000
9 *Portrait of Johannes Uyittenbogaert* Rembrandt Sotheby's, London July 8, 1992	7,296,000
10 *Argonauts in Colchis* Bartolomeo di Giovanni (15th C) Sotheby's, London December 6, 1989	7,268,000

TOP 10
MOST EXPENSIVE PAINTINGS BY AMERICAN ARTISTS

Artist/work/sale	Price ($)
1 *Interchange* Willem de Kooning (b.1904) Sotheby's, New York November 8, 1989	18,800,000
2 *False Start* Jasper Johns (b.1930) Sotheby's, New York November 10, 1988	15,500,000
3 *Two Flags* Jasper Johns Sotheby's, New York November 8, 1989	11,000,000
4 *Number 8, 1950* Jackson Pollock (1912–56) Sotheby's, New York May 2, 1989	10,500,000
5 *July* Willem de Kooning Christie's, New York November 7, 1990	8,000,000
6 *Home by the Lake, Scene in the Catskill Mountains* Frederic Edwin Church (1826–1900), Sotheby's, New York May 24, 1989	7,500,000
7 *Spanish Dancer* John Singer Sargent (1856–1925) Sotheby's, New York May 25, 1994	6,900,000
8 *Rebus*, Robert Rauschenberg (b.1925) Sotheby's, New York April 30, 1991	6,600,000
9 *Palisade* Willem de Kooning Sotheby's, New York May 8, 1990	6,500,000
10 *White Flag* Jasper Johns Christie's, New York November 9, 1988	6,400,000

While living painters Willem de Kooning and Jasper Johns dominate this world list, two earlier artists, Frederic Edwin Church and John Singer Sargent, are represented: Church was notable as a painter of naturalistic landscapes, while Sargent worked mainly in Europe where he was influenced by the French Impressionists.

TOP 10
MOST EXPENSIVE PAINTINGS BY WOMEN ARTISTS

Work/artist/sale	Price ($)
1 *The Conversation* Mary Cassatt (American; 1845–1926) Christie's, New York May 11, 1988	4,100,000
2 *Mother, Sara and the Baby* Mary Cassatt, Christie's, New York, May 10, 1989	3,500,000
3 *Augusta Reading to her Daughter* Mary Cassatt, Sotheby's, New York, May 9, 1989	2,800,000
4 *Sara Holding her Dog* Mary Cassatt Sotheby's, New York November 11, 1988	2,500,000
5 *Young Lady in a Loge, Gazing to the Right* Mary Cassatt Sotheby's, New York November 10, 1992	2,300,000
6 *Madame H. de Fleury and her Child* Mary Cassatt Sotheby's, New York May 25, 1988	1,900,000
7= *Adam et Eve*, Tamara de Lempicka (Polish; 1898–1980) Christie's, New York March 3, 1994	1,800,000
7= *Black Hollyhocks with Blue Larkspur*, Georgia O'Keeffe (American; 1887–1986) Sotheby's, New York December 3, 1987	1,800,000
9 *Balskorna – Dancing Shoe* Helene Schjerfbeck (Finnish; 1862–1946), Sotheby's, London, March 27, 1990	1,630,000
10= *Jules Standing by his Mother* Mary Cassatt Christie's, New York November 14, 1989	1,500,000
10= *Dark Iris, No. 2*, Georgia O'Keeffe, Sotheby's, New York, May 24, 1989	1,500,000
10= *Autorretrato con Pelo Suelto* Frida Kahlo (Mexican; 1907–54), Christie's, New York, May 15, 1991	1,500,000

MODERN ARTISTS

The twentieth-century artists represented here share the comparatively rare ability to command auction prices in excess of $1,000,000. In the case of Picasso, he holds the unique distinction of four of his paintings achieving places among the ten highest-priced paintings of all time.

TOP 10

MOST EXPENSIVE PAINTINGS BY JASPER JOHNS

	Work/sale	Price ($)
1	False Start Sotheby's, New York, November 10, 1988	15,500,000
2	Two Flags Sotheby's, New York, November 8, 1989	11,000,000
3	White Flag Christie's, New York, November 9, 1988	6,400,000
4	Jubilee Sotheby's, New York, November 13, 1991	4,500,000
5	Device Circle Christie's, New York, November 12, 1991	4,000,000
6	Gray Rectangles Sotheby's, New York, November 10, 1988	3,900,000
7	Diver Christie's, New York, May 3, 1988	3,800,000
8	Small False Start Christie's, New York, November 9, 1989	3,700,000
9	Out of the Window Sotheby's, New York, November 10, 1986	3,300,000
10	Colored Alphabet Christie's, New York, May 3, 1989	3,200,000

The work of US artist Jasper Johns (b.1930) is the most expensive of any living painter. Considered in the vanguard of Pop Art, it typically features flags, targets, and numbers, often with 3-D objects on the canvas.

TOP 10

MOST EXPENSIVE PAINTINGS BY PABLO PICASSO

	Work/sale	Price ($)
1	Les Noces de Pierrette Binoche et Godeau, Paris, November 30, 1989	51,671,920 (FF315,000,000)
2	Self Portrait: Yo Picasso Sotheby's, New York, May 9, 1989	43,500,000
3	Au Lapin Agile Sotheby's, New York, November 15, 1989	37,000,000
4	Angel Fernandez De Soto Sotheby's, New York May 8, 1995	28,152,500
5	Le Miroir Sotheby's, New York, November 15, 1989	24,000,000 (£15,483,872)
6	Maternité Christie's, New York, June 14, 1988	22,500,000
7	Les Tuileries Christie's, London, June 25, 1990	22,000,000 (£12,500,000)
8	Acrobate et Jeune Arlequin Christie's, London, November 28, 1988	19,000,000
9	Mère et Enfant Sotheby's, New York, November 15, 1989	17,000,000
10=	Famille de l'Arlequin Christie's, New York, November 14, 1989	14,000,000
10=	La Cage d'Oiseaux Sotheby's, New York, November 10, 1988	14,000,000

By the late 1950s the Spanish artist Pablo Picasso (1881–1973) was being hailed as the twentieth century's foremost artist. When *Mother and Child* sold in 1957 for $185,000, it was the top price ever paid for a work by a living artist. *Self Portrait: Yo Picasso* made $5,300,000 in 1981 – an amazing price at the time, but outsold many times since both by itself and the other top three works. Picasso's top four are in the World Top 10 and he holds the record for the most paintings sold for over $1,000,000. *Angel Fernando De Soto*, sold in 1995, was the most expensive painting sold since 1990.

TOP 10

MOST EXPENSIVE PAINTINGS BY DAVID HOCKNEY

	Work/sale	Price ($)
1	Grand Procession of Dignitaries in the semi-Egyptian Style Sotheby's, New York, May 2, 1989	2,000,000
2	Deep and Wet Water Sotheby's, New York, November 8, 1989	1,300,000
3	Henry Geldzahler and Christopher Scott Sotheby's, New York, November 17, 1992	1,000,000
4	California Art Collector Sotheby's, New York, November 10, 1993	925,000
5	The Room, Manchester Street Christie's, New York, May 3, 1989	800,000
6	A Neat Lawn Sotheby's, London, December 1, 1988	598,400
7	Different Kinds of Water Pouring into Swimming Pool, Santa Monica Sotheby's, New York, May 2, 1989	460,000
8	The Room, Tarzana Christie's, London, December 3, 1987	447,200
9	The Actor Sotheby's, London, June 27, 1991	386,400
10	Fall Pool with Two Flat Blues Christie's, New York, November 12, 1991	380,000

David Hockney (born in Bradford, July 9, 1937) studied at the Royal College of Art and achieved early acclaim in England as a representative of Pop Art before settling in California, where the colorful urban landscape ideally suited his evolving style. In addition to his paintings, which are avidly collected by the fashionable wealthy, he has produced stage sets and worked in a variety of novel media such as Polaroid photocollages and even faxes. Many of his popular subjects have become widely known at a more affordable level through reproduction as decorative posters.

TOP 10

MOST EXPENSIVE PAINTINGS BY GEORGIA O'KEEFFE

	Work/sale	Price ($)
1	*Black Hollyhocks with Blue Larkspur* Sotheby's, New York, December 3, 1987	1,800,000
2	*Dark Iris, No. 2* Sotheby's, New York, May 24, 1989	1,500,000
3	*At the Rodeo, New Mexico* Sotheby's, New York, December 3, 1987	1,430,000
4	*Yellow Cactus Flowers* Sotheby's, New York, May 24, 1989	1,200,000
5	*White Rose, New Mexico* Sotheby's, New York, December 5, 1985	1,150,000
6=	*Two Jimson Weeds* Sotheby's, New York, December 3, 1987	1,100,000
6=	*Ritz Tower, Night* Christie's, New York, December 4, 1992	1,100,000
8=	*Red Poppy, No. VI* Christie's, New York, May 23, 1990	1,000,000
8=	*Cow's Skull on Red* Christie's, New York, November 30, 1994	1,000,000
10=	*Black Petunia and White Morning Glory II* Sotheby's, New York, May 24, 1990	950,000
10=	*Jimson Weed* Sotheby's, New York, December 1, 1994	950,000

Georgia O'Keeffe (1887–1986) is acknowledged as the leading US female painter of the twentieth century. Much of her work was based on natural organic forms, microscopic detail, and landscapes.

TOP 10

MOST EXPENSIVE PAINTINGS BY FRANCIS BACON

	Work/sale	Price ($)
1	*Triptych May–June* Sotheby's, New York, May 2, 1989	5,700,000
2	*Study for Portrait of Van Gogh II* Sotheby's, New York, May 2, 1989	5,300,000
3	*Study for Pope* Christie's, New York, November 7, 1989	5,200,000
4	*Study for Portrait* Sotheby's, New York, May 8, 1990	5,000,000
5	*Study for Portrait VIII* Sotheby's, London, December 5, 1991	3,358,000
6	*Portrait of Lucian Freud* Sotheby's, New York, May 8, 1990	3,300,000
7	*Turning Figure* Sotheby's, New York, November 8, 1989	3,000,000
8=	*Portrait of George Dyer Staring into Mirror* Christie's, New York, November 7, 1989	1,900,000
8=	*Study for Figure in Room* Sotheby's, New York, May 2, 1989	1,900,000
10	*Study for Portrait of Lucian Freud* Christie's, New York, November 9, 1993	1,600,000

Irish-born Francis Bacon (1909–92) became famous as one of the principal figures in post-war British art, notorious for the sensational and horrific content of his paintings. These include smeared, convoluted portraits, such as his "screaming Popes," often juxtaposed with slabs of meat, which evoke anger and terror.

TOP 10

MOST EXPENSIVE PAINTINGS BY SALVADOR DALI

	Work/sale	Price ($)
1	*Assumpta Corpuscularia Lapislazulina* Christie's, New York, May 15, 1990	3,700,000
2=	*The Battle of Tetuan* Sotheby's, New York, November 11, 1987	2,200,000
2=	*L'Ascension de Christ – Pieta* Christie's, New York, November 2, 1993	2,200,000
4	*La Bataille de Tetouan* Christie's, New York, May 10, 1994	2,000,000
5	*Portrait of Paul Eluard* Christie's, New York, November 14, 1989	1,900,000
6	*Bataille autour d'un Pissenlit* Guy Loudmer, Paris, March 21, 1988	1,061,185
7	*Le Christ de Gala* Christie's, New York, May 10, 1994	950,000
8	*Le Someil* Christie's, London, March 30, 1981	806,000
9	*L'Enigme de Desir – Ma Mère* Christie's, London, March 29, 1982	760,200
10	*Instrument Masochiste* Sotheby's, London, December 1, 1992	647,800

In the late 1920s the Spanish artist Salvador Dali became one of the principal figures in the Surrealism movement. His work usually features dreamlike and psychologically disturbing images set in realistic landscapes. The best known are the "melting" watches in his *The Persistence of Memory* (1931), as well as various symbolic paintings on religious themes.

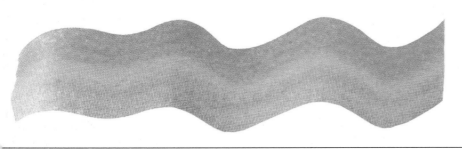

ART ON SHOW

BEST-ATTENDED EXHIBITIONS
AT THE METROPOLITAN MUSEUM
OF ART, NEW YORK

	Exhibition	Year	Attendance
1	The Treasures of Tutankhamun	1978–79	1,226,467
2	The Mona Lisa	1963	1,077,000
3	The Vatican Collection: The Papacy and Art	1983	896,743
4	Seurat	1991–92	642,408
5	Van Gogh in St. Rémy and Auvers	1986–87	630,699
6	Van Gogh in Arles	1984	624,120
7	Mexico: Splendor of Thirty Centuries	1990–91	584,528
8	Masterpieces of Impressionism and Post-Impressionism: The Annenberg Collection	1991	560,734
9	Velazquez	1989–90	556,394
10	Degas	1988–89	540,363

BEST-ATTENDED EXHIBITIONS
AT THE ART INSTITUTE
OF CHICAGO

	Exhibition	Year	Attendance
1	A Century of Progress	1933	1,538,103
2	The Vatican Collection	1983	616,134
3	Pompeii AD 79	1978	489,118
4	Monet in the Nineties	1990	456,217
5	Paintings by Claude Monet	1975	384,458
6	The Art of Paul Gauguin	1988	374,477
7	A Day in the Country	1985–86	369,766
8	Half a Century of American Art	1939–40	363,093
9	Paintings by Renoir	1973	352,987
10	The Search for Alexander	1981	319,892

Some of the Art Institute's most successful exhibits have featured paintings by French Impressionists and Post-Impressionists. Its own collection of such works is one of the world's finest, and includes many famous works, such as Seurat's *Sunday Afternoon at the Grande Jatte*.

BEST-ATTENDED EXHIBITIONS
AT THE NATIONAL GALLERY,
WASHINGTON, D.C.

	Exhibition	Year	Attendance
1	Rodin Rediscovered	1981–82	1,053,223
2	Treasure Houses of Britain	1985–86	990,474
3	Treasures of Tutankhamun	1976–77	835,924
4	Archaeological Finds of the People's Republic of China	1974–75	684,238
5	Ansel Adams: Classic Images	1985–86	651,652
6	The Splendor of Dresden	1978	620,089
7	The Art of Paul Gauguin	1988	596,058
8	Circa 1492: Art in the Age of Exploration	1991–92	568,192
9	Post-Impressionism: Cross Currents in European & American Painting	1980	557,533
10	Great French Paintings from The Barnes Foundation	1993	520,924

PHARAOH RULES
The Tutankhamun exhibition attracted the biggest-ever crowds at both the Metropolitan Museum of Art, New York, and the British Museum, London. The solid-gold burial mask, weighing over 22.5 lb (10.2 kg), was the highlight

BEST-ATTENDED
EXHIBITIONS AT THE FINE
ARTS MUSEUM, BOSTON

	Exhibition	Year	Attendance
1	Monet in the Nineties	1990	537,502
2	Renoir	1985	515,795
3	Pompeii AD 79	1978	432,080
4	New World: American Painting	1983	264,640
5	Pissarro	1981	235,012
6	Masters From The Cone Collection	1991	221,886
7	The Age of Rubens	1993	218,010
8	Living National Treasures of Japan	1982	197,456
9	Great Bronze Age of China	1981	192,175
10	Goya	1989	185,765

TOP 10

MOST EXPENSIVE PHOTOGRAPHS EVER SOLD AT AUCTION

	Photographer/photograph/sale	Price ($)
1	Edward S. Curtis (American, 1868–1952), *The North American Indian** (1907–30), Sotheby's, New York, October 7, 1993	662,500
2	Edward S. Curtis, *The North American Indian**, (1907–30), Christie's, New York, April 6, 1995	464,500
3	Alfred Stieglitz (American, 1864–1946), *Georgia O'Keeffe: A Portrait – Hands with Thimble* (1930), Christie's, New York, October 8, 1993	398,500
4=	Alfred Stieglitz, *Equivalents (21)**, 1920s Christie's, New York, October 30, 1989	396,000
4=	Edward S. Curtis, *The North American Indian** (1907–30) Christie's, New York, October 13, 1992	396,000
6	Man Ray (American, 1890–1976), *Noir et Blanche** (1926) Christie's, New York, April 21, 1994	354,500
7	Man Ray, *Hier, Demain, Aujourd'hui* (triptych) (1930–32) Christie's, New York, October 8, 1993	222,500
8	Man Ray, *Glass Tears*, c.1930 Sotheby's, London, May 7, 1993 (£122,500)	195,000
9	Tina Modotti (Mexican, 1896–1942), *Two Callas*, 1925 Christie's, New York, October 8, 1993	189,500
10	Alexander Rodchenko (Russian, 1891–1956), *Girl with Leica*, 1934 Christie's, London, October 29, 1992 (£115,500)	181,450

* *Collections; all others are single prints*

SYMBOL OF FREEDOM
Standing on a massive pedestal, Liberty bears a book of law and a burning torch that reaches 305 ft (93 m) above sea level.

TOP 10

TALLEST FREE-STANDING STATUES IN THE WORLD

	Statue	Height m	ft
1	*Chief Crazy Horse*, Thunderhead Mountain, South Dakota	172	563

Started in 1948 by Polish-American sculptor Korczak Ziolkowski, and continued after his death in 1982 by his widow and eight of his children, this gigantic equestrian statue is even longer than it is high (641 ft/195 m). It is not expected to be completed until the next century.

| 2 | *Buddha*, Tokyo, Japan | 120 | 394 |

This Japan-Taiwanese project, unveiled in 1993, took seven years to complete and weighs more than 1,000 tons.

| 3 | *The Indian Rope Trick*, Riddersberg Säteri, Jönköping, Sweden | 103 | 337 |

Sculptor Calle Örnemark's 159-ton wooden sculpture depicts a long strand of "rope" held by a fakir, while another figure ascends.

| 4 | *Motherland, 1967*, Volgograd, Russia | 82 | 270 |

Unveiled in 1967, this concrete statue of a woman with raised sword commemorates the Soviet victory at the Battle of Stalingrad (1942–43).

| 5 | *Buddha*, Bamian, Afghanistan | 53 | 173 |

Near this 3rd–4th century AD statue lie the remains of the even taller Sakya Buddha, said to have measured 1,000 ft/305 m.

| 6 | *Kannon*, Otsubo-yama, near Tokyo, Japan | 52 | 170 |

The immense statue of the goddess of mercy was unveiled in 1961 in honor of the dead of World War II.

| 7 | *Statue of Liberty*, New York | 46 | 151 |

Designed by Auguste Bartholdi and presented to the US by the people of France, the statue was shipped in sections to Liberty (formerly Bedloes) Island where it was assembled. It was unveiled on October 28, 1886, and restored and reinaugurated on July 4, 1986. It consists of sheets of copper on an iron frame, and weighs 252 tons in total.

| 8 | *Christ*, Rio de Janeiro, Brazil | 38 | 125 |

The work of sculptor Paul Landowski and engineer Heitor da Silva Costa, the figure of Christ weighs 1,282 tons. It was unveiled in 1931 and has recently been restored.

| 9 | *Tian Tan (Temple of Heaven) Buddha* Po Lin Monastery, Lantau Island, Hong Kong | 34 | 112 |

Completed after 20 years of work and unveiled on December 29, 1993, the bronze statue weighs 275 tons and cost $9,000,000 (£6,000,000).

| 10 | *Colossi of Memnon*, Karnak, Egypt | 21 | 70 |

Two seated sandstone figures of Pharaoh Amenhotep III.

MUSIC

TOP 10
SINGLES OF ALL TIME WORLDWIDE

	Artist/title	Sales exceed
1	Bing Crosby *White Christmas*	30,000,000
2	Bill Haley & His Comets *Rock Around The Clock*	17,000,000
3	The Beatles, *I Want To Hold Your Hand*	12,000,000
4=	Elvis Presley *It's Now Or Never*	10,000,000
4=	Whitney Houston *I Will Always Love You*	10,000,000
6=	Elvis Presley *Hound Dog/ Don't Be Cruel*	9,000,000
6=	Paul Anka, *Diana*	9,000,000
8=	The Beatles, *Hey Jude*	8,000,000
8=	The Monkees *I'm A Believer*	8,000,000
10=	The Beatles *Can't Buy Me Love*	7,000,000
10=	Band Aid *Do They Know It's Christmas?*	7,000,000
10=	USA For Africa *We Are The World*	7,000,000

TOP 10
SINGLES – THE FIRST CHART IN THE US

1	Tommy Dorsey, *I'll Never Smile Again*	6	Charlie Barnet, *Where Was I*
2	Jimmy Dorsey, *The Breeze And I*	7	Glenn Miller, *Pennsylvania 6-5000*
3	Glenn Miller, *Imagination*	8	Tommy Dorsey, *Imagination*
4	Kay Kyser, *Playmates*	9	Bing Crosby, *Sierra Sue*
5	Glenn Miller, *Fools Rush In*	10	Mitchell Ayres, *Make-Believe Island*

This was the first singles Top 10 compiled by *Billboard* magazine, for its issue dated July 20, 1940. Since the 7-inch 45-rpm single was still nearly a decade away, all these would have been 10-inch 78-rpm disks. Note the almost total domination of big-name big bands.

TOP 10
ARTISTS WITH THE LONGEST CHART CAREER RUNS, 1955–1995*

	Artist	Chart span Years	Months		Artist	Chartspan Years	Months
1	Four Seasons	38	2	6	Roy Orbison	32	11
2	Tokens	33	6	7	Stevie Wonder	32	8
3	Aretha Franklin	33	3	8	Ray Charles	32	4
4	Tina Turner	33	2	9	Smokey Robinson	32	1
5	Paul Simon	33	0	10	B.B. King	31	8

* To April 1995

Thanks to a remix in 1994 of their December '63 hit, *Oh, What A Night*, The Four Seasons top the list with a career that began in the week ending May 26, 1956. Roy Orbison's fifth place is remarkable since his chart career, which began in 1956, stalled in 1967, and he did not chart again until 1980. It was another nine years until *You Got It*, just before his death.

TOP 10

SINGLES OF ALL TIME IN THE US

	Artist/title	Released
1	Bing Crosby, *White Christmas*	1942
2	The Beatles *I Want To Hold Your Hand*	1964
3	Elvis Presley, *Hound Dog/Don't Be Cruel*	1956
4	Elvis Presley *It's Now Or Never*	1960
5	Whitney Houston *I Will Always Love You*	1992
6	The Beatles, *Hey Jude*	1968
7	USA For Africa *We Are The World*	1985
8	Tag Team *Whoomp! There It Is*	1993
9	Bryan Adams *Everything I Do (I Do It for You)*	1991
10	The Chipmunks *The Chipmunk Song*	1958

White Christmas is still the US's all-time most-charted single, having been a major Yuletide seller every Christmas since its original release in 1942. Total US sales are thought to be somewhere in the region of 15,000,000 disks, more than twice the number for The Beatles' biggest seller at No. 2, *I Want to Hold Your Hand*. The Whitney Houston release became the first single to exceed sales of 4,000,000 in the 1990s, joined in 1993 by the equally quadruple-platinum rap novelty hit by Tag Team.

THE KING
Elvis Presley's international success is exemplified by his two appearances among the world's 10 bestselling singles of all time.

TOP 10

SINGLES IN THE US, 1994

	Artist	Title
1	Boyz II Men	*I'll Make Love To You*
2	All-4-One	*I Swear*
3	R. Kelly	*Bump 'N' Grind*
4	Ace of Base	*The Sign*
5	69 Boyz	*Tootsee Roll*
6	Coolio	*Fantastic Voyage*
7	Warren G & Nate Dogg	*Regulate*
8	Celine Dion	*The Power Of Love*
9	Lisa Loeb & Nine Stories	*Stay (I Missed You)*
10	Ini Kamoze	*Here Comes The Hotstepper*

TOP 10

YOUNGEST ARTISTS TO HAVE NO. 1 SINGLES IN THE US

	Artist/year	Age* yrs	mths
1	Michael Jackson (1970)	11	5
2	Jimmy Boyd (1952)	12	11
3	Stevie Wonder (1963)	13	2
4	Donny Osmond (1971)	13	9
5	Laurie London (1958)	14	3
6	Little Peggy March (1963)	15	1
7	Brenda Lee (1960)	15	7
8=	Paul Anka (1957)	16	1
8=	Tiffany (1987)	16	1
10=	Little Eva (1962)	17	1
10=	Lesley Gore (1963)	17	1

* *During first week of debut No. 1 US single*

TOP 10

SINGLES THAT STAYED LONGEST AT NO. 1 IN THE US*

	Artist/title	Year released	Weeks at No. 1
1=	Whitney Houston, *I Will Always Love You*	1992	14
1=	Boyz II Men, *I'll Make Love To You*	1994	14
3	Boyz II Men, *End Of The Road*	1992	13
4=	Elvis Presley, *Don't Be Cruel/Hound Dog*	1956	11
4=	All-4-One, *I Swear*	1994	11
6=	Perez Prado, *Cherry Pink And Apple Blossom White*	1955	10
6=	Debby Boone, *You Light Up My Life*	1977	10
6=	Olivia Newton-John, *Physical*	1981	10
9=	Bobby Darin, *Mack The Knife*	1959	9
9=	The Beatles, *Hey Jude*	1968	9
9=	Diana Ross and Lionel Richie, *Endless Love*	1981	9
9=	Kim Carnes, *Bette Davis Eyes*	1981	9
9=	Guy Mitchell, *Singing The Blues*	1956	9
9=	Percy Faith, Theme from *"A Summer Place"*	1960	9

* *Based on Billboard charts from 1955 when Billboard's US Top 100 was inaugurated for singles*

SINGLES OF THE DECADES

SINGLES OF THE 1950s IN THE UK

	Title	Artist	Year
1	*Rock Around The Clock*	Bill Haley & His Comets	1955
2	*Diana*	Paul Anka	1957
3	*Mary's Boy Child*	Harry Belafonte	1957
4	*The Harry Lime Theme (The Third Man)*	Anton Karas	1950
5	*Living Doll*	Cliff Richard	1959
6	*Jailhouse Rock*	Elvis Presley	1958
7	*What Do You Want To Make Those Eyes At Me For?*	Emile Ford	1959
8	*All I Have To Do Is Dream/ Claudette*	Everly Brothers	1958
9	*What Do You Want?*	Adam Faith	1959
10	*All Shook Up*	Elvis Presley	1957

In 1955–56 record sales boomed with the advent of rock 'n' roll. The top three represent the first three singles (and the only ones of the 1950s) to sell over 1,000,000 copies apiece in the UK. Anton Karas's zither instrumental theme from the film *The Third Man* predates the first UK charts, but sold 900,000 copies between 1950 and 1954 – virtually all of which were on 78-rpm singles.

ROCK LEGEND
Bill Haley's (1925–81), Rock Around The Clock became the bestselling single of the 1950s.

SINGLES OF THE 1950s IN THE US

	Title	Artist	Year
1	*Hound Dog/Don't Be Cruel*	Elvis Presley	1956
2	*The Chipmunk Song*	Chipmunks	1958
3	*Love Letters In The Sand*	Pat Boone	1957
4	*Rock Around The Clock*	Bill Haley & His Comets	1955
5	*Tom Dooley*	Kingston Trio	1958
6	*Love Me Tender*	Elvis Presley	1956
7	*Tennessee Waltz*	Patti Page	1951
8	*Volare (Nel Blu Dipintu Di Blu)*	Domenico Modugno	1958
9	*Jailhouse Rock*	Elvis Presley	1957
10	*All Shook Up*	Elvis Presley	1957

SINGLES OF THE 1960s IN THE UK

	Title	Artist	Year
1	*She Loves You*	The Beatles	1963
2	*I Want To Hold Your Hand*	The Beatles	1963
3	*Tears*	Ken Dodd	1965
4	*Can't Buy Me Love*	The Beatles	1964
5	*I Feel Fine*	The Beatles	1964
6	*We Can Work It Out/ Day Tripper*	The Beatles	1965
7	*The Carnival Is Over*	Seekers	1965
8	*Release Me*	Engelbert Humperdinck	1967
9	*It's Now Or Never*	Elvis Presley	1960
10	*Green, Green Grass Of Home*	Tom Jones	1966

The Beatles' domination of the 1960s is clear, with five singles in the decade's top six. Intriguingly, the other five in this Top 10 are all ballads to varying degrees of what, in those days, would have been termed "squareness." The majority of occasional record-buyers in this era purchased singles, not albums, and Messrs. Dodd, Humperdinck, *et al.* were the lucky recipients of this custom.

SINGLES OF THE 1960s IN THE US

	Title	Artist	Year
1	*I Want To Hold Your Hand*	The Beatles	1964
2	*It's Now Or Never*	Elvis Presley	1960
3	*Hey Jude*	The Beatles	1968
4	*The Ballad Of The Green Berets*	S/Sgt. Barry Sadler	1966
5	*Love Is Blue*	Paul Mauriat	1968
6	*I'm A Believer*	The Monkees	1966
7	*Can't Buy Me Love*	The Beatles	1964
8	*She Loves You*	The Beatles	1964
9	*Sugar Sugar*	Archies	1969
10	*The Twist*	Chubby Checker	1960

Though the 1960s are recalled as the decade in which British music invaded America, the only UK representatives among the decade's 10 biggest sellers in the United States are by the leaders of that invasion, The Beatles – although they do completely dominate the list. Elvis Presley's *It's Now Or Never*, with sales of around 5,000,000, almost equaled his total on *Hound Dog/Don't Be Cruel*, the previous decade's biggest single.

T O P 1 0

SINGLES OF THE 1970s IN THE UK

	Title	Artist	Year
1	*Mull Of Kintyre*	Wings	1977
2	*Rivers Of Babylon/ Brown Girl In The Ring*	Boney M	1978
3	*You're The One That I Want*	John Travolta and Olivia Newton-John	1978
4	*Mary's Boy Child/ Oh My Lord*	Boney M	1978
5	*Summer Nights*	John Travolta and Olivia Newton-John	1978
6	*Y.M.C.A.*	Village People	1979
7	*Bohemian Rhapsody*	Queen	1975
8	*Heart Of Glass*	Blondie	1979
9	*Merry Xmas Everybody*	Slade	1973
10	*Don't Give Up On Us*	David Soul	1977

Most of the 1970s best-sellers were released between December 1977 and May 1979. *Mull Of Kintyre* was the first single to top 2,000,000 copies in the UK, surpassing The Beatles' *She Loves You*, which held the record for 14 years. It was not overtaken until 1991, when Freddie Mercury died and *Bohemian Rhapsody* nearly doubled its sales.

T O P 1 0

SINGLES OF THE 1970s IN THE US

	Title	Artist	Year
1	*You Light Up My Life*	Debby Boone	1977
2	*Le Freak*	Chic	1978
3	*Night Fever*	The Bee Gees	1978
4	*Stayin' Alive*	The Bee Gees	1978
5	*Shadow Dancing*	Andy Gibb	1978
6	*Disco Lady*	Johnnie Taylor	1976
7	*I'll Be There*	The Jackson Five	1970
8	*Star Wars Theme/ Cantina Band*	Meco	1977
9	*Car Wash*	Rose Royce	1976
10	*Joy To The World*	Three Dog Night	1971

During the last four years of the 1970s, singles sales in the United States rose to their highest-ever level, and chart-topping records were almost routinely selling over 2,000,000 copies. Also at their commercial peak in the US during this period were The Bee Gees, who appropriately have the biggest presence on this chart, both with two of their own songs and as writer/producers of younger brother Andy Gibb's *Shadow Dancing*.

T O P 1 0

SINGLES OF THE 1980s IN THE UK

	Title	Artist	Year
1	*Do They Know It's Christmas?*	Band Aid	1984
2	*Relax*	Frankie Goes To Hollywood	1984
3	*I Just Called To Say I Love You*	Stevie Wonder	1984
4	*Two Tribes*	Frankie Goes To Hollywood	1984
5	*Don't You Want Me?*	Human League	1981
6	*Last Christmas*	Wham!	1984
7	*Karma Chameleon*	Culture Club	1983
8	*Careless Whisper*	George Michael	1984
9	*The Power Of Love*	Jennifer Rush	1985
10	*Come On Eileen*	Dexy's Midnight Runners	1982

Singles from the boom year of 1984 dominate this Top 10, two by newcomers Frankie Goes To Hollywood and two by Wham!/George Michael (one of the Band Aid lead singers, like Boy George from Culture Club). Stevie Wonder and Jennifer Rush, the sole US entrants, were the only Americans to have UK million-sellers during the 1980s.

T O P 1 0

SINGLES OF THE 1980s IN THE US

	Title	Artist	Year
1	*We Are The World*	USA For Africa	1985
2	*Physical*	Olivia Newton-John	1981
3	*Endless Love*	Diana Ross and Lionel Richie	1981
4	*Eye Of The Tiger*	Survivor	1982
5	*I Love Rock 'n' Roll*	Joan Jett & The Blackhearts	1982
6	*When Doves Cry*	Prince	1984
7	*Celebration*	Kool & The Gang	1981
8	*Another One Bites The Dust*	Queen	1980
9	*Wild Thing*	Tone Loc	1989
10	*Islands In The Stream*	Kenny Rogers and Dolly Parton	1983

America's top-selling single of the 1980s was, rather fittingly, a record that included contributions from many of those artists who had become the recording elite during the decade – the charity single for Africa's famine victims, *We Are The World*. Meanwhile, three of the close runners-up, *Endless Love* (from the same film), *Eye Of The Tiger* (from *Rocky III*), and *When Doves Cry* (from Prince's *Purple Rain*) were all taken from movies.

THE BEATLES

TOP 10

MOST VALUABLE RECORDS IN THE UK

	Title Special feature/ label/cat. no.	Year	Estimated value (£)
1	*Please Please Me* First UK stereo album with gold label/Parlophone PCS 3042	1963	1,000
2	*The Beatles At The Beeb* BBC Transcription disk for broadcasters only/CN 3970	1982	400
3	*From Then To You* Fan club album compiling Xmas flexis/Apple LYN 2153	1970	260
4	*Abbey Road* Limited-edition picture disk LP/Parlophone PHO 7088	1978	250
5=	*First HMV Boxed Set* First four albums on CD, in exclusive box/HMV BEACD 25	1987	200
5=	*Please Please Me* Mono version of (1) above Parlophone PMC 1202	1963	200
7	*Let It Be* Original UK LP release with book and box/Apple PXS 1	1970	160
8	*The Beatles Mono* Mono versions of first 10 LPs Collection in a box/Parlophone BMC 10	1984	120
9	*The Beatles Collection* Stereo versions of 13 LPs in a box/Parlophone BC 13	1986	110
10	*Sweet Georgia Brown* 7" single made with Tony Sheridan/Polydor NH 52906	1964	80

These are all UK releases, and mint condition is assumed for the quoted prices. Items such as acetates and demonstration disks, which can fetch higher sums still, have not been included. All of those in the Top 10 had at least some degree of public availability, although *From Then to You* was, strictly speaking, available only to members of The Beatles' official fan club as the traditional Christmas free gift, just prior to the club's permanent closure following the group's split early in 1970. Inevitably, the release was later widely bootlegged, and there will be few Beatles collectors around the world who do not possess a copy in some form, which in no way detracts from the desirability and value of the original pressing.

TOP 10

MOST VALUABLE ALBUMS IN THE US

	Title Special feature/ label/cat. no.	Year	Estimated value ($)
1=	*Introducing The Beatles* "Ad back" cover/ Vee Jay SR 1062 (mono)	1963	9,000
1=	*Hear The Beatles Tell All* White label promotional LP/ Vee Jay PRO 202	1964	9,000
3=	*The Beatles And Frank Ifield* Full-color painted Beatles portrait cover/ On Stage Vee Jay LPS 1085 (stereo)	1964	7,500
3=	*Yesterday And Today* Initial state "butcher" cover/ Capitol ST 2553 (stereo)	1966	7,500
5=	*Introducing The Beatles* "Ad back" cover/ Vee Jay LP 1062 (stereo)	1963	3,000
5=	*Introducing The Beatles* Blank back cover/ Vee Jay SR 1062 (stereo)	1963	3,000
5=	*Yesterday And Today* Initial state "butcher" cover/ Capitol T 2553 (mono)	1966	3,000
8=	*The Beatles And Frank Ifield* Portrait cover/ Vee Jay LP 1085 (mono)	1964	2,500
8=	*The Beatles Vs The Four Seasons* Double-LP/ Vee Jay DXS 30*	1964	2,500
10	*A Hard Day's Night* White label promotional LP/ United Artists UAL 3366	1964	2,000

* *This double set combined the contents of* Introducing The Beatles *with* The Golden Hits Of The Four Seasons, *and, if found with a fold-open poster, is worth an additional $300.*

Source: Goldmine/Neal Umphred

The Vee Jay label, a US independent that held the rights to release a limited number of Beatles tracks during 1963 and 1964, was demonstrably skilled in making a little go a long way.

PAUL AND JOHN
The songwriting team of Paul McCartney and John Lennon was the driving force behind the unmatched global success of The Beatles during almost 10 years from their first hit record in 1962.

THE 10

FIRST ALBUMS RELEASED IN THE US

	Title	Label	Cat. no.
1	*Introducing The Beatles*	Vee Jay	VJLP 1062
2	*Meet The Beatles*	Capitol	ST 2047
3	*The Beatles With Tony Sheridan*	MGM	SE 4215
4	*Jolly What!*	Vee Jay	VJLP 1085
5	*The Beatles' Second Album*	Capitol	ST 2080
6	*A Hard Day's Night*	United Artists	UAS 6366
7	*Something New*	Capitol	ST 2108
8	*The Beatles Vs The Four Seasons*	Vee Jay	VJDX 30
9	*Ain't She Sweet*	Atco	SD 33-169
10	*Songs, Pictures & Stories Of The Fabulous Beatles*	Vee Jay	VJLP 1092

TOP 10

LONGEST US SINGLE CHART RUNS

	Title	Year	Weeks in charts
1	*Twist And Shout*	1964/1986	28
2	*Hey Jude*	1968–9	19
3	*I Want To Hold Your Hand*	1964	18
4	*Got To Get You Into My Life*	1976	17
5=	*Come Together/Something*	1969–70	16
5=	*She Loves You*	1964	16
7	*Love Me Do*	1964	16
8=	*A Hard Day's Night*	1964	14
8=	*Help!*	1965	14
8=	*Please Please Me*	1964	14
8=	*Let It Be*	1970	14

TOP 10

BEATLES SINGLES IN THE US

	Title	Year
1	*I Want To Hold Your Hand*	1964
2	*Hey Jude*	1968
3	*Can't Buy Me Love*	1964
4	*She Loves You*	1964
5	*Help!*	1965
6	*I Feel Fine*	1964
7	*Get Back*	1969
8	*Yesterday*	1965
9	*We Can Work It Out/Day Tripper*	1965
10	*A Hard Day's Night*	1964

The Beatles never managed to quite equal the sales of the single which first broke them in America, though *Hey Jude*, almost five years later, came close. Numbers one to four were all 2,000,000-plus US sellers.

SGT. PEPPER
Designed by British Pop artists Peter Blake and Jann Haworth, the collage sleeve for The Beatles' 1967 album was the first to print the tracks' lyrics.

THE SUPERGROUPS

TOP 10

ALL-TIME SINGLES BY GROUPS IN THE UK

1	Queen, *Bohemian Rhapsody*
2	Wings, *Mull Of Kintyre*
3	Boney M, *Rivers Of Babylon/Brown Girl In The Ring*
4	Frankie Goes To Hollywood, *Relax*
5	The Beatles, *She Loves You*
6	Boney M, *Mary's Boy Child/ Oh My Lord*
7	Wet Wet Wet, *Love Is All Around*
8	The Beatles, *I Want To Hold Your Hand*
9	The Beatles, *Can't Buy Me Love*
10	Frankie Goes To Hollywood, *Two Tribes*

Paul McCartney appears four times, three times with The Beatles and once with Wings. Further high-level consistency sees both Boney M and Frankie Goes To Hollywood represented twice among these 10 titles.

ALL-TIME ALBUMS BY GROUPS IN THE UK

1	The Beatles, *Sgt. Pepper's Lonely Hearts Club Band*
2	Dire Straits, *Brothers In Arms*
3	Queen, *Greatest Hits*
4	Simply Red, *Stars*
5	Fleetwood Mac, *Rumours*
6	Pink Floyd, *Dark Side Of The Moon*
7	Fleetwood Mac, *Tango In The Night*
8	R.E.M., *Automatic For The People*
9	U2, *The Joshua Tree*
10	Abba, *Greatest Hits*

The definition of "group" here excludes duos such as Simon and Garfunkel, the Eurythmics, and the Carpenters. Most of these albums still sell regularly today on CD – notably the most recent entry to the list, the 1992 release *Automatic for the People* by the US group R.E.M.

ALL-TIME SINGLES BY GROUPS IN THE US

1	The Beatles, *I Want To Hold Your Hand*
2	The Beatles, *Hey Jude*
3	The Chipmunks, *The Chipmunk Song*
4	Chic, *Le Freak*
5	The Monkees, *I'm A Believer*
6	The Beatles, *Can't Buy Me Love*
7	The Beatles, *She Loves You*
8	Archies, *Sugar Sugar*
9	Bill Haley & The Comets, *Rock Around The Clock*
10	The Bee Gees, *Stayin' Alive*

The Beatles appear no fewer than four times in this Top 10, making them the only group that are listed more than once. Each of the first eight singles sold more than 3,000,000 copies in the US, while *I Want To Hold Your Hand* sold an amazing 8,000,000 copies.

ALL-TIME ALBUMS BY GROUPS IN THE US

1	Fleetwood Mac, *Rumours*
2	Pink Floyd, *Dark Side Of The Moon*
3	Boston, *Boston*
4	Def Leppard, *Hysteria*
5	The Beatles, *Abbey Road*
6	Bon Jovi, *Slippery When Wet*
7	The Beatles, *Sgt. Pepper's Lonely Hearts Club Band*
8	Guns N' Roses, *Appetite For Destruction*
9	Def Leppard, *Pyromania*
10	Pink Floyd, *The Wall*

British groups, interestingly, slightly outnumber their American cousins on this list, with the Beatles, Def Leppard, and Pink Floyd all appearing twice, and Fleetwood Mac being 60 percent British at the time of *Rumours*.

GROUPS OF THE 1960s IN THE UK

1	The Beatles
2	The Rolling Stones
3	The Shadows
4	The Hollies
5	The Beach Boys
6	The Kinks
7	The Four Tops
8	Manfred Mann
9	Seekers
10	Bachelors

Based on comparative UK singles chart performance

The Beatles outsold every other act by a large margin during the 1960s – notably in the album field, where their LPs sold in the sort of numbers others could achieve only with singles. Six of this list are British, with the US, Australia, and Ireland also represented.

GROUPS OF THE 1960s IN THE US

1	The Beatles
2	The Supremes
3	Four Seasons
4	The Beach Boys
5	The Rolling Stones
6	Miracles
7	The Temptations
8	Tommy James & The Shondells
9	Dave Clark Five
10	Herman's Hermits

Based on comparative US singles chart performance

Despite the 1960s being remembered in the US as the decade of the "British Invasion," only four groups here are British. Motown, with The Supremes, The Miracles, and The Temptations, was almost as consistent.

T O P   1 0

GROUPS OF THE 1970s IN THE US

1	The Bee Gees	**6**	Gladys Knight & The Pips
2	Carpenters	**7**	Dawn
3	Chicago	**8**	Earth, Wind & Fire
4	The Jackson Five	**9**	Eagles
5	Three Dog Night	**10**	Fleetwood Mac

Based on comparative US singles chart performance

There was less apparent rock n' roll influence among America's top groups of the 1970s than is evident in the surrounding decades, thanks to the growth of the mellow, adult-oriented rock genre that sustained the Eagles, Fleetwood Mac, and Chicago. Black music also prospered, bringing success to the Jacksons, Earth, Wind & Fire, and Gladys Knight and the Pips, while The Bee Gees became superstars by switching from ballads to disco.

T O P   1 0

GROUPS OF THE 1970s IN THE UK

1	Abba	**6**	Showaddywaddy
2	Slade	**7**	Mud
3	T. Rex	**8**	Wings
4	Bay City Rollers	**9**	Electric Light Orchestra
5	Sweet	**10**	Osmonds

Based on comparative UK singles chart performance

T O P   1 0

GROUPS OF THE 1980s IN THE UK

1	Police
2	Wham!
3	Dire Straits
4	U2
5	Queen
6	Simple Minds
7	Pet Shop Boys
8	Duran Duran
9	Adam & The Ants
10	Madness

Based on comparative UK single and album chart performance

It should be noted that, apart from U2 – who are from Ireland – all 10 of these groups are British. With the exception of Queen, none of them had achieved any success prior to the tail-end of the 1970s.

T O P   1 0

GROUPS OF THE 1980s IN THE US

1	Wham!
2	Kool & The Gang
3	Huey Lewis & The News
4	Journey
5	Duran Duran
6	U2
7	The Rolling Stones
8	Alabama
9	Pointer Sisters
10	Starship

Based on comparative US single and album chart performance

BAND AID
Irish band U2 was a success story of the 1980s on both sides of the Atlantic. Aptly for a loud rock band, lead singer Bono (Paul Hewson) took his name from an advertisement for Bono Vox, a hearing-aid company.

LONG PLAYERS

ARTISTS WITH THE MOST CHART ALBUMS IN THE US

	Artist	Chart albums
1	Elvis Presley	93
2	Frank Sinatra	67
3	Johnny Mathis	63
4=	James Brown	49
4=	Ray Conniff	49
6	Mantovani	45
7	Barbra Streisand	44
8=	Beach Boys	41
8=	Temptations	41
8=	Lawrence Welk	41

Elvis' total will not be matched this century, and could pass 100 chart albums by the year 2000 if RCA Records carry on releasing at least one Elvis album every year.

78 – A RECORD NUMBER

Before the advent of the grooved record in the 1950s, the definition of "long player" was a collection of 78 rpm disks. Any piece of music that was over about three minutes long was beyond the capacity of a single disk. Therefore, a recording of an orchestral symphony, for instance, would be a boxed collection of 78 rpm disks, with the music interrupted every so often by the need for changeover (these boxed sets were the origin of the term "album"). No wonder the 12-inch LP, with a playing capacity of nearly one hour over two sides, was so welcomed. Today, with the latest in CD techology, it is possible to cram a full 78 minutes of music time onto a single disk of laser-readable disk. By the end of the century, 78 hours perhaps? In another 40 years, who knows?

ALBUMS LONGEST AT NO.1 IN THE US CHARTS

(Based on Billboard charts)

	Artist/album/year	Weeks at No. 1
1	Michael Jackson, *Thriller* (1982)	37
2=	Harry Belafonte, *Calypso* (1956)	31
2=	Fleetwood Mac, *Rumours* (1977)	31
4=	Various, *Saturday Night Fever* (1978), Soundtrack	24
4=	Prince & The Revolution *Purple Rain* (1984), Soundtrack	24
6	MC Hammer, *Please Hammer Don't Hurt 'Em* (1990)	21
7=	Whitney Houston/Various *The Bodyguard* (1992), Soundtrack	20
7=	Elvis Presley *Blue Hawaii* (1962), Soundtrack	20
9=	Monkees, *More of the Monkees* (1967)	18
9=	Various, *Dirty Dancing* (1988) Soundtrack	18
9=	Garth Brooks *Ropin' The Wind* (1991)	18

ARTISTS WITH THE MOST NO. 1 CHART ALBUMS IN THE US

	Artist	No. 1 Albums
1	Beatles	15
2=	Elvis Presley	9
2=	Rolling Stones	9
4	Elton John*	8
5=	Paul McCartney	7
5=	Barbra Streisand	7
7	Led Zeppelin	6
8=	Kingston Trio	5
8=	Herb Alpert & The Tijuana Brass	5
8=	Chicago	5
8=	Eagles	5

* *Including* The Lion King *soundtrack (1994)*

The Rolling Stones missed the opportunity for a sole ranking in second position when their most recent release, *Voodoo Lounge*, peaked at No. 2 upon release in July 1994. A similar fate befell Frank Sinatra's last outing, his 1993 *Duets*.

ALBUMS OF ALL TIME IN THE US

	Artist/album	Estimated US sales		Artist/album	Estimated US sales
1	Michael Jackson, *Thriller*	24,000,000	**7=**	Pink Floyd, *Dark Side Of The Moon*	13,000,000
1	Fleetwood Mac, *Rumours*	17,000,000	**7=**	Guns N' Roses, *Appetite For Destruction*	13,000,000
3=	Boston, *Boston*	15,000,000	**7=**	Garth Brooks *No Fences*	13,000,000
3=	Bruce Springsteen *Born In The USA*	15,000,000	**10=**	Carole King, *Tapestry*	12,000,000
5=	Eagles, *Eagles – Their Greatest Hits 1971–1975*	14,000,000	**10=**	Whitney Houston *Whitney Houston*	12,000,000
5=	Soundtrack *The Bodyguard*	14,000,000			

Many of these albums were originally released before the CD age, so have benefitted from "second copy" buying as people replace old vinyl copies with compact disks. A good example of such an album is Carole King's *Tapestry*, the only album on the list not to be officially certified for its 12,000,000-plus sales accomplishment. Two of the albums here, Garth Brooks's *No Fences* and the soundtrack for *The Bodyguard*, were released in the current decade (1990 and 1992 respectively), and both are still selling actively. The latter is largely a Whitney Houston record, and makes her the only artist with two entries in this Top 10.

TOP 10

ALBUMS OF ALL TIME WORLDWIDE

	Artist	Album	Estimated sales
1	Michael Jackson	*Thriller*	40,000,000
2	Soundtrack	*The Bodyguard*	26,000,000
3	Soundtrack	*Saturday Night Fever*	25,000,000
4	Beatles	*Sgt. Pepper's Lonely Hearts Club Band*	24,000,000
5	Carole King	*Tapestry*	22,500,000
6=	Simon and Garfunkel	*Bridge Over Troubled Water*	22,000,000
6=	Soundtrack	*Grease*	22,000,000
8	Bruce Springsteen	*Born In The USA*	21,500,000
9	Soundtrack	*The Sound Of Music*	21,000,000
10	Fleetwood Mac	*Rumours*	20,500,000

Total worldwide sales of albums have traditionally been notoriously hard to gauge, but even with the huge expansion of the album market during the 1980s, and multiple million sales of many major releases, this Top 10 is still élite territory. In recent years reassessments of sales have elevated certain albums, such as The Beatles' *Sgt. Pepper's Lonely Heart's Club Band* and Carole King's *Tapestry* in a list that presents the oddest of bedfellows, Bruce Springsteen and *The Sound of Music* in adjacent positions.

THE 10

FIRST MILLION-SELLING ALBUMS IN THE US

	Artist/title	Year
1	Various, *Oklahoma!* (original cast recording)	1949
2	Various, *South Pacific* (original cast recording)	1949
3	Various, Soundtrack, *An American in Paris*	1952
4	Mantovani, *Strauss Waltzes*	1953
5	Mantovani, *Christmas Carols*	1953
6	Mario Lanza, *Songs from "The Student Prince"*	1954
7	Glenn Miller Band, *The Glenn Miller Story*	1954
8	Mantovani, *Mantovani Plays the Immortal Classics*	1954
9	Bing Crosby, *Merry Christmas*	1954
10	Kermit Schafer, *Radio Bloopers*	1954

Albums in the usual modern sense – 12" or 10" vinyl disks that are played at 33⅓ rpm – first appeared in the US in 1948. Nos. 1 and 9 in this Top 10 were both originally issued prior to the dates listed as boxed-set collections of 78-rpm records. *The Glenn Miller Story* was a posthumous hit achieved 10 years after the bandleader's mysterious disappearance during a wartime flight in Europe. Although 1964, when the Beatles "conquered" America, is generally regarded as the first year of notable British influence in American popular music, it is worth noting that the act represented most frequently among these earlier million-selling albums is the British Mantovani orchestra, more than a decade before Beatlemania.

ON THE RECORD
The long-playing record has undergone notable improvements in the postwar era, from vinyl LPs to modern CDs that represent a significant leap forward in both capacity and quality.

DID YOU KNOW

SLOW MOVERS

The Tyrannosaurus Rex album *My People Were Fair And Had Sky In Their Hair, But Now They're Content To Wear Stars On Their Brows* is not only the album with the longest title ever to chart in the UK, but is also the slowest album ever to rise to their No. 1 position. Originally charting in July 1968, it had to wait until the heyday of T. Rex (as they had then become) in May 1972 to rechart as one-half of a double album repackage with *Prophets, Seers And Sages, The Angels Of The Ages*. It finally hit No. 1 199 weeks (nearly four years) after its first chart appearance. Only three other albums have taken longer than a year to hit pole position after they first appeared on the UK charts: Elvis Presley's *40 Greatest Hits* (114 weeks), *Fame: The Original Soundtrack* (98 weeks), and Mike Oldfield's *Tubular Bells* (65 weeks). The latter is also the most successful pop instrumental album of all time. Two other slow climbers to No. 1 in the UK, Fleetwood Mac's *Rumours* (49 weeks) and Bruce Springsteen's *Born In The USA* (36 weeks), also appear in the Top 10 Albums Of All Time Worldwide.

ALBUMS OF THE DECADES

TOP 10

US ALBUMS OF THE 1950s

	Artist/title	Year
1	Various artists, *South Pacific* (Original Soundtrack)	1958
2	Various artists, *My Fair Lady* (Original Cast)	1956
3	Various artists, *The Music Man* (Original Soundtrack)	1958
4	Various artists, *Gigi* (Original Soundtrack)	1958
5	Various artists, *Oklahoma* (Original Soundtrack)	1955
6	Harry Belafonte, *Calypso*	1956
7	Elvis Presley, *Elvis Presley*	1956
8	Nat "King" Cole *Love Is The Thing*	1957
9	Johnny Mathis *Johnny's Greatest Hits*	1958
10	Doris Day, *Love Me Or Leave Me* (Original Soundtrack)	1955

Soundtracks ruled the day until the advent of Elvis and his contemporaries.

TOP 10

UK ALBUMS OF THE 1960s

	Artist/title	Year
1	The Beatles, *Sgt. Pepper's Lonely Hearts Club Band*	1967
2	Various, *The Sound of Music* (Original Soundtrack)	1965
3	The Beatles, *With The Beatles*	1963
4	The Beatles, *Abbey Road*	1969
5	Various, *South Pacific* (Original Soundtrack)	1958
6	The Beatles, *Beatles For Sale*	1964
7	The Beatles, *A Hard Day's Night*	1964
8	The Beatles, *Rubber Soul*	1965
9	The Beatles, *The Beatles* ("*White Album*")	1968
10	Various, *West Side Story*	1962

Not only did the Beatles dominate the Top 10, but three further albums of theirs, *Revolver*, *Please Please Me*, and *Help!*, were also the 11th, 12th, and 13th bestselling albums of a decade that belonged to the most successful group in pop history.

WALL OF SOUND
Pink Floyd's last multimillion-selling album was The Wall, *which took them to No. 1 in 1980 and carried them to 10th place overall in the following decade.*

TOP 10

US ALBUMS OF THE 1960s

	Artist/title	Year
1	Various, *West Side Story* (Soundtrack)	1961
2	The Beatles, *Meet The Beatles*	1964
3	Various, *The Sound of Music* (Soundtrack)	1965
4	The Beatles *Sgt. Pepper's Lonely Hearts Club Band*	1967
5	The Monkees, *The Monkees*	1966
6	The Monkees, *More of The Monkees*	1967
7	Various, *Hair* (Broadway cast)	1968
8	Herb Alpert & The Tijuana Brass *Whipped Cream and Other Delights*	1965
9	Various, *Mary Poppins* (Soundtrack)	1964
10	Documentary *John Fitzgerald Kennedy: A Memorial Album*	1963

While Beatles, Monkees, and Presley albums sold huge quantities over a short period of time, successful movie soundtracks had less dramatic sales peaks but often stayed on the charts for years – *The Sound of Music* eventually accrued more than five years.

TOP 10

US ALBUMS OF THE 1970s

	Artist/title	Year
1	Fleetwood Mac, *Rumours*	1977
2	Various, *Saturday Night Fever* (Soundtrack)	1977
3	Various, *Grease* (Soundtrack)	1978
4	Carole King, *Tapestry*	1971
5	Pink Floyd, *The Dark Side of the Moon*	1973
6	Boston, *Boston*	1976
7	Peter Frampton, *Frampton Comes Alive!*	1976
8	Stevie Wonder, *Songs in the Key of Life*	1976
9	Elton John, *Goodbye Yellow Brick Road*	1973
10	Eagles, *Hotel California*	1976

In the decade when album sales really took off (*Rumours* alone sold over 13,000,000 copies), it is notable that five of these Top 10 titles were double albums.

TOP 10

UK ALBUMS OF THE 1970s

	Artist/title	Year
1	Simon and Garfunkel, *Bridge Over Troubled Water*	1970
2	Simon and Garfunkel, *Simon And Garfunkel's Greatest Hits*	1972
3	Fleetwood Mac, *Rumours*	1977
4	Pink Floyd, *Dark Side Of The Moon*	1973
5	Mike Oldfield, *Tubular Bells*	1973
6	Abba, *Greatest Hits*	1976
7	Meat Loaf, *Bat Out Of Hell*	1978
8	Various, *Saturday Night Fever* (Original Soundtrack)	1978
9	Perry Como, *And I Love You So*	1973
10	Carpenters, *The Singles 1969–1973*	1974

Each of the top five albums of the 1970s clocked up over 250 weeks on the British chart, with Fleetwood Mac's *Rumours* outdistancing them all with an astonishing 443 weeks on the survey. *Tubular Bells*, recorded by Mike Oldfield for a pittance, proved to be the business building block upon which Virgin label boss Richard Branson would create his Virgin empire.

TOP 10

US ALBUMS OF THE 1980s

	Artist/title	Year
1	Michael Jackson, *Thriller*	1982
2	Bruce Springsteen, *Born In The USA*	1984
3	Various, Soundtrack, *Dirty Dancing*	1987
4	Prince & The Revolution, *Purple Rain* (Soundtrack)	1984
5	Lionel Richie, *Can't Slow Down*	1983
6	Whitney Houston, *Whitney Houston*	1985
7	Def Leppard, *Hysteria*	1987
8	Bon Jovi, *Slippery When Wet*	1986
9	Guns N' Roses, *Appetite For Destruction*	1988
10	Pink Floyd, *The Wall*	1979

On October 30, 1984, *Thriller* became the first album to receive its 20th platinum sales certificate, for sales of 20,000,000 copies in the US alone. It dominated the US charts in 1983 and early 1984, and seven of the tracks became Top 10 singles in the US; far from detracting from the album's sales, the success of each single served to reinforce its popularity. *The Wall*, although included in this list as a 1980s album, was actually released during the week ending December 15, 1979, but accumulated most of its sales during the following decade.

TOP 10

UK ALBUMS OF THE 1980s

	Artist/title	Year
1	Dire Straits, *Brothers In Arms*	1985
2	Michael Jackson, *Bad*	1987
3	Michael Jackson, *Thriller*	1982
4	Queen, *Greatest Hits*	1981
5	Kylie Minogue, *Kylie*	1988
6	Whitney Houston, *Whitney*	1987
7	Fleetwood Mac *Tango In The Night*	1987
8	Phil Collins *No Jacket Required*	1985
9	Madonna, *True Blue*	1986
10	U2, *The Joshua Tree*	1987

While Michael Jackson's *Thriller* was his bestselling album in most countries around the world (and, of course, the bestselling global album of all time), British buyers eventually preferred *Bad*. Fleetwood Mac is the only group to feature on the bestseller lists in two decades, their achievement with *Rumours* in the 1970s being followed by success with *Tango in the Night*. As the 1990s commenced, and for the first time ever, classical albums began to sell in sufficient numbers to enable violinist Nigel Kennedy and tenors José Carreras, Plácido Domingo, and Luciano Pavarotti to rub shoulders with pop stars.

BORN IN THE USA
Bruce Springsteen had the second bestselling album of the 1980s in the US.

ALBUM GREATS

BOXED-SET ALBUMS OF THE 1990s IN THE US
(*To March 31, 1994*)

	Title	Artist	Year of release
1	*Led Zeppelin/Remasters*	Led Zeppelin	1990/2*
2	*Just For The Record*	Barbra Streisand	1991
3	*Boats Beaches Bars And Ballads*	Jimmy Buffett	1992
4	*Songs Of Freedom*	Bob Marley	1992
5	*Pandora's Box*	Aerosmith	1991
6	*The Complete Recordings*	Robert Johnson	1990
7	*Live Shit: Binge And Purge*	Metallica	1993
8	*Crossroads*	Eric Clapton	1988
9	*Storyteller*	Rod Stewart	1989
10	*The King Of Rock 'n' Roll – The Complete '50s Masters*	Elvis Presley	1992

* Remasters *is a 1992 edited version of the original* Led Zeppelin, *which had already sold more than 1,000,000 by the time* Remasters *came out.*

Overall back-catalog CD sales have kept the record industry alive over the past decade, and boxed-set collections in particular have proved both popular and highly profitable. Inexpensive to produce, boxed-set compilations can begin to make a profit for record companies after selling only 25,000 copies. The phenomenal success of Led Zeppelin's digitally remastered boxed set prompted the issue of the definitive 10-CD *Complete Studio Recordings*, in November 1993.

INSTRUMENTAL ALBUMS OF ALL TIME IN THE US

1	Ernest Gold and the Sinfonia of London Orchestra, Soundtrack, *Exodus*
2	Enoch Light and the Light Brigade/Terry and the All-Stars, *Persuasive Percussion*
3	Henry Mancini, Soundtrack, *Breakfast At Tiffany's*
4	Lawrence Welk, *Calcutta!*
5	Victor Young, Soundtrack, *Around The World In 80 Days*
6	Henry Mancini, *The Music From Peter Gunn*
7	Herb Alpert & The Tijuana Brass, *What Now My Love*
8	Herb Alpert & The Tijuana Brass, *Whipped Cream And Other Delights*
9	Enoch Light and the Light Brigade, *Stereo 33/MM*
10	Van Cliburn, *Tchaikovsky: Piano Concerto No. 1*

All of these albums hit No. 1, and between them logged a total of 1,076 weeks on the US Albums survey. All 10 albums were released between 1957 (*Around The World In 80 Days*) and 1966 (*What Now My Love*), a 10-year window when instrumental albums were more popular than at any other time in chart history.

HEAVY SELLERS
In 1968 Robert Plant, seen here, was invited to become the vocalist with the New Yardbirds, soon after renamed Led Zeppelin. From 1969 until the band's breakup in 1980, it scored six No. 1 albums in the US, although paradoxically Led Zeppelin IV *was not one of these. Once the bestselling heavy metal album in the US, but latterly relegated to 4th place, it achieved the remarkable feat of spending 259 consecutive weeks on the charts but never reached No. 1.*

TOP 10
COUNTRY ALBUMS OF ALL TIME IN THE US

1 Garth Brooks, *No Fences*

2 Garth Brooks, *Ropin' the Wind*

3 Billy Ray Cyrus, *Some Gave All*

4 Garth Brooks, *Garth Brooks*

5 Garth Brooks, *The Chase*

6 Patsy Cline, *Greatest Hits*

7 Garth Brooks, *In Pieces*

8 Brooks and Dunn, *Brand New Man*

9 Garth Brooks, *The Hits*

10 Alabama, *Feels So Right*

Each of these albums has sold more than 4,000,000 domestic copies, but Garth Brooks is in a league of his own. Exploding onto the country scene in 1990, he has become his own industry, selling over 35,000,000 albums in under four years in the US alone. He is the first country artist to sell 10,000,000 copies of one album (*No Fences* and *Ropin' the Wind*).

TOP 10
ALBUMS IN THE US, 1994

1 Soundtrack, *The Lion King*

2 Ace of Base, *The Sign*

3 Boyz II Men, *II*

4 Counting Crows, *August And Everything After*

5 Green Day, *Dookie*

6 Tim McGraw, *Not a Moment Too Soon*

7 Stone Temple Pilots, *Purple*

8 Kenny G, *Miracles: The Holiday Album*

9 Offspring, *Smash*

10 Mariah Carey, *Music Box*

Each of these albums sold over 2,500,000 copies in the US during the year.

GARTH BROOKS
Booming record sales during the 1990s have made Brooks a giant among country artists.

TOP 10
HEAVY METAL ALBUMS OF ALL TIME IN THE US

1 Boston, *Boston*

2 Guns N' Roses, *Appetite For Destruction*

3 Meat Loaf, *Bat Out Of Hell*

4 Led Zeppelin, *Led Zeppelin IV (Untitled)*

5 Bon Jovi, *Slippery When Wet*

6 Def Leppard, *Hysteria*

7 Def Leppard, *Pyromania*

8 Journey, *Escape*

9 AC/DC, *Back In Black*

10 Metallica, *Metallica*

All of these albums have sold more than 8,000,000 copies each in the US alone, with *Boston* recently certified for sales over 15,000,000. *Hysteria's* sales performance is a noteworthy achievement for Def Leppard, the British band whose lineup has suffered a death (Steve Clark in 1991) and a car accident (drummer Rick Allen lost his left arm in 1984, but continues to perform).

TOP 10
ORIGINAL CAST RECORDINGS OF ALL TIME IN THE US

1 *My Fair Lady* (Broadway)   1956

2 *The Sound Of Music* (Broadway)   1959

3 *The Music Man* (Broadway)   1958

4 *The Phantom Of The Opera* (London)   1988

5 *Camelot* (Broadway)   1961

6 *West Side Story* (Broadway)   1958

7 *Jesus Christ Superstar**   1970

8 *Fiddler On The Roof* (Broadway) 1964

9 *Hair* (Broadway)   1968

10 *Hello, Dolly!* (Broadway)   1964

* *Although an original Broadway cast version appeared in 1972, the album that outperformed it here was a studio cast recording made in 1970 with Deep Purple vocalist Ian Gillan playing Jesus.*

The 1950s and early 1960s were clearly the golden era of musicals, when cast albums regularly outperformed the burgeoning number of rock 'n' roll artist releases.

TOP 10
RAP ALBUMS OF ALL TIME IN THE US

1 MC Hammer, *Please Hammer Don't Hurt 'Em*

2 Vanilla Ice, *To The Extreme*

3 Beastie Boys, *Licence To Ill*

4 Snoop Doggy Dogg, *Doggy Style*

5 Kriss Kross, *Totally Krossed Out*

6 Dr. Dre, *The Chronic*

7 R. Kelly, *12 Play*

8 Run D.M.C., *Raising Hell*

9 L.L. Cool J, *Bigger And Deffer*

10 Tone Loc, *Loc'ed After Dark*

On March 7, 1987, No. 3 became the first rap album to top the US Albums Chart, while in 1990 M.C. Hammer's 10,000,000-plus selling album spent 21 weeks at No. 1. Numbers 1 to 8 have all sold over 3,000,000 copies in the US, with the 1990s' hottest rap-producer Dr. Dre also responsible for the quadruple-platinum No. 4, *Doggy Style*.

IS THIS A RECORD?

TOP 10

HIGHEST GROSSING TOURS IN NORTH AMERICA, 1994

	Act	Total gross ($)
1	Rolling Stones	124,175,506
2	Pink Floyd	104,567,057
3	Billy Joel	75,821,767
4	Eagles	73,692,859
5	Barbra Streisand	58,935,825
6	Elton John	56,822,911
7	Grateful Dead	48,826,066
8	Phil Collins	26,223,660
9	Aerosmith	23,256,297
10	Michael Bolton	19,668,870

The Lollapalooza '94 tour grossed $27,001,185. Of this year's Top 10, only Billy Joel and Grateful Dead were in the previous year's tour Top 10 list.

TOP 10

KARAOKE SONGS IN THE US

	Song	Original artist
1	New York, New York	Frank Sinatra
2	My Way	Frank Sinatra
3	Love Shack	B52s
4	Mack The Knife	Bobby Darin
5	The Rose	Bette Midler
6	Takin' Care Of Business	Bachman-Turner Overdrive
7	Hello Dolly!	Louis Armstrong
8	Friends In Low Places	Garth Brooks
9	Greatest Love Of All	George Benson
10	Crazy	Patsy Cline

This Top 10, based on data supplied by American Karaoke Magazine, was assembled from a survey of Karaoke DJs (or "KJs") across the US, where bars and clubs often specialize in one music genre, usually standards, pop, rock, or country.

TOP 10

JUKEBOX SINGLES OF ALL TIME IN THE US

1	Patsy Cline, Crazy	1962
2	Bob Seger Old Time Rock 'n' Roll	1979
3	Elvis Presley Hound Dog/Don't Be Cruel	1956
4	Marvin Gaye, I Heard It Through The Grapevine	1968
5	Bobby Darin, Mack The Knife	1959
6	Bill Haley & His Comets Rock Around The Clock	1955
7	Doors, Light My Fire	1967
8	Otis Redding, (Sittin' On) The Dock Of The Bay	1968
9	Temptations, My Girl	1965
10	Frank Sinatra New York, New York	1980

This list was last compiled in 1992 by the Amusement and Music Operators Association, whose members service and operate over 250,000 jukeboxes in the US. It is based on the estimated popularity of jukebox singles from 1950 to the present. In 1989 the chart-topper was Hound Dog/Don't Be Cruel, while the Righteous Brothers' Unchained Melody was the highest new entry into the Top 40 in 1992, due in part to its rebirth as the featured song in the hit movie Ghost.

TOP 10

ONE-HIT WONDERS OF ALL TIME IN THE US

1	USA For Africa, We Are The World
2	Bobby McFerrin, Don't Worry Be Happy
3	M, Pop Muzik
4	Zager & Evans, In The Year 2525 (Exordium And Terminus)
5	Jan Hammer, Miami Vice (theme)
6	Elegants, Little Star
7	Hollywood Argyles, Alley-Oop
8	Laurie London, He's Got The Whole World (In His Hands)
9	Morris Stoloff, Moonglow (theme from Picnic)
10	Silhouettes, Get A Job

TOP 10

FIRST ARTISTS TO FEATURE IN A COCA-COLA TV COMMERCIAL

	Act/jingle	Year
1	McGuire Sisters, Pause For A Coke	1958
2=	Brothers Four* Refreshing New Feeling	1960
2=	Anita Bryant Refreshing New Feeling	1960
2=	Connie Francis Refreshing New Feeling	1960
5=	Fortunes Things Go Better With Coke	1963
5=	Limelighters* Things Go Better With Coke	1963
7	Ray Charles Things Go Better With Coke	1969
8=	Bobby Goldboro It's The Real Thing	1971
8=	New Seekers*, It's The Real Thing	1971
10	Dottie West*, It's The Real Thing (Country Sunshine)	1972

*   Artist provided only the audio soundtrack

Coke has used music artists in its promotion since the 1900s. In the 1950s they sponsored music TV shows for the likes of Eddie Fisher and Mario Lanza. 1980s ads featured Robert Plant and Chuck Berry, and recent ads include George Michael and Paula Abdul.

All of these acts hit US No. 1 with their only American chart appearance, but never followed up with any other rock chart disc. The charity ensemble USA For Africa's only single release is by far the most successful one-hit wonder, with over 4,000,000 copies sold, while numbers two to four all sold in excess of 1,000,000 – earning the artists enough to retire without another chart appearance. Honorable mention to Tag Team's 1993 smash Whoomp! There It Is: although it peaked only at No. 2 on the Hot 100, it sold more than 4,000,000 copies and, as a rap novelty, seems destined to become a notable one-off success.

T O P 1 0

MOST FREQUENTLY RECORDED SONGS IN THE US, 1900–50

	Title	Year first recorded
1	*St. Louis Blues*	1914
2	*Tea For Two*	1924
3	*Body And Soul*	1930
4	*After You've Gone*	1918
5	*How High The Moon*	1940
6	*Blue Skies*	1927
7	*Dinah*	1925
8	*Ain't Misbehavin'*	1929
9	*Honeysuckle Rose*	1929
10	*Stardust*	1929

T O P 1 0

WORST RECORDS OF ALL TIME?

1	Jimmy Cross *I Want My Baby Back*
2	Zara Leander, *Wunderbar*
3	Legendary Stardust Cowboy, *Paralysed*
4	Pat Campbell, *The Deal*
5	Nervous Norvus, *Transfusion*
6	Jess Conrad, *This Pullover*
7	Mel & Dave, *Spinning Wheel*
8	Dickey Lee, *Laurie*
9	Mrs. Miller *A Lover's Concerto*
10	Tania Day, *I Get So Lonely*

In 1978 London Capital Radio DJ Kenny Everett polled his listeners on their least favorite songs from the disks he regularly played in a "ghastly records" spot. From 6,000 replies, these were the Top (or Bottom) 10, which went on to headline a special "All-Time Worst" show. Mostly obscure before Everett dragged them up, several of these have since become bywords of bad taste on vinyl, particularly Jimmy Cross's 1965 tale of necrophiliac love which proudly tops this grisly list.

T O P 1 0

FIRST WORDS OF POPULAR SONGS

	Word	Incidence			Word	Incidence
1	I	226		9	Oh	48
2	My	115		10=	If	46
3	I'm	94		10=	I'll	46
4	When	93				
5	You	72				
6=	It's	58				
6=	Little	58				
8	In	55				

This Top 10 is based on a survey of about 6,500 popular songs published or released as records in the period 1900–75. If all the variants of "I" (I, I'd, I'll, I'm, and I've) are combined, the total goes up to 405.

T O P 1 0

US CHART SINGLES WITH THE LONGEST TITLES

	Title	Artist	Highest position	Year	No. of letters*
1	*Anaheim, Azusa & Cucamonga Sewing Circle, Book Review And Timing Association*	Jan & Dean	77	1964	66
2	*What Can You Get A Wookie For Christmas (When He Already Owns A Comb)?*	Star Wars Intergalactic Droid Choir & Chorale	69	1980	57
3	*Breaking Up Is Hard On You (a.k.a. Don't Take Ma Bell Away From Me)*	American Comedy Network	70	1984	53
4=	*Does Your Chewing Gum Lose Its Flavor On The Bedpost Over Night*	Lonnie Donegan	5	1961	52
4=	*Objects In The Rear View Mirror May Appear Closer Than They Are*	Meat Loaf	38	1994	52
4=	*Rhythm 'n' Blues (Mama's Got The Rhythm – Papa's Got The Blues)*	McGuire Sisters	5	1955	52
7=	*If I Said You Have A Beautiful Body Would You Hold It Against Me*	Bellamy Brothers	39	1979	51
7=	*(Sartorial Eloquence) Don't Ya Wanna Play This Game No More?*	Elton John	39	1980	51
9=	*Pink Cookies In A Plastic Bag Getting Crushed By Buildings*	L.L. Cool J	96	1993	49
9=	*First Thing Ev'ry Morning (And The Last Thing Ev'ry Night)*	Jimmy Dean	91	1965	49

* *Punctuation, excluding spaces, is counted as a single letter.*

Lonnie Donegan's 1961 single was based on a 1924 hit by Ernest Hare and Billy Jones entitled *Does The Spearmint Lose Its Flavor On The Bedpost Over Night.*

MUSIC ON RADIO & TV

FIRST MUSIC VIDEOS BROADCAST BY MTV IN THE US

1	Buggles, *Video Killed The Radio Star*	**6**	Cliff Richard, *We Don't Talk Anymore*
2	Pat Benatar, *You Better Run*	**7**	Pretenders, *Brass In Pocket*
3	Rod Stewart, *She Won't Dance With Me*	**8**	Todd Rundgren, *Time Heals*
4	Who, *You Better You Bet*	**9**	REO Speedwagon, *Take It On The Run*
5	PhD, *Little Susie's On The Up*	**10**	Styx, *Rockin' The Paradise*

This varied lineup inaugurated the world's first 24-hour music video network on August 1, 1981. Six of the 10 are British acts, there are no R & B videos, and little-known British duo PhD, who never had a US chart record, make an incongruous appearance at No. 5.

BMI "MILLION-AIRS"

	Songwriter(s)	No. of Million-Airs		Songwriter(s)	No. of Million-Airs
1	Lennon & McCartney	26	**8=**	Daryl Hall	7
2	Barry Gibb	22	**8=**	Carole Bayer-Sager	7
3	Paul Simon	15	**8=**	Gamble & Huff	7
4	Norman Gimbel	12	**8=**	John & Taupin	7
5	Holland, Dozier, Holland	10			
6	Barry Mann	9			
7	Cynthia Weil	8			

These are songwriters with the greatest number of songs broadcast more then 1,000,000 times. In the repertoire of songs in the BMI (Broadcast Music Incorporated) nearly 1,000 have achieved "Million-Air" status – that is, they have been broadcast over 1,000,000 times in the United States. With each song averaging three minutes, this is equal to over 50,000 hours of broadcasting, or 5.7 years of continuous airplay. It is estimated that, at any given time, there is a Lennon & McCartney composition being played on at least one US radio station – a graphic reminder of the partnership's colossal and ongoing royalty income.

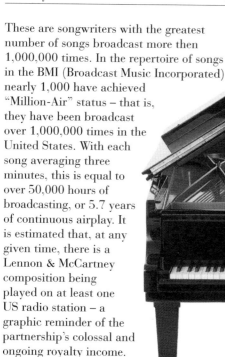

MOVIE SOUNDTRACKS IN THE US, 1994

	Artist/title
1	Elton John/Various *The Lion King*
2	Various, *Forrest Gump*
3	Various, *Above The Rim*
4	Various, *Reality Bites*
5	Various, *The Crow*
6	Whitney Houston/Various *The Bodyguard*
7	Various, *Murder Was The Case*
8	Various, *Philadelphia*
9	Tina Turner, *Jason's Lyric*
10	Various, *Sleepless In Seattle*

The Lion King was the biggest-selling album of the year, with 4,900,000 units sold. *The Bodyguard*, the bestseller of 1993 and prominent in the all-time albums Top 10, maintained a place in the 1994 list despite hot competition.

FIRST ACTS TO APPEAR ON SOUL TRAIN

1	Gladys Knight & The Pips
2	Bobby Hutton
3	Honeycones
4	Eddie Kendricks
5	Watts 103rd Street Band
6	Carla Thomas
7	General Cook
8	Chairmen Of The Board
9	Rufus Thomas
10	Laura Lee

Soul Train, which was conceived and hosted by Don Cornelius, made its American television broadcast debut on August 17, 1972. It quickly became the definitive soul/disco/dance showcase for R & B acts and generated the annual Soul Train Music Awards.

T O P 1 0

HIGHEST-RATED TV MUSIC SHOWS IN THE US, 1980–90

	Show	Broadcast date	% of TV audience*
1	*The Grammy Awards*	Feb 28, 1984	30.8
2	*American Music Awards*	Jan 16, 1984	27.4
3	*American Music Awards*	Jan 28, 1985	25.8
4=	*American Music Awards*	Jan 17, 1983	24.4
4=	*Country Music Awards*	Oct 11, 1982	24.4
6	*The Grammy Awards*	Feb 27, 1980	23.9
7	*The Grammy Awards*	Feb 26, 1985	23.8
8	*Country Music Awards*	Oct 13, 1980	22.9
9	*Country Music Awards*	Oct 10, 1983	22.6
10	*American Music Awards*	Jan 26, 1987	22.2

* *Percentage of US households with TV sets watching the broadcast. There are now more than 93,000,000 such households in the US.*

The Grammy Awards is primarily a music industry voting affair, while the *American Music Awards* is based on votes cast by the public and therefore tends to be a more teen-oriented broadcast. Annual music awards shows dominate American network music programming and are far more popular than, say, *Soul Train* or *Casey Kasem's American Top 10* weekly programs; they also include the *MTV Music Awards* (broadcast on cable).

T O P 1 0

SONGS ON *YOUR HIT PARADE*, 1935-58

	Composer/title	Year
1	Sid Lippman, *Too Young*	1951
2	Irving Berlin, *White Christmas*	1942
3	Arthur Hammerstein and Dudley Wilson, *Because Of You*	1951
4	Harry Warren, *You'll Never Know*	1953
5	Sammy Fain, *I'll Be Seeing You*	1938
6	Dorothy Stewart and Clement Scott, *Now Is The Hour*	1946
7	Fred Fisher, *Peg o' My Heart*	1947
8	Richard Rodgers, *People Will Say We're In Love*	1943
9	Billie Reid *A Tree In The Meadow*	1948
10	Richard Rodgers *Some Enchanted Evening*	1949

Your Hit Parade, a popular syndicated US weekly radio program featuring the most successful sheet-music sales, began in 1935.

T H E 1 0

FIRST ARTISTS TO APPEAR ON *AMERICAN BANDSTAND*

	Artist/song performed	Date
1	Billy Williams, *I'm Gonna Sit Right Down And Write Myself A Letter*	Aug 5, 1957
2	Chordettes, *Just Between You And Me*	Aug 5, 1957
3	Dale Hawkins, *Susie Q*	Aug 6, 1957
4	Don Rondo *White Silver Sands*	Aug 6, 1957
5	Paul Anka, *Diana*	Aug 7, 1957
6	Lee Andrews & The Hearts *Long Lonely Nights*	Aug 9, 1957
7	Gene Vincent & His Blue Caps *Lotta Lovin'/ Wear My Ring*	Aug 12, 1957
8	Four Coins, *Shangri-La*	Aug 12, 1957
9	Jodi Sands *All My Heart*	Aug 13, 1957
10	Sal Mineo, *Start Movin'/ Lasting Love*	Aug 13, 1957

T O P 1 0

MOST PERFORMED BMI SONGS OF ALL TIME IN THE US

	Title/Composer(s)
1	*Yesterday*, Lennon & McCartney
2	*Never My Love* Donald & Richard Addrisi
3	*By The Time I Get to Phoenix* Jim Webb
4	*Gentle on My Mind*, John Hartford
5	*You've Lost That Lovin' Feelin'* Phil Spector, Barry Mann, & Cynthia Weil
6	*More*, Norman Newell, Nino Oliviero, Riz Ortalani, & Marcello Ciorcioloni
7	*Georgia on My Mind* Hoagy Carmichael & Stuart Gorrell
8	*Bridge Over Troubled Water* Paul Simon
9	*Something*, George Harrison
10	*Mrs. Robinson*, Paul Simon

This list represents the most broadcast songs of all time on American radio and television, for those titles represented by the BMI (Broadcast Music Incorporated). The first five songs have all been broadcast over 5,000,000 times in the US alone.

MUSIC IN THE SALEROOM

RECORD SLEEVES
John Lennon's 30-year-old jacket brought $47,900 at auction.

MOST EXPENSIVE ITEMS OF ROCK STARS' CLOTHING SOLD AT AUCTION IN THE UK

Item/sale	Price ($)*
1 Elvis Presley's one-piece "Shooting Star" stage outfit, *c.*1972 Phillips, London, August 24, 1988	48,000
2 John Lennon's black leather jacket, *c.*1960–62 Christie's, London, May 7, 1992	47,900
3 Four "superhero"-style costumes worn by glam rock group Kiss in the film *Kiss Meets the Phantom* (1978) Christie's, London, May 14, 1993	31,400
4 Michael Jackson's white rhinestone glove Christie's, London, December 19, 1991	27,900
5 Elvis Presley's one-piece stage costume, as shown on the cover of his *Burning Love* album Phillips, London, August 25, 1992	26,100
6 Elvis Presley's blue stage costume, *c.*1972 Phillips, London, August 24, 1988	25,900
7 Jimi Hendrix's black felt hat Sotheby's, London, August 22, 1991	24,200
8 Elton John's giant Dr. Marten boots from the film *Tommy* Sotheby's, London, September 6, 1988	20,300
9= Michael Jackson's black sequinned jacket Sotheby's, London, August 22, 1991	18,600
9= Prince's *Purple Rain* stage costume, 1984 Christie's, London, December 19, 1991	18,600

* Including 10 percent buyer's premium

MOST EXPENSIVE ITEMS OF POP MEMORABILIA EVER SOLD AT AUCTION

(Excluding rock stars' clothing – see previous list)

Item/sale	Price ($)*
1 John Lennon's 1965 Rolls-Royce Phantom V touring limousine, finished with a psychedelic paint job Sotheby's, New York, June 29, 1985	2,299,000
2 Jimi Hendrix's Fender Stratocaster electric guitar Sotheby's, London, April 25, 1990	370,000 (£198,000)
3 Acoustic guitar owned by David Bowie, Paul McCartney, and George Michael Christie's, London, May 18, 1994	330,000 (£220,000)
4 Buddy Holly's Gibson acoustic guitar, *c.*1945, in a tooled leather case made by Holly Sotheby's, New York, June 23, 1990	242,000
5 John Lennon's 1970 Mercedes-Benz 600 Pullman four-door limousine Christie's, London, April 27, 1989	213,000 (£137,500)
6 Elvis Presley's 1942 Martin D-18 guitar (used to record his first singles, 1954–56) Red Baron Antiques, Atlanta, Georgia October 3, 1991. The same guitar was resold by Christie's, London, May 14, 1993 for $167,300.	180,000
7 Elvis Presley's 1963 Rolls-Royce Phantom V touring limousine Sotheby's, London, August 28, 1986	161,700 (£110,000)
8= Recording of 16-year-old John Lennon singing at a 1957 church fair in Liverpool Sotheby's London, September 15, 1994	121,300 (£78,500)
8= Tape recording of John Lennon and the Quarry Men, 1957, Sotheby's, London September 15, 1994	121,300 (£78,500)
9 Buddy Holly's Fender Stratocaster electric guitar, 1958 Sotheby's, New York, June 23, 1990	110,000

* Including 10 percent buyer's premium, where appropriate

Pioneered particularly by Sotheby's in London, pop memorabilia has become big business – especially if it involves personal association with megastars such as the Beatles and, more recently, Buddy Holly (whose eyeglasses were sold by Sotheby's, New York, on June 23, 1990 for $45,100). In addition to the Top 10, high prices have also been paid for other musical instruments once owned by notable rock stars, such as a guitar belonging to John Entwistle of the Who and pianos formerly owned by Paul McCartney and John Lennon.

T O P 1 0
MOST EXPENSIVE MUSIC MANUSCRIPTS EVER SOLD AT AUCTION

	Manuscript/sale	Price ($)*
1	Nine symphonies by Wolfgang Amadeus Mozart Sotheby's, London, May 22, 1987	3,854,000 (£2,350,000)
2	Schumann's Second Symphony Sotheby's, London, December 1, 1994	2,085,000 (£1,350,000)
3	Ludwig van Beethoven's Piano Sonata in E Minor, Opus 90 Sotheby's, London, December 6, 1991	1,690,000 (£1,000,000)
4	Wolfgang Amadeus Mozart's Fantasia in C Minor and Sonata in C Minor Sotheby's, London, November 21, 1990	1,496,000 (£800,000)
5	Robert Schumann's Piano Concerto in A Minor, Opus 54 Sotheby's, London, November 22, 1989	1,240,000 (£800,000)
6	Ludwig van Beethoven's first movement of the Sonata for Violoncello and Piano in A Major, Opus 69 Sotheby's, London, May 17, 1990	897,000 (£480,000)
7	Johann Sebastian Bach's cantata *Auf Christi Himmelfahrt allein* Sotheby's, London, November 22, 1989	604,500 (£390,000)
8	Igor Stravinsky's *Rite of Spring* Sotheby's, London, November 11, 1982	570,000 (£300,000)
9	Franz Schubert's Quartet in B flat Major (No. 8) D.112, Opus 168 Christie's, London, June 24, 1992	534,500 (£270,000)
10	Henry Purcell, 21 pieces for the harpsichord (the highest price for a British manuscript) Sotheby's, London, May 26, 1994	414,750 (£220,500)

* *"Hammer prices," excluding premiums*

The collection of nine symphonies by Mozart not only holds the record for the highest price ever paid for a music manuscript, but also for any postmedieval manuscript.

T O P 1 0
MOST EXPENSIVE MUSICAL INSTRUMENTS EVER SOLD AT AUCTION

	Instrument/sale	Price ($)*
1	"Mendelssohn" Stradivarius violin Christie's, London, November 21, 1990	1,686,700 (£902,000)
2	"Cholmondley" Stradivarius violoncello Sotheby's, London, June 22, 1988	1,145,800 (£682,000)
3	Steinway grand piano, decorated by Lawrence Alma-Tadema and Edward Poynter for Henry Marquand, 1884–87 Sotheby Parke Bernet, New York, March 26, 1980	390,000
4	Jimi Hendrix's Fender Stratocaster electric guitar Sotheby's, London, April 25, 1990	370,000 (£198,000)
5	Acoustic guitar owned by David Bowie, Paul McCartney, and George Michael Christie's, London, May 18, 1994	330,000 (£220,000)
6	Verne Powell platinum flute Christie's, New York, October 18, 1986	187,000
7	Flemish single-manual harpsichord made by Johan Daniel Dulken of Antwerp, 1755 Sotheby's, London, March 27, 1990	153,900 (£82,280)
8	Kirkman double-manual harpsichord Christie's, London, June 26, 1987	126,000 (£77,000)
9	Columnar alto recorder made by Hans van Schratt, mid-16th century Christie's, London, March 16, 1988	73,900 (£44,000)
10	"Portable Grand Piano" made by John Isaac Hawkins, *c*.1805 (a very early example of an upright piano, considerably predating the modern type, and one of only three examples known) Sotheby's, London, July 4, 1985	15,000 (£14,300)

* *Including 10 percent buyer's premium, where appropriate*

This list shows the most expensive example of each type of instrument. The harpsichords and pianos are of different types, but from the same family, so perhaps numbers 8 and 10 should be disqualified. If so, 9 and 10 would be a silver horn made by Johann Wilhelm Haas of Nuremburg in 1681, sold at Sotheby's, Geneva, on May 5, 1981 for $21,660/SF46,200 and a pair of German kettle drums, *c*.1700, sold at Sotheby's, London, on November 21, 1974 for $9,000.

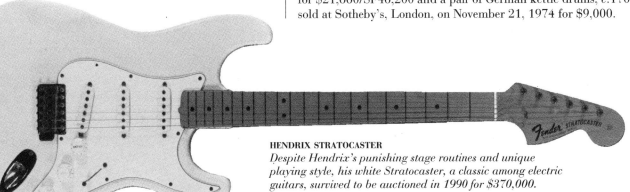

HENDRIX STRATOCASTER
Despite Hendrix's punishing stage routines and unique playing style, his white Stratocaster, a classic among electric guitars, survived to be auctioned in 1990 for $370,000.

CLASSICAL & OPERA

LAST WINNERS OF THE "BEST CLASSICAL ALBUM" GRAMMY AWARD

Year	Artist/title/performer
1995	Béla Bartók, *Concerto for Orchestra; Four Orchestral Pieces op.12*/Pierre Boulez, Chicago Symphony Orchestra
1994	Béla Bartók, *The Wooden Prince* Pierre Boulez, Chicago Symphony Orchestra and Chorus
1993	Gustav Mahler, *Symphony No. 9* Leonard Bernstein, Berlin Philharmonic Orchestra
1992	Leonard Bernstein, *Candide* Leonard Bernstein, London Symphony Orchestra
1991	Charles Ives, *Symphony No. 2 (And Three Short Works)* Leonard Bernstein, New York Philharmonic Orchestra
1990	Béla Bartók, *Six String Quartets*/Emerson String Quartet
1989	Giuseppi Verdi, *Requiem and Operatic Choruses* Robert Shaw, Atlanta Symphony Orchestra
1988	*Horowitz in Moscow*/Vladimir Horowitz
1987	*Horowitz: The Studio Recordings, New York*/Vladimir Horowitz
1986	Hector Berlioz, *Requiem* Robert Shaw, Atlanta Symphony Orchestra

The three consecutive awards to Leonard Bernstein in 1991–93 brought his overall Grammy tally to 15. Despite Pierre Boulez and the Chicago Symphony Orchestra's winning in successive years, Sir Georg Solti is easily the leading Grammy winner in any category and is unlikely to be overtaken in the near future.

POPULAR OPERA
Opera diva Maria Ewing takes the title role in Bizet's romantic opera Carmen, *first staged in Paris in 1875 and the Royal Opera House's all-time most performed work.*

OPERAS MOST FREQUENTLY PERFORMED AT THE METROPOLITAN OPERA HOUSE, NEW YORK

	Opera	Composer	Performances
1	*La Bohème*	Giacomo Puccini	728
2	*Aïda*	Giuseppe Verdi	709
3	*La Traviata*	Giuseppe Verdi	579
4	*Tosca*	Giacomo Puccini	559
5	*Carmen*	Georges Bizet	548
6	*Madama Butterfly*	Giacomo Puccini	517
7	*Rigoletto*	Giuseppe Verdi	510
8	*I Pagliacci*	Ruggero Leoncavallo	460
9	*Faust*	Charles Gounod	436
10	*Cavalleria Rusticana*	Pietro Mascagni	428

The Metropolitan Opera House opened on October 22, 1883, with a performance of Charles Gounod's *Faust*. Such is the universality of opera that no fewer than eight of the Met's top operas also appear (though in a somewhat different order) in the Top 10 performed at London's principal venue, the Royal Opera House, Covent Garden, London, UK, where *Carmen* tops the list of "most performed."

MOST PROLIFIC CLASSICAL COMPOSERS

	Composer	Dates	Nationality	Hrs
1	Joseph Haydn	1732–1809	Austrian	340
2	George Handel	1685–1759	German/English	303
3	Wolfgang Amadeus Mozart	1656–91	Austrian	202
4	Johann Sebastian Bach	1685–1750	German	175
5	Franz Schubert	1797–1828	German	134
6	Ludwig van Beethoven	1770–1827	German	120
7	Henry Purcell	1659–95	English	116
8	Giuseppe Verdi	1813–1901	Italian	87
9	Antonín Dvořák	1841–1904	Czechoslovakian	79
10=	Franz Liszt	1811–86	Hungarian	76
10=	Peter Tchaikovsky	1840–93	Russian	76

This list is based on a survey conducted by *Classical Music* magazine which ranked classical composers by the total number of hours of music each composed. If the length of the composer's working life is brought into the calculation, Schubert wins: his 134 hours were composed in a career of 18 years, giving an average of 7 hours 27 minutes per annum. The same method would put Tchaikovsky ahead of Liszt: although both composed 76 hours of music, Tchaikovsky worked for 30 years and Liszt for 51, giving them respective annual averages of 2 hours 32 minutes and 1 hour 29 minutes.

T O P 1 0

OPERAS MOST FREQUENTLY PERFORMED AT THE ROYAL OPERA HOUSE, COVENT GARDEN, LONDON 1833–1994

	Opera	Total		Opera	Total
1	*Carmen*	495	6	*Don Giovanni*	373
2	*La Bohème*	493	7	*Tosca*	363
3	*Aïda*	459	8	*Norma*	353
4	*Faust*	428	9	*La Traviata*	348
5	*Rigoletto*	423	10	*Madama Butterfly*	342

T O P 1 0

LARGEST OPERA HOUSES IN THE WORLD

	Opera house	Location	seating	Capacity standing	total
1	The Metropolitan Opera	New York, NY	3,800	265	4,065
2	Cincinnati Opera	Cincinnati, OH	3,630	–	3,630
3	Lyric Opera of Chicago	Chicago, IL	3,563	–	3,563
4	San Francisco Opera	San Francisco, CA	3,176	300	3,476
5	The Dallas Opera	Dallas, TX	3,420	–	3,420
6	Canadian Opera Company	Toronto, Canada	3,167	–	3,167
7	Los Angeles Music Center Opera	Los Angeles, CA	3,098	–	3,098
8	San Diego Opera	San Diego, CA	2,992	84	3,076
9	Seattle Opera	Seattle, WA	3,017	–	3,017
10	L'Opéra de Montréal	Montreal, Canada	2,874	–	2,874

T O P 1 0

LARGEST OPERA HOUSES IN EUROPE

	Opera house	Location	seating	Capacity standing	total
1	Opéra Bastille	Paris, France	2,716	–	2,716
2	Gran Teatre del Liceu	Barcelona, Spain	2,700	–	2,700
3	English National Opera	London, UK	2,356	75	2,431
4	Staatsoper	Vienna, Austria	1,709	567	2,276
5	Teatro alla Scala	Milan, Italy	2,015	150	2,165
6	Bolshoi Theatre	Moscow, Russia	2,153	*	2,153
7	The Royal Opera	London, UK	2,067	42	2,109
8	Bayerische Staatsoper	Munich, Germany	1,773	328	2,101
9	Bayreuth Festspielhaus	Bayreuth, Germany	1,925	–	1,925
10	Teatro Comunale	Florence, Italy	1,890	–	1,890

* *Standing capacity unspecified*

T H E 1 0

LAST WINNERS OF THE "BEST OPERA RECORDING" GRAMMY AWARD

Year	Artist/title/principal soloists
1995	Carlisle Floyd, *Susannah*/Jerry Hadley, Samuel Ramey, Cheryl Studer, Kenn Chester
1994	Handel, *Semele*/Kathleen Battle, Marilyn Horne, Samuel Ramey, Sylvia McNair, Michael Chance
1993	Richard Strauss, *Die Frau Ohne Schatten*/Placido Domingo, Jose Van Dam, Hildegard Behrens
1992	Richard Wagner, *Götterdämmerung* Hildegard Behrens, Ekkehard Wlashiha
1991	Richard Wagner, *Das Rheingold* James Morris, Kurt Moll, Christa Ludwig
1990	Richard Wagner, *Die Walküre*/Gary Lakes, Jessye Norman, Kurt Moll
1989	Richard Wagner, *Lohengrin*/Placido Domingo, Jessye Norman, Eva Randova
1988	Richard Strauss, *Ariadne Auf Naxos* Anna Tomowa-Sintow, Katleen Battle, Agnes Baltsa, Gary Lakes
1987	Leonard Bernstein, *Candide*/Ernie Mills, David Eisler, John Lankston
1986	Arnold Schoenberg, *Moses und Aron* Franz Mazura, Philip Landridge

OPERA'S LONDON HOME
Built in 1858, on a site occupied by a succession of theaters since 1732, the Royal Opera House is home to the Royal Opera and Royal Ballet Companies.

STAGE & SCREEN

TOP 10

LONGEST-RUNNING SHOWS OF ALL TIME IN THE UK

	Show	Performances
1	*The Mousetrap* (1952–)	17,630*
2	*No Sex, Please – We're British* (1971–87)	6,761
3	*Cats* (1981–)	5,765*
4	*Starlight Express* (1984–)	4,606*
5	*Oliver!* (1960–69)	4,125
6	*Oh! Calcutta!* (1870–80)	3,918
7	*Les Misérables* (1985–)	3,868*
8	*The Phantom of the Opera* (1986–)	3,586*
9	*Jesus Christ, Superstar* (1972–80)	3,357
10	*Evita* (1978–86)*	2,900

* *Still running; total at March 31, 1995*

These are all London productions. Like many of the shows in these lists, several closed briefly to move to another theater.

TOP 10

LONGEST-RUNNING COMEDIES OF ALL TIME IN THE UK

	Show	Performances
1	*No Sex, Please – We're British* (1971–87)	6,761
2	*Run for Your Wife* (1983–91)	2,638
3	*There's a Girl in My Soup* (1966–72)	2,547
4	*Pyjama Tops* (1969–75)	2,498
5	*Worm's Eye View* (1945–51)	2,245
6	*Boeing Boeing* (1962–67)	2,035
7	*Blithe Spirit* (1941–46)	1,997
8	*Dirty Linen* (1976–80)	1,667
9	*Reluctant Heroes* (1950–54)	1,610
10	*Seagulls Over Sorrento* (1950–54)	1,551

No Sex Please – We're British is the world's longest-running comedy. It opened at the Strand Theatre on June 3, 1971, transferred to the Garrick and Duchess Theatres, and finally closed on September 5, 1987.

TOP 10

LONGEST-RUNNING NONMUSICALS OF ALL TIME IN THE UK

	Show	Performances
1	*The Mousetrap* (1952–)	17,630*
2	*No Sex, Please – We're British* (1971–87)	6,761
3	*Oh! Calcutta!* (1970–80)	3,918
4	*Run for Your Wife* (1983–91)	2,638
5	*There's a Girl in My Soup* (1966–72)	2,547
6	*Pyjama Tops* (1965–75)	2,498
7	*Sleuth* (1970–75)	2,359
8	*Worm's Eye View* (1945–51)	2,245
9	*Boeing Boeing* (1962–67)	2,035
10	*Blithe Spirit* (1941–46)	1,997

* *Still running; total at March 31, 1995*

Oh! Calcutta! is regarded as a revue with music, rather than a musical.

NINE LIVES
Cats *has been a huge success both in the UK and worldwide.*

T O P 1 0

LONGEST-RUNNING MUSICALS OF ALL TIME IN THE UK

	Show	Performances
1	Cats (1981–)	5,765*
2	Starlight Express (1984–)	4,606*
3	Les Misérables (1985–)	3,868*
4	The Phantom of the Opera (1986–)	3,586*
5	Jesus Christ, Superstar (1972–80)	3,357
6	Evita (1978–86)	2,900
7	Miss Saigon (1989–)	2,407*
8	The Sound of Music (1961–67)	2,386
9	Salad Days (1954–60)	2,283
10	My Fair Lady (1958–63)	2,281

* *Still running; total at March 1, 1995*

T O P 1 0

LONGEST-RUNNING COMEDIES OF ALL TIME ON BROADWAY

	Comedy	Performances
1	Life With Father (1939–47)	3,224
2	Abie's Irish Rose (1922–27)	2,327
3	Gemini (1977–81)	1,788
4	Harvey (1944–49)	1,775
5	Born Yesterday (1946–49)	1,642
6	Mary, Mary (1961–64)	1,572
7	Voice of the Turtle (1943–48)	1,558
8=	Barefoot in the Park (1963–67)	1,532
9	Brighton Beach Memoirs (1975–78)	1,444
10	Same Time Next Year (1983–86)	1,299

T O P 1 0

LONGEST-RUNNING SHOWS OF ALL TIME ON BROADWAY

	Show	Performances
1	A Chorus Line (1975–90)	6,137
2	Oh! Calcutta! (1976–89)	5,959
3	Cats (1982–)	5,210*
4	42nd Street (1980–89)	3,486
5	Grease (1972–80)	3,388
6	Les Misérables (1987–)	3,298*
7	Fiddler on the Roof (1964–72)	3,242
8	Life with Father (1939–47)	3,224
9	Tobacco Road (1933–41)	3,182
10	The Phantom of the Opera (1988–)	2,850*

* *Still running; total at March 31, 1995*

T O P 1 0

LONGEST-RUNNING MUSICALS OF ALL TIME ON BROADWAY

	Show	Performances
1	A Chorus Line (1975–90)	6,137
2	Cats (1982–)	5,210*
3	42nd Street (1980–89)	3,486
4	Grease (1972–80)	3,388
5	Les Misérables (1987–)	3,298*
6	Fiddler on the Roof (1964–72)	3,242
7	The Phantom of the Opera (1988–)	2,850*
8	Hello Dolly! (1964–71)	2,844
9	My Fair Lady (1956–62)	2,717
10	Annie (1977–83)	2,377

* *Still running; total at March 31, 1995*

Off Broadway, the musical show *The Fantasticks* by Tom Jones and Harvey Schmidt has been performed continuously at the Sullivan Street Playhouse, New York, since May 3, 1960 – a total of 14,451 performances as of March 31, 1995.

BEHIND THE MASK
Michael Crawford in the title role of the box office smash musical The Phantom of the Opera.

T O P 1 0

LONGEST-RUNNING NONMUSICALS OF ALL TIME ON BROADWAY

	Show	Performances
1	Oh! Calcutta! (1976–89)	5,959
2	Life With Father (1939–47)	3,224
3	Tobacco Road (1933–41)	3,182
4	Abie's Irish Rose (1922–27)	2,327
5	Deathtrap (1978–82)	1,792
6	Gemini (1977–81)	1,788
7	Harvey (1944–49)	1,775
8	Born Yesterday (1946–49)	1,642
9	Mary, Mary (1961–65)	1,572
10	Voice of the Turtle (1943–47)	1,557

More than half the longest-running nonmusical shows on Broadway began their runs before World War II; the others all date from the period up to the 1970s, before the long-running musical completely dominated the Broadway stage. Off Broadway, these records have all been broken by *The Drunkard*, which was performed at the Mart Theatre, Los Angeles, from July 6, 1933 to September 6, 1953, and then reopened with a musical adapation and continued its run from September 7, 1953 until October 17, 1959 – a grand total of 9,477 performances seen by some 3,000,000 people.

THEATER AWARDS

LAST NEW YORK DRAMA DESK AWARDS FOR AN ACTOR

1994	Stephen Spinella	Angels in America Part II: Perestroika
1993	Ron Leibman	Angels in America Part I: Millennium Approaches
1992	Brian Bedford	Two Shakespearean Actors
1991	Ron Rifkin	The Substance of Fire
1990	Nathan Lane	The Lisbon Traviata
1989	Philip Bosco	Lend Me a Tenor
1988	Ron Silver	Speed-the-Plow
1987	James Earl Jones	Fences
1986	Ed Harris	Precious Sons
1985	John Lithgow	Requiem for a Heavyweight

LAST NEW YORK DRAMA DESK AWARDS FOR AN ACTRESS

1994	Myra Carter	Three Tall Women
1993	Jane Alexander	The Sisters Rosensweig
1992	Laura Esterman	Marvin's Room
1991	Irene Worth	Lost in Yonkers
1990	Geraldine Page	The Merchant of Venice
1989	Pauline Collins	Shirley Valentine
1988	Stockard Channing	Woman in Mind
1987	Linda Lavin	Broadway Bound
1986	Lily Tomlin	The Search for Signs of Intelligent Life in the Universe
1985	Rosemary Harris	Pack of Lies

MOST RECENT PULITZER DRAMA AWARDS

1994	Three Tall Women by Edward Albee
1993	Angels in America: Millennium Approaches by Tony Kushner
1992	The Kentucky Cycle by Robert Schenkkan
1991	Lost in Yonkers by Neil Simon
1990	The Piano Lesson by August Wilson
1989	The Heidi Chronicles by Wendy Wasserstein
1988	Driving Miss Daisy by Alfred Uhry
1987	Fences by August Wilson
1985	Sunday in the Park with George by Stephen Sondheim and James Lapine
1984	Glengarry Glenn Ross by David Mamet

No award in 1986

LAST NEW YORK DRAMA DESK AWARDS FOR A DIRECTOR

1994	Stephen Daldry	An Inspector Calls
1993	George C. Wolfe	Angels in America Part I: Millennium Approaches
1992	Patrick Mason	Dancing at Lughnasa
1991	Jerry Zaks	Six Degrees of Separation
1990	Frank Galati	The Grapes of Wrath
1989	Jerry Zaks	Lend Me a Tenor
1988	John Dexter	M. Butterfly
1987	Howard Davies	Les Liaisons Dangereuses
1986	Jerry Zaks	The Marriage Of Bette and Boo/The House of Blue Leaves
1985	John Malkovich	Balm In Gilead

The National Theatre's production of Stephen Daldry's revival of J.B. Priestley's 1944 play *An Inspector Calls* stunned audiences and critics, preventing George C. Wolfe from winning two years in a row.

LAST NEW YORK DRAMA DESK AWARDS FOR A PLAY

1994	Angels in America Part II: Perestroika by Tony Kushner
1993	Angels in America Part I: Millennium Approaches by Tony Kushner
1992	Marvin's Room by Scott McPherson
1991	The Substance Of Fire by Jon Robin Baitz
1990	The Piano Lesson by August Wilson
1989	The Heidi Chronicles by Wendy Wasserstein
1988	M. Butterfly by Henry Hwang
1987	Fences by August Wilson
1986	A Lie of the Mind by Sam Shepard
1985	As Is by William M. Hoffman

Tony Kushner's *Angels in America* Parts I and II and Scott McPherson's *Marvin's Room* have all brought AIDS awareness into mainstream theater. Both plays have been performed often in regional theater.

LAST NEW YORK DRAMA DESK AWARDS FOR A MUSICAL

1994	Passion
1993	Kiss of the Spider Woman
1992	Crazy for You
1991	The Will Rogers Follies
1990	City of Angels
1989	Jerome Robbins's Broadway
1988	Into the Woods
1987	Les Misérables
1986	The Mystery of Edwin Drood
1983	Sunday in the Park with George

No award 1984–5

The first New York Drama Desk Award was presented 50 years ago for a 1945 production of Richard Rodgers and Oscar Hammerstein II's *Carousel*. Winners over successive years include popular post-war musicals like *Brigadoon*, *South Pacific*, *Guys and Dolls*, and *My Fair Lady*. Stephen Sondheim is the only multiple Award winner.

THE 10

LAST TONY AWARDS FOR AN ACTOR

1995	Ralph Fiennes	Hamlet
1994	Stephen Spinella	Angels in America Part II: Perestroika
1993	Ron Leibman	Angels in America Part I: Millenium Approaches
1992	Judd Hirsch	Conversations with My Father
1991	Nigel Hawthorne	Shadowlands
1990	Robert Morse	Tru
1989	Philip Bosco	Lend Me a Tenor
1988	Ron Silver	Speed-the-Plow
1987	James Earl Jones	Fences
1986	Judd Hirsch	I'm Not Rappaport

THE 10

LAST TONY AWARDS FOR AN ACTRESS

1995	Cherry Jones	The Heiress
1994	Diana Rigg	Medea
1993	Madeline Kahn	The Sisters Rosensweig
1992	Glenn Close	Death and the Maiden
1991	Mercedes Ruehl	Lost in Yonkers
1990	Maggie Smith	Lettice and Lovage
1989	Pauline Collins	Shirley Valentine
1988	Joan Allen	Burn This
1987	Linda Lavin	Broadway Bound
1986	Lily Tomlin	The Search for Signs of Intelligent Life in the Universe

THE 10

LAST TONY AWARDS FOR A MUSICAL

1995	Sunset Boulevard		1990	City of Angels
1994	Passion		1989	Jerome Robbins's Broadway
1993	Kiss of the Spider Woman		1988	The Phantom of the Opera
1992	Crazy for You		1987	Les Misérables
1991	The Will Rogers Follies		1986	The Mystery of Edwin Drood

THE 10

LAST TONY AWARDS FOR A DIRECTOR

1994	Stephen Daldry	An Inspector Calls
1993	George C. Wolfe	Angels in America Part I: Millennium Approaches
1992	Patrick Mason	Dancing at Lughnasa
1991	Jerry Zaks	Six Degrees of Separation
1990	Frank Galati	The Grapes of Wrath
1989	Jerry Zaks	Lend Me a Tenor
1988	John Dexter	M. Butterfly
1987	Lloyd Richards	Fences
1986	Jerry Zaks	House of Blue Leaves

THE 10

LAST TONY AWARDS FOR A PLAY

1995	Love! Valour! Compassion! by Terence McNally
1994	Angels in America Part II: Perestroika by Tony Kushner
1993	Angels in America Part I: Millenium Approaches by Tony Kushner
1992	Dancing at Lughnasa by Brian Friel
1991	Lost in Yonkers by Neil Simon
1990	The Grapes of Wrath by Frank Galati
1989	The Heidi Chronicles by Wendy Wasserstein
1988	M. Butterfly by Henry Hwang
1987	Fences by August Wilson
1986	I'm Not Rappaport by Herb Gardner

Broadway veteran Jerry Zaks is the only director to have won more than one Tony over the last decade, receiving a total of three, all for comedies – which surprisingly have been shared equally with drama over that period.

The Tony Awards, founded in 1947 by the American Theater Wing to honor Broadway plays and musicals, are named for the actress/director Antoinette Perry (1888–1946), who ran the Wing in World War II.

THE IMMORTAL BARD

SHAKESPEARE'S MOST DEMANDING ROLES

	Role	Play	Lines
1	Hamlet	*Hamlet*	1,422
2	Falstaff	*Henry IV, Parts I and II*	1,178
3	Richard III	*Richard III*	1,124
4	Iago	*Othello*	1,097
5	Henry V	*Henry V*	1,025
6	Othello	*Othello*	860
7	Vincentio	*Measure for Measure*	820
8	Coriolanus	*Coriolanus*	809
9	Timon	*Timon of Athens*	795
10	Antony	*Antony and Cleopatra*	766

Hamlet speaks over 36 percent of the play – 11,610 words – the most of any character in Shakespeare. But Falstaff, appearing in *Henry IV, Parts I* and *II*, and *The Merry Wives of Windsor*, wins with 1,614 lines.

"ALAS, POOR YORICK"
Hamlet's encounter with the skull of Yorick the court jester is often misquoted – he says "Alas, poor Yorick! I knew him, Horatio," not ". . . I knew him well."

POLONIUS'S PRECEPTS FOR LAERTES

1 Give thy thoughts no tongue, Nor any unproportioned thought his act.

2 Be thou familiar, but by no means vulgar.

3 Those friends thou hast, and their adoption tried, Grapple them to thy soul with hoops of steel;

4 But do not dull thy palm with entertainment Of each new-hatch'd, unfledged comrade.

5 Beware of entrance to a quarrel, but being in, Bear't that the opposed may beware of thee.

6 Give every man thy ear, but few thy voice;

7 Take each man's censure, but reserve thy judgment.

8 Costly thy habit as thy purse can buy, But not express'd in fancy; rich, not gaudy; For the apparel oft proclaims the man, And they in France of the best rank and station Are of a most select and generous chief in that.

9 Neither a borrower nor a lender be; For loan oft loses both itself and friend, And borrowing dulls the edge of husbandry.

10 This above all: to thine ownself be true, And it must follow, as the night the day, Thou canst not then be false to any man.

In Act I, Scene iii of *Hamlet*, Polonius, the Lord Chamberlain and father of Hamlet's friend Laertes, gives his son these 10 pieces of advice before Laertes sets sail for France.

MOST PRODUCED SHAKESPEARE PLAYS

	Play	Productions
1	*As You Like It*	65
2=	*The Merchant of Venice*	59
2=	*Twelfth Night*	59
4	*Hamlet*	58
5=	*Much Ado About Nothing*	56
5=	*The Taming of the Shrew*	56
7	*A Midsummer Night's Dream*	50
8=	*Macbeth*	49
8=	*The Merry Wives of Windsor*	47
8=	*Romeo and Juliet*	47

* To January 1, 1995

This list, which is based on an analysis of Shakespearean productions from December 31, 1878 to January 1, 1995 at Stratford-upon-Avon and by the Royal Shakespeare Company in London, provides a reasonable picture of his most popular plays. Records do not, however, indicate the total number of individual performances during each production.

SHAKESPEARE'S LONGEST PLAYS

	Play	Lines
1	*Hamlet*	3,901
2	*Richard III*	3,886
3	*Coriolanus*	3,820
4	*Cymbeline*	3,813
5	*Othello*	3,672
6	*Antony and Cleopatra*	3,630
7	*Troilus and Cressida*	3,576
8	*Henry VIII*	3,450
9	*Henry V*	3,368
10	*The Winter's Tale*	3,354

WILLIAM SHAKESPEARE (1564–1616)
England's best-known poet, actor, and playwright was born in Stratford-upon-Avon, Warwickshire, the town to which he returned at the end of a life spent in the theatrical world of London.

THE 10
FIRST SHAKESPEARE PLAYS

	Play	Approx. year written
1	*Titus Andronicus*	1588–90
2	*Love's Labour's Lost*	1590
3	*Henry VI, Parts I–III*	1590–91
4=	*The Comedy of Errors*	1591
4=	*Richard III*	1591
4=	*Romeo and Juliet*	1591
7	*The Two Gentlemen of Verona*	1592–93
8	*A Midsummer Night's Dream*	1593–94
9	*Richard II*	1594
10	*King John*	1595

Precise dating of Shakespeare's plays is problematic. Contemporary records of early performances are rare, and only half the plays were published before Shakepeare died in 1616. Even these were much altered from the originals. It was only after 1623, when the "Folios" were published, that the complete works of Shakespeare were published progressively. *Romeo and Juliet* is especially difficult because it may date from as early as 1591 or as late as 1596–97. If the latter, it would be predated by numbers 7–10 and by *The Merchant of Venice* (c. 1596).

TOP 10
WORDS USED BY SHAKESPEARE

	Word	Frequency
1	The	27,457
2	And	26,285
3	I	21,206
4	To	19,938
5	Of	17,079
6	A	14,675
7	You	14,326
8	My	13,075
9	That	11,725
10	In	11,511

In his complete works, William Shakespeare wrote a total of 884,647 words – 118,406 lines comprising 31,959 separate speeches. He used a total vocabulary of 29,066 words, some – such as "America" – appearing only once (*The Comedy of Errors*, III.ii). At the other end of the scale the Top 10 lists all those words used on more than 10,000 occasions. Perhaps surprisingly, their frequency is not dissimilar to modern usage, with words such as is, not, me, and for.

DID YOU KNOW
APING SHAKESPEARE

As an explanation of probability, it has often been said that, given an infinite amount of time, a chimpanzee with a typewriter could by chance type the complete works of Shakespeare. However, in a recently published discussion, one correspondent calculated that it might take 140,000 years of nonstop random typing before a chimp stumbled on just the first three words of Hamlet's soliloquy "To be or not to be." Therefore, to achieve the full complement of 884,647 words, with spaces and punctuation, in the right order, would take longer than the period during which the universe has existed. Even simplifying the task by issuing a keyboard with only 26 letters and a space bar, at a rate of one key per second it would take 12 years to type "Macbet." Since the chances of hitting the letters in the correct sequence decrease the longer the word gets, 331 years would be required to achieve the complete name "Macbeth."

YESTERDAY'S STARS

TOP 10

MOVIE REMAKES

	Original movie	Remake
1	*Father of the Bride* (1950)	1991
2	*The Ten Commandments* (1923)	1956
3	*A Star is Born* (1954)	1976
4	*Ben Hur* (1926)	1959
5	*King Kong* (1933)	1976
6	*Dragnet* (1954)	1987
7	*The Three Musketeers* (1948)	1974
8	*Hamlet* (1964)	1990
9	*The Postman Always Rings Twice* (1946)	1981
10	*King Solomon's Mines* (1950)	1985

This Top 10 includes only remakes with the identical title, and hence such retitled remakes as *Anna and the King of Siam* (1946)/*The King and I* (1956) and *Dracula* (1979)/*Bram Stoker's Dracula* (1992) are ineligible. The "original" movie is the last significant Hollywood version, but many subjects have been remade more than once – *The Three Musketeers* and *Hamlet* being notable examples.

TOP 10

MOVIES OF THE SILENT ERA

	Movie	Year
1	*The Birth of a Nation*	1915
2	*The Big Parade*	1925
3	*Ben Hur*	1926
4	*The Ten Commandments*	1923
5=	*What Price Glory?*	1926
5=	*The Covered Wagon*	1923
7=	*Way Down East*	1921
7=	*Hearts of the World*	1918
9=	*Wings*	1927
9=	*The Four Horsemen of the Apocalypse*	1921

The Birth of a Nation is not only at the top of the list, but, having earned almost twice as much as *The Big Parade*, is ranked as the most successful movie made before 1937, when *Snow White and the Seven Dwarfs* took the crown. All the movies in this list were black and white, with the exception of *Ben Hur*, which, despite its early date, contains a color sequence.

TOP 10

BLACK-AND-WHITE MOVIES

	Movie	Year
1	*Young Frankenstein*	1974
2	*Schindler's List*	1993
3	*Paper Moon*	1973
4	*Manhattan*	1979
5	*Mom and Dad*	1944
6	*Who's Afraid of Virginia Woolf?*	1966
7	*Easy Money*	1983
8	*The Last Picture Show*	1971
9	*From Here to Eternity*	1953
10	*Lenny*	1974

Perhaps surprisingly, all the most successful black-and-white movies date from the modern era, when the choice of filming in color or monochrome was available and, consequently, the decision to use the latter was deliberate.

TOP 10

MOST EXPENSIVE ITEMS OF MOVIE MEMORABILIA SOLD AT AUCTION

	Item/sale	Price ($)*
1	James Bond's Aston Martin DB5 from *Goldfinger* Sotheby's, New York, June 28, 1986	275,000
2	Herman J. Mankiewicz's scripts for *Citizen Kane* and *The American* Christie's, New York, June 21, 1989	231,000
3	Judy Garland's ruby slippers from *The Wizard of Oz* Christie's, New York, June 21, 1988	165,000
4	Piano from the Paris scene in *Casablanca* Sotheby's, New York, December 16, 1988	154,000
5	Charlie Chaplin's hat and cane Christie's, London, December 11, 1987 (resold at Christie's, London, December 17, 1993)	135,300 82,500
6	Clark Gable's script from *Gone With the Wind* Sotheby's, New York, December 16, 1988	77,000
7	Charlie Chaplin's boots Christie's, London, December 11, 1987	63,100
8	A 1932 Universal poster for *The Old Dark House*, starring Boris Karloff Christie's, New York, December 9, 1991	48,400
9	A special effects painting of the Emerald City from *The Wizard of Oz* Camden House, Los Angeles, April 1, 1991	44,000
10	16mm film of the only meeting between Danny Kaye and George Bernard Shaw Christie's, London, April 27, 1989	32,400

* *$/£ conversion at rate then prevailing*

This list excludes the hand-painted scenes used in animations. These now attain huge prices: one of Donald Duck in *Orphan's Benefit* (1934) sold for $286,000 in 1989.

T O P 1 0
AUDREY HEPBURN MOVIES

	Movie	Year
1	*My Fair Lady*	1964
2	*Always*	1989
3	*Wait until Dark*	1967
4	*Charade*	1963
5	*War and Peace*	1956
6	*The Nun's Story*	1959
7	*Bloodline*	1979
8	*How to Steal a Million*	1966
9	*Breakfast at Tiffany's*	1961
10=	*Sabrina*	1954
10=	*Robin and Marian*	1976

T O P 1 0
HUMPHREY BOGART MOVIES

	Movie	Year
1	*The Caine Mutiny*	1954
2	*Casablanca*	1942
3	*The African Queen*	1951
4=	*Sabrina*	1954
4=	*The Left Hand of God*	1955
6	*To Have and Have Not*	1945
7=	*Key Largo*	1948
7=	*The Barefoot Contessa*	1954
9=	*Dark Passage*	1947
9=	*The Big Sleep*	1946

YOU MUST REMEMBER THIS
Ingrid Bergman and Humphrey Bogart in the poignant Paris flashback scene in Casablanca.

T O P 1 0
JOHN WAYNE MOVIES

	Movie	Year
1	*How the West was Won*	1962
2	*The Longest Day*	1962
3	*True Grit*	1969
4	*The Green Berets*	1968
5	*The Alamo*	1960
6=	*The Cowboys*	1972
6=	*Big Jake*	1971
8	*Rooster Cogburn*	1975
9	*Hatari!*	1962
10	*The Greatest Story Ever Told*	1965

John Wayne (born Marion Michael Morrison) was one of the most prolific Hollywood actors, making more than 150 movies during a career that spanned 48 years. He is chiefly remembered for his tough-guy roles as a soldier or cowboy – often, curiously, with a Scottish name, such as his title roles in *Big Jim McLain* (1952), *McLintock* (1963), and *McQ* (1974). Occasionally he found himself badly miscast, for example, as Genghis Khan in *The Conqueror* (1955) and in the 10th film on this list, in which he appeared, (mercifully briefly) as the Roman centurion who gazes at the crucified Jesus and, in a Western drawl, recites his single line, "Truly, this man was the son of God."

T O P 1 0
INGRID BERGMAN MOVIES

	Movie	Year		Movie	Year
1	*Murder on the Orient Express*	1974	6	*Notorious*	1946
2	*Cactus Flower*	1969	7	*Casablanca*	1942
3	*The Bells of St Mary's*	1945	8	*The Yellow Rolls Royce*	1964
4	*For Whom the Bell Tolls*	1943	9	*The Inn of the Sixth Happiness*	1958
5	*Spellbound*	1945	10	*Anastasia*	1956

T O P 1 0
PETER SELLERS MOVIES

	Movie	Year
1	*The Revenge of the Pink Panther*	1978
2	*The Return of the Pink Panther*	1974
3	*The Pink Panther Strikes Again*	1976
4	*Murder by Death*	1976
5	*Being There*	1979
6	*Casino Royale*	1967
7	*What's New Pussycat?*	1965
8	*A Shot in the Dark*	1964
9	*The Pink Panther*	1963
10=	*Dr. Strangelove*	1963
10=	*The Fiendish Plot of Dr. Fu Manchu*	1963

T O P 1 0
MARILYN MONROE MOVIES

	Movie	Year
1	*Some Like it Hot*	1959
2	*How to Marry a Millionaire*	1953
3	*The Seven Year Itch*	1955
4	*Gentlemen Prefer Blondes*	1953
5	*There's No Business Like Show Business*	1954
6	*Bus Stop*	1956
7	*The Misfits*	1961
8	*River of No Return*	1954
9	*All About Eve*	1950
10	*Let's Make Love*	1960

MOVIE HITS & MISSES

Movies in these lists are ranked according to the total rental fees paid to the distributors by movie theaters in the US and Canada. The movie industry regards this as a reliable guide to what a movie has earned in these markets. Doubling these receipts is also accepted as a very rough guide to the world total. Rental income is not the same as "box office gross," another way of comparing the success of movies. While valid over a short time, such as when comparing recent releases, it indicates the movie theaters' earnings rather than the movie's, and depends on ticket price. Recent movies tend to earn the most money because as inflation rises, so too do ticket prices, box office income, and distributors' fees. If inflation were taken into account, *Gone With the Wind* (1939), now placed 40th, would be the most successful movie with rental fees of almost $80,000,000, equivalent over the years to $500,000,000 today.

T O P 1 0
BIGGEST MOVIE FLOPS OF ALL TIME

	Movie	Year	Loss ($)
1	*The Adventures of Baron Münchhausen*	1988	48,100,000
2	*Ishtar*	1987	47,300,000
3	*Hudson Hawk*	1991	47,000,000
4	*Inchon*	1981	44,100,000
5	*The Cotton Club*	1984	38,100,000
6	*Santa Claus – The Movie*	1985	37,000,000
7	*Heaven's Gate*	1980	34,200,000
8	*Billy Bathgate*	1991	33,000,000
9	*Pirates*	1986	30,300,000
10	*Rambo III*	1988	30,000,000

Since the figures here are based upon North American rental earnings balanced against the movies' original production cost, some may recoup a proportion of their losses via overseas earnings, video, and TV revenue, although for others, such as *Inchon* and *Pirates*, time has run out. The recent entry of *Hudson Hawk* and *Billy Bathgate* means that *Raise the Titanic* (1980), said to have lost $29,200,000, has finally sunk from the Top 10.

T O P 1 0
MOST EXPENSIVE MOVIES EVER MADE

	Movie*	Year	Estimated cost ($)
1	*True Lies*	1994	110,000,000
2	*Inchon* (US/Korea)	1981	102,000,000
3	*War and Peace* (USSR)	1967	100,000,000
4	*Terminator 2: Judgement Day*	1991	95,000,000
5	*Total Recall*	1990	85,000,000
6	*The Last Action Hero*	1993	82,500,000
7	*Batman Returns*	1992	80,000,000
8	*Alien 3*	1992	75,000,000
9=	*Who Framed Roger Rabbit*	1988	70,000,000
9=	*Die Hard 2*	1990	70,000,000
9=	*Hook*	1991	70,000,000
9=	*Wyatt Earp*	1994	70,000,000

* All US-made unless otherwise stated

T O P 1 0
MOVIE RENTAL BLOCKBUSTERS OF ALL TIME

1	*E.T.: The Extra-Terrestrial*	1982
2	*Jurassic Park*	1993
3	*Star Wars*	1977
4	*The Lion King*	1995
5	*Forrest Gump*	1995
6	*Return of the Jedi*	1983
7	*Batman*	1989
8	*The Empire Strikes Back*	1980
9	*Home Alone*	1990
10	*Ghostbusters*	1984

E.T.: The Extra-Terrestrial and *Jurassic Park* have each earned in excess of $200,000,000 in North American rentals alone, while the rest have all earned more than $100,000,000. Only nine other movies have ever earned over $100,000,000: *Jaws* (1975), *Indiana Jones and the Last Crusade* (1989), *Terminator 2* (1991), *Indiana Jones and the Temple of Doom* (1984), *Beverly Hills Cop* (1984), *Back to the Future* (1985), *Home Alone 2: Lost in New York* (1993), and *Batman Returns* (1992).

T O P 1 0
MOVIE SEQUELS THAT EARNED MORE THAN THE ORIGINAL*

	Original	Outearned by
1	*Terminator*	*Terminator 2: Judgment Day*
2	*First Blood*	*Rambo: First Blood Part II/Rambo III*
3	*Lethal Weapon*	*Lethal Weapon 2 / Lethal Weapon 3*
4	*Die Hard*	*Die Hard 2*
5	*Patriot Games*	*Clear and Present Danger*
6	*Rocky*	*Rocky III/Rocky IV*
7	*The Pink Panther*	*Return of the Pink Panther/ The Pink Panther Strikes Again/ Revenge of the Pink Panther*
8	*48 Hours*	*Another 48 Hours*
9	*A Nightmare on Elm Street*	*A Nightmare on Elm Street 2, 3, 4, 5*
10	*Alien*	*Aliens*

* Ranked according to the greatest differential between the original and the highest-earning sequel

TOP 10

MOVIE SEQUELS OF ALL TIME

1 *Star Wars/The Empire Strikes Back/Return of the Jedi*

2 *Raiders of the Lost Ark/Indiana Jones and the Temple of Doom/Indiana Jones and the Last Crusade*

3 *Rocky I–VI*

4 *Star Trek I–VI*

5 *Batman /Batman Returns*

6 *Home Alone 1–2*

7 *Back to the Future I–III*

8 *Jaws I–IV*

9 *Ghostbusters I–II*

10 *Superman I–IV*

Based on total earnings of the original movie and all its sequels up to the end of 1993, the *Star Wars* trilogy stands head and shoulders above the rest, having made more than $500,000,000 in the North American market alone. All the other movies in the Top 10 have achieved total earnings of around $200,000,000 or more, with *Lethal Weapon 1–3* and *Beverly Hills Cop I–II* lagging just outside the Top 10. A successful movie does not guarantee a successful sequel, however: although their total earns them a place in the Top 10, each of the four *Superman* movies actually earned less than the previous one, with *Superman IV* earning just one-tenth of the original. *Smokey and the Bandit Part III* earned just one-seventeenth of the original, and while the 1973 movie *The Sting* was a box-office blockbuster, its 1983 sequel earned less than one-fifteenth as much, and *Grease 2* less than one-tenth of the original *Grease*. On the other hand, *Terminator 2* has already earned six times as much as its "prequel." The James Bond movies are not presented as sequels, but if they were taken into account their total earnings would place them in 2nd position in this list.

"LIFE'S LIKE A BOX OF CHOCOLATES"

The homespun "Gumpisms" uttered by the eponymous hero of Forrest Gump *endeared it to audiences the world over. It won Oscars for Best Picture, Best Director, and Best Screenplay, and for Tom Hanks as Best Actor.*

THE 10

HIGHEST-GROSSING FILMS OF ALL TIME IN THE UK

	Film	Year	Approx. gross (£)
1	*Jurassic Park*	1993	32,000,000
2	*Four Weddings and a Funeral*	1994	27,400,000
3	*Ghost*	1990	23,300,000
4	*E.T.: The Extra-Terrestrial*	1983	21,700,000
5	*Crocodile Dundee*	1987	21,500,000
6	*Mrs. Doubtfire*	1994	20,900,000
7	*The Flintstones*	1994	20,200,000
8	*Robin Hood: Prince of Thieves*	1991	20,500,000
9	*The Lion King*	1994	18,500,000
10	*Terminator 2: Judgment Day*	1991	18,400,000

Inevitably, owing to inflation, the top-grossing films ever are those of the 1980s and 1990s. From the low point of the late 1960s and 1970s, today's films (even excluding video) are more widely viewed than those 15 to 25 years ago, as well as grossing much more at the box office.

TOP 10

MOVIES OF 1994 IN THE US

	Movie	release	Box office gross ($)*		Movie	release	Box office gross ($)*
1	*Forrest Gump*	Jul 6	323,602,990	8	*Speed*	Jun 10	121,248,145
2	*The Lion King*	Jun 15	312,844,232	9	*The Mask*	Jul 29	119,938,730
3	*True Lies*	Jul 15	146,282,411	10	*Interview With the Vampire*	Nov 11	105,264,608
4	*Santa Claus*	Nov 11	144,810,923				
5	*The Flintstones*	May 27	130,531,208				
6	*Clear and Present Danger*	Aug 3	122,012,656				
7	*Dumb and Dumber*	Dec 16	121,923,234				

* *Ongoing earnings through April 9, 1995*
Source: © 1995 Entertainment Data, Inc.

MOVIES OF THE DECADES

T O P 1 0

MOVIES OF THE 1930s

	Movie	Year
1	Gone With the Wind*	1939
2	Snow White and the Seven Dwarfs	1937
3	The Wizard of Oz	1939
4	King Kong	1933
5	San Francisco	1936
6=	Mr. Smith Goes to Washington	1939
6=	Lost Horizon	1937
6=	Hell's Angels	1930
9	Maytime	1937
10	City Lights	1931

* *Winner of "Best Picture" Academy Award*

Both *Gone With the Wind* and *Snow White and the Seven Dwarfs* have generated considerably more income than any other prewar movies, appearing respectively within the Top 40 and the Top 60 movies of all time – although if the income of *Gone With the Wind* is adjusted to allow for inflation in the period since its release, it could with some justification be regarded as the most successful movie ever. *Gone With the Wind* and *The Wizard of Oz* both celebrated their 50th anniversaries in 1989, and the extra publicity generated by these events further enhanced their rental income. The Academy Award-winning *Cavalcade* (1932) is a potential contender for a place in this Top 10, but its earnings have been disputed.

T O P 1 0

MOVIES OF THE 1940s

	Movie	Year
1	Bambi	1942
2	Fantasia	1940
3	Cinderella	1949
4	Pinocchio	1940
5	Song of the South	1946
6	Mom and Dad	1944
7	Samson and Delilah	1949
8=	The Best Years of Our Lives*	1946
8=	Duel in the Sun	1946
10	This is the Army	1943

* *Winner of "Best Picture" Academy Award*

With the top four movies of the decade classic Disney cartoons (and *Song of the South* being part animated/part live action), the 1940s may truly be regarded as the "golden age" of the animated movie. The genre was especially appealing in this era as colorful escapism during and after the drabness and grim realities of the war years. The songs from two of these movies – *When You Wish Upon a Star* from *Pinocchio* and *Zip-A-Dee-Doo-Dah* from *Song of the South* – won "Best Song" Academy Awards. The cumulative income of certain of the Disney cartoons has increased as a result of their systematic re-release in movie theaters and as bestselling videos. *Samson and Delilah* heralded the epic movies of the 1950s.

T O P 1 0

MOVIES OF THE 1950s

	Movie	Year
1	The Ten Commandments	1956
2	Lady and the Tramp	1955
3	Peter Pan	1953
4	Ben Hur*	1959
5	Around the World in 80 Days*	1956
6	Sleeping Beauty	1959
7=	South Pacific	1958
7=	The Robe	1953
9	Bridge on the River Kwai*	1957
10	This is Cinerama	1952

* *Winner of "Best Picture" Academy Award*

While the popularity of animated movies continued with *Lady and the Tramp*, *Peter Pan*, and *Sleeping Beauty*, the 1950s were outstanding as the decade of the "big" picture. Many of the most successful movies were enormous in terms of cast (*Around the World in 80 Days* boasted no fewer than 44 stars, most in cameo performances) and scale (*Ben Hur*, with its vast sets, broke all previous records by costing a staggering $4,000,000 to make, while *The Robe* was the first picture to offer the wide screen of Cinemascope). They were also enormous in the magnitude of the subjects they tackled. Three of these were major biblical epics. *Bridge on the River Kwai* was unusual in that it was a British-made success, with primarily British stars.

WIND-FALL!
Vivien Leigh and Clark Gable are shown in a scene from Gone With the Wind. *In cash terms, the movie has earned almost 20 times the then record $4,230,000 it cost to make – but indexing its earnings over the 56 years since its release would establish it as Hollywood's all-time money earner.*

MOVIES OF THE 1960s

	Movie	Year
1	*The Sound of Music**	1965
2	*101 Dalmatians*	1961
3	*The Jungle Book*	1967
4	*Doctor Zhivago*	1965
5	*Butch Cassidy and the Sundance Kid*	1969
6	*Mary Poppins*	1964
7	*The Graduate*	1968
8	*My Fair Lady**	1964
9	*Thunderball*	1965
10	*Funny Girl*	1968

During the 1960s the growth in popularity of soundtrack record albums and featured singles often matched the commercial success of the movies from which they were derived: four of the Top 10 movies of the decade were avowed musicals, while all had a high musical content, every one of them generating either an album or a hit single or two. *The Sound of Music*, the highest-earning movie of the decade, produced the fastest-selling album ever, with over half a million sold in two weeks – as well as the first million-selling tape cassette. *Mary Poppins* was a No. 1 album, as were albums of *The Jungle Book* and *Doctor Zhivago*.

* Winner of "Best Picture" Academy Award

MOVIES OF THE 1970s

	Movie	Year
1	*Star Wars*	1977
2	*Jaws*	1975
3	*Grease*	1978
4	*The Exorcist*	1973
5	*The Godfather**	1972
6	*Superman*	1978
7	*Close Encounters of the Third Kind*	1977/80
8	*The Sting**	1973
9	*Saturday Night Fever*	1977
10	*National Lampoon's Animal House*	1978

* Winner of "Best Picture" Academy Award

In the 1970s the arrival of the two prodigies, Steven Spielberg and George Lucas, set the scene for the high adventure blockbusters whose domination has continued ever since. Lucas directed his first science-fiction movie, *THX 1138*, in 1970 and went on to write and direct *Star Wars* (and wrote the two sequels, *The Empire Strikes Back* and *Return of the Jedi*). Spielberg directed *Jaws* and wrote and directed *Close Encounters* (which derives its success from the original release and the 1980 "Special Edition").

MOVIES OF THE 1980s

	Movie	Year
1	*E.T.: The Extra-Terrestrial*	1982
2	*Return of the Jedi*	1983
3	*Batman*	1989
4	*The Empire Strikes Back*	1980
5	*Ghostbusters*	1984
6	*Raiders of the Lost Ark*	1981
7	*Indiana Jones and the Last Crusade*	1989
8	*Indiana Jones and the Temple of Doom*	1984
9	*Beverly Hills Cop*	1984
10	*Back to the Future*	1985

Adventure movies proliferated during the 1980s, with George Lucas and Steven Spielberg sharing the Top 10 between them. Lucas was producer of 2 and 4 and Spielberg director of 1, 6, 7, 8, and 10. Despite their financial success, they failed to win a "Best Picture" Academy Award, although *E.T.* and *Raiders of the Lost Ark* were nominated. None of the high-earning movies of the 1980s won this Oscar. Each one, however, made more than $100,000,000 in North American rentals.

MOVIES OF THE 1990s

	Movie	Year
1	*Jurassic Park*	1993
2	*The Lion King*	1994
3	*Forrest Gump*	1994
4	*Home Alone*	1990
5	*Mrs. Doubtfire*	1993
6	*Terminator 2*	1992
7	*Home Alone 2: Lost in New York*	1992
8	*Batman Returns*	1992
9	*Ghost*	1990
10	*The Fugitive*	1993

Just four years into the decade, all 10 of these movies have amassed rental income from the North American market alone in excess of $80,000,000, an achievement matched by only 15 movies in the whole of the 1980s and just seven in the 1970s. *Home Alone* has been so successful that it now ranks as one of the Top 10 movies of all time. The sequel, *Home Alone 2: Lost in New York*, which was made in 1992, is now ranked 16th in the list of all-time top movies. A further 30 movies released since 1990, including several released in 1994, have each earned more than $50,000,000.

CAPED CRUSADER
Exactly 50 years after his first appearance as a comic-book superhero, Batman became one of the top movies of the 1980s, with Batman Returns among the highest-earning movies of the 1990s to date.

MOVIE GENRES

TOP 10

WAR MOVIES

1	*Platoon*	1986
2	*Good Morning, Vietnam*	1987
3	*Apocalypse Now*	1979
4	*Schindler's List*	1993
5	*M*A*S*H*	1970
6	*Patton*	1970
7	*The Deer Hunter*	1978
8	*Full Metal Jacket*	1987
9	*Midway*	1976
10	*The Dirty Dozen*	1967

High-earning war movies have been rare in recent years, suggesting that the days of big-budget movies in this genre may be over. However, this list excludes successful movies with military, rather than war themes, such as *A Few Good Men* (1992), *The Hunt for Red October* (1990), and *An Officer and a Gentleman* (1982), which would otherwise have been in the top five; or *Top Gun* (1986), which would top the list, just beating *Rambo: First Blood 2*, a post-Vietnam War action movie, which is also disqualified.

TOP 10

SCIENCE-FICTION AND FANTASY MOVIES

1	*E.T.:The Extra-Terrestrial*	1982
2	*Star Wars*	1977
3	*Return of the Jedi*	1983
4	*Batman*	1989
5	*The Empire Strikes Back*	1980
6	*Ghostbusters*	1984
7	*Terminator 2*	1991
8	*Back to the Future*	1985
9	*Batman Returns*	1992
10	*Ghost*	1990

The first six movies are also in the all-time Top 10, and all 10 are among the 21 most successful movies ever, having earned over $80,000,000 each from North American rentals alone. Just outside the Top 10 another eight have had a rental income of over $60,000,000: *Close Encounters of the Third Kind*; *Gremlins*; *Honey, I Shrunk the Kids*; *Back to the Future, Part II*; *Teenage Mutant Ninja Turtles*; *Superman II*; *Total Recall*; and *Ghostbusters II*.

TOP 10

COMEDY MOVIES

1	*Forrest Gump*	1994
2	*Home Alone*	1990
3	*Mrs. Doubtfire*	1993
4	*Beverly Hills Cop*	1984
5	*Ghost*	1990
6	*Home Alone 2: Lost in New York*	1992
7	*Tootsie*	1982
8	*Pretty Woman*	1990
9	*Three Men and a Baby*	1987
10	*Beverly Hills Cop II*	1987

If the two *Beverly Hills Cop* movies are excluded as "action thrillers" rather than comedies, Nos. 9 and 10 would be *National Lampoon's Animal House* (1978) and *Crocodile Dundee* (1986). If *Ghost* and *Pretty Woman*, arguably either comedies or romances with comic elements, are also left out, the next two are *Look Who's Talking* (1989) and *Coming to America* (1988). High earners also include: *Sister Act* (1992), *City Slickers* (1991), and *Nine to Five* (1980).

TOP 10

MOVIES IN WHICH THE STAR WEARS DRAG

	Movie	Star
1	*Mrs. Doubtfire* (1994)	Robin Williams
2	*Tootsie* (1983)	Dustin Hoffman
3	*Rocky Horror Picture Show* (1974)	Tim Curry
4	*Under Siege* (1992)	Gary Busey
5	*The Crying Game* (1993)	Jaye Davidson
6	*Dressed to Kill* (1980)	Michael Caine
7	*Psycho* (1960)	Anthony Perkins
8	*Some Like It Hot* (1959)	Tony Curtis/ Jack Lemmon
9	*La Cage aux Folles* (1979)	Michel Serrault
10	*Jo Jo Dancer, Your Life Is Calling* (1986)	Richard Pryor

TOP 10

HORROR FILMS

1	*Jurassic Park*	1993
2	*Jaws*	1975
3	*The Exorcist*	1973
4	*Jaws II*	1978
5	*Interview With the Vampire*	1994
6	*Bram Stoker's Dracula*	1992
7	*Aliens*	1986
8	*Alien*	1979
9	*Poltergeist*	1982
10	*King Kong*	1976

This list encompasses supernatural and science-fiction horror and monsters (including dinosaurs, gorillas, and oversized sharks), but omits science-fiction movies that do not have a major horrific component.

TOP 10

BIBLICAL MOVIES

1	*The Ten Commandments*	1956
2	*Ben Hur*	1959
3	*The Robe*	1953
4	*Jesus Christ Superstar*	1973
5	*Quo Vadis*	1951
6	*Samson and Delilah*	1949
7	*Jesus*	1979
8	*The Greatest Story Ever Told*	1965
9	*King of Kings*	1961
10	*Solomon and Sheba*	1959

Biblical subjects have been standard Hollywood fare since the pioneer days but are now less fashionable – Martin Scorsese's controversial *The Last Temptation of Christ* (1988) actually earned less than the silent versions of *Ben Hur* (1926) and *The Ten Commandments* (1923).

LICENCE TO THRILL
Roger Moore almost reaches the end of the line in Octopussy, *the most successful of the long series of James Bond movies, made by the MGM Studios.*

T O P 1 0
JAMES BOND MOVIES

	Movie	Bond actor
1	*Octopussy* (1983)	Roger Moore
2	*Moonraker* (1979)	Roger Moore
3	*Thunderball* (1965)	Sean Connery
4	*Never Say Never Again* (1983)	Sean Connery
5	*The Living Daylights* (1987)	Timothy Dalton
6	*For Your Eyes Only* (1981)	Roger Moore
7	*A View to a Kill* (1985)	Roger Moore
8	*The Spy Who Loved Me* (1977)	Roger Moore
9	*Goldfinger* (1964)	Sean Connery
10	*Diamonds Are Forever* (1967)	Sean Connery

T O P 1 0
WESTERNS

1	*Dances With Wolves*	1990
2	*Maverick*	1994
3	*Butch Cassidy and the Sundance Kid*	1969
4	*Unforgiven*	1992
5	*Jeremiah Johnson*	1972
6	*How the West Was Won*	1962
7	*Pale Rider*	1985
8	*Young Guns*	1988
9	*Young Guns II*	1990
10	*Bronco Billy*	1980

Clint Eastwood is in the unusual position of directing and starring in a movie that has forced another of his own movies out of the Top 10, since the recent success of *Unforgiven* has ejected *The Outlaw Josey Wales* (1976). Although it has a Western setting, Steven Spielberg's *Back to the Future, Part III* (1990) is essentially a science-fiction film (if it were a true Western, it would rate in 2nd place). According to some criteria, *The Last of the Mohicans* (1992) qualifies as a Western; if included, it would be in 4th position.

T O P 1 0
MUSICAL MOVIES

1	*Grease*	1978
2	*The Sound of Music*	1965
3	*Saturday Night Fever*	1977
4	*American Graffiti*	1973
5	*The Best Little Whorehouse in Texas*	1982
6	*Mary Poppins*	1964
7	*Fiddler on the Roof*	1971
8	*Annie*	1982
9	*A Star Is Born*	1976
10	*Flashdance*	1983

Traditional musicals (movies in which the cast actually sing) and movies in which a musical soundtrack is a major component of the movie are included. Several other musical movies have also each earned in excess of $30,000,000 in North American rentals; among them *Coalminer's Daughter* (1980), *The Rocky Horror Picture Show* (1975), *Footloose* (1984), *The Blues Brothers* (1980), and *Purple Rain* (1984), but it would appear that the era of the blockbuster musical movie is over.

T O P 1 0
DISASTER MOVIES

1	*Die Hard 2*	1990
2	*The Towering Inferno*	1975
3	*Airport*	1970
4	*The Poseidon Adventure*	1972
5	*Die Hard*	1988
6	*Earthquake*	1974
7	*Airport 1975*	1974
7	*Airport '77*	1977
9	*The Hindenburg*	1975
10	*Black Sunday*	1977

Disasters involving blazing buildings, natural disasters such as volcanoes, earthquakes, and tidal waves, train and air crashes, sinking ships and terrorist attacks have long been a staple of Hollywood movies, of which these are the most successful. Firemen fighting fires are also part of the theme of *Backdraft* (1991), which, if included, would enter at No. 5. *The China Syndrome* (1979) would appear in seventh place, except that the threatened nuclear diasaster which provides the storyline is actually averted.

KIDS' STUFF

T O P 1 0
ANIMATED MOVIES

1	*The Lion King*	1994
2	*Aladdin*	1992
3	*Who Framed Roger Rabbit?**	1988
4	*Snow White and the Seven Dwarfs*	1937
5	*Beauty and the Beast*	1991
6	*One Hundred and One Dalmatians*	1961
7	*Jungle Book*	1967
8	*Bambi*	1942
9	*Fantasia*	1940
10	*Cinderella*	1949

* Part animated, part live-action

The 1990s have already given us the two most successful animated movies of all time, but they descend from a long and glittering line of predecessors. For almost 60 years the popularity of the genre has been so great that animated movies stand out among the leading money-makers of each decade: *Snow White* was the second highest earning movie of the 1930s (after *Gone With the Wind*); *Bambi*, *Fantasia* and *Cinderella* – and through the success of its recent re-release joined by *Pinocchio* – were the most successful movies of the 1940s. Like the latter, *Lady and the Tramp* falls just outside the Top 10, but was the second most successful of the 1950s (after *The Ten Commandments*). In the 1960s, *One Hundred and One Dalmatians* was the second and *Jungle Book* the third most successful movie of the 1960s (after *The Sound of Music*). Among runners-up are, in descending order: *Pinocchio* (1940); *Lady and the Tramp* (1955); *The Little Mermaid* (1989); *Peter Pan* (1953); *The Rescuers* (1977); *The Fox and the Hound* (1981); the part-animated *Song of the South* (1946); *The Aristocats* (1970); *Oliver & Company* (1988); *The Land Before Time* (1988), *An American Tail* (1986), and *Sleeping Beauty* (1989).

KING OF THE JUNGLE
Disney's hit, The Lion King, *won Oscars for Best Original Score (Hans Zimmer) and Best Original Song,* Can You Feel The Love Tonight? *(Elton John and Tim Rice).*

T O P 1 0
MOVIES STARRING ANIMALS*

	Film	Animal
1	*Jaws* (1975)	Shark
2	*Jaws II* (1978)	Shark
3	*Free Willy* (1993)	Orca whale
4	*Arachnophobia* (1990)	Spiders
5	*Jaws 3-D* (1983)	Shark
6	*Oliver & Company* (1988)	Cats (and dogs)
7	*The Life and Times of Grizzly Adams* (1975)	Bear
8	*The Black Stallion* (1979)	Horse
9	*White Fang* (1991)	Wolf/dog
10	*Never Cry Wolf* (1983)	Wolves

* Except dogs – see The Top 10 Movies Starring Dogs

This is a list of movies (other than animated) where an animal is acknowledged as a central character, rather than a peripheral. Hence, it excludes, for example, the wolves in *Dances with Wolves*, the fish in *A Fish Called Wanda*, and omits fantasy animals such as dragons and the giant gorilla in *King Kong* (1976), which would otherwise rank 3rd. Without the sharks and whales, Nos. 7 to 10 are taken by *The Bear* (1989), *That Darn Cat* (1965), *Gorillas in the Mist* (1988), and *Gus* (1976), starring a mule.

T O P 1 0
CHILDREN'S MOVIES*

1	*Honey, I Shrunk the Kids*	1989
2	*Hook*	1991
3	*Teenage Mutant Ninja Turtles*	1990
4	*The Karate Kid Part II*	1986
5	*Mary Poppins*	1964
6	*The Karate Kid*	1984
7	*Teenage Mutant Ninja Turtles II*	1991
8	*War Games*	1983
9	*The Muppet Movie*	1979
10	*The Goonies*	1985

* Excluding animated movies

Some of the most successful movies of all time, such as *E.T.*, *Star Wars* and its two sequels, the two Ghostbusters films, *Home Alone* and *Home Alone 2: Lost in New York*, all of which would be eligible for this list, have been those that are unrestricted by classification, appeal to the broadest possible base of the "family audience," and consequently attract the greatest revenue. This Top 10, however, is of movies that are aimed primarily at a young audience – although some are no doubt also appreciated by the accompanying adults.

© DISNEY

TOP 10

MOVIES FEATURING DINOSAURS

1	*Jurassic Park*	1993
2	*Fantasia*	1940
3	*The Land Before Time**	1988
4	*Baby. . . Secret of the Lost Legend*	1985
5	*One of Our Dinosaurs is Missing*	1975
6	*Journey to the Center of the Earth*	1959
7	*King Kong*	1933
8	*At the Earth's Core*	1976
9	*One Million Years BC*	1966
10	*When Dinosaurs Ruled the Earth*	1970

TOP 10

YOUNGEST OSCAR WINNERS

	Actor/actress	Award/movie	Year	Age
1	Shirley Temple	Special Award – outstanding contribution in 1934	1934	6
2	Margaret O'Brien	Special Award (*Meet Me in St. Louis*, etc.)	1944	8
3	Vincent Winter	Special Award (*The Little Kidnappers*)	1954	8
4	Jon Whitely	Special Award (*The Little Kidnappers*)	1954	9
5	Ivan Jandl	Special Award (*The Search*)	1948	9
6	Tatum O'Neal	Best Supporting Actress (*Paper Moon*)	1973	10
7	Anna Paquin	Best Supporting Actress (*The Piano*)	1993	11
8	Claude Jarman, Jr.	Special Award (*The Yearling*)	1946	12
9	Bobby Driscoll	Special Award (*The Window*)	1949	13
10	Hayley Mills	Special Award (*Pollyanna*)	1960	13

The Academy Awards ceremony usually takes place at the end of March in the year after that in which the movie was released, so the winners are generally at least a year older when they receive their Oscars than when they acted in their award-winning movies. Hayley Mills, the 12th and last winner of the "Special Award" miniature Oscar (presented to her by its first winner, Shirley Temple), won her award one day before her 14th birthday. Subsequent winners have had to compete on the same basis as adult actors and actresses for the major awards of "Best Actor," "Best Actress," "Best Supporting Actor," and "Best Supporting Actress." Tatum O'Neal is the youngest nominee, and winner, of an "adult" Oscar. Jackie Cooper was nine when he was nominated "Best Actor" for his part in *Skippy* (1930–31 Awards), but the youngest winner was more than 20 years older, Richard Dreyfuss (for *The Goodbye Girl* in the 1977 Awards). Eight-year-old Justin Henry is the youngest ever Oscar nominee for "Best Supporting Actor," for *Kramer vs Kramer* (1979), but the youngest winner is Timothy Hutton, aged 20 when he won in 1980 for *Ordinary People*. The youngest "Best Actress" Award winner is Marlee Matlin, aged 21, for *Children of a Lesser God* (1986), and the youngest nominee Isabelle Adjani, 20, for *The Story of Adèle H* (1975).

TOP 10

MOVIES STARRING DOGS

1	*One Hundred and One Dalmatians**	1961
2	*Lady and the Tramp**	1955
3	*Turner & Hooch*	1989
4	*The Fox and the Hound**	1981
5	*Beethoven*	1992
6	*Oliver & Company*	1988
7	*Beethoven's 2nd*	1993
8	*K-9*	1989
9	*Benji*	1974
10	*Homeward Bound: The Incredible Journey*	1993

* *Animated*

Man's best friend has been stealing scenes since the earliest years of movie-making, with the 1905 low-budget *Rescued by Rover* outstanding as one of the most successful productions of the pioneer period. The numerous silent era films starring Rin Tin Tin, an ex-German army dog who emigrated to the US, and his successor Lassie, whose long series of feature and TV films date from the 1940s onward, are among the most enduring in cinematic history. Since the 1950s, dogs – both real and animated – have been a consistently popular mainstay of the Disney Studios, who were responsible for the first four, the 6th and the last entry in this Top 10.

DID YOU KNOW

TOP OF THE CLASS

The saying may be "never act with animals or children," but many of the most successful movies are family movies and include child actors with whom the younger viewers may identify. In fact, seven of the 20 highest-earning movies ever feature child actors. They include *E.T.: The Extra-Terrestrial* (1982), with Henry Thomas (Elliott) and Drew Barrymore (Gertie), and *Home Alone* (1990) and *Home Alone 2: Lost in New York* (1992), both starring Macaulay Culkin.

OSCAR WINNERS – MOVIES

MOVIES NOMINATED FOR THE MOST OSCARS

(Oscar ® is a registered trademark)

	Movie	Year	Awards	Nominations
1	All About Eve	1950	6	14
2=	Gone With the Wind	1939	8*	13
2=	From Here to Eternity	1953	8	13
2=	Mary Poppins	1964	5	13
2=	Who's Afraid of Virginia Woolf?	1966	5	13
2=	Forrest Gump	1994	6	13
7=	Mrs. Miniver	1942	6	12
7=	The Song of Bernadette	1943	4	12
7=	Johnny Belinda	1948	1	12
7=	A Streetcar Named Desire	1951	4	12
7=	On the Waterfront	1954	8	12
7=	Ben Hur	1959	11	12
7=	Becket	1964	1	12
7=	My Fair Lady	1964	8	12
7=	Reds	1981	3	12
7=	Dances With Wolves	1990	7	12
7=	Schindler's List	1993	7	12

* Plus two special awards

While Johnny Belinda and Becket at least had the consolation of winning once out of their 11 nominations, both The Turning Point (1977) and The Color Purple (1985) suffered the ignominy of receiving 11 nominations without a single win.

"BEST PICTURE" OSCAR WINNERS OF THE 1930s

Year	Movie
1930	All Quiet on the Western Front
1931	Cimarron
1932	Grand Hotel
1933	Cavalcade
1934	It Happened One Night*
1935	Mutiny on the Bounty
1936	The Great Ziegfeld
1937	The Life of Emile Zola
1938	You Can't Take It With You
1939	Gone With the Wind

* Winner of Oscars for "Best Director," "Best Actor," "Best Actress," and "Best Screenplay"

The first Academy Awards, popularly known as Oscars, were presented at a ceremony at the Hollywood Roosevelt Hotel on May 16, 1929, and were for movies released in the period 1927–28. A second ceremony held at the Ambassador Hotel on October 31 of the same year was for movies released in 1928–29.

MOVIES TO WIN MOST OSCARS

	Movie	Year	Awards
1	Ben Hur	1959	11
2	West Side Story	1961	10
3=	Gigi	1958	9
3=	The Last Emperor	1987	9
5=	Gone With the Wind	1939	8
5=	From Here to Eternity	1953	8
5=	On the Waterfront	1954	8
5=	My Fair Lady	1964	8
5=	Cabaret	1972	8
5=	Gandhi	1982	8
5=	Amadeus	1984	8

"BEST PICTURE" OSCAR WINNERS OF THE 1940s

Year	Movie
1940	Rebecca
1941	How Green was my Valley
1942	Mrs. Miniver
1943	Casablanca
1944	Going My Way
1945	The Lost Weekend
1946	The Best Years of Our Lives
1947	Gentleman's Agreement
1948	Hamlet
1949	All the King's Men

"BEST PICTURE" OSCAR WINNERS OF THE 1950s

Year	Movie
1950	All About Eve
1951	An American in Paris
1952	The Greatest Show on Earth
1953	From Here to Eternity
1954	On the Waterfront
1955	Marty
1956	Around the World in 80 Days
1957	The Bridge on the River Kwai
1958	Gigi
1959	Ben Hur

TOP 10

HIGHEST-EARNING "BEST PICTURE" OSCAR WINNERS

	Movie	Year
1	Forrest Gump	1994
2	Rain Man	1988
3	The Godfather	1972
4	Dances With Wolves	1990
5	The Sound of Music	1965
6	Gone With the Wind	1939
7	The Sting	1973
8	Platoon	1986
9	Kramer vs Kramer	1979
10	One Flew Over the Cuckoo's Nest	1975

Winning the "Best Picture" Academy Award is no guarantee of box-office success: the award is given for a picture released the previous year, and by the time the Oscar ceremony takes place the movie-going public has already effectively decided on the winning picture's fate. An Oscar may enhance a successful picture's continuing earnings, but it is usually too late to revive a movie that has not been popular.

TOP 10

"BEST PICTURE" OSCAR WINNERS OF THE 1960s

Year	Movie
1960	The Apartment
1961	West Side Story
1962	Lawrence of Arabia
1963	Tom Jones
1964	My Fair Lady
1965	The Sound of Music
1966	A Man for All Seasons
1967	In the Heat of the Night
1968	Oliver!
1969	Midnight Cowboy

The Apartment (1960), was the last black-and-white movie to receive a "Best Picture" Oscar until Steven Spielberg's Schindler's List in 1993, which won seven Oscars.

GOLDEN IDOL
Standing 13.5 in (34 cm) high, gold plated "Oscar" was reputedly named for his resemblance to a movie-librarian's Uncle Oscar.

TOP 10

"BEST PICTURE" OSCAR WINNERS OF THE 1970s

Year	Movie
1970	Patton
1971	The French Connection
1972	The Godfather
1973	The Sting
1974	The Godfather, Part II
1975	One Flew Over the Cuckoo's Nest*
1976	Rocky
1977	Annie Hall
1978	The Deer Hunter
1979	Kramer vs Kramer

* Winner of Oscars for "Best Director," "Best Actor," "Best Actress," and "Best Screenplay"

TOP 10

"BEST PICTURE" OSCAR WINNERS OF THE 1980s

Year	Movie
1980	Ordinary People
1981	Chariots of Fire
1982	Gandhi
1983	Terms of Endearment
1984	Amadeus
1985	Out of Africa
1986	Platoon
1987	The Last Emperor
1988	Rain Man
1989	Driving Miss Daisy

The winners of "Best Picture" Oscars during the 1990s are: 1990 Dances With Wolves; 1991 The Silence of the Lambs – which also won Oscars for "Best Director," "Best Actor," "Best Actress," and "Best Screenplay"; 1992 Unforgiven; 1993: Schindler's List – which also won six other awards, for "Best Director," "Best Adapted Screenplay," "Best Film Editing," "Best Art Direction," "Best Cinematography," and "Best Original Score," and 1994: Forrest Gump, which also won six Oscars in total.

OSCAR WINNERS – STARS & DIRECTORS

THE 10

"BEST DIRECTOR" OSCAR WINNERS OF THE 1970s

Year	Movie	Director
1970	*Patton**	Franklin J. Schaffner
1971	*The French Connection**	William Friedkin
1972	*Cabaret*	Bob Fosse
1973	*The Sting**	George Roy Hill
1974	*The Godfather Part II**	Francis Ford Coppola
1975	*One Flew Over the Cuckoo's Nest**	Milos Forman
1976	*Rocky**	John G. Avildsen
1977	*Annie Hall**	Woody Allen
1978	*The Deer Hunter**	Michael Cimino
1979	*Kramer vs Kramer**	Robert Benton

* *Winner of "Best Picture" Oscar*

THE 10

"BEST DIRECTOR" OSCAR WINNERS OF THE 1980s

Year	Movie	Director
1980	*Ordinary People**	Robert Redford
1981	*Reds*	Warren Beatty
1982	*Gandhi**	Richard Attenborough
1983	*Terms of Endearment**	James L. Brooks
1984	*Amadeus**	Milos Forman
1985	*Out of Africa**	Sydney Pollack
1986	*Platoon**	Oliver Stone
1985	*The Last Emperor**	Bernardo Bertolucci
1988	*Rain Man**	Barry Levinson
1989	*Born on the Fourth of July*	Oliver Stone

* *Winner of "Best Picture" Oscar*

The "Best Director" Oscars for the 1990s are, 1990: Kevin Costner for *Dances With Wolves*; 1991: Jonathan Demme for *The Silence of the Lambs*; 1992: Clint Eastwood for *Unforgiven*; 1993: Steven Spielberg for *Schindler's List*; and 1994: Robert Zemeckis for *Forrest Gump*.

THE 10

"BEST ACTRESS" OSCAR WINNERS OF THE 1970s

Year	Movie	Actress
1970	*Women in Love*	Glenda Jackson
1971	*Klute*	Jane Fonda
1972	*Cabaret*	Liza Minelli
1973	*A Touch of Class*	Glenda Jackson
1974	*Alice Doesn't Live Here Any More*	Ellen Burstyn
1975	*One Flew Over the Cuckoo's Nest*#*	Louise Fletcher
1976	*Network***	Faye Dunaway
1977	*Annie Hall*#	Diane Keaton
1978	*Coming Home***	Jane Fonda
1979	*Norma Rae*	Sally Field

* *Winner of "Best Picture" Oscar*
# *Winner of "Best Director," "Best Actor," and "Best Screenplay" Oscars*
** *Winner of "Best Actor" Oscar*

THE 10

"BEST ACTOR" OSCAR WINNERS OF THE 1970s

Year	Movie	Actress
1970	*Patton**	George C. Scott
1971	*The French Connection**	Gene Hackman
1972	*The Godfather**	Marlon Brando
1973	*Save the Tiger*	Jack Lemmon
1974	*Harry and Tonto*	Art Carney
1975	*One Flew Over the Cuckoo's Nest*#*	Jack Nicholson
1976	*Network***	Peter Finch
1977	*The Goodbye Girl*	Richard Dreyfuss
1978	*Coming Home***	John Voight
1979	*Kramer vs Kramer**	Dustin Hoffman

* *Winner of "Best Picture" Oscar*
# *Winner of "Best Director," "Best Actress," and "Best Screenplay" Oscars*
** *Winner of "Best Actress" Oscar*

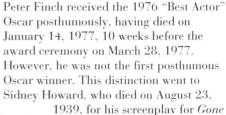

Peter Finch received the 1976 "Best Actor" Oscar posthumously, having died on January 14, 1977, 10 weeks before the award ceremony on March 28, 1977. However, he was not the first posthumous Oscar winner. This distinction went to Sidney Howard, who died on August 23, 1939, for his screenplay for *Gone With the Wind*. The Nobel Prize-winning novelist Sinclair Lewis received the Oscar on his behalf on February 29, 1940. The oldest "Best Actor" and "Best Actress" Oscar winners were Henry Fonda, aged 76, for *On Golden Pond* (1981), and Jessica Tandy, aged 79, for *Driving Miss Daisy* (1989). George Burns, aged 80, for *The Sunshine Boys* (1975), and Peggy Ashcroft aged 77, for *A Passage to India* (1984), were the oldest "Best Supporting Actor and Actress." Ralph Richardson was 82 when he was nominated as "Best Supporting Actor" for *Greystoke: The Legend of Tarzan* (1984), as was Eva Le Gallienne, nominated as "Best Supporting Actress" for *Resurrection* (1980).

THE 10

"BEST ACTOR" OSCAR WINNERS OF THE 1980s

Year	Movie	Actor
1980	*Raging Bull*	Robert De Niro
1981	*On Golden Pond**	Henry Fonda
1982	*Gandhi#*	Ben Kingsley
1983	*Tender Mercies*	Robert Duvall
1984	*Amadeus#*	F. Murray Abraham
1985	*Kiss of the Spider Woman*	William Hurt
1986	*The Color of Money*	Paul Newman
1987	*Wall Street*	Michael Douglas
1988	*Rain Man#*	Dustin Hoffman
1989	*My Left Foot*	Daniel Day-Lewis

* *Winner of "Best Actress" Oscar*
\# *Winner of "Best Picture" Oscar*

The 1990s winners to date are 1990: Jeremy Irons for *Reversal of Fortune*; 1991: Anthony Hopkins for *The Silence of the Lambs* (which also won "Best Picture" and "Best Actress" Oscars); 1992: Al Pacino for *Scent of a Woman*; 1993: Tom Hanks for *Philadelphia* – who also won the award in 1994 for *Forrest Gump*. Hanks' achievement in winning in consecutive years is unique; Marlon Brando, Gary Cooper, Dustin Hoffman, and Spencer Tracy each won the award twice.

THE 10

"BEST SUPPORTING ACTOR"
OSCAR WINNERS OF THE 1980s

Year	Actor	Movie
1980	Timothy Hutton	*Ordinary People*
1981	John Gielgud	*Arthur*
1982	Louis Gossett, Jr	*An Officer and a Gentleman*
1983	Jack Nicholson	*Terms of Endearment*
1984	Haing S. Ngor	*The Killing Fields*
1985	Don Ameche	*Cocoon*
1986	Michael Caine	*Hannah and Her Sisters*
1987	Sean Connery	*The Untouchables*
1988	Kevin Kline	*A Fish Called Wanda*
1989	Denzel Washington	*Glory*

The winners of "Best Supporting Actor" Oscars during the 1990s are 1990: Joe Pesci for *Goodfellas*; 1991: Jack Palance for *City Slickers*; 1992: Gene Hackman for *Unforgiven*; 1993: Tommy Lee Jones for *The Fugitive*; and 1994: Martin Landau for *Ed Wood*. Only three films have received three nominations for "Best Supporting Actor": *On the Waterfront*, *The Godfather*, and *The Godfather, Part II*.

THE 10

"BEST ACTRESS" OSCAR WINNERS OF THE 1980s

Year	Movie	Actress
1980	*The Coal Miner's Daughter*	Sissy Spacek
1981	*On Golden Pond**	Katharine Hepburn
1982	*Sophie's Choice*	Meryl Streep
1983	*Terms of Endearment#*	Shirley MacLaine
1984	*Places in the Heart*	Sally Field
1985	*The Trip to Bountiful*	Geraldine Page
1986	*Children of a Lesser God*	Marlee Matlin
1987	*Moonstruck*	Cher
1988	*The Accused*	Jodie Foster
1989	*Driving Miss Daisy#*	Jessica Tandy

* *Winner of "Best Actor" Oscar*
\# *Winner of "Best Picture" Oscar*

The 1990s winners are 1990: Kathy Bates for *Misery*; 1991: Jodie Foster for *The Silence of the Lambs*; 1992: Emma Thompson for *Howard's End*; 1993: Holly Hunter for *The Piano*; and 1994: Jessica Lange for *Blue Sky*. Only Katherine Hepburn won in consecutive years, 1967 and 1968. A further 10 have won twice: Ingrid Bergman, Bette Davis, Olivia De Havilland, Sally Field, Jane Fonda, Jodie Foster, Glenda Jackson, Vivien Leigh, Louise Rainer, and Elizabeth Taylor.

THE 10

"BEST SUPPORTING ACTRESS"
OSCAR WINNERS OF THE 1980s

Year	Actress	Movie
1980	Mary Steenburgen	*Melvin and Howard*
1981	Maureen Stapleton	*Reds*
1982	Jessica Lange	*Tootsie*
1983	Linda Hunt	*The Year of Living Dangerously*
1984	Peggy Ashcroft	*A Passage to India*
1985	Anjelica Huston	*Prizzi's Honor*
1986	Diane Wiest	*Hannah and Her Sisters*
1987	Olympia Dukakis	*Moonstruck*
1988	Geena Davis	*The Accidental Tourist*
1989	Brenda Fricker	*My Left Foot*

The winners of "Best Supporting Actress" Oscars during the 1990s are 1990: Whoopi Goldberg for *Ghost*; 1991: Mercedes Ruehl for *The Fisher King*; 1992: Marisa Tomei for *My Cousin Vinny*; 1993: Anna Paquin for *The Piano*; and 1994: Dianne Wiest for *Bullets Over Broadway*. *Tom Jones* is the only film that has received three nominations for "Best Supporting Actress."

AND THE WINNER IS . . .

THE 10

LAST WINNERS OF THE CANNES *PALME D'OR* FOR BEST MOVIE

Year	Movie	Country of Origin
1995	*Underground*	Yugoslavia
1994	*Pulp Fiction*	US
1993*	*Farewell My Concubine/*	China
	The Piano	Australia
1992	*Best Intentions*	Sweden
1991	*Barton Fink*	US
1990	*Wild at Heart*	US
1989	*sex, lies, and videotape*	US
1988	*Pelle the Conqueror*	Denmark
1987	*Under the Sun of Satan*	France
1986	*The Mission*	UK

* *Shared the prize*

THE 10

FIRST WINNERS OF THE CANNES *PALME D'OR* FOR BEST MOVIE

Year	Movie	Country of Origin
1949	*The Third Man*	UK
1951*	*Miracle in Milan*	Italy
	Miss Julie	Sweden
1952*	*Othello*	Morocco
	Two Cents Worth of Hope	Italy
1953	*Wages of Fear*	France
1954	*Gates of Hell*	Japan
1955	*Marty*	US
1956	*World of Silence*	France
1957	*Friendly Persuasion*	US
1958	*The Cranes Are Flying*	USSR
1959	*Black Orpheus*	France

* *Shared the prize*

In 1946 and 1947 there was no single "Best Film" prize; several films were honored jointly. These included such unlikely bedfellows as David Lean's *Brief Encounter* and Walt Disney's *Dumbo*. There was no Festival in 1948 or 1950.

THE 10

FIRST AMERICAN FILM INSTITUTE LIFETIME ACHIEVEMENT AWARD WINNERS

Year	Recipient
1973	John Ford
1974	James Cagney
1975	Orson Welles
1976	William Wyler
1977	Henry Fonda
1978	Bette Davis
1979	Alfred Hitchcock
1980	James Stewart
1981	Fred Astaire
1982	Frank Capra

DID YOU KNOW

THE GOLDEN GLOBE AWARDS

The Hollywood Foreign Press Association, a group of US-based journalists who report on the entertainment industry for the world press, present the Golden Globe Awards annually. Although the categories differ in some respects from those of the "Oscars," they are often a prediction of Oscars to come: in the "Best Picture" category their awards were identical on six out of 10 occasions in the first 10 years, a coincidence rate that it has continued to maintain ever since.

THE 10

LAST GOLDEN GLOBE AWARDS FOR BEST MUSICAL/ COMEDY MOVIE

Year	Movie
1995	*The Lion King*
1994	*Mrs. Doubtfire*
1993	*The Player*
1992	*Beauty and the Beast*
1991	*Green Card*
1990	*Driving Miss Daisy*
1989	*Working Girl*
1988	*Hope and Glory*
1987	*Hannah and Her Sisters*
1986	*Prizzi's Honor*

THE 10

LAST AMERICAN FILM INSTITUTE LIFETIME ACHIEVEMENT AWARD WINNERS

Year	Recipient
1995	Steven Spielberg
1994	Jack Nicholson
1993	Elizabeth Taylor
1992	Sidney Poitier
1991	Kirk Douglas
1990	David Lean
1989	Gregory Peck
1988	Jack Lemmon
1987	Barbara Stanwyck
1986	Billy Wilder

THE 10

LAST GOLDEN GLOBE AWARDS FOR "BEST DRAMA MOVIE"

Year	Movie
1995	*Forrest Gump*
1994	*Schindler's List*
1993	*Scent of a Woman*
1992	*Bugsy*
1991	*Dances With Wolves*
1990	*Born on the Fourth of July*
1989	*Rain Man*
1988	*The Last Emperor*
1987	*Platoon*
1986	*Out of Africa*

THE 10

LAST GOLDEN GLOBE AWARDS FOR "BEST ACTOR IN A MOTION PICTURE – DRAMA"

Year	Actor	Movie
1995	Tom Hanks	*Forrest Gump*
1994	Tom Hanks	*Philadelphia*
1993	Al Pacino	*Scent of a Woman*
1992	Nick Nolte	*The Prince of Tides*
1991	Jeremy Irons	*Reversal of Fortunes*
1990	Tom Cruise	*Born on the Fourth of July*
1989	Dustin Hoffman	*Rain Man*
1988	Michael Douglas	*Wall Street*
1987	Bob Hoskins	*Mona Lisa*
1986	Jon Voight	*Runaway Train*

THE 10

LAST GOLDEN GLOBE AWARDS FOR "BEST ACTOR IN A MUSICAL/COMEDY MOVIE"

Year	Actor	Movie
1995	Hugh Grant	*Four Weddings and a Funeral*
1994	Robin Williams	*Mrs. Doubtfire*
1993	Tim Robbins	*The Player*
1992	Robin Williams	*The Fisher King*
1991	Gerard Depardieu	*Green Card*
1990	Morgan Freeman	*Driving Miss Daisy*
1989	Tom Hanks	*Big*
1988	Robin Williams	*Good Morning Vietnam*
1987	Paul Hogan	*Crocodile Dundee*
1986	Jack Nicholson	*Prizzi's Honor*

THE 10

LAST GOLDEN GLOBE AWARDS FOR "BEST ACTRESS IN A MOTION PICTURE – DRAMA"

Year	Actress	Movie
1995	Jessica Lange	*Blue Skies*
1994	Holly Hunter	*The Piano*
1993	Emma Thompson	*Howard's End*
1992	Jodie Foster	*The Silence of the Lambs*
1991	Kathy Bates	*Misery*
1990	Michele Pfeiffer	*The Fabulous Baker Boys*
1989*	Jodie Foster Shirley MacLaine	*The Accused* *Madame Sousatzka*
1988	Shirley Kirkland	*Anna*
1987	Marlee Matlin	*Children of a Lesser God*
1986	Whoopi Goldberg	*The Color Purple*

* *Prize shared*

THE 10

LAST GOLDEN GLOBE AWARDS FOR "BEST ACTRESS IN A MUSICAL/COMEDY MOVIE"

Year	Actress	Movie
1995	Jamie Lee Curtis	*True Lies*
1994	Angela Bassett	*What's Love Got To Do With It*
1993	Miranda Richardson	*Enchanted April*
1992	Bett Midler	*For the Boys*
1991	Julia Roberts	*Pretty Woman*
1990	Jessica Tandy	*Driving Miss Daisy*
1989	Melanie Griffith	*Working Girl*
1988	Cher	*Moonstruck*
1987	Sissy Spacek	*Crimes of the Heart*
1986	Kathleen Turner	*Prizzi's Honor*

THE 10

FIRST GOLDEN GLOBE AWARDS FOR "BEST PICTURE"

Year	Movie	Year	Movie
1943	*The Song of Bernadette*	1949	*All the King's Men*
1944	*Going My Way* *	1950	*Sunset Boulevard*
1945	*The Lost Weekend* *	1951	*A Place in the Sun*
1946	*The Best Years of Our Lives* *	1952	*The Greatest Show on Earth*
1947	*Gentleman's Agreement* *		
1948	*Treasure of Sierra Madre* and *Johnny Belinda* #		

* *Also won "Best Picture" Academy Award*
# *Shared the prize*

148

MOVIE STARS – ACTORS

L ike the other Movie Top 10s, the Top 10 movies of actors are ranked according to the total rental fees paid to distributors by movie theaters in the US and Canada. This is regarded by the industry as a reliable guide to earnings in those markets. As a rule of thumb, doubling these rental figures roughly corresponds to world totals. Rental income is not the same as "box-office gross." While this is valid over a short period, comparing movies distributed in the same year for example, it only indicates the theater's earnings, which varies according to ticket price.

TOP 10
HARRISON FORD MOVIES

1	Star Wars	1977
2	Return of the Jedi	1983
3	The Empire Strikes Back	1980
4	Raiders of the Lost Ark	1981
5	Indiana Jones and the Last Crusade	1989
6	Indiana Jones and the Temple of Doom	1984
7	The Fugitive	1993
8	Clear and Present Danger	1994
9	American Graffiti	1973
10	Presumed Innocent	1990

TOP 10
SEAN CONNERY MOVIES

1	Indiana Jones and the Last Crusade	1989
2	The Hunt for Red October	1990
3	The Untouchables	1987
4	Rising Sun	1993
5	Thunderball	1965
6	Never Say Never Again	1983
7	Goldfinger	1964
8	Medicine Man	1992
9	Time Bandits	1981
10	A Bridge Too Far	1977

TOP 10
TOM CRUISE MOVIES

1	Rain Man	1988
2	Top Gun	1986
3	The Firm	1993
4	A Few Good Men	1992
5	Interview With the Vampire	1994
6	Days of Thunder	1990
7	Born on the Fourth of July	1989
8	Cocktail	1988
9	Risky Business	1983
10	Far and Away	1992

TOP 10
TOM HANKS MOVIES

1	Forrest Gump	1994
2	Sleepless in Seattle	1993
3	A League of Their Own	1992
4	Big	1988
5	Turner & Hooch	1989
6	Splash!	1984
7	Philadelphia	1993
8	Dragnet	1987
9	Bachelor Party	1984
10	Joe Versus the Volcano	1990

TOP 10
ANTHONY HOPKINS MOVIES

1	The Silence of the Lambs	1991
2	Bram Stoker's Dracula	1992
3	A Bridge Too Far	1977
4	Magic	1978
5	Howard's End	1992
6	The Elephant Man	1980
7	Shadowlands	1993
8	The Remains of the Day	1993
9	The Lion in Winter	1968
10	Freejack	1992

TOP 10
SYLVESTER STALLONE MOVIES

1	Rambo: First Blood 2	1985
2	Rocky IV	1985
3	Rocky III	1982
4	The Specialist	1994
5	Rocky	1976
6	Cliffhanger	1993
7	Rocky II	1979
8	Tango and Cash	1989
9	Cobra	1986
10	Demolition Man	1993

TOP 10
AL PACINO MOVIES

1	The Godfather	1972
2	Dick Tracy	1990
3	The Godfather Part III	1990
4	The Godfather Part II	1974
5	Sea of Love	1989
6	Scent of a Woman	1992
7	Scarface	1983
8	Dog Day Afternoon	1975
9	Carlito's Way	1993
10	Serpico	1973

TOP 10
ROBIN WILLIAMS MOVIES

1	Mrs. Doubtfire	1993
2	Hook	1991
3	Good Morning, Vietnam	1987
4	Dead Poets Society	1989
5	Popeye	1980
6	Awakenings	1990
7	The Fisher King	1991
8	Dead Again	1991
9	The World According to Garp	1982
10	Cadillac Man	1990

T O P 1 0

ARNOLD SCHWARZENEGGER MOVIES

1	Terminator 2: Judgment Day	1991
2	True Lies	1994
3	Total Recall	1990
4	Twins	1988
5	Kindergarten Cop	1990
6	Predator	1987
7	Last Action Hero	1993
8	Conan the Barbarian	1981
9	Commando	1985
10	The Terminator	1984

T O P 1 0

JACK NICHOLSON MOVIES

1	Batman	1989
2	A Few Good Men	1992
3	One Flew Over the Cuckoo's Nest	1975
4	Terms of Endearment	1983
5	Wolf	1994
6	The Witches of Eastwick	1987
7	The Shining	1980
8	Broadcast News	1987
9	Reds	1981
10	Easy Rider	1969

T O P 1 0

MEL GIBSON MOVIES

1	Lethal Weapon 3	1992
2	Lethal Weapon 2	1989
3	Maverick	1994
4	Bird on a Wire	1990
5	Lethal Weapon	1987
6	Forever Young	1992
7	Tequila Sunrise	1988
8	Mad Max Beyond Thunderdome	1985
9	Air America	1990
10	Mad Max 2: The Road Warrior	1981

T O P 1 0

RICHARD GERE MOVIES

1	Pretty Woman	1990
2	An Officer and a Gentleman	1982
3	Sommersby	1993
4	Looking for Mr Goodbar	1977
5	Final Analysis	1992
6	The Cotton Club	1984
7	American Gigolo	1980
8	Internal Affairs	1990
9	Breathless	1983
10	No Mercy	1986

T O P 1 0

KEVIN COSTNER MOVIES

1	Robin Hood: Prince of Thieves	1991
2	Dances With Wolves	1990
3	The Bodyguard	1992
4	The Untouchables	1987
5	JFK	1991
6	Field of Dreams	1989
7	The Big Chill	1983
8	Bull Durham	1988
9	Silverado	1985
10	No Way Out	1987

ACT OF MURDER
After two huge successes in the late 1970s, in Grease *and* Saturday Night Fever, *John Travolta's roles were unmemorable until his Oscar-nominat ed return as the killer Vincent Vega in Quentin Tarantino's* Pulp Fiction.

T O P 1 0

CLINT EASTWOOD MOVIES

1	Every Which Way But Loose	1978
2	In the Line of Fire	1993
3	Unforgiven	1992
4	Any Which Way You Can	1980
5	Sudden Impact	1983
6	Firefox	1982
7	The Enforcer	1976
8	Tightrope	1984
9	Heartbreak Ridge	1986
10	Escape from Alcatraz	1979

T O P 1 0

JOHN TRAVOLTA MOVIES

1	Grease	1978
2	Saturday Night Fever	1977
3	Look Who's Talking	1989
4	Staying Alive	1983
5	Pulp Fiction	1994
6	Urban Cowboy	1980
7	Look Who's Talking Too	1990
8	Carrie	1976
9	Two of a Kind	1983
10	Blow Out	1981

MOVIE STARS – ACTRESSES

TOP 10

SIGOURNEY WEAVER MOVIES

1	Ghostbusters	1984
2	Ghostbusters II	1989
3	Aliens	1986
4	Alien	1979
5	Alien³	1992
6	Dave	1993
7	Working Girl	1988
8	Gorillas in the Mist	1988
9	The Deal of the Century	1983
10	The Year of Living Dangerously	1982

Sigourney Weaver also had a fleeting minor part in *Annie Hall* (1977). If included, this would appear in 7th position.

TOP 10

DEMI MOORE MOVIES

1	Ghost	1990
2	A Few Good Men	1992
3	Indecent Proposal	1993
4	St. Elmo's Fire	1985
5	About Last Night	1986
6	Young Doctors in Love	1982
7	Blame it on Rio	1984
8	Mortal Thoughts	1991
9	The Seventh Sign	1988
10	One Crazy Summer	1986

Demi Moore has progressed from working as a teenaged model, through the TV soap *General Hospital*, to Hollywood movies. She is married to the actor Bruce Willis.

TOP 10

MELANIE GRIFFITH MOVIES

1	Working Girl	1988
2	Pacific Heights	1990
3	One-on-One	1977
4	Shining Through	1992
5	Paradise	1991
6	The Bonfire of the Vanities	1990
7	The Milagro Beanfield War	1988
8	Body Double	1984
9	Something Wild	1986
10	The Harrad Experiment*	1973

* Appeared as an extra only

TOP 10

CARRIE FISHER MOVIES

1	Star Wars	1977
2	Return of the Jedi	1983
3	The Empire Strikes Back	1980
4	When Harry Met Sally	1989
5	The Blues Brothers	1980
6	Shampoo	1975
7	Hannah and Her Sisters	1986
8	The 'Burbs	1989
9	Soapdish	1991
10	Sibling Rivalry	1990

TOP 10

MICHELLE PFEIFFER MOVIES

1	Batman Returns	1992
2	Wolf	1994
3	The Witches of Eastwick	1987
4	Scarface	1983
5	Tequila Sunrise	1988
6	Dangerous Liaisons	1988
7	The Age of Innocence	1993
8	Frankie and Johnny	1991
9	The Russia House	1990
10	The Fabulous Baker Boys	1989

TOP 10

MEG RYAN MOVIES

1	Top Gun	1986
2	Sleepless in Seattle	1993
3	When Harry Met Sally	1989
4	When a Man Loves a Woman	1994
5	Joe Versus the Volcano	1990
6	The Doors	1991
7	Innerspace	1987
8	The Presido	1988
9	Rich and Famous	1981
10	D.O.A.	1988

TOP 10

KATHLEEN TURNER MOVIES

1	Who Framed Roger Rabbit*	1988	7	Prizzi's Honour	1985
2	The War of the Roses	1989	8	Body Heat	1981
3	The Jewel of the Nile	1985	9	V.I. Warshawski	1991
4	Romancing the Stone	1984	10	The Man with Two Brains	1983
5	Peggy Sue Got Married	1986			
6	The Accidental Tourist	1988			

* Speaking voice of Jessica Rabbit; if excluded, the 10th movie in which she acted is Serial Mom *(1994).*

TOP 10

KIM BASINGER MOVIES

1	*Batman*	1989
2	*9½ Weeks*	1986
3	*Never Say Never Again*	1983
4	*Wayne's World 2*	1993
5	*The Natural*	1984
6	*Blind Date*	1987
7	*Final Analysis*	1992
8	*The Getaway*	1994
9	*No Mercy*	1986
10	*The Marrying Man*	1991

TOP 10

DIANE KEATON MOVIES

1	*The Godfather*	1972
2	*The Godfather, Part II*	1974
3	*Father of the Bride*	1991
4	*The Godfather, Part III*	1990
5	*Reds*	1981
6	*Annie Hall*	1977
7	*Manhattan*	1979
8	*Looking for Mr. Goodbar*	1977
9	*Baby Boom*	1987
10	*Crimes of the Heart*	1986

TOP 10

SHARON STONE MOVIES

1	*Total Recall*	1990
2	*Basic Instinct*	1992
3	*Last Action Hero*	1993
4	*Sliver*	1993
5	*Police Academy 4: Citizens on Patrol*	1987
6	*Intersection*	1994
7	*Action Jackson*	1988
8	*Above The Law/Nico*	1988
9	*Irreconcilable Differences*	1984
10	*King Solomon's Mines*	1985

TOP 10

MERYL STREEP MOVIES

1	*Kramer vs Kramer*	1979
2	*Out of Africa*	1985
3	*Death Becomes Her*	1992
4	*The Deer Hunter*	1978
5	*Silkwood*	1983
6	*Manhattan*	1979
7	*Postcards from the Edge*	1990
8	*Sophie's Choice*	1982
9	*Julia*	1982
10	*Heartburn*	1986

It is perhaps surprising that *Sophie's Choice*, the movie for which Meryl Streep won an Oscar, scores so far down this list, while one of her most celebrated movies, *The French Lieutenant's Woman* (1981), does not make her personal Top 10 at all.

TOP 10

WHOOPI GOLDBERG MOVIES

1	*Ghost*	1990
2	*Sister Act*	1992
3	*The Color Purple*	1985
4	*Star Trek: Generations*	1994
5	*Sister Act 2: Back in the Habit*	1993
6	*Made in America*	1993
7	*Soapdish*	1993
8	*National Lampoon's Loaded Weapon 1**	1993
9	*Jumpin' Jack Flash*	1986
10	*Corrina, Corrina*	1994

* *Uncredited cameo appearance*

Whoopi Goldberg also provided the voice of Shenzi in *The Lion King* (1994). If this were taken into account, it would appear in No. 1 position in her Top 10.

THE COLOR PURPLE
Suitably dressed, Whoopi Goldberg won "Best Actress" Golden Globe Award and an Oscar nomination for The Color Purple.

TOP 10

JODIE FOSTER MOVIES

1	*The Silence of the Lambs*	1990
2	*Maverick*	1994
3	*Sommersby*	1993
4	*The Accused*	1988
5	*Taxi Driver*	1976
6	*Freaky Friday*	1976
7	*Little Man Tate**	1991
8	*Alice Doesn't Live Here Any More*	1975
9	*Candleshoe*	1977
10	*Tom Sawyer*	1973

* *Also directed*

THE STUDIOS

T O P 1 0

20TH CENTURY-FOX MOVIES OF ALL TIME

1	*Star Wars*	1977
2	*Return of the Jedi*	1983
3	*The Empire Strikes Back*	1980
4	*Home Alone*	1990
5	*Mrs. Doubtfire*	1993
6	*Home Alone 2*	1992
7	*The Sound of Music*	1965
8	*True Lies*	1994
9	*Speed*	1994
10	*Die Hard 2*	1990

In 1912 William Fox, a nickelodeon owner from New York, founded a production company in California. Fox was a pioneer in the use of sound, particularly through the medium of Fox Movietone newsreels. In 1935 the Fox company was merged with 20th Century Pictures. 20th Century-Fox, as it was then called, achieved some of its greatest successes in the 1940s, especially a series of musicals starring Betty Grable, while under the control of Darryl F. Zanuck and Joseph M. Schenck. The 1950s and 1960s were less lucrative, however, and despite the box-office success of *The Sound of Music* (1965) the studio suffered a series of setbacks, including the failure of the vastly expensive *Cleopatra* (1963). Its return to prosperity began with *The French Connection* (1971) and was consolidated by the outstanding success of *Star Wars* (1977) and its sequels. In 1985 20th Century-Fox was acquired by Rupert Murdoch, thereby allowing Fox television stations to show the company's productions.

T O P 1 0

WARNER BROTHERS MOVIES OF ALL TIME

1	*Batman*	1989
2	*Batman Returns*	1992
3	*The Fugitive*	1993
4	*The Exorcist*	1973
5	*Robin Hood: Prince of Thieves*	1991
6	*Superman*	1978
7	*Lethal Weapon 3*	1993
8	*Gremlins*	1984
9	*Lethal Weapon 2*	1989
10	*Superman II*	1981

Warner Brothers' *The Jazz Singer* (1927), took its place in cinema history as the first successful movie with sound. The 1940s were a successful decade for the company, when cartoons such as Bugs Bunny became popular. Concentrating on TV production in the 1960s, movies again came to the fore in the 1970s. The company merged with Time, Inc. in 1989 to become Time Warner.

T O P 1 0

BUENA VISTA/WALT DISNEY MOVIES OF ALL TIME

1	*The Lion King*	1994
2	*Aladdin*	1992
3	*Pretty Woman*	1990
4	*Three Men and a Baby*	1987
5	*Who Framed Roger Rabbit?*	1988
6	*Snow White and the Seven Dwarfs**	1937
7	*Honey, I Shrunk the Kids*	1989
8	*Beauty and the Beast*	1991
9	*101 Dalmatians*	1961
10	*The Santa Clause*	1994

* *Originally released by RKO*

Walt Disney began his business in 1923, but did not distribute his movies until 1953 when Buena Vista was set up. Touchstone Pictures was established in 1966 to produce movies for a more adult audience.

T O P 1 0

MGM MOVIES OF ALL TIME

1	*Rain Man*	1988
2	*Gone With the Wind*	1939
3	*Rocky IV*	1985
4	*Rocky III*	1982
5	*Doctor Zhivago*	1965
6	*The Goodbye Girl*	1977
7	*War Games*	1983
8	*Poltergeist*	1982
9	*Ben Hur*	1959
10	*Moonstruck*	1987

With "more stars than there are in heaven," Metro Goldwyn Mayer enjoyed huge success in the 1930s and 1940s. However, after the departure of its head Louis B. Mayer in 1951, it suffered mixed fortunes. Taken over by airline tycoon Kirk Kerkorian in 1969, production ceased until the early 1980s, when it was merged with United Artists and relaunched with the very successful James Bond movies.

T O P 1 0

ORION MOVIES OF ALL TIME

1	*Dances With Wolves*	1990
2	*Platoon*	1986
3	*The Silence of the Lambs*	1991
4	*Arthur*	1981
5	*Back to School*	1986
6	*10*	1979
7	*Throw Momma from the Train*	1987
8	*Robocop*	1987
9	*Amadeus*	1984
10	*First Blood*	1982

TOP 10

PARAMOUNT MOVIES
OF ALL TIME

1	*Forrest Gump*	1994
2	*Raiders of the Lost Ark*	1981
3	*Indiana Jones and the Last Crusade*	1989
4	*Indiana Jones and the Temple of Doom*	1984
5	*Beverly Hills Cop*	1984
6	*Ghost*	1990
7	*Grease*	1978
8	*The Godfather*	1972
9	*Beverly Hills Cop II*	1987
10	*Top Gun*	1986

Founded in 1921 with its heyday in the 1930s and 1940s, Paramount's success began to fade in the 1950s. Taken over in 1966, the studio's forturnes did not improve until 1972 and *The Godfather*.

TOP 10

TRI-STAR MOVIES OF ALL TIME

1	*Terminator 2*	1991
2	*Rambo: First Blood 2*	1985
3	*Look Who's Talking*	1989
4	*Hook*	1991
5	*Sleepless in Seattle*	1993
6	*Total Recall*	1990
7	*Basic Instinct*	1992
8	*Cliffhanger*	1993
9	*Steel Magnolias*	1989
10	*Rambo 3*	1988

TOP 10

UNIVERSAL MOVIES
OF ALL TIME

1	*E.T.: The Extra-Terrestrial*	1982
2	*Jurassic Park*	1993
3	*Jaws*	1975
4	*Back to the Future*	1985
5	*The Sting*	1973
6	*Back to the Future, Part II*	1989
7	*National Lampoon's Animal House*	1978
8	*The Flintstones*	1994
9	*On Golden Pond*	1981
10	*Smokey and the Bandit*	1977

Founded in 1912, Universal Pictures, the world's largest movie studio, changed hands in 1936, 1952, and 1962, when it was developed as a TV production company. It is now owned by Matsushita, a Japanese multinational.

TOP 10

UNITED ARTISTS MOVIES
OF ALL TIME

1	*One Flew Over the Cuckoo's Nest*	1975
2	*Rocky*	1976
3	*Rocky II*	1979
4	*Fiddler on the Roof*	1971
5	*Apocalypse Now*	1979
6	*Moonraker*	1979
7	*Thunderball*	1965
8	*Revenge of the Pink Panther*	1978
9	*The Spy Who Loved Me*	1977
10	*Around the World in 80 Days*	1956

United Artists was formed in 1919 by actors including Charlie Chaplin and Douglas Fairbanks, together with director D.W. Griffith, to provide an independent means of producing and distributing their movies. It never actually owned a studio, but rented production facilities. After many vicissitudes, and a successful run in the 1970s with the consistently successful James Bond movies, it was merged with MGM in 1981.

TOP 10

COLUMBIA MOVIES
OF ALL TIME

1	*Ghostbusters*	1984
2	*Tootsie*	1982
3	*Close Encounters of the Third Kind*	1977/80
4	*A Few Good Men*	1992
5	*City Slickers*	1991
6	*Ghostbusters II*	1989
7	*Kramer vs Kramer*	1979
8	*Stir Crazy*	1980
9	*The Karate Kid Part II*	1986
10	*A League of Their Own*	1992

Harry Cohn and his brother Jack founded Columbia in 1924, building it up to rival the established giants MGM and Paramount. In 1934 Frank Capra's *It Happened One Night*, starring Clark Gable and Claudette Colbert, won Best Picture, Director, Actor, and Actress Oscars. The studio's success was further consolidated by stars such as Rita Hayworth, movies ranging from *Lost Horizon* (1937) to *The Jolson Story* (1946), and serials such as *Batman*. The 1950s saw such award-winning movies as *The Bridge on the River Kwai* (1957), *On the Waterfront* (1954), and *From Here to Eternity* (1953). Classics of the 1960s included *Lawrence of Arabia* (1962) and *A Man For All Seasons* (1966), and the Columbia-distributed *Easy Rider*. Taken over by Coca-Cola after an uneasy period in the 1970s, the 1980s saw many hits such as *Ghostbusters* (1984). Under the control of English producer David Puttnam for two years, Columbia took over Tri-Star Pictures before being acquired by Sony Corporation.

RADIO, TV, & VIDEO

TOP 10

LONGEST-RUNNING PROGRAMS ON NATIONAL PUBLIC RADIO

1	*All Things Considered*
2	*National Press Club*
3	*BBC News and Science Magazines*
4	*Weekend All Things Considered*
5	*Marian McPartland's Piano Jazz*
6	*Morning Edition*
7	*Horizons*
8	*NPR Playhouse*
9	*NPR World of Opera*
10	*St. Louis Symphony*

National Public Radio and Public Broadcasting Service television were born out of the Public Broadcasting Act signed by President Johnson on November 7, 1967. The first known radio program in the US, consisting of two selections of music, the reading of a poem, and a short talk, went out on Christmas Eve, 1906. Broadcast by Reginald Aubrey Fessenden from his experimental radio station in Brant Rock, Massachusetts, the program was heard by radio operators on ships within a radius of several hundred miles. The first commercial radio station was KDKA in Pittsburgh, which started broadcasting on November 2, 1920: the following decade saw huge increases in the sales of radio receiving equipment, matched by a rapid growth in the number of transmitting stations. However, unlike the UK, where the longest-running radio program (*The Week's Good Cause*) started on January 24, 1926, and is still on the air, most of the oldest American programs have been going for less than a quarter of a century. *All Things Considered*, the longest-running National Public Radio program, was first broadcast on May 3, 1971. Nos. 2 to 7 date from the 1970s, and Nos. 8 to 10 from the early 1980s. (It is interesting to note that a British radio program from the BBC appears at No. 3 on the NPR list.)

THE 10

LAST GEORGE FOSTER PEABODY BROADCASTING AWARDS WON BY NATIONAL PUBLIC RADIO*

	Radio Programs	Year
1	*Tobacco Stories and Wade in the Water: African American Sacred Music Traditions* (NPR/Smithsonian Institution)	1994
2	*Health Reform Coverage*	1993
3	*Prisoners in Bosnia*	1992
4	*The Coverage of the Judge Clarence Thomas Confirmation*	1991
5	*Manicu's Story: The War in Mozambique*	1990
6	Scott Simon's Radio Essays on *Weekend Edition Saturday*	1989
7	*Cowboys on Everest*	1988
8	*The Sunday Show* and *Taylor Made Piano: A Jazz History*	1983
9	*Jazz Alive*	1981
10	*Dialogues on a Tightrope: An Italian Mosaic*	1979

* *Includes only programs made or coproduced by NPR.*

T O P 1 0
MOST LISTENED-TO RADIO STATIONS IN THE US

	Station	City	Format	Listeners*
1	WRKS-FM	New York	Black	163,300
2	WABC	New York	Talk	147,000
3	WLTW-FM	New York	Soft Adult Contemporary	143,700
4	WCBS-FM	New York	Oldies	133,100
5	WBLS-FM	New York	Black	128,600
6	KFI	New York	Talk	119,800
7	WXRK-FM	New York	Classic Adult Oriented Albums	119,700
8	WPLJ-FM	New York	Contemporary Hit Radio	116,800
9	KOST-FM	Los Angeles	Adult Contemporary	110,200
10	WOR	New York	Talk	105,500

* Average for listeners aged 12+ listening at any time

Source: Duncan's American Radio, Inc.

T O P 1 0
RADIO-OWNING COUNTRIES IN THE WORLD

	Country	Radios per 1,000 population
1	US	2,118
2	Guam	1,403
3	Australia	1,273
4	Bermuda	1,260
5	Gibraltar	1,173
6	Netherlands Antilles	1,165
7	UK	1,146
8	Monaco	1,126
9	Denmark	1,033
10	Canada	1,030

The prevalence of radios in island communities is understandable as a method of maintaining contact with the outside world. Apart from South Korea (1,002 radios per 1,000), a country occupying a peninsula, two other islands – American Samoa (1,007) and Norfolk Island (1,000) – have ratios equivalent to at least one per inhabitant. These levels contrast with those of certain African countries with one radio for every 20 or more people.

T O P 1 0
RADIO FORMATS IN THE US

	Format	Share (%)*
1	News/Talk	16.0
2	Adult Contemporary	15.2
3	Country	12.6
4	Top 40	9.1
5=	Urban	8.9
5=	Album Rock	8.9
7	Oldies	7.7
8	Spanish	5.0
9	Classic Rock	3.2
10	Adult Standards	3.0

* Of all radio listening during an average week, 6 am to midnight, Oct–Dec 1994, for listeners aged 12+

News/Talk tops the survey for the first time since spring of 1989.

T O P 1 0
US RADIO STATIONS BY AUDIENCE SHARE

	Station	City	Share (%)*
1	WIVX-FM	Knoxville Tennessee	32.7
2	WXBQ-FM	Johnson City Tennessee	28.5
3	WTCR-FM	Huntington West Virginia	28.1
4	KLLL-FM	Lubbock Texas	27.7
5	WJBC	Bloomington Illinois	26.9
6	WFGY-FM	Altoona Iowa	24.6
7	WWNC	Asheville North Carolina	24.2
8	WQBE-FM	Charleston West Virginia	24.1
9	WUSY-FM	Chattanooga Tennessee	23.9
10	KCCY-FM	Pueblo Colorado	23.2

* Of all radio listening for listeners aged 12+

All the stations listed specialize in country music, with the exception of WJBC, which is a "full service" station, broadcasting talk, news, and middle-of-the-road music. Country music has been growing in popularity – and in radio terms in market share – for the past decade. Many of these stations in America's heartland have ridden that wave of popularity.

Source: Duncan's American Radio, Inc.

TV FIRSTS

TEN US TV FIRSTS

1 The first President to appear on TV

Franklin D. Roosevelt was seen opening the World's Fair, New York, on April 30, 1939.

2 The first king and queen televised in the US

The UK's King George VI and Queen Elizabeth were shown visiting the World's Fair on June 10, 1939.

3 The first televised NFL baseball game

The match between the Brooklyn Dodgers (a major league team from 1930 to 1943) and the Philadelphia Eagles, at Ebbets Field, Brooklyn, New York, was broadcast on August 26, 1939.

4 The first televised professional football game

The Brooklyn Dodgers v Philadelphia Eagles match at Ebbets Field was shown on October 22, 1939.

5 The first TV commercial

A 20-second commercial for a Bulova clock was broadcast by WNBT New York on July 1, 1941.

6 The first soap opera on TV

The first regular daytime serial, DuMont TV network's A Woman to Remember, began its run on February 21, 1947.

7 The first broadcast of a current TV show

NBC's Meet the Press was first broadcast on November 6, 1947.

8 The first televised atomic bomb explosion

An "Operation Ranger" detonation at Frenchman Flats, Nevada, on February 1, 1951, was televised by KTLA, Los Angeles.

9 The first networked coast-to-coast color TV show

The Tournament of Roses parade at Pasadena, California, hosted by Don Ameche, was seen in color in 21 cities nationwide on January 1, 1954.

10 The first presidential news conference televised live

President John F. Kennedy was shown in a live broadcast from the auditorium of the State Department Building, Washington, DC, on January 25, 1961. (A filmed conference with President Eisenhower had been shown on January 19, 1955.)

THE 10

FIRST PROGRAMS ON BBC TELEVISION

Time	Program
Monday November 2, 1936	
1 15:02	Opening ceremony by Postmaster General G.C. Tryon
2 15:15	British Movietone News No. 387 (repeated several times during the next few days)
3 15:23	*Variety* – Adele Dixon (singer), Buck and Bubbles (comic dancers), and the Television Orchestra
	(15.31 close; 15.32 Television Orchestra continues in sound only with music.)
4 21:05	Film: *Television Comes to London*
5 21:23	*Picture Page* (magazine program featuring interviews with transatlantic flyer Jim Mollison, tennis champion Kay Stammers, King's Bargemaster Bossy Phelps, and others, ghost stories from Algernon Blackwood, and various musical interludes)
6 22:11	Speech by Lord Selsdon, followed by close
Tuesday November 3, 1936	
7 15:04	Exhibits from the Metropolitan and Essex Canine Society's Show – "Animals described by A. Croxton Smith, OBE"
8 15:28	*The Golden Hind* – "a model of Drake's famous ship, made by L.A. Stock, a bus driver"
9 15:46	*Starlight* with comedians Bebe Daniels and Ben Lyon (followed by repeat of items 7 and 8)
10 21:48	*Starlight* with Manuela Del Rio

Although there were earlier low-definition experimental broadcasts, BBC television's high-definition public broadcasting service – the first in the world – was inaugurated on a daily basis on November 2, 1936. During the first three months, two parallel operating systems were in use: the opening programs were thus broadcast twice, first on the Baird system, and repeated slightly later on the Marconi-EMI system.

MTV LOGO
Another first on American TV was the inauguration of MTV, the world's first 24-hour music video network, on August 1, 1981. It has largely taken over music programming from the four major US networks.

THE 10

FIRST COUNTRIES TO HAVE TELEVISION

(High-definition regular public broadcasting service)

	Country	Year
1	UK	1936
2=	US	1939
2=	USSR	1939
4	France	1948
5=	Brazil	1950
5=	Cuba	1950
5=	Mexico	1950
8=	Argentina	1951
8=	Denmark	1951
8=	Netherlands	1951

TOP 10

LONGEST-RUNNING PROGRAMS ON BRITISH TELEVISION

	Program	First shown
1	*Come Dancing*	Sep 29, 1950
2	*Panorama*	Nov 11, 1953
3	*What the Papers Say*	Nov 5, 1956
4	*The Sky at Night*	Apr 24, 1957
5	*Grandstand*	Oct 11, 1958
6	*Blue Peter*	Oct 16, 1958
7	*Coronation Street*	Dec 9, 1960
8	*Songs of Praise*	Oct 1, 1961
9	*Dr. Who*	Nov 23, 1963
10	*Top of the Pops*	Jan 1, 1964

Only programs appearing every year since their first screenings are listed, and all are BBC programs except the Lancashire TV soap opera *Coronation Street*. *The Sky at Night*, a popular series on astronomy, has the additional distinction of having had the same host, Patrick Moore, since its first program. Although *The Sooty Show* has been screened intermittently, Sooty, a teddy-bear glove puppet, is the longest-serving TV personality. Several US imports have also enjoyed lasting success; one of the most notable is *Dallas*, which does not make it onto this list but ran from 1978 to 1991.

TOP 10

WAYS THE NEW SHOW WILL BE BETTER *LATE NIGHT WITH DAVID LETTERMAN*

10	Kids watch free
9	No more relying on cheap G.E. jokes (unless we're really stuck)
8	My new "Rappin' Dave" character
7	Inhaling asbestos particles from renovation makes me extra "wacky"
6	If they applaud really loudly, everyone in tonight's audience gets a brand-new car!
5	No more pressure to book NBC president Robert C. Wright's son-in-law, Marv Albert
4	It's the same show, better time, new sta. . . – Oh, for the love of God, stop saying that!
3	I'm more focused since my breakup with Loni
2	Every Friday, Paul and I swap medication
1	A whole new wardrobe for Vanna!

Now part of US popular culture, Letterman's "Top 10" list made its bow on September 18, 1985 on NBC-TV's *Late Night With David Letterman* and has endured as one of the most popular features on his show, making the move with him to CBS in 1993 with its nightly inclusion on *The Late Show With David Letterman*.

The Top 10 of Everything pays tribute to Mr. Letterman's contribution to Top 10s by publishing this, his first list broadcast on his first CBS show on August 30, 1993.

Source: CBS Broadcast Group

TOP 10 DAVE
Master of the humorous Top 10 list, David Letterman's show is now aptly celebrating its first 10 years.

THE 10

FIRST GUESTS ON *THE TONIGHT SHOW* – STARRING JOHNNY CARSON

1	Groucho Marx	Comic actor
2	Joan Crawford	Actress
3	Rudy Vallee	Singer/actor
4	Tony Bennett	Singer
5	Mel Brooks	Comic
6	Tom Pedi	Actor
7	The Phoenix Singers	Vocal trio
8	Tallulah Bankhead	Actress
9	Shelley Berman	Comedian
10	Artie Shaw	Band leader

Originally a two-hour weeknightly show taped in New York, Carson took over *The Tonight Show* from Jack Parr on October 1, 1962, and became America's late-night TV legend for almost three decades, his final show airing on May 22, 1992. Groucho Marx was actually the surprise host for the first 15 minutes of the broadcast, flying in from Hollywood to introduce Carson as the *The Tonight Show*'s new permanent host.

Source: Carson Productions

TOP TV

TOP 10

TV-OWNING COUNTRIES IN THE WORLD

	Country	Homes with TV
1	China	227,500,000
2	US	94,200,000
3	Russia	48,269,000
4	Japan	41,328,000
5	Brazil	38,880,000
6	Germany	36,295,000
7	India	35,000,000
8	UK	22,446,000
9	France	21,667,000
10	Italy	20,812,000

Taking population into account, China disappears from the list and the US comes at the top with 790 sets per 1,000 people.

TOP 10

NIELSEN'S DAYTIME SOAP OPERAS IN THE US, 1993–94

	Program	Households viewing total	%
1	*Young and Restless*	8,084,000	8.6
2	*All My Children*	6,204,000	6.6
3	*General Hospital*	5,828,000	6.2
4	*Bold and the Beautiful*	5,730,000	6.1
5	*As the World Turns*	5,452,000	5.8
6=	*Days of Our Lives*	5,364,000	5.6
6=	*One Life to Live*	5,264,000	5.6
8	*Guiding Light*	5,076,000	5.4
9	*Another World*	3,290,000	3.5
10	*Loving*	2,538,000	2.7

© Copyright 1994 Nielsen Media Research

TOP 10

NIELSEN'S TV AUDIENCES OF ALL TIME IN THE US

	Program	Date	Households viewing total	%
1	*M*A*S*H* Special	Feb 28, 1983	50,150,000	60.2
2	*Dallas*	Nov 21, 1980	41,470,000	53.3
3	*Roots* Part 8	Jan 30, 1977	36,380,000	51.1
4	Super Bowl XVI	Jan 24, 1982	40,020,000	49.1
5	Super Bowl XVII	Jan 30, 1983	40,500,000	48.6
6	XVII Winter Olympics	Feb 23, 1994	45,690,000	48.5
7	Super Bowl XX	Jan 26, 1986	41,490,000	48.3
8	*Gone With the Wind* Pt. 1	Nov 7, 1976	33,960,000	47.7
9	*Gone With the Wind* Pt. 2	Nov 8, 1976	33,750,000	47.4
10	Super Bowl XII	Jan 15, 1978	34,410,000	47.2

© Copyright 1994 Nielsen Media Research

As more and more households have television sets, the most recently screened programs naturally tend to be watched by larger audiences, which distorts the historical picture. By listing the Top 10 according to percentage of households viewing, we get a clearer picture of who watches what. The last-ever episode of *M*A*S*H* had both the largest number and highest percentage of households watching. The last episode of *Cheers* (broadcast May 20, 1993; 42,360,000 households/45.5 percent) only just failed to gain a place in the Top 10.

SUPERBOWL 1982
Bengals's Pete Johnson (top) is stopped by the 49ers 3rd quarter goal line stand.

TOP 10

NIELSEN'S MOVIES OF ALL TIME ON PRIME-TIME NETWORK TV

	Film	Year released	Broadcast	Rating %*
1	*Gone With the Wind* Pt. 1	1939	Nov 7, 1976	47.7
2	*Gone With the Wind* Pt. 2	1939	Nov 8, 1976	47.4
3=	*Love Story*	1970	Oct 1, 1972	42.3
3=	*Airport*	1970	Nov 11, 1973	42.3
5	*The Godfather, Part II*	1974	Nov 18, 1974	39.4
6	*Jaws*	1975	Nov 4, 1979	39.1
7	*The Poseidon Adventure*	1972	Oct 27, 1974	39.0
8=	*True Grit*	1969	Nov 12, 1972	38.9
8=	*The Birds*	1963	Jan 6, 1968	38.9
10	*Patton*	1970	Nov 19, 1972	38.5

* *Of households viewing*

© *Copyright 1994 Nielsen Media Research*

All the movies listed are dramas made for theatrical release, but if such productions were included, the controversial 1983 made-for-TV post-nuclear war movie, *The Day After* (screened on November 20, 1983) would rank in 3rd place with a rating of 46.0 percent. It is significant that all the most watched movies on TV were broadcast before the dawn of the video era, and attracted substantial audiences to whom this was the only opportunity to see a particular movie that they might have missed or wished to see again.

BIG STARS OF THE SMALL SCREEN
Roseanne, starring Roseanne Barr and John Goodman, is hugely popular both in the US and worldwide. It is one of the most-watched of all current TV programs, although it is not on Nielsen's Top 10 list.

TOP 10

MOST WATCHED PROGRAMS ON PBS TELEVISION*

	Program	Viewers
1	*National Geographic Special: The Sharks*	24,100,000
2	*National Geographic Special: Land of the Tiger*	22,400,000
3	*National Geographic Special: The Grizzlies*	22,300,000
4	*Great Moments With National Geographic*	21,300,000
5	*Best of Wild America: The Babies*	19,300,000
6	*National Geographic Special: The Incredible Machine*	19,000,000
7	*The Music Man*	18,700,000
8	*National Geographic Special: Polar Bear Alert*	18,400,000
9	*National Geographic Special: Lions of the African Night*	18,100,000
10	*National Geographic Special: Rain Forest*	18,000,000

TOP 10

NIELSEN'S DOCUMENTARIES IN THE US, 1993–94

	Program	Households viewing total	%
1	*60 Minutes*	19,720,000	20.9
2	*20/20*	19,910,000	14.8
3	*Turning Point*	13,020,000	13.8
4	*48 Hours*	10,910,000	11.6
5	*Dateline NBC*	10,150,000	10.8
6	*Now with Tom Brokaw and Katie Curic*	10,080,000	10.7
7	*Eye to Eye with Connie Chung*	9,780,000	10.4
8	*Cops 2*	7,720,000	8.2
9	*Cops*	7,060,000	7.5
10	*National Geographic on Assignment*	6,820,000	7.2

© *Copyright 1994 Nielsen Media Research*

TOP 10

NIELSEN'S ANIMATED TV PROGRAMS IN THE US, 1993–94

	Program	Households viewing total	%
1	*X-Men*	4,700,000	5.0
2	*Terrible Thunderlizards*	3,984,000	4.2
3	*Power Rangers (Saturday)*	3,854,000	4.1
4=	*Garfield and Friends*	3,760,000	4.0
4=	*Taz-Mania*	3,760,000	4.0
4=	*Tiny Toons (Saturday)*	3,760,000	4.0
7	*Animaniacs*	3,384,000	3.6
8=	*Batman*	3,290,000	3.5
8=	*Carmen Sandiego*	3,290,000	3.5
8=	*Power Rangers*	3,290,000	3.5

© *Copyright 1994 Nielsen Media Research*

* *As of May 1994*

CABLE TV & VIDEO

TOP 10

MOVIE RENTALS ON VIDEO, 1994

	Movie	1994 release	Video earnings($)*
1	The Fugitive	Mar 10	50,200,000
2	Mrs. Doubtfire	Apr 26	41,900,000
3	Ace Ventura: Pet Detective	Jun 14	39,600,000
4	The Pelican Brief	Jun 15	37,300,000
5	Jurassic Park	Oct 4	34,500,000
6	In The Line of Fire	Feb 9	34,300,000
7	Philadelphia	Jun 29	30,500,000
8	Grumpy Old Men	Jul 6	29,700,000
9	Tombstone	Jun 22	28,300,000
10	Speed	Nov 16	27,600,000

* Spent by US consumers renting the title during its first four months of release

TOP 10

BESTSELLING CHILDREN'S VIDEOS OF 1994 IN THE US

1 *The Return of Jafar*

2 *Mighty Morphin Power Rangers Vol. 1*

3 *Barney & Gang: Let's Pretend*

4 *Mighty Morphin Power Rangers Vol. 4*

5 *Mighty Morphin Power Rangers Vol. 5*

6 *Barney's Alphabet Zoo*

7 *Mighty Morphin Power Rangers Vol. 2*

8 *Mighty Morphin Power Rangers Vol. 3*

9 *Barney Live: In New York City*

10 *Dr. Seuss: How the Grinch Stole Christmas*

Such has been the success of both the *Barney* and *Power Rangers* videos that in 1993 five of each dominated the Top 10, and a year on the *Power Rangers* tapes continued their success. However, Disney's *The Return of Jafar*, a video-only release, capitalized on the international popularity of both the *Aladdin* film and tape, reaching the top slot.

TOP 10

REGIONAL CABLE CHANNELS IN THE US

	Channel	Subscribers*
1	Madison Square Garden Network	5,100,000
2	Home Sports Entertainment	4,300,000
3	Prime Sports#	4,200,000
4	Sport South	3,837,000
5	Sunshine Network	3,573,200
6	The California Channel	3,555,634
7	Home Team Sports	2,700,000
8	SportsChannel Chicago	2,245,472
9	KBL Sports Network	2,100,000
10	SportsChannel Philadelphia	1,900,000

* As of December 31, 1994
\# Formerly known as Prime Ticket

TOP 10

CABLE DELIVERY SYSTEMS IN US CITIES

	Location	Operator	Subscribers*
1	New York, New York	Time Warner Cable	1,007,036
2	Long Island, New York	Cablevision Systems	610,717
3	Orlando, Florida	Time Warner Cable	492,684
4	Puget Sound, Washington	Viacom	424,500
5	Phoenix, Arizona	Times Mirror	372,201
6	Tampa/St. Petersburg, Florida	Paragon	327,954
7	San Diego, California	Cox Cable	326,525
8	Bronx/Brooklyn, New York	Cablevision Systems	320,261
9	Los Angels, California	Continental	279,672
10	San Antonio, Texas	KBLCOM	260,700

* Ranked by locations with most subscribers to one system, as of December 31, 1994

The purchase of Tele Cable will further enhance the market share of Denver-based TCI (Telecommunications, Inc.), America's largest cable operator (Time Warner Cable is ranked second). Owned by media visionary John Malone, TCI delivers cable TV to more than 11,000,000 homes. The first threat to cable-based systems comes from DirecTV. Owned by GM and Hughes Electronics, it uses DBS (Digital Broadcast Satellite) to deliver high-quality programming via inexpensive 18-inch satellite dishes, and is aimed initially at uncabled rural areas where large and expensive dishes have previously been the norm.

TOP 10

PAY CABLE CHANNELS IN THE US

	Channel	Subscribers*
1	Home Box Office	18,000,000
2	The Disney Channel	7,830,000
3	Showtime	7,600,000
4	Cinemax	6,700,000
5	Encore	5,100,000
6	The Movie Channel	2,700,000
7	Starz	1,000,000
8	Flix	900,000
9	TV-Japan	25,000
10	ANA Television Network	10,000

* As of December 31, 1994

TOP 10

NETWORK CABLE CHANNELS IN THE US

	Channel	Subscribers*
1	USA Network	63,193,000
2	ESPN	63,104,000
3	The Discovery Channel	62,968,000
4	TBS Superstation	61,896,000
5	TNT	60,960,000
6	Nickelodeon	60,929,000
7	Cable News Network	60,742,000
8	C-SPAN	60,600,000
9	Arts & Entertainment	60,114,000
10	The Family Channel	59,502,000

* As of December 31, 1994

Numbers 4, 5, and 7 are all owned by Turner Broadcasting System, based in Atlanta, Georgia, from where in 1993 he also successfully launched the Cartoon Network – which already has more than 11,000,000 subscribers.

TOP 10

HORROR MOVIE RENTALS ON VIDEO

	Movie	1994 release	Video earnings($)*
1	Jason Goes to Hell	Jan 19	6,060,000
2	The Stand	Aug 17	3,150,000
3	Body Snatchers	Jul 13	2,890,000
4	Leprechaun 2	Sept 7	2,120,000
5	Brainscan	Nov 2	1,620,000
6	When a Stranger Calls Back	Feb 9	1,370,000
7	Pumpkinhead 2: Bloodwings	Oct 19	1,020,000
8	The Dark	Jun 8	820,000
9	Return of the Living Dead 3	Apr 27	750,000
10	The Hidden 2	Jul 20	760,000

* Spent by US consumers renting the title during its first four months of release

TOP 10

DRAMA MOVIE RENTALS ON VIDEO

	Movie	1994 release	Video earnings($)*
1	Philadelphia	Jun 29	30,500,000
2	A Perfect World	May 4	22,300,000
3	The Man Without a Face	Feb 16	19,600,000
4	Schindler's List	Aug 17	18,200,000
5	What's Love Got To Do With It	Mar 23	16,600,000
6	Rudy	May 25	15,100,000
7	My Life	Jun 8	15,300,000
8	Intersection	Aug 10	14,400,000
9	In the Name of the Father	Jun 29	14,400,000
10	The Joy Luck Club	Mar 30	13,700,000

* Spent by US consumers renting the title during its first four months of release

TOP 10

ACTION RENTALS ON VIDEO

	Movie	1994 release	Video earnings ($)*
1	The Fugitive	Mar 10	50,200,000
2	Speed	Nov 16	27,600,000
3	Demolition Man	Mar 2	25,100,000
4	Striking Distance	Mar 2	19,100,000
5	The Last Action Hero	Jan 26	20,300,000
6	Hard Target	Jan 26	17,900,000
7	Carlito's Way	Apr 6	17,000,000
8	The Program	Feb 16	15,100,000
9	Judgement Night	Mar 9	13,200,000
10	True Romance	Jan 5	12,700,000

* Spent by US consumers renting the title during its first four months of release

TOP 10

COMEDY RENTALS ON VIDEO

	Movie	1994 release	Video earnings ($)*
1	Mrs. Doubtfire	Apr 26	41,900,000
2	Ace Ventura: Pet Detective	Jun 14	39,600,000
3	Grumpy Old Men	Jul 6	29,700,000
4	Cool Runnings	Apr 13	25,900,000
5	Beethoven's 2nd	Aug 9	21,100,000
6	Sister Act 2	Jul 13	20,100,000
7	Rookie of the Year	Jan 26	19,800,000
8	Son-in-Law	Feb 23	19,600,000
9	Hocus Pocus	Jan 5	19,400,000
10	Robin Hood: Men in Tights	Jan 12	18,600,000

* Spent by US consumers renting the title during its first four months of release

THE COMMERCIAL WORLD

TOP 10

PAPER CONSUMERS IN THE WORLD

	Country	Total tonnes	Annual consumption per capita lb	Annual consumption per capita kg
1	US	77,502,000	679	308
2	Sweden	2,574,000	659	299
3	Denmark	1,337,000	571	259
4	Japan	29,091,000	518	235
5	Belgium/ Luxembourg	2,345,000	500	227
6	Netherlands	3,322,000	487	221
7	Finland	1,103,000	485	220
8	Switzerland	1,455,000	474	215
9	Germany	16,629,000	459	208
10	Canada	5,583,000	456	207

So much for the "paperless office": the coming of computers, with their relative ease of printing, has increased – rather than reduced – international paper consumption, while the proliferation of junk mail, packaging, and newspaper publishing has contributed to the world's voracious appetite for paper. Currently, the average US citizen consumes the equivalent of five times his own weight in paper annually, and despite various curbs, such as recycling, the United Nations has predicted that by the year 2010 the nation's total demand will have reached 113,422,000 tonnes, or 858 lb/389 kg for each member of the 291,290,000 population projected for that year.

TOP 10

EMPLOYERS IN THE US

	Industry	Employees
1	Retail trade*	19,346,300
2	Durable goods manufacturing	10,235,400
3	Education (public and private)	9,718,100
4	Health services	9,612,900
5	Government#	9,544,900
6	Nondurable goods manufacturing	7,804,100
7	Wholesale trade	6,045,100
8	Business services	5,312,600
9	Construction	4,471,200
10	Transportation	3,486,600

* Includes eating and drinking places
\# Includes Postal Service and federal, state, and local governments

TOP 10

COUNTRIES WITH MOST WORKERS

	Country	Economically active population*
1	China	584,569,000
2	India	314,904,000
3	US	128,458,000
4	Indonesia	75,508,000
5	Russia	73,809,000
6	Japan	65,780,000
7	Brazil	64,468,000
8	Bangladesh	50,744,000
9	Germany	39,405,000
10	Pakistan	33,829,000

* Excluding unpaid groups, such as students, housewives, and retired people

TOP 10

FAIRS IN THE US

	Fair	Attendance (1994)
1	State Fair of Texas, Dallas	3,298,070
2	New Mexico State Fair, Albuquerque	1,891,415
3	State Fair of Oklahoma, Oklahoma City	1,860,355
4	Houston (Texas) Livestock Show	1,616,113
5	Minnesota State Fair, St. Paul	1,561,930
6	Los Angeles County Fair, Pomona	1,365,631
7	Western Washington Fair, Puyallup	1,358,614
8	Florida State Fair, Tampa	1,298,383
9	Colorado State Fair, Pueblo	1,116,978
10	The Big E (Eastern States Exposition), West Springfield	1,115,714

TOP 10

MOST DANGEROUS JOBS IN THE US

	Job	Deaths per 100,000
1	Fishers	155.0
2	Timber-cutters and loggers	133.0
3	Aircraft pilots and navigators	103.0
4	Structural metal workers	76.0
5	Taxicab drivers and chauffeurs	50.0
6	Electric power line and cable installers and repairers	38.0
7	Farm operators, managers, and supervisors	36.0
8	Construction laborers	33.0
9	Truck drivers	26.0
10	Driver-sales workers	23.0

Together with the 11th-placed Farm workers (distinct from No. 7 "Farm operators"), the top 11 job categories account for nearly one third of the some 6,300 fatalities reported in 1993. The risk attached to most "white-collar" jobs is under 10 per 100,000, with some being placed extremely low – chances of death at work among embalmers and librarians, for example, is put at zero. The work of such specialists as bomb-disposal experts, astronauts, and deep-sea divers would qualify them for inclusion, but the actual numbers of persons engaged in these activities are relatively small and the risk assessment thus statistically undetermined. Since four out of 42 US Presidents have been killed in office, this profession might also be considered "high risk."

TOP 10

LEAST STRESSFUL JOBS IN THE US

1	Musical instrument repairer
2	Industrial machine repairer
3	Medical records technician
4	Pharmacist
5	Software engineer
6	Typist/word processor
7	Librarian
8	Janitor
9	Book keeper
10	Forklift operator

TOP 10

MOST STRESSFUL JOBS IN THE US

1	US President
2	Firefighter
3	Racing car driver
4	Astronaut
5	Surgeon
6	National Football League player
7	Police officer
8	Osteopath
9	Highway patrol officer
10	Air traffic controller

Source: Les Krantz, The Jobs Rated Almanac

WATER PRESSURE
The stress level of a firefighter is ranked second only to that of the US President.

COMPANIES & PRODUCTS

TOP 10

US COMPANIES BY MARKET VALUE

	Corporation	Principal products/ activity	Market value ($)
1	General Electric	Electrical household goods, electronic equipment	89,953,000,000
2	Exxon	Petroleum products	80,550,000,000
3	AT&T	Telecommunications	71,001,000,000
4	Wal-Mart Stores	Department stores	65,221,000,000
5	Coca-Cola	Soft drinks	55,371,000,000
6	Philip Morris	Foodstuffs, beer, cigarettes	49,117,000,000
7	General Motors	Motor vehicles	41,946,000,000
8	Merck	Pharmaceutical products	40,596,000,000
9	Procter & Gamble	Soap and other detergents	39,272,000,000
10	Dupont	Petroleum refining	36,062,000,000

Source: Business Week

THE 10

LARGEST LIFE INSURANCE COMPANIES IN THE US

	Company	Assets ($)
1	Prudential of America	154,779,400,000
2	Metropolitan Life	118,178,300,000
3	Teachers Insurance & Annuity	61,776,700,000
4	Aetna Life	50,896,500,000
5	New York Life	46,925,000,000
6	Equitable Life Assurance	46,624,000,000
7	Connecticut General Life	44,075,500,000
8	Northwestern Mutual Life	39,663,300,000
9	John Hancock Mutual Life	39,146,100,000
10	Principal Mutual Life	35,124,800,000

The huge assets of the major US life insurance companies are greater than the entire gross domestic product of most countries (i.e. the value of the output of all goods and services produced within their borders). Indeed, only 21 of the world's leading industrialized countries have GDPs in excess of the No. 1 company on this list, Prudential of America. The total assets of the Top 50 companies are $1,141,431,900,000, a sum equivalent to approximately one-fifth of the GDP of the whole United States.

Source: Fortune *magazine,* Fortune's Service 500

TOP 10

GOODS IMPORTED TO THE US

	Product	Total value of imports in 1993 ($)
1	Road vehicles and parts	79,471,000,000
2	Electrical machinery	46,752,000,000
3	Office and ADP machines	43,182,000,000
4	Crude oil	38,438,000,000
5	Clothing	33,787,000,000
6	Telecommunications equipment	27,303,000,000
7	Power-generating machinery	17,163,000,000
8	General industrial machinery	17,084,000,000
9	Specialized industrial machinery	13,546,000,000
10	Toys, games, and sporting goods	11,640,000,000

Source: US Department of Commerce, International Trade Administration

The total value of US imports in 1993 was $580,511,000,000. The value of imports of road vehicles – especially cars – first exceeded that of vehicles exported in 1968 (when imports stood at $4,295,000,000), and have been rising relentlessly ever since.

TOP 10

GOODS EXPORTED FROM THE US

	Product	Total value of exports in 1993 ($)
1	Electrical machinery	36,639,000,000
2	Road vehicles and parts	35,800,000,000
3	Office and ADP machines	27,167,000,000
4	Airplanes	21,297,000,000
5	General industrial machinery	19,519,000,000
6	Power-generating machinery	19,132,000,000
7	Specialized industrial machinery	17,635,000,000
8	Scientific instruments	15,213,000,000
9	Telecommunications equipment	13,071,000,000
10	Organic chemicals	11,090,000,000

Source: US Department of Commerce, International Trade Administration

The US exported commodities to the total value of $464,767,000,000 in 1993. Foreign sales of US-manufactured airplanes has long been a strong sector of the economy, with exports first exceeding $1,000,000,000 during World War II.

THE 10

LARGEST BANKS IN THE WORLD

	Bank	Assets ($)
1	Bank of Tokyo/ Mitsubishi Bank	703,000,000,000
2	Fuji Bank Ltd Tokyo	509,000,000,000
3	Dai-Ichi Kangyo Bank, Tokyo	508,000,000,000
4	Sumitomo Bank Ltd Osaka	499,000,000,000
5	Sakura Bank Ltd Tokyo	498,000,000,000
6	Sanwa Bank Ltd Osaka	495,000,000,000
7	Norinchukin Bank Tokyo	431,000,000,000
8	Industrial Bank of Japan, Tokyo	388,000,000,000
9	Mitsubishi Trust & Banking, Tokyo	344,000,000,000
10	Credit Lyonnais Paris	338,000,000,000

TOP 10

BANKS WITH MOST BRANCHES IN THE US

	Bank	Assets ($)
1	CitiCorp	213,701,000,000
2	Bank America Corp.	180,646,000,000
3	Chemical Banking Corp.	139,655,000,000
4	NationsBank Corp.	118,059,300,000
5	J.P. Morgan & Co.	102,941,000,000
6	Chase Manhattan Corp.	95,862,000,000
7	Bankers Trust New York Corp.	72,448,000,000
8	Banc One Corp.	61,417,400,000
9	Wells Fargo & Co.	52,537,000,000
10	PNC Bank Corp.	51,379,900,000

Source: Fortune *magazine*

TOP 10

DUTY-FREE PRODUCTS

	Product	Sales (US$)
1	Cigarettes	2,010,000,000
2	Women's fragrances	1,855,000,000
3	Scotch whisky	1,420,000,000
4	Women's cosmetics and toiletries	1,400,000,000
5	Cognac	1,175,000,000
6	Men's fragrances and toiletries	890,000,000
7	Accessories	780,000,000
8	Confectionery	770,000,000
9	Watches	765,000,000
10	Leather goods (handbags, belts, etc.)	715,000,000

CHANEL NO.1
Women's fragrances figure in second place among the world's top duty-free products, with Chanel established as the leading brand.

Duty-free sales began in 1951 at Shannon Airport in Ireland, where transatlantic flights stopped to refuel on their way to New York. Dr. Brendan O'Regan is credited with the idea of selling goods to people waiting in the transit lounge, (not technically part of Irish soil, and therefore exempt from taxes). By the end of the 1950s, airport shops had opened in Amsterdam, Brussels, London, and Frankfurt. In 1993 total world duty-free sales were estimated to have reached $17,000,000,000, of which the Top 10 comprise $11,580,000,000, or 68 percent. In terms of sales, the world's biggest duty-free shop is that at Honolulu International Airport, with a total of $400,000,000, closely followed by London Heathrow with $395,000,000. Overall, the UK is the most important country in the duty-free world, its various airport, airline, and ferry outlets achieving total sales approaching $1,200,000,000.

TOP 10

SOURCES OF IMPORTS TO THE US

	Country	Total value of imports in 1993 ($)
1	Canada	110,922,000,000
2	Japan	107,268,000,000
3	Mexico	35,211,000,000
4	China	31,535,000,000
5	Germany	28,605,000,000
6	Taiwan	25,105,000,000
7	UK	21,736,000,000
8	South Korea	17,123,000,000
9	France	15,244,000,000
10	Italy	13,223,000,000

Source: US Department of Commerce, International Trade Administration

TOP 10

EXPORT MARKETS FOR GOODS FROM THE US

	Country	Total value of exports in 1993 ($)
1	Canada	100,177,000,000
2	Japan	47,950,000,000
3	Mexico	27,162,000,000
4	UK	26,376,000,000
5	Germany	18,957,000,000
6	Taiwan	16,250,000,000
7	South Korea	14,776,000,000
8	France	13,267,000,000
9	Netherlands	12,839,000,000
10	Singapore	11,676,000,000

Source: US Department of Commerce, International Trade Administration

PATENTS & INVENTIONS

THE 10

FIRST PATENTS IN THE US

	Patentee	Patent	Date
1	Samuel Hopkins	Making pot and pearl ash	July 31, 1790
2	Joseph S Sampson	Candle making	Aug 6, 1790
3	Oliver Evans	Flour and meal making	Dec 18, 1790
4=	Francis Bailey	Punches for type	Jan 29, 1791
4=	Aaron Putnam	Improvement in distilling	Jan 29, 1791
6	John Stone	Driving piles	Mar 10, 1791
7=	Samuel Mullikin	Threshing machine	Mar 11, 1791
7=	Samuel Mullikin	Breaking hemp	Mar 11, 1791
7=	Samuel Mullikin	Polishing marble	Mar 11, 1791
7=	Samuel Mullikin	Raising nap on cloth	Mar 11, 1791

After pressure from American inventors who sought legal protection for their creations, Congress set up the US Patent Office on April 10, 1790, basing it on the British Patent Office. Samuel Hopkin of Philadelphia had the honor of being the first to register a patent under the new system, although the sequential numbering of patents was not in fact introduced until a later date.

TOP 10

CATEGORIES OF PATENTS IN 1900

	Category	Number*
1	Metals, cutting, etc.	614
2	Mechanism, etc.	475
3	Electricity, regulating	471
4	Furnaces, etc.	431
5	Furniture, etc.	430
6	Railways, vehicles	426
7	Steam engines	370
8	Velocipedes	354
9	Lamps, etc.	353
10	Locomotives, etc.	345

* Based on number of patents granted in that year

Unlike its US counterpart, the British Patent Office issues a summary that classifies the patents it registers by subject. Examination of the subject group suggests the state of invention in each era, with heavy industrial equipment and steam engines dominating the turn-of-the-century list, just as electronic and computer components feature most prominently among today's patents.

WHEELS OF FORTUNE
The bizarrely named Starley Psycho Safety Bicycle, built in Coventry, UK, in about 1887. The growth in cycling's popularity in the late 1800s mean that "Velocipedes" were among the most common patent categories of 1900.

TOP 10

COUNTRIES THAT REGISTER THE MOST PATENTS

	Category	Patents
1	US	97,443
2	Japan	92,100
3	Germany	46,520
4	France	38,215
5	UK	37,827
6	Italy	27,228
7	Netherlands	20,346
8	Sweden	18,672
9	Switzerland	18,642
10	Canada	18,332

A patent is an exclusive license to manufacture and exploit a unique product or process for a fixed period. The figures refer to the number of patents actually granted during 1992 – which is only a fraction of the patents applied for: a total of 384,456 applications were registered in Japan, for example, but many are refused after investigations show that the product is too similar to one already patented.

THE 10

FIRST US TRADEMARKS *

	Issued to	Invention or discovery
1	Averill Chemical-Paint Company	Liquid paint
2	J.B. Baldy & Co	Mustard
3	Ellis Branson	Retail coal
4	Tracy Coit	Fish
5	William Lanfair Ellis & Co	Oyster packing
6	Evans, Clow, Dalzell & Co	Wrought-iron pipe
7	W.E. Garrett & Sons	Snuff
8	William G. Hamilton	Car wheel
9	John K. Hogg, Frederick	Soap
10	Abraham P. Olzendam	Woolen hose

* All of these trademarks were registered on the same day, October 25th, 1870. They are distinguished in rank only by the trademark numbers assigned to them.

STRANGE INVENTIONS

The late 19th century produced some odd inventions, including the Dimple Drill patented in Germany; the Self-raising Hat, a "Saluting device" that was devised to enable gentlemen carrying armloads of packages still to politely doff their hat to ladies; and perhaps most bizarre of all, a coffin designed by one Count Karnice-Karnicki of Russia, to avoid death in the event of premature burial. At the slightest movement, a ball that was placed on the occupant's chest and connected to a tube passing to the surface, activated a spring that made an iron box on top of the tube fly open, light a lamp, raise a flag, and ring a bell. The tube could also be used to offer encouraging words to the occupant until he or she could be disinterred.

MOST PROLIFIC PATENTEES IN THE US

	Patentee	No. of patents*
1	Thomas A. Edison	1,093
2	Francis H. Richards	619
3	Edwin Herbert Land	533
4=	Marvin Camras	500
4=	Jerome H. Lemelson	500
6	Elihu Thomson	444
7	Charles E. Scribner	374
8	Philo Taylor Farnsworth	300
9	Lee deForest	300
10	Luther Childs Cromwell	293

* Minimum number credited to each inventor.

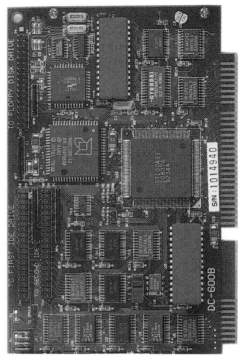

PATENTLY OBVIOUS
Increasingly, patents are being granted for electronic parts, such as those for computers.

TRADE NAMES THAT HAVE ENTERED THE LANGUAGE

1 Bic

Hungarian sculptor, painter, hypnotist, and journalist, László J. and his brother Georg Biró, a chemist, developed the idea of the ballpoint pen in the 1930s and 1940s from their base in Argentina. The French BiC company (its name derives from its founder, Marcel Bich) today owns the rights to the trade name "Biro."

2 Escalator

The moving staircases developed in the 1890s and patented in 1900 were made in the US for the Manhattan Elevated Railway by the Otis Elevator Company and originally bore the name "Escalator" (from "escalading elevator"), a word that rapidly entered everyday usage.

3 Hoover

In 1908 American leather goods and harness manufacturers William Henry "Boss" Hoover (1849–1932) and his son set up the Hoover Suction Co. to sell a vacuum cleaner that had been invented by J. Murray Spangler, first exporting them from their Canadian factory to the UK after World War I. The British company was established in the 1930s and expanded into other domestic appliances after World War II. Although the name Hoover is a trademark, the word has come into use as both noun and verb equivalent to "vacuum cleaner" and "vacuum cleaning."

4 Jacuzzi

The "whirlpool bath" is named after Candido Jacuzzi (1903–86), an Italian immigrant to the US and manufacturer of hydraulic pumps. His son was crippled with rheumatoid arthritis, so he used one of the firm's jet pumps for hydromassage. Developed in the 1950s, the revolutionary bath, which became known as the "Jacuzzi," began the cult of the hot tub, particularly in California, and was the basis of a multimillion dollar manufacturing empire.

5 Linoleum

Linoleum was patented in the UK in 1863 by Frederick Walton, and the following year the Linoleum Manufacturing Company was formed. The word, and its abbreviation "lino," soon became so widely used that in 1878 it was removed from the Trade Marks Register.

6 Plasticine

The modeling clay invented by William Harbutt (1844–1922) was originally made on a small scale for art students, then for children. Commercial manufacturing began in 1900 in a converted flour mill near Bath.

7 Pullman carriages

In 1864, after several years of experimentation with converted railroad carriages, American inventor George Mortimer Pullman (1831–97) built the first railroad sleeping car that bears his name. They first came into use in the UK in 1874 and continued to be manufactured by Pullman's British company, but the name became applied to any train with sleeping accommodation.

8 Thermos flask

"Thermos" became a registered trademark after a competition held in Germany by the firm that produced vacuum flasks for their British inventor, Sir James Dewar (1843–1923). The firm, Thermos Ltd., was set up in the UK in 1907, when the name was registered internationally.

9 Vaseline

"Petroleum jelly" was developed and patented in 1870 by US chemist Robert Chesebrough (1837–1933) as a byproduct of the oil industry; it was patented in the UK in 1874. Chesebrough reputedly ate a spoonful of Vaseline every day – and lived to the age of 96.

10 Xerox

The name comes from the Greek xeros, dry, because the Xerox copying process patented by US inventor Chester Carlson (1906–68) does not involve liquid developer. It was registered in 1952 as a trademark by the Rochester, New York, Haloid Company, which later became the Xerox Corporation.

TOYS & GAMES

BESTSELLING TOYS OF 1994 IN THE US

	Toy	Manufacturer
1	*Mighty Morphin Power Rangers America*	Bandai
2	*Barbie*	Mattel
3	*The Lion King*	Mattel
4	*Genesis*	Sega
5	*Batman*	Kenner
6	*Jennie Gymnast*	Mattel
7	*Super Nintendo Entertainment System*	Nintendo
8	*G.I. Joe*	Hasbro
9	*Bumble Ball*	Ertl
10	*Cool Tools*	Playskool

The 1990s have already proved to be boom years for toy sales in the US. A long period of only steady growth averaging some two percent a year brought the industry to total 1991 sales of $15,150,000,000, but in 1992 this rocketed by an unprecedented 12 percent to almost $17,000,000,000, an expansion that continued in 1993, with character merchandising maintaining its grip on the market. The mega-selling Mighty Morphin Power Rangers products, derived from the cult Japanese TV series, continued this trend in 1994.

	Word/play	Score
1	QUARTZY	
	(i) Play across a triple-word-score (red) square with the Z on a double-letter-score (light blue) square	*164*
	(ii) Play across two double-word-score (pink) squares with Q and Y on light blue squares	*162*
2=	BEZIQUE	
	(i) Play across a red square with either the Z or the QU on a light blue square	*161*
	(ii) Play across two pink squares with the B and second E on two light blue squares	*158*
2=	CAZIQUE	
	(i) Play across a red square with either the Z or the Q on a light blue square	*161*
	(ii) Play across two pink squares with the C and E on two light blue squares	*158*
4=	ZINKIFY	
	Play across a red square with the Z on a light blue square	*158*
5=	QUETZAL	
	Play across a red square with either the Q or the Z on a light blue square	*155*

HIGHEST SCORING WORDS IN SCRABBLE

Word/play	Score
5= JAZZILY	
Using a blank as one of the Zs, play across a red square with the nonblank Z on a light blue square	*155*
5= QUIZZED	
Using a blank as one of the Zs, play across a red square with the nonblank Z or the Q on a light blue square	*155*
8= ZEPHYRS	
Play across a red square with the Z on a light blue square	*152*
8= ZINCIFY	
Play across a red square with the Z on a light blue square	*152*
8= ZYTHUMS	
Play across a red square with the Z on a light blue square	*152*

All the Top 10 words contain seven letters and therefore earn the premium of 50 if the player uses all the letters in the rack. Being able to play them depends on there already being suitable words on the board to which they can be added. In an actual game, the face values of the perpendicular words to which they are joined would also be counted, but they are discounted here since the total score variations would be infinite. Scrabble was invented in the US during the Depression by a jobless architect, Alfred Butts. It was developed in the late 1940s by James Brunot, who chose the name Scrabble.

MOST EXPENSIVE TOYS EVER SOLD AT AUCTION BY CHRISTIE'S EAST, NEW YORK

	Toy/sale	Price ($)*
1	"The Charles," a fire hose-reel made by American manufacturer George Brown & Co, c.1875 December 1991	231,000
2	Märklin fire station December 1991	79,200
3	Horse-drawn double-decker tram December 1991	71,500
4	Mikado mechanical bank December 1993	63,000

	Toy/sale	Price ($)*
5	Märklin Ferris wheel June 1994	55,200
6	Girl skipping rope mechanical bank, June 1994	48,300
7	Märklin battleship June 1994	33,350
8	Märklin battleship June 1994	32,200
9=	Bing keywind open phaeton tinplate automobile December 1991	24,200

	Toy/sale	Price ($)*
9=	Märklin fire pumper December 1991	24,200

* Including 10% buyer's premium

The fire hose-reel at No. 1 in this list is the record price paid at auction for a toy other than a doll. Models by the German tinplate maker Märklin, regarded by collectors as the Rolls-Royce of toys, similarly feature among the record prices of auction houses in the UK and other countries, where high prices have also been attained.

TOP 10

MOST EXPENSIVE TEDDY BEARS SOLD AT AUCTION IN THE UK

	Bear/sale	Price (£)*
1	"Teddy Girl," Steiff Teddy bear, 1904, Christie's, London, December 5, 1994	110,000

Teddy Girl doubled the world record for a Teddy bear when she was acquired by Yoshiro Sekiguchi, who plans to display her at his teddy bear museum near Tokyo.

	Bear/sale	Price (£)*
2	"Happy," dual-plush Steiff Teddy bear, 1926 Sotheby's, London, September 19, 1989	55,000

Although Happy's value was originally estimated at £700–£900, competitive bidding pushed the price up to the world record when the bear was bought by collector Paul Volpp.

	Bear/sale	Price (£)*
3	"Eliot," a blue Steiff bear, 1908 Christie's, London, December 6, 1993	49,500

Eliot was produced as a sample for Harrods but was never manufactured commercially.

	Bear/sale	Price (£)*
4	Black Steiff Teddy bear, c.1912, Sotheby's, London, May 18, 1990	24,200

	Bear/sale	Price (£)*
5	"Alfonzo," a red Steiff Teddy bear, c.1906–09 Christie's, London, May 18, 1989	12,100

This bear was once owned by Princess Xenia of Russia.

	Bear/sale	Price (£)*
6	Rod-jointed Steiff apricot plush Teddy bear, c.1904 Sotheby's, London, May 9, 1991	11,770
7	Black Steiff Teddy bear, c.1912, Phillips, London, October 19, 1990	8,800
8	Apricot-colored Steiff Teddy bear, c.1904 Sotheby's, London, January 31, 1990	7,700
9=	White plush Steiff Teddy bear, c.1904 Sotheby's, London, January 31, 1990	6,050
9=	White plush Steiff Teddy bear, c.1905 Sotheby's, London, May 18, 1990	6,050

* *Prices include buyer's premium.*

While on a hunting trip, US President Theodore ("Teddy") Roosevelt refused to shoot a young bear, a story that promptly became the subject of a famous cartoon by Clifford K. Berryman, published in the *Washington Post* on November 16, 1902. Soon afterward, Morris Michtom, a New York shopkeeper (later founder of the Ideal Toy and Novelty Company) made stuffed bears and – with Roosevelt's permission – advertised them as "Teddy's Bears." At about the same time, Margarete Steiff, a German toymaker, started to make her first toy bears, exporting them to the US to meet the demand "Teddy Bears" had created. In 1903 Steiff's factory produced 12,000 bears; by 1907 this had risen to 974,000. Steiff bears, recognizable by their distinctive ear tags, are still made and sold internationally, but it is the early ones that are most prized among collectors, with the result that all the Top 10 are Steiffs.

BEAR THE COST
Certain rare teddy bears have attained amazing prizes at auction.

TOP 10

MOST LANDED-ON SQUARES IN MONOPOLY®

1	Illinois Avenue
2	Go
3	B & Q Railroad
4	Free Parking
5	Tennessee Avenue
6	New York Avenue
7	Reading Railroad
8	St. James Place
9	Water Works
10	Pennsylvania Railroad

Monopoly® is a registered trademark of Parker Brothers division of Tonka Corporation.

Monopoly has sold over 100,000,000 sets in 23 languages and 34 countries and is the bestselling copyrighted game of all time. It was created in Philadelphia during the Depression by an unemployed heating engineer called Charles Darrow. He patented it on February 7, 1936 after sales rocketed to 20,000 in 1934. Althought real estate board games already existed, some even featuring a "Go to Jail" square and "Chance" and "Community Chest" cards, none was commercially successful.

TOP 10

BESTSELLING CD-ROM TITLES IN THE US, 1994

	Title	Manufacturer
1	*Myst*	Broderbund
2	*Doom II*	GT
3	*Quicken Deluxe*	Intuit
4	*Lion King*	Disney
5	*Print Shop Deluxe Ensemble*	Broderbund
6	*X-Wing Collector's CD*	Lucasarts
7	*Encarta*	Microsoft
8	*One Stop CD Shop*	Softkey
9	*Wing Commander III*	Origin
10	*Aladdin Activity Center*	Disney

SHOPPING LISTS

TOP 10

DRUG STORE ITEMS IN THE US
(*Not including private label and miscellaneous items*)

	Product	Annual sales ($)
1	Prescriptions	38,000,000,000
2	General merchandise	9,978,000,000
3	Food, drinks, tobacco products	8,345,000,000
4	General health care	5,969,000,000
5	Toiletries/ Beauty care	4,701,000,000
6	Other grocery products	2,344,000,000
7	Cosmetics/fragrances	1,879,000,000
8	Cough/cold/allergy/ sinus remedies	1,590,000,000
9	Internal analgesics	1,097,000,000
10	Oral care products	1,071,000,000

TOP 10

RETAILERS IN THE US

	Retailer	Annual sales ($)
1	Wal-Mart Stores	83,412,000,000
2	Sears, Roebuck & Co.	54,559,000,000
3	KMart Corp.	34,313,000,000
4	The Kroger Co.	22,959,600,000
5	Dayton-Hudson Corp.	21,311,000,000
6	J.C. Penney Co., Inc.	21,082,000,000
7	American Stores Co.	18,355,000,000
8	Safeway Stores	15,627,000,000
9	May Department Stores	12,223,000,000
10	Albertson's, Inc.	11,895,000,000

Sears Roebuck, previously No. 1 in this list, was established in Chicago in 1892 by Richard Warren Sears, a railroad worker turned watch salesman, and Alvah C. Roebuck, a watchmaker, exclusively as a mail order company.

TOP 10

SUPERMARKET GROUPS WITH MOST OUTLETS IN THE US

	Retailer	No. of outlets
1	The Kroger Co.	2,214
2	The Great Atlantic & Pacific Tea Co., Inc.	1,193
3	Winn-Dixie Stores Inc.	1,164
4	Safeway Inc.	1,103
5	Food Lion Inc.	1,050
6	American Stores Company	930
7	Albertson's, Inc.	656
8	Publix Super Markets Inc.	407
9	The Vons Companies Inc.	346
10	Pathmark Supermarkets General Corp.	147

Unlike other countries, where a small number of supermarket chains have established a virtually nationwide spread, the US industry is highly regionalized – companies that have a high profile in one part of the country are unknown elsewhere.

TOP 10

FOOD AND DRUG STORES IN THE US

	Retailer	Annual sales ($)
1	The Kroger Co.	22,959,000,000
2	American Stores	18,355,000,000
3	Safeway	15,627,000,000
4	Albertson's	11,895,000,000
5	Winn-Dixie Stores	11,082,000,000
6	The Great Atlantic & Pacific Tea Co.	10,384,000,000
7	Walgreen	9,235,000,000
8	Publix Super Markets	8,742,000,000
9	Supermarkets General Holdings	7,226,000,000
10	Vons	4,997,000,000

Source: Fortune 500

TOP 10

SHOPPING STREETS IN THE WORLD

	Street	Location
1	The Ginza	Tokyo, Japan
2	Pedder Street/ Chater Street	Hong Kong
3	East 57th Street	New York, US
4	5th Avenue	New York, US
5	Madison Avenue	New York, US
6	Kaufinger Strasse	Munich, Germany
7	Hohe Strasse	Cologne, Germany
8	Kurfürstendamm	Berlin, Germany
9	Königsallee	Dusseldorf, Germany
10	Königstrasse	Stuttgart, Germany

Based on prime retail rents at end of 1992

TOP 10

DRUG STORE BRANDS IN THE US

	Product	Sales ($)*
1	Tylenol analgesics	327,900,000
2	Revlon cosmetics	220,100,000
3	Cover Girl cosmetics	199,500,000
4	Maybelline cosmetics	149,600,000
5	Advil	129,400,000
6	L'Oreal cosmetics	123,200,000
7	Lifescan	121,200,000
8	Robitussin	115,400,000
9	Trojan	109,800,000
10	J&J first aid products	98,600,000

* *12 months to March 1994*

Source: Towne-Oller & Associates/ Information Resources, Inc.

TOP 10

SPORTSWEAR RETAILERS IN THE US

	Company	Average sales per store ($)
1	Sportmart	9,657,143
2	The Sports Authority	9,400,000
3	Sports & Recreation	8,500,000
4	Academy Corp.	8,100,000
5	SportsTown	7,700,000
6	Sport Chalet	7,500,000
7	MVP Sports Stores	5,178,105
8	Olympic Sports	4,700,000
9	Modell's	4,127,000
10	Herman's	3,250,000

TOP 10

SPORTS FOOTWEAR RETAILERS IN THE US

	Retailer	Sales (1993)
1	Foot Locker	1,900,000,000
2	The Athlete's Foot	388,000,000
3	Lady Foot Locker	326,000,000
4	Foot/Action	260,000,000
5	The Finish Line	153,000,000
6	Athletic X-Press	95,000,000
7	Athletic Attic	60,000,000
8	Kids Foot Locker	54,000,000
9	Just For Feet	42,000,000
10	Fleet Feet	23,000,000

Figures for all except Nos. 2 and 9 are minimum estimates for sales in 1993; precise amounts may be even greater, and the relentless growth in the US sports footwear market continues: in 1993, total sales of the Top 10 retailers alone accounted for $3,301,000,000, 19 percent up from the $2,777,000,000 of the previous year – which was 35 percent up from 1991's $2,051,000,000.

Source: National Sporting Goods Association

TOP 10

DEPARTMENT STORE CHAINS IN THE US

	Chain	Annual sales ($)
1	Sears Roebuck, Chicago, Illinois	59,101,100,000
2	Wal-Mart Stores, Bentonville, Arkansas	55,483,800,000
3	KMart, Troy, Michigan	37,724,000,000
4	J.C. Penney, Plano, Texas	19,085,000,000
5	Dayton Hudson, Minneapolis, Minnesota	17,927,000,000
6	May Department Stores, St. Louis, Missouri	11,170,000,000
7	Woolworth, New York, New York	9,962,000,000
8	Federated Department Stores, Cincinnati, Ohio	7,079,900,000
9	R.H. Macy, New York, New York	6,648,900,000
10	Dillard Department Stores, Little Rock, Arizona	4,883,200,000

TOP 10

LARGEST SHOPPING MALLS IN THE US

	Mall	Gross leasable area (sq ft)*
1	Del Amo Fashion Center, Torrance, California	3,000,000
2	South Coast Plaza/Crystal Court, Costa Mesa, California	2,918,236
3	Mall of America, Bloomington, Minnesota	2,472,500
4	Lakewood Center Mall, Lakewood, California	2,390,000
5	Roosevelt Field Mall, Garden City, New York	2,300,000
6	Gurnee Mills, Gurnee, Illinois	2,200,000
7	The Galleria, Houston, Texas	2,100,000
8	Randall Park Mall, North Randall, Ohio	2,097,416
9	Oakbrook Shopping Center, Oak Brook, Illinois	2,006,688
10=	Sungrass Mills, Sunrise, Florida	2,000,000
10=	The Woodlands Mall, The Woodlands, Texas	2,000,000
10=	Woodfield, Schaumburg, Illinois	2,000,000

* As of March 1995

Gross leasable area is defined as "the floor area designated for tenant occupancy," and includes square footage occupied by anchor stores.

Source: Blackburn Marketing Services Inc.

COMMUNICATION

TOP 10

COUNTRIES THAT MAKE THE MOST INTERNATIONAL PHONE CALLS

	Country	Calls per head p.a.	Total calls
1	US	6.5	1,651,913,000
2	Germany	12.6	1,011,600,000
3	UK	8.3	480,000,000*
4	Italy	6.9	396,000,000
5	Netherlands	22.0	334,000,000
6	Switzerland	44.3	304,940,000
7	Canada	11.1	302,500,000*
8	Japan	2.3	290,000,000
9	Belgium	24.7	243,906,000
10	Hong Kong	40.6	241,023,000

* *Estimated*

TOP 10

COUNTRIES WITH THE MOST PUBLIC TELEPHONES

	Country	Telephones
1	US	1,761,407
2	Japan	830,000
3	Italy	406,532
4	Republic of Korea	271,927
5	Brazil	263,643
6	Germany	200,000
7	France	190,497
8	Canada	172,049
9	India	145,577
10	Mexico	125,073

TOP 10

COMMEMORATIVE STAMPS OF THE US POST OFFICE

	Stamp	Year	Approx. sales
1	Elvis Presley	1993	517,000,000
2	John F. Kennedy	1964	511,000,000
3	Rock and Roll	1993	488,000,000
4	Dinosaurs	1989	407,000,000
5	Wildflowers	1992	275,000,000
6	Winter Olympics	1994	179,000,000
7=	Winter Olympics	1992	160,000,000
7=	Summer Olympics	1992	160,000,000
9	Moon landing	1994	155,000,000
10	Lyndon B. Johnson	1973	150,000,000

TOP 10

COUNTRIES WITH THE MOST TELEPHONES

	Country	Telephones
1	US	143,325,389
2	Japan	58,520,000
3	Germany	35,420,843
4	France	29,521,000
5	UK	26,880,000
6	Italy	23,708,388
7	Russia	22,778,601
8	Canada	16,227,000
9	Republic of Korea	15,865,381
10	Spain	13,792,156

It is estimated that there are some 574,860,000 telephone lines in use in the world, of which 234,083,000 are in Europe, 193,053,000 in North and South America, 127,290,000 in Asia, 10,336,000 in Oceania, and 10,098,000 in Africa. It is remarkable that, given its population, the whole of China has only 11,469,100 telephones – which is fewer than half the total for Italy. India, similarly, has 6,696,748 telephones, fewer than half as many as Spain but with more than twenty times as many inhabitants.

TOP 10

COUNTRIES WITH THE MOST TELEPHONES PER 100 PEOPLE

	Country	Telephones per 100 inhabitants
1	Sweden	68.43
2	Switzerland	60.83
3	Canada	59.24
4	Denmark	58.30
5	US	56.12
6	Luxembourg	55.07
7	Finland	54.57
8	Iceland	54.28
9	Norway	53.00
10	France	51.52
	UK	*46.75*

Contrasting with the Top 10 countries, where the ratio is around two people per telephone or better, there are many countries in the world with fewer than one telephone per 100 inhabitants. The overall ratio for Africa is 1.54 telephones per 100, with many countries falling well below even this level – Tanzania's for example, is equivalent to one telephone for every 280 people.

TOP 10

COUNTRIES SENDING AND RECEIVING THE MOST MAIL

	Country	Items of mail handled p.a.
1	US	165,228,428,000
2	Japan	22,723,628,000
3	France	22,344,900,000
4	UK	16,364,000,000
5	Russia	15,075,068,000
6	India	13,314,660,000
7	Canada	9,004,547,000
8	Germany	8,839,012,000
9	Italy	7,711,808,000
10	Netherlands	6,105,000,000

TOP 10

MOST POPULAR TYPES OF GREETING CARDS MAILED IN THE US

	Holiday	Estimated no. sent
1	Christmas	2,700,000,000
2	Valentine's Day	1,000,000,000
3	Easter	160,000,000
4	Mother's Day	150,000,000
5	Father's Day	101,000,000
6	Thanksgiving	40,000,000
7	Halloween	35,000,000
8	St. Patrick's Day	19,000,000
9	Jewish New Year	12,000,000
10	Hanukkah	11,000,000

Some 50 percent of all personal mail is greeting cards. Of these, cards given during the major holidays dominate the market. Greeting cards for these occasions – as well as birthday, anniversary, and graduation cards (81,000,000 alone), and cards for such modern inventions as Secretary's Day (1,600,000) and National Boss Day (1,000,000) – combine to a projected 1994 sales of $5,900,000,000.

TOP 10

FIRST CITIES/COUNTRIES TO ISSUE POSTAGE STAMPS

	City/country	Stamps first issued
1	UK	May 1840
2	New York City	February 1842
3	Zurich, Switzerland	March 1843
4	Brazil	August 1843
5	Geneva, Switzerland	October 1843
6	Basle, Switzerland	July 1845
7	US	July 1847
8	Mauritius	September 1847
9	France	January 1849
10	Belgium	July 1849

The first adhesive postage stamps issued in the US were designed for local delivery (as authorized by an 1836 Act of Congress) and produced by the City Despatch Post, New York City, which was inaugurated on February 15, 1842, and later that year incorporated into the US Post Office Department. After a further Act in 1847, the rest of the United States followed suit, and the Post Office Department issued its first national stamps: a 5-cent Benjamin Franklin stamp and a 10-cent George Washington stamp, both of which first went on sale in New York City on July 1, 1847.

SUPERHIGHWAY
With access to international information resources and electronic mail, the Internet is the communications phenomenon of the 1990s.

TOP 10

WORDS USED ON THE INTERNET

	Word	% of use
1	the	4.02
2	to	2.44
3	of	2.06
4	a	1.96
5	I	1.70
6	and	1.68
7	is	1.32
8	in	1.23
9	that	1.15
10	it	0.81

By analyzing a database of 343,945,617 words used during a year of USENET traffic, infonaut Rick Walker compiled a list of the 1,000 most common words on the Internet. Of these, nine are common to the Top 10 words used in English. Surprisingly, the word "Internet" appears in a lowly 772nd place, together with words such as BBS (bulletin board system), buffer, science, and interface.

FUEL & POWER

TOP 10

COAL CONSUMERS
IN THE WORLD

	Country	Consumption 1992 (tonnes)
1	China	1,090,809,000
2	US	808,346,000
3	Germany	327,500,000
4	Russia	316,058,000
5	India	256,750,000
6	Poland	176,682,000
7	Ukraine	138,915,000
8	South Africa	132,260,000
9	Japan	116,813,000
10	Australia	103,486,000
	UK	*100,388,000*

TOP 10

COAL PRODUCERS
IN THE WORLD

	Country	Annual production (tonnes)
1	China	1,116,369,000
2	US	904,959,000
3	Germany	458,102,000
4	Russia	313,960,000
5	India	254,600,000
6	Australia	225,788,000
7	Poland	198,449,000
8	South Africa	174,910,000
9	Ukraine	133,597,000
10	Kazakhstan	131,033,000
	UK	*84,874,000*

DID YOU KNOW

RUNNING OUT?

The world's oil supplies will be exhausted before 2040 at the current rate of consumption. And some countries will run out more quickly – China's in 23 and that of the US in just nine years, although Saudi Arabia's supplies may last for 88, Kuwait's 141 years, and Iraq's 629 years. But growing populations and industrialization will deplete supplies at a greater rate. This must be offset by using improved energy efficiency methods, nonfossil fuels such as nuclear energy, and renewable resources such as biofuels, solar, water, and wind power.

TOP 10

COUNTRIES WITH THE
GREATEST COAL RESERVES
IN THE WORLD

	Country	Reserves (tonnes)
1	Russia	265,657,000,000
2	US	240,116,000,000
3	China	114,500,000,000
4	Australia	90,940,000,000
5	Germany	80,069,000,000
6	India	62,548,000,000
7	South Africa	55,333,000,000
8	Poland	41,200,000,000
9	Indonesia	32,063,000,000
10	Kazakhstan	25,000,000,000

TOP 10

ELECTRICITY PRODUCING
COUNTRIES

	Country	Production (kw/hr)
1	US	3,074,504,000,000
2	Russia	1,008,450,000,000
3	Japan	895,336,000,000
4	China	753,940,000,000
5	Germany	537,134,000,000
6	Canada	520,857,000,000
7	France	462,263,000,000
8	India	327,913,000,000
9	UK	326,879,000,000
10	Ukraine	252,524,000,000

TOP 10

ENERGY CONSUMERS
IN THE WORLD

	Country	Annual consumption coal equivalent (tonnes)
1	US	2,757,800,000
2	Former USSR	1,867,300,000
3	China	933,000,000
4	Japan	589,600,000
5	Germany	509,200,000
6	France	311,000,000
7	UK	309,300,000
8	Canada	299,500,000
9	India	273,300,000
10	Italy	230,900,000

STANDARD ELECTRIC LIGHTBULB
The incandescent lightbulb has a tungsten filament that glows yellow-white when electricity is passed through it. This type of bulb is very inefficient, converting only eight percent of the electric energy to light.

TOP 10

COUNTRIES PRODUCING THE MOST ELECTRICITY FROM NUCLEAR SOURCES

	Country	Nuclear power stations in operation	Nuclear power as % of total power use	Output (megawatt-hours)
1	US	109	22.3	98,729
2	France	55	72.9	57,688
3	Japan	44	27.7	34,238
4	Germany	21	30.1	22,559
5	Russia	28	11.8	18,893
6	Canada	21	15.2	14,874
7	Ukraine	15	25.0	13,020
8	UK	37	23.2	12,066
9	Sweden	12	43.2	10,002
10	South Korea	9	53.2	7,220
	World total	*412*		*323,497*

TOP 10

COUNTRIES CONSUMING THE MOST OIL

	Country	Consumption 1992 (barrels)
1	US	4,873,000,000
2	Russia	1,924,000,000
3	Japan	1,532,000,000
4	China	963,000,000
5	Germany	729,000,000
6	UK	602,000,000
7	Saudi Arabia	573,000,000
8	Italy	559,000,000
9	France	543,000,000
10	South Korea	511,000,000

TOP 10

STATES CONSUMING THE GREATEST AMOUNT OF GASOLINE

	State	Consumption 1994 (gallons)
1	California	13,164,099
2	Texas	8,649,661
3	Florida	6,496,641
4	New York	5,525,044
5	Ohio	4,886,312
6	Pennsylvania	4,764,539
7	Illinois	4,758,985
8	Michigan	4,628,524
9	Georgia	3,970,202
10	North Carolina	3,606,653

TOP 10

COUNTRIES WITH THE LARGEST CRUDE OIL RESERVES

	Country	Reserves (barrels)*
1	Saudi Arabia	261,203,000,000
2	Russia	156,700,000,000
3	Iraq	100,000,000,000
4	Iran	99,840,000,000
5	United Arab Emirates	98,100,000,000
6	Kuwait	96,500,000,000
7	Venezuela	63,330,000,000
8	Mexico	50,925,000,000
9	China	24,000,000,000
10	US	23,745,000,000
	UK	*4,554,000,000*

* *A barrel contains 42 US gallons/34.97 UK gallons*

TOP 10

CRUDE OIL PRODUCERS IN THE WORLD

	Country	Production (barrels per annum)
1	Saudi Arabia	2,979,000,000
2	Russia	2,595,000,000
3	US	2,517,000,000
4	Iran	1,329,000,000
5	China	1,057,000,000
6	Mexico	972,000,000
7	Venezuela	851,000,000
8	Norway	820,000,000
9	United Arab Emirates	799,000,000
10	Nigeria	692,000,000
	UK	*681,000,000*

Despite its huge output, the US produces barely half the 4,873,000,000 barrels of oil it consumes every year – an energy consumption that is equivalent to 19 barrels per capita. The average US citizen thus uses one barrel of oil every 20 days. This compares with the UK's consumption of 602,000,000 barrels per annum – 10 per capita, or one barrel every 36 days.

SAVING THE PLANET

TOP 10

USERS OF UNLEADED GASOLINE IN EUROPE

	Country	Total gasoline consumption (tons)*, 1994	Unleaded as % of market
1	Austria	2,800,000	100
2	Germany	34,000,000	93
3	Finland	2,100,000	92#
4	Sweden	4,500,000	89#
5	Switzerland	4,100,000	83#
6	Netherlands	3,300,000	82
7	Denmark	2,000,000	78
8	Luxembourg	550,000	77
9	Norway	1,900,000	76#
10	Belgium	2,400,000	67

* *Estimated*
\# *For countries not in the EU in 1994, sales data estimated for 1993*

Based on data supplied by the UK Petroleum Industry Association.

The use of unleaded gasoline in Europe has increased: in 1988 the total consumption was 18,900,000 tons (17,180,000 tonnes), and by 1994 the Top 10 countries alone accounted for 50,200,000 tons (45,500,000 tonnes). Like Austria, there are a few other countries around the world that only use unleaded gasoline, among them Brazil, Canada, and Japan.

BACK TO BASICS
Today's typical shopping basket includes an increasing proportion of paper, glass, metal, and plastic packaging that can be recycled.

TOP 10

GARBAGE PRODUCERS IN THE WORLD

	Country	Domestic waste per head per annum kg	lb
1	US	721	1,590
2	Finland	624	1,376
3	Canada	601	1,325
4	The Netherlands	497	1,096
5	Denmark	475	1,047
6	Norway	472	1,041
7	Hungary	463	1,021
8	Luxembourg	445	981
9	Switzerland	441	972
10	Japan	411	906
	UK	*348*	*767*

TOP 10

CARBON DIOXIDE EMITTERS IN THE WORLD

	Country	CO_2 emissions (tons of carbon) per capita	total
1	US	11.7508	2,967,350,570
2	Former USSR	7.4029	2,154,787,670
3	China	1.3305	1,530,345,220
4	Japan	5.2940	722,193,200
5	Germany	7.3041	583,424,600
6	India	0.4907	423,325,620
7	UK	6.0111	347,273,510
8	Canada	9.1531	247,073,390
9	Italy	4.1936	242,191,930
10	France	3.9516	225,102,130

The Carbon Dioxide Information Analysis Center, located in Oak Ridge, Tennessee, calculates the CO_2 emissions that result from fossil fuel burning, gas flaring, and cement manufacturing. Statistics show that increasing industrialization has led to huge increases in carbon dioxide. Many countries are trying to reverse this trend through laws such as the Clean Air Act.

TOP 10

DEFORESTING COUNTRIES IN THE WORLD

	Country	Average annual forest loss in 1980s (sq miles)
1	Brazil	14,170
2	Indonesia	4,290
3	Zaïre	2,830
4	Mexico	2,620
5	Bolivia	2,410
6	Venezuela	2,310
7	Thailand	1,990
8	Sudan	1,860
9	Tanzania	1,690
10	Paraguay	1,560

The loss of Brazilian forest at an annual average of 14,170 sq miles means that over the decade of the 1980s the total loss was equivalent to the entire area of Germany, or half the area of Texas.

THE 10

STATES WITH THE MOST TOXIC CHEMICAL ACCIDENTS, 1982–92

	State	Accidents
1	California	4,820
2	Texas	4,532
3	Louisiana	2,505
4	Pennsylvania	1,395
5	Ohio	1,269
6	Kentucky	1,166
7	Illinois	1,085
8	Florida	905
9	Michigan	869
10	New Jersey	857

A study made by the US Environmental Protection Agency determined that more than 680,000,000 pounds of toxic materials were released from a total of some 34,500 toxic accidents during the four-year period.

THE 10
LEAST-POLLUTED CITIES IN THE WORLD*

1 Craiova, Poland
2 Melbourne, Australia
3 Auckland, New Zealand
4 Cali, Colombia
5 Tel Aviv, Israel
6 Bucharest, Romania
7 Vancouver, Canada
8 Toronto, Canada
9 Bangkok, Thailand
10 Chicago, US

* *Based on levels of atmospheric sulfur dioxide*

THE 10
STATES WITH THE HIGHEST WASTE RECYCLING TARGETS

	State*/target year	Target %
1	Rhode Island (not stated)	70
2	New Jersey (1995)	60
3=	California (2000)	50
3=	Hawaii (2000)	50
3=	Indiana (2001)	50
3=	Iowa (2000)	50
3=	Maine (1994)	50
3=	Massachusetts (2000)	50
3=	Nebraska (2002)	50
3=	New Mexico (2000)	50
3=	New York (1997)	50
3=	Oregon (2000)	50
3=	South Dakota (2001)	50
3=	Washington (1995)	50
3=	West Virginia (2010)	50

* *Ten states have not stated their target for recycling*

TOP 10
MOST POLLUTED CITIES IN THE WORLD*

1 Milan, Italy
2 Shengyang, China
3 Tehran, Iran
4 Seoul, South Korea
5 Rio de Janeiro, Brazil
6 São Paulo, Brazil
7 Xian, China
8 Paris, France
9 Peking, China
10 Madrid, Spain

* *Based on levels of atmospheric sulfur dioxide*

Assessments made by the World Health Organization in the 1980s lacked information from Soviet bloc countries, where pollution levels may be even higher. Many countries have since taken steps to

TOP 10
SULFUR DIOXIDE EMITTERS IN THE WORLD

	Country	SO$_2$ emissions per head per annum kg	lb
1	Canada	118.7	261.7
2	US	81.2	179.0
3	Germany	70.7	155.9
4	UK	61.8	136.2
5	Spain	56.1	123.7
6	Ireland	52.9	116.6
7	Belgium	41.8	92.2
8	Finland	38.3	84.4
9	Denmark	35.0	77.2
10	Italy	34.4	75.8

Sulfur dioxide, the principal cause of acid rain, is produced by fuel combustion in factories and power stations. During the 1980s, emissions by all countries declined.

TOP 10
STATES WITH THE MOST SOLID WASTE

	State	recycled	Disposal % incinerated	landfilled	Total (tons per annum)
1	California	11	2	87	44,535,000
2	New York	21	17	62	22,800,000
3	Florida	27	23	49	19,400,000
4	Ohio	19	6	75	16,400,000
5	Texas	11	1	88	14,469,000
6	Illinois	11	2	87	14,140,000
7	Michigan	26	17	57	13,000,000
8	Pennsylvania	11	30	59	8,984,000
9	Indiana	8	17	25	8,400,000
10	North Carolina	4	1	95	7,788,000

* *Totals for some states include quantities of industrial waste*

Estimates put the total amount of solid waste generated by the entire United States in 1992 at 291,742,000 tons (more than one ton per head of the population), of which the top 10 states were responsible for 169,916,000 tons, or 58 percent. Of this total, an average of 17 percent was recycled, 11 percent incinerated, and 72 percent disposed of by burial in landfill sites. The state recycling the greatest proportion of its solid waste in 1992 was Minnesota, at 38 percent, with Hawaii, Montana, North Carolina, and Wyoming tied for the lowest place at 4 percent.

INDUSTRIAL & OTHER ACCIDENTS

WORST EXPLOSIONS IN THE WORLD

(Excluding mining disasters, and terrorist and military bombs)

	Location/incident	Date	Killed
1	Lanchow, China (arsenal)	October 26, 1935	2,000
2	Halifax, Nova Scotia (ammunition ship *Mont Blanc*)	December 6, 1917	1,635
3	Memphis, Tennessee (*Sultana* boiler explosion)	April 27, 1865	1,547
4	Bombay, India (ammunition ship *Fort Stikine*)	April 14, 1944	1,376
5	Cali, Colombia (ammunition trucks)	August 7, 1956	1,200
6	Salang Tunnel, Afghanistan (gasoline tanker collision)	November 2, 1982	over 1,100
7	Chelyabinsk, USSR (liquid gas beside railroad)	June 3, 1989	up to 800
8	Texas City, Texas (ammonium nitrate on *Grandcamp* freighter)	April 16, 1947	752
9	Oppau, Germany (chemical plant)	September 21, 1921	561
10	Mexico City, Mexico (PEMEX gas plant)	November 20, 1984	540

All these "best estimate" figures should be treated with caution, since, as with fires and shipwrecks, body counts are notoriously unreliable.

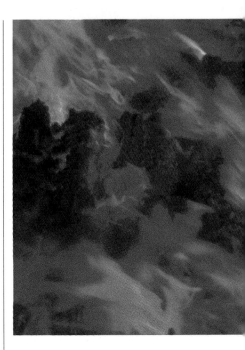

WORST INDUSTRIAL DISASTERS

(Excluding mining disasters, and marine and other transportation disasters)

	Location/incident	Date	Killed
1	Bhopal, India, gas escape at Union Carbide plant	December 3, 1984	over 2,500
2	Oppau, Germany, chemical plant explosion	September 21, 1921	561
3	Mexico City, Mexico, explosion at a gas plant.	November 20, 1984	540
4	Brussels, Belgium, fire in L'Innovation department store	May 22, 1967	322
5	Guadalajara, Mexico, explosions after gas leak into sewers	April 22, 1992	230
6	São Paulo, Brazil, fire in Joelma bank and office building	February 1, 1974	227
7	Bangkok, Thailand, fire engulfed a four-story doll factory	May 10, 1993	187
8	North Sea, Piper Alpha oil rig explosion and fire	July 6, 1988	173
9	New York City, fire in Triangle Shirtwaist Factory	March 25, 1911	145
10	Eddystone, Pennsylvania, munitions plant explosion	April 10, 1917	133

MOST COMMON CAUSES OF INJURY AT WORK IN THE US

	Cause	% of total injuries
1	Overexertion	31.3
2	Contact with objects or equipment	27.0
3	Falls	15.0
4	Other/nonclassifiable	13.0
5	Exposure to harmful substances	5.0
6	Repetitive motion	4.0
7	Slips, trips	3.5
8	Transportation accidents	3.0
9	Assaults and other violent acts	1.0
10	Fires, explosions	0.2

Source: US Department of Labor, Bureau of Labor Statistics

MOST COMMON CAUSES OF FATAL ACCIDENTS AT WORK IN THE US

	Cause	% of total fatalities		Cause	% of total injuries		Cause	% of total injuries
1	Motor vehicle	35.6	**5**	Poison (liquid/solid)	3.5	**9**	Water transportation	1.7
2	Other*	33.9	**6**	Fires/burns	3.2	**10**	Poison (gas/vapor)	1.3
3	Falls	12.2	**7**	Air transportation	2.5			
4	Electric current	3.7	**8**	Drowning	2.4			

* Includes machinery, being struck by a falling object, mechanical suffocation, and railroads.
Source: National Safety Council

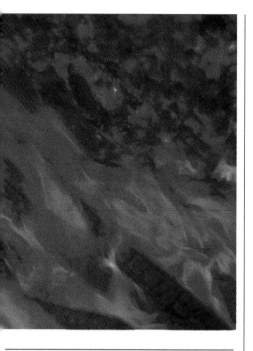

THE 10

WORST FIRES IN THE WORLD

(Excluding sports and entertainment venues, mining disasters, and the results of military action)

	Location/incident	Date	Killed
1	Kwanto, Japan (following earthquake)	September 1, 1923	60,000
2	Cairo, Egypt (city fire)	1824	4,000
3	London Bridge, England	July 1212	3,000
4	Peshtigo, Wisconsin (forest)	October 8, 1871	2,682
5	Santiago, Chile (church of La Compañía)	December 8, 1863	2,500
6	Chungking, China (docks)	September 2, 1949	1,700
7	Constantinople, Turkey (city fire)	June 5, 1870	900
8	Cloquet, Minnesota (forest)	October 12, 1918	800
9	Hinckley, Minnesota (forest)	September 1, 1894	480
10	Hoboken, New Jersey (docks)	June 30, 1900	326

TOP 10

CAUSES OF FATAL INJURIES AT WORK IN THE US

	Event or exposure	Fatalities (1993)
1	Shooting	874
2	Highway collision between vehicles/mobile equipment	652
3	Falls to lower level	530
4	Nonhighway transportation accident (farm/industrial premises)	392
5	Struck by vehicle	361
6	Struck by falling object	345
7	Highway noncollision accident	333
8	Contact with electrical current	324
9	Caught in or compressed by equipment or objects	308
10	Aircraft	280

Total (incl. others not in Top 10) 6,271

Death by shooting (such as the homicide of police and security officers and workers as a result of armed robbery incidents) and highway collisions sadly feature as prominently among the most common causes of occupational fatalities as they do in daily life in modern America. Of the 1993 total, 5,790 victims were men and 481 women – vastly out of proportion to a labor force that comprises some 66,029,000 men and 54,761,000 women.

THE 10

WORST MINING DISASTERS IN THE WORLD

	Location	Date	Killed
1	Hinkeiko, China	April 26, 1942	1,549
2	Courrières, France	March 10, 1906	1,060
3	Omuta, Japan	November 9, 1963	447
4	Senghenydd, UK	October 14, 1913	439
5	Coalbrook, South Africa	January 21, 1960	437
6	Wankie, Rhodesia	June 6, 1972	427
7	Dharbad, India	May 28, 1965	375
8	Chasnala, India	December 27, 1975	372
9	Monongah, West Virginia	December 6, 1907	362
10	Barnsley, UK	December 12, 1866	361*

The Fushun mines, Manchuria, were the site of a mining disaster on February 12, 1931 that may have resulted in 3,000 deaths, but information was suppressed by the Chinese government. Soviet security was responsible for obscuring details of an explosion at the East German Johanngeorgendstadt uranium mine on November 29, 1949, when 3,700 may have died.

* Including 27 killed the following day while searching for survivors

TOP 10

OCCUPATIONS FOR FATAL INJURIES AT WORK IN THE US

	Occupation	Fatalities (1993)
1	Motor vehicle operators	917
2	Construction trades	565
3	Sales occupations	556
4	Executives, administrators and managers	427
5	Farming operators and managers	409
6	Mechanics and repairers	317
7	Protective service occupations	288
8	Professional specialists	254
9	Construction laborers	218
10	Farm workers	209

Total (incl. others not in Top 10) 6,271

Truck drivers (731) comprise most of the No. 1 category.

THE WORLD'S RICHEST

TOP 10

HIGHEST-EARNING ENTERTAINERS IN THE WORLD*

MONEY TALKS
*Oprah Winfrey has transformed her
daytime talk show into a multimillion
dollar production company.*

	Entertainer	Profession	1993–94 income ($)
1	Steven Spielberg	Movie producer/director	335,000,000
2	Oprah Winfrey	TV host/producer	105,000,000
3	Barney	Singer/dancer/children's educator	84,000,000
4	David Copperfield	Illusionist	55,000,000
5	Charles M. Schulz	"Peanuts" cartoonist	37,000,000
6	Michael Crichton	Novelist	35,000,000
7	Siegfried & Roy	Illusionists	34,000,000
8=	Tom Clancy	Novelist	33,000,000
8=	John Grisham	Novelist	33,000,000
8=	Stephen King	Novelist/screenwriter	33,000,000

* Other than actors and pop stars
Used by permission of Forbes Magazine

The global success of the blockbuster *Jurassic Park* accounts for two prominent placings in this Top 10: the producer/director Steven Spielberg, whose $250,000,000 take from the movie represents the greatest amount any individual has ever earned from a single movie, and Michael Crichton, the author. Barney, the US public TV children's dinosaur/character, scored too, with sales of 23,000,000 videos, 2,000,000 records, and more than $500,000,000 in merchandise from which his creators earned substantial royalties.

TOP 10

HIGHEST-EARNING POP STARS IN THE WORLD

	Artist(s)	1993–94 income ($)
1	Pink Floyd	62,000,000
2	Barbra Streisand	57,000,000
3	Eagles	56,000,000
4	The Rolling Stones	53,000,000
5	Garth Brooks	41,000,000
6	Billy Joel	40,000,000
7	Michael Jackson	38,000,000
8	Aerosmith	36,000,000
9=	Grateful Dead	33,000,000
9=	Elton John	33,000,000
9=	Whitney Houston	33,000,000

Used by permission of Forbes Magazine

Forbes Magazine's survey of top entertainers' income covers a two-year period in order to iron out fluctuations, especially those caused by successful tours. Pink Floyd's earnings in 1993, for example, were estimated at $6,000,000, but through a sell-out tour in 1994 they increased to $56,000,000. If the five groups are excluded on the ground that they have to share their income, their places would be taken by three British stars (Eric Clapton, Paul McCartney, and Rod Stewart), Julio Iglesias, and Jimmy Buffet. Previous top slot holder Michael Jackson has fallen from grace; his income once peaked at $125,000,000. Jackson is not the only artist to see his income decline in the past five years: various stars who were formerly prominent fixtures within or just outside the Top 10, but who have fallen from the *Forbes* reckoning, include George Michael, Madonna, and Bruce Springsteen, all of whom were once in the over-$40,000,000 bracket, together with Bon Jovi, Prince, The Who, Def Leppard, Van Halen, Frank Sinatra, and Kenny Rogers. Of course, a new sell-out tour could easily reinstate any of them to their former glory.

TOP 10

STATE LOTTERY WINNERS

	State/date	Winners	Jackpot ($)
1	California Apr 1991	10	118,500,000
2	Pennsylvania Apr 1989	14	115,500,000
3	Wisconsin Jul 1993	1	111,000,000
4	Florida, Sep 1990	6	106,500,000
5	Indiana/Nebraska Nov 1994	2	101,000,000
6	New York Jan 1991	9	90,000,000
7	Florida, Oct 1991	6	89,700,000
8	District of Columbia Dec 1993	2	89,500,000
9	Idaho, Jun 1995	1	87,300,000
10	Texas, Mar 1994	3	86,000,000

TOP 10

RICHEST PEOPLE OUTSIDE THE US
(Excluding royalty)

	Name	Country	Business	Assets ($ Millions)
1	Yoshiaki Tsutsumi	Japan	Property	9,000*
2	Family of late Taikichiro Mori	Japan	Property	7,500
3=	Haniel family	Germany	Food wholesaling	6,200
3=	Erivan Haub	Germany	Supermarkets	6,200
5=	Hans and Gad Rausing	Sweden	Packaging	6,000
5=	Shin Kyuk-ho	Korea	Candy, retailing	6,000
7	Theo and Karl Albrecht	Germany	Supermarkets	5,700
8	Kenneth Thomson	Canada	Publishing	5,400
9	Emilio Azcarraga Milmo	Mexico	TV, bullrings	5,100
10	Henkel family	Germany	Consumer products	4,900

* *Some sources suggest a figure as high as $22,500,000,000*
Based on data published in Forbes Magazine

TOP 10

RICHEST MEN IN THE UK

	Name	Profession/source	Assets ($)
1	Paul Raymond	Publishing/property	2,558,000,000
2	David Sainsbury	Retailing	2,139,000,000
3	Sir Evelyn Rothschild	Merchant banker	2,093,000,000
4	Viscount Rothermere	Newspaper publisher	1,891,000,000
5	Duke of Westminster	Landowner	1,395,000,000
6	Lord Jacob Rothschild	Banking/investment	1,201,000,000
7	Sir James Goldsmith	Financier	1,132,000,000
8	Viscount Cowdray	Publishing/banking	1,085,000,000
9=	Richard Branson	Leisure, airline	1,008,000,000
9=	Garry Weston	Food	1,008,000,000

TOP 10

RICHEST WOMEN IN THE UK

	Name	Assets ($ Millions)		Name	Assets ($ Millions)
1	Chryss Goulandris	465	6	Patricia Martin	277
2	Lady Brigid Ness	411	7	HM The Queen	245
3	Viscountess Boyd	364	8	Lady Elizabeth Nugent	229
4	Donatella Moores	338	9	Lady Virginia Stanhope	167
5	Lady Grantchester	287	10	Baroness W. de Eresby	164

TOP 10

HIGHEST-EARNING ACTORS IN THE WORLD

	Actor	1993–94 income ($)
1	Bill Cosby	60,000,000
2	Harrison Ford	44,000,000
3=	Kevin Costner	37,000,000
3=	Sylvester Stallone	37,000,000
5	Tom Cruise	33,000,000
6	Eddie Murphy	30,000,000
7	Clint Eastwood	28,000,000
8	Bruce Willis	26,000,000
9	Tom Hanks	24,000,000
10	Roseanne Barr	23,000,000

Used by permission of Forbes Magazine

Between 1993 and 1994, Bill Cosby kept the lead he has held for several years through extensive serialization of *The Cosby Show*. The success of *The Fugitive* and *Clear and Present Danger* put Harrison Ford into 1st place among movie actors, while Sylvester Stallone in his 8th consecutive year in the Top 10 rose in the rankings. A year is a long time in show business, as a comparison with 1992–93 rankings shows: Bruce Willis, Tom Hanks, and Roseanne have entered the list, while former No. 3 Arnold Schwarzenegger, Mel Gibson, Robin Williams, and Jack Nicholson have disappeared.

TOP 10

HIGHEST-EARNING MODELS IN THE WORLD

	Model/age	Nationality	1994 income ($)
1	Cindy Crawford (28)	American	6,500,000
2	Claudia Schiffer (24)	German	5,300,000
3	Christy Turlington (26)	American	4,800,000
4=	Linda Evangelista (29)	Canadian	3,000,000
4=	Elle Macpherson (30)	Australian	3,000,000
6	Nicki Taylor (20)	American	2,400,000
7	Isabella Rossellini (42)	Italian	2,300,000
8	Kate Moss (21)	British	2,200,000
9	Naomi Campbell (24)	British	2,100,000
10	Bridget Hall (17)	American	2,000,000

RICHEST IN THE US

T O P   1 0

RICHEST PEOPLE IN THE US

Name(s)	Assets ($)
1 William Henry Gates III	9,350,000,000

In 1975, at the age of 19, Gates left law school to co-found (with Paul G. Allen, who rates 11th place in this list) the Microsoft Corporation of Seattle, now one of the world's leading computer software companies and one that has experienced phenomenal growth: a $2,000 investment in 1986 was worth nearly $70,000 in 1993. Gates, a self-described "hard-core technoid" was placed in No. 1 position in 1992. Formerly a bachelor devoted only to his business and fast cars, in 1994 he married Microsoft executive Melinda French.

Name(s)	Assets ($)
2 Warren Edward Buffett	9,200,000,000

Buffet was born and still lives in Omaha, Nebraska. His professional career started as a pinball service engineer, after which he published a horse race tip sheet. His diverse business interests include the New England textile company, Berkshire Hathaway which has in turn acquired major stakes in the Washington Post, Coca-Cola, and other companies. In 1992 Buffett was ranked fourth in the Forbes 400, in 1993 was elevated to first place, and in 1994 dropped back behind Bill Gates.

Name(s)	Assets ($)
3 John Werner Kluge	5,900,000,000

Founder of the Metromedia Company of Charlottesville, Virginia. The family of German-born Kluge settled in Detroit in 1922, where he worked on the Ford assembly line. He won a scholarship to Columbia University and gained a degree in economics. He started a radio station and in 1959, with partners, acquired the Metropolitan Broadcasting Company, developing it into Metromedia, a corporation that owns TV and radio stations and cellular telephone franchises and other varied properties; he also owns an 80,000-acre estate and castle in Scotland. Kluge, who was placed as America's richest man in 1989, has diversified his interests into such areas as movies (Orion Pictures), printing, and a chain of steak houses.

Name(s)	Assets ($)
4 Edward Crosby Johnson III and family	5,100,000,000

Boston-born Edward Johnson derived his wealth from his role as chief executive of Fidelity Investments as well as real estate and newspaper and magazine publishing interests.

Name(s)	Assets ($)
5= Richard Marvin De Vos and Jay Van Andel ($9,000,000,000 shared)	4,500,000,000

Newcomers to the Top 10, De Vos and Van Andel are partners in the Amway Corporation, the success of which is founded on its hugely successful soap distribution operation, but is also involved in real estate, jewelry, and hotels. De Vos owns the Orlando Magic basketball team.

Name(s)	Assets ($)
5= Ronald Owen Perelman	4,500,000,000

Perelman is a wide-ranging entrepreneur who acquired Revlon, Max Factor, and other cosmetics businesses, was the former owner of Technicolor, and has professional interests that encompass firms from Marvel Comics and cigars to a camping supplies company, with TV assets under the control of newly-formed New World Communications.

Name(s)	Assets ($)
7 Helen Walton, S. Robson Walton, John T. Walton, Jim C. Walton, and Alice L. Walton ($21,700,000,000 shared)	4,300,000,000

Samuel Moore Walton, the founder of Wal-Mart Stores, headed the list of America's richest people for several years. One of the largest retail chains in the US, its more than 2,000 stores achieved sales of $55,500,000,000 in 1992, the year in which Sam Walton died. His widow Helen and four children share the fortune he created.

Name(s)	Assets ($)
8= Samuel Irving Newhouse, Jr. and brother Donald Edward Newhouse ($8,000,000,000 shared)	4,000,000,000

The New York City-based Newhouse brothers are owners of America's largest privately owned chain of newspapers, and with interests that include cable television and book publishing. Samuel ("Si") Newhouse runs book publishers Random House and magazine publishers Condé Nast, the publishers of Vogue, bought by their father in 1959 as an anniversary gift for his wife. ("She asked for a fashion magazine and I went out and got her Vogue.") Donald controls their newspaper group.

Name(s)	Assets ($)
8= (Keith) Rupert Murdoch	4,000,000,000

Son of Melbourne Herald owner Sir Keith Murdoch, Australian-born newspaper tycoon Rupert Murdoch, now a US citizen, has expanded his News Corporation empire to encompass magazines, book publishing, cinema (Twentieth Century Fox) and broadcasting interests, including Sky satellite TV.

Name(s)	Assets ($)
8= Sumner Murray Redstone	4,000,000,000

Formerly in 6th place, Redstone, who comes from a theater-owning family, built up his own movie theater company, National Amusements, Inc., which now has more than 750 screens across the US, coining the word "multiplex" for his multiscreen movie theater complexes, and acquired the company Viacom.

Close runners-up in the two-billion-plus dollars league include Paul G. Allen, ($3,900,000,000), co-founder of Microsoft, and the four Mars family members (of Mars candy fame) sharing $10,000,000,000.

T O P   1 0

FOOD, DRINK, & CANDY FORTUNES IN THE US

Name/main interests	Assets ($)
1 Mars family (4 members)/candy and pet food	10,000,000,000
2 Dorrance family/Campbell's soup	3,600,000,000
3 Edgar Miles Bronfman/Seagram Co.	2,500,000,000
4 Bacardi family/liquor	1,800,000,000
5= Joan Beverly Kroc/McDonald's	1,400,000,000

Name/main interests	Assets ($)
5= John Simplot and family/potatoes	1,400,000,000
6 William Wrigley/Wrigley's chewing gum	1,360,000,000
6 Busch family/Budweiser beer	1,300,000,000
7 Brown family/liquor	1,100,000,000
10 Donald Tyson/food processing	925,000,000

T O P 1 0

COMPUTER FORTUNES IN THE US

	Name	Main interests	Assets ($)
1	William Henry Gates III	Microsoft	9,350,000,000
2	Paul G. Allen	Microsoft	3,910,000,000
3	Lawrence J. Ellison	Oracle Corp.	2,900,000,000
4	David Packard	Hewlett-Packard	2,200,000,000
5=	Steven Anthony Ballmer	Microsoft	1,750,000,000
5=	William Redington Hewlett	Hewlett-Packard	1,750,000,000
7	Gordon Earle Moore	Intel Corp.	1,500,000,000
8	Robert N. Miner	Oracle Corp.	685,000,000
9	Stuart Robert Levine	Cabletron Systems	580,000,000
10	Craig Robert Benson	Cabletron Systems	490,000,000

T O P 1 0

CLOTHING & SHOE FORTUNES IN THE US

	Name/main interests	Assets ($)
1	Philip Hampson Knight/Nike	1,700,000,000
2	Nordstrom family/Clothing and shoe stores	1,500,000,000
3=	Leslie Herbert Wexner/The Limited	1,400,000,000
3=	Peter E. Haas Sr. and family/Levi Strauss	1,400,000,000
5	Donald George Fisher and family/The Gap	1,400,000,000
6	Gore family/Gore-Tex	700,000,000
7	Paul B. Fireman/Reebok International	670,000,000
8	Bean family/L.L. Bean	600,000,000
9	Ralph Lauren/Polo, Ralph Lauren	500,000,000
10	Gary Campbell Comer/Land's End	460,000,000

T O P 1 0

STORE FORTUNES IN THE US

	Name	Main interests	Assets ($)
1	Walton family	Wal-Mart Stores	21,700,000,000
2	Davis family	Winn-Dixie Stores	1,700,000,000
3	Meijer family	Supermarkets	1,200,000,000
4	Kathryn McCurry Albertson and family	Albertson's	1,100,000,000
5	Jenkins family	Publix Super Markets	1,000,000,000
6	Milton Petrie	Petrie Stores	940,000,000
7	Charles Feeney	Duty Free Shoppers	900,000,000
8	Edward John DeBartolo and family	Shopping centers	860,000,000
9	Bernard Marcus	Home Depot	700,000,000
10	Wilmot family	Wilmorite shopping centers	660,000,000

Published by permission of Forbes Magazine

T O P 1 0

BROADCAST & MEDIA FORTUNES IN THE US

	Name/main interests	Assets ($)
1	John Werner Kluge/Metromedia, Orion	5,900,000,000
2	Sumner Murray Redstone/Viacom movie theaters, TV	4,000,000,000
3	Robert Edward (Ted) Turner/Turner Broadcasting	1,600,000,000
4	David Geffen/Asylum Records	1,000,000,000
5	Frank Batten, Sr. and family/TV stations	820,000,000
6	Amos Barr Hostetter, Jr./Continental Cablevision	800,000,000
7	Edward Lewis Gaylord/TV, radio	735,000,000
8	Charles Dolan/HBO, cable TV	715,000,000
9	Harry Wayne Huizenga/Blockbuster Entertainment	700,000,000
10=	Alan Gerry/Cablevision	600,000,000
10=	Steven Spielberg/Movies	600,000,000

DIAMONDS & GOLD

T O P 1 0

MOST EXPENSIVE SINGLE DIAMONDS SOLD AT AUCTION

	Diamond/sale	Price (US$)
1	*Mouawad Splendor* Pear-shaped 11-sided 101.84 carat diamond Sotheby's, Geneva, November 14, 1990 (SF15,950,000)	12,760,000
2	Unnamed pear-shaped 85.91 carat diamond Sotheby's, New York, April 19, 1988	9,130,000
3	Rectangular-cut 52.59 carat diamond Christie's, New York, April 20, 1988	7,480,000
4	*Jeddah Bride* Rectangular-cut 80.02 carat diamond Sotheby's, New York, October 24, 1991	7,150,000
5	*Agra* Cushion-cut light pink 32.24 carat diamond Christie's, London, June 20, 1990 (£4,070,000)	6,959,700

	Diamond/sale	Price (US$)
6	Pear-shaped 64.83 carat diamond Christie's, New York, October 21, 1987	6,380,000
7	*Mouawad Pink* Cushion-cut fancy pink 21.06 carat diamond Christie's, Geneva, May 11, 1989 (SF10,230,000)	6,053,254
8	*Star of Abdel Aziz* Pear-shaped 59.00 carat diamond Christie's, New York, April 19, 1988	5,560,500
9	Unnamed rectangular-cut fancy blue 19.41 carat diamond Christie's, New York, October 23, 1990	5,500,000
10	*Polar Star* Cushion-cut 41.28 carat diamond Christie's, Geneva, November 19, 1980 (SF8,800,000)	5,086,705

Allegedly worn by Babur (1483–1530), the first Mogul emperor, it is said that the Agra was smuggled out of Delhi by British officers in 1857 – inside a horse. Sold in London at Christie's on February 22, 1905, it brought $24,786 and still holds the world record price for a pink diamond.

Said to be the brightest diamond known, it probably came from India and was once owned by Joseph Bonaparte, Emperor Napoleon's brother. After changing hands several times, it entered the possession of Lady Deterding, widow of oil magnate Sir Henry Deterding.

T O P 1 0

LARGEST UNCUT DIAMONDS IN THE WORLD

DID YOU KNOW

A DIAMOND IS NOT FOREVER

In 1796, English chemist Smithson Tennant discovered the chemical composition of diamond. He burned diamonds, producing only carbon and carbon dioxide gas. Tennant thus showed that diamonds, the rarest of commodities, are composed of carbon, one of the most common elements.

	Diamond	Carats
1	*Cullinan*	3,106.00

Found in the Premier Mine, South Africa in 1905, the Cullinan is the largest diamond ever found. It was cut into 105 separate gems, some of which are now in the British Crown Jewels.

	Diamond	Carats
2	*Braganza*	1,680.00

Found in Brazil in the eighteenth century, its position is dubious since all trace of this stone has been lost. Most authorities believe it was a white sapphire, a topaz, or an aquamarine.

	Diamond	Carats
3	*Excelsior*	995.20

The native worker who found this diamond (in 1893 – in a shovelful of gravel at the South African Jagersfontein Mine) hid it and took it directly to the mine manager, who rewarded him with a horse, a saddle, and £500.

	Diamond	Carats
4	*Star of Sierra Leone*	968.80

Found in Sierra Leone on St. Valentine's Day, 1972, the uncut diamond weighed 8 oz/225 g and measured 2½ x 1½ in/6.5 x 4 cm.

	Diamond	Carats
5	*Zale Corporation "Golden Giant"*	890.00

Its origin is so shrouded in mystery that it is not even known from which country it came.

	Diamond	Carats
6	*Great Mogul*	787.50

When found in 1650 in the Gani Mine, India, this diamond was presented to Shah Jehan, the builder of the Taj Mahal.

	Diamond	Carats
7	*Woyie River*	770.00

Found in 1945 beside the river in Sierra Leone.

	Diamond	Carats
8	*Presidente Vargas*	726.60

Discovered in the Antonio River, Brazil, in 1938, it was named after the President.

	Diamond	Carats
9	*Jonker*	726.00

In 1934 Jacobus Jonker, a previously unsuccessful diamond prospector, found this massive diamond after it had been exposed by a heavy storm.

	Diamond	Carats
10	*Reitz*	650.80

Like the Excelsior, the Reitz was found in the Jagersfontein Mine in South Africa in 1895.

A diamond's weight is measured in "carats." There are roughly 142 carats to the ounce. Fewer than 1,000 diamonds of over 100 carats have ever been recorded.

TOP 10

LARGEST POLISHED GEM DIAMONDS IN THE WORLD

	Diamond/(last known whereabouts or owner)	Carats
1	*"Unnamed Brown"* (De Beers)	545.67
2	*Great Star of Africa/Cullinan I* (British Crown Jewels)	530.20
3	*Incomparable/Zale* (auctioned in New York, 1988)	407.48
4	*Second Star of Africa/Cullinan II* (British Crown Jewels)	317.40
5	*Centenary* (De Beers)	273.85
6	*Jubilee* (Paul-Louis Weiller)	245.35
7	*De Beers* (sold in Geneva, 1982)	234.50
8	*Red Cross* (sold in Geneva, 1973)	205.07
9	*Black Star of Africa* (unknown)	202.00
10	*Anon* (unknown)	200.87

TOP 10

GOLD PRODUCERS IN THE WORLD

	Country	1994 production (tonnes)
1	South Africa	583.9
2	US	331.0
3	Australia	256.2
4	Russia	164.7
5	Canada	146.1
6	China	130.0
7	Brazil	75.4
8	Uzbekistan	64.4
9	Papua New Guinea	60.6
10	Indonesia	55.3

South Africa's output fell slightly in 1994, as did US production for the first time in 15 years. But Australia has seen a dramatic rise since 1988 when it rocketted to 152 tonnes, after staying static at 119 tonnes since 1903.

TOP 10

GOLD RESERVES IN THE WORLD

	Country	Reserves (tonnes)*
1	US	8,141
2	Germany	2,960
3	Switzerland	2,590
4	France	2,546
5	Italy	2,074
6	Netherlands	1,081
7	Belgium	779
8	Japan	754
9	UK	574
10	Austria	570

* *As of March 8, 1995; Belgium subsequently disposed of 175 tonnes, moving it to 8th position*

Gold reserves are the government holdings of gold in each country – which are often far greater than the gold owned by private individuals. In the days of the "Gold Standard," this provided a tangible measure of a country's wealth, guaranteeing the convertibility of its currency and determining such factors as exchange rates. Although less significant today, gold reserves remain part of calculating a country's international reserves, alongside its holdings of foreign exchange and SDRs (Special Drawing Rights).

TOP 10

MAKERS OF GOLD JEWELRY IN THE WORLD

	Country	Gold used in jewelry (tonnes p.a.)
1	Italy	441.0
2	India	259.0
3	China	173.1
4	Saudi Arabia and Yemen	147.5
5	US	140.0
6	Turkey	130.5
7	Taiwan	127.8
8	Japan	87.0
9	Hong Kong	85.0
10	Malaysia	82.0

Demand for gold jewelry has more than doubled since 1985. By 1993, the Top 10 gold jewelry manufacturing nations were using over twice as much gold as South's Africa produced annually , and not far short of the Western world annual total. The remaining gold used in electronics (183.4 tonnes), dentistry (63.4 tonnes) and other industrial or decorative purposes. Official coins comprise 121.8 tonnes, but as the gold supply is relatively limited, a single special issue coin can use up a large part of the world supply. In 1986, for example, the Japanese use 182 tonnes when a coin was issued to celebrate the 60th anniversary of the Emperor Hirohito's accession.

DID YOU KNOW

100 YEARS AGO: GOLD FEVER!

In August 1896, 35-year-old George Washington Carmack struck gold while panning the Rabbit Creek, south of the Yukon at Klondike near the Canadian/Alaskan border. When news of his discovery reached the US, it sparked the world's biggest gold rush since the Californian stampede of 1849. More than 100,000 prospectors traveled to the region to seek their fortunes, and in the first year some $22,000,000-worth of Klondike gold was shipped out. Most of the gold-seekers failed – many dying in freezing winter conditions or returning home empty-handed. In 1976 much of the area was designated the Klondike Gold Rush Historical Park, where visitors can see the sites, buildings, and trails associated with the rush, including the Pioneer Square Historic District in Seattle, Washington, from where the prospectors departed on their quest.

THE WORLD OF WEALTH

TOP 10

COINS AND NOTES IN CIRCULATION IN THE US*

	Unit	Total value($)	Units in circulation
1	penny	171,000,000	171,000,000,000
2	dime	2,679,000,000	26,790,000,000
3	quarter	918,800,000	22,970,000,000
4	nickel	923,500,000	18,470,000,000
5	$1 bill	5,824,163,172	5,824,163,172
6	$20 bill	76,156,047,740	3,807,802,387
7	$100 bill	228,683,199,100	2,286,831,991
8	$5 bill	6,956,197,830	1,391,239,566
9	$10 bill	13,001,827,370	1,300,182,737
10	$50 bill	42,299,423,700	845,988,474

* As of January 1995

At number 11 is the $2 bill with a total of $998,041,528 in circulation. The number of coins being minted annually is declining for each denomination. Congress began discussing the withdrawal of the penny in 1994.

THE 10

POOREST COUNTRIES IN THE WORLD

	Country	GDP per capita (US$)
1	Sudan	55
2	Mozambique	62
3	Tanzania	99
4	Somalia	100
5	Cambodia	103
6	Ethiopia	113
7	Vietnam	130
8	Nepal	165
8	Afghanistan	195
9	Sierra Leone	167
10	Uganda	169

TOP 10

COUNTRIES WITH MOST CURRENCY IN CIRCULATION 100 YEARS AGO

	Country	Total currency in circulation (US$)
1	US	2,142,000,000
2	France	2,104,000,000
3	India	960,000,000
4	Germany	900,000,000
5	UK	845,000,000
6	Russia	720,000,000
7	China	700,000,000
8	Italy	510,000,000
9	Austria	460,000,000
10	Spain	390,000,000

It is interesting to consider that, as a result of inflation during the past century, there are now individuals in these countries who – on paper at least – own more than the entire country's money supply in the 1890s. In excess of $1,000,000,000,000 is in circulation in the US today.

TOP 10

COUNTRIES IN WHICH IT IS EASIEST TO BE A MILLIONAIRE

	Country	Currency unit	Value of 1,000,000 units in $
1	Angola	New Kwanza	10.54
2	Turkey	Lira	29.32
3	Poland	Zloty	43.50
4	Ukraine	Karbovanets	48.78
5	Guinea-Bissau	Peso	81.38
6	Vietnam	Dông	91.05
7	Mozambique	Metical	159.58
8	Madagascar	Franc	284.47
9	Cambodia	Riel	285.87
10	Somalia	Shilling	381.87

Runaway inflation in many countries has made their currencies virtually worthless. Occasionally currencies are realigned (effectively devalued): in 1993, for example, there were 5,789,293 Zaïres to the dollar; in 1994 the exchange rate was 1,289.81 Zaïre/$1.00.

THE 10

RICHEST COUNTRIES IN THE WORLD

	Country	GDP per capita (US$)
1	Switzerland	36,231
2	Luxembourg	35,260
3	Japan	28,217
4	Sweden	26,784
5	Bermuda	26,600
6	Denmark	25,927
7	Norway	25,805
8	Iceland	23,667
9	US	23,119
10	Finland	22,977

Gross Domestic Product (GDP) is the total value of all the goods and services produced annually within the country. (Gross National Product – GNP – includes income from overseas.) Dividing GDP by the country's population produces GDP per capita, which is often used as a measure of how "rich" a country is.

RICHEST STATES IN THE US

	State	Average income per head ($)
1	District of Columbia	29,438
2	Connecticut	28,110
3	New Jersey	26,967
4	New York	24,623
5	Massachusetts	24,563
6	Maryland	24,044
7	Hawaii	23,354
8	Alaska	22,846
9	Nevada	22,729
10	New Hampshire	22,659

The median income of US citizens in 1993 was put at $18,177, so the average for the residents of the District of Columbia, (treated as a state for these calculations) is about 62 percent higher than the average.

COUNTRIES WITH THE HIGHEST INFLATION

	Country	Annual inflation rate (%)
1	Zaïre	23,773.0
2	Brazil	2,668.5
3	Romania	255.2
4	Zambia	189.0
5	Turkey	106.3
6	Mongolia	87.6
7	Venezuela	60.8
8	Estonia	47.7
9	Uruguay	44.7
10	Haiti	40.2

Calculated by the International Monetary Fund, these 1994 figures indicate the rise in prices over 1993–94 (except for Romania and Zambia, which are for 1992–93). Inflation of 100 percent means that prices have doubled. Rates may vary over a year – in October 1994, for example, Zaïre's rate hit a modern record of 87,745 percent. Some countries have "improved" their rates – Peru, for example, went down from an annual rate of 3,399 percent in 1989 to 23.7 percent in 1994. The worst inflation ever experienced occurred in Germany in 1923 and Hungary in 1946, and ran into millions of percent.

RICHEST CITIES IN THE US

	Location	Population	Average household income ($)
1	Bloomfield Hills (city), MI	4,288	150,001
2	King's Point (village), NY	4,843	140,838
3	Old Westbury (village), NY	3,897	137,518
4	Saddle River (borough), NJ	2,950	135,662
5	Hunters Creek Village (city), TX	3,954	134,961
6	Village of Indian Hill (city), OH	5,383	132,244
7	Atherton (town), CA	7,163	130,734
8	Lloyd Harbor (village), NY	3,343	130,720
9	Blackhawk (town), CA	6,199	129,135
10	Belle Meade (city), TN	2,830	125,459

1989 US Department of Commerce figures indicate that the richest places have between 2,500 and 9,999 inhabitants; the richest with more than 50,000 people is West Bloomfield, MI (median family income $68,661).

POOREST STATES IN THE US

	State	Average income per head ($)
1	Mississippi	14,894
2	Arkansas	16,143
3	Utah	16,180
4	West Virginia	16,209
5	New Mexico	16,297
6	Louisiana	16,667
7	South Carolina	16,923
8	Oklahoma	17,020
9	Kentucky	17,173
10	Alabama	17,234

The southern states have always been among the poorest, with all 10 here falling below the national average. In 1980, when the latter was put at $8,569, that of Mississippians was calculated at $6,122, then, as now, the lowest of all 50 states.

SWEET TEETH

TOP 10

CANDY-CONSUMING NATIONS IN THE WORLD

| | Country | Annual consumption (lb per head) | | |
		chocolate	other candy	total
1	Netherlands	18.10	12.52	30.63
2	Denmark	15.24	14.09	29.33
3	Switzerland	22.12	6.39	28.51
4	UK	16.36	11.40	27.76
5	Belgium/Luxembourg	16.82	10.72	27.54
6	Ireland	14.66	12.74	27.40
7	Norway	17.40	9.63	27.03
8	Germany	14.49	12.52	27.01
9	Sweden	12.24	11.57	23.81
10	Austria	16.14	6.28	22.42
	US	*10.28*	*7.58*	*17.86*

DID YOU KNOW

HERSHEY – THE MAN, THE TOWN, AND THE CANDY BAR

Milton Snavely Hershey (1857–1945) created the first Hershey's bar in 1894, following a visit to the Chicago State Fair where he had been so impressed with German chocolate-making machines that he ordered them for his Lancaster Caramel Company. After selling the company for $2,000,000 in 1900, he returned to his birthplace of Derry Church, Pennsylvania, and in 1903 set up a new factory, together with houses for his workers. The town was later renamed after Hershey himself. Although it had steadily shrunk in size, the Hershey's bar continued to cost a nickel from 1894 until 1968, when it was enlarged but also doubled in price. Despite its huge success and the familiarity of the Hershey's name, the company did not advertise its products during its first 68 years.

TOP 10

ICE CREAM BRANDS IN THE US

	Brand	Sales ($)*
1	Private labels	610,200,000
2	Good Humor-Breyers	269,100,000
3	Blue Bell	144,700,000
4	Dreyer's/Edy's	142,800,000
5	Häagen-Dazs	131,100,000
6	Ben & Jerry's	114,200,000
7	Sealtest	60,000,000
8	Borden	49,600,000
9	Kemps	45,900,000
10	Turkey Hill	40,200,000

* Year to October 15, 1994
Source: Dairy Foods Magazine

TOP 10

COCOA-CONSUMING NATIONS IN THE WORLD

	Country	Total cocoa consumption (tonnes)
1	US	587,400
2	Germany	263,400
3	UK	189,200
4	France	157,300
5	Russia	117,400
6	Japan	111,200
7	Brazil	76,000
8	Italy	68,300
9	Canada	55,800
10	Spain	53,100

Cocoa is the principal ingredient of chocolate, and its consumption is therefore closely linked to the production of chocolate in each consuming country. Like coffee, the consumption of chocolate occurs mainly in the West and in more affluent countries. Since some of the Top 10 consuming nations also have large populations, the figures for cocoa consumption per head present a somewhat different picture, dominated by those countries with the long-established tradition of manufacturing high-quality chocolate product.

TOP 10

COCOA-CONSUMING NATIONS IN THE WORLD (PER HEAD)

| | Country | Consumption per head | | |
		kg	lb	oz
1	Belgium/Luxembourg	4.794	10	9
2	Switzerland	4.161	9	2
3	Iceland	3.627	8	0
4=	UK	3.266	7	3
4=	Austria	3.266	7	3
6	Germany	3.245	7	2
7	Netherlands	2.985	6	9
8	Denmark	2.741	6	0
9	France	2.728	6	0
10	Norway	2.621	5	12

TOP 10

CANDY BRANDS IN THE US

	Brand	Sales 1993 ($)*
1	M&M's	185,881,472
2	Brach's	181,870,852
3	Hershey	169,958,497
4	Reese's	152,339,870
5	Snickers	122,144,324
6	Hershey Kisses	119,178,840
7	Kit Kat	61,144,354
8	Butterfinger	51,361,624
9	Milky Way	48,005,216
10	Lifesavers	46,340,416

* Through grocery stores only – total sales of some brands through drug stores, mass merchandisers, and other outlets (vending machines, gas stations, etc.) may more than double these figures.

Source: Information Resources Inc.

TOP 10

BEN & JERRY'S ICE CREAM FLAVORS

1 Chocolate Chip Cookie Dough

2 Cherry Garcia

3 Chocolate Fudge Brownie

4 New York Super Fudge Chunk

5 English Toffee Crunch

6 Chocolate Fudge Brownie Frozen Yogurt

7 Chunky Monkey

8 Cherry Garcia Frozen Yogurt

9 Wavy Gravy

10 Mint with Cookies

Grateful Dead founder Jerry Garcia is believed to be the only rock musician ever to have two bestselling ice cream flavors named in his honor.

TOP 10

GUM BRANDS IN THE US

	Brand	Sales 1993 ($)*
1	Wrigley's Extra	108,288,122
2	Trident	76,374,560
3	Carefree	73,746,912
4	Wrigley's Doublemint	39,397,616
5	Freedent	36,320,686
6	Wrigley's Big Red	25,086,000
7	Wrigley's	22,593,408
8	Wrigley's Juicy Fruit	21,305,330
9	Dentyne Cinn A Burst	19,077,312
10	Bubblicious	15,117,924

* Through grocery stores only – total sales of some brands through drug stores, mass merchandisers, and other outlets (vending machines, gas stations, etc.) may more than double these figures.

Source: Information Resources Inc.

TOP 10

FROZEN YOGURT BRANDS IN THE US

	Brand	Sales ($)*
1	Dreyer's/Edy's	80,700,000
2	Private label	72,200,000
3	Kemps	68,200,000
4	Häagen-Dazs	40,900,000
5	Ben & Jerry's	39,300,000
6	Breyers	28,100,000
7	Colombo	25,200,000
8	Wells' Blue Bunny	21,800,000
9	Crowley	21,300,000
10	Turkey Hill	20,400,000

* Year to October 15, 1994

Source: Dairy Foods Magazine

TOP 10

ICE CREAM CONSUMERS IN THE WORLD

	Country	Production per capita (US pints)
1	US	47.04
2	New Zealand	37.70
3	Denmark	36.02
4	Australia	32.64
5	Belgium/Luxembourg	31.50
6	Sweden	30.09
7	Canada	27.02
8	Norway	25.65
9	Ireland	19.32
10	Switzerland	15.79

Global statistics for ice cream consumption are hard to come by. This list presents the International Ice Cream Association's most recent and reliable estimates for per capita production of ice cream and related products (frozen yogurt, sherbert, sorbet, popsicles, etc.) – and since only small amounts of such products are exported, consumption figures can be presumed to be similar. In 1992 US production of all ice cream products was put at a remarkable 1,492,517,000 gallons.

FOOD – WORLD

TOP 10

CONSUMERS OF KELLOGG'S CORN FLAKES*

1	Ireland
2	UK
3	Australia
4	Denmark
5	Sweden
6	Norway
7	Canada
8	US
9	Mexico
10	Venezuela

* Based on per capita consumption

In 1894, while attempting to devise healthy food products for the patients in their "Sanatorium," a health resort in Battle Creek, Michigan, the brothers Will Keith and Dr. John Harvey Kellogg experimented with wheat dough , which they boiled and passed through rollers. By accident, they discovered that if the dough was left overnight it came out as flakes, and that when baked they turned into a tasty cereal. The Kellogg brothers started making their new product on a small scale, providing cereal by mail order to former patients. In 1898 they replaced wheat with corn, thereby creating the Corn Flakes we know today. Will Keith left the Sanatorium in 1906 and set up a business manufacturing Corn Flakes with his distinctive signature on the packet. Corn Flakes, first exported to England in 1922 along with All Bran, followed in 1928 by Rice Krispies, remain Kellogg's bestselling product. The company's corn mill in Seaforth, Liverpool, is Europe's largest and processes 1,000 tons of grain a day.

TOP 10

CALORIE-CONSUMING NATIONS IN THE WORLD

	Country	Average daily per capita consumption
1	Ireland	3,952
2	Belgium/Luxembourg	3,925
3	Greece	3,775
4	Former East Germany	3,710
5	Bulgaria	3,695
6	US	3,642
7	Denmark	3,639
8	Hungary	3,608
9	France	3,593
10	Former Czechoslovakia	3,574
	World average	2,697

A Calorie is a unit of heat (defined as the amount of heat needed to raise one kilogram of water 1° Celcius in temperature). Calories are used by nutritionists as a means of expressing the energy-producing value of foods. The daily Calorie requirement of the average man is 2,700 and, of a woman, 2,500. Inactive people need fewer, while those engaged in heavy labor might have to consume much more, perhaps even double this amount of energy. Calories that are not consumed as energy turn to fat – which is why Calorie-counting is one of the key aspects of most diets. The high Calorie intake of certain countries, measured over the period 1988–90, reflects the high proportion of starchy foods, such as potatoes, bread, and pasta, in the national diet. In many Western countries the high figures simply reflect over-eating – especially since these figures are averages that include men, women, and children, suggesting that large numbers in each country are greatly exceeding them. While weight-watchers of the West guzzle their way through 30 percent more than they need, every country in Europe (except Sweden) consuming more than 3,000 Calories per head, the Calorie consumption in Bangladesh and some of the poorest African nations falls below 2,000. In the Congo it is 1,760 – less than half that of the nations in the world Top 10.

TOP 10

MEAT-EATING NATIONS IN THE WORLD

	Country	Consumption per head per annum		
		kg	lb	oz
1	US	118.8	261	14
2	France	111.5	245	13
3	Denmark	108.5	239	3
4	Belgium/ Luxembourg	102.6	226	3
5	Australia	101.7	224	3
6	New Zealand	100.8	222	3
7	Austria	100.6	221	12
8	Hungary	97.5	214	15
9	Canada	96.4	212	8
10	Germany	95.4	210	5

Meat consumption reflects factors such as wealth, culture, and religion. In general, more meat is eaten in richer countries. New Zealand, a lamb-producer, and Argentina and Uruguay, both beef-producers, are among those that eat the most lamb and beef. Pork, forbidden under religious dietary laws, is rarely eaten in the Middle East.

TOP 10

CONSUMERS OF HEINZ BAKED BEANS IN THE WORLD

	Consumer	Sales (cans per annum)*
1	UK	451,000,000
2	Sweden	2,066,000
3	Singapore	444,000
4	United Arab Emirates	441,000
5	West Africa	339,000
6	Hong Kong	276,000
7	Greece	275,000
8	Saudi Arabia	226,800
9	NAAFI, Germany	216,000
10	Finland	190,476

Based on 1 lb/450 g can

These figures are not a mistake: the United Kingdom really does munch its way through 451,000,000 cans of Heinz baked beans a year – equivalent to 10 cans for every inhabitant, and 224 times as many as the next most important international market, Sweden (where the annual consumption is just 0.28 cans per head).

Of all their "57 Varieties," baked beans are Heinz's most famous product. They were originally test-marketed in northern England in 1901 and imported from the US up until 1928, when they were first canned in the UK. The slogan "Beanz Meanz Heinz" was invented in 1967 over a drink in the Victoria pub in Mornington Terrace, London, by Young and Rubicam advertising agency executive Maurice Drake.

In 1995 H. J. Heinz celebrates 100 years of baked bean production and the opening of the company's first London office.

TOP 10

HEINZ PRODUCTS IN THE WORLD

1	Ketchup
2	Tuna and seafood
3	Pet food
4	Baby food
5	Frozen potatoes and vegetables
6	Frozen meals and snacks
7	Soup
8	Baked beans and canned pasta
9	Sauces and pastes
10	Bakery products

Henry John Heinz, the founder of the Heinz food processing and canning empire, was born in 1844, in Pittsburgh, Pennsylvania, of German immigrant parents. In 1869 he formed a partnership with L.C. Noble, selling horseradish in clear glass jars (previously, green glass disguised the dishonest practice of filling out the horseradish with turnip), beginning the Heinz reputation for quality and integrity. Their products were also sold on their lack of artificial flavorings and colorings long before this was thought desirable. Heinz & Noble steadily added other lines, including pickles. In 1876, with his brother John and cousin Frederick, H.J. formed the firm of F. & J. Heinz. One of their first products was ketchup, a staple in every American household, but one made on a domestic scale, involving the entire family stirring a cauldron over an open fire for a whole day. By 1886 the business was sufficiently well established for the Heinz family to visit Europe. H.J. sold the first Heinz products in Britain to Fortnum & Mason, the upscale Piccadilly food emporium, astonishing them by his audacity at entering through the front door, rather than the tradesman's entrance. The first branch office in London was opened in 1895.

Why "57 Varieties"? In 1896, on the New York Third Avenue El, H.J. saw a sign that advertised "21 Styles" of shoe. "I said to myself, 'We do not have styles of products, but we do have varieties of products.' I counted well beyond 57, but '57' kept coming back into my mind . . . 58 Varieties or 59 Varieties did not appeal to me at all." Henry went straight to the printers and designed the first "Heinz 57" advertisement.

TOP 10

SUGAR-CONSUMING NATIONS IN THE WORLD

	Country	Consumption per head per annum kg	lb
1	Cuba	88.9	196.0
2	Swaziland	70.9	156.3
3	Singapore	70.4	155.2
4	Fiji	60.7	133.8
5	Costa Rica	58.0	127.9
6	Iceland	57.7	127.2
7	Israel	57.5	126.8
8	Netherlands	55.4	122.1
9	Belize	55.3	121.9
10	Austria	54.6	120.4
	UK	*43.7*	*96.3*
	US	*28.9*	*63.7*

Each Cuban citizen would appear to consume a quantity equal to the familiar 2.2 lb/1 kg bag of sugar every four days.

DID YOU KNOW

FOOD FROM THE FREEZER

Working as a fur-trader, Brooklyn-born Clarence Birdseye observed Eskimos keeping fish and caribou meat for months in sub-zero conditions. Back in the US, he set up General Seafoods in 1924 and began to preserve fish by rapid freezing – experimenting with anything from whales to alligators. Soon he was also freezing 500 tons of fruit and vegetables each year. In 1930 it first marketed individual packs of frozen food in the US, and the domestic frozen food industry was born. In Britain, Smedley of Wisbech first sold frozen asparagus in 1937. Birds Eye sold its first individual frozen meals – chicken fricassée and steak – in 1939.

FOOD – US

FAST FOOD CHAINS IN THE US

	Chain*	Revenue ($)#		Chain*	Revenue ($)#
1	McDonald's	23,587,000,000	6	Taco Bell	3,720,000,000
2	KFC	7,100,000,000	7	Hardee's	3,550,000,000
3	Burger King	6,700,000,000	8	Dairy Queen	2,400,000,000
4	Pizza Hut	6,300,000,000	9=	Subway	2,200,000,000
5	Wendy's	3,924,000,000	9=	Domino's Pizza	2,200,000,000

* Excluding fast-food contractors such as ARA Services and Marriott Management Services, which would otherwise appear at numbers 8 and 9
 # Worldwide, 1993

McDonald's staggering worldwide sales includes $9,400,000,000 in revenue from its 4,710 overseas outlets, scattered throughout some 80 countries. The chain is adding between 600 and 700 new sites in foreign countries each year and is expecting overseas revenue to top domestic volume by the turn of the century.

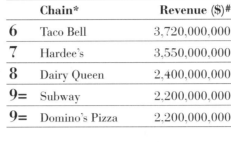

Source: Restaurants & Institutions: *The Top 400 List*

FOOD AND DRINK ADVERTISERS IN THE US

	Company	Adspend ($)*
1	Kelloggs	101,782,800
2	McDonald's	100,354,700
3	Budweiser	62,632,400
4	Kraft	58,960,100
5	General Mills Cereals	58,891,000
6	Coke/Diet Coke	55,057,000
7	Pizza Hut	44,323,700
8	Miller Beer	43,266,200
9	Post Cereals	41,011,900
10	Burger King	40,055,900

* First quarter of 1994

Source: Advertising Age

Half of the company names in this Top 10 are eponymous: Kelloggs (brothers John Harvey and Will Keith), McDonalds (Maurice and Richard), Kraft (James L.), and Post Cereals (Charles William). Budweiser's name derives not from a person but from the German name for the Czech town from which the company's founder emigrated.

FOOD COMPANIES IN THE US

	Company	Main products	Annual sales ($)		Company	Main products	Annual sales ($)
1	Philip Morris	Cheese, cereals, beer	53,776,000,000	8	CPC International	Sweeteners, corn oil, mayonnaise, pasta, peanut butter	7,425,000,000
2	Conagra	Frozen foods, processed meats, potato products	23,512,000,000	9	H.J. Heinz	Ketchup, baby food, pickles	7,047,000,000
3	Sara Lee	Bakery goods, processed meats	15,536,000,000	10	Campbell Soup	Canned soups	6,691,000,000
4	IBP	Beef and pork	12,075,000,000				
5	Archer Daniels Midland	Refined oils, food additives	11,374,000,000				
6	General Mills	Cereals, flour, cake mixes, dessert items	8,517,000,000				
7	Ralston Purina	Bakery goods, pet food	7,705,000,000				

American food giant Philip Morris is a division of a company that can trace its origins back to 1847, when Philip Morris opened his shop in Oxford, England, with a sign that read "Philip Morris, Esquire, Tobacconist and Importer of Fine Seegars." Exploiting the new fashion for cigarettes, in 1854 Morris expanded with a shop in London's Bond Street, and in 1872 an agency was established to sell his products in New York. This business grew rapidly, soon eclipsing its English parent company, and developed interests in industries far beyond tobacco.

TOP 10

SUPERMARKET DELI SALES IN THE US

	Products	Percentage of sales*
1	Sliced meats	34.4
2	Cheese	13.3
3	Salads	12.0
4	Prepared chicken	10.1
5	Pizza	8.4
6	Sandwiches	7.8
7=	Refrigerated entrées	6.3
7=	Hot entrées	6.3
9	Barbecued ribs	1.7
10	Other	0.7

* The total amounts to more than 100% due to rounding off

TOP 10

POULTRY PRODUCERS IN THE US

	Company	Average weekly poultry slaughter
1	Tyson Foods, Inc.	26,500,000
2	Gold Kist, Inc.	12,600,000
3	ConAgra, Inc.	11,250,000
4	Perdue Farms, Inc.	7,510,000
5	Pilgrim's Pride Corp.	7,500,000
6	Hudson Food, Inc.	4,350,000
7	Wayne Poultry Div.	4,030,000
8	Seaboard Farms, Inc.	3,800,000
9	Sanderson Farms, Inc.	2,880,000
10	Foster Farms	2,850,000

The Top 10 companies alone slaughter 83,270,000 birds (mostly chickens) a week, or 4,330,040,000 a year – equivalent to more than 16 per annum for every US inhabitant. Perdue Farms' Frank Perdue has achieved nationwide celebrity by appearing in his own TV commercials.

TOP 10

SNACKS IN THE US

	Snack	Consumption* volume (lb)	sales ($)
1	Potato chips	6.69	17.80
2	Tortilla chips	4.56	11.30
3	Snack nuts	1.71	5.70
4	Pretzels	2.30	4.27
5	Microwavable popcorn	1.46	3.07
6	Extruded snacks	1.11	2.98
7	Cornchips	0.97	2.45
8	Meat snacks	0.17	2.10
9	Ready-to-eat popcorn	0.64	1.81
10	Party mix	0.38	1.12

* Average per capita 1993, ranked by value

In 1993 the average American ate 21.42 pounds of snacks at a cost of $56.88. The total includes both those in the Top 10 and various additional categories outside it, such as pork rinds, multigrain chips, and unpopped popcorn.

TOP 10

BRANDS OF POPCORN*

	Brand	Sales ($)
1	Orville Redenbacher	243,700,000
2	Betty Crocker Pop-Secret	170,700,000
3	Golden Valley	85,600,000
4	Private labels	69,800,000
5	Pop Weaver's	39,600,000
6	Jolly Time	32,900,000
7	Newman's Own	9,300,000
9	Cousin Willie's	8,900,000
10	Pops-Rile	800,000,000

* Unpopped only

TOP 10

HONEY-PRODUCING STATES IN THE US

	State	Honey production (lb p.a.)
1	California	45,000,000
2	South Dakota	24,010,000
3	Florida	22,600,000
4	North Dakota	19,800,000
5	Minnesota	14,400,000
6	Idaho	9,443,000
7	Texas	8,610,000
9	Wisconsin	8,200,000
10	Michigan	6,930,000

The US as a whole produces 198,416,960 lbs of honey a year but is in second place behind the world's leading producer China, with 451,946,880 lbs. The total annual world production is 2,593,395,840 lbs.

TOP 10

DESSERTS IN RESTAURANTS IN THE US

	Dessert	Percentage of restaurants with dessert menu
1	Cheesecake	64.0
2	Apple pie	61.5
3	Chocolate cake	51.8
4	Carrot cake	47.6
5	Brownies	45.4
6	Cookies	43.8
7	Cherry pie	43.5
9	Fresh fruit	41.7
10	Cream pie	40.1

While homemade apple pie has become a virtual icon of American culture, pumpkin pie was already a traditional Thanksgiving dish when the first American cookbook was published in 1796 and included the recipe.

ALCOHOL

TOP 10

ALCOHOL-DRINKING NATIONS IN THE WORLD

	Country	Annual consumption per head (100% alcohol) liters	pints
1	Luxembourg	12.6	26.6
2	France	11.5	24.3
3	Austria	10.6	22.4
4=	Germany	10.4	22.0
4=	Portugal	10.4	22.0
6	Hungary	10.2	21.6
7=	Spain	10.0	21.1
7=	Switzerland	10.0	21.1
9	Denmark	9.2	19.4
10	Greece	9.1	19.2
23=	*UK*	*6.8*	*12.0*
23=	*US*	*6.8*	*12.0*

France, which headed the list for many years, peaking at 36.8 pints/17.4 liters per head, has been overtaken by Luxembourg.

TOP 10

CHAMPAGNE IMPORTERS IN THE WORLD

	Country	Bottles imported
1	Germany	18,844,853
2	UK	17,023,214
3	US	11,992,434
4	Switzerland	7,524,137
5	Italy	6,616,110
6	Belgium	6,552,579
7	The Netherlands	1,925,883
8	Japan	1,459,353
9	Australia	1,107,295
10	Spain	1,086,809

The UK fell from first position in 1991 but even now consumes more per head (0.33 bottles) than does Germany (0.25 bottles). France, champagne's domestic market, consumed 157,147,534 bottles in 1994 – equivalent to 2.5 bottles per head.

TOP 10

BEER-PRODUCING COUNTRIES IN THE WORLD

	Country	Annual production liters	pints
1	US	23,716,800,000	41,735,200,000
2	Germany	12,015,800,000	21,144,800,000
3	China	10,206,400,000	17,960,700,000
4	Japan	7,010,600,000	12,336,900,000
5	Brazil	5,730,000,000	10,833,800,000
6	UK	5,588,700,000	9,834,700,000
7	Mexico	4,253,300,000	7,487,600,000
8	Russia	2,790,000,000	4,909,700,000
9	Spain	2,608,200,000	4,589,800,000
10	South Africa	2,250,000,000	3,959,400,000
	World total	*118,080,000,000*	*207,792,000,000*

The production of beer throughout the world is almost sufficient to allow every person on the planet to drink 1.2 pints/0.57 liters every 9 days of the year. In relation to their populations, the beer production of the US and the UK is similar in that it is sufficient to provide each of the inhabitants of both countries with 1.2 pints/0.57 liters every two days.

TOP 10

BEER-DRINKING NATIONS IN THE WORLD

	Country	Annual consumption per head liters	pints
1	Czech Republic	140.0	295.9
2	Germany	137.5	290.6
3	Ireland	130.8	276.4
4	Slovakia	130.0	274.7
5	Denmark	127.6	269.7
6	Austria	125.0	264.2
7	Luxembourg	122.0	257.8
8	Belgium	110.5	233.5
9	Hungary	103.8	219.4
10	Australia	102.1	215.8

Perhaps surprisingly, despite its position as the world's leading producer of beer, the US is ranked 13th in terms of consumption (180 pints/ 85.2 liters per head).

DID YOU KNOW

NOT A GOOD YEAR

After surviving for over 200 years, the first and eighth entries in the "Most Expensive Bottles of Wine" list – both of which were initialed by America's third president Thomas Jefferson – suffered disastrous fates in New York. The world's most expensive single bottle was exhibited in a cabinet where the heat from the display light dried out the cork, allowing the contents to evaporate. No. 8 had been bought by Jefferson when he was ambassador to France, and had his initials scratched into the glass. This association had increased its post-auction price tag to $500,000, and an offer approaching $300,000 had been refused. On April 25, 1989 it was on show at a tasting in the Four Seasons restaurant, New York, when it was inadvertently smashed by a waiter's tray. A small quantity of the wine was salvaged, but, as the wine merchant who drank it reported, "It tasted like it still had wine taste, but not very good." Fortunately, it was insured.

CHAMPAGNE
BRUT
PERRIER-JOUET
EPERNAY-FRANCE
GRAND BRUT

T O P 1 0

BRANDS OF IMPORTED BEER IN THE US

	Brand/nationality	Imports 1993 (gallons)
1	Heineken (German)	52,300,000
2	Corona (Mexican)	27,100,000
3	Molsen (Canadian)	22,600,000
4	Becks (German)	21,600,000
5	LaBatt's (Canadian)	14,400,000
6	Amstel Light (Dutch)	9,900,000
7	Tecate (Mexican)	8,000,000
8	Moosehead (Canadian)	6,700,000
9	Foster's (Australian)	6,000,000
10	Dos Equis (Mexican)	5,600,000

The total amount of imported beer brands in 1993 was 236,000,000 gallons.

T O P 1 0

BREWERIES IN THE US

	Brewery	Total sales 1993 (barrels)*
1	Anheuser-Busch	87,300,000
2	Miller Brewing Company	42,700,000
3	Coors	19,900,000
4	Stroh	13,000,000
5	G. Heileman	9,000,000
6	S&P Industries	8,200,000
7	Genesee	2,000,000
8	Latrobe Brewing	1,000,000
9	Pittsburgh Brewing	600,000
10	Hudepohl-Schoenling	400,000

Wholesale sales; a barrel contains 31.5 US gallons.

The Anheuser-Busch total annual sales account for 2,749,950,000 gallons – equivalent to more than 10 gallons for every inhabitant of the US.

T O P 1 0

MOST EXPENSIVE BOTTLES OF WINE EVER SOLD AT AUCTION

	Wine	Price ($)
1	Château Lafite 1787 Christie's, London, December 5, 1985	140,700 (£105,000)

The highest price ever paid for a bottle of red wine resulted from the bottle having been initialed by the third US President, Thomas Jefferson. It was purchased by Christopher Forbes and is now on display in the Forbes Magazine Galleries, New York.

	Wine	Price ($)
2	Château d'Yquem 1784 Christie's, London, December 4, 1986	58,500 (£39,600)

The highest price ever paid for a bottle of white wine.

	Wine	Price ($)
3	Château Mouton-Rothschild 1945 (jeroboam – equivalent to four bottles) Christie's, Geneva, May 14, 1995	54,400 (SF68,200)

The highest price ever paid for a postwar wine.

	Wine	Price ($)
4	Château Lafite Rothschild 1832 (double magnum) International Wine Auctions, London, April 9, 1988	40,300 (£24,000)
5	Château Lafite 1806 Sotheby's, Geneva, November 13, 1988	36,100 (SF57,200)

	Wine	Price ($)
6	Château Lafite 1811 (tappit-hen – equivalent to three bottles) Christie's, London, June 23, 1988	33,600 (£20,000)
7	Cheval-blanc 1947 (imperial – equivalent to eight bottles) Christie's, London, December 1, 1994	33,100 (£19,250)
8	Château Lafite 1822 Sold at a Heublein Auction San Francisco, May 28, 1980	31,000
9	Cheval-blanc 1947 (jeroboam) Christie's, London, November 3, 1994	29,700 (£17,300)
10	Château Margaux 1784 (half-bottle) Christie's, at Vin Expo, Bordeaux, France, June 26, 1987	29,500 (FF176,400)

The highest price ever paid for a half-bottle.

As well as these prices at auction, rare bottles of wine have also been sold privately for sums in excess of $30,000.

T O P 1 0

WINE-DRINKING NATIONS IN THE WORLD

	Country	Liters per head per annum	Equiv. 75 cl bottles
1	France	63.5	84.7
2	Luxembourg	61.0	81.3
3	Italy	58.0	77.3
4	Argentina	47.8	63.7
5	Portugal	46.8	62.4
6	Switzerland	46.0	61.3
7	Greece	35.2	46.9
8	Austria	34.5	46.0
9	Hungary	31.8	42.4
10	Spain	31.3	41.7

T O P 1 0

WINE-PRODUCING COUNTRIES IN THE WORLD

	Country	Annual production (tonnes)
1	Italy	5,700,000
2	France	5,398,000
3	Spain	2,709,000
4	US	1,700,000
5	Germany	1,340,000
6	Argentina	1,200,000
7	South Africa	930,000
8	Portugal	900,000
9	Romania	800,000
10	Russia	750,000
	World total	26,349,000

SOFT SELL

T O P 1 0

READY-TO-DRINK TEA BRANDS IN THE US

	Brand	1994 sales (cases)*
1	Lipton	44,200,000
2	Snapple	41,100,000
3	Nestea	24,900,000
4	Arizona	22,000,000
5	Private Label	7,800,000
6	Ssips	4,400,000
7	Tetley	3,100,000
8	Mistic	1,800,000
9	Celestial Seasoning	400,000
10	Best Health	300,000

* *Wholesale sales – one case = 24 x 16 oz cans*

The latest soft drink fad in the US, ready-to-drink iced tea is the most popular new nonalcoholic beverage of the 1990s.

Source: Beverage Marketing Corporation

T O P 1 0

TEA-DRINKING NATIONS

	Country	Annual consumption per head		
		kg	lb oz	cups*
1	Irish Republic	3.33	7 5	1,465
2	UK	2.61	5 12	1,148
3	Qatar	2.30	5 1	1,012
4	Turkey	2.14	4 11	942
5=	Hong Kong	1.74	3 13	766
5=	Iran	1.74	3 13	766
7	Kuwait	1.69	3 12	744
8	Syria	1.66	3 11	730
9	Tunisia	1.42	3 2	625
10	Bahrain	1.41	3 2	620
	US	0.34	0 12	150

* *Based on 440 cups per 2 lb 3 oz/kg*

Tea consumption in Qatar has fallen from its former world record of 8 lb 12 oz/3.97 kg (1,747 cups) per head. In Italy just 3 oz/ 0.09 kg (40 cups) are drunk annually per head, while Thailand's 0.4 oz/0.01 kg (4 cups) is one of the lowest.

T O P 1 0

COFFEE-DRINKING NATIONS

	Country	Annual consumption per head			
		kg	lb	oz	cups*
1	Finland	13.32	29	5	1,998
2	Sweden	11.10	24	8	1,665
3	Austria	10.03	22	2	1,505
4=	Denmark	9.61	21	3	1,442
4=	Norway	9.61	21	3	1,442
6	Netherlands	9.34	20	10	1,401
7	Germany	7.91	17	7	1,187
8	Switzerland	7.51	16	9	1,127
9	Cyprus	6.25	13	13	938
10	France	5.73	12	10	860
	US	4.28	9	7	642
	UK	2.63	5	13	395

* *Based on 150 cups per 2 lb 3 oz/kg*

The total coffee consumption of many countries declined during the 1980s. That of Belgium and Luxembourg dropped almost 70 percent, from 15 lb 13 oz/7.17 kg (1,076 cups) in 1986 to 5 lb 0 oz/2.27 kg (341 cups) in 1990, but has recently risen again. However, that of Finland and Sweden has remained high – the average Finn drinks more than five cups of coffee a day compared with just over one for the UK. The Irish drink the least amount of coffee in the European Community at 4 lb/1.82 kg (273 cups) – but as the comparative table shows, the country more than compensates with its preeminence in tea-drinking.

T O P 1 0

SOFT DRINKS IN THE US

	Brand	1993 market share (%)
1	Coca-Cola Classic	19.3
2	Pepsi	16.1
3	Diet Coke	9.8
4	Diet Pepsi	6.2
5	Dr. Pepper	5.3
6	Mountain Dew	4.3
7	Sprite	3.9
8	7-Up	2.9
9	Caffeine-Free Coke	2.2
10	Caffeine-Free Pepsi	1.3

T O P 1 0

COCA-COLA CONSUMERS IN THE WORLD

1	Iceland
2	US
3	Mexico
4	Australia
5	Norway
6	Germany
7	Canada
8	Spain
9	Argentina
10	Japan

This ranking is based on consumption per capita in these countries – although the actual volumes are secret. The figures for many small countries are distorted by the influx of large numbers of tourists.

T O P 1 0

CONSUMERS OF PERRIER WATER

1	France
2	US
3	UK
4	Belgium
5	Canada
6	Germany
7	Greece
8	Hong Kong
9	Switzerland
10	Reunion Island

In 1903 St. John Harmsworth, a wealthy Englishman on a tour of France, visited Vergèze, a spa town near Nîmes. Its spring, Les Bouillens (which was believed to have been discovered by the Carthaginian soldier Hannibal in *c.*218 BC), was notable for the occurrence of carbon dioxide, which is released from the surrounding rock, permeating the water and making it "naturally sparkling." Harmsworth recognized the potential for selling the spa water and proceeded to buy the spring, naming it after its former owner, Dr. Louis Perrier, a local doctor, and bottling it in distinctive green bottles – said to have been modeled on the Indian clubs with which he exercised. The company was sold back to the French in 1948 (and in 1992 the firm was bought by the Swiss company Nestlé). Perrier water has maintained a reputation as a popular beverage in sophisticated circles. In 1960 in *For Your Eyes Only* Ian Fleming even has James Bond drink it –

"He always stipulated Perrier. . . . " In the late 1970s a combination of increased health consciousness and ingenious advertising and marketing enabled Perrier to broaden its appeal and to achieve its world dominance of the burgeoning mineral water business. Perrier is now drunk in 145 countries around the world, and its name has become virtually synonymous with mineral water. In the US, Perrier is outsold by many of the domestic brands, and it commands a share of the market that is little more than 2 percent. However, it is the mineral water of choice and is ordered by name in many of the country's leading restaurants, a cachet and brand name profile that are all the more remarkable when one considers the economics of transporting bottled mineral water across the Atlantic.

T O P 1 0

SOFT DRINK BRANDS IN THE US

	Brand	1994 sales (gallons)*
1	Coca-Cola Classic	2,621,000,000
2	Pepsi	2,066,000,000
3	Diet Coke	1,268,000,000
4	Dr. Pepper	768,000,000
5	Diet Pepsi	760,000,000
6	Mountain Dew	683,000,000
7	Sprite	581,000,000
8	7-Up	381,000,000
9	Caffeine-Free Diet Coke	265,000,000
10	Caffeine-Free Diet Pepsi	153,000,000

* Wholesale sales

Source: Beverage Marketing Corporation

In 1994, 13,275,000,000 gallons of soft drinks were sold in the US – equivalent to 50 gallons for every US citizen.

T O P 1 0

BOTTLED WATER BRANDS IN THE US

	Brand	1994 sales ($)		Brand	1994 sales ($)
1	Arrowhead	235,400,000	**6**	Ozarka	79,300,000
2	Poland Spring	167,000,000	**7**	Zephyrhills	75,100,000
3	Evian	154,500,000	**8**	Alpine Springs	67,500,000
4	Sparklets	152,000,000	**9**	Mountain Valley	59,800,000
5	Hinckley-Schmitt	108,000,000	**10**	Perrier	56,600,000

Source: Beverage Marketing Corporation

Total sales of bottled water in the US in 1994 were 2,685,000,000 gallons, representing $3,122,100,000 in wholesale sales, of which the Top 10 were responsible for 50 percent.

T O P 1 0

FRUIT DRINK COMPANIES IN THE US

	Company	1994 sales ($)*		Company	1994 sales ($)*
1	Coca-Cola Foods	1,827,700,000	**7**	Dole	225,000,000
2	Tropicana	1,480,400,000	**8**	Tree Top	180,000,000
3	Ocean Spray	991,000,000	**9**	Mott's USA	159,700,000
4	Proctor & Gamble	580,000,000	**10**	Del Monte	140,000,000
5	Welch's	352,000,000			
6	Veryfine	262,000,000			

* Wholesale sales

Source: Beverage Marketing Corporation

TOWN & COUNTRY

TOP 10

LONGEST FRONTIERS IN THE WORLD

	Country	km	miles
1	China	22,143	13,759
2	Russia	20,139	12,514
3	Brazil	14,691	9,129
4	India	14,103	8,763
5	US	12,248	7,611
6	Zaïre	10,271	6,382
7	Argentina	9,665	6,006
8	Canada	8,893	5,526
9	Mongolia	8,114	5,042
10	Sudan	7,697	4,783

The 7,611 miles/12,248 km of the US's frontiers include those shared with Canada (3,987 miles/6,416 km of which compose the longest continuous frontier in the world), the 1,539-mile/2,477-km boundary between Canada and Alaska, that with Mexico (2,067 miles/3,326 km), and between the US naval base at Guantánamo and Cuba (18 miles/29 km).

TOP 10

SMALLEST COUNTRIES IN THE WORLD

	Country	Area sq km	sq miles
1	Vatican City	0.44	0.17
2	Monaco	1.81	0.7
3	Gibraltar	6.47	2.5
4	Macao	16.06	6.2
5	Nauru	21.23	8.2
6	Tuvalu	25.90	10.0
7	Bermuda	53.35	20.6
8	San Marino	59.57	23.0
9	Liechtenstein	157.99	61.0
10	Antigua	279.72	108.0

SMALLEST COUNTRY
St. Peter's is at the heart of the Vatican City, which is the world's smallest country.

TOP 10

LARGEST COUNTRIES IN THE WORLD

	Country	Area sq km	sq miles
1	Russia	17,070,289	6,590,876
2	Canada	9,970,537	3,849,646
3	China	9,596,961	3,705,408
4	US	9,372,614	3,618,787
5	Brazil	8,511,965	3,286,488
6	Australia	7,686,848	2,967,909
7	India	3,287,590	1,269,346
8	Argentina	2,766,889	1,068,302
9	Kazakhstan	2,716,626	1,048,895
10	Sudan	2,505,813	967,500
	World total	*136,597,770*	*52,740,700*

The breakup of the former USSR has effectively introduced two new countries to this list of the world's largest. Russia thus takes the preeminent position, while Kazakhstan, which enters in the 9th position, ousts Algeria from the bottom of the list.

TOP 10

COUNTRIES WITH MOST NEIGHBORS

Country/neighbors	No. of neighbors
1 China	16

Afghanistan, Bhutan, Hong Kong, India, Kazakhstan, Kyrgyzstan, Laos, Macao, Mongolia, Myanmar (Burma), Nepal, North Korea, Pakistan, Russia, Tajikistan, Vietnam

2 Russia	14

Azerbaijan, Belarus, China, Estonia, Finland, Georgia, Kazakhstan, Latvia, Lithuania, Mongolia, North Korea, Norway, Poland, Ukraine

3 Brazil	10

Argentina, Bolivia, Colombia, French Guiana, Guyana, Paraguay, Peru, Suriname, Uruguay, Venezuela

4= Germany	9

Austria, Belgium, Czech Republic, Denmark, France, Luxembourg, Netherlands, Poland, Switzerland

4= Sudan	9

Central African Republic, Chad, Egypt, Eritrea, Ethiopia, Kenya, Libya, Uganda, Zaïre

4= Zaïre	9

Angola, Burundi, Central African Republic, Congo, Rwanda, Sudan, Tanzania, Uganda, Zambia

7= Austria	8

Czech Republic, Germany, Hungary, Italy, Liechtenstein, Slovakia, Slovenia, Switzerland

7= France	8

Andorra, Belgium, Germany, Italy, Luxembourg, Monaco, Spain, Switzerland

7= Saudi Arabia	8

Iraq, Jordan, Kuwait, Oman, People's Democratic Republic of Yemen, Qatar, United Arab Emirates, Yemen Arab Republic

7= Tanzania	8

Burundi, Kenya, Malawi, Mozambique, Rwanda, Uganda, Zaïre, Zambia

7= Turkey	8

Armenia, Azerbaijan, Bulgaria, Georgia, Greece, Iran, Iraq, Syria

TOP 10

COUNTRIES WITH THE LONGEST COASTLINES

	Country	km	miles
1	Canada	243,791	151,485
2	Indonesia	54,716	33,999
3	Greenland	44,087	27,394
4	Russia	37,653	23,396
5	Philippines	36,289	22,559
6	Australia	25,760	16,007
7	Norway	21,925	13,624
8	US	19,924	12,380
9	New Zealand	15,134	9,404
10	China	14,500	9,010

TOP 10

LARGEST COUNTRIES IN ASIA

	Country	Area sq km	sq miles
1	China	9,596,961	3,705,408
2	India	3,287,590	1,269,346
3	Kazakhstan	2,716,626	1,049,155
4	Saudi Arabia	2,149,640	830,000
5	Indonesia	1,904,569	735,358
6	Iran	1,648,000	636,296
7	Mongolia	1,565,000	604,250
8	Pakistan	803,950	310,407
9	Turkey (in Asia)	790,200	305,098
10	Myanmar (Burma)	676,552	261,218

TOP 10

LARGEST COUNTRIES IN AFRICA

	Country	Area sq km	sq miles
1	Sudan	2,505,813	967,500
2	Algeria	2,381,741	919,595
3	Zaïre	2,345,409	905,567
4	Libya	1,759,540	679,362
5	Chad	1,284,000	495,755
6	Niger	1,267,080	489,191
7	Angola	1,246,700	481,354
8	Mali	1,240,000	478,791
9	Ethiopia	1,221,900	471,778
10	South Africa	1,221,031	471,445

TOP 10

LARGEST COUNTRIES IN EUROPE

	Country	Area sq km	sq miles
1	Russia (in Europe)	4,710,227	1,818,629
2	Ukraine	603,700	233,090
3	France	547,026	211,208
4	Spain	504,781	194,897
5	Sweden	449,964	173,732
6	Germany	356,999	137,838
7	Finland	337,007	130,119
8	Norway	324,220	125,182
9	Poland	312,676	120,725
10	Italy	301,226	116,304

WORLD POPULATIONS

THE GROWTH OF WORLD POPULATION SINCE 1000 AD

Year	Estimated total
1000	254,000,000
1500	460,000,000
1600	579,000,000
1700	679,000,000
1800	954,000,000
1850	1,094,000,000
1900	1,633,000,000
1950	2,515,312,000
1960	3,019,376,000
1970	3,697,918,000
1980	4,450,210,000
1985	4,853,848,000
1995	5,692,210,000

World population is believed to have exceeded 5,000,000 before 8000 BC, and surpassed 5,000,000,000 in 1987. The United Nations has estimated the future growth of world population within three ranges – "low," "medium," and "high," depending on the extent of birth control measures and other factors during the coming decades. The high scenario, which assumes that few additional checks are placed on population expansion, implies a 78 percent global increase by the year 2025. Estimates suggest that by the turn of the century more than 60 percent of the world's population will be in Asia.

Year	Low	Medium	High
2000	6,088.506,000	6,251,055,000	6,410,707,000
2005	6,463,211,000	6,728,574,000	6,978,754,000
2010	6,805,064,000	7,190,762,000	7,561,301,000
2015	7,109,736,000	7,639,547,000	8,167,357,000
2020	7.368,995,000	8,062,274,000	8,791,432,000
2025	7,589,731,000	8,466,516,000	9,422,749,000

TOP 10

MOST HIGHLY POPULATED COUNTRIES 100 YEARS AGO

	Country	Population
1	China	303,241,969
2	India	289,187,316
3	Russia	129,211,113
4	US	62,981,000
5	Germany	52,244,503
6	Austria	41,345,329
7	Japan	40,072,020
8	UK	39,824,563
9	Turkey	39,500,000
10	France	38,517,975

In the late 1890s many national boundaries were different from their present form: for example, India encompassed what are now Pakistan and Bangladesh, Poland was part of Russia, and Austria and Turkey were extensive empires that included all their territories in their censuses. Censuses taken in 1891 put the estimated population of the entire British Empire at 340,220,000, making it second only to China's, with the UK's population 37,888,153; by 1897 this had reached almost 40,000,000.

TOP 10

MOST HIGHLY POPULATED COUNTRIES IN THE WORLD

	Country	Population 1985*	Population 1995#
1	China	1,008,175,288	1,193,332,000
2	India	685,184,692	934,228,000
3	US	231,106,727	263,119,000
4	Indonesia	153,030,000	192,543,000
5	Brazil	119,098,922	161,374,000
6	Russia	142,117,000	148,940,000
7	Pakistan	83,780,000	129,704,000
8	Japan	119,430,000	125,213,000
9	Bangladesh	94,700,000	121,110,000
10	Nigeria	82,390,000	111,273,000
	Total		5,692,210,000

* Based on closest censuses
 # Based on World Bank estimates

The population of China is now more than four times that of the US and 20 times that of the UK. It represents over 21 percent of the total population of the world in 1995, proving the commonly stated statistic that "one person in five is Chinese." Although differential rates of population increase result in changes in the order, the members of the Top 10 remain largely the same from year to year: the population of Pakistan, for example, only recently overtook that of Japan. The Top 10 accounts for all the world's countries that have populations of more than 100,000,000 – that of the closest runner-up, Mexico, was estimated to be 90,464,000 in 1995.

TOP 10

COUNTRIES WITH THE HIGHEST ESTIMATED POPULATION IN THE YEAR 2000

	Country	Population*
1	China	1,255,054,000
2	India	1,016,242,000
3	US	275,636,000
4	Indonesia	206,213,000
5	Brazil	172,228,000
6	Russia	149,844,000
7	Pakistan	148,012,000
8	Bangladesh	132,417,000
9	Nigeria	127,806,000
10	Japan	126,840,000

* Based on World Bank 1994 estimates

Asia contains many of the countries with the highest estimated populations in the year 2000. The part of the former USSR located within Asia previously placed the USSR as one of the most populated countries in Asia. Following the breakup of the Soviet Union, no one of its individual states has such a high population. The largest country at present, Uzbekistan, has a population of 22,128,000.

THE 10

LEAST POPULATED COUNTRIES IN THE WORLD

	Country	Population
1	Vatican City	738
2	Niue	2,239
3	Tuvalu	9,000
4	Nauru	9,500
5	Wallis and Futuna	14,800
6	Cook Islands	18,300
7	San Marino	23,942
8	Gibraltar	28,848
9	Liechtenstein	29,868
10	Monaco	29,972

TOP 10

MOST DENSELY POPULATED COUNTRIES AND COLONIES IN THE WORLD

	Country/colony	Area sq km	sq miles	Estimated population 1995	Population per sq mile
1	Macau	16.06	6.2	415,000	66,928
2	Monaco	1.81	0.7	29,972	42,888
3	Hong Kong	1,037.29	400.5	5,962,000	14,877
4	Singapore	619.01	239.0	2,943,000	12,313
5	Gibraltar	6.47	2.5	28,848	11,549
6	Vatican City	0.44	0.17	738	4,343
7	Malta	313.39	121.0	367,000	3,033
8	Bermuda	53.35	20.6	59,549	1,115
9	Bahrein	675.99	261.0	572,000	2,178
10	Bangladesh	143,998.15	55,598.0	121,110,000	2,178
	US	9,372,614.90	3,618,787.0	263,119,000	73
	World total*	135,994,014.00	52,488,283.0	5,692,210,000	average 108

* These figures exclude Antarctica, which is virtually uninhabited.

TOP 10

COUNTRIES WITH THE HIGHEST BIRTH RATE

	Country	Birth rate*
1	Malawi	54.5
2	Afghanistan	52.8
3	Rwanda	52.1
4=	Angola	51.3
4=	Niger	51.3
6	Uganda	51.0
7	Mali	50.7
8	Guinea	50.6
9	Somalia	50.2
10	Côte d'Ivoire	49.9

* Live births per annum per 1,000 population during the period 1990–95

The 10 countries with the highest birth rate during the 1990s to date correspond very closely with those countries – mostly in Africa – that have the highest fertility rate (the average number of children born to each woman in that country). In the case of Rwanda, the fertility rate is 8.49.

THE 10

COUNTRIES WITH THE LOWEST BIRTH RATE

	Country	Birth rate*
1	Italy	10.0
2	Greece	10.4
3	Spain	10.8
4	Japan	11.2
5	Germany	11.3
6=	Austria	11.6
6=	Portugal	11.6
8	Belgium	12.1
9=	Hungary	12.3
9=	Luxembourg	12.3

* Live births per annum per 1,000 population during the period 1990–95

As with high birth rate countries, those with low birth rates usually have low fertility rates. Italy, for example, has the lowest with 1.31 births per woman. When the rate is under 2.0 the population is declining – the situation in almost 30 countries – in effect, couples are not replacing themselves.

WORLD CITIES

Calculating the populations of the world's cities is fraught with difficulties, not least of which is determining whether the city is defined by its administrative boundaries or by its continuously expanding built-up areas or conurbations. Since different countries adopt different methods, and some have populations concentrated in city centers while others are spread out in suburbs sprawling over hundreds of square miles, it has been impossible to compare them meaningfully. In order to resolve this problem, the US Bureau of the Census has adopted the method of defining a city as a population cluster or "urban agglomeration" with a density of more than 5,000 inhabitants per square mile (1,931 per sq km). Totals based on this system will differ considerably from those of other methods: according to this system,

for example, the hugely spread-out city of Shanghai has a population of 7,194,000, compared with the total of 12,670,000 estimated for its metropolitan area. On this basis, the city in the Top 10 with the greatest area is New York (1,274 sq miles/3,300 sq km) and the smallest is Bombay (95 sq miles/246 sq km) – which also means that Bombay has the greatest population density: 127,379 inhabitants per sq mile/55,008 per sq km – more than 12 times that of London.

One recent change to note in the Top 10 is the inexorable rise in the population of Brazil's second-largest city, Rio de Janeiro, the total of which has now overtaken that of Buenos Aires. These two remain the most populous cities in the Southern Hemisphere, with Jakarta, Indonesia, the runner-up (11,151,000 in 1995, using this method of calculation).

TOP 10

MOST HIGHLY POPULATED CITIES IN EUROPE

	City	Country	Population
1	Moscow*	Russia	10,769,000
2	London*	UK	8,897,000
3	Paris*	France	8,764,000
4	Essen	Germany	7,364,000
5	Istanbul#	Turkey	7,624,000
6	Milan	Italy	4,795,000
7	St. Petersburg	Russia	4,694,000
8	Madrid*	Spain	4,772,000
9	Barcelona	Spain	4,492,000
10	Manchester	UK	3,949,000

* Capital city
\# Located in Turkey in Europe

This list is produced using the US Bureau of the Census method, which means that suburbs are often included in the population figures. A list of cities without their suburbs would show a very different picture. Using the US Bureau method, Athens, Rome, and Berlin have populations of over 3,000,000.

THE 10

FIRST CITIES IN THE WORLD WITH POPULATIONS OF MORE THAN ONE MILLION

	City	Country
1	Rome	Italy
2	Angkor	Cambodia
3	Hangchow (Hangzhou)	China
4	London	UK
5	Paris	France
6	Peking	China
7	Canton	China
8	Berlin	Prussia
9	New York	US
10	Vienna	Austria

Rome's population is thought to have exceeded 1,000,000 sometime in the second century BC, while both Angkor and Hangchow had reached this figure by about AD 900 and 1200 respectively. All three cities subsequently declined (Angkor was completely abandoned in the fifteenth century). No other city attained 1,000,000 until London did so in the early nineteenth century. The next cities to pass the million mark did so between about 1850 and the late 1870s. Now at least 130 cities have populations of 1,000,000 or more.

TOP 10

MOST HIGHLY POPULATED CITIES IN THE WORLD 100 YEARS AGO

	City	Population
1	London	4,231,431
2	Paris	2,423,946
3	Peking (Beijing)	1,648,814
4	Canton (Guangzhou))	1,600,000
5	Berlin	1,579,244
6	Tokyo	1,552,457
7	New York	1,515,301
8	Vienna	1,364,548
9	Chicago	1,099,850
10	Philadelphia	1,046,964

In 1890 Nanking, China, was the only other city in the world with a population of more than 1,000,000, with another Chinese city, Tientsin (Tianjin), close behind. Several other cities, including Constantinople, St. Petersburg, and Moscow, had populations in excess of 850,000. It is remarkable that in 1890 Brooklyn, which had a population of 806,343, was slightly larger than Bombay (804,470 in 1891), whereas Bombay's present population of 12,571,720 is more than five times that of the whole of King's County (which encompasses Brooklyn).

TOP 10

MOST HIGHLY POPULATED CITIES IN NORTH AMERICA

	City	Country	Population
1	Mexico City	Mexico	23,913,000
2	New York	US	14,638,000
3	Los Angeles	US	10,414,000
4	Chicago	US	6,541,000
5	San Francisco	US	4,104,000
6	Philadelphia	US	3,988,000
7	Guadalajara	Mexico	3,839,000
8	Miami	US	3,679,000
9	Monterrey	Mexico	3,385,000
10	Toronto	Canada	3,296,000

The method used by the US Bureau of the Census for calculating city populations (see introduction, above) takes account of often widely spread "urban agglomerations."

T O P 1 0

LARGEST CITIES IN THE WORLD IN THE YEAR 2000

	City/Country	Estimated population 2000*
1	Tokyo–Yokohama, Japan	29,971,000
2	Mexico City, Mexico	27,872,000
3	São Paulo, Brazil	25,354,000
4	Seoul, South Korea	21,976,000
5	Bombay, India	15,357,000
6	New York, US	14,648,000
7	Osaka–Kobe–Kyoto, Japan	14,287,000
8	Tehran, Iran	14,251,000
9	Rio de Janeiro, Brazil	14,169,000
10	Calcutta, India	14,088,000

* *Based on US Bureau of the Census method of calculating city populations; this gives a list that differs from that calculated by other methods, such as those used by the United Nations.*

T O P 1 0

MOST HIGHLY POPULATED CITIES IN THE WORLD

	City/Country	Population
1	Tokyo–Yokohama Japan	28,447,000
2	Mexico City, Mexico	23,913,000
3	São Paulo, Brazil	21,539,000
4	Seoul, South Korea	19,065,000
5	New York, US	14,638,000
6	Osaka–Kobe–Kyoto Japan	14,060,000
7	Bombay, India	13,532,000
8	Calcutta, India	12,885,000
9	Rio de Janeiro, Brazil	12,788,000
10	Buenos Aires, Argentina	12,232,000

SIX MILLION'S A CROWD
Technically a British colony, the island of Hong Kong is so highly urbanized that it ranks as the world's most densely populated city.

T O P 1 0

LARGEST NONCAPITAL CITIES IN THE WORLD

	City	Country	Population	Capital	Population
1	Shanghai	China	12,670,000	Beijing	10,860,000
2	Bombay	India	12,571,000	Delhi	8,375,188
3	Calcutta	India	10,916,272	Delhi	8,375,188
4	São Paulo	Brazil	10,063,110	Brasília	1,803,478
5	New York	US	7,322,564	Washington, D.C.	604,000
6	Karachi*	Pakistan	7,183,000	Islamabad	350,000
7	Rio de Janeiro*	Brazil	6,603,388	Brasília	1,803,478
8	Tianjin	China	5,700,000	Beijing	10,860,000
9	St. Petersburg*	Russia	5,020,000	Moscow	8,967,000
10	Alexandria	Egypt	5,000,000	Cairo	14,000,000

* *Former capital city*

Based on a comparison of populations within administrative boundaries, this list differs from the Most Highly Populated Cities list. A city's position varies depending on the method used.

T O P 1 0

MOST DENSELY POPULATED CITIES IN THE WORLD

	City	Country	Population per sq mile		City	Country	Population per sq mile
1	Hong Kong	Hong Kong	247,501	6	Ahmadabad	India	115,893
2	Lagos	Nigeria	142,821	7	Shenyang	China	109,974
3	Jakarta	Indonesia	130,026	8	Tianjin	China	98,990
4	Bombay	India	127,379	9	Cairo	Egypt	97,106
5	Ho Chi Minh City	Vietnam	120,168	10	Bangalore	India	96,041

THE STATES OF THE UNION

TOP 10

LARGEST STATES IN THE US

	State	Area* sq km	Area* sq miles
1	Alaska	1,700,139	656,427
2	Texas	695,676	268,602
3	California	424,002	163,708
4	Montana	380,850	147,047
5	New Mexico	314,939	121,599
6	Arizona	295,276	114,007
7	Nevada	286,368	110,567
8	Colorado	269,620	104,101
9	Oregon	254,819	98,386
10	Wyoming	253,349	97,819

* *Total, including water*

Alaska, the largest state, has the second smallest population (587,000; Wyoming is the smallest with 453,588). Alaska also has the greatest area of inland water of any state: 222,871 sq miles/86,051 sq km.

TOP 10

SMALLEST STATES IN THE US

	State	Area* sq km	Area* sq miles
1	Rhode Island	4,002	1,545
2	Delaware	6,447	2,489
3	Connecticut	14,358	5,544
4	New Jersey	22,590	8,722
5	New Hampshire	24,219	9,351
6	Vermont	24,903	9,615
7	Massachusetts	27,337	10,555
8	Hawaii	28,313	10,932
9	Maryland	32,135	12,407
10	West Virginia	62,759	24,231

* *Total, including water*

The District of Columbia has a total area of 69 sq miles/179 sq km.

THE 10

FIRST STATES OF THE US

	State	Entered Union		State	Entered Union
1	Delaware	December 7, 1787	6	Massachusetts	February 6, 1788
2	Pennsylvania	December 12, 1787	7	Maryland	April 28, 1788
3	New Jersey	December 18, 1787	8	South Carolina	May 23, 1788
4	Georgia	January 2, 1788	9	New Hampshire	June 21, 1788
5	Connecticut	January 9, 1788	10	Virginia	June 25, 1788

The names of two of these states commemorate early colonists. Delaware was named after Thomas West, Lord De La Warr, a governor of Virginia. Pennsylvania was called "Pensilvania," or "Penn's woodland," in its original charter, issued in 1681 to the Quaker leader William Penn. He had acquired the territory as part settlement of a debt of £16,000 owed to his father by King Charles II. Two states were named after places with which their founders had associations: New Jersey was the subject of a deed issued in 1644 by the Duke of York to John Berkeley and Sir George Carteret, who came from Jersey in the Channel Islands, and New Hampshire was called after the English county by settler Captain John Mason. Two names are of Native American origin: Connecticut after the Algonquin Indian name "kuenihtekot," meaning "long river at"; and Massachusetts, which is believed to be Native American for "high hill, little plain," the name of a place and of a tribe. The remaining four states' names have royal connections. Virginia was named after Queen Elizabeth I, the "Virgin Queen," and Georgia in honor of King George II. Maryland was named after Queen Henrietta Maria, wife of Charles I. South Carolina was originally a French settlement called La Caroline after the French king Charles IX, but was renamed Carolana after the English king Charles I.

THE 10

LAST STATES OF THE US

	State	Entered Union		State	Entered Union
1	Hawaii	August 21, 1959	6	Utah	January 4, 1896
2	Alaska	January 3, 1959	7	Wyoming	July 10, 1890
3	Arizona	February 24, 1912	8	Idaho	July 3, 1890
4	New Mexico	January 6, 1912	9	Washington	November 11, 1889
5	Oklahoma	November 16, 1907	10	Montana	November 8, 1889

TOP 10

COUNTRIES OUTSIDE THE US WITH THE MOST RESIDENT US CITIZENS

	Country	US citizens*		Country	US citizens*
1	Mexico	463,500	6	Germany	120,188
2	Canada	422,035	7	Greece	67,000
3	UK	215,530	8	Australia	66,570
4	Philippines	123,000	9	Japan	64,311
5	Italy	121,500	10	Spain	49,800

* *As of December 31, 1994*

T O P 1 O

ANCESTRIES OF THE US POPULATION

	Ancestry group	Number
1	German	57,947,873
2	Irish	38,735,539
3	English	32,651,788
4	African–American	23,777,098
5	Italian	14,664,550
6	American	12,395,999
7	Mexican	11,586,983
8	French	10,320,935
9	Polish	9,366,106
10	Native American	8,708,220

The 1990 US Census asked people to identify the ancestry group to which they believed they belonged: while 23.3 percent claimed German ancestry, 15.6 Irish, and so on, 5 percent were unable to define their family origin more precisely than "American." Many claimed multiple ancestry, and some reported broad racial origins, such as "White" (1,799,711 replies), "European" (466,718), and "Asian" (107,172).

T O P 1 O

FOREIGN BIRTHPLACES OF THE US POPULATION*

	Birthplace	Number
1	Mexico	4,298,014
2	Philippines	912,674
3	Canada	744,830
4	Cuba	736,971
5	Germany	711,929
6	UK	640,145
7	Italy	580,592
8	Korea	568,397
9	Vietnam	543,262
10	China	529,837

* US Bureau of the Census 1990 figures

T O P 1 O

LARGEST AMERICAN INDIAN TRIBES

	Tribe	Population
1	Cherokee	308,132
2	Navajo	219,198
3	Chippewa	103,826
4	Sioux	103,255
5	Choctaw	82,299
6	Pueblo	52,939
7	Apache	50,051
8	Iroquois	49,038
9	Lumbee	48,444
10	Creek	43,550

The total Native American population was 1,878,285 according to the 1990 Census. Different authorities have estimated that at the time of the first European arrivals in 1492, it was anything from 1,000,000 to 10,000,000. This declined to a low of some 90,000 in 1890 but has increased over the past century: according to the Census it had risen to 357,000 in 1950, 793,000 in 1970, and 1,479,000 in 1980.

T O P 1 O

COUNTRIES OF ORIGIN OF US IMMIGRANTS, 1820–1993

	Country	Number
1	Germany	7,117,192
2	Italy	5,419,285
3	Great Britain	5,178,264
4	Mexico*	5,177,422
5	Ireland	4,755,172
6	Canada/Newfoundland	4,380,955
7	Austria/Hungary#	4,354,085
8	Former USSR**	3,572,281
9	West Indies	3,035,898
10	Sweden##	1,288,763

* Unreported 1886–93
 # Unreported before 1861; combined 1861–1905; separately 1905–, but cumulative total included here; Austria included with Germany 1938–45
**Russia before 1917
##Figures combined with Norway 1820–68

T O P 1 O

LARGEST NATIVE AMERICAN RESERVATIONS

	Reservation	State	Population
1	Navajo	Arizona/New Mexico/Utah	143,405
2	Pine Ridge	Nevada/South Dakota	11,182
3	Fort Apache	Arizona	9,825
4	Gila River	Arizona	9,116
5	Papago	Arizona	8,480
6	Rosebud	South Dakota	8,043
7	San Carlos	Arizona	7,110
8	Zuni Pueblo	Arizona/New Mexico	7,073
9	Hopi	Arizona	7,061
10	Blackfeet	Montana	7,025

T O P 1 O

MOST HIGHLY POPULATED STATES IN THE US

	State	Population 1900	1994*
1	California	1,485,053	31,431,000
2	Texas	3,048,710	18,378,000
3	New York	7,268,894	18,169,000
4	Florida	528,542	13,953,000
5	Pennsylvania	6,302,115	12,052,000
6	Illinois	4,821,550	11,752,000
7	Ohio	4,157,545	11,102,000
8	Michigan	2,420,982	9,496,000
9	New Jersey	1,883,669	7,904,000
10	North Carolina	1,893,810	7,070,000

PLACE NAMES

LONGEST PLACE NAMES IN THE WORLD
(Including single-word, hyphenated, and multiple names)

	Name	Letters
1	Krung thep mahanakhon bovorn ratanakosin mahintharayutthaya mahadilok pop noparatratchathani burirom udomratchanivetma hasathan amornpiman avatarnsa thit sakkathattiyavisnukarmprasit	167

When the poetic name of Bangkok, capital of Thailand, is used, it is usually abbreviated to "Krung Thep" (City of Angels).

	Name	Letters
2	Taumatawhakatangihangakoauau-otamateaturipukakapikimaunga-horonukupokaiwhenuakitanatahu	85

This is the longer version (the other has a mere 83 letters) of the Maori name of a hill in New Zealand. It translates as "The place where Tamatea, the man with the big knees, who slid, climbed, and swallowed mountains, known as land-eater, played on the flute to his loved one."

	Name	Letters
3	Gorsafawddacha'idraigodanhed-dogleddollônpenrhynareur-draethceredigion	67

A name contrived by the Fairbourne Steam Railway, Gwynedd, North Wales, for publicity purposes and in order to outdo its rival, No. 4. It means "The Mawddach station and its dragon teeth at the Northern Penrhyn Road on the golden beach of Cardigan Bay."

	Name	Letters
4	Llanfairpwllgwyngyllgogerychwyrn-drobwllllantysiliogogogoch	58

This is the place in Gwynedd famed especially for the length of its railroad tickets. It means "St. Mary's Church in the hollow of the white hazel near to the rapid whirlpool of Llantysilio of the Red Cave." Its authenticity is suspect, since its official name consists of only the first 20 letters, and the full name appears to have been invented as a hoax in the 19th century by local inhabitant John Evans.

	Name	Letters
5	El Pueblo de Nuestra Señora la Reina de los Angeles de la Porciuncula	57

The site of a Franciscan mission and the full Spanish name of Los Angeles; it means "the town of Our Lady the Queen of the Angels of the Little Portion." Now it is customarily known by its initial letters "LA," making it also one of the shortest-named cities in the world.

	Name	Letters
6	Chargoggagoggmanchauggagogg-chaubunagungamaugg	45

America's longest place name, a lake near Webster, Massachusetts. Its Indian name, loosely translated, means "You fish on your side, I'll fish on mine, and no one fishes in the middle." It is pronounced "Char-gogg-a-gogg (pause) man-chaugg-a-gogg (pause) chau-bun-a-gung-a-maugg."

	Name	Letters
7=	Lower North Branch Little Southwest Miramichi	40

The longest place name in Canada belongs – rather incongruously – to a short river in New Brunswick.

	Name	Letters
7=	Villa Real de la Santa Fe de San Francisco de Asis	40

The full Spanish name of Santa Fe, New Mexico, translates as "Royal city of the holy faith of St. Francis of Assisi."

	Name	Letters
9	Te Whakatakangaotengarehuote-ahiatamatea	38

The Maori name of Hammer Springs, New Zealand; like the second name in this list, it refers to a legend of Tamatea, explaining how the springs were warmed by "the falling of the cinders of the fire of Tamatea."

	Name	Letters
10	Meallan Liath Coire Mhic Dhubhghaill	32

The longest multiple name in Scotland belongs to this place near Aultanrynie, Highland. The alternative spelling is Meallan Liath Coire Mhic Dhughaill.

LONGEST PLACE NAMES IN THE UK
(Single and hyphenated only)

	Name	Letters
1	Gorsafawddacha'idraigodanhed-dogleddollônpenrhynareur-draethceredigion (*see* Top 10 Longest Place Names in the World)	67
2	Llanfairpwllgwyngyllgogerych-wyrndrobwllllantysiliogogogoch (*see* Top 10 Longest Place Names in the World)	58
3	Sutton-under-Whitestonecliffe, North Yorkshire	27
4	Llanfihangel-yng-Ngwynfa, Powys	22
5=	Llanfihangel-y-Creuddyn, Dyfed	21
5=	Llanfihangel-y-traethau, Gwynedd	21
7	Cottonshopeburnfoot, Northumberland	19
8=	Blakehopeburnhaugh, Northumberland	18
8=	Coignafeuinternich, Inverness-shire	18
10=	Claddach-baleshare, North Uist, Outer Hebrides	17
10=	Claddach-knockline, North Uist, Outer Hebrides	17

Runners-up include Combeinteignhead, Doddiscombsleigh, Moretonhampstead, Stokeinteignhead, and Woolfardisworthy (pronounced "Woolsery"), all of which are in Devon and have 16 letters. The longest multiple name in England is North Leverton with Habblesthorpe, Nottinghamshire (30 letters), followed by Sulhampstead Bannister Upper End, Berkshire (29). In Wales the longest are Lower Llanfihangel-y-Creuddyn, Dyfed (26) followed by Llansantffraid Cwmdeuddwr, Powys (24), and in Scotland Meallan Liath Coire Mhic Dhughaill, Highland, (32), a loch on the island of Lewis called Loch Airidh Mhic Fhionnlaidh Dhuibh (31), and Huntingtower and Ruthvenfield (27). If the parameters are extended to include Ireland, Castletownconyersmaceniery (26), Co. Limerick, Muikeenachidirdhashaile (24), and Muckanaghederdauhalia (21), both in Co. Galway, are scooped into the net. The shortest place name in the UK is Ae in Dumfries and Galloway, Scotland.

TOP 10

COUNTRIES WITH THE LONGEST OFFICIAL NAMES

	Official name	Common English name	Letters
1	al-Jamāhīrīyah al-'Arabīya al-Lībīyah ash-Sha'bīyah al-Ishtirākīyah	Libya	56
2	al-Jumhūrīyah al-Jazā'irīyah ad-Dīmuqrāṭīyah ash-Sha'bīyah	Algeria	49
3	United Kingdom of Great Britain and Northern Ireland	United Kingdom	45
4	Sri Lankā Prajathanthrika Samajavadi Janarajaya	Sri Lanka	43
5	Jumhūrīyat al-Qumur al-Ittihādīyah al-Islāmīyah	The Comores	41
6=	al-Jumhūrīyah al-Islāmīyah al-Mūrītānīyah	Mauritania	36
6=	The Federation of St. Christopher and Nevis	St. Kitts and Nevis	36
8	Jamhuuriyadda Dimuqraadiga Soomaaliya	Somalia	35
9	al-Mamlakah al-Urdunnīyah al-Hāshimīyah	Jordan	34
10	Repolika Demokratika n'i Madagaskar	Madagascar	32

TOP 10

MOST COMMON STREET NAMES IN THE US

1	Second Street	6	First Street
2	Park Street	7	Sixth Street
3	Third Street	8	Seventh Street
4	Fourth Street	9	Washington Street
5	Fifth Street	10	Maple Street

The list continues with Oak, Eighth, Elm, Lincoln, Ninth, Pine, Walnut, Tenth, and Cedar. Curiously, First is not first, because many streets that would be so designated are instead called Main.

TOP 10

MOST COMMON PLACE NAMES IN THE US

	Name	No. of occurrences		Name	No. of occurrences
1	Midway	207	6	Centerville	109
2	Fairview	192	7	Mount Pleasant	108
3	Oak Grove	150	8	Riverside	106
4	Five Points	145	9	Bethel	105
5	Pleasant Hill	113	10	New Hope	98

TOP 10

MOST COMMON PLACE NAMES OF BIBLICAL ORIGIN IN THE US

	Name/meaning/ original location	US occurrences
1	Salem	95

"Peace"; this was the kingdom of Melchizidek, supposedly Jerusalem.

2	Eden	61

"Pleasure"; principally meaning the place where mankind began, it is also the name given to a market in Mesopotamia.

3	Bethel	47

"House of God"; this was a city in Palestine, or a town in South Judah.

4	Lebanon	39

"White"; in the Bible this was originally the name of two mountain ranges. Today it is the name of a country.

5	Sharon	38

"Plain"; this was the plain on the Mediterranean coast between Judah and Caesarea. It was also the name of a place in east Jordan.

6	Goshen	33

"Drawing near"; as well as being the northern province of Egypt, this was also the name of part of southern Palestine, and of a city in Judah.

7	Jordan	27

"Descender"; this was the principal river of Palestine.

8	Hebron	26

"Friendship"; this could be either a person or a place. In the Bible, the son of Kohath was called Hebron, and this was also the name of a city in Judah.

9	Zion	24

"Mount, sunny"; this was a mountain in Jerusalem, or the sacred capital of the Jewish people generally.

10=	Antioch	18

Named for Antiochus, king of Syria, this was the capital of the Greek kings of Syria. There was also a city of Pisidia with the same name.

10=	Paradise	18

"Pleasure ground"; this is another name for the Garden of Eden, or heaven.

10=	Shiloh	18

"Peace"; this possibly signified the Messiah, and was the name of a city in Ephraim.

Research conducted by John Leighley surveyed a substantial sampling (61,742) of US place names, from which he concluded that 101 different names, comprising a total of 803 occurrences, were of biblical origin.

US CITIES

TOP 10

CITIES WITH THE GREATEST AREA

	City	State	Area sq km	sq miles		City	State	Area sq km	sq miles
1	Anchorage	Alaska	4,397.0	1,697.7	**6**	Los Angeles	California	1,215.5	469.3
2	Jacksonville	Florida	1,965.0	758.7	**7**	Phoenix	Arizona	1,087.5	419.9
3	Oklahoma City	Oklahoma	1,575.2	608.2	**8**	Indianapolis	Indiana	936.8	361.7
4	Houston	Texas	1,398.3	539.9	**9**	Dallas	Texas	886.8	342.4
5	Nashville–Davidson	Tennessee	1,225.8	473.5	**10**	Chesapeake	Virginia	882.4	340.7

TOP 10

MOST DENSELY POPULATED CITIES IN THE US*

(Cities with populations of 100,000+ only)

	City	Population per sq km	sq mile
1	New York, New York	9,151	23,701
2	Patterson, New Jersey	6,445	16,693
3	San Francisco, California	5,985	15,502
4	Jersey City, New Jersey	5,922	15,337
5	Chicago, Illinois	4,730	12,251
6	Inglewood, California	4,626	11,952
7	Boston, Massachusetts	4,579	11,860
8	Philadelphia Pennsylvania	4,531	11,734
9	Newark, New Jersey	4,461	11,554
10	El Monte, California	4,315	11,175

The New York figure is for the metropolitan area as a whole. Three boroughs, though – Manhattan, Brooklyn, and the Bronx – have even higher population densities.

TOP 10

HIGHEST CITIES IN THE US

	City	Highest point m	ft
1	Colorado Spings, Colorado	1,873	6,145
2	Denver, Colorado	1,667	5,470
3	Albuquerque, New Mexico	1,632	5,354
4	Los Angeles, California	1,549	5,081
5	Salt Lake City, Utah	1,319	4,327
6	Honolulu, Hawaii	1,227	4,025
7	El Paso, Texas	1,147	3,762
8	Lubbock, Texas	988	3,241
9	Phoenix, Arizona	835	2,740
10	Tucson, Arizona	728	2,390

This list is based on the highest points of US cities with populations of more than 150,000. Some cities are otherwise low-lying. Smaller towns lie entirely at higher elevations, such as Climax, CO, at 11,560 ft/3,523 m.

TOP 10

US CITIES WITH THE MOST HISTORIC PLACES

	City	Historic places*
1	New York, New York	624
2	Philadelphia, Pennsylvania	470
3	Washington, D.C.	336
4	Chicago, Illinois	223
5	Cincinnati, Ohio	222
6	Boston, Massachusetts	196
7=	Baltimore, Maryland	176
7=	Cleveland, Ohio	176
9	Providence, Rhode Island	126
10	Richmond, Virginia	120

* *As designated in the* National Register *of Historic Places*

NEW YORK SKYLINE
Although its skyscrapers give it a sharply modern look, New York has a wealth of historic locations.

T O P 1 0

LARGEST CITIES IN THE US

	City	State	Population
1	New York	New York	7,311,966
2	Los Angeles	California	3,489,779
3	Chicago	Illinois	2,768,483
4	Houston	Texas	1,690,180
5	Philadelphia	Pennsylvania	1,552,572
6	San Diego	California	1,148,851
7	Dallas	Texas	1,022,497
8	Phoenix	Arizona	1,012,230
9	Detroit	Michigan	1,012,110
10	San Antonio	Texas	966,437

Based on the 1992 Census update, these are estimates for central city areas only, not for the metropolitan areas that surround them, which may be several times as large. The populations of both Dallas and Phoenix have overtaken that of Detroit (which, like New York and Chicago, has actually declined) since there is a general shift toward the southern and western Sun Belt states.

T O P 1 0

LARGEST CITIES IN THE US IN 1900

Rank 1900	1990	City	State	1900 population
1	(1)	New York	New York	3,437,202
2	(3)	Chicago	Illinois	1,698,575
3	(5)	Philadelphia	Pennsylvania	1,293,697
4	(34)	St. Louis	Missouri	575,238
5	(20)	Boston	Massachusetts	560,892
6	(13)	Baltimore	Maryland	508,957
7	(24)	Cleveland	Ohio	381,768
8	(50)	Buffalo	New York	352,387
9	(14)	San Francisco	California	342,782
10	(45)	Cincinnati	Ohio	325,902

Only the first three cities are in the present Top 10, the rest having been overtaken by seven others that had relatively small populations at the turn of the century: Los Angeles (102,479 in 1900), Houston (44,633), San Diego (17,700), Detroit (285,704), Dallas (42,638), Phoenix (5,444), and San Antonio (53,321). The population of Buffalo has declined from 352,387 in 1900 to 328,123 today.

T O P 1 0

US CITIES WITH THE GREATEST POPULATION DECLINE, 1980–1990

	City	Population 1980	1990	Percentage decline
1	Gary, Indiana	151,968	116,646	23.2
2	Newark, New Jersey	329,248	275,221	16.4
3	Detroit, Michigan	1,203,368	1,027,974	14.6
4	Pittsburgh, Pennsylvania	423,960	369,879	12.8
5	St. Louis, Missouri	452,801	396,685	12.4
6	Cleveland, Ohio	573,822	505,616	11.9
7	Flint, Michigan	159,611	140,761	11.8
8	New Orleans, Louisiana	557,927	496,638	10.9
9	Warren, Michigan	161,134	144,864	10.1
10	Chattanooga, Tennessee	169,514	152,494	10.0

During the 1980s, many of the great industrial cities suffered shrinkage as the country's manufacturing base declined in favor of high-tech businesses, service industries, and imports – especially of motor vehicles. Detroit, Philadelphia, and Chicago may still be numbered among the 10 largest cities in the US, but the populations of all three dwindled between 1980 and 1990, whereas the populations of cities such as Los Angeles and Dallas expanded during the same period.

T O P 1 0

FASTEST-GROWING CITIES IN THE US, 1980–1990

	City	Population 1980	1990	Percentage increase
1	Moreno Valley, California	28,309	118,779	319.6
2	Mesa, Arizona	152,404	288,104	89.0
3	Rancho Cucamonga, California	55,250	101,409	83.5
4	Plano, Texas	72,231	128,885	78.5
5	Irvine, California	62,134	110,330	77.6
6	Escondido, California	64,355	108,635	66.8
7	Oceanside, California	76,698	128,154	67.1
8	Santa Clarita, California	66,730	110,690	65.9
9	Bakersfield, California	105,611	174,820	65.5
10	Arlington, Texas	160,113	261,721	63.5

The majority of fastest-growing US cities (seven of the Top 10 and 11 in the Top 20) are located in California, with Texas the closest runner-up. The enduring appeal of the Golden State to those relocating, plus natural increase, added 6,092,257 to its population between the 1980 and 1990 censuses, and as a result it now has 11.97 percent of the entire US population.

NATIONAL PARKS

THE 10
FIRST NATIONAL MONUMENTS IN THE US

	National Monument	Established
1	Devils Tower, Wyoming	Sep 24, 1906
2	Montezuma Castle, Arizona	Dec 8, 1906
3	Gila Cliff Dwellings, New Mexico	Nov 16, 1907
4	Tonto, Arizona	Dec 19, 1907
5	Muir Woods, California	Jan 9, 1908
6	Grand Canyon, Arizona	Jan 11, 1908
7	Pinnacles, California	Jan 16, 1908
8	Jewel Cave, South Dakota	Feb 7, 1908
9	Natural Bridges, Utah	Apr 16, 1908
10	Navajo, Arizona	Mar 20, 1909

There are some 76 National Monuments in the US, covering a total of 4,787,744 acres. Some sites were identified as of special historical importance earlier than those in the Top 10, but were not officially designated as National Monuments until later dates, among them the Custer Battlefield, Montana (the site of the Battle of Little Big Horn, June 25–26, 1876), which was established as a national cemetery on January 29, 1879, but did not become a National Monument until an Act of Congress dated March 22, 1946.

THE 10
FIRST NATIONAL HISTORIC SITES IN THE US

	National historic site	Established*
1	Ford's Theatre, Washington D.C.	Apr 7, 1866
2	Abraham Lincoln Birthplace, Kentucky	Jul 17, 1916
3	Andrew Johnson Memorial, Tennessee	Aug 29, 1935
4	Jefferson National Expansion Memorial, Missouri	Dec 20, 1935
5	Whitman Mission, Washington	Jun 29, 1936
6	Salem Maritime, Massachusetts	Mar 17, 1938
7	Fort Laramie, Wyoming	Jul 16, 1938
8	Hopewell Furnace, Pennsylvania	Aug 3, 1938
9	Vanderbilt Mansion, New York	Dec 18, 1940
10	Fort Raleigh, North Carolina	Apr 5, 1941

* *Or subsequently designated as a Historic Site*

A site commemorating the 1954 Brown v Board of Education case, which established that racial segregation in public schools was unconstitutional, was designated as a National Historic Site in 1992.

THE 10
FIRST NATIONAL PARKS IN THE US

	National Park	Established
1	Yellowstone, Wyoming/ Montana/Idaho	Mar 1, 1872
2	Sequoia, California	Sep 25, 1890
3=	Yosemite, California	Oct 1, 1890
3=	General Grant, California*	Oct 1, 1890
5	Mount Rainier, Washington	Mar 2, 1899
6	Crater Lake, Oregon	May 22, 1902
7	Wind Cave, South Dakota	Jan 9, 1903
8	Mesa Verde, Colorado	Jun 29, 1906
9	Glacier, Montana	May 11, 1910
10	Rocky Mountain, Colorado	Jan 26, 1915

* *Name changed to Kings Canyon National Park, March 4, 1940*

These are the first National Parks established as such in the US. Several others, founded under different appellations at earlier dates, and later redesignated as National Parks, could also claim a place in the list. For example, Hot Springs, Arkansas, established as early as April 20, 1832 as Hot Springs Reservation, became a public park on June 16, 1880, but was not made a National Park until March 4, 1921. Similarly, Petrified Forest, Arizona, was made a National Monument on December 8, 1906, but it did not become a National Park until December 9, 1962.

THE 10
FIRST NATIONAL BATTLEFIELDS IN THE US

	National Battlefield	Battle	Established*
1	Chickamauga and Chattanooga, Georgia/Tennessee	Sep 19–20, 1863	Aug 19, 1890
2	Antietam, Maryland	Sep 17, 1862	Aug 30, 1890
3	Shiloh, Tennessee	Apr 6–7, 1862	Dec 27, 1894
4	Gettysburg, Pennsylvania	Jul 1–3, 1863	Feb 11, 1895
5	Vicksburg, Mississippi	Jan 9–Jul 4, 1863	Feb 21, 1899
6	Big Hole, Montana	Aug 9, 1877	Jun 23, 1910
7	Guilford Courthouse, North Carolina	Mar 15, 1781	Mar 2, 1917
8	Kennesaw Mountain, Georgia	Jun 20–Jul 2, 1864	Apr 22, 1917
9	Moores Creek, North Carolina	Feb 27, 1776	Jun 2, 1926
10	Petersburg, Virginia	Jun 15, 1864–Apr 3, 1865	Jul 3, 1926

There are 24 National Battlefields, National Battlefield Parks, and National Military Parks, but just one National Battlefield Site – Brices Cross Roads, Mississippi. The scene of a Civil War engagement on Jun 10, 1864, the Site was established on Feb 21, 1929. The earliest battle to be so commemorated is Fort Necessity, Pennsylvania (July 3, 1754; National Battlefield established Mar 4, 1931), the opening hostility in the French and Indian War, in which the militia led by George Washington, then a 22-year-old Lt.-Colonel, was defeated and captured.

* *Dates include those for locations originally assigned other designations but later authorized as National Battlefields, National Battlefield Parks, and National Military Parks.*

T O P 1 0

LARGEST NATIONAL PARKS IN THE US

National Park	Established	Area sq km	sq miles
1 Wrangell-St. Elias, Alaska	Dec 2, 1980	33,716	13,018
2 Gates of the Arctic, Alaska	Dec 2, 1980	30,448	11,756
3 Denali (formerly Mt. McKinley), Alaska	Feb 26, 1917	19,088	7,370
4 Katmai, Alaska	Dec 2, 1980	15,037	5,806
5 Glacier Bay, Alaska	Dec 2, 1980	13,054	5,040
6 Lake Clark, Alaska	Dec 2, 1980	10,671	4,120
7 Yellowstone, Wyoming/Montana/Idaho	Mar 1, 1872	8,982	3,468
8 Kobuk Valley, Alaska	Dec 2, 1980	7,084	2,735
9 Everglades, Florida	May 30, 1934	5,662	2,186
10 Grand Canyon, Arizona	Feb 26, 1919	4,931	1,904

Yellowstone National Park was established on March 1, 1872 as the first national park in the world with its role "as a public park or pleasuring ground for the benefit and enjoyment of the people." There are now some 1,200 national parks in more than 100 countries. There are 49 National Parks in the US, with a total area of more than 73,816 sq miles/191,183 sq km. This is more than double the area they covered before 1980 (when large tracts of Alaska were added). With the addition of various National Monuments, National Historic Parks, National Preserves, and other specially designated areas under the aegis of the National Park Service, the total area is 124,378 sq miles/322,138 sq km, and is visited by almost 300,000,000 people a year.

T O P 1 0

MOST-VISITED NATIONAL PARKS IN THE US

Park/location	Visitors (1994)
1 Great Smoky Mountains National Park, North Carolina/Tennessee	8,628,174
2 Grand Canyon National Park, Arizona	4,364,316
3 Yosemite National Park, California	3,962,117
4 Olympic National Park, Washington	3,381,573
5 Yellowstone National Park, Wyoming	3,046,145
6 Rocky Mountain National Park, California	2,968,450
7 Acadia National Park, Maine	2,710,749
8 Grand Teton National Park, Wyoming	2,540,699
9 Zion National Park, Utah	2,270,871
10 Glacier National Park, Montana	2,152,989

The total number of visitors to US National Parks in 1994 was 62,984,052. The number of recreational visits to National Parks is smaller than those to National Historic Sites (including battlefields and other military sites), but nonetheless has risen steadily during the 20th century: in 1904, the first year for which records exists, there were 121,000 visits. The figure topped 1,000,000 for the first time in 1921 and 10,000,000 by 1940, and exceeded 50,000,000 by 1980. More than 18,000,000 people a year also make overnight stays in the camping facilities provided within the National Parks.

WORLD'S TALLEST BUILDINGS

T O P 1 0

TALLEST BUILDINGS ERECTED MORE THAN 100 YEARS AGO

	Building	Location	Year completed	Height m	ft
1	Eiffel Tower	Paris, France	1889	300	984
2	Washington Monument	Washington D.C.	1885	169	555
3	Ulm Cathedral	Ulm, Germany	1890	161	528
4	Lincoln Cathedral	Lincoln, England	c.1307 (destroyed 1548)	160	525
5	Cologne Cathedral	Cologne, Germany	1880	156.4	513
6	Rouen Cathedral	Rouen, France	1530 (destroyed 1822)	156	512
7	St. Pierre Church	Beauvais, France	1568 (collapsed 1573)	153	502
8	St. Paul's Cathedral	London, England	1315 (destroyed 1561)	149	489
9	Rouen Cathedral	Rouen, France	1876	148	485
10	Great Pyramid	Giza, Egypt	c.2580 BC	146.5	481

T O P 1 0

TALLEST HABITABLE BUILDINGS IN THE WORLD

	Building	Location	Year completed	Stories	Height m	ft
1	Sears Tower with spires	Chicago, Illinois	1974	110	443 520	1,454 1,707
2	World Trade Center*	New York, New York	1973	110	417	1,368
3	Empire State Building with spire	New York, New York	1931	102	381 449	1,250 1,472
4	Amoco Building	Chicago, Illinois	1973	80	346	1,136
5	John Hancock Center with spire	Chicago, Illinois	1968	100	343 450	1,127 1,476
6	Chrysler Building	New York, New York	1929	77	319	1,046
7	Central Plaza with spire	Hong Kong	1992	78	309 374	1,015 1,228
8	First Interstate World Center	Los Angeles, California	1990	73	310	1,017
9	Texas Commerce Tower	Houston, Texas	1981	75	305	1,002
10	Bank of China Tower with spires	Hong Kong	1989	70	305 368	1,001 1,209

Twin towers; the second tower, completed in 1973, has the same number of stories but is slightly smaller at 1,362 ft/415 m – although its spire takes it up to 1,710 ft/521 m.

Heights do not include TV and radio antennae and uninhabited extensions. By 2000, several more will be added. The tallest will be the Chonging Tower, China (1,500 ft/ 457 m, due 1997), and the Nina Tower, Hong Kong (1,534 ft/468 m, 1998).

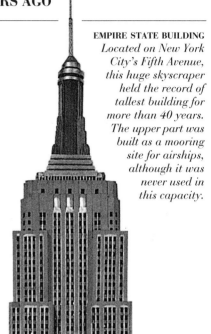

EMPIRE STATE BUILDING
Located on New York City's Fifth Avenue, this huge skyscraper held the record of tallest building for more than 40 years. The upper part was built as a mooring site for airships, although it was never used in this capacity.

TOP 10

TALLEST CHIMNEYS IN THE WORLD

	Chimney/location	Height m	ft
1	Ekibastuz Power Station Kazakhstan	420	1,377
2	International Nickel Company, Sudbury, Ontario, Canada	381	1,250
3	Pennsylvania Electric Company, Homer City, Pennsylvania	371	1,216
4	Kennecott Copper Corporation, Magna, Utah	370	1,215
5	Ohio Power Company Cresap, West Virginia,	368	1,206
6	Zasavje Power Station Trboulje, Yugoslavia	360	1,181
7	Empresa Nacional de Electricidad SA Puentes de Garcia Rodriguez, Spain	356	1,169
8	Appalachian Power Company, New Haven, West Virginia	336	1,103
9	Indiana & Michigan Electric Company Rockport, Indiana	316	1,037
10	West Penn Power Company, Reesedale, Pennsylvania	308	1,012

Nos. 2 to 5 and 7 to 10 were all built by Pullman Power Products Corporation (formerly a division of M.W. Kellogg), an American engineering company that has been in business since 1902 and has built many of the world's tallest chimneys. The largest internal volume is No. 7: 6,700,000 cubic feet. The diameter of No. 1, completed in 1991, tapers from 144 ft/44 m at the base to 47 ft/14 m at the top; the outside diameter of No. 4, built in 1974 and formerly the world's largest, is 124 ft/38 m at the base, tapering to 40 ft/12 m.

TOP 10

WORLD CITIES WITH MOST SKYSCRAPERS*

	City	Skyscrapers
1	New York, New York	131
2	Chicago, Illinois	47
3	Houston, Texas	27
4	Los Angeles, California	21
5	Hong Kong	20
6	Dallas, Texas	17
7	Melbourne, Australia	16
8	San Francisco, California	15
9	Boston, Massachusetts	14
10=	Atlanta, Georgia	13
10=	Singapore	13
10=	Sydney, Australia	13

* Habitable buildings of over 500 ft/152 m

The word "skyscraper" was first used in the 18th century to mean a high-flying flag on a ship, and later to describe a tall horse or person. It was not used to describe buildings until the 1880s when the first tall office buildings of 10 stories or more were built in Chicago and New York, with the Eiffel Tower following at the end of the decade. The first modern skyscraper was the Woolworth Building, New York, built in 1913.

TOP 10

CITIES OUTSIDE THE US WITH MOST SKYSCRAPERS*

	City	Skyscrapers
1	Hong Kong	20
2	Melbourne, Australia	16
3	Singapore	13
4	Sydney, Australia	13
5	Toronto, Ontario, Canada	11
6	Tokyo, Japan	10
7	Frankfurt, Germany	4
8=	Caracas, Venezuela	3
8=	Johannesburg, South Africa	3
8=	London, UK	3
8=	Moscow, Russia	3
8=	Paris, France	3
8=	Perth, Australia	3

TOP 10

TALLEST STRUCTURES THAT ARE NO LONGER STANDING

	Structure	Location	Completed	Destroyed	Height m	ft
1	Warszawa Radio Mast	Konstantynow, Poland	1974	1991	646	2,120
2	KSWS TV Mast	Roswell, New Mexico,	1956	1960	491	1,610
3	IBA Mast	Emley Moor, UK	1965	1969	385	1,265
4	No. 6 Flue (chimney), Matla Power Station	Kriel, South Africa	1980	1981	275	902
5	Singer Building	New York, New York	1908	1970	200	656
6	New Brighton Tower	Merseyside, UK	1900	1919	171	562
7	Lincoln Cathedral	Lincoln, UK	c.1307	1548	160	525
8	Rouen Cathedral	Rouen, France	1530	1822	156	512
9	St. Pierre Church	Beauvais, France	1568	1573	153	502
10	St. Peter's	Louvain, Flanders	1497	1606	152	500

The Matla Power Station chimney was never fully operational and, following an accident that resulted in two fatalities, it was demolished. If excluded for this reason, the 10th entry is the 492-ft/150-m Lin He Pagoda, Hang Zhou, China, built in 970 and destroyed in a military conflict in 1121.

BIGGEST BUILDINGS – US

TOP 10

NORTH AMERICAN CITIES WITH MOST SKYSCRAPERS

	City	Skyscrapers
1	New York, New York	131
2	Chicago, Illinois	47
3	Houston, Texas	26
4	Los Angeles, California	21
5	Dallas, Texas	17
6	San Francisco, California	15
7	Boston, Massachusetts	14
8	Atlanta, Georgia	13
9=	Seattle, Washington	11
9=	Toronto, Ontario, Canada	11

This list covers habitable buildings of more than 500 ft/152 m. A US-only version of this list would eliminate Toronto, replacing it with Pittsburgh and Philadelphia, each of which has nine buildings over 500 ft/152 m, while Minneapolis, with seven skyscrapers, would just fail to make the list.

TOP 10

TALLEST BUILDINGS IN CHICAGO

	Building/ date built	Stories	Height m	ft
1	Sears Tower (1974) *with spires*	110	443 *520*	1,454 *1,707*
2	Amoco Building (1973)	80	346	1,136
3	John Hancock Center (1968) *with spires*	100	343 *449*	1,127 *1,476*
4	311 South Wacker Drive (1990)	65	296	970
5	2 Prudential Plaza (1990) *with spire*	64	275 *303*	901 *994*
6	AT&T Corporate Center (1991)	60	271	891
7	900 North Michigan Avenue (1990)	66	265	871
8	Water Tower Place (1975)	74	262	859
9	First National Bank (1968)	60	260	852
10	Three First National Plaza (1981)	57	236	775

TOP 10

TALLEST BUILDINGS IN HOUSTON

	Building/ date built	Stories	Height m	ft
1	Texas Commerce Tower (1981)	75	305	1,002
2	First Interstate Plaza (1983)	71	302	992
3	Transco Tower (1985)	64	275	901
4	NationsBank Center (1989)	56	238	780
5	Heritage Plaza (1989)	53	232	762
6	InterFirst Plaza (1982)	55	227	744
7	1600 Smith Street (1982)	54	222	729
8	Chevron Tower (1982)	52	221	725
9	One Shell Plaza (1970) *with TV tower*	50	218 *305*	714 *999*
10	Enron Building (1983)	50	211	692

TOP 10

TALLEST BUILDINGS IN NEW YORK CITY

	Building/ date built	Stories	Height m	ft
1	World Trade Center (1973)	110	417	1,368
2	Empire State Building (1931) *with spire*	102	381 *449*	1,250 *1,472*
3	Chrysler Building (1930) *with spire*	77	282 *319*	925 *1,046*
4	Citicorp Center (1977)	59	279	915
5	40 Wall Tower (1929) *with spire*	71	260 *282*	854 *927*
6	G.E. Building (1933)	70	259	850
7	American Int'l. (1932) *with spire*	67	252 *28*	826 *950*
8	Chase Manhattan Plaza (1960)	60	248	813
9	MetLife Building (1963)	59	246	808
10	Cityspire (1989)	72	245	802

TOP 10

TALLEST REINFORCED CONCRETE BUILDINGS IN THE US

	Building	Location	Year completed	Stories	Height m	ft
1	311 South Wacker Drive	Chicago	1990	65	296	970
2	2 Prudential Plaza *with spire*	Chicago	1990	64	275 *303*	901 *994*
3	NationsBank Corporation Center	Charlotte	1992	60	265	871
4	Water Tower Place	Chicago	1975	74	262	859
5	Cityspire	New York	1989	72	245	802
6	Carnegie Hall Tower	New York	1990	59	230	756
7	Texas Commerce Tower	Dallas	1987	55	225	738
8	Olympia Centre	Chicago	1981	63	222	727
9	Peachtree Hotel	Atlanta	1973	71	221	723
10	Renaissance Hotel	Detroit	1977	71	220	720

Reinforced concrete was patented in France by Joseph Monier (1823–1906) on March 16, 1867, and developed by another Frenchman, François Hennebique (1842–1921). The first American buildings constructed from it date from a century ago, since when it has become one of the most important building materials. Steel bars set within concrete slabs expand and contract at the same rate as the concrete, providing great tensile strength and fire resistance, making it ideal for huge structures such as bridge spans and skyscrapers.

TOP 10

HIGHEST PUBLIC OBSERVATORIES IN THE US

	Observatory/location	Year completed	Height m	ft
1	World Trade Center, New York (rooftop Tower B)	1973	415	1,360
2	Sears Tower, Chicago (103rd floor)	1974	412	1,353
3	Empire State Building, New York (102nd floor)	1931	381	1,250
4	John Hancock Center, Chicago (94th floor)	1968	322	1,056
5	Columbia Seafirst Center, Seattle (74th floor)	1986	280	918
6	Transco Tower, Houston (64th floor)	1986	260	852
7	Stratosphere Tower, Las Vegas (Turret Level 9) *(Thrill Ride)*	1995	260 *278*	852 *913*
8	RCA Center, New York (70th floor)	1933	259	850
9	John Hancock Tower, Boston (59th floor)	1973	236	775
10	Westin Hotel, Detroit (70th floor)	1977	210	688

From the 1930s US observatories dominated the world, and currently North America is home to seven of the world's 10 highest observatories. However, buildings in Asia such as the KL Tower, Kuala Lumpur, Malaysia, whose public observatory will be at 906 ft/276 m when finished, are fast gaining ground. Before the opening of the Empire State Building in 1931, the Eiffel Tower, built between 1887 and 1889 and now eighth in world ranking, was the world's highest viewing platform in a man-made structure for 42 years.

TOP 10

LARGEST HOTELS IN THE US

	Hotel	Rooms
1	MGM Grand Casino Las Vegas	5,012
2	Excalibur, Las Vegas	4,032
3	Hilton Flamingo, Las Vegas	3,530
4	Mirage, Las Vegas	3,049
5	Treasure Island, Las Vegas	2,900
6	Hilton Hotel, Las Vegas	2,877
7	Bally Grand Hotel, Las Vegas	2,832
8	Circus Circus, Las Vegas	2,793
9	Imperial Palace, Las Vegas	2,637
10	Lumor Hotel, Las Vegas	2,533

Source: American Hotel/ Motel Association

JOHN HANCOCK CENTER
Reinforcing girders can be seen in the external walls of this highly distinctive building.

BRIDGES & TUNNELS

LONGEST SUSPENSION BRIDGES IN THE WORLD

	Bridge	Completed	Length of main span	
			m	**ft**
1	Akashi-Kaikyo, Japan	UC/1998	1,990.0	6,529
2	Great Belt East Bridge, Denmark	UC/1997	1,624.0	5,328
3	Humber Estuary, UK	1980	1,410.0	4,626
4	Verrazano Narrows, New York, New York	1964	1,298.5	4,260
5	Golden Gate, San Francisco, California	1937	1,280.2	4,200
6	Mackinac Straits, Michigan	1957	1,158.2	3,800
7	Bosphorus, Istanbul, Turkey	1973	1,074.1	3,524
8	George Washington, New York, New York	1931	1,066.8	3,500
9	Ponte 25 Abril (Ponte Salazar) Lisbon, Portugal	1966	1,012.9	3,323
10	Forth Road Bridge, UK	1964	1,005.8	3,300

UC *Under construction/expected completion year*

The Messina Strait Bridge, planned to stretch between Sicily and Calabria in southern Italy, remains a speculative project, but if constructed according to plan it will have by far the longest center span of any bridge (although at 12,828 ft/3,910 m the Akashi-Kaikyo bridge will be the world's longest overall). If only completed bridges are included, the Humber Estuary Bridge heads the list. No. 9 then becomes another British structure, the Severn Bridge (completed 1966; 3,240 ft/987.6 m). The Tacoma Narrows II, Washington (completed 1950; 2,800 ft/853.4 m) takes 10th place.

LONGEST CANTILEVER BRIDGES IN THE WORLD

	Bridge	Completed	Longest span	
			m	**ft**
1	Pont de Québec, Canada	1917	548.6	1,800
2	Firth of Forth, Scotland	1890	521.2	1,710
3	Minato, Osaka, Japan	1974	509.9	1,673
4	Commodore John Barry, New Jersey/Pennsylvania	1974	494.4	1,622
5	Greater New Orleans Louisiana	1958	480.1	1,575
6	Howrah, Calcutta, India	1943	457.2	1,500
7	Transbay, San Francisco	1936	426.7	1,400
8	Baton Rouge, Louisiana	1969	376.4	1,235
9	Tappan Zee, Tarrytown New York	1955	369.4	1,212
10	Longview Oregon/Washington	1930	365.8	1,200

LONGEST BRIDGES IN THE US

	Bridge	Year completed	Length of main span	
			m	**ft**
1	Verrazano Narrows, New York	1964	1,298	4,260
2	Golden Gate, San Francisco, California	1937	1,280	4,200
3	Mackinac Straits, Michigan, Missouri	1957	1,158	3,800
4	George Washington, New York	1931	1,067	3,500
5	Tacoma Narrows II, Washington	1950	853	2,800
6	Transbay, San Francisco, California	1936	704	2,310
7	Bronx-Whitestone, New York	1939	701	2,300
8=	Delaware Memorial, Wilmington Delaware (twin)	1951/68	655	2,150
8=	Seaway Skyway, Ogdensburg, New York	1960	655	2,150
10=	Melville Gas Pipeline Atchafalaya River, Louisiana	1951	610	2,000
10=	Walt Whitman, Philadelphia Pennsylvania	1957	610	2,000

T O P 1 0

LONGEST ROAD AND RAILROAD TUNNELS IN THE US

(Excluding subways)

	Tunnel/location	Type	Completed	Length km	miles
1	Cascade, Washington	Rail	1929	12.54	7.79
2	Flathead, Montana	Rail	1970	12.48	7.78
3	Moffat, Colorado	Rail	1928	10.00	6.21
4	Hoosac, Massachusetts	Rail	1875	7.56	4.70
5	BART Trans-Bay Tubes, San Francisco, California	Rail	1974	5.79	3.60
6	Brooklyn-Battery, New York	Road	1950	2.78	1.73
7	E. Johnson Memorial, Colorado	Road	1979	2.74	1.70
8	Eisenhower Memorial, Colorado*	Road	1973	2.72	1.69
9	Holland Tunnel, New York	Road	1927	2.61	1.62
10	Lincoln Tunnel I, New York	Road	1937	2.51	1.56

* *The highest-elevation highway tunnel in the world*

At 9.13 miles/14.70 km, Canadian Mount McDonald railroad tunnel, on the Canadian Pacific line, is the longest transportation tunnel in North America. The US Air Force is reported to have built an experimental missile transportation tunnel 3.73 miles/6 km long beneath the Arizona desert. The New York City West Delaware water tunnel (105 miles/168.98 km) is the longest tunnel of any kind in the world.

GOLDEN GATE BRIDGE
This magnificent suspension bridge spans the Golden Gate waterway that links San Francisco Bay with the Pacific Ocean.

T O P 1 0

LONGEST ROAD TUNNELS IN THE WORLD

	Tunnel/country	Year completed	Length km	miles
1	St. Gotthard, Switzerland	1980	16.32	10.14
2	Arlberg, Austria	1978	13.98	8.69
3	Fréjus, France/Italy	1980	12.90	8.02
4	Mont-Blanc, France/Italy	1965	11.60	7.21
5	Gudvangen, Norway	1992	11.40	7.08
6	Leirfjord, Norway	UC	11.11	6.90
7	Kan-Etsu, Japan	1991	11.01	6.84
8	Kan-Etsu, Japan	1985	10.93	6.79
9	Gran Sasso, Italy	1984	10.17	6.32
10	Plabutsch, Austria	1987	9.76	6.06

UC *Under construction*

All the road tunnels in the Top 10 were built during the past 30 years. Previously, the record for "world's longest" had been held by the 3.13-mile/5.04-km Viella Tunnel, Cataluña, Spain, which was opened in 1941. This tunnel overtook the 2.13-mile/3.43-km Mersey Tunnel connecting Liverpool and Birkenhead, built in 1925–34.

T O P 1 0

LONGEST RAILROAD TUNNELS IN THE WORLD

	Tunnel/country	Year completed	Length km	miles
1	Seikan, Japan	1988	53.90	33.49
2	Channel Tunnel, France/England	1994	49.94	31.03
3	Moscow Metro (Medvedkovo/Belyaevo section), Russia	1979	30.70	19.07
4	London Underground (East Finchley/Morden Northern Line), UK	1939	27.84	17.30
5	Dai-Shimizu, Japan	1982	22.17	13.78
6	Simplon II, Italy/Switzerland	1922	19.82	12.31
7	Simplon I, Italy/Switzerland	1906	19.80	12.30
8	Shin-Kanmon, Japan	1975	18.68	11.61
9	Apennine, Italy	1934	18.49	11.49
10	Rokko, Japan	1972	16.25	10.10

The first specifically-built passenger rail tunnel was the 2,514-ft/766-m Tyler Hill Tunnel, Kent, UK, opened on May 4, 1830. The longest rail tunnel built in the 19th century is the 9.32-mile/15-km St. Gotthard Tunnel, Switzerland, opened on May 20, 1882.

OTHER STRUCTURES

T O P 1 0

LARGEST ARTIFICIAL LAKES IN THE WORLD

(Includes only those formed as a result of dam construction)

	Dam/lake	Location	Year completed	Volume (m³)
1	Owen Falls	Uganda	1954	204,800,000,000
2	Kariba	Zimbabwe	1959	181,592,000,000
3	Bratsk	Russia	1964	169,270,000,000
4	High Aswan	Egypt	1970	168,000,000,000
5	Akosombo	Ghana	1965	148,000,000,000
6	Daniel Johnson	Canada	1968	141,852,000,000
7	Guri (Raul Leoni)	Venezuela	1986	136,000,000,000
8	Krasnoyarsk	Russia	1967	73,300,000,000
9	Bennett	Canada	1967	70,309,000,000
10	Zeya	Russia	1978	68,400,000,000

T O P 1 0

LARGEST BELLS IN THE WESTERN WORLD

	Bell/location	Year cast	Weight (tons)
1	*Tsar Kolokol*, Kremlin, Moscow, Russia	1735	222.56
2	*Voskresenskiy (Resurrection)*, Ivan the Great Bell Tower, Kremlin, Moscow, Russia	1746	72.20
3	*Petersglocke*, Cologne Cathedral, Germany	1923	28.00
4	Lisbon Cathedral, Portugal	post-1344	26.90
5	St. Stephen's Cathedral, Vienna, Austria	1957	23.58
6	Bourdon, Strasbourg Cathedral, France	1521	22.05
7	*Savoyarde*, Sacre-Coeur Basilica, Paris, France	1891	20.78
8	Bourdon, Riverside Church, New York, US	1931	20.44
9	Olmütz, Czech Republic	1931	20.05
10	*Campana gorda*, Toledo Cathedral, Spain	1753	19.04

Outside the West, large bells are struck with a beam, not rung with a clapper. In 1942 a 181-ton bell in Osaka, Japan, was destroyed, but there is a 170-ton bell in the Shi-Tenno-Ji Temple in Kyoto and a 83-ton bell in Chonan, both in Japan. The Mingun bell, just outside Mandalay in Myanmar (Burma), cast in 1780, weighs approximately 97 tons. There is also a 60-ton bell in Beijing in China.

T O P 1 0

HIGHEST DAMS IN THE US

	Dam/location	Completed	Height ft
1	Oroville Feather, CA	1968	755
2	Hoover Colorado, AZ/NV	1936	725
3	Dworshak North Fork of Clearwater, ID	1973	717
4	Glen Canyon Colorado, AZ	1966	709
5	New Bullard's Bar North Yuba, CA	1970	637
6	New Melones Stanislaus, CA	1979	625
7	Swift Lewis, WA	1958	610
8	Mossyrock Cowlitz, WA	1968	607
9	Shasta Sacramento, CA	1945	602
10	Don Pedro Tuolummne, CA	1971	568

Hailed as one of the great engineering achievements of the era, the Boulder Dam, built in 21 months at a cost of $175,000,000, was renamed Hoover in 1947, in honor of the President who authorized its construction. It was the tallest in the world until the 778-ft/237-m Mauvoisin, Switzerland, was completed in 1957. The Grand Coulee, on the Columbia River, Washington (completed 1942; 551 ft/168 m), is the largest concrete dam, and the largest concrete construction of any kind in the world. Currently, the world's tallest dam is the Nurek on the River Vakhsh, Tajikstan, completed in 1980 and measuring 984 ft/300 m; under construction on the same river, but behind schedule as a result of financial problems consequent to the breakup of the former Soviet Union, the Rogun is planned to attain 1,099 ft/335 m.

THE BELL THAT NEVER RANG
A 12.7-ton fragment broke off the Tsar Kolokol bell when water was thrown on it during a fire in 1737.

LARGEST CONVENTION CENTERS IN THE US

	Center/city	sq ft
1	McCormick Place, Chicago, IL	1,900,000
2	International Exposition Center, Cleveland, OH	1,700,000
3	Las Vegas Convention Center, Las Vegas, NV	1,300,000
4	Georgia World Congress Center, Atlanta, GA	1,200,000
5	Astrodome/Astrohall, Houston, TX	1,100,000
6	Javits Convention Center, New York, NY	900,000
7=	Kentucky Exposition Center, Louisville, KY	800,000
7=	Cobo Convention/Exhibit Center, Detroit, MI	800,000
9=	Anaheim Convention Center, Anaheim, CA	700,000
9=	Morial Convention Center, New Orleans, LA	700,000

GREAT BARRIER
The complex engineering project of damming the Indus River produced the world's fourth most massive earth and rockfill structure.

OLDEST CHURCHES IN THE US

	Church/location	Built
1	Cervento de Porta Coeli San German, PR*	1609
2	San Estevan del Rey Mission Valencia County, NM	1629
3	St. Luke's Church Isle of Wight County, VA	1632
4	First Church of Christ and the Ancient Burying Ground Hartford County, CT	1640
5	St. Ignatius Catholic Church St. Mary's County, MD	1641
6	Merchant's Hope Church Prince George County, VA	1657
7	Flatlands Dutch Reformed Church King's County, NY	1660
8=	Claflin-Richards House Essex County, MA	1661
8=	Church San Blas de Illesces of Coamo, Ponce, PR*	1661
8=	St. Mary's Whitechapel Lancaster County, VA	1661

* Not US territory when built, but now US National Historic Sites

LARGEST DAMS IN THE WORLD

(Ranked according to the volume of material used in construction)

	Dam	Location	Completed	Volume (m³)
1	Syncrude Tailings	Alberta, Canada	1992	540,000,000
2	Pati	Paraná, Argentina	1990	230,180,000
3	New Cornelia Tailings	Ten Mile Wash, Arizona, US	1973	209,500,000
4	Tarbela	Indus, Pakistan	1976	105,922,000
5	Fort Peck	Missouri, Montana, US	1937	96,050,000
6	Lower Usuma	Usuma, Nigeria	1990	93,000,000
7	Atatürk	Euphrates, Turkey	1990	84,500,000
8	Yacyreta-Apipe	Paraná, Paraguay/ Argentina	1991	81,000,000
9	Guri (Raul Leoni)	Caroni, Venezuela	1986	77,971,000
10	Rogun	Vakhsh, Tajikstan	1987	75,500,000

Despite the recent cancellation of several dams on environmental grounds, such as two in the Cantabrian Mountains, Spain, numerous major projects are in development for completion by the end of the century, when this Top 10 will contain some notable new entries. Among several in Argentina is the Chapeton dam under construction on the Paraná and scheduled for completion in 1998; it will have a volume of 296,200,000 m³ and will thus become the second largest dam in the world. The Pati, also on the Paraná, will be 238,180,000 m³. The Cipasang dam under construction on the Cimanuk, Indonesia, will have a volume of 90,000,000 m³.

TRAVEL & TOURISM

TOP 10

MODELS OF CAR IN THE US

	Make/model	Total 1994 sales ($)
1	Ford Taurus	397,037
2	Honda Accord	367,815*
3	Ford Escort	336,967
4	Toyota Camry	321,979*
5	GM Saturn	286,003
6	Honda Civic	267,023*
7	Pontiac Grand Am	262,310
8	Chevrolet Corsica/Beretta	222,129
9	Toyota Corolla	210,926*
10	Chevrolet Cavalier	187,263

* Includes imports

The Top 10 car models remain similar from year to year, with some jostling for position: the Ford Taurus has held on to the No. 1 slot, and the Ford Escort has steadily gained ground. The Pontiac Grand Am has risen from its former 10th placing against the general trend toward more compact vehicles.

TOP 10

MOTOR VEHICLE MANUFACTURERS IN THE WORLD

	Production company	Country	Cars	Commercial vehicles	Total
1	General Motors	US	4,989,938	1,875,890	6,865,828
2	Ford Motor Company	US	3,685,415	2,058,879	5,744,294
3	Toyota	Japan	3,649,640	838,251	4,487,891
4	Volkswagen	Germany	3,119,997	165,699	3,285,696
5	Nissan	Japan	2,222,985	675,200	2,437,726
6	PSA (Peugeot-Citroën)	France	2,252,121	185,605	2,437,726
7	Renault	France	1,929,858	334,473	2,264,331
8	Chrysler	US	727,928	1,254,748	1,982,676
9	Fiat	Italy	1,557,556	242,844	1,800,400
10	Honda	Japan	1,629,666	132,531	1,762,197
	World total		*35,322,375*	*12,369,371*	*47,691,746*

Figures are for 1992 production, amalgamating worldwide production in all companies owned by the manufacturers, as compiled by the American Automobile Manufacturers Association. Two other Japanese companies, Mitsubishi and Mazda, actually produced more cars than Chrysler (1,116,791 and 1,205,073 respectively – the only other companies in the world to produce more than 1,000,000), but Chrysler's disproportionate commercial vehicle production moved the US company up from 10th place in 1991, while Honda dropped from 8th position. In this year, the output of the Rover Group, the only British-owned company in the world Top 40, a total of 399,661 vehicles, meant that it was placed 22nd in the world league.

CAR MANUFACTURERS IN THE US

	Company	Production
1	Ford	1,220,512
2	Chevrolet	651,647
3	Pontiac	597,137
4	Honda	498,710
5	Buick	483,029
6	Oldsmobile	481,452
7	Toyota	399,341
8	Nissan	312,675
9	Dodge	303,678
10	Lincoln-Mercury	440,838

Based on group totals, General Motors (which encompasses Buick, Cadillac, Chevrolet, Oldsmobile, and Pontiac) is the largest manufacturer by a considerable margin, with US production of 2,719,764 to Ford's total (Ford plus Lincoln-Mercury) of 1,661,350.

VEHICLE-OWNING COUNTRIES IN THE WORLD

	Country	Cars	Commercial vehicles	Total
1	US	144,213,429	46,148,799	190,362,228
2	Japan	38,963,793	22,694,351	61,658,144
3	Germany	39,086,000	2,923,000	42,009,000
4	Italy	29,497,000	2,763,050	32,260,050
5	France	24,020,000	5,040,000	29,060,000
6	UK	23,008,342	3,643,398	26,651,740
7	CIS (Commonwealth of Independent States)	18,000,000	8,000,000	26,000,000
8	Canada	13,322,457	3,688,433	17,010,890
9	Spain	13,102,385	2,773,371	15,875,756
10	Brazil	12,974,991	1,371,127	14,346,118

Between 1960 and 1992 world vehicle ownership increased more than fourfold from 126,954,817, while the ratio of vehicles to people has risen from 1:23 to 1:9. In affluent countries the ratio is higher: 1:1.4 in the US and 1:2.2 in the UK. San Marino and a few other small countries claim a ratio of 1:1. The biggest disparities occur in poor economies, such as India with a ratio of 1:170, China with 1:83, Ethiopia 1:869, and Bangladesh 1:915.

MAKES OF CAR IMPORTED TO THE US

	Manufacturer	Country	Total 1993 sales ($)
1	Toyota	Japan	373,773
2	Honda	Japan	298,512
3	Nissan	Japan/Spain	232,802
4	Mazda	Japan	159,452
5	Hyundai	South Korea	93,376
6	Mitsubishi	Japan/Australia	92,222
7	BMW	Germany	78,010
8	Volvo	Sweden/Netherlands/Belgium	72,955
9	Chrysler	Mexico	67,988
10	Mercedes-Benz	Germany/Austria	61,899

COUNTRIES PRODUCING THE MOST MOTOR VEHICLES

	Country	Cars	Commercial vehicles	Total
1	Japan	8,497,094	2,730,451	11,227,545
2	US	5,981,046	4,883,157	10,864,203
3	Germany	3,753,341	237,309	3,990,650
4	France	2,836,280	319,437	3,155,717
5	Canada	1,349,081	888,652	2,237,733
6	South Korea	1,592,669	457,389	2,050,058
7	CIS (Commonwealth of Independent States	1,207,500	599,500	1,807,000
8	Spain	1,505,949	261,691	1,767,640
9	UK	1,375,524	193,410	1,568,934
10	Brazil	1,102,119	288,142	1,390,261
	World total	*33,843,533*	*13,012,660*	*46,856,193*

Brazil replaced Italy as No. 10 in 1993. Italy's output dropped to 1,267,195 vehicles (No. 12), below China's output of 1,310,000.

ROADS & PUBLIC TRANSPORTATION

TOP 10

TYPES OF LOST PROPERTY ON PUBLIC TRANSPORTATION

NYC METROPOLITAN TRANSIT AUTHORITY		LONDON TRANSPORT (1993–94)
Backpacks	1	Books, checkbooks and credit cards
Radios/Walkmen	2	"Value items" (handbags, pocketbooks, wallets, etc.)
Eyeglasses	3	Clothing
Wallets and pocketbooks	4	Umbrellas
Cameras	5	Cases and bags
Keys	6	Keys
Attaché cases	7	Eyeglasses
Watches	8	Cameras, electronic articles, and jewelry
Shoes	9	Gloves (pairs)
Jewelry	10	Gloves (odd)

Although the Metropolitan Transit Authority does not keep itemized records of lost items in the same meticulous detail as London Transport, a comparison of the ranking of the two lists reveals both interesting similarities (keys feature at No. 6 in both lists) and differences (where are the umbrellas in the New York version?). In the London list, it raises further questions, most notably what accounts for the remarkable consistency in the numbers and order of most

categories of items handed in to London Transport's Lost Property Office from year to year? Alongside the mysterious pattern that emerges, a clear decline in the total can also be discerned, raising the question of whether the traveling public are becoming more careful with their property or less scrupulous about handing in finds. Books have figured in the No. 1 position for several years, but changes in fashion have meant that hats, once one of the most common lost items, no longer even warrant a separate category, while often expensive electronic calculators, laptop computers, and mobile phones are now lost in increasing numbers in both New York and London. A June 1994 auction of the New York MTA's unclaimed property included such bizarre items as five wheelchairs (prompting the thought that healers are at work in the New York subways), while false teeth and artificial limbs feature among the stranger items that have been lost in recent years in both cities. London's weird list includes a skeleton, a box of glass eyes, breast implants, an outboard motor, a complete double bed, a theatrical coffin, 280 pounds of currants and sultanas, a stuffed gorilla, and an urn containing human ashes (the latter was never claimed and the ashes were ceremoniously scattered in a flowerbed in a nearby park). However, this is chicken-feed, when compared with the odd items left on Japanese trains in one year, among which were no fewer than 500,000 umbrellas, $15,000,000 in cash, 29 small dogs, one live snake in a bag, 150 sets of false teeth, and 15 urns containing ashes of the dead.

TOP 10

COUNTRIES WITH THE LONGEST ROAD NETWORKS

	Country	km	miles
1	USA	6,243,103	3,879,284
2	India	1,970,000	1,224,101
3	Brazil	1,670,148	1,037,782
4	France	1,510,750	938,736
5	Japan	1,115,609	693,207
6	China	1,029,000	639,391
7	Russia	893,000	554,884
8	Canada	884,272	549,461
9	Australia	837,872	520,629
10	Germany	625,600	388,730

TOP 10

STATES WITH THE GREATEST ROAD NETWORKS

	State	Total length*	
		km	miles
1	Texas	473,456	294,142
2	California	272,203	169,201
3	Illinois	220,424	136,965
4	Kansas	214,455	133,256
5	Minnesota	209,149	129,959
6	Missouri	195,997	121,787
7	Michigan	189,354	117,659
8	Pennsylvania	188,354	117,038
9	Ohio	183,180	113,823
10	Florida	181,547	112,808

Interstate, rural and urban

Source: Federal Highway Administration

US Department of Transportation Federal Highway Administration figures show that Texas has both the greatest road network overall and the greatest length of interstate highways (3,229 miles/5,197 km). Total US public road and street mileage as of December 31, 1993 was 3,904,721 miles/6,284,039 km.

COUNTRIES DRIVING ON THE LEFT

	Country	Total vehicles registered
1	Japan	68,658,144
2	UK	26,651,740
3	Australia	9,954,000
4	South Africa	5,338,291
5	India	5,203,271
6	Indonesia	3,008,651
7	Thailand	3,016,453
8	Malaysia	2,833,111
9	New Zealand	1,902,803
10	Nigeria	1,425,000

While more countries drive on the right than on the left, there are 42 countries in the world that drive on the left, including the UK and most members of the British Commonwealth. The last country in Europe to change over from driving on the left to the right was Sweden, on September 3, 1967. At the time it was estimated to have cost $63,000,000 to do so. There are innumerable explanations for keeping to the left, one being that it is common practice, especially among sword-wearing riders, to mount a horse from the left, and it is then simplest to remain on the left. Similarly, riding on the left facilitates right-handed sword defense against approaching riders. This does not explain, however, why other nations drive on the right.

ON THE BUSES

Paris had the first public buses, eight-seater horse-drawn carriages, from 1662, but they were not a success and soon abandoned. A service was not reintroduced until the early 1980s. In London an omnibus service was set up in 1829 by George Shillibeer. The first steam buses operated in London in 1833, and the first double-decker horse buses in 1847. There were gasoline-powered buses in Germany from 1895, and Britain from 1897.

STATES WITH THE MOST LICENSED DRIVERS

	State	Drivers female	male	total
1	California	9,609,000	10,822,000	20,431,000
2	Texas	5,670,000	5,949,000	11,619,000
3	Florida	5,235,000	5,470,000	10,705,000
4	New York	4,964,000	5,561,000	10,525,000
5	Ohio	4,604,000	4,711,000	9,315,000
6	Pennsylvania	3,954,000	4,192,000	8,146,000
7	Illinois	3,721,000	3,808,000	7,529,000
8	Michigan	3,309,000	3,274,000	6,583,000
9	New Jersey	2,517,000	2,852,000	5,369,000
10	Virginia	2,376,000	2,396,000	4,772,000
	US total	*86,092,000*	*89,786,000*	*175,878,000*

Compared with 1992, when there were nine, 14 states now have more female than male drivers, while one state – Utah – has identical numbers (581,000 women and 581,000 men).

LONGEST HIGHWAYS IN THE US

	Highway	Total length km	miles
1	US-20	5,415	3,365
2	US-6	5,229	3,249
3	US-30	5,020	3,119
4	US-50	4,889	3,038
5	I-80	4,649	2,889
6	I-90	4,480	2,784
7	US-60	4,422	2,748
8	US-70	4,390	2,728
9	US-2	4,253	2,643
10	US-1	4,173	2,593

Source: Federal Highway Administration

The Interstate road system began with the introduction of the 1956 Highway Act, after which "I" shields began appearing on new highways that ran through more than one state. An Interstate differs from a US Route in that it is a full freeway, with no "Stop" signs – although some older US Routes still retain a few.

ON THE RIGHT TRACK

TOP 10

LONGEST RAILROAD PLATFORMS IN THE WORLD

	Station	Platform length m	ft
1	State Street Center Subway, Chicago Illinois	1,067	3,500
2	Khargpur, India	833	2,733
3	Perth, Australia	762	2,500
4	Sonepur, India	736	2,415
5	Bournemouth UK	720	2,362
6	Bulawayo Zimbabwe	702	2,302
7	New Lucknow, India	686	2,250
8	Bezwada, India	640	2,100
9	Gloucester, UK	624	2,047
10	Jhansi, India	617	2,025

TOP 10

LONGEST RAILROAD NETWORKS IN THE WORLD

	Country	Total rail length km	miles
1	US	240,000	149,129
2	Russia	158,100	98,239
3	Canada	146,444	90,996
4	China	64,000	39,768
5	India	61,850	38,432
6	Germany	45,468	28,253
7	Australia	40,478	25,152
8	France	34,322	21,327
9	Argentina	34,172	21,233
10	Brazil	30,133	18,724

US rail mileage has declined since its peak of 254,000 miles/408,773 km in 1916.

TOP 10

FIRST COUNTRIES WITH RAILROADS

	Country	First railroad established
1	UK	1825
2	US	1834
3=	Belgium	1835
3=	Germany	1835
5=	Canada	1836
5=	Russia	1836
7=	Austria	1837
7=	France	1837
9=	Italy	1839
9=	Netherlands	1839

Although there were earlier, horse-drawn railroads, the UK had the first steam service.

TOP 10

BUSIEST AMTRAK RAIL STATIONS IN THE US

	Station	Boardings (1994)
1	New York-Penn	5,894,036
2	Washington-Union	3,343,792
3	Philadelphia-30th St.	3,314,070
4	Chicago-Union	2,429,048
5	Los Angeles-Union	1,109,447
6	Baltimore-Penn	953,614
7	Boston-South	770,577
8	San Diego	615,196
9	Wilmington (Delaware)	602,105
10	Newark-Penn	514,667

On May 1, 1970, Amtrak, the National Railroad Passenger Corporation, took over the passenger system previously controlled by 22 of the principal railroads in the US. It now operates services over some 23,560 miles/38,000 km of track.

TOP 10

FASTEST RAILROAD JOURNEYS IN THE WORLD

	Journey	Train	Distance miles	Speed (mph)
1	Massy – St. Pierre, France	TGV 8501	128.4	152.6
2	Hiroshima – Kokuru, Japan	27 Nozomi	119.3	143.2
3	Madrid – Ciudad Real, Spain	4 AVE	106.1	135.4
4	Hannover – Göttingen, Germany	23 ICE	61.8	119.6
5	Skövde – Alingsås, Sweden	X2000 421	61.6	108.8
6	Doncaster – Grantham, UK	InterCity 225	40.5	106.3
7	Rome – Florence, Italy	Cristoforo Colombo	162.7	101.7
8	Philadelphia, PA – Wilmington, DE	Metroliner	31.4	99.3
9	Toronto – Dorval, Canada	Metropolis	323.7	90.3
10	St. Petersburg – Moscow, Russia	ER200	403.8	81.0

This list comprises the fastest journey for each country; all have other similarly – occasionally equally – fast services.

TRAIN A GRANDE VITESSE
The current world rail speed record is held by the French TGV, which on May 18, 1990 clocked 320.0 mph/515.0 km/h.

LATTER-DAY LABYRINTH
Trains run 24 hours a day, 365 days a year on most of the New York subway routes. This network is among the oldest and longest underground railroad systems in the world.

TOP 10

OLDEST SUBWAY SYSTEMS IN THE WORLD

	City	Year construction commenced
1	London	1863
2	New York	1868
3	Chicago	1892
4=	Budapest	1896
4=	Glasgow	1896
6	Boston	1897
7	Paris	1900
8	Wuppertal	1901
9	Berlin	1902
10	Philadelphia	1907

TOP 10

BUSIEST AMTRAK STATES IN THE US

	State	Boardings (1994)
1	New York	7,422,288
2	California	6,723,788
3	Pennsylvania	4,040,609
4	District of Columbia	3,343,792
5	Illinois	3,116,888
6	Maryland	1,448,824
7	New Jersey	1,369,231
8	Massachusetts	1,239,032
9	Florida	1,124,956
10	Connecticut	1,108,306

TOP 10

LONGEST SUBWAY NETWORKS IN THE US

	City	First built/ extended	No. of stations	Total track length km	miles
1	New York	1868/1968	461	370	230
2	Washington, D.C.	1976/93	86	612	380
3	Chicago	1892/1983	142	156	97
4	San Francisco	1972	34	115	71
5	Boston	1897/1980	51	70	43
6	Cleveland	1955/68	18	47	29
7	Atlanta	1979	20	41	25
8	Philadelphia	1907	68	63	39
9	Miami	1984	20	33	21
10	Baltimore	1983	9	22	14

A 17-mile/27-km subway currently under construction in Honolulu, is scheduled to open in 1997. Several Canadian cities (Toronto, Montreal, and Vancouver) have subways, and certain US cities, such as Los Angeles and Detroit, have short sytems.

TOP 10

LONGEST UNDERGROUND RAILROAD NETWORKS IN THE WORLD

	City	Built	Stations	Total track length km	miles
1	Washington, D.C.	1976–1993	86	612	380
2	London	1863–1979	272	430	267
3	New York	1868–1968	461	370	230
4	Paris (Metro & RER)	1900–1985	430	301	187
5	Moscow	1935–1979	115	225	140
6	Tokyo	1927–1980	192	218	135
7	Berlin	1902–1980	134	167	104
8	Chicago	1892–1953	142	156	97
9	Copenhagen	1934	61	134	83
10	Mexico City	1969–1982	57	125	78

The extension of Washington, D.C.'s subway, completed in 1993, has lifted it from 10th to 1st place. Other underground systems being developed include Seoul, Korea, currently 72 miles/116 km long and due to gain 21 miles/33 km, which will put it into the Top 10.

LAND TRANSPORTATION DISASTERS

WORST RAILROAD DISASTERS IN THE US

	Incident	No. killed
1	July 9, 1918, Nashville Tennessee	101

On the Nashville, Chattanooga, and St. Louis Railroad, a head-on collision led to the worst death-toll in US history, with 171 injured.

	Incident	No. killed
2	November 2, 1918, Brooklyn New York	97

A subway train was derailed in the Malbone Street tunnel.

	Incident	No. killed
3=	August 7, 1904, Eden, Colorado	96

The "World's Fair Express" was derailed when Steele's Hollow Bridge collapsed as it crossed.

	Incident	No. killed
3=	March 1, 1910, Wellington Washington	96

An avalanche swept two trains into a canyon.

	Incident	No. killed
5	September 8, 1900, Bolivar, Texas	85

A train traveling from Beaumont encountered a hurricane that killed 6,000 in Galveston. Attempts to load the train onto a ferry were abandoned, and it set back but was destroyed by the storm.

	Incident	No. killed
6	February 6, 1951, Woodbridge New Jersey	84

A Pennsylvania Railroad commuter train crashed while speeding around a bend.

	Incident	No. killed
7	August 10, 1887, Chatsworth Illinois	82

A trestle bridge caught fire and collapsed as the Toledo, Peoria & Western train was passing over. As many as 372 were injured.

	Incident	No. killed
8	December 29, 1876, Ashtabula, Ohio	80

A bridge collapsed in a snowstorm, and the Lake Shore train fell into the Ashtabula River. The death toll may have been as high as 92.

	Incident	No. killed
9=	September 6, 1943, Frankford Junction, Pennsylvania	79

Pennsylvania's worst railroad accident since Camp Hill in 1856, when two trains met head-on, killing 66 children on an outing.

	Incident	No. killed
9=	November 22, 1950, Richmond Hill New York	79

STATES WITH THE FEWEST AND THE MOST MOTOR VEHICLE FATALITIES

	FEWEST State	Total fatalities (1994)
1	Rhode Island	63
2	District of Columbia	68
3	Vermont	77
4	Alaska	84
5	North Dakota	88
6	Delaware	112
7	New Hampshire	119
8	Hawaii	122
9	Wyoming	144
10	South Dakota	154

	MOST State	Total fatalities (1994)
1	California	4,230
2	Texas	3,124
3	Florida	2,735
4	New York	1,615
5	Illinois	1,520
6	Pennsylvania	1,440
7=	Michigan	1,418
7=	North Carolina	1,418
9	Georgia	1,404
10	Ohio	1,322

While they have the greatest number of motor vehicle deaths, most of the states appearing in the "Most" Top 10 are also among the nation's foremost vehicle users, and if this is taken into account, they have fatality rates below the national average. The highest rates actually occur in states with relatively few vehicles, including Alaska, Arkansas, Mississippi, Nevada, and New Mexico. Connecticut and Massachusetts have the lowest rates of all.

WORST RAIL DISASTERS IN THE WORLD

	Incident	Killed
1	June 6, 1981, Bagmati River, India	c.800

The carriages of a train plunged off a bridge when the driver braked, apparently to avoid a sacred cow. Rescuers recovered 268 bodies, but it has been claimed that the train was so full that in reality over 800 died, making it probably the worst rail disaster of all time.

	Incident	Killed
2	June 3, 1989, Chelyabinsk, Russia	up to 800

Two Trans-Siberian passenger trains, going to and from the Black Sea, were destroyed when liquid gas from a nearby pipeline exploded.

	Incident	Killed
3	January 18, 1915, Guadalajara, Mexico	600+

A train derailed on a steep incline, but details of the disaster were suppressed.

	Incident	Killed
4	December 12, 1917, Modane, France	573

A troop-carrying train ran out of control and was derailed. It was probably overloaded, and as many as 1,000 people may have died.

	Incident	Killed
5	March 2, 1944, Balvano, Italy	521

Passengers were asphyxiated when a train stalled in the Armi Tunnel. Wartime secrecy prevented true figures from being published.

	Incident	Killed
6	January 3, 1944, Torre, Spain	500+

A double collision and fire in a tunnel caused many deaths. Wartime secrecy prevented full details from being published.

	Incident	Killed
7	January 13, 1985, Awash Ethiopia	428

A derailment hurled a train laden with some 1,000 passengers into a ravine.

	Incident	Killed
8	January 7, 1917, Cireau Romania	374

An overcrowded passenger train crashed into a military train and was derailed. As well as the high death toll, 756 were injured.

	Incident	Killed
9	May 31, 1993, Quipungo, Angola	355

A trail was derailed by UNITA guerrilla action.

	Incident	Killed
10	January 4, 1990, Sangi, Pakistan	306

A train diverted onto the wrong line, resulted in a fatal collision.

Casualty figures for rail accidents are often very imprecise, especially during wartime.

THE 10

WORST MOTOR VEHICLE AND ROAD DISASTERS IN THE WORLD

	Country/incident	Killed
1	Afghanistan, November 3, 1982	2,000+

Following a collision with a Soviet army truck, a gasoline tanker exploded in the 1.7-mile-/2.7-km-long Salang Tunnel. Some authorities have put the death toll as high as 3,000.

2	Colombia, August 7, 1956	1,200

Seven army ammunition trucks exploded at night in the center of Cali, destroying eight city blocks.

3	Thailand, February 15, 1990	150+

A dynamite truck exploded.

4	Nepal, November 23, 1974	148

Hindu pilgrims were killed when a suspension bridge over the Mahahali River collapsed.

5	Egypt, August 9, 1973	127

A bus drove into an irrigation canal.

6	Togo, December 6, 1965	125+

Two trucks collided with dancers during a festival at Sotouboua.

7	Spain, July 11, 1978	120+

A liquid gas tanker exploded in a camping site at San Carlos de la Rapita.

8	Gambia, November 12, 1992	c.100

A bus plunged into a river when its brakes failed.

9	Kenya, early December 1992	nearly 100

A bus carrying 112 skidded, hit a bridge, and plunged into a river.

10=	Lesotho, December 16, 1976	90

A bus fell into the Tsoaing River.

10=	India, March 16, 1988	90

In the state of Madhya Pradesh, the driver of a bus carrying a wedding party lost control and crashed while trying to change a tape cassette.

The worst-ever racing car accident occurred on June 11, 1955 at Le Mans, France, when, in attempting to avoid other cars, French driver Pierre Levegh's Mercedes-Benz 300 SLR went out of control, hit a wall, and exploded in midair, showering wreckage into the crowd and killing a total of 82 (*see also* The 10 Worst Disasters at Sports Venues, p.35).

THE 10

LEAST BAD YEARS FOR ROAD FATALITIES IN THE US

	Year	Total fatalities*
1	1899	26
2	1900	36
3	1901	54
4	1902	79
5	1903	117
6	1904	172
7	1905	252
8	1906	338
9	1907	581
10	1908	751

* Deaths occurring within 30 days of accident

From 1899, when the recording of road deaths began, the annual toll has risen at a fairly steady rate, retreating marginally due to restrictions on driving during the Depression years and in World War II. Fatalities exceeded 10,000 for the first time in 1918, and 50,000 in 1966. Until the 1940s, pedestrians were the principal victims of fatal accidents, and collisions with railroad trains, streetcars, and animals figured prominently in the early decades. In the past 50 years, other vehicles have been the main objects of collision.

TOP 10

CARS WITH THE HIGHEST DRIVER DEATH RATES IN THE US*

1	Chevrolet Corvette
2	Pontiac LeMans
3	Isuzu Amigo
4	Ford Mustang
5	Ford Festiva
6	Nissan pickup
7	Ford Escort
8	Geo Metro
9	Chevrolet S10
10	Dodge Ram 50

* During the period 1989–93

THE 10

WORST YEARS FOR ROAD FATALITIES IN THE US

	Year	Fatalities per 100,000,000 VMT*	Total fatalities#
1	1972	4.3	54,589
2	1973	4.1	54,052
3	1969	5.0	53,543
4	1968	5.2	52,725
5	1970	4.7	52,627
6	1971	4.5	52,542
7	1979	3.3	51,093
8	1980	3.3	51,091
9	1966	5.5	50,894
10	1967	5.3	50,724

* Vehicle Miles of Travel
 # Deaths occurring within 30 days of accident

Although 1972 was the worst year on record for total fatalities, it is important to take into account the progressive increases in population and numbers of vehicles on the road, so the ratio of fatalities to vehicle miles of travel is more significant. This has steadily declined since 1921, the first year it was recorded, when there were 24.1 deaths per 100,000,000 VMT. By 1993 this figure had plunged to 1.7 per 100,000,000 VMT.

WATER TRANSPORTATION

LONGEST PASSENGER LINERS IN THE WORLD

	Ship/year built country	Length m	ft	in
1	*France/ Norway** 1961, France	315.53	1,035	2
2	*QEII* 1969, UK	293.53	963	0
3=	*Majesty of the Seas* 1992, France	268.32	880	4
3=	*Monarch of the Seas* 1991, France	268.32	880	4
3=	*Sovereign of the Seas* 1987, France	268.32	880	4
6	*Sensation* 1993, Finland	262.00	859	7
7	*Ecstasy* 1991, Finland	262.00	859	7
8	*Fantasy* 1990, Finland	260.60	855	0
9	*Oriana* 1995, Germany	260.00	853	0
10	*Canberra* 1961, UK	249.49	818	6

* *Renamed*

"THE BIGGEST SHIP IN THE WORLD"

The 692-ft/211-m steamship *Great Eastern*, designed by Isambard Kingdom Brunel, was five times bigger than any vessel ever built, a record held for nearly 50 years. Built in Millwall, London, and almost as long as the Thames was wide, it was decided to launch it sideways. Thousands turned out for the event but the ship would not budge. She was finally launched in 1858 and in 1866 laid the first commercially successful transatlantic telegraph cable. However, dogged by misfortune, thirty years after her launch, she was broken up for scrap.

FIRST SHIPS LAUNCHED BY THE QUEEN

	Ship	Location	Date launched
1	HMY *Britannia*	Clydebank	April 16, 1953
2	SS *Southern Cross*	Belfast	August 17, 1954
3	SS *Empress of Britain*	Govan	June 22, 1955
4	HMS *Dreadnought*	Barrow	October 21, 1960
5	SS *British Admiral*	Barrow	March 17, 1965
6	*Queen Elizabeth II*	Clydebank	September 20, 1967
7	HMS *Sheffield**	Barrow	June 10, 1971
8	*The Royal British Legion Jubilee*#	Henley-on-Thames	July 17, 1972
9	HMS *Invincible*	Barrow	May 3, 1977
10	HMS *Lancaster*	Scotstoun	May 24, 1990

* *Sunk May 8, 1982 after being struck by an Exocet missile during the Falklands conflict*
\# *Lifeboat*

LARGEST PASSENGER LINERS IN THE WORLD

	Ship	Year	Country built in	Passenger capacity	Gross tonnage
1	*France/Norway (renamed)*	1961	France	2,565	76,049
2=	*Majesty of the Seas*	1992	France	2,766	73,937
2=	*Monarch of the Seas*	1991	France	2,764	73,937
4	*Sovereign of the Seas*	1987	France	2,600	73,192
5=	*Sensation*	1993	Finland	2,634	70,367
5=	*Ecstasy*	1991	Finland	2,634	70,367
5=	*Fantasy*	1990	Finland	2,634	70,367
8=	*Crown Princess*	1990	Italy	1,590	69,845
8=	*Regal Princess*	1991	Italy	1,900	69,845
10	*Oriana*	1995	Germany	1,975	69,153

The *Oriana* has pushed the *QEII* from tenth position. Currently under construction in Italy, for a P&O subsidiary is the 77,000-ton *Sun Princess*. Another as yet unnamed liner, weighing 100,000 tons, is scheduled for 1997, and will be 935 ft/285 m long.

TOP 10

COUNTRIES WITH THE LONGEST INLAND WATERWAY NETWORKS*

	Country	km	miles
1	China	138,600	86,122
2	Russia	100,000	62,137
3	Brazil	50,000	31,069
4	US#	41,009	25,482
5	Indonesia	21,579	13,409
6	Vietnam	17,702	11,000
7	India	16,180	10,054
8	Zaïre	15,000	9,321
9	France	14,932	9,278
10	Colombia	14,300	8,886

* Canals and navigable rivers
# Excluding Great Lakes

TOP 10

SHIPPING COUNTRIES IN THE WORLD

	Country	No. of ships	Total GRT*
1	Panama	5,564	57,618,623
2	Liberia	1,611	53,918,534
3	Greece	1,929	29,134,435
4	Japan	9,950	24,247,525
5	Cyprus	1,591	22,842,009
6	Bahamas	1,121	21,224,164
7	Norway	785	19,383,417
8	Russia	5,335	16,813,761
9	China	2,501	14,944,999
10	Malta	1,037	14,163,357

* GRT or Gross Registered Tonnage is not
   the actual weight of a ship but its cubic
   capacity (1 ton = 100 cubic feet). The list
   includes only ships of more than 100 GRT.

BLUE RIBAND
On her maiden voyage in 1952, United States
set the still unbeaten record for the fastest
commercial transatlantic crossing, thereby
winning the Hales Trophy or "Blue Riband."

TOP 10

LARGEST OIL TANKERS IN THE WORLD

	Ship	Year built	Country	Deadweight tonnage
1	Jahre Viking	1979	Japan	564,650
2	Kapetan Giannis	1977	Japan	516,895
3	Kapetan Michalis	1977	Japan	516,423
4	Nissei Maru	1975	Japan	484,276
5	Stena King	1978	Taiwan	457,927
6	Stena Queen	1977	Taiwan	457,841
7	Kapetan Panagiotis	1977	Japan	457,062
8	Kapetan Giorgis	1976	Japan	456,368
9	Sea Empress	1976	Japan	423,677
10	Mira Star	1975	Japan	423,642

THE 10

"BLUE RIBAND" HOLDERS IN THE 20TH CENTURY
(The 10 fastest transatlantic crossings by passenger liners.)

	Ship	Year	Route	Weight (tons)	days	Time hrs	mins
1	United States	1952	Ambrose Light to Bishop Rock	51,988	3	10	40
2	Queen Mary	1938	Ambrose Light to Bishop Rock	81,237	3	20	42
3	Queen Mary	1938	Bishop Rock to Ambrose Light	81,237	3	21	45
4	Normandie	1937	Bishop Rock to Ambrose Light	80,000	3	23	2
5	Queen Mary	1936	Ambrose Light to Bishop Rock	81,237	3	23	57
6	Queen Mary	1936	Bishop Rock to Ambrose Light	81,237	4	0	27
7	Normandie	1935	Bishop Rock to Ambrose Light	80,000	4	3	2
8	Empress of Britain	1934	Quebec to Cherbourg	42,348	4	6	58
9	Europa	1932	From Cherbourg	51,656	4	15	56
10	Europa	1930	From Cherbourg	51,656	4	17	6

MARINE DISASTERS

SINKING THE UNSINKABLE
The collision of the supposedly unsinkable British liner Titanic with an iceberg was one of the worst marine disasters in peacetime.

DID YOU KNOW

PASSENGER FERRY DISASTERS

The presence of the *Dona Paz* in the Top 10 Marine Disasters of the 20th Century list is a reminder that in modern times many of the most serious accidents at sea have involved passenger ferries. Among the worst since World War II are the loss of the *Toya Maru* off Japan on September 26, 1954, with 1,172 killed, and the *Don Juan* off the Philippines on April 22, 1980, with at least 1,000 killed. Although ferry passengers usually travel unregistered, so precise numbers are often vague, the *Neptune*, a ferry that went down off Haiti on February 17, 1992 probably resulted in the loss of about 1,800 lives. The December 8, 1966 sinking in the Aegean of the *Heraklion*, with 217 casualties, and, more recently, the March 6, 1987 sinking of the *Herald of Free Enterprise* at Zeebrugge with 193 victims and the *Estonia* in the Gulf of Finland on September 27, 1994, killing 912 passengers and crew, are notable among the worst-ever roll-on roll-off ferry disasters, putting the safety of such vessels under scrutiny. In the postwar period as many as 20 such ferries have capsized, with the loss of more than 1,500 lives in total.

THE 10

WORST MARINE DISASTER BEFORE THE 20TH CENTURY

	Incident	Killed
1	Spanish Armada – Military conflict and storms combined to destroy the Spanish fleet in the English Channel and elsewhere off the British coast, August to October 1588.	c.4,000
2=	British fleet – Eight ships sunk in storms off Egg Island, Labrador, Canada, August 22, 1711.	c.2,000
2=	*St. George, Defence,* and *Hero* – British warships stranded off the Jutland coast, Denmark, December 4, 1811.	c.2,000
4	*Sultana* – A Mississippi River steamboat destroyed by a boiler explosion near Memphis, April 27, 1865 – the US's worst ever marine accident, although the official death toll may be an underestimate.	1,547
5	*Capitanas* – Twin Spanish treasure vessels sunk in a hurricane off the Florida coast, July 31, 1715.	c.1,000
6	*Royal George* – British warship wrecked off Spithead, August 29, 1782, the worst ever single shipwreck off the British coast.	c.900
7	*Princess Alice* – Pleasure steamer in collision with *Bywell Castle* on the Thames near Woolwich, September 3, 1878.	786
8	*Queen Charlotte* – British warship burned in Leghorn harbor, March 17, 1800.	c.700
9	*Ertogrul* – Turkish frigate wrecked off the Japanese coast, September 19, 1890.	587
10	*Utopia* – British steamer collided with British warship *Amson* off Gibraltar, March 17, 1891.	576

THE 10

WORST OIL TANKER SPILLS OF ALL TIME

	Tanker/location	Date	Spillage (tonnes approx.)
1	*Atlantic Empress* and *Aegean Captain*, Trinidad	July 19, 1979	300,000
2	*Castillio de Bellver*, Cape Town, South Africa	Augus t 6, 1983	255,000
3	*Olympic Bravery*, Ushant, France	January 24, 1976	250,000
4	*Showa-Maru*, Malacca, Malaya	June 7, 1975	237,000
5	*Amoco Cadiz*, Finistère, France	March 16, 1978	223,000
6	*Odyssey*, Atlantic, off Canada	November 10, 1988	140,000
7	*Torrey Canyon*, Scilly Isles, UK	March 18, 1967	120,000
8	*Sea Star*, Gulf of Oman	December 19, 1972	115,000
9	*Irenes Serenada*, Pilos, Greece	February 23, 1980	102,000
10	*Urquiola*, Corunna, Spain	May 12, 1976	101,000

It is estimated that an average of 2,000,000 tonnes is spilled into the world's seas every year. All these accidents were caused by collision, grounding, fire, or explosion. Military action has caused worse tanker oil spills: during the Gulf War tankers sunk in the Persian Gulf spilled more than 1,000,000 tonnes of oil. The *Exxon Valdez* grounding in Alaska on March 24, 1989 spilled about 35,000 tonnes, resulting in major ecological damage.

THE 10
WORST MARINE DISASTERS
OF THE 20TH CENTURY

Incident	Approx no. killed
1 *Wilhelm Gustloff* The German liner, laden with refugees, was torpedoed off Danzig by a Soviet submarine, *S-13*, January 30, 1945. The precise death toll remains uncertain, but is in the range of 5,348–7,700.	up to 7,700
2 Unknown vessel An unidentified Chinese troopship carrying Nationalist soldiers from Manchuria sank off Yingkow, November 1947.	6,000+
3 *Cap Arcona* A German ship carrying concentration camp survivors was bombed and sunk by British aircraft in Lübeck harbor, May 3, 1945.	4,650
4 *Lancastria* A British troop ship sunk off St. Nazaire, June 17, 1940.	4,000+
5 *Yamato* A Japanese battleship sunk off Kyushu Island, April 7, 1945.	3,033
6 *Dona Paz* The ferry *Dona Paz* was struck by oil tanker MV *Victor* in the Tabias Strait, Philippines, December 20, 1987.	3,000+
7 *Kiangya* An overloaded steamship carrying refugees struck a Japanese mine off Woosung, China, December 3, 1948.	2,750+
8 *Thielbeck* A refugee ship sunk during the British bombardment of Lübeck harbor in the closing weeks of World War II, May 1945.	2,750
9 *Arisan Maru* A Japanese vessel carrying American prisoners-of-war was torpedoed by a US submarine in the South China Sea, October 24, 1944.	1,790+
10 *Mont Blanc* A French ammunition ship collided with Belgian steamer *Imo* and exploded, Halifax, Nova Scotia, December 6, 1917.	1,600

Due to a reassessment of the death tolls in some of the World War II marine disasters, the most famous of all, the sinking of the *Titanic* (the British liner that struck an iceberg in the North Atlantic on April 15, 1912 and went down with the loss of 1,517 lives) no longer ranks in the Top 10. However, the *Titanic* tragedy remains one of the worst-ever peacetime disasters.

THE 10
WORST SUBMARINE DISASTERS
(Excluding those as a result of military action)

Incident	Killed
1 *Le Surcouf* – A French submarine accidentally rammed by a US merchant ship, *Thomas Lykes*, in the Gulf of Mexico on February 18, 1942.	159
2 *Thresher* – A three-year-old US nuclear submarine, worth $45,000,000, sank in the North Atlantic, 220 miles (350 km) east of Boston on April 10, 1963.	129
3 *I-12* – A Japanese submarine sunk the Central Pacific in circumstances unknown during January 1945.	114
4 *I-174* – A Japanese submarine sunk the Central Pacific in circumstances unknown on April 3, 1944.	107
5 *I-26* – A Japanese submarine sunk East of Leyte, cause unknown, during October 1944.	105
6 *I-169* – A Japanese submarine flooded and sunk on April 4, 1994 while in harbor at Truk.	103
7 *I-22* – A Japanese submarine sunk off the Solomon Islands in October 1942.	100
8= *Seawolf* – A US submarine sunk in error by USS Rowell off Morotai, October 3, 1944.	99
8= *Thetis* – A British submarine sank on June 1, 1939 during trials in Liverpool Bay, with civilians on board. Her captain and three crew members escaped. *Thetis* was later salvaged and renamed *Thunderbolt*. On March 13, 1943 she was sunk by an Italian ship with the loss of 63 lives.	99
8= *Scorpion* – A US nuclear submarine was lost in the North Atlantic, south-west of the Azores, on May 21, 1968. The wreck was located on October 31 of that year.	99

* *Excluding those as a result of military action*

The loss of the *Thresher* is the worst accident ever involving a nuclear submarine. It sank while undertaking tests off the US coast and after an exhaustive search was eventually located by the bathyscaphe *Trieste*. It found the remains of the submarine scattered over the ocean floor at a depth of 8,400 ft/ 2,560m. The cause of the disaster, if it was indeed ever established, remains a military secret.

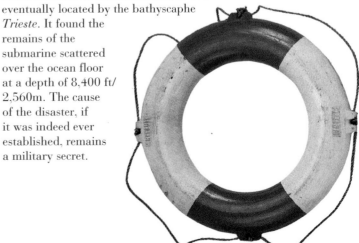

THE FIRST TO FLY

FIRST MANNED BALLOON FLIGHTS*

1 November 21, 1783

François Laurent, Marquis d'Arlandes, and Jean-François Pilâtre de Rozier took off from the Bois de Boulogne, Paris, in a hot-air balloon designed by Joseph and Etienne Montgolfier. This first-ever manned flight covered a distance of about 5½ miles/9 km in 23 minutes, landing safely near Gentilly. (On June 15, 1785 de Rozier and his passenger were killed near Boulogne when their hydrogen balloon burst into flames during an attempted Channel crossing, making them the first air fatalities.)

2 December 1, 1783

A crowd of 400,000 watched as Jacques Alexandre César Charles and Nicholas-Louis Robert made the first-ever flight in a hydrogen balloon. They took off from the Tuileries, Paris, and traveled approximately 27 miles/ 43 km north to Nesle in about two hours. Charles then took off again alone, thus becoming the first solo flier.

3 January 19, 1784

La Flesselle, a 131-ft-/40-m-high Montgolfier hot-air balloon named after its sponsor, the local Governor, ascended from Lyons piloted by Pilâtre de Rozier with Joseph Montgolfier, Prince Charles de Ligne, and the Comtes de La Porte d'Anglefort, de Dampierre, and de Laurencin – and the first aerial stowaway, a man called Fontaine, who leaped in as it was taking off.

4 February 25, 1784

Chevalier Paolo Andreani and the brothers Augustino and Carlo Giuseppi Gerli (the builders of the balloon) made the first-ever flight outside France, at Moncuco near Milan, Italy.

5 March 2, 1784

Jean-Pierre François Blanchard made his first flight in a hydrogen balloon from the Champ de Mars, Paris, after making experimental hops during the preceding months.

6 April 14, 1784

A Mr. Rousseau and an unnamed 10-year-old drummer boy flew from Navan to Ratoath in Ireland, the first ascent in the British Isles.

7 April 25, 1784

Guyton de Morveau, a French chemist, and L'Abbé Bertrand flew at Dijon.

8 May 8, 1784

Bremond and Maret flew at Marseilles.

9 May 12, 1784

Brun ascended at Chambéry.

10 May 15, 1784

Adorne and an unnamed passenger took off, but crash-landed near Strasbourg.

* *The first 10 flights of the ballooning pioneers all took place within a year. Several of the balloonists listed also made subsequent flights, but in each instance only their first flight is included.*

Joseph and Etienne Montgolfier conducted the first unmanned hot-air balloon test in the French town of Annonay on June 5, 1783. They were then invited to demonstrate it to Louis XVI at Versailles. On September 19, 1783 it took off with the first-ever airborne passengers – a sheep, a rooster, and a duck.

After the first 10 manned flights, the pace of ballooning accelerated rapidly. On June 4, 1784 Monsieur Fleurant took as his passenger in a flight at Lyons Mme. Elisabeth Thiblé, an opera singer, who was thus the first woman to fly (the Marchioness de Montalembert and other aristocratic ladies had ascended on May 20, 1784, but in a tethered balloon). On August 27, James Tytler (known as "Balloon Tytler"), a doctor and newspaper editor, took off from Comely Gardens, Edinburgh, achieving an altitude of 350 ft/107 km in a ½-mile/0.8-km hop in a homemade balloon – the first (and until Smeath in 1837, the only) hot-air balloon flight in the UK. On September 15, watched by a crowd of 200,000, Vincenzo Lunardi ascended from the Artillery Company Ground, Moorfields, London, flying to Standon near Ware in Hertfordshire, the first balloon flight in England. (An attempt the previous month by Dr. Moret ended with the balloon catching fire and the crowd rioting.) Lunardi went on to make further flights in Edinburgh and Glasgow. On October 4, 1784 James Sadler flew a Montgolfier balloon at Oxford, thereby becoming the first English pilot.

FIRST PEOPLE TO FLY IN HEAVIER-THAN-AIR AIRCRAFT

1 Orville Wright (1871–1948), USA

On December 17, 1903 at Kitty Hawk, North Carolina, Wright made the first-ever manned flight in his Wright Flyer I. It lasted 12 seconds and covered a distance of 120 ft/37 m.

2 Wilbur Wright (1867–1912), USA

On the same day, Orville's brother made his first flight in the Wright Flyer I (59 sec).

3 Alberto Santos-Dumont (1873–1932), Brazilian

At Bagatelle, Bois de Boulogne, Paris, Santos-Dumont made a 193-ft/60-m hop on October 23, 1906 in his clumsy No. 14-bis.

4 Charles Voisin (1882–1912), France

Voisin made a short 6-second hop of 197 ft/60 m at Bagatelle on March 30, 1907 in a plane built by himself and his brother Gabriel, commissioned by Léon Delagrange.

5 Henri Farman (1874–1958), British, (later a French citizen)

Farman first flew on October 7, 1907 and by October 26 had achieved 2,530 ft/771 m.

6 Léon Delagrange (1873–1910), France

On November 5, 1907 at Issy-les-Moulineaux, France, Delagrange flew his Voisin-Delagrange I (see 4) for 40 seconds.

7 Robert Esnault-Pelterie (1881–1957), France

On November 16, 1907 at Buc, France, he first flew his REP 1 (55 sec; 1,969 ft/600 m).

8 Charles W. Furnas (1880–1941), USA

On May 14, 1908 at Kitty Hawk, Wilbur Wright took Furnas, his mechanic, for a spin in the Wright Flyer III (29 sec; 1,968 ft/ 600 m). Furnas was thus the first passenger in the US.

9 Louis Blériot (1872–1936), France

After some earlier short hops, on June 29, 1908 at Issy, France, Blériot flew his Blériot VIII; on July 25, 1909 he became the first to fly across the English Channel.

10 Glenn Hammond Curtiss (1878–1930), USA

On July 4, 1908 at Hammondsport, New York, Curtiss flew an AEA June Bug (1 min 42.5 sec; 5,090 ft/1,551 m), the first "official" flight in the US watched by a large crowd.

THE 10

FIRST FLIGHTS OF MORE THAN ONE HOUR

	Pilot	Location	Duration hr	min	sec	Date
1	Orville Wright	Fort Meyer, US	1	2	15.0	Sep 9, 1908
2	Orville Wright	Fort Meyer, US	1	5	52.0	Sep 10, 1908
3	Orville Wright	Fort Meyer, US	1	10	0.0	Sep 11, 1908
4	Orville Wright	Fort Meyer, US	1	15	20.0	Sep 12, 1908
5	Wilbur Wright	Auvours, France	1	31	25.8	Sep 21, 1908
6	Wilbur Wright	Auvours, France	1	7	24.8	Sep 28, 1908
7	Wilbur Wright*	Auvours, France	1	4	26.0	Oct 6, 1908
8	Wilbur Wright	Auvours, France	1	9	45.4	Oct 10, 1908
9	Wilbur Wright	Auvours, France	1	54	53.4	Dec 18, 1908
10	Wilbur Wright	Auvours, France	2	20	23.2	Dec 31, 1908

* *First-ever flight of more than one hour with a passenger (M.A. Fordyce)*

The first pilot other than one of the Wright Brothers to remain airborne for longer than an hour was Paul Tissandier, who on May 20, 1909 flew for 1 hr 2 min 13 sec at Pont-Lond, near Pau, France. He was followed by Hubert Latham, an Anglo-French aviator, who on June 1909 at Châlons, France, flew an *Antoinette IV* for 1 hr 7 min 37 sec, and by Henry Farman (July 20, 1909, at Châlons), with a flight of 1 hr 23 min 3.2 sec duration, Roger Sommer (who broke Wilbur Wright's record on August 7, 1909 with a flight of 2 hr 27 min 15 sec), and Louis Paulhan. The first flight lasting over an hour in the UK was by Samuel Franklin Cody (a naturalized British citizen born in the US, and the first person in the UK to fly), in London on September 8, 1909; the flight lasted 1 hr 3 min 0 sec.

THE 10

FIRST TRANSATLANTIC FLIGHTS

1 May 16–27, 1919*
Trepassy Harbor,
Newfoundland to Lisbon, Portugal
US Navy/Curtiss flying boat *NC-4*

Lt.-Cdr. Albert Cushing Read and a crew of five (Elmer Fowler Stone, Walter Hinton, James Lawrence Breese, Herbert Charles Rodd, and Eugene Saylor Rhoads) crossed the Atlantic in a series of hops, refueling at sea.

2 June 14–15, 1919
St. John's, Newfoundland to Galway, Ireland
Twin Rolls-Royce-engined converted Vickers Vimy bomber

British pilot Capt. John Alcock and Navigator Lt. Arthur Whitten Brown achieved the first nonstop flight, ditching in Derrygimla bog after their epic 16 hr 28 min journey.

3 July 2–6, 1919
East Fortune, Scotland to Roosevelt Field, New York
British *R-34* airship

Major George Herbert Scott and a crew of 30 (including the first-ever transatlantic air stowaway, William Ballantyne) made the first east–west crossing. It was the first airship to do so and, when it returned to Pulham, England, on July 13, the first to complete a double crossing.

4 March 30–June 5, 1922
Lisbon, Portugal to Recife, Brazil
Fairey IIID seaplane *Santa Cruz*

Portuguese pilots Admiral Gago Coutinho and Commander Sacadura Cabral were the first to fly the South Atlantic in stages, although they replaced one damaged plane with another.

5 August 2–31, 1924
Orkneys, Scotland to Labrador, Canada
Two Douglas seaplanes, *Chicago* and *New Orleans*

Lt. Lowell H. Smith and Leslie P. Arnold in one biplane and Erik Nelson and John Harding in another set out and crossed the North Atlantic together in a series of hops via Iceland and Greenland.

6 October 12–15, 1924
Friedrichshafen, Germany to Lakehurst, New Jersey
Los Angeles, a renamed German-built *ZR 3* airship

Piloted by its inventor, Dr. Hugo Eckener, with 31 passengers and crew.

7 January 22–February 10, 1926
Huelva, Spain to Recife, Brazil
Plus Ultra, a Dornier Wal twin-engined flying boat

The Spanish crew – General Franco's brother Ramón with Julio Ruiz De Alda, Ensign Beran, and mechanic Pablo Rada – crossed in stages.

8 February 8–24, 1927
Cagliari, Sardinia to Recife, Brazil
Santa Maria, a Savoia-Marchetti S.55 flying boat

Francesco Marquis de Pinedo, Capt. Carlo del Prete, and Lt. Vitale Zacchetti crossed in stages as part of a goodwill trip to South America from Fascist Italy.

9 March 16–17, 1927
Lisbon, Portugal to Natal, Brazil
Dornier Wal flying boat

Portuguese flyers Sarmento de Beires and Jorge de Castilho took the route via Casablanca.

10 April 28–May 14, 1927
Genoa, Italy to Natal, Brazil
Savoia-Marchetti flying boat

A Brazilian crew of João De Barros, João Negrão, Newton Braga, and Vasco Cinquini set out on October 17, 1926, flying in stages via the Canaries and Cape Verde Islands.

* *All dates refer to the actual Atlantic legs of the journeys; some started earlier and ended beyond their first transatlantic landfalls.*

AIRPORTS & AIRLINES

TOP 10
BUSIEST AIRPORTS IN THE WORLD

	Airport	Location	Terminal passengers per annum*
1	Chicago O'Hare	Chicago, Illinois	65,091,000
2	DFW International	Dallas/Fort Worth, Texas	49,655,000
3	LA International	Los Angeles, California	47,845,000
4	Hartsfield Atlanta International	Atlanta, Georgia	47,775,000
5	London Heathrow	London, UK	47,602,000
6	Tokyo-Haneda International	Tokyo, Japan	41,507,000
7	San Francisco International	San Francisco, California	32,769,000
8	Stapleton International	Denver, Colorado	32,627,000
9	Frankfurt	Frankfurt, Germany	31,945,000
10	Miami International	Miami, Florida	28,660,000

* International and domestic flights

CHICAGO O'HARE
Like the other six US airports in the world's ten busiest, O'Hare handles mainly domestic passengers. Only JFK sees enough international flights to put it in the international Top Ten.

TOP 10
COMPLAINTS AGAINST AIRLINES IN THE US

	Complaint	Total (1994)
1	Flight problems (delay, etc.)	1,778
2	Baggage	1049
3	Customer service	909
4	Refunds	781
5	Ticketing/boarding	757
6	Tours	508
7	Oversales/bumping	421
8	Fares	331
9	Advertising	110
10	Smoking	33
	Others	*284*

Since the US forbid smoking on domestic flights in 1992, the most common source of smoking complaints are those who would like to smoke but cannot.

TOP 10
US AIRLINES WITH THE FEWEST COMPLAINTS

	Airline	Complaints per 100,000 passengers boarded (1994)
1	Southwest	0.23
2	Delta	0.45
3	Alaska	0.51
4	Northwest	0.63
5	American	0.70
6	United	0.71
7	USAir	0.76
8	America West	1.28
9	TWA	1.58
10	Continental	2.15

Southwest's impressive customer service performance resulted in only 104 complaints against the airline in 1994.

TOP 10
BUSIEST INTERNATIONAL AIRPORTS IN THE WORLD

	Airport/Country	Passengers P/A
1	London Heathrow, UK	40,844,000
2	Frankfurt, Germany	25,195,000
3	Hong Kong	24,421,000
4	Charles de Gaulle, France	22,336,000
5	Schiphol, Netherlands	20,659,000
6	Tokyo/Narita, Japan	18,947,000
7	Singapore International	18,796,000
8	London Gatwick, UK	18,660,000
9	JFK International, US	15,014,000
10	Bangkok, Thailand	12,755,000

TOP 10
BUSIEST AIRPORTS IN THE US

	Airport	Total passengers (1993)
1	Chicago O'Hare, Illinois	29,133,604
2	Dallas/Fort Worth, Texas	24,655,922
3	Hartsfield Atlanta Georgia	22,294,571
4	Los Angeles, California	18,456,714
5	Denver, Colorado	14,328,068
6	San Francisco, California	14,003,254
7	Phoenix, Arizona	11,294,603
8	Detroit, Michigan	11,027,172
9	Newark, New Jersey	10,965,362
10	Minneapolis, St. Paul Minnesota	10,377,577

TOP 10

AIRLINE-USING COUNTRIES

	Country	Passenger-miles flown per annum*
1	US	480,513,000,000
2	UK	74,533,000,000
3	Japan	66,089,000,000
4	Russia	47,500,000,000
5	France	36,786,000,000
6	Australia	35,744,000,000
7	Germany	32,896,000,000
8	China	27,962,000,000
9	Singapore	25,639,000,000
10	Canada	25,120,000,000

* Total distance traveled by aircraft of national airlines multiplied by number of passengers carried

TOP 10

US SCHEDULED AIRLINES WITH THE GREATEST NUMBER OF PILOT DEVIATIONS, 1992

	Airline	Scheduled flight hours	Pilot Deviations
1	American	1,921,972	52
2	US Air	1,194,058	30
3	Delta	1,694,292	27
4	United	1,531,780	26
5	Continental	943,243	15
6	Northwest	1,049,034	14
7	TWA	519,308	10
8	Southwest	422,512	7
9	America West	312,939	3
10	Federal Express*	369,720	2

* Cargo carrier classified as scheduled airline

A "pilot deviation" is "the action of a pilot that may result in the violation of a Federal Aviation Regulation or a North American Airspace Air Defense Identification Zone Tolerance."

HIGH FLIERS
American Airlines has more aircraft than any other airline in the world, but is just beaten to the passenger-mile post by United Airlines.

CONCORDE
The only supersonic passenger aircraft, Concorde flies at twice the speed of sound.

TOP 10

AIRLINES IN THE WORLD

	Airline/country	Aircraft in service	Passenger-miles flown per annum*
1	United Airlines (US)	539	100,968,000,000
2	American Airlines (US)	672	97,039,900,000
3	Delta Airlines (US)	554	82,866,500,000
4	Northwest Airlines (US)	373	58,019,500,000
5	British Airways (UK)	215	49,026,000,000
6	Aeroflot (Russia)	n/a	47,499,500,000
7	USAir (US)	502	35,231,100,000
8	JAL (Japan)	116	33,936,100,000
9	Lufthansa (Germany)	219	32,722,500,000
10	Air France (France)	144	27,049,100,000

* Total distance traveled by aircraft of these airlines multiplied by number of passengers carried

TOP 10

AIRLINES IN THE US

	Airline	Total passengers (1993)
1	Delta	80,416,268
2	American	75,175,859
3	United	63,027,704
4	USAir	52,982,127
5	Northwest	39,592,069
6	Southwest	37,636,098
7	Continental	35,334,709
8	TWA	17,964,791
9	America West	14,710,610
10	Alaska	6,157,673

The total includes passengers for scheduled and unscheduled flights. The total on all such US flights in 1993 was 468,313,029.

AIR DISASTERS

DOWN IN FLAMES
The Hindenburg *was the ultimate in luxury air travel, but the explosion of the airship, which contained 7,000,000 cubic feet/200,000 cubic meters of hydrogen gas, put an end to plans to expand the use of lighter-than-air craft.*

THE 10
FIRST AIRCRAFT FATALITIES

	Name	Nationality	Location	Date
1	Lt. Thomas Etholen Selfridge	American	Fort Myer, Virginia	Sep 17, 1908
2	Eugène Lefèbvre	French	Juvisy, France	Sep 7, 1909
3	Captain Ferdinand Ferber	French	Boulogne, France	Sep 22, 1909
4	Antonio Fernandez	Spanish	Nice, France	Dec 6, 1909
5	Aindan de Zoseley	Hungarian	Budapest, Hungary	Jan 2, 1910
6	Léon Delagrange	French	Croix d'Hins, France	Jan 4, 1910
7	Hubert Leblon	French	San Sebastián, Spain	Apr 2, 1910
8	Hauvette-Michelin	French	Lyons, France	May 13, 1910
9	Thaddeus Robl	German	Stettin, Germany	Jun 18, 1910
10	Charles Louis Wachter	French	Rheims, France	Jul 3, 1910

Following the Wright Brothers' first flights in 1903, the first four years of powered flying remained surprisingly accident-free. Although there had been many fatalities in the early years of ballooning and among pioneer parachutists, it was not until 1908 that anyone was killed in an airplane. On September 17, at Fort Myer, Virginia, Orville Wright was demonstrating his Type A *Flyer* to the US Army. On board was a passenger, 26-year-old Lieutenant Thomas Etholen Selfridge of the Army Signal Corps. At a height of just 75 feet/ 23 m, one of the propellers struck a wire, sending the plane out of control. It crash-landed, injuring Wright and killing Lt. Selfridge, who thus became powered flying's first victim.

THE 10
WORST AIRSHIP DISASTERS IN THE WORLD

	Incident	killed
1	April 3, 1933, off the Atlantic coast of the US	73

US Navy airship Akron *crashed into the sea in a storm, leaving only three survivors in the world's worst airship tragedy.*

	Incident	killed
2	December 21, 1923, over the Mediterranean	52

French airship Dixmude, *which was assumed to have been struck by lightning, broke up and crashed into the sea; wreckage, believed to be from the airship, was found off Sicily 10 years later.*

	Incident	killed
3	October 5, 1930, near Beauvais, France	50

British airship R101 *crashed into a hillside leaving 48 dead, with two dying later, and six saved.*

	Incident	killed
4	August 24, 1921, off the coast near Hull, UK	44

Airship R38, *sold by the British Government to the US and thereafter renamed USN* ZR-2, *broke in two on a training and test flight.*

	Incident	killed
5	May 6, 1937, Lakehurst, New Jersey	36

German Zeppelin Hindenburg *caught fire when mooring.*

	Incident	killed
6	February 21, 1922, Hampton Roads, Virginia	34

Roma, *an Italian airship bought by the US Army, crashed killing all but 11 men on board.*

	Incident	killed
7	October 17, 1913, Berlin, Germany	28

German airship LZ18 *crashed after engine failure during a test flight at Berlin-Johannisthal.*

	Incident	killed
8	March 30, 1917, Baltic Sea	23

German airship SL9 *was struck by lightning on a flight from Seerappen to Seddin, and crashed into the sea.*

	Incident	killed
9	September 3, 1915, mouth of the River Elbe, Germany	19

German airship L10 *was struck by lightning and plunged into the sea.*

	Incident	killed
10=	September 9, 1913, off Heligoland	14

German navy airship L1 *crashed into the sea, leaving six survivors out of the 20 on board.*

	Incident	killed
10=	September 3, 1925, Caldwell, Ohio	14

US dirigible Shenandoah, *the first airship built in the US and the first to use safe helium instead of inflammable hydrogen, broke up in a storm, scattering sections over many miles of the Ohio countryside.*

THE 10

WORST AIR DISASTERS IN THE WORLD

Incident	Killed
1 March 27, 1977, Tenerife, Canary Islands	583

Two Boeing 747s (Pan Am and KLM, carrying 364 passengers and 16 crew and 230 passengers and 11 crew, respectively) collided and caught fire on the runway of Los Rodeos airport after the pilots received incorrect control-tower instructions.

2 August 12, 1985, Mt. Ogura, Japan	520

A JAL Boeing 747 on an internal flight from Tokyo to Osaka crashed, killing all but four on board in the worst-ever disaster involving a single aircraft.

3 March 3, 1974, Paris, France	346

A Turkish Airlines DC-10 crashed at Ermenonville, north of Paris, immediately after takeoff for London, with many English rugby supporters among the dead.

4 June 23, 1985, off the Irish coast	329

An Air India Boeing 747 on a flight from Vancouver to Delhi exploded in midair, perhaps as a result of a terrorist bomb.

5 August 19, 1980, Riyadh, Saudi Arabia	301

A Saudia (Saudi Arabian) Airlines Lockheed Tristar caught fire during an emergency landing.

6 July 3, 1988, off the Iranian coast	290

An Iran Air A300 airbus was shot down in error by a missile fired by the USS Vincennes.

7 May 25, 1979, Chicago, Illinois	275

The worst air disaster in the US occurred when an engine fell off a DC-10 as it took off from Chicago O'Hare airport. The plane plunged out of control, killing all 273 on board and two on the ground.

8 December 21, 1988, Lockerbie, Scotland	270

Pan Am Flight 103 from London Heathrow to New York exploded in midair as a result of a terrorist bomb, killing 243 passengers, 16 crew, and 11 on the ground in the UK's worst-ever air disaster.

9 September 1, 1983, Sakhalin Island, off the Siberian coast	269

A Korean Air Lines Boeing 747 that had strayed into Soviet airspace was shot down by a Soviet fighter.

10 April 26, 1994, Nagoya airport, Japan	262

A China Airlines Airbus A300-600R, on a flight from Taipai, Taiwan, stalled and crashed while landing at Nagoya airport, Japan.

Three further air disasters have resulted in the deaths of more than 250 people: on July 11, 1991 a DC-8 carrying Muslim pilgrims from Mecca to Nigeria crashed on takeoff, killing 261; on November 28, 1979 an Air New Zealand DC-10 crashed near Mount Erebus, Antarctica, while on a sightseeing trip, killing 257 passengers and crew; and on December 12, 1985 an Arrow Air DC-8 crashed on takeoff at Gander, Newfoundland, killing all 256 on board, including 248 members of the 101st US Airborne Division.

THE 10

WORST AIR DISASTERS IN THE US

Incident	Killed
1 May 25, 1979, Chicago, Illinois	275

In the world's worst single aircraft disaster to date, an American Airlines DC-10 crashed on takeoff from Chicago O'Hare airport, killing all 273 on board and two on the ground after an engine fell off. As a result, all DC-10s were temporarily grounded.

2 August 16, 1987, Romulus, Michigan	156

A Northwest Airlines McDonnell Douglas MD-80 crashed onto a road following an engine fire after takeoff from Detroit. Only a four-year-old girl survived.

3 July 9, 1982, Kenner, Louisiana	154

A Pan American Boeing 727 crashed after takeoff from New Orleans, killing all 138 passengers, the crew of eight, and eight on the ground.

4 September 25, 1978, San Diego, California	144

A Pacific Southwest Boeing 727 crashed midair with a Cessna 172 light aircraft. Seven died on the ground, two in the Cessna, and 135 in the plane.

5 December 16, 1960, New York	135

A United Air Lines DC-8 with 77 passengers and a crew of seven collided in a snow storm with a TWA Super Constellation carrying 39 passengers and a crew of four. The DC-8 crashed in Brooklyn, killing eight on the ground; the Super Constellation crashed in Staten Island harbor, killing all on board.

6 August 2, 1985, Dallas-Ft. Worth Airport, Texas	133

A Delta Airlines TriStar crashed when a severe downdraft affected it during landing.

7 September 8, 1994, Pittsburgh, Pennsylvania	132

A USAir Boeing 737-400 en route from Chicago to West Palm Beach, Florida, crashed seven miles from Pittsburgh airport, killing all on board.

8 June 30, 1956, Grand Canyon, Arizona	128

A United Airlines DC-7 and a TWA Super Constellation collided midair, killing all on board in the worst civil aviation disaster to that date.

9 June 24, 1975, JFK Airport, New York	113

An Eastern Air Lines Boeing 727 on a flight from New Orleans crashed while attempting to land in a storm.

10 September 4, 1971, Mount Fairweather, Alaska	109

An Alaska Airlines Boeing 727 crashed in a storm as it approached Juneau Airport.

The 1988 Lockerbie crash (see Worst Air Disasters in the World) is the worst US air disaster outside US territory. Prior to that, the worst was the crash on December 12, 1985 of a chartered Arrow Air DC-8 as it took off from Gander, Newfoundland. All 256 on board died, including 248 members of the 101st US Airborne Division. A domestic incident that could have caused many casualties, but in fact killed only 14 with a further 25 injured, was the crash of a US Army B-25 bomber into the 78th and 79th floors of the Empire State Building on July 28, 1945. Blazing wreckage hurtled through the building, killing the crew of three and four office workers.

TOURISM IN THE US

FINAL RESTING PLACE?
Graceland, in Memphis, the palatial former home of Elvis Presley, attracts 600,000 visitors a year – more than any other historical house in the US. Many people come to pay their respects at Elvis's grave – that is, if they believe that he is really dead . . .

T O P 1 0

AMUSEMENT PARKS IN THE US

	Park	Visitors (1994 estimate)
1	The Magic Kingdom of Walt Disney World Lake Buena Vista, Florida	11,200,000
2	Disneyland, Anaheim, California	10,300,000
3	EPCOT at Walt Disney World Florida	9,700,000
4	Disney-MGM Studios at Walt Disney World Florida	8,000,000
5	Universal Studios Florida Orlando, Florida	7,700,000
6=	Sea World of Florida, Orlando, Florida	4,600,000
6=	Universal Studios Hollywood Universal City, California	4,600,000
8	Knott's Berry Farm, Buena Park, California	3,800,000
9=	Busch Gardens, Tampa, Florida	3,700,000
9=	Sea World of California San Diego, California	3,700,000

T O P 1 0

HISTORIC HOUSES IN THE US

1	Graceland, Memphis Tennessee
2	Isabella Stewart Gardner Museum Boston, Massachusetts
3	Gallier House Museum New Orleans, Louisiana
4	Bonnet House Ft. Lauderdale, Florida
5	Falling Water, Mill Run Pennsylvania
6	Victoria Mansion Portland, Maine
7	Melrose, Natchez Mississippi
8	Bayou Bend Houston, Texas
9	Olana, Hudson New York
10	Gamble House Pasadena, California

T O P 1 0

COUNTRIES OF ORIGIN OF TOURISTS TO THE US

	Country*	Annual visitors
1	Japan	3,486,000
2	UK	2,395,000
3	Germany	1,487,000
4	Mexico	1,238,000
5	France	667,000
6	Australia	581,000
7	Italy	508,000
8	Brazil	380,000
9	Argentina	302,000
10	Spain	295,000

* Excluding Canada

Though originally declared in a quite different context, the phrase "the British are coming!" might have been coined to describe the modern "invasion" of the US by tourists from the UK.

T O P 1 0

ZOOS IN THE US

	Zoo	1994 visitors
1	Lincoln Park Zoo Chicago, IL	4,000,000
2	Busch Gardens, Tampa Bay, FL	3,500,000
3=	San Diego Zoo, San Diego, CA	3,000,000
3=	National Zoo Washington, D.C.	3,000,000
5	St Louis Zoo St. Louis, MO	2,600,000
6	Bronx Zoo, New York, NY	2,000,000
7	Brookfield Zoo Chicago, IL	1,950,000
8=	Houston Zoo Houston, TX	1,500,000
8=	Cleveland Metroparks Zoo, Cleveland, OH	1,500,000
10=	San Diego Wildlife Park Escondido, CA	1,400,000

TOP 10

MARINE ATTRACTIONS IN THE US

	Attraction	1994 visitors
1	Living Seas, Lake Buena Vista, FL	6,000,000
2	Sea World, Orlando, FL	4,600,000
3	Sea World, San Diego, CA	3,000,000
4	Marine World Africa USA, Vallejo, CA	1,900,000
5	Shedd Aquarium, Chicago, IL	1,859,000
6	Monterey Bay Aquarium, Monterey, CA	1,558,000
7=	National Aquarium, Baltimore, MD	1,500,000
7=	Sea World, Aurora, OH	1,500,000
7=	Sea World, San Antonio, TX	1,500,000
10	Aquarium of the Americas, New Orleans, LA	1,400,000

TOP 10

TRAVEL-SPENDING STATES

	State	Travel expenditures* ($)		State	Travel expenditures ($)
1	California	40,489,200,000	6	Nevada	10,980,400,000
2	Florida	26,094,700,000	7	New Jersey	9,758,300,000
3	New York	19,311,900,000	8	Pennsylvania	9,097,200,000
4	Texas	16,834,600,000	9	Virginia	8,086,400,000
5	Illinois	11,641,000,000	10	Ohio	7,822,100,000

* *Excludes spending within the states by foreign visitors and US residents living abroad*

TOP 10

MOST-VISITED STATES

	State	Annual visitors		State	Annual visitors
1	California	6,192,000	6	Washington	2,108,000
2	New York	5,382,000	7	Arizona	1,982,000
3	Texas	5,032,000	8	Nevada	1,267,000
4	Florida	3,853,000	9	Massachusetts	1,253,000
5	Hawaii	2,203,000	10	Michigan	1,172,000

A NATIONAL TREASURE
The National Gallery of Art (below) and the Hirschhorn Museum and Sculpture Garden are both part of the Smithsonian Institution, Washington, DC. The Smithsonian encompasses centers of excellence in many areas of human endeavor, including the visual and performing arts, the sciences, and technology.

TOP 10

ART MUSEUMS IN THE US

	Art museum	Annual visitors
1	National Gallery of Art Washington, D.C.	7,500,000
2	Metropolitan Museum of Art, New York, NY	3,700,000
3	Art Institute of Chicago, IL	1,800,000
4	Museum of Modern Art New York, NY	1,600,000
5	Hirshhorn Museum and Sculpture Garden Washington, D.C.	1,300,000
6	Detroit Institute of Art, MI	1,000,000
7	Museum of Fine Arts Boston, MA	894,000
8	Los Angeles County Museum of Art, CA	880,000
9	Whitney Museum of Art New York, NY	837,000
10	Museum of Fine Arts Houston, TX	631,000

WORLD TOURISM

EIFFEL TOWER
When the Eiffel Tower was erected for the Universal Exhibition of 1889, it was meant to be a temporary addition to the Paris skyline. In fact, it outraged many Parisians who felt it was an eyesore. The world's tallest building until New York's Empire State Building was completed in 1931, the Eiffel Tower has become the symbol of Paris.

T O P 1 0

COUNTRIES WITH THE MOST TOURISTS

	Country	Annual arrivals/ departures
1	France	59,590,000
2	US	44,647,000
3	Spain	39,638,000
4	Italy	26,113,000
5	Hungary	20,188,000
6	Austria	19,098,000
7	UK	18,535,000
8	Mexico	17,271,000
9	China	15,512,000
10	Germany	15,147,000

Spain has fallen from first position, while China, a newcomer, has overtaken Germany (which became popular after the collapse of the Berlin Wall). Former Yugoslavia, once high in the Top 10, had fallen to 62nd place by 1992 as a result of military conflict with just 700,000 intrepid tourists visiting. It is now considered a no-go area.

T O P 1 0

DESTINATIONS OF JAPANESE TOURISTS

	Country	Trips (%)
1	US	28.0
2	Korea	12.2
3	Hong Kong	10.6
4	Singapore	7.5
5	Taiwan	6.9
6=	Germany	5.6
6=	Italy	5.6
8	China	5.4
9	Guam	4.9
10	Thailand	4.7

In recent years tourism by Japanese nationals has become one of the most important contributors to the international travel industry. Japanese subjects are especially welcomed by the retail trade as the highest spending per head of any travelers. Almost 12,000,000, some 10 percent of the entire population, went abroad in 1992, and it is predicted that, by the year 2005 their expenditure and that of Germany, another major overseas spending nation, will together exceed that of the current world leader, the US.

T O P 1 0

AMUSEMENT AND THEME PARKS IN EUROPE

	Park/location	Estimated visitors (1994)
1	EuroDisney, Marne-la-Vallée, France	8,800,000
2	Blackpool Pleasure Beach, Blackpool, UK	7,200,000
3	Alton Towers, Staffordshire, UK	3,011,000
4	Tivoli Gardens, Copenhagen, Denmark	3,000,000
5	De Efteling, Kaatsheuvel, The Netherlands	2,550,000
6	Europa Park, Rust, Germany	2,450,000
7	Bakken, Klampenborg, Denmark	2,300,000

	Park/location	Estimated visitors (1994)
8	Liseberg, Gothenburg, Sweden	2,200,000
9=	Pleasure Beach, Great Yarmouth, Norfolk, UK	2,000,000
9=	Pleasureland, Southport, Merseyside, UK	2,000,000

Despite appearing at the top of this list, EuroDisney continues to lose money at an alarming rate (though in the first half of 1995 this was reduced to FF 241,000,000/ $49,000,000 from FF 1,055,000,000/ $213,000,000). Meanwhile, competition is mounting both from existing theme parks, among which the UK is especially well represented, and from newly opened complexes, such as Spain's Port Aventura.

TOP 10
TOURIST SPENDERS

	Tourist country of origin	Annual expenditure ($)
1	US	39,872,000,000
2	Germany	37,309,000,000
3	Japan	26,837,000,000
4	UK	19,831,000,000
5	Italy	16,617,000,000
6	France	13,910,000,000
7	Canada	11,265,000,000
8	Netherlands	9,330,000,000
9	Taiwan	7,098,000,000
10	Austria	6,895,000,000

TOP 10
TOURIST EARNERS

	Country	Annual receipts ($)
1	US	53,861,000,000
2	France	25,000,000,000
3	Spain	22,181,000,000
4	Italy	21,577,000,000
5	UK	13,683,000,000
6	Austria	13,250,000,000
7	Germany	10,982,000,000
8	Switzerland	7,650,000,000
9	Hong Kong	6,037,000,000
10	Mexico	5,997,000,000

TOP 10
TRAVEL SHOPPERS

	Country of origin	Average spend per head ($)*
1	Japan	389.83
2	Korea	360.00
3	Australia	340.91
4	Qatar	312.50
5	South Africa	300.00
6	Norway	260.00
7	Kuwait	250.00
8	New Zealand	237.50
9	Israel	216.67
10	Oman	200.00
	US	*190.48*

* *Shopping during travel overseas, including duty-free purchases*

Shopping by travelers was estimated to be $50,000,000,000 in 1992. The United Arab Emirates received the highest average spend per traveler with an estimated $848.38.

TOP 10
AMUSEMENT AND THEME PARKS IN THE WORLD

	Park/location	Estimated annual visitors 1994
1	Disneyland, Tokyo, Japan	16,000,000
2	Magic Kingdom, Disney World, Florida	11,200,000
3	Disneyland, Anaheim, California	10,300,000
4	Jaya Ancol Dreamland, Jakarta, Indonesia	9,800,000
5	EPCOT, Disney World, Florida	9,700,000
6	EuroDisney, Marne-la-Vallée, France	8,800,000
7	Yokohama Hakkeijima Sea Paradise, Japan	8,737,000
8	Disney-MGM Studios Theme Park, Florida	8,000,000
9	Universal Studios Florida, Orlando, Florida	7,700,000
10	Blackpool Pleasure Beach, Blackpool, UK	7,200,000

TOP 10
BLUE FLAG COUNTRIES IN EUROPE*

	Country	Beaches	Marinas
1	Spain	229	51
2	Italy	215	39
3	Greece	237	6
4	France	193	43
5	Denmark	125	43
6	Portugal	102	1
7	Ireland	61	0
8	Germany	0	27
9	Netherlands	19	3
10	UK	20	0

* *A Blue Flag is awarded to beaches or marinas according to European Community water quality directives.*

ON THE BEACH
The exceptionally high standard of Spain's many beaches and marinas lures enormous numbers of tourists.

LIFE ON EARTH

T O P   1 0

LARGEST DINOSAURS

1 *"Seismosaurus"*
Length: 98–119 ft/30–36 m
Estimated weight: 50–80 tons

A single skeleton of this colossal plant-eater was excavated in 1985 near Albuquerque, New Mexico, by US paleontologist David Gillette and given an unofficial name (i.e. one that is not yet an established scientific name) that means "earth-shaking lizard." It is currently being studied by the New Mexico Museum of Natural History.

2 *Supersaurus*
Length: 80–100 ft/24–30 m
Height: 54 ft/16 m
Estimated weight: 50 tons

The remains of Supersaurus *were found in Colorado in 1972 (like those of* Ultrasaurus, *by James A. Jensen). Some scientists have suggested a length of up to 138 ft/42 m and a weight of 75–100 tons.*

3 *Antarctosaurus*
Length: 60–98 ft/18–30 m
Estimated weight: 40–50 tons

Named Antarctosaurus *("southern lizard") by German paleontologist Friedrich von Huene in 1929, this creature's thigh bone alone measures 7 ft 6 in/2.3 m.*

4 *Barosaurus*
Length: 75–90 ft/23–27.5 m
Height and weight uncertain

Barosaurus *(meaning "heavy lizard," so named by US paleontologist Othniel C. Marsh in 1890) has been found in both North America and Africa, thus proving the existence of a land link in Jurassic times (205–140 million years ago).*

5 *Mamenchisaurus*
Length: 89 ft/27 m
Height and weight uncertain

An almost complete skeleton discovered in 1972 showed it had the longest neck of any known animal, comprising more than half its total body length – perhaps up to 49 ft/15 m. It was named by Chinese paleontologist Young Chung Chien after the place in China where it was found.

6 *Diplodocus*
Length: 75–89 ft/23–27 m
Estimated weight: 12 tons

Since it was long and thin, Diplodocus *was a relative lightweight in the dinosaur world. It was also probably one of the most stupid dinosaurs, having the smallest brain in relation to its body size.* Diplodocus *was given its name (which means "double beam") in 1878 by Marsh. One skeleton was named* Diplodocus carnegii, *in honor of Andrew Carnegie, who financed the excavations that discovered it.*

7 *"Ultrasaurus"*
Length: Over 82 ft/25 m
Height: 52 ft/16 m
Estimated weight: 50 tons

Discovered by US paleontologist James A. Jensen in Colorado in 1979, it has not yet been fully studied. Some authorities put its weight at an unlikely 100–140 tons. Confusingly, although its informal name (which means "ultra lizard") was widely recognized, another, smaller dinosaur has been given the same official name.

8 *Brachiosaurus*
Length: 82 ft/25 m
Height: 52 ft/16 m
Estimated weight: 50 tons

Its name (given to it in 1903 by US paleontologist Elmer S. Riggs) means "arm lizard." Some have put the weight of Brachiosaurus *as high as 190 tons, but this seems improbable, in light of theories of maximum weights of terrestrial animals.*

9 *Pelorosaurus*
Length: 80 ft/24 m
Weight uncertain

The first fragments of Pelorosaurus ("monstrous lizard") were found in Sussex and named by British doctor and geologist Gideon Algernon Mantell as early as 1850.

10 *Apatosaurus*
Length: 66–70 ft/20–21m
Estimated weight: 20–30 tons

Apatosaurus (its name, coined by Marsh, means "deceptive lizard") is better known by its former name of Brontosaurus ("thunder reptile"). The bones of the first one ever found, in Colorado in 1879, caused great confusion for many years because its discoverer attached a head from a different species to the rest of the skeleton.

This list is based on the most reliable recent evidence of dinosaur lengths and indicates the probable ranges, although these undergo constant revision. Lengths are often estimated from a few fossilized bones. Experts dispute these and, even more, the weights of most dinosaurs. Some, such as *Diplodocus*, were long but not immensely heavy.

The popular *Tyrannosaurus rex* does not appear in the list because, although one of the fiercest meat-eaters, at 39 ft/12 m and 6 tons, it was not as large as many of the herbivores. To compare with still-living animals, the largest recorded crocodile measured 20 ft 4 in/6.2 m and the largest elephant 35 ft/10.7 m from trunk to tail and weighed about 12 tons. The largest living creature is the blue whale at 110 ft/33.6 m – slightly smaller than the size claimed for *Seismosaurus*.

JURASSIC MONSTER
The 82-ft/25-m Brachiosaurus was a gigantic plant-eating dinosaur of the late Jurassic period. Fossil specimens have been found as far apart as Colorado and Tanzania.

FINAL DATES WHEN 10 ANIMALS WERE LAST SEEN ALIVE

1 Aurochs   1627

This giant wild ox was last recorded in central Europe, after the advance of agriculture forced it to retreat from its former territory, which once stretched to the West as far as Britain.

2 Aepyornis   1649

Also known as the "Elephant bird," the 10 ft/3 m wingless bird was a native of Madagascar.

3 Dodo   1681

Discovered by European travelers in 1507, the last dodo seen alive was on the island of Mauritius in 1681. Its name comes from the Portuguese for "stupid," and its lack of flight, tameness, and tastiness made it extremely vulnerable to being caught and eaten.

4 Steller's sea cow   1768

A large marine mammal named after its 1741 discoverer, German naturalist Georg Wilhelm Steller, it was hunted to extinction. The spectacled cormorant, which Steller also found, became extinct at about the same time.

5 Great auk   1844

The last example of this flightless North Atlantic seabird breeding in Britain was in 1812, when one was nesting in the Orkneys, and the last seen in Britain in 1821 when one was killed for food on St. Kilda. The last surviving pair in the world was killed on June 4, 1844 on Eldey island on behalf of a collector named Carl Siemsen. A stuffed example was sold at Sotheby's, London, in 1971.

6 Tarpan   1851

The European wild horse was last seen in the Ukraine. Another wild horse thought to be extinct, Przewalski's horse, has been rediscovered in Mongolia and new captive-bred stock has been reintroduced into its former range around the Gobi Desert.

7 Quagga   1883

This zebralike creature found in South Africa, first recorded in 1685, was hunted by European settlers for food and leather to such an extent that by 1870 the last specimen in the wild had been killed. The last example, a female in Amsterdam Zoo, died on August 12, 1883.

8 Guadalupe Island caracara   1900

On December 1, 1900, the last-ever example of this large brown hawk was sighted.

9 Passenger pigeon   1914

The last moment of this creature can be stated precisely: at 1:00 pm on September 1, 1914 at the Cincinnati Zoo, a 29-year-old bird named Martha expired. Her stuffed body is now on display at the Smithsonian Institution, Washington, DC. Totals ran to a staggering five to nine billion in the 19th century, but they were remorselessly killed for food and to protect farm crops in the US.

10 Carolina parakeet   1918

The last of this colorful species, which was the only parrot native to North America, died, like Martha the passenger pigion at the Cincinnati Zoo, on February 21, 1918.

FIRST DINOSAURS TO BE NAMED

	Name	Meaning	Named by	Year
1	*Megalosaurus*	Great lizard	William Buckland	1824
2	*Iguanodon*	Iguana tooth	Gideon Mantell	1825
3	*Hylaeosaurus*	Woodland lizard	Gideon Mantell	1832
4	*Macrodontophion*	Large tooth snake	A. Zborzewski	1834
5=	*Thecodontosaurus*	Socket-toothed lizard	Samuel Stutchbury and H. Riley	1836
5=	*Palaeosaurus*	Ancient lizard	Samuel Stutchbury and H. Riley	1836
7	*Plateosaurus*	Flat lizard	Hermann von Meyer	1837
8=	*Cladeiodon*	Branch tooth	Richard Owen	1841
8=	*Cetiosaurus*	Whale lizard	Richard Owen	1841
10	*Pelorosaurus*	Monstrous lizard	Gideon Mantell	1850

COMMON & RARE

TOP 10

MOST ABUNDANT CLASSES OF ANIMAL

5   Mollusks

Includes snails, slugs, most shellfish, squids and octopus, and many tiny animals in the plankton horde.

6   Amphibians

Frogs, toads, newts, and the like: an estimated trillion (1,000,000,000,000) creatures.

7   Birds

Many birds share human habitats yet avoid conflict with us, so they have the advantage in numbers over most other larger wildlife outside the oceans. There are probably about 100,000,000,000 birds in the world and the most common must include poultry species and town inhabitants such as the sparrows.

8   Mammals (excluding humans)

Despite exploding human numbers and heavy pressures on many rare mammal species in the wild, other mammals probably still outnumber humans by at least four to one, boosted by the huge numbers of herd animals, pets, and "commensal" or scavenging animals such as rats and mice that share our habitat.

9   Humans

The baby that pushed the world's human population meter past the 5,000,000,000 mark was in all probability born in 1987.

10   Reptiles

Reptiles never recovered from the unknown cataclysm that finished off the dinosaurs, well before Homo sapiens arrived on the scene. Now largely through conflict and competition with humans, the world's snakes, lizards, turtles, crocodiles, and other scaly skinned beasts are once more in decline and may number fewer than 2,000,000,000 individuals at present.

1   Insects and spiders

At least 5,000,000,000,000,000 individuals. Among the most common insects are ants, fleas, flies, and the little-known springtails, which inhabit moist topsoil the world over. The latter alone probably outnumber the human race.

2   Crustaceans

Besides crabs, sowbugs, and so on, this class also includes krill and other tiny shrimplike creatures that form a major component of plankton, the mainstay of life in the oceans.

3   Worms

Earthworms and other tubelike animals, including parasitic worms, can occur in great numbers in some habitats: more than 1,000,000 earthworms were counted in 1 acre/0.4 hectare of British farmland. But their distribution is variable compared with the teeming arthropods higher up the list.

4   Fish

The total fish population of the world's oceans has been estimated at around 838,000,000 tons – numbering at least 100,000,000,000,000 individuals.

Microbes exist in staggering numbers: some nine trillion (9,000,000,000,000) of medium size could be packed into a box with sides 1 in/2.5 cm long. But whether they are animals or they belong to another kingdom is a matter of endless debate and we shall therefore disregard them.

Of animals that can be seen without a microscope, insects unquestionably top the numbers league: there are at least 1,000,000 insects for each of the Earth's 5,554,552,000 humans. Put together, they would weigh at least 12 times as much as the human race and at least three times more than the combined weight of all other living animals.

Estimates of the populations of other classes are at best "guesstimates," and this Top 10 should be viewed as a general picture of the relative numbers of each type of animal.

TOP 10

GROUPS WITH MOST KNOWN SPECIES

	Group	Approx. no. of known species
1	Insects	750–800,000
2	Higher plants	248,000
3	Noninsect arthropods (crustaceans, spiders, etc.)	123,000
4	Fungi	69,000
5	Mollusks	50,000
6	Algae	27,000
7=	Roundworms	12,000
7=	Flatworms	12,000
7=	Earthworms	12,000
10	Birds	9,000

The total number of known species is about 1,400,000. Approximately 27,000 species become extinct annually, principally inhabitants of rainforests.

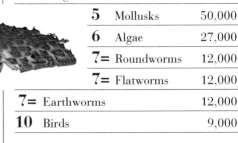

TOP 10

MOST ENDANGERED MAMMALS IN THE WORLD

Mammal	Number
1= Tasmanian wolf	?
1= Halcon fruit bat	?
1= Ghana fat mouse	?
4 Kouprey	10
5 Javan rhinoceros	50
6 Iriomote cat	60
7 Black lion tamarin	130
8 Pygmy hog	150
9 Tamaraw	200
10 Indus dolphin	400

The first three mammals on the list have not been seen for many years and may well be extinct, but zoologists are hopeful of the possibility of their survival: the Tasmanian wolf, for example, has been technically extinct since the last specimen died in a zoo in 1936, but occasional unconfirmed sightings suggest that there may still be animals in the wild, and a 1,601,240-acre/648,000-hectare nature reserve has been set aside for it in Tasmania in the expectation that it will be found again. The only Halcon fruit bat that has ever been seen is one that was discovered in the Philippines in 1937. (Another bat, the Tanzanian woolly bat, was discovered in the 1870s but has not been observed since, and is assumed to be extinct.) All the species on this list, which is ranked in order of rarity, face global extinction – unlike many species that may be at serious risk in one area but flourishing elsewhere. Some species that would once have been on the "most endangered" list, such as the Arabian oryx, were "extinct" in the wild, but have been successfully bred in captivity and reintroduced into their natural habitats.

TOP 10

RAREST MARINE MAMMALS

Mammal	Estimated no.
1 Caribbean monk seal	200
2 Mediterranean monk seal	300–400
3 Juan Fernandez fur seal	750
4 West Indian manatee	1,000
5 Guadeloupe fur seal	1,600
6 New Zealand fur seal	2,000
7= Hooker's sea lion	4,000
7= Right whale	4,000
9 Fraser's dolphin	7,800
10 Amazon manatee	8,000

The hunting of seals for their fur and of whales for oil and other products, combined in many instances with the depletion of their natural food resources by the fishing industry, has resulted in a sharp decline in the population of many marine mammals. Populations of some species of seal formerly numbering in the millions have shrunk to a few thousand and it has been estimated that the world population of humpback whales has dwindled from 100,000 to 10,000.

TOP 10

COUNTRIES WITH THE MOST ELEPHANTS

Country	Elephants
1 Zaïre	195,000
2 Tanzania	100,000
3 Gabon	76,000
4 Congo	61,000
5 Botswana	51,000
6 Zimbabwe	43,000
7 Zambia	41,000
8 Sudan	40,000
9 Kenya	35,000
10 Cameroon	21,000

All the countries in the Top 10 are in Africa, which in 1987 was believed to have a total elephant population of 764,410. India's 20,000 Asian elephants just fail to enter the list and the entire surviving population of Asian elephants in the wild is only a fraction of that of Africa at between 30,000 and 55,000. In addition, about 16,000 tame elephants are found in Myanmar (Burma), India, Thailand, Vietnam, and Cambodia. Estimates of Asian elephant populations are notoriously unreliable as this species is exclusively a forest animal and its numbers cannot be sampled using aerial survey techniques. The same is true of the forest variety of African elephant, distributed in heavily wooded countries such as Gabon or Zaïre, as distinct from the savanna elephant found in the wide-open spaces of scantily wooded countries including Tanzania and Zimbabwe, and this problem may account for widely varying estimates of elephant populations in such countries.

AFRICAN ELEPHANT

CREATURES GREAT & SMALL

Diversity is one of the most impressive features of the animal kingdom, and even within a single species huge variations can be encountered. There are practical problems that make measurement difficult – it is virtually impossible to weigh an elephant in the wild or to estimate a bird's air speed minus the wind factor, for example. Most of the lists, therefore, represent "likely averages" based on the informed observations of scientific researchers, rather than one-time assessments or rare and extreme record-breaking cases.

TOP 10

HEAVIEST PRIMATES

	Primate	Length* cm	in	Weight kg	lb
1	Gorilla	200	79	220	485
2	Man	177	70	77	170
3	Orangutan	137	54	75	165
4	Chimpanzee	92	36	50	110
5=	Baboon	100	39	45	99
5=	Mandrill	95	37	45	99
7	Gelada baboon	75	30	25	55
8	Proboscis monkey	76	30	24	53
9	Hanuman langur	107	42	20	44
10	Siamang gibbon	90	35	13	29

* Excluding tail

The largest primates (including man) and all the apes originated in the Old World (Africa, Asia, and Europe): only one member of a New World species of monkeys (the Guatemalan howler at 36 in/91 cm; 20 lb/9 kg) is a close contender for the Top 10. The difference between the prosimians (primitive primates), great apes, lesser apes, and monkeys has more to do with shape than size, although the great apes top most of the list anyway. Lower down the list, the longer, skinnier, and lighter forms of the lemurs, langurs, gibbons, and monkeys, designed for serious monkeying around in trees, send the length column haywire.

TOP 10

HEAVIEST TERRESTRIAL MAMMALS

	Mammal	Length m	ft	Weight kg	lb
1	African elephant	7.2	23.6	5,000	11,023
2	Great Indian rhinoceros	4.2	13.8	4,000	8,818
3	Hippopotamus	4.9	16.1	2,000	4,409
4	Giraffe	5.8	19.0	1,200	2,646
5	American bison	3.9	12.8	1,000	2,205
6	Grizzly bear	3.0	9.8	780	1,720
7	Arabian camel (dromedary)	3.0	9.8	600	1,323
8	Moose	3.0	9.8	595	1,312
9	Tiger	2.8	9.2	300	661
10	Gorilla	2.0	6.6	220	485

The list excludes domesticated cattle and horses. It also avoids comparing close kin such as the African and Indian elephants, highlighting instead the sumo stars within distinctive large mammal groups such as the bears, deer, big cats, primates, and bovines (oxlike mammals). Sizes are not necessarily the top of the known range: records exist, for instance, of African elephant specimens weighing more than 13,228 lb/6,000 kg.

TOP 10

LARGEST CARNIVORES

	Animal	Length m	ft	in	Weight kg	lb
1	Southern elephant seal	6.5	21	4	3,500	7,716
2	Walrus	3.8	12	6	1,200	2,646
3	Steller sea lion	3.0	9	8	1,100	2,425
4	Grizzly bear	3.0	9	8	780	1,720
5	Polar bear	2.5	8	2	700	1,543
6	Tiger	2.8	9	2	300	661
7	Lion	1.9	6	3	250	551
8	American black bear	1.8	6	0	227	500
9	Giant panda	1.5	5	0	160	353
10	Spectacled bear	1.8	6	0	140	309

Of the 273 species in the mammalian order Carnivora, or meat-eaters, many (including its largest representatives on land, the bears) are in fact omnivorous and around 40 specialize in eating fish or insects. All, however, share a common ancestry indicated by the butcher's-knife form of their canine teeth. Since the Top 10 would otherwise consist exclusively of seals and related marine carnivores, only three representatives have been included in order to enable the terrestrial heavyweight division to make an appearance. The polar bear is probably the largest land carnivore if shoulder height (when the animal is on all fours) is taken into account: it tops an awesome 5 ft 3 in/1.60 m, compared with the 4 ft/1.20 m of its nearest rival, the grizzly. The common (or least) weasel is probably the smallest carnivore: small specimens are less than 7 in/17 cm long, not counting the tail, and can weigh less than 3 oz (about 80 g).

TOP 10

LONGEST ANIMALS

	Animal	Length m	ft	in
1	Blue whale	33.5	110	0
2	Royal python	10.7	35	0
3	Tapeworm	10.0	32	10
4	Whale shark	9.8	32	2
5	African elephant	7.2*	23	7
6	Crocodile	5.9	19	5
7	Giraffe	5.8	19	0
8	Hippopotamus	4.9	16	1
9	Arabian camel (dromedary)	4.1	13	6
10=	Indian bison	3.4	11	2
10=	White rhinoceros	3.4	11	2

* Trunk to tail

The lion's mane jellyfish, which lives in the Arctic Ocean, has tentacles as long as 131 ft/40 m trailing behind it, but its "body" is relatively small, and it has thus not been included. Only one fish (the whale shark is a fish, not a true whale) and one snake have been included.

TOP 10

SMALLEST MAMMALS

	Mammal	Weight g	oz	Length cm	in
1	Kitti's hognosed bat	2.0	0.07	2.9	1.1
2	Pygmy shrew	1.5	0.05	3.6	1.4
3	Pipistrelle bat	3.0	0.11	4.0	1.6
4	Little brown bat	8.0	0.28	4.0	1.6
5	Masked shrew	2.4	0.08	4.5	1.8
6	Southern blossom bat	12.0	0.42	5.0	2.0
7	Harvest mouse	5.0	0.18	5.8	2.3
8	Pygmy glider	12.0	0.42	6.0	2.4
9	House mouse	12.0	0.42	6.4	2.5
10	Common shrew	5.0	0.18	6.5	2.5

The pygmy glider and another that does not quite make the Top 10, the pygmy possum, are marsupials, more closely related to kangaroos than to anything else in this list. Some classifications exclude marsupials from the mammal class. Among other contenders for the small world are the water shrew (0.42 oz/12.0 g; 2.8 in/7.0 cm) and bank vole (0.53 oz/15.0 g; 3.2 in/8.0 cm). The Kitti's hognosed bat is represented only by a few specimens in museum collections, so it may well have been short-changed.

TOP 10

LONGEST SNAKES

	Snake	Maximum length m	ft
1	Royal python	10.7	35
2	Anaconda	8.5	28
3	Indian python	7.6	25
4	Diamond python	6.4	21
5	King cobra	5.8	19
6	Boa constrictor	4.9	16
7	Bushmaster	3.7	12
8	Giant brown snake	3.4	11
9	Diamondback rattlesnake	2.7	9
10	Indigo or gopher snake	2.4	8

Although the South American anaconda is sometimes claimed to be the longest snake, this has not been authenticated and it seems that the python remains entitled to claim preeminence.

GIANT OF THE SEAS
Probably the largest animal that ever lived, the blue whale dwarfs even the other whales.

TOP 10

HEAVIEST MARINE MAMMALS

	Mammal	Length m	ft	Weight (tons)
1	Blue whale	33.5	110.0	145.0
2	Fin whale	25.0	82.0	50.0
3	Right whale	17.5	57.4	45.0
4	Sperm whale	18.0	59.0	40.0
5	Gray whale	14.0	46.0	36.0
6	Humpback whale	15.0	49.2	29.0
7	Baird's whale	5.5	18.0	12.0
8	Southern elephant seal	6.5	21.3	4.0
9	Northern elephant seal	5.8	19.0	3.7
10	Pilot whale	6.4	21.0	3.2

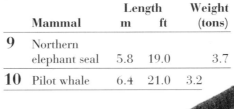

ANIMAL RECORD-BREAKERS

DEADLIEST SNAKES IN THE WORLD

Most people fear snakes, but only a few dozen of the 3,000-odd snake species that exist can cause serious harm, and many more are beneficial because they prey on vermin and other snake species of worse repute. The strength of a snake's venom can be measured, but this does not indicate how dangerous it may be: the Australian smooth-scaled snake, for example, is believed to be the most venomous land snake, but no human victims have ever been recorded. The Top 10 takes into account the degree of threat posed by those snakes that have a record of causing fatalities. This is approximate, since factors such as the amount of venom injected and the victim's resistance can vary greatly.

	Species	Native region
1=	Taipan	Australia and New Guinea

Mortality is nearly 100 percent unless antivenin is administered promptly.

	Species	Native region
1=	Black mamba	Southern and Central Africa

Mortality nearly 100 percent without antivenin.

	Species	Native region
3	Tiger snake	Australia

Very high mortality without antivenin.

	Species	Native region
4	Common krait	South Asia

Up to 50 percent mortality even with antivenin.

	Species	Native region
5	Death adder	Australia

Over 50 percent mortality without antivenin.

	Species	Native region
6	Yellow or Cape cobra	Southern Africa

The most dangerous type of cobra, with high mortality.

	Species	Native region
7	King cobra	India and Southeast Asia

At 16 ft/4.9 m long, the king cobra is the largest poisonous snake in the world. It also injects the most venom into its victims.

	Species	Native region
8=	Bushmaster	Central and South America
8=	Green mamba	Africa
10	Coral snake	North, Central, and South America

MAMMALS WITH THE LARGEST LITTERS

	Mammal	Average litter
1	Malagasy tenrec	25
2	Virginia opossum	22
3	Golden hamster	11
4	Ermine	10
5	Prairie vole	9
6	Coypu	8.5
7=	European hedgehog	7
7=	African hunting dog	7
9=	Meadow vole	6.5
9=	Wild boar	6.5

Individual litters may be larger than these averages. The record for the most offspring produced in a season probably goes to the prairie vole, which gives birth to up to 17 litters and 150 young. The tiny tenrec can produce up to 31 in a single litter and domestic pigs often produce 30 or more. In spite of these peaks, mammals have smaller litters than many other animal groups. Many fish can lay more than 10,000 eggs at a time and many amphibians over 1,000. The giant clam is most staggering of all, laying up to 1,000,000,000 eggs at a time.

MAMMALS WITH THE LONGEST GESTATION PERIODS

	Mammal	Average gestation (days)
1	African elephant	660
2	Asian elephant	600
3	Baird's beaked whale	520
4	White rhinoceros	490
5	Walrus	480
6	Giraffe	460
7	Tapir	400
8	Arabian camel (dromedary)	390
9	Fin whale	370
10	Llama	360

The 480-day gestation of the walrus includes a delay of up to five months while the fertilized embryo is held as a blastocyst (a sphere of cells) but is not implanted until later in the wall of the uterus. This option enables offspring to be produced at the most favorable time of the year. Human gestation (ranging from 253 to 303 days) is exceeded not only by the Top 10 mammals but also by others including the porpoise, horse, and water buffalo.

MAMMALS WITH THE SHORTEST GESTATION PERIODS

	Mammal	Average gestation (days)
1	Short-nosed bandicoot	12
2	Opossum	13
3	Shrew	14
4	Golden hamster	16
5	Lemming	20
6	Mouse	21
7	Rat	22
8	Gerbil	24
9	Rabbit	30
10	Mole	38

Newborn marsupials, such as the short-nosed bandicoot and opossums, are not fully developed at birth and transfer to a pouch in their mother's body to complete their development. Tiny at birth, the opossum is smaller than a bee. The ratio between the size of a newborn kangaroo (another marsupial), at under 1 in./2.5cm long, and the adult is the greatest of all the mammals.

TOP 10

FASTEST MAMMALS IN THE WORLD

Mammal	Maximum recorded speed km/h	mph		Mammal	Maximum recorded speed km/h	mph
1 Cheetah	105	65		5= Thomson's gazelle	76	47
2 Pronghorn antelope	89	55		7 Brown hare	72	45
3= Mongolian gazelle	80	50		8 Horse	69	43
3= Springbok	80	50		9= Greyhound	68	42
5= Grant's gazelle	76	47		9= Red deer	68	42

As well as these speeds estimated over distances of up to ¼ mile/0.4 km, charging lions can achieve 500 mph/80 km/h over short distances, while some antelopes, wildebeests, elks, dogs, coyotes, foxes, hyenas, zebras, and Mongolian wild asses have been credited with spurts of 40 mph/64 km/h or more. The Sei whale, the fastest of the large sea mammals, just misses the list at 40.2 mph/64 km/h.

FLEET-FOOTED
Unbeatable over a short course, the cheetah is one of the most feared carnivores in Africa.

TOP 10

FASTEST FISH IN THE WORLD

Fish	Maximum recorded speed km/h	mph
1 Sailfish	110	68
2 Marlin	80	50
3 Bluefin tuna	74	46
4 Yellowfin tuna	70	44
5 Blue shark	69	43
6 Wahoo	66	41
7= Bonefish	64	40
7= Swordfish	64	40
9 Tarpon	56	35
10 Tiger shark	53	33

TOP 10

LONGEST-LIVED ANIMALS
(Excluding humans)

Animal	Maximum age (years)
1 Quahog (marine clam)	up to 200
2 Giant tortoise	150
3 Greek tortoise	110
4 Killer whale	90
5 European eel	88
6 Lake sturgeon	82
7 Sea anemone	80
8 Elephant	78
9 Freshwater mussel	75
10 Andean condor	70

The ages of animals in the wild are difficult to determine with accuracy since the precise birth and death dates of relatively few long-lived animals have ever been recorded. There are clues, such as annual growth of shells, teeth, and, in the case of whales, even ear wax. The Top 10 represents documented maximum ages of animals attained by more than one individual – although there may well be extreme cases of animals exceeding these life spans. Although there are alleged instances of parrots living to ages of 80 years or more, few stand up to scrutiny.

TOP 10

LAZIEST ANIMALS IN THE WORLD

Animal	Average hours of sleep
1 Koala	22
2 Sloth	20
3= Armadillo	19
3= Opossum	19
5 Lemur	16
6= Hamster	14
6= Squirrel	14
8= Cat	13
8= Pig	13
10 Spiny anteater	12

The list excludes periods of hibernation, which can last up to several months among creatures such as the ground squirrel, marmot, and brown bear. At the other end of the scale comes the frantic shrew, which has to hunt and eat constantly or perish: it literally has no time for sleep. The incredible swift contrives to sleep on the wing, "turning off" alternate halves of its brain for shifts of two hours or more. Flight control is entrusted to whichever hemisphere is on duty at the time.

TOP 10

MOST INTELLIGENT MAMMALS

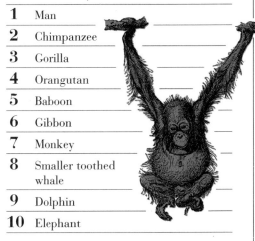

1	Man
2	Chimpanzee
3	Gorilla
4	Orangutan
5	Baboon
6	Gibbon
7	Monkey
8	Smaller toothed whale
9	Dolphin
10	Elephant

This list is based on research conducted by Edward O. Wilson, Professor of Zoology at Harvard University, who defined intelligence as speed and extent of learning performance over a wide range of tasks, also taking into account the ratio of the animal's brain size to its body bulk. It may come as a surprise that the dog does not make the Top 10, and that if man is excluded, No. 10 becomes the pig.

BIRDS

FASTEST BIRDS IN THE WORLD

	Bird	Maximum recorded speed km/h	mph
1	Spine-tailed swift	171	106
2	Magnificent frigatebird	153	95
3	Spur-winged goose	142	88
4	Red-breasted merganser	129	80
5	White-rumped swift	124	77
6	Canvasback	116	72
7	Common eider	113	70
8	Green-winged teal	109	68
9=	Mallard	105	65
9=	Northern pintail	105	65

Until airplane pilots cracked 190 mph/ 306 km/h in 1919, birds were the fastest animals on Earth. Stooping (diving) peregrine falcons have been clocked at speeds approaching 185 mph/298 km/h. However, most comparisons of air speed in birds rule out diving or wind-assisted flight; most migratory small birds can manage a ground speed of 60 to 70 mph/97 to 113 km/h if there is even a moderate tailwind. This list therefore picks out star performers among the medium- to large-sized birds (mainly waterfowl) that do not need help from wind or gravity to hit their top speed.

RAREST BIRDS IN THE WORLD

	Bird	Pairs reported*
1	Echo parakeet (Mauritius)	1
2	Mauritius parakeet	4
3	White-eyed river martin (Thailand)	5
4	Cuban ivory-billed woodpecker	8
5	Madagascar sea eagle	10
6	Pink pigeon (Mauritius)	11
7	Magpie robin (Seychelles)	12
8	Imperial Amazon parrot	15
9	Mauritius kestrel	16
10	Kakapo (New Zealand)	21

Since 1986

Several rare species are known from old records or a single specimen but must be assumed to be extinct without recent sightings or records of breeding pairs. Rare birds are in most danger on islands, such as Mauritius, where they have nowhere to seek refuge. The Mauritius kestrel – formerly second rarest – is now ninth thanks to measures to set aside part of its habitat as a reserve.

LARGEST FLIGHTED BIRDS

	Bird	Weight kg	lb	oz
1	Great bustard	20.9	46	1
2	Trumpeter swan	16.8	37	1
3	Mute swan	16.3	35	15
4=	Wandering albatross	15.8	34	13
4=	Whooper swan	15.8	34	13
6	Manchurian crane	14.9	32	14
7	Kori bustard	13.6	30	0
8	Gray pelican	13.0	28	11
9	Black vulture	12.5	27	8
10	Griffon vulture	12.0	26	7

Wing size does not necessarily correspond to weight in flighted birds. The 13-ft/4-m wingspan of the marabou stork beats all the birds listed here, yet its body weight is usually no heavier than any of these. When laden with a meal of carrion, however, the marabou can double its weight and needs all the lift it can get to take off. It usually has to wait until dinner is digested.

TOP 10

LARGEST FLIGHTLESS BIRDS

	Bird	Weight			Height	
		kg	lb	oz	cm	in
1	Ostrich	156.5	345	0	274.3	108.0
2	Emu	40.0	88	3	152.4	60.0
3	Southern cassowary	33.5	73	14	152.4	60.0
4	Greater rhea	25.0	55	2	137.1	54.0
5	Great spotted kiwi	29.0	63	15	114.3	45.0
6	Emperor penguin	29.4	64	13	114.0	44.9
7	King penguin	15.8	34	13	94.0	37.0
8	Gentoo penguin	5.4	11	14	71.0	28.0
9=	Adelie penguin	4.9	10	13	71.0	28.0
9=	Magellanic penguin	4.9	10	13	71.0	28.0

There are 46 living and 16 recently extinct flightless birds on record. The largest bird in recorded history was the flightless "elephant bird" (*Aepyornis*) of Madagascar. It weighed around 966 lb/438 kg and stood 10 ft/3 m tall. Its eggs were nearly 15 in/ 38 cm long and weighed over 40 lb/18 kg. The smallest known bird, the bee hummingbird, weighs 0.06 oz/1.7 g and measures 2.5 in/6.4 cm from beak to tail. Almost 100,000 bee hummingbirds would be needed to balance one ostrich on a pair of scales.

OSTRICH
An ostrich, when running, can reach a speed of 40 mph/64 km/h.

HIGH FLYER
The bald eagle is protected under the National Emblem Act of 1940, and is the lucky recipient of the greatest level of funding of any bird recovery program, raising hopes that its status may be reclassified from "endangered" to "threatened".

TOP 10

MOST ENDANGERED BIRDS IN THE US

1	Golden-cheeked Warbler
2	Kirtland's Warbler
3	Bachman's Warbler
4	Black-capped Vireo
5	Cerulean Warbler
6	Colima Warbler
7	Golden-winged Warbler
8	Black Swift
9	Baird's Sparrow
10	Cassin's Sparrow

Source: US Fish and Wildlife Service

TOP 10

MOST COMMON BREEDING BIRDS IN THE US

1	Red-winged blackbird
2	House sparrow
3	Mourning dove
4	European starling
5	American robin
6	Horned lark
7	Common grackle
8	American crow
9	Western meadowlark
10	Brown-headed cowbird

This list, based on research carried out by the Breeding Bird Survey of the US Fish and Wildlife Service, ranks birds breeding in the US, with the red-winged blackbird (*Agelaius phoeniceus*) heading the list. Found throughout the United States, except in extreme desert and mountain regions, its population has grown from 25,600,000 estimated in 1983 to more than 30,000,000 today.

CATS, DOGS, & OTHER PETS

TOP 10

PETS IN THE US

	Pet	% of US households
1	Dogs	36.5
2	Cats	30.9
3	Birds	5.7
4=	Fish	2.8
4=	Horses	2.8
6	Rabbits	1.5
7	Hamsters	1.0
8	Guinea pigs	0.5
9	Gerbils	0.3
10	Ferrets	0.2

While this survey indicates numbers of households owning companion pets, owners often have more than one: the average is 1.5 in the case of dogs, and 2.0 for cats, and hence the estimated populations for each are 52,500,000 and 57,000,00 respectively, cats thereby outnumbering dogs.

Source: American Veterinary Medical Association

TOP 10

PETS' NAMES IN THE UK
(*Based on the RSPCA's 1993* Animal World *magazine survey*)

1	Fluffy	6	Gizmo
2	Sooty	7	Charlie
3	Ben	8	Flopsy
4	Sammy	9	Max
5	Snowy	10	Sandy

TOP 10

DOGS' NAMES IN THE UK

Female		Male
Holly	1	Ben
Lucy	2	Max
Tess	3	Bruno
Ellie	4	Oscar
Sophie	5	Lucky
Bonnie	6	Barney
Cassie	7	Benji
Daisy	8	Sam
Lady	9	Charlie
Bess	10	Patch

During the 1980s, there was a move away from traditional canine names such as Shep, Brandy, Whisky, Rex, Lassie, and Rover, and an increasing tendency toward human first names. The latest research by the National Canine Defence League shows that this fashion has continued, with Ben holding on at No. 1 among male names, and Holly hurtling in from nowhere to take first position among female names.

TOP 10

DOG BREEDS IN THE UK

	Breed	No. registered by Kennel Club
1	Labrador	29,118
2	German Shepherd (Alsatian)	22,026
3	Golden Retriever	14,418
4	West Highland White Terrier	14,057
5	Cavalier King Charles Spaniel	13,772
6	Cocker Spaniel	12,808
7	Yorkshire Terrier	12,343
8	English Springer Spaniel	11,904
9	Boxer	8,360
10	Staffordshire Bull Terrier	5,971

The Top 10 dog breeds registered by the Kennel Club have remained the same for the last few years, although the order has changed. Independent surveys show a similar picture, though other popular breeds (including Jack Russells, Border Collies, and Poodles) make a stronger showing.

TOP 10

DOGS' NAMES IN THE US

1	Lady
2	King
3	Duke
4	Peppy
5	Prince
6	Pepper
7	Snoopy
8	Princess
9	Heidi
10=	Sam
10=	Coco

A recent study of male and female names appearing on dog licenses in the US produced a list that has only "Lady" and "Sam" in common with the British Top 10. The same American list also revealed a number of bizarre dogs' names, including Beowulf, Bikini, Fag, Rembrandt, and Twit. Lassie, popularized by films from 1942 onward, has declined to 82nd position, while Rover is in a humble 161st place.

TOP 10

DOG BREEDS IN THE US

	Breed	No. registered by American Kennel Club (1994)
1	Labrador Retriever	126,393
2	Rottweiler	102,596
3	German Shepherd	78,999
4	Golden Retriever	64,322
5	Poodle	61,775
6	Cocker Spaniel	60,888
7	Beagle	59,215
8	Dachshund	46,129
9	Dalmation	42,621
10	Pomeranian	39,947

TOP 10

MOST INTELLIGENT DOG BREEDS

1	Border Collie
2	Poodle
3=	German Shepherd (Alsatian)
3=	Golden Retriever
5	Doberman Pinscher
6	Shetland Sheepdog
7	Labrador Retriever
8	Papillon
9	Rottweiler
10	Australian Cattle Dog

For his 1994 book *The Intelligence of Dogs*, American psychology professor and pet trainer Stanley Coren put 133 breeds through obedience and work tests, ranking them accordingly. His canine IQ exams produced some surprising – and to their devotees, controversial – results. The Bloodhound, the doggy Sherlock Holmes, was in 128th place; the bulldog, symbol of British might, in 131st place; and the Afghan Hound, bottom of the class.

TOP 10

PEDIGREE CAT BREEDS IN THE UK

(Based on a total of 30,013 cats registered with the Governing Council of the Cat Fancy in 1994; 1993: 33,436)

		No. registered by Cat Fancy	
	Breed	**1993**	**1994**
1	Persian	10,991	9,091
2	Siamese	5,471	4,728
3	British Shorthair	3,727	3,894
4	Burmese	3,947	3,590
5	Birman	2,152	1,982
6	Oriental Shorthair	1,360	1,186
7	Maine Coon	1,123	1,049
8	Exotic Shorthair	646	581
9	Abyssinian	603	561
10	Devon Rex	455	455

TOP 10

TRICKS PERFORMED BY DOGS IN THE US

	Trick	**Dogs performing**
1	Sit	5,313,105
2	Shake paw	3,795,075
3	Roll over	2,884,257
4	"Speak"	2,681,853
5=	Lie down	1,872,237
5=	Stand on hind legs	1,872,237
7	Beg	1,821,636
8	Dance	1,543,331
9	"Sing"	759,015
10	Fetch newspaper	430,508

A survey conducted by the Pet Food Institute and a US pet food manufacturer produced these astonishingly precise statistics for the tricks performed by 25,300,500 of the alleged 41,361,183 dogs in the country. Why exactly the same number lie down and stand on their hind legs was not explained. Surprisingly for such a religious nation, only 379,508 were claimed to "say prayers."

TOP 10

PEDIGREE CAT BREEDS IN THE US

	Breed	**Total registered**
1	Persian	47,022
2	Maine coon	3,852
3	Siamese	2,881
4	Abyssinian	2,447
5	Exotic Shorthair	1,507
6	Scottish fold	1,250
7	American Shorthair	1,143
8	Oriental Shorthair	1,123
9	Birman	957
10	Burmese	884

Of the 39 different breeds and 71,036 individual cats listed with the Cat Fancier's Association, these were the Top 10 registered in 1994. Since 1982 the Exotic Shorthair has leapt from 14th place to its current No. 5.

TOP 10

CATS' NAMES IN THE US

Femal		**Male**
Samantha	**1**	Tiger/Tigger
Misty	**2**	Smokey
Patches	**3**	Pepper
Cali/Calico	**4**	Max/Maxwell
Muffin	**5**	Simon
Angel/Angela	**6**	Snoopy
Ginger	**7**	Morris
Tiger/Tigger	**8**	Mickey
Princess	**9**	Rusty/Rusti
Punkin/Pumpkin	**10**	Boots/Bootsie

TOP 10

CATS' NAMES IN THE UK

(Based on an RSPCA survey conducted during National Pet Week, 1991)

1	Sooty
2	Tigger
3	Tiger
4	Smokey
5	Ginger
6	Tom
7	Fluffy
8	Lucy
9	Sam
10	Lucky

LIVESTOCK

TOP 10

TYPES OF LIVESTOCK IN THE WORLD

	Animal	World total
1	Chickens	11,868,000,000
2	Cattle	1,277,793,000
3	Sheep	1,110,782,000
4	Pigs	870,705,000
5	Ducks	662,000,000
6	Goats	591,802,000
7	Turkeys	248,000,000
8	Buffaloes	148,876,000
9	Horses	60,376,000
10	Donkeys	43,863,000

The world chicken population is more than double the human population, while the world's cattle population outnumbers the population of China. There are more pigs in the world than the entire population of India, enough turkeys for every US citizen to have one each for Thanksgiving, and sufficient horses for everyone in the UK to go riding.

TOP 10

CHICKEN COUNTRIES

	Country	Chickens
1	China	2,688,000,000
2	US	1,486,000,000
3	Russia	625,000,000
4=	Indonesia	620,000,000
4=	Brazil	620,000,000
6	India	435,000,000
7	Japan	334,000,000
8	Mexico	285,000,000
9	France	210,000,000
10	Ukraine	180,000,000
	World total	*11,868,000,000*

The Top 10 countries have 61 percent of the world's chicken population. In the UK the estimated chicken population of 124,000,000 outnumbers the human population more than twice over.

TOP 10

DUCK COUNTRIES

	Country	Ducks
1	China	430,000,000
2=	Indonesia	30,000,000
2=	Vietnam	30,000,000
4	Ukraine	25,000,000
5	France	19,000,000
6	Thailand	16,000,000
7	Bangladesh	14,000,000
8	Malaysia	13,000,000
9=	Philippines	8,000,000
9=	Egypt	8,000,000
9=	Mexico	8,000,000
	World total	*662,000,000*

While it is extraordinary to consider that 66 percent of the world's domestic ducks live in China, an examination of the menu of any Chinese restaurant reveals the duck's major role in oriental cuisine. In contrast, British ducks number barely 2,000,000.

TOP 10

GOAT COUNTRIES

	Country	Goats
1	India	117,547,000
2	China	97,812,000
3	Pakistan	40,225,000
4	Bangladesh	25,967,000
5	Nigeria	24,500,000
6	Iran	23,500,000
7	Ethiopia	16,700,000
8	Sudan	16,200,000
9	Brazil	12,500,000
10	Indonesia	11,800,000
	World total	*591,802,000*

The goat is one of the most widely distributed of all domesticated animals. Its resilience to diseases, such as the tuberculosis that affects cattle, and its adaptability to harsh conditions make it ideally suited to less developed countries.

TOP 10

BUFFALO COUNTRIES

	Country	Buffaloes
1	India	78,555,000
2	China	22,217,000
3	Pakistan	18,740,000
4	Thailand	4,747,000
5	Egypt	3,466,000
6	Indonesia	3,452,000
7	Nepal	3,073,000
8	Vietnam	2,956,000
9	Philippines	2,561,000
10	Myanmar	2,110,000
	World total	*148,876,000*

More than 95 percent of the world's total buffalo population resides in the Top 10 countries. Only two European countries have significant herds: Romania with 180,000 and Italy (where buffalo milk is used to make mozzarella cheese) with 83,000.

TOP 10

TURKEY COUNTRIES

	Country	Turkeys
1	US	90,000,000
2	France	32,000,000
3	Russia	24,000,000
4	Italy	22,000,000
5	UK	11,000,000
6=	Brazil	6,000,000
6=	Canada	6,000,000
6=	Mexico	6,000,000
9	Portugal	5,000,000
10=	Argentina	4,000,000
10=	Germany	4,000,000
10=	Israel	4,000,000
	World total	*248,000,000*

Some 88 percent of the world's turkeys are found in the Top 10 countries – with the largest number, appropriately, in North America, their area of origin.

TOP 10

SHEEP COUNTRIES

	Country	Sheep
1	Australia	138,102,000
2	China	109,720,000
3	New Zealand	51,000,000
4	Russia	48,183,000
5	Iran	45,200,000
6	India	44,608,000
7	Turkey	39,416,000
8	Kazakhstan	33,000,000
9	South Africa	30,000,000
10	UK	29,333,000
	World total	*1,110,782,000*

This is one of the few world lists in which the UK ranks considerably higher than the US, which has only 10,750,000 head of sheep. The Falkland Islands have 713,000 sheep to a human population of 2,121 (336 sheep per person), followed by New Zealand (16 sheep per person).

TOP 10

PIG COUNTRIES

	Country	Pigs
1	China	393,965,000
2	US	59,815,000
3	Russia	31,520,000
4	Brazil	31,050,000
5	Germany	26,466,000
6	Poland	18,860,000
7	Spain	18,000,000
8	Mexico	16,832,000
9	Ukraine	16,175,000
10	Netherlands	13,709,000
	World total	*870,705,000*

The distribution of the world's pig population is determined by cultural, religious, and dietary factors – few pigs are found in African and Islamic countries, for example – so there is a disproportionate concentration of pigs in those countries that do not have such prohibitions.

TOP 10

CATTLE COUNTRIES

	Country	Cattle
1	India	192,700,000
2	Brazil	153,350,000
3	US	100,611,000
4	China	82,641,000
5	Russia	52,226,000
6	Argentina	50,320,000
7	Mexico	30,649,000
8	Ethiopia	29,450,000
9	Colombia	25,324,000
10	Australia	24,062,000
	World total	*1,277,793,000*

The Top 10 countries own almost 60 percent of the world's cattle. The cattle population in the UK is 11,623,000, equivalent to more than one animal for every five people.

TOP 10

HORSE COUNTRIES

	Country	Horses
1	China	10,018,000
2	Brazil	6,310,000
3	Mexico	6,185,000
4	US	5,480,000
5	Argentina	3,300,000
6	Ethiopia	2,750,000
7	Russia	2,556,000
8	Mongolia	2,200,000
9	Colombia	2,000,000
10	Kazakhstan	1,500,000
	World total	*60,376,000*

Mongolia makes an appearance in few Top 10 lists – but here it scores doubly since it is also the only country in the world where humans are outnumbered by horses. Throughout the world the horse population has declined since they have been replaced by motor vehicles.

TOP 10

DONKEY COUNTRIES

	Country	Donkeys
1	China	10,983,000
2	Ethiopia	5,200,000
3	Pakistan	3,775,000
4	Mexico	3,190,000
5	Iran	1,900,000
6=	Egypt	1,550,000
6=	India	1,550,000
8	Brazil	1,364,000
9	Afghanistan	1,180,000
10	Nigeria	1,000,000
	World total	*43,863,000*

The donkey is widely used throughout the world as a beast of burden, although its role in Western countries has been greatly reduced. It should not be confused with the mule (the progeny of a horse and donkey), of which there is a world population of over 15,000,000, one-third living in China.

DID YOU KNOW

"PIGS MIGHT FLY"

It is hard to imagine a creature less likely to fly than a pig – hence the expression ". . . and pigs might fly!" has come to signify an event that will never happen – and yet it has, thanks to Lord Brabazon (1884–1964). He had already achieved fame as a skilled motor racer, regularly bobsledded down the Cresta run at St. Moritz, and in 1909 became the first Briton to fly an aircraft. On November 4 of the same year he took off from the Isle of Sheppey, Kent, in his *Voisin* biplane and, determined to prove the old adage wrong, took a pig in a basket to which was attached a sign reading, "I am the first pig to fly." After a journey of 3½ miles, the world's first flying pig was returned to land and the more familiar comfort of its sty. The next year Lord Brabazon received the first-ever pilot's licence, but never again carried such an unusual passenger.

FRUIT SALAD

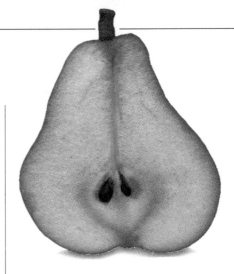

TOP 10

FRUIT-PRODUCING COUNTRIES
(Excluding melons)

	Country	Annual production (metric tonnes)
1	Brazil	32,737,000
2	India	31,850,000
3	US	28,565,000
4	China	23,093,000
5	Italy	18,630,000
6	Spain	12,649,000
7	France	9,953,000
8	Turkey	9,645,000
9	Mexico	9,462,000
10	Uganda	9,104,000
	World total	*371,278,000*

TOP 10

BANANA-PRODUCING COUNTRIES

	Country	Annual production (metric tonnes)
1	India	7,200,000
2	Brazil	5,593,000
3	Ecuador	3,990,000
4	Philippines	3,100,000
5	Indonesia	2,550,000
6	China	2,399,000
7	Colombia	1,950,000
8	Costa Rica	1,827,000
9=	Thailand	1,650,000
9=	Mexico	1,650,000

TOP 10

MANGO-PRODUCING COUNTRIES

	Country	Annual production (metric tonnes)
1	India	10,000,000
2	Mexico	1,120,000
3	Pakistan	794,000
4	Indonesia	750,000
5	Thailand	620,000
6	China	613,000
7	Nigeria	500,000
8	Brazil	394,000
9	Philippine	350,000
10	Haiti	230,000
	World total	*17,744,000*

TOP 10

GRAPE-PRODUCING COUNTRIES

	Country	Annual production (metric tonnes)
1	Italy	9,773,000
2	France	6,741,000
3	US	5,117,000
4	Spain	4,453,000
5	Turkey	3,700,000
6	Argentina	1,821,000
7	Iran	1,680,000
8	South Africa	1,490,000
9	Germany	1,440,000
10	Greece	1,400,000

TOP 10

PEAR-PRODUCING COUNTRIES

	Country	Annual production (metric tonnes)
1	China	2,915,000
2	Italy	856,000
3	US	848,000
4	Spain	459,000
5	Germany	432,000
6	Turkey	420,000
7	Japan	396,000
8	Argentina	370,000
9	South Africa	260,000
10	France	237,000
	World total	*10,333,000*

TOP 10

COCONUT-PRODUCING COUNTRIES

	Country	Annual production (metric tonnes)
1	Indonesia	14,219,000
2	Philippines	9,300,000
3	India	7,700,000
4	Sri Lanka	1,597,000
5	Thailand	1,379,000
6	Vietnam	1,207,000
7	Malaysia	1,030,000
8	Mexico	990,000
9	Brazil	826,000
10	Papua New Guinea	790,000
	World total	*43,385,000*

TOP 10

APPLE-PRODUCING COUNTRIES

	Country	Annual production (metric tonnes)
1	China	5,018,000
2	US	4,813,000
3	Italy	2,084,000
4	Turkey	2,080,000
5	France	2,027,000
6	Poland	1,842,000
7	Ukraine	1,774,000
8	Russia	1,700,000
9	Iran	1,550,000
10	India	1,200,000
	World total	*42,388,000*

Romania (1,097,000 tonnes), Germany (1,094,000 tonnes), and Japan (1,027,000 tonnes) are the only other countries in the world with annual apple production of more than 1,000,000 tonnes. Having steadily declined during the 1980s in the face of cheap imports, the UK's commercial production of apples has recently increased again and in 1993 totaled 368,000 tonnes.

TOP 10

ORANGE-PRODUCING COUNTRIES

	Country	Annual production (metric tonnes)
1	Thailand	2,674,000
2	Philippines	1,200,000
3	Brazil	820,000
4=	India	800,000
4=	Nigeria	800,000
6	China	709,000
7	Vietnam	519,000
8	Indonesia	383,000
9	Colombia	347,000
10	US	336,000
	World total	*11,740,000*

During the 1980s, orange production progressively increased from a world total of less than 40,000,000 metric tonnes. China's, in particular, rocketed up almost sevenfold during the decade from less than 800,000 tonnes to its present third position in the league table, while that of Iran has more than trebled over the same period.

TOP 10

PINEAPPLE-PRODUCING COUNTRIES

	Country	Annual production (metric tonnes)
1	Thailand	2,674,000
2	Philippines	1,200,000
3	Brazil	820,000
4=	India	800,000
4=	Nigeria	800,000
6	China	709,000
7	Vietnam	519,000
8	Indonesia	383,000
9	Colombia	347,000
10	US	336,000
	World total	*11,740,000*

TOP 10

PEACH- & NECTARINE-PRODUCING COUNTRIES

	Country	Annual production (metric tonnes)
1	Italy	1,597,000
2	US	1,418,000
3	Greece	1,123,000
4	China	993,000
5	Spain	855,000
6	France	403,000
7	Turkey	370,000
8	Chile	237,000
9	Argentina	236,000
10	Japan	173,000
	World total	*9,785,000*

TOP 10

PLANTAIN-PRODUCING COUNTRIES

	Country	Annual production (metric tonnes)
1	Uganda	8,488,000
2	Rwanda	2,700,000
3	Colombia	2,682,000
4	Zaïre	2,291,000
5	Nigeria	1,400,000
6	Ghana	1,322,000
7	Cote d'Ivoire	1,199,000
8	Ecuador	950,000
9	Cameroon	860,000
10	Tanzania	800,000
	World total	*27,902,000*

TOP OF THE CROPS

FOOD CROPS IN THE WORLD

	Country	Annual production (metric tonnes)
1	Sugarcane	1,040,600,000
2	Wheat	564,457,000
3	Rice	527,413,000
4	Corn	470,570,000
5	Potatoes	288,183,000
6	Sugar beet	281,682,000
7	Barley	170,364,000
8	Cassava	153,628,000
9	Sweet potatoes	123,750,000
10	Soybeans	111,011,000

SUGARCANE-GROWING COUNTRIES IN THE WORLD

	Country	Annual production (metric tonnes)
1	Brazil	251,408,000
2	India	230,832,000
3	China	68,419,000
4	Cuba	44,000,000
5	Mexico	41,652,000
6	Pakistan	38,743,000
7	Thailand	34,710,000
8	Indonesia	32,400,000
9	Australia	31,700,000
10	Colombia	30,500,000
	World total	*1,040,600,000*

WHEAT-GROWING COUNTRIES IN THE WORLD

	Country	Annual production (metric tonnes)
1	China	105,005,000
2	US	65,374,000
3	India	56,762,000
4	Russia	42,480,000
5	France	29,324,000
6	Canada	27,825,000
7	Ukraine	21,831,000
8	Turkey	21,016,000
9	Australia	18,203,000
10	Pakistan	16,157,000
	World total	*564,457,000*

CORN-GROWING COUNTRIES IN THE WORLD

	Country	Annual production (metric tonnes)
1	US	161,145,000
2	China	103,380,000
3	Brazil	29,967,000
4	Mexico	18,600,000
5	France	14,966,000
6	Argentina	10,897,000
7	India	9,700,000
8	South Africa	9,425,000
9	Romania	7,988,000
10	Italy	7,738,000
	World total	*470,570,000*

RICE-GROWING COUNTRIES IN THE WORLD

	Country	Annual production (metric tonnes)
1	China	187,211,000
2	India	111,011,000
3	Indonesia	47,885,000
4	Bangladesh	28,000,000
5	Vietnam	22,300,000
6	Thailand	19,090,000
7	Myanmar (Burma)	17,434,000
8	Brazil	10,193,000
9	Japan	9,793,000
10	Philippines	9,530,000
	World total	*527,413,000*

World rice production has risen dramatically during the century; China's has more than trebled since 1950. Rice remains the staple diet for a large proportion of the global population, especially in Asia, as well as several countries in South America and Africa. Relatively small quantities are grown elsewhere: Europe's production is 2,060,000 tonnes, with Italy producing more than half.

TOP 10

SUGAR BEET-GROWING COUNTRIES IN THE WORLD

	Country	Annual production (metric tonnes)
1	Ukraine	33,717,000
2	France	31,748,000
3	Germany	28,610,000
4	Russia	25,500,000
5	US	23,946,000
6	Poland	15,621,000
7	Turkey	15,563,000
8	China	12,100,000
9	Italy	11,867,000
10	UK	8,988,000
	World total	*281,682,000*

TOP 10

SWEET POTATO-GROWING COUNTRIES IN THE WORLD

	Country	Annual production (metric tonnes)
1	China	105,185,000
2	Vietnam	2,620,000
3	Indonesia	2,277,000
4	Uganda	1,894,000
5	India	1,102,000
6	Japan	1,033,000
7	Rwanda	700,000
8	Burundi	680,000
9	Philippines	650,000
10	Brazil	603,000
	World total	*123,750,000*

TOP 10

BARLEY-GROWING COUNTRIES IN THE WORLD

	Country	Annual production (metric tonnes)
1	Russia	26,628,000
2	Ukraine	13,550,000
3	Canada	13,342,000
4	Germany	11,900,000
5	Spain	9,520,000
6	France	8,995,000
7	US	8,714,000
8	Turkey	7,500,000
9	Kazakhstan	6,850,000
10	Australia	6,815,000
	World total	*170,364,000*

TOP 10

POTATO-GROWING COUNTRIES IN THE WORLD

	Country	Annual production (metric tonnes)
1	Russia	38,000,000
2	Poland	36,271,000
3	China	35,050,000
4	Ukraine	21,009,000
5	US	19,024,000
6	India	15,718,000
7	Germany	12,074,000
8	Belarus	11,600,000
9	Netherlands	7,699,000
10	UK	7,069,000
	World total	*288,183,000*

TOP 10

CASSAVA-GROWING COUNTRIES IN THE WORLD

	Country	Annual production (metric tonnes)
1	Brazil	21,719,000
2	Nigeria	21,000,000
3	Zaïre	20,835,000
4	Thailand	19,610,000
5	Indonesia	16,356,000
6	Tanzania	6,833,000
7	India	5,340,000
8	Ghana	4,200,000
9	Uganda	3,982,000
10	Mozambique	3,511,000
	World total	*153,628,000*

TOP 10

SOYBEAN-GROWING COUNTRIES IN THE WORLD

	Country	Annual production (metric tonnes)
1	US	49,221,000
2	Brazil	22,710,000
3	China	13,007000
4	Argentina	10,673,000
5	India	4,500,000
6	Canada	1,900,000
7	Paraguay	1,750,000
8	Indonesia	1,630,000
9	Italy	1,006,000
10	Mexico	520,000
	World total	*111,011,000*

Dividing a country's population by the weight of potatoes grown will not reveal who eats the most since a great deal of the world harvest is used in the manufacture of alcohol and other products. Nonetheless, large populations of the world depend on potatoes for their nutrition: the destruction of the Irish crop by blight in 1845–47 caused widespread famine and the beginning of mass emigration, especially to the United States.

TREE TOPS

TOP 10

LARGEST NATIONAL FORESTS IN THE US

	Forest	Location	Acres
1	Tongass National Forest	Sitka Alaska	16,719,874
2	Chugach National Forest	Anchorage Alaska	5,404,414
3	Toiyabe National Forest	Sparks Nevada	3,212,229
4	Tonto National Forest	Phoenix Arizona	2,874,593
5	Boise National Forest	Boise Idaho	2,647,740
6	Humboldt National Forest	Elko Nevada	2,478,102
7	Challis National Forest	Challis Idaho	2,464,524
8	Shoshone National Forest	Cody Wyoming	2,436,834
9	Flathead National Forest	Montana	2,354,511
10	Payette National Forest	McCall Idaho	2,323,232

This list's No. 1 is actually larger than the District of Columbia as well as all of the 10 smallest states. Even the much smaller No. 2 is larger than Massachusetts, and No. 10 covers an area greater than that of Delaware and Rhode Island combined.

TOP 10

COUNTRIES WITH THE LARGEST AREAS OF FOREST

	Country	Area hectares	Acres
1	Russia	778,500,000	1,923,712,000
2	Brazil	488,000,000	1,205,872,000
3	Canada	361,000,000	892,049,000
4	US	286,200,000	707,215,000
5	Zaïre	173,800,000	429,468,000
6	China	130,495,000	322,460,000
7	Indonesia	108,600,000	268,356,000
8	Australia	106,000,000	261,931,000
9	India	68,500,000	169,267,000
10	Peru	68,000,000	168,031,000
	World total	*3,879,796,000*	*9,587,170,000*

TOP 10

BIGGEST TREES IN THE US

(The biggest known example of each of the 10 biggest species)

	Species	Location	Points
1	General Sherman giant sequoia	Sequoia National Park California	1,300
2	Coast redwood	Humboldt Redwoods State Park, California	1,017
3	Western redcedar	Forks, Washington	924
4	Sitka spruce	Olympic National Forest Washington	922
5	Coast Douglas fir	Coos County, Oregon	762
6	Common bald cypress	Cat Island, Louisiana	748
7	Sycamore	Jeromesville, Ohio	737
8	Port-Orford cedar	Siskiyou National Forest Oregon	680
9	Sugar pine	Yosemite National Park California	635
10	Incense cedar	Marble Mountains Wilderness, California	626

The American Forestry Association operates a *National Register of Big Trees* that is constantly updated as new "champion trees" are nominated by enthusiastic tree-spotters across the United States. Their method of measurement, which gives this Top 10 by species, is based not solely on height, but also takes into account the thickness of the trunk and the spread of the upper branches and leaves, or crown. The formula adds the circumference in inches of the tree at 4½ feet above the ground to the total height in feet and to one-quarter of the average crown spread in feet. The General Sherman giant sequoia is 998 inches in circumference, 275 feet tall, and has an average crown spread of 107 feet, hence 998 + 275 + 27 = 1,300 points.

DID YOU KNOW

THE LARGEST LIVING THING ON EARTH

Founded in 1890, the Sequoia National Park in Northern California is the home of General Sherman, a Giant Sequoia, which is thought to be the planet's biggest living thing, nine percent bigger than its nearest competitor, the Sequoia, the General Grant. Weighing 1,400 tons/ 1,270 tonnes (as much as nine blue whales or 360 elephants), it is calculated to be 266,000,000,000 times heavier than the seed from which it grew, 2,600 years ago, and is gaining 40 cubic feet, or 1 ton/0.9 tonne a year, making it the world's fastest growing organism.

TOP 10

MOST FORESTED COUNTRIES IN THE WORLD

(By percent forest cover)

1 Suriname	91%	
2 Solomon Islands	89%	
3 Papua New Guinea	83%	
4 French Guiana	81%	
5 Guyana	76%	
6= Gabon	74%	
6= North Korea	74%	
8 Finland	69%	
9 Japan	67%	
10 South Korea	65%	

TOP 10

TALLEST TREES IN THE UK

(The tallest known example of each of the 10 tallest species)

	Tree	Location	m	ft
1	Grand fir	Strone House, Argyll Strathclyde	63.4	208
2	Douglas fir	The Hermitage, Dunkeld Tayside	62.5	205
3	Sitka spruce	Private estate, Strath Earn Tayside	61.6	202
4=	Giant sequoia	Castle Leod, Strathpeffer Highland	53.0	174
4=	Low's fir	Diana's Grove, Blair Castle Strathclyde	53.0	174
6	Norway spruce	Moniack Glenn Highland	51.8	170
7=	Western hemlock	Benmore Younger Botanic Gardens Argyll, Strathclyde	51.0	167
7=	Noble fir	Ardkinglas House Argyll, Strathclyde	51.0	167
9	European silver fir	Armadale Castle, Skye Highland	50.0	164
10	London plane	Bryanston School Blandford, Dorset	48.0	157

Based on data supplied by *The Tree Register of the British Isles*

TOP 10

TALLEST TREES IN THE US

(The tallest known example of each of the 10 tallest species)

	Tree	Location	m	ft
1	Coast redwood	Humboldt Redwoods State Park, California	110.6	363
2	Coast Douglas fir	Coos County, Oregon	100.27	329
3	General Sherman giant sequoia	Sequoia National Park California	83.8	275
4	Noble fir	Mount St. Helens National Monument Washington	82.9	272
5	Sugar pine	Yosemite National Park California	82.3	270
6	Western hemlock	Olympic National Park Washington	73.5	241
7	Port-Orford cedar	Siskiyou National Forest Oregon	66.8	219
8	Sitka spruce	Seaside, Oregon	62.8	206
9	Swamp chestnut (Basket) oak	Fayette County, Alabama	61.0	200
10	Pignut hickory	Robbinsville North Carolina	57.9	190

The champion Coast Redwood is two-thirds the size of the Washington Monument and over twice the size of London's Nelson Column. A close rival, the Dyerville Giant (from Dyerville, California), stood 362 ft/110.3 m high but fell in a storm on March 27, 1991. Several trees no longer standing, including various Australian eucalyptus trees, exceeded 400 ft/122 m.

THE UNIVERSE & EARTH

THE 10

STARS NEAREST TO THE EARTH
(Excluding the Sun)

	Star	Light-years*	km	miles
1	Proxima Centauri	4.22	39,923,310,000,000	24,792,500,000,000
2	Alpha Centauri	4.35	41,153,175,000,000	25,556,250,000,000
3	Barnard's Star	5.98	56,573,790,000,000	35,132,500,000,000
4	Wolf 359	7.75	73,318,875,000,000	45,531,250,000,000
5	Lalande 21185	8.22	77,765,310,000,000	48,292,500,000,000
6	Luyten 726-8	8.43	79,752,015,000,000	49,526,250,000,000
7	Sirius	8.65	81,833,325,000,000	50,818,750,000,000
8	Ross 154	9.45	89,401,725,000,000	55,518,750,000,000
9	Ross 248	10.40	98,389,200,000,000	61,100,000,000,000
10	Epsilon Eridani	10.80	102,173,400,000,000	63,450,000,000,000

* *One light-year = 5.875 x 10^{12} miles/9.4605 x 10^{12} km*

A spaceship traveling at 25,000 mph/40,237 km/h – which is faster than any human has yet reached in space – would take more than 113,200 years to reach the Earth's closest star, Proxima Centauri.

TOP 10

MOST FREQUENTLY SEEN COMETS

	Comet	Orbit period (years)
1	Encke	3.302
2	Grigg–Skjellerup	4.908
3	Honda–Mrkós–Pajdusáková	5.210
4	Tempel 2	5.259
5	Neujmin 2	5.437
6	Brorsen	5.463
7	Tuttle–Giacobini–Kresák	5.489
8	Tempel–L. Swift	5.681
9	Tempel 1	5.982
10	Pons–Winnecke	6.125

NATURAL PHENOMENON
This painting depicts the sighting of a comet in 1858.

COMETS COMING CLOSEST TO THE EARTH

	Comet	Date*	Distance (AU)#
1	Lexell	Jul 1, 1770	2.3
2	Tempel–Tuttle	Oct 26, 1366	3.4
3	Halley	Apr 10, 837	5.0
4	Biela	Dec 9, 1805	5.5
5	Grischow	Feb 8, 1743	5.8
6	Pons–Winnecke	Jun 26, 1927	5.9
7	La Hire	Apr 20, 1702	6.6
8	Schwassmann–Wachmann	May 31, 1930	9.3
9	Cassini	Jan 8, 1760	10.2
10	Schweizer	Apr 29, 1853	12.6

* Of closest approach to the Earth
\# Astronomical units: 1AU = mean distance from the Earth to the Sun (92,955,900 miles/149,598,200 km)

MOST RECENT OBSERVATIONS OF HALLEY'S COMET

1 1986
Japanese, Soviet, and European probes were sent to investigate the comet. All were heavily battered by dust particles, and it was concluded that Halley's comet is composed of dust bonded by water and carbon dioxide ice.

2 1910
Predictions of disaster were widely published, with many people convinced that the world would come to an end.

3 1835
Widely observed, but dimmer than in 1759.

4 1759
The comet's first return, as predicted by Halley, proving his calculations correct.

5 1682
Observed in Africa and China, and in Europe, where it was observed from September 5 to 19 by Edmund Halley, who successfully calculated its orbit and predicted its return.

6 1607
Seen extensively in China, Japan, Korea, and Europe; described by German astronomer Johannes Kepler; and its position accurately measured by amateur Welsh astronomer Thomas Harriot.

7 1531
Observed in China, Japan, and Korea, and in Europe, where Peter Appian, a German geographer and astronomer, noted that comets' tails point away from the Sun.

8 1456
Observed in China, Japan, Korea, and Europe. When Papal forces defeated the invading Turks, it was seen as a portent of their victory.

9 1378
Observed in China, Japan, Korea, and Europe.

10 1301
Seen in Iceland, parts of Europe, China, Japan, and Korea.

LARGEST REFLECTING TELESCOPES IN THE WORLD

	Telescope name	Location	Opened*	(m)
1	Keck Telescope	Mauna Kea Observatory, Hawaii	1992	10.0
2	Bolshoi Teleskop Azimutal'ny	Special Astrophysical Observatory of the Russian Academy of Sciences, Mount Pastukhov, Russia	1976	6.0
3	Hale Telescope	Palomar Observatory, California	1948	5.0
4	William Herschel Telescope	Observatorio del Roque de los Muchachos, La Palma, Canary Islands	1987	4.2
5=	Mayall Telescope#	Kitt Peak National Observatory, Arizona	1973	4.0
5=	4-meter Telescope#	Cerro Tololo Inter-American Observatory, Chile	1976	4.0
7	Anglo-Australian Telescope	Siding Spring Observatory, New South Wales, Australia	1974	3.9
8=	ESO 3.6-meter Telescope	European Southern Observatory, La Silla, Chile	1975	3.6
8=	Canada–France–Hawaii Telescope	Mauna Kea Observatory, Hawaii	1970	3.6
8=	United Kingdom Infrared Telescope	Mauna Kea Observatory, Hawaii	1979	3.6

* Dedicated or regular use commenced
\# Northern/southern hemisphere "twin" telescopes

THE KECK TELESCOPE
The world's largest optical telescope is the Keck, with a 394-inch/10-m mirror comprising 36 separate segments. It is planned as the first of a pair, Keck I and Keck II, at Mauna Kea, Hawaii.

If the Keck Telescope at No. 1 is discounted because its "mirror" is not in one piece, but consists of 36 hexagonal segments slotted together, then the 10th entry in the list becomes the 3.5-meter New Technology Telescope at the European Observatory, La Silla, Chile, which started operations in 1990. The Multiple Mirror Telescope at the Fred Lawrence Whipple Observatory, Arizona, opened in 1979, has six linked 1.8-meter mirrors, together equivalent to a 4.5-meter telescope. These are being replaced by a single 6.5-meter mirror which is currently under construction.

THE PLANETS

TOP 10

LONGEST DAYS IN THE SOLAR SYSTEM

	Body	Length of day* days	hours	mins
1	Venus	244	0	0
2	Mercury	58	14	0
3	Sun	25#	0	0
4	Pluto	6	9	0
5	Mars		24	37
6	Earth		23	56
7	Uranus		17	14
8	Neptune		16	7
9	Saturn		10	39
10	Jupiter		9	55

* Period of rotation, based on Earth day
\# Variable

TOP 10

LONGEST YEARS IN THE SOLAR SYSTEM

	Body	Length of year* years	days
1	Pluto	247	256
2	Neptune	164	298
3	Uranus	84	4
4	Saturn	29	168
5	Jupiter	11	314
6	Mars	1	322
7	Earth		365
8	Venus		225
9	Mercury		88
10	Sun		0

* Period of orbit around the Sun, in Earth years/days

INHOSPITABLE
The surface of Venus is extremely hot, with high atmospheric pressure and clouds of sulfuric acid.

TOP 10

BODIES FARTHEST FROM THE SUN
(In the Solar System, excluding satellites and asteroids)

	Body	Average distance from the Sun km	miles
1	Pluto	5,914,000,000	3,675,000,000
2	Neptune	4,497,000,000	2,794,000,000
3	Uranus	2,871,000,000	1,784,000,000
4	Chiron	2,800,000,000	1,740,000,000
5	Saturn	1,427,000,000	887,000,000
6	Jupiter	778,300,000	483,600,000
7	Mars	227,900,000	141,600,000
8	Earth	149,600,000	92,900,000
9	Venus	108,200,000	67,200,000
10	Mercury	57,900,000	36,000,000

GAS GIANT
Jupiter, seen here with two of its moons, is composed almost entirely of hydrogen and helium.

DID YOU KNOW

NAMING THE PLANETS

As the discovery of new asteroids, stars, moons, and craters have proliferated, astronomers have had to resort to increasingly strange appellations. In 1781 Sir William Herschel discovered the seventh planet, which was finally named after the Greek god Uranus. The features on one of Uranus's moons, Oberon, all have Shakespearean names including Hamlet, Romeo, and Macbeth. Mercury's craters are named after the poets Milton, Byron, and Coleridge, composers Beethoven, Chopin, and Wagner, artists van Gogh, Gainsborough, and Matisse, and writers such as Dickens, Shakespeare, and Proust. On Venus, the large craters are named after mythological figures and small craters of 62 miles/ 100 km or less in width after famous women, such as nurse Florence Nightingale.

TOP 10

LARGEST BODIES IN THE SOLAR SYSTEM

	Name	Maximum diameter km	miles
1	Sun	1,392,140	865,036
2	Jupiter	142,984	88,846
3	Saturn	120,536	74,898
4	Uranus	51,118	31,763
5	Neptune	49,532	30,778
6	Earth	12,756	7,926
7	Venus	12,103	7,520
8	Mars	6,794	4,222
9	Ganymede	5,268	3,273
10	Titan	5,150	3,200

Most of the planets are visible with the naked eye and have been observed since ancient times. The exceptions are Uranus, discovered on March 13, 1781 by the British astronomer Sir William Herschel; Neptune, found by German astronomer Johann Galle on September 23, 1846 (Galle was led to his discovery by the independent calculations of the French astronomer Urbain Leverrier and the British mathematician John Adams); and, outside the Top 10, Pluto, located using photographic techniques by American astronomer Clyde Tombaugh. The announcement of its discovery came on March 13, 1930; its diameter remains uncertain, but it is thought to be approximately 1,430 miles/2,302 km.

T O P 1 0

LARGEST PLANETARY MOONS

	Moon	Planet	Diameter km	miles
1	Ganymede	Jupiter	5,268	3,273

Discovered by Galileo in 1609–10 and believed to be the largest moon in the Solar System, Ganymede – one of Jupiter's 16 satellites – is thought to have a surface of ice about 60 miles/97 km thick.

2	Titan	Saturn	5,150	3,200

Titan, the largest of Saturn's 18 confirmed moons, is actually larger than Mercury or Pluto. It was discovered by the Dutch astronomer Christian Huygens in 1655.

3	Callisto	Jupiter	4,820	2,995

Similar in composition to Ganymede, Callisto is heavily pitted with craters, perhaps more so than any other body in the Solar System.

4	Io	Jupiter	3,632	2,257

Most of what we know about Io was reported back by the 1979 Voyager probe, which revealed a crust of solid sulfur with massive volcanic eruptions in progress.

5	Moon	Earth	3,475	2,159

Our own satellite is a quarter of the size of the Earth and the 5th largest in the Solar System. To date it is the only one that has been explored by humans.

6	Europa	Jupiter	3,126	1,942

Europa's fairly smooth, icy surface is covered with mysterious black lines, some of them 40 miles/64 km wide and resembling canals.

7	Triton	Neptune	2,750	1,708

Discovered in 1846 by British brewer and amateur astronomer William Lassell, Triton is unique in that it revolves around its planet in the opposite direction to the planet's rotation.

8	Titania	Uranus	1,580	982

The largest of Uranus's 15 moons, Titania was discovered by William Herschel (who had discovered the planet six years earlier) in 1787 and has a snowball-like surface of ice.

9	Rhea	Saturn	1,530	951

Saturn's second largest moon was discovered in the 17th century by Italian-born French astronomer Giovanni Cassini.

10	Oberon	Uranus	1,516	942

Oberon was discovered by Herschel and given the name of the fairy king husband of Queen Titania; both are characters in Shakespeare's A Midsummer Night's Dream.

T O P 1 0

LARGEST ASTEROIDS

	Name	Year discovered	Diameter km	miles
1	Ceres	1801	936	582
2	Pallas	1802	607	377
3	Vesta	1807	519	322
4	Hygeia	1849	450	279
5	Euphrosyne	1854	370	229
6	Interamnia	1910	349	217
7	Davida	1903	322	200
8	Cybele	1861	308	192
9	Europa	1858	288	179
10	Patienta	1899	275	171

Asteroids, sometimes known as "minor planets," are fragments of rock orbiting between Mars and Jupiter. There are perhaps 45,000 of them, but fewer than 10 percent have been named. The first (and largest) to be discovered was Ceres, which was found by Giuseppe Piazzi (1746–1826), director of the Palermo observatory in Sicily, on New Year's Day, 1801. All have been numbered according to the order in which they were discovered. Some have only code numbers, but most also have names: women's names are especially popular and include Hilda (No. 153), Bertha (No. 154), Marilyn (No. 1,486), Sabrina (No. 2,264), and Samantha (No. 3,147). Among asteroids named after men are Mark Twain (No. 2,362) and Mr. Spock from *Star Trek* (No. 2,309).

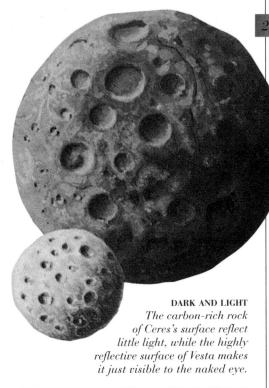

DARK AND LIGHT
The carbon-rich rock of Ceres's surface reflect little light, while the highly reflective surface of Vesta makes it just visible to the naked eye.

T O P 1 0

COLDEST BODIES IN THE SOLAR SYSTEM*

	Planet	Lowest temperature °F	°C
1	Pluto	–382	–230
2	Uranus	–369	–223
3	Neptune	–364	–220
4	Mercury	–328	–200
5	Saturn	–256	–160
6	Jupiter	–229	–145
7	Mars	–220	–140
8	Earth	–128	–89
9	Venus	+867	+464
10	Sun	+9,932	+5,500

* *Excluding satellites*

Absolute zero, which has almost been reached on Earth under laboratory conditions, is –459.67°F/–273.15°C, only 100°F/38.15°C below the surface temperature of Triton, a moon of Neptune. At the other extreme, it has been calculated theoretically that the core of Jupiter attains 54,032°F, more than five times the boiling point of tungsten, while the Sun's core reaches almost 28,000,000°F.

SATURN'S LARGEST MOON
NASA and the European Space Agency plan to send a space probe to Titan in April 1996. It should reach Titan in October 2002.

REACHING FOR THE MOON

THE 10

FIRST ANIMALS IN SPACE

	Animal	Country of origin	Date
1	Laika	USSR	Nov 3, 1957

Name used by Western press – actually the name of the breed to which the dog named Kudryavka, a female Samoyed husky, belonged. Died in space.

2=	Laska and		
2=	Benjy (mice)	US	Dec 13, 1958

Reentered the Earth's atmosphere, but not recovered.

4=	Able (female rhesus monkey) and		
4=	Baker (female squirrel monkey)	US	May 28, 1959

Successfully returned to Earth.

6=	Otvazhnaya (female Samoyed husky) and		
6=	An unnamed rabbit	USSR	Jul 2, 1959

Recovered.

8	Sam (male rhesus monkey)	US	Dec 4, 1959

Recovered.

9	Miss Sam (female rhesus monkey)	US	Jan 21, 1960

Recovered.

10=	Belka and		
10=	Strelka (female Samoyed huskies)	USSR	Aug 19, 1960

First to orbit and return safely.

The first animal sent up in a rocket – but not into space – was Albert, a male rhesus monkey, in a US Air Force converted German V2 rocket in 1948. He died during the test, as did a monkey and 11 mice in a US *Aerobee* rocket in 1951. The earliest Soviet experiments involved launching monkeys, dogs, rabbits, cats, and mice, most of whom died. Laika, the first dog in space, went up with no hope of coming down alive. Able and Baker, launched in a *Jupiter* missile, were the first animals to return (although Able died a few days later). Before the first US manned spaceflight, on November 29, 1961, Enos, a male chimpanzee, completed two orbits and returned safely to the Earth.

TOP 10

LARGEST CRATERS ON THE MOON
(Near, or visible side only)

	Crater	Diameter km	miles
1	Bailly	303	188
2	Deslandres	234	145
3	Schickard	227	141
4	Clavius	225	140
5	Grimaldi	222	138
6	Humboldt	207	129
7	Belkovich	198	123
8	Janssen	190	118
9	Schiller	179	111
10=	Gauss	177	110
10=	Petavius	177	110

The most characteristic features of the lunar landscape are its craters, many of which are named after famous astronomers and scientists. On the near side of the Moon there are some 300,000 craters with diameters greater than 0.6 mile/1 km, 234 of them larger than 62 miles/100 km. Those larger than about 37 miles/60 km are referred to as "walled plains." The walled plains and smaller craters have been continually degraded by meteorite bombardment over millions of years and, as a result, many contain numerous further craters within them. Bailly (named after Jean Sylvain Bailly, astronomer and Mayor of Paris, who was guillotined soon after the French Revolution) is the largest crater on the visible side, with walls rising to 14,000 ft/4,267 m.

THE 10

FIRST PEOPLE IN SPACE

	Name	Age	Orbits	Duration hr:min	Spacecraft/ country of origin	Date
1	Fl. Major Yuri Alekseyivich Gagarin	27	1	1:48	*Vostok I* USSR	Apr 12, 1961
2	Major Gherman Stepanovich Titov	25	17	25:18	*Vostok II* USSR	Aug 6–7, 1961
3	Lt.-Col. John Herschel Glenn	43	3	4:56	*Friendship 7* US	Feb 20, 1962
4	Lt.-Col. Malcolm Scott Carpenter	37	3	4:56	*Aurora 7* US	May 24, 1962
5	Major Andrian Grigoryevich Nikolayev	32	64	94:22	*Vostok III* USSR	Aug 11–15, 1962
6	Col. Pavel Romanovich Popovich	31	48	70:57	*Vostok IV* USSR	Aug 12–15, 1962
7	Cdr. Walter Marty Schirra	39	6	9:13	*Sigma 7* US	Oct 3, 1962
8	Major Leroy Gordon Cooper	36	22	34:19	*Faith 7* US	May 15–16, 1963
9	Lt.-Col. Valeri Fyodorovich Bykovsky	28	81	119:60	*Vostok V* USSR	Jun 14–19, 1963
10	Jr. Lt. Valentina Vladimirovna Tereshkova	26	48	70:50	*Vostok VI* USSR	Jun 16–19, 1963

No. 10 was the first woman in space. Among early pioneering flights, neither Alan Shepard (May 5, 1961: *Freedom 7*) nor Gus Grissom (July 21, 1961: *Liberty Bell 7*) actually entered space, achieving altitudes of only 115 miles/185 km and 118 miles/190 km respectively, and neither flight lasted more than 15 minutes. Glenn was the first American to orbit the Earth.

LUNAR, COMMAND,
AND SERVICE MODULES

THE 10

FIRST MOONWALKERS

	Astronaut	Birthdate	Spacecraft	Total EVA* hr:min	Mission dates
1	Neil A. Armstrong	Aug 5, 1930	Apollo 11	2:32	Jul 16–24, 1969
2	Edwin E. ("Buzz") Aldrin	Jan 20, 1930	Apollo 11	2:15	Jul 16–24, 1969
3	Charles Conrad Jr.	Jun 2, 1930	Apollo 12	7:45	Nov 14–24, 1969
4	Alan L. Bean	Mar 15, 1932	Apollo 12	7:45	Nov 14–24, 1969
5	Alan B. Shepard	Nov 18, 1923	Apollo 14	9:23	Jan 31–Feb 9, 1971
6	Edgar D. Mitchell	Sep 17, 1930	Apollo 14	9:23	Jan 31–Feb 9, 1971
7	David R. Scott	Jun 6, 1932	Apollo 15	19:08	Jul 26–Aug 7, 1971
8	James B. Irwin	Mar 17, 1930	Apollo 15	18:35	Jul 26–Aug 7, 1971
9	John W. Young	Sep 24, 1930	Apollo 16	20:14	Apr 16–27, 1972
10	Charles M. Duke	Oct 3, 1935	Apollo 16	20:14	Apr 16–27, 1972

* Extra-vehicular Activity (i.e., time spent out of the lunar module on the Moon's surface)

Six US Apollo missions resulted in successful Moon landings (Apollo 13, April 11–17, 1970, was aborted after an oxygen tank exploded). During the last of these (Apollo 17, December 7–19, 1972), Eugene A. Cernan (b. March 14, 1934) and Harrison H. Schmitt (b. July 3, 1935) became the only other astronauts to date who have walked on the surface of the Moon, both spending a total of 22:04 hours in EVA. No further Moon landings are planned by the US. Although Russian scientists recently proposed sending a series of unmanned probes to land on Mars, which, if successful, would have led to a follow-up manned mission between 2005 and 2010, the entire Russian space program is suffering from such severe financial problems that its current missions appear to be in jeopardy.

SATURN V
This launch vehicle was built to send astronauts to the Moon.

THE 10

FIRST ARTIFICIAL SATELLITES

	Satellite	Country of origin	Launch date
1	Sputnik 1	USSR	Oct 4, 1957
2	Sputnik 2	USSR	Nov 3, 1957
3	Explorer 1	US	Feb 1, 1958
4	Vanguard 1	US	Mar 17, 1958
5	Explorer 3	US	Mar 26, 1958
6	Sputnik 3	USSR	May 15, 1958
7	Explorer 4	US	Jul 26, 1958
8	Score	US	Dec 18, 1958
9	Vanguard 2	US	Feb 17, 1959
10	Discoverer 1	US	Feb 28, 1959

Artificial satellites for use as radio relay stations were first proposed by the British science-fiction writer Arthur C. Clarke, in the October 1945 issue of Wireless World, but it was 12 years before his fantasy became reality with the launch of Sputnik 1, the first-ever artificial satellite to enter the Earth's orbit. A 184-lb/83.6-kg metal sphere, it transmitted signals back to the Earth for three weeks before its batteries failed, although it continued to be tracked until it fell back to the Earth and burned up on January 4, 1958. Its early successors were similarly short-lived, destroyed on reentry (although Vanguard 1 is destined to remain in orbit for the next 275 years and Vanguard 2 for 125 years). Sputnik 2 carried the first animal into space, and Explorer 1 first detected the radiation zone known as the Van Allen belts. Explorer 2 failed to enter the Earth's orbit. Score (the Signal Communications Orbit Relay Experiment) transmitted a prerecorded Christmas message from President Eisenhower. Discoverer 1, the first to be launched in a polar orbit, was a military satellite.

THE 10

FIRST UNMANNED MOON LANDINGS

	Name	Country of origin	Date (launch/impact)
1	Lunik 2	USSR	Sep 12/14, 1959
2	Ranger 4*	US	Apr 23/26, 1962
3	Ranger 6	US	Jan 30/Feb 2, 1964
4	Ranger 7	US	Jul 28/31, 1964
5	Ranger 8	US	Feb 17/20, 1965
6	Ranger 9	US	Mar 21/24, 1965
7	Luna 5*	USSR	May 9/12, 1965
8	Luna 7*	USSR	Oct 4/8, 1965
9	Luna 8*	USSR	Dec 3/7, 1965
10	Luna 9	USSR	Jan 31/Feb 3, 1966

In addition to these 10 craft, debris left on the Moon includes the remains of several more Luna craft, including unmanned sample-collectors and Lunakhod 1 and 2 (1966–71; all Soviet), seven Surveyors (1966–68), five Lunar Orbiters (1966–67), and the descent stages of six Apollo modules (all US) – to which one may add the world's most expensive used cars, the three Lunar Rovers used on Apollo missions Nos. 15 to 17 and worth $6,000,000 each.

* Crash landing

ASTRONAUTS & COSMONAUTS

COUNTRIES WITH MOST SPACEFLIGHT EXPERIENCE
(To January 14, 1994)

	Country	Missions	Host country	days	hr	min	sec
				Total duration of missions			
1	USSR	72	–	3,835	8	16	44
2	US	89	–	738	3	57	18
3	Russia*	4	–	710	6	23	5
4	France	5	1 US/3 USSR/1 Russia	74	4	43	36
5	Germany	5	3 US/2 USSR	41	4	33	3
6	Canada	3	US	26	3	34	31
7	Japan	2	1 US/1 USSR	15	20	26	11
8	Bulgaria	2	USSR	11	19	11	6
9	Belgium	1	US	8	22	9	25
10	Afghanistan	1	USSR	8	20	27	0

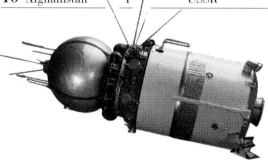

* Russia became a separate independent state on December 25, 1991

FIRST MANNED ORBIT
On April 12, 1961 Soviet cosmonaut Yuri Gagarin became the first person in space when he completed one orbit of the Earth in his capsule, Vostok 1.

FIRST SPACEWALKERS

	Astronaut	Spacecraft	EVA* hr:min	Launch date
1	Alexei Leonov	*Voskhod 2*	0:12	Mar 18, 1965
2	Edward H. White	*Gemini 4*	0:23	Jun 3, 1965
3	Eugene A. Cernan#	*Gemini 9*	2:08	Jun 3, 1966
4	Michael Collins	*Gemini 10*	1:30	Jul 18, 1966
5	Richard F. Gordon	*Gemini 11*	1:57	Sep 12, 1966
6	Edwin E. ("Buzz") Aldrin**	*Gemini 12*	5:37	Nov 11, 1966
7	Alexei Yeleseyev	*Soyuz 5*	##	Jan 15, 1969
8	Yevgeny Khrunov	*Soyuz 5*	##	Jan 15, 1969
9	David R. Scott‡	*Apollo 9*	1:01	Mar 3, 1969
10	*Russell L. Schweickart*	*Apollo 9*	*1:07*	*Mar 3, 1969*

* Extra-vehicular Activity
 # Short-duration EVA transfer to Soyuz 4
**July 16, 1969 – first to walk in space twice
##Short-duration transfer to Soyuz 4
‡ July 26, 1971 – first to walk in space three times

FIRST IN-FLIGHT SPACE FATALITIES

1 Vladimir M. Komarov (1927–1967)

Launched on April 24, 1967, Soviet spaceship Soyuz 1 experienced various technical problems during its eighteenth orbit. After a successful reentry, the capsule parachute was deployed at 23,000 ft/7,010 m but its lines became tangled, and it crash-landed near Orsk in the Urals, killing Komarov (the survivor of a previous one-day flight on October 12, 1964), and thus became the first-ever space fatality.

2= Georgi T. Dobrovolsky (1928–1971)
2= Viktor I. Patsayev (1933–1971)
2= Vladislav N. Volkov (1933–1971)

After a then-record 23 days in space and a link-up with the Salyut space station, the Soviet Soyuz 9 mission ended in disaster on June 29, 1971 when the capsule depressurized during reentry. Although it landed intact, all three cosmonauts – who were not wearing spacesuits – were found dead. Their ashes were buried, along with those of cosmonauts Yuri Gagarin and Vladimir Komarov, at the Kremlin, Moscow. Spacesuits have been worn during reentry on all subsequent missions.

5= Gregory B. Jarvis (1944–1986)
5= Sharon C. McAuliffe (1948–1986)
5= Ronald E. McNair (1950–1986)
5= Ellison S. Onizuka (1946–1986)
5= Judith A. Resnik (1949–1986)
5= Francis R. Scobee (1939–1986)
5= Michael J. Smith (1945–1986)

Challenger STS-51-L, the 25th Space Shuttle mission, exploded shortly after takeoff from Cape Canaveral, Florida, on January 28, 1986. The cause was determined to have been leakage of seals in the joint between rocket sections. The disaster, watched by thousands on the ground and millions on television, halted the US space program until a full review of engineering problems and safety methods had been undertaken, and it was not until September 29, 1988 that the next Space Shuttle, Discovery STS-26, was launched.

The 11 cosmonauts and astronauts in this list are, to date, the only in-flight space fatalities, although not the only victims of accidents during the space programs of the former USSR and the US. On October 24, 1960, five months before the first manned flight, Field Marshal Mitrofan Nedelin, the commander of the USSR's Strategic Rocket Forces, and an unknown number of other personnel (a total of 165 according to some authorities) were killed in the catastrophic launchpad explosion of an unmanned space rocket at the Baikonur cosmodrome, but the precise circumstances remain secret. Another explosion, during the refueling of a *Vostok* rocket at the Plesetsk Space Center on March 18, 1980, left some 50 dead. During a test countdown of *Apollo 1* on January 27, 1967, Roger B. Chaffee, Virgil I. "Gus" Grissom, veteran of the US's second and seventh space missions, and Edward H. White (who flew in the eighth US mission) were killed in a fire, probably caused by an electrical fault. This tragedy led to greatly improved capsule design and safety procedures. A number of former astronauts and cosmonauts have also been killed in accidents during other activities: Yuri Gagarin, the first man in space, was killed on March 27, 1968 in an airplane crash. The same fate befell a number of US astronauts who trained for, but were killed before, their space missions: Charles A. Bassett, Theodore C. Freeman, Elliot M. See, and Clifton C. Williams all died during training in T-38 jet crashes in 1964–67. Stephen D. Thorne was killed in a 1986 airplane accident, and Edward G. Givens in a 1967 car crash. John L. Swigert, who had survived the ill-fated *Apollo 13* mission in 1970, died of cancer on December 27, 1982, thus becoming the first American space explorer to die of natural causes. James B. Irwin, who died on August 8, 1991 as a result of a heart attack, became the first moonwalker to die.

THE 10

MOST EXPERIENCED SPACEMEN
(To March 31, 1995)

	Name	Missions	Total duration of missions			
			days	hr	min	sec
1	Valeri Polyakov	2	677	40	36	0
2	Musa Manarov	2	541	0	31	18
3	Sergei Krikalyov*	2	463	7	11	0
4	Yuri Romanenko	3	430	18	21	30
5	Alexander Volkov	3	391	11	54	0
6	Anatoli Solovyov	3	377	20	0	0
7	Leonid Kizim	3	374	17	57	42
8	Vladimir Titov	2	367	22	56	48
9	Vladimir Solovyov	2	361	22	50	0
10	Valeri Ryumin	3	361	21	31	57

* *During February 3–11, 1994, Krikalyov flew a third mission on board the US shuttle* Discovery STS–60, *adding 7 days, 8 min 50 secs to his space log*

All the missions listed were undertaken by the USSR (and, more recently, Russia). The durations of Soviet/Russian cosmonauts' space missions are far ahead of those of the US, whose closest rivals are the three *Skylab 4* astronauts Gerald P. Carr, Edward G. Gibson, and William R. Pogue. Each of them clocked up a total of 84 days 1 hr 15 min 31 sec in space (November 16, 1973 to February 8, 1974) giving all three the equal US record for space experience. The four Space Shuttle missions of Daniel C. Brandenstein (*SST-8, STS-51-G, STS-32,* and *STS-49*) make him the most experienced Shuttle astronaut, with a total time in space of 32 days 21 hr 5 min 16 sec.

THE 10

MOST EXPERIENCED SPACEWOMEN
(To January 1, 1995)

	Name*	Missions	Total duration of missions			
			days	hr	min	sec
1	Tamara Kondakova	1	169	5	22	0
2	Shannon W. Lucid	4	34	22	53	14
3	Bonnie J. Dunbar	3	31	17	15	33
4	Kathryn C. Thornton	3	23	41	15	30
5	Marsha S. Ivins	3	31	7	32	40
6	Margaret Rhea Seddon	2	23	2	27	54
7	Kathryn D. Sullivan	3	22	4	48	39
8	Ellen Ochoa	2	20	4	43	10
9	Svetlana Savitskaya	2	19	17	7	0
10	Tamara E. Jernigan	2	18	23	10	33

* *All US except 1 and 9 (USSR)*

THE FACE OF THE EARTH

TOP 10

LARGEST METEORITE CRATERS IN THE WORLD

Crater	Diameter km	miles
1= Sudbury Ontario, Canada	140	87
1= Vredefort, South Africa	140	87
3= Manicouagan Québec, Canada	100	62
3= Popigai, Russia	100	62
5 Puchezh-Katunki Russia	80	50
6 Kara, Russia	60	37
7 Siljan, Sweden	52	32
8 Charlevoix Québec, Canada	46	29
9 Araguainha Dome Brazil	40	25
10 Carswell Saskatchewan, Canada	37	23

Unlike collision sites on other planets and moons, those on Earth have been obscured by time, making it hard to know if craters are of meteoric origin or the remains of long-extinct volcanoes. The International Union of Geological Sciences Commission on Comparative Planetology recognize only 107 meteoric craters, and even these are in dispute. Arizona's relatively small Barringer Crater (0.79 mile/1.265 km wide) is the largest that *all* scientists agree upon. A newly-found site, 199-mile/320-km wide, near Prague, may be Europe's largest crater.

DID YOU KNOW

THE WORLD'S BIGGEST METEORITES

The 54.4-tonne Hoba meteorite is the largest in the world. Found at Grootfontein, South Africa, in 1920, it measures 9 ft/2.73 m by 8 ft/2.43 m and is 82 percent iron and 16 percent nickel. "The Tent," which is the next largest, weighs 30.9 tonnes and was discovered in Greenland in 1897 by the US explorer Admiral Robert Peary. This meteorite is now on exhibit at the American Museum of Natural History, in New York.

TOP 10

LARGEST ISLANDS IN THE WORLD

	Island	Location	Approx. area* sq km	sq miles
1	Greenland (Kalaatdlit Nunaat)	Arctic Ocean	2,175,590	840,000
2	New Guinea	West Pacific	789,900	304,980
3	Borneo	Indian Ocean	751,000	289,961
4	Madagascar (Malagasy Republic)	Indian Ocean	587,041	226,657
5	Baffin Island, Canada	Arctic Ocean	507,451	195,926
6	Sumatra, Indonesia	Indian Ocean	422,200	163,011
7	Honshu, Japan	Northwest Pacific	230,092	88,839
8	Great Britain	North Atlantic	218,041	84,186
9	Victoria Island, Canada	Arctic Ocean	217,290	83,896
10	Ellesmere Island, Canada	Arctic Ocean	196,236	75,767

* Mainlands, including areas of inland water, but excluding offshore islands

Australia is regarded as a continental land mass rather than an island; otherwise it would rank 1st, at 2,941,517 sq miles/7,618,493 sq km, or 35 times the size of Great Britain. Several islands that are also countries fall just outside the Top 10, among them the South and North Islands of New Zealand (58,093 sq miles/151,460 sq km and 44,281 sq miles/114,687 sq km respectively) and Cuba (42,804 sq miles/110,861 sq km).

TOP 10

LARGEST DESERTS IN THE WORLD

	Desert	Location	Approx. area sq km	sq miles
1	Sahara	North Africa	9,000,000	3,500,000
2	Australian	Australia	3,800,000	1,470,000
3	Arabian	Southwest Asia	1,300,000	502,000
4	Gobi	Central Asia	1,040,000	401,500
5	Kalahari	Southern Africa	520,000	201,000
6	Turkestan	Central Asia	450,000	174,000
7	Takla Makan	China	327,000	125,000
8=	Sonoran	US/Mexico	310,000	120,000
8=	Namib	Southwest Africa	310,000	120,000
10=	Thar	Northwest India/Pakistan	260,000	100,000
10=	Somali	Somalia	260,000	100,000

This Top 10 presents the approximate areas and ranking of the world's great deserts. These are often broken down into smaller desert regions – the Australian Desert into the Gibson, Simpson, and Great Sandy Desert, for example. Of the total land surface of the Earth, as much as one-third may be considered "desert," or land where more water is lost through evaporation than is acquired through precipitation. However, deserts may range from the extremely arid and typical barren sandy desert, through arid to semiarid, and most exhibit features that encompass all these degrees of aridity without a precise line of demarcation.

T O P 1 0

LONGEST CAVES IN THE WORLD

	Cave	Location	Total Known Length m	ft
1	Mammoth cave system	Kentucky, US	560,000	1,837,270
2	Optimisticeskaja	Ukraine	178,000	583,989
3	Hölloch	Switzerland	137,000	449,475
4	Jewel Cave	South Dakota, US	127,000	416,667
5	Siebenhengsteholensystem	Switzerland	110,000	360,892
6	Ozernaya	Ukraine	107,300	352,034
7	Réseau de la Coume d'Hyouernede	France	90,500	296,916
8	Sistema de Ojo Guarena	Spain	89,100	292,323
9	Wind Cave	South Dakota, US	88,500	290,354
10	Fisher Ridge cave system	Kentucky, US	83,000	273,950

T O P 1 0

DEEPEST DEPRESSIONS IN THE WORLD

	Depression	Maximum depth below sea level m	ft
1	Dead Sea Israel/Jordan	400	1,312
2	Turfan Depression China	154	505
3	Qattâra Depression Egypt	133	436
4	Poluostrov Mangyshlak Kazakhstan	132	433
5	Danakil Depression Ethiopia	117	383
6	Death Valley US	86	282
7	Salton Sink US	72	235
8	Zapadny Chink Ustyurta Kazakhstan	70	230
9	Prikaspiyskaya Nizmennost' Kazakhstan/Russia	67	220
10	Ozera Sarykamysh Turkmenistan/Uzbekistan	45	148

The shore of the Dead Sea is the lowest exposed ground below sea level. However, the bed of the Sea, at 2,388 ft/728 m below sea level, is only half as deep as that of Lake Baikal, Russia, which is 4,872 ft/1,485 m below sea level. Much of Antarctica is also below sea level (some as low as 8,326 ft/2,538 m), but the land there is covered by an ice cap.

T O P 1 0

LARGEST ISLANDS IN THE US

	Island	Approx area sq km	sq miles
1	Hawaii Hawaii	4,037	10,456
2	Kodiak Alaska	3,672	9,510
3	Puerto Rico	3,459	8,959
4	Prince of Wales Alaska	2,587	6,700
5	Chicagof Alaska	2,085	5,400
6	Saint Lawrence Alaska	1,710	4,430
7	Admiralty Alaska	1,649	4,270
8	Nunivak Alaska	1,625	4,210
9	Unimak Alaska	1,606	4,160
10	Baranof Alaska	1,598	4,140

Long Island, New York (1,396 sq miles/ 3,630 sq km), falls just outside the Top 10. Manhattan, New York, measures just 22 sq miles/57 sq km.

DEATH VALLEY
The lowest-lying place in the Western Hemisphere, and one of the hottest with a US record 134°F/57°C, California's Death Valley is almost rainless. It contains fascinating desert plants and animals, and since 1933 has been a US National Monument.

ON TOP OF THE WORLD

TOP 10

HIGHEST MOUNTAINS IN THE WORLD

(Height of principal peak; lower peaks of the same mountain are excluded)

	Mountain	Country	m	ft
1	Everest	Nepal/Tibet	8,846	29,022
2	K2	Kashmir/China	8,611	28,250
3	Kanchenjunga	Nepal/Sikkim	8,598	28,208
4	Lhotse	Nepal/Tibet	8,501	27,890
5	Makalu I	Nepal/Tibet	8,470	27,790
6	Dhaulagiri I	Nepal	8,172	26,810
7	Manaslu I	Nepal	8,156	26,760
8	Cho Oyu	Nepal	8,153	26,750
9	Nanga Parbat	Kashmir	8,126	26,660
10	Annapurna I	Nepal	8,078	26,504

Many of the Top 10 mountains have alternative names: in Tibetan, Everest is known as Chomolungma ("Goddess Mother of the World"). K2 (so called because it was the second mountain in the Karakoram range counting from the Kashmir end) is also referred to by the local name Chogori, and sometimes as Godwin-Austen (after Lieutenant Henry Haversham Godwin-Austen [1834–1923], who first surveyed it in 1865). Manaslu is also known as Kutang I, and Nanga Parbat as Diamir.

TOP 10

HIGHEST MOUNTAINS IN EUROPE

	Mountain/Country	m	ft
1	Mont Blanc, France/Italy	4,810	15,770
2	Monte Rosa, Italy/Switzerland	4,630	15,200
3	Dom, Switzerland	4,540	14,910
4	Liskamm, Italy/Switzerland	4,540	14,890
5	Weisshorn, Switzerland	4,500	14,780
6	Taschorn, Switzerland	4,490	14,730
7	Matterhorn, Italy/Switzerland	4,480	14,690
8	La Dent Blanche, Switzerland	4,360	14,300
9	Nadelhorn, Switzerland	4,327	14,196
10	Le Grand Combin, Switzerland	4,314	14,154

All 10 of Europe's highest mountains are in the Alps; there are, however, at least 15 mountains in the Caucasus (the mountain range that straddles Europe and Asia) that are taller than Mont Blanc. The highest of them, the west peak of Mt. Elbrus, is 18,480 ft/5,630 m, which was climbed in 1963 by 107-year-old mountaineer Tschokka Zalichanov.

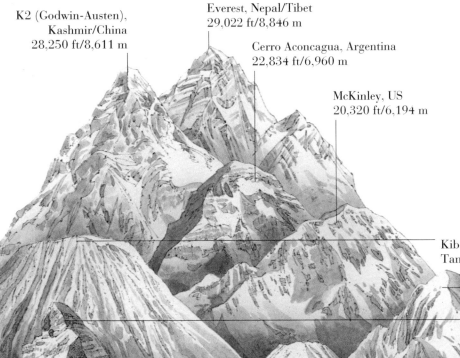

K2 (Godwin-Austen), Kashmir/China 28,250 ft/8,611 m

Everest, Nepal/Tibet 29,022 ft/8,846 m

Cerro Aconcagua, Argentina 22,834 ft/6,960 m

McKinley, US 20,320 ft/6,194 m

Kibo (Kilimanjaro), Tanganyika/Tanzania 19,340 ft/5,895 m

Mont Blanc, France/Italy 15,770 ft/4,807m

Matterhorn, Italy/Switzerland 14,691 ft/4,478 m

Fujiyama, Japan 12,388 ft/3,776 m

TOP 10
HIGHEST MOUNTAINS IN AFRICA

	Mountain	Country	m	ft
1	Kibo (Kilimanjaro)	Tanganyika/Tanzania	5,895	19,340
2	Batian (Kenya)	Kenya	5,199	17,058
3	Ngaliema	Uganda/Zaïre	5,109	16,763
4	Duwoni	Uganda	4,896	16,062
5	Baker	Uganda	4,843	15,889
6	Emin	Zaïre	4,798	15,741
7	Gessi	Uganda	4,715	15,470
8	Sella	Uganda	4,627	15,179
9	Ras Dashen	Ethiopia	4,620	15,158
10	Wasuwameso	Zaïre	4,581	15,030

AFRICAN SUMMIT
The crater of an extinct volcano, snow-capped Kibo, the higher of two peaks of Tanzania's Mt. Kilimanjaro (the other is Mawenzi), is the highest mountain on the African continent.

TOP 10
HIGHEST MOUNTAINS IN OCEANIA

	Mountain	m	ft
1	Jaya	5,030	16,500
2	Daam	4,920	16,150
3	Pilimsit	4,800	15,750
4	Trikora	4,750	15,580
5	Mandala	4,700	15,420
6	Wilhelm,	4,690	15,400
7	Wisnumurti,	4,590	15,080
8	Yamin,Indonesia	4,530	14,860
9	Kubor, Indonesia	4,360	14,300
10	Herbert	4,270	14,000

TOP 10
HIGHEST MOUNTAINS IN SOUTH AMERICA

	Mountain	Country	m	ft
1	Cerro Aconcagua	Argentina	6,960	22,834
2	Ojos del Salado	Argentina/Chile	6,885	22,588
3	Bonete	Argentina	6,873	22,550
4	Pissis	Argentina/Chile	6,780	22,244
5	Huascarán	Peru	6,768	22,205
6	Llullaillaco	Argentina/Chile	6,723	22,057
7	Libertador	Argentina	6,721	22,050
8	Mercadario	Argentina/Chile	6,670	21,884
9	Yerupajá	Peru	6,634	21,765
10	Tres Cruces	Argentina/Chile	6,620	21,720

TOP 10
HIGHEST MOUNTAINS IN NORTH AMERICA

	Mountain	Country	m	ft
1	McKinley	US	6,194	20,320
2	Logan	Canada	6,050	19,850
3	Citlaltépetl (Orizaba)	Mexico	5,700	18,700
4	St. Elias	US/Canada	5,489	18,008
5	Popocatépetl	Mexico	5,452	17,887
6	Foraker	US	5,304	17,400
7	Ixtaccihuatl	Mexico	5,286	17,343
8	Lucania	Canada	5,226	17,147
9	King	Canada	5,173	16,971
10	Steele	Canada	5,073	16,644

RIVERS & WATERFALLS

T O P 1 0

LONGEST RIVERS IN EUROPE

(Excluding former USSR)

	River	Countries	km	miles
1	Danube	Germany/Austria/Slovakia/ Hungary/Serbia/Romania/Bulgaria	2,842	1,766
2	Rhine	Switzerland/Germany/Holland	1,368	850
3	Elbe	Czech Republic/Slovakia/Germany	1,167	725
4	Loire	France	1,014	630
5	Tagus	Portugal	1,009	627
6	Meuse	France/Belgium/Holland	950	590
7	Ebro	Spain	933	580
8	Rhône	Switzerland/France	813	505
9	Guadiana	Spain/Portugal	805	500
10	Seine	France	776	482

T O P 1 0

LONGEST RIVERS IN THE WORLD

	River	Countries	km	miles
1	Nile	Tanzania/Uganda/Sudan/Egypt	6,670	4,145
2	Amazon	Peru/Brazil	6,448	4,007
3	Yangtze–Kiang	China	6,300	3,915
4	Mississippi–Missouri– Red Rock	US	5,971	3,710
5	Yenisey–Angara–Selenga	Mongolia/Russia	5,540	3,442
6	Huang Ho (Yellow River)	China	5,464	3,395
7	Ob'–Irtysh	Mongolia/Kazakhstan/Russia	5,410	3,362
8	Zaïre (Congo)	Angola/Zaïre	4,700	2,920
9	Lena–Kirenga	Russia	4,400	2,734
10	Mekong	Tibet/China/Myanmar /Laos/ Cambodia/Vietnam	4,350	2,703

T O P 1 0

LONGEST RIVERS IN NORTH AMERICA

	River	Country	km	miles
1	Mackenzie– Peace	Canada	4,241	2,635
2	Missouri– Red Rock	US	4,088	2,540
3	Mississippi	US	3,779	2,348
4	Missouri	US	3,726	2,315
5	Yukon	US	3,185	1,979
6	St. Lawrence	Canada	3,130	1,945
7	Rio Grande	US	2,832	1,760
8	Nelson	Canada	2,575	1,600
9	Arkansas	US	2,348	1,459
10	Colorado	US	2,334	1,450

The principal reaches of the Mississippi, Missouri, and Red Rock Rivers are often combined, thus becoming the 4th longest river in the world at 3,710 miles/5,971 km.

T O P 1 0

LONGEST RIVERS IN THE UK

	River	km	miles
1	Severn	354	220
2	Thames	346	215
3	Trent	298	185
4	Aire	259	161
5	Great Ouse	230	143
6	Wye	217	135
7	Tay	188	117
8	Nene	161	100
9	Clyde	159	98.5
10	Spey	158	98

During their courses, some of these rivers change their names. For example, the Trent becomes the Humber and the Thames becomes the Isis.

BRINGER OF LIFE
For thousands of years, since the time of the ancient Egyptians, the Nile has attracted the peoples of northeast Africa to its fertile banks.

GREATEST WATERFALLS IN THE WORLD

(Based on volume of water)

	Waterfall	Country	Average flow (m³/sec)
1	Boyoma (Stanley)	Zaïre	17,000
2	Khône	Laos	11,610
3	Niagara (Horseshoe)	Canada/US	5,830
4	Grande	Uruguay	4,500
5	Paulo Afonso	Brazil	2,890
6	Urubupungá	Brazil	2,750
7	Iguaçu	Argentina/ Brazil	1,700
8	Maribondo	Brazil	1,500
9	Churchill (Grand)	Canada	1,390
10	Kabalega (Murchison)	Uganda	1,200

"THE SMOKE THAT THUNDERS"

Journeying up the Zambezi river 140 years ago, Scottish missionary David Livingstone encountered one of the world's most spectacular waterfalls, known locally as *Mosi-oa-tunya* ("smoke that thunders"). He wrote in his diary on November 17, 1855: "We came in sight for the first time of the columns of vapour appropriately called smoke, rising at a distance of five or six miles, exactly as when large tracts of grass are burned in Africa. Five columns now arose and, bending in the direction of the wind, they seemed placed against a low ridge covered with trees; the tops of the columns at this distance appeared to mingle with the clouds." Livingstone promptly "claimed" them for Britain, naming them after Queen Victoria. Commemorating his discovery by carving his initials on a nearby tree, Livingstone continued up the river.

LONGEST RIVERS IN AFRICA

	River	Countries	Length km	miles
1	Nile	Tanzania/ Uganda/ Sudan/ Egypt	6,670	4,145
2	Zaïre (Congo)	Angola/ Zaïre	4,700	2,920
3	Niger	Guinea/ Nigeria	4,100	2,550
4	Zambezi	Zambia/ Mozambique	2,650	1,650
5	Shebeli	Somalia	2,490	1,550
6	Ubangi	Zaïre	2,460	1,530
7	Orange	Namibia/ South Africa	2,250	1,400
8	Kasai	Zaïre	1,930	1,200
9	Senegal– Bafing	Mauritania/ Senegal	1,700	1,050
10	Blue Nile	Sudan	1,610	1,000

HIGHEST WATERFALLS IN THE WORLD

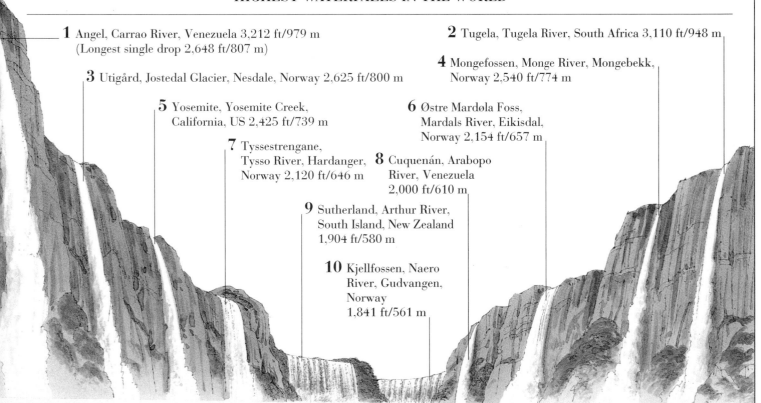

1 Angel, Carrao River, Venezuela 3,212 ft/979 m (Longest single drop 2,648 ft/807 m)

2 Tugela, Tugela River, South Africa 3,110 ft/948 m

3 Utigård, Jostedal Glacier, Nesdale, Norway 2,625 ft/800 m

4 Mongefossen, Monge River, Mongebekk, Norway 2,540 ft/774 m

5 Yosemite, Yosemite Creek, California, US 2,425 ft/739 m

6 Østre Mardøla Foss, Mardals River, Eikisdal, Norway 2,154 ft/657 m

7 Tyssestrengane, Tysso River, Hardanger, Norway 2,120 ft/646 m

8 Cuquenán, Arabopo River, Venezuela 2,000 ft/610 m

9 Sutherland, Arthur River, South Island, New Zealand 1,904 ft/580 m

10 Kjellfossen, Naero River, Gudvangen, Norway 1,841 ft/561 m

SEAS & LAKES

T O P 1 0

DEEPEST DEEP-SEA TRENCHES

	Name	Ocean	Deepest point m	ft
1	Marianas	Pacific	10,924	35,837
2	Tonga*	Pacific	10,800	35,430
3	Philippine	Pacific	10,497	34,436
4	Kermadec*	Pacific	10,047	32,960
5	Bonin	Pacific '	9,994	32,786
6	New Britain	Pacific	9,940	32,609
7	Kuril	Pacific	9,750	31,985
8	Izu	Pacific	9,695	31,805
9	Puerto Rico	Atlantic	8,605	28,229
10	Yap	Pacific	8,527	27,973

* Some authorities consider these parts of the same feature

The eight deepest ocean trenches would be deep enough to submerge Mount Everest, which is 29,022 ft/8,846 m above sea level.

T O P 1 0

LARGEST OCEANS AND SEAS IN THE WORLD

	Ocean/sea	Approx. area sq km	sq miles
1	Pacific Ocean	165,241,000	63,800,000
2	Atlantic Ocean	82,439,000	31,830,000
3	Indian Ocean	73,452,000	28,360,000
4	Arctic Ocean	13,986,000	5,400,000
5	Arabian Sea	3,864,000	1,492,000
6	South China Sea	3,447,000	1,331,000
7	Caribbean Sea	2,753,000	1,063,000
8	Mediterranean Sea	2,505,000	967,000
9	Bering Sea	2,269,000	876,000
10	Bay of Bengal	2,173,000	839,000

T O P 1 0

DEEPEST OCEANS AND SEAS IN THE WORLD

	Ocean/sea	Average depth m	ft		Ocean/sea	Average depth m	ft
1	Pacific Ocean	4,028	13,215	6	Bering Sea	1,547	5,075
2	Indian Ocean	3,963	13,002	7	Gulf of Mexico	1,486	4,874
3	Atlantic Ocean	3,926	12,880	8	Mediterranean Sea	1,429	4,688
4	Caribbean Sea	2,647	8,685	9	Japan Sea	1,350	4,429
5	South China Sea	1,652	5,419	10	Arctic Ocean	1,205	3,953

The deepest point in the deepest ocean is the Marianas Trench in the Pacific at a depth of 35,837 ft/10,924 m according to a recent hydrographic survey, although a depth of 35,814 ft/10,916 m was recorded by Jacques Piccard and Donald Walsh in the 58-ft/17.7-m long bathyscaphe *Trieste 2* during their descent of January 23, 1960. Whichever is correct, it is close to seven miles down, or almost 29 times the height of the Empire State Building.

T O P 1 0

LAKES WITH THE GREATEST VOLUME OF WATER

	Lake	Location	Volume cubic km	cubic miles
1	Caspian Sea	Azerbaijan/Iran/Kazakhstan/Russia/Turkmenistan	89,600	21,497
2	Baikal	Russia	22,995	5,517
3	Tanganyika	Burundi/Tanzania/Zaïre/Zambia	18,304	4,392
4	Superior	Canada/US	12,174	2,921
5	Nyasa (Malawi)	Malawi/Mozambique/Tanzania	6,140	1,473
6	Michigan	US	4,874	1,169
7	Huron	Canada/US	3,575	858
8	Victoria	Kenya/Tanzania/Uganda	2,518	604
9	Great Bear	Canada	2,258	542
10	Great Slave	Canada	1,771	425

DID YOU KNOW

IN DEEP WATER

The world's 10 deepest freshwater lakes are deep enough to submerge easily all the tallest towers and habitable buildings in the world. At its deepest point, Lake Baikal is so deep that it could comfortably accommodate all four of the tallest buildings in the world – the Sears Tower, the tallest of the two World Trade Center towers, the Empire State Building, and the Amoco Building – standing one on top of another. Lake Tanganyika could submerge the three tallest buildings in the world. Even the 20th deepest lake in the world, the 1,454-ft-/443-m-deep Manapouri on the South Island of New Zealand, would be sufficiently deep to cover every one of the world's tallest buildings.

THE GREAT LAKES
The vast expanse of the Great Lakes as viewed from space. Superior and Huron are partly within Canada, making Michigan the largest lake situated entirely within the United States.

T O P 1 0

LARGEST FRESHWATER LAKES IN THE US

(Excluding those partly in Canada)

	Lake	State	Approx. area sq km	sq miles
1	Michigan	Illinois/Indiana/ Michigan/Wisconsin	57,700	22,278
2	Iliamna	Alaska	2,590	1,000
3	Okeechobee	Florida	1,813	700
4	Becharof	Alaska	1,186	458
5	Red	Minnesota	1,168	451
6	Teshepuk	Alaska	816	315
7	Naknek	Alaska	627	242
8	Winnebago	Wisconsin	557	215
9	Mille Lacs	Minnesota	536	207
10	Flathead	Montana	510	97

Broadening the compass of this list to include those lakes that lie within the borders of Canada as well as the United States would draw in the even larger 31,820-sq mile/ 82,414-sq km Lake Superior, which is the world's largest area of freshwater; Lake Huron (23,010 sq miles/59,596 sq km); and Lake Ontario (7,520 sq miles/19,477 sq km), which is larger than all those in the US Top 10 with the exception of Lake Michigan. On a global scale, Lake Victoria (Kenya/Tanzania/Uganda), at 26,828 sq miles/69,485 sq km, also exceeds the area of Lake Michigan.

T O P 1 0

LARGEST LAKES IN THE UK

	Lake	Area sq km	sq miles
1	Lough Neagh, Northern Ireland	381.74	147.39
2	Lower Lough Erne, Northern Ireland	105.08	40.57
3	Loch Lomond, Scotland	71.22	27.50
4	Loch Ness, Scotland	56.64	21.87
5	Loch Awe, Scotland	38.72	14.95
6	Upper Lough Erne, Northern Ireland	31.73	12.25
7	Loch Maree, Scotland	28.49	11.00
8	Loch Morar, Scotland	26.68	10.30
9	Loch Tay, Scotland	26.39	10.19
10	Loch Shin, Scotland	22.53	8.70

WEATHER EXTREMES

COLDEST CITIES IN THE US

	City	Mean temperature °C	°F
1	International Falls, Minnesota	2.4	36.4
2	Duluth, Minnesota	3.4	38.2
3	Caribou, Maine	3.8	38.9
4	Marquette, Michigan	4.0	39.2
5	Sault Ste. Marie, Michigan	4.3	39.7
6	Fargo, North Dakota	4.7	40.5
7	Williston, North Dakota	4.9	40.8
8	Alamosa, Colorado	5.1	41.2
9	Bismarck, Nevada	5.2	41.3
10	Saint Cloud, Minnesota	5.3	41.4

These are constantly updated mean figures kept by individual climatic data centers from the beginning of their records, the origins of which vary (some centers began collecting data over 100 years ago), and include readings complete up to November 1993. (The figures are for the contiguous states, and therefore do not include Hawaii and Alaska.)

WETTEST CITIES IN THE US

	City	Mean annual precipitation mm	in
1	Quillayute, WA	2,654	104.50
2	Astoria, OR	1,768	69.60
3	Blue Canyon, CA	1,724	67.87
4	Mobile, AL	1,642	64.64
5	Tallahassee, FL	1,641	64.59
6	Pensacola, FL	1,553	61.16
7	New Orleans, LA	1,517	59.74
8	West Palm Beach, FL	1,516	59.72
9	Miami, FL	1,513	59.55
10	Tupelo, MS	1,425	56.12

WARMEST CITIES IN THE US

	City	Mean temperature °C	°F
1	Key West, Florida	25.4	77.7
2	Miami, Florida	24.2	75.6
3	West Palm Beach, Florida	23.7	74.6
4=	Fort Myers, Florida	23.3	73.9
4=	Yuma, Arizona	23.3	73.9
6	Brownsville, Texas	23.1	73.6
7=	Orlando, Florida	22.4	72.4
7=	Vero Beach, Florida	22.4	72.4
9	Corpus Christi, Texas	22.3	72.1
10	Tampa, Florida	22.2	72.0

With seven out of the 10 warmest cities located in the state of Florida, it is fitting that its nickname since 1970 should be the "Sunshine State."

WINDIEST CITIES IN THE US

	City	Mean wind speed km/h	mph
1	Blue Hill, Massachusetts	24.8	15.4
2	Dodge City, Kansas	22.5	14.0
3	Amarillo, Texas	21.7	13.5
4	Rochester, Minnesota	21.1	13.1
5=	Cheyenne, Wyoming	20.8	12.9
5=	Casper, Wyoming	20.8	12.9
7	Great Falls, Montana	20.4	12.7
8	Goodland, Kansas	20.3	12.6
9	Boston, Massachusetts	20.1	12.5
10	Lubbock, Texas	20.0	12.4

Source: National Climatic Data Center

DRIEST CITIES IN THE US

	City	Mean annual precipitation mm	in
1	Yuma, Arizona	67	2.65
2	Las Vegas, Nevada	106	4.19
3	Bishop, California	142	5.61
4	Bakersfield, California	145	5.72
5	Phoenix, Arizona	180	7.11
6	Alamosa, Colorado	181	7.13
7	Reno, Nevada	190	7.49
8	Winslow, Arizona	194	7.64
9	El Paso, Texas	199	7.82
10	Winnemucca, Nevada	200	7.87

The presence of three Nevadan cities among the 10 driest is in keeping with Nevada's claim to be the driest state in the US, with an average rainfall of just 9 inches/229 mm.

SNOWIEST CITIES IN THE US

	City	Mean annual snowfall mm	in
1	Blue Canyon, California	6,116	240.8
2	Marquette, Michigan	3,266	128.6
3	Sault Ste. Marie, Michigan	2,964	116.7
4	Syracuse, New York	2,835	111.6
5	Caribou, Maine	2,804	110.4
6	Mount Shasta, California	2,664	104.9
7	Lander, Wyoming	2,604	102.5
8	Flagstaff, Arizona	2,537	99.9
9	Sexton Summit, Oregon	2,484	97.8
10	Muskegon, Michigan	2,464	97.0

Marquette, Michigan, achieves a place in both this list and that of the 10 Coldest Places (p.279).

T O P 1 0

WETTEST INHABITED PLACES IN THE WORLD

	Location	Average annual rainfall mm	in
1	Buenaventura, Colombia	6,743	265.47
2	Monrovia, Liberia	5,131	202.01
3	Pago Pago, American Samoa	4,990	196.46
4	Moulmein, Myanmar (Burma)	4,852	191.02
5	Lae, Papua New Guinea	4,465	182.87
6	Baguio, Luzon Island, Philippines	4,573	180.04
7	Sylhet, Bangladesh	4,457	175.47
8	Conakry, Guinea	4,341	170.91
9=	Padang, Sumatra Island, Indonesia	4,225	166.34
9=	Bogor, Java, Indonesia	4,225	166.34

The total annual rainfall of the Top 10 wettest locations is equivalent to 26 6-ft/1.83-m adults standing on top of each other.

T O P 1 0

DRIEST INHABITED PLACES IN THE WORLD

	Location	Average annual rainfall mm	in
1	Aswan, Egypt	0.5	0.02
2	Luxor, Egypt	0.7	0.03
3	Arica, Chile	1.1	0.04
4	Ica, Peru	2.3	0.09
5	Antofagasta, Chile	4.9	0.19
6	Minya, Egypt	5.1	0.20
7	Asyut, Egypt	5.2	0.20
8	Callao, Peru	12.0	0.47
9	Trujilo, Peru	14.0	0.54
10	Fayyum, Egypt	19.0	0.75

The total annual rainfall of the Top 10 driest inhabited places is just 2½ inches/64.8 mm – the length of an adult little finger.

T O P 1 0

COLDEST AND HOTTEST INHABITED PLACES IN THE WORLD

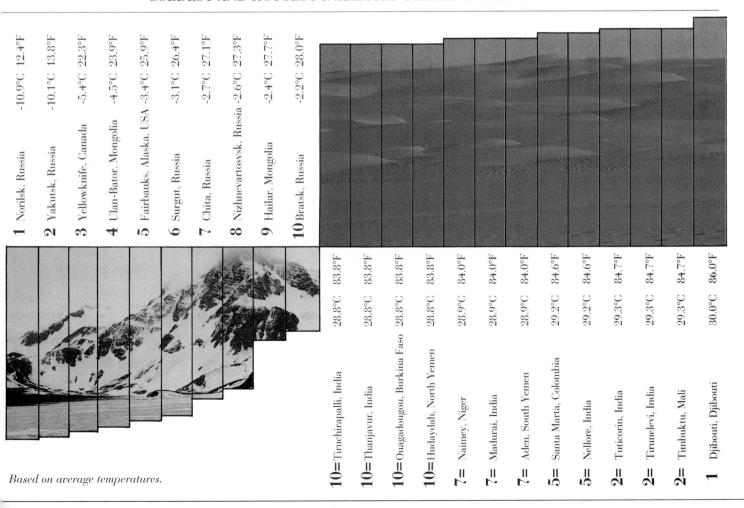

Coldest:

1	Norilsk, Russia	-10.9°C	12.4°F
2	Yakutsk, Russia	-10.1°C	13.8°F
3	Yellowknife, Canada	-5.4°C	22.3°F
4	Ulan-Bator, Mongolia	-4.5°C	23.9°F
5	Fairbanks, Alaska, USA	-3.4°C	25.9°F
6	Surgut, Russia	-3.1°C	26.4°F
7	Chita, Russia	-2.7°C	27.1°F
8	Nizhnevartovsk, Russia	-2.6°C	27.3°F
9	Hailar, Mongolia	-2.4°C	27.7°F
10	Bratsk, Russia	-2.2°C	28.0°F

Hottest:

10=	Tiruchirapalli, India	28.8°C	83.8°F
10=	Thanjavur, India	28.8°C	83.8°F
10=	Ouagadougou, Burkina Faso	28.8°C	83.8°F
10=	Hudaydah, North Yemen	28.8°C	83.8°F
7=	Naimey, Niger	28.9°C	84.0°F
7=	Madurai, India	28.9°C	84.0°F
7=	Aden, South Yemen	28.9°C	84.0°F
5=	Santa Marta, Colombia	29.2°C	84.6°F
5=	Nellore, India	29.2°C	84.6°F
2=	Tuticorin, India	29.3°C	84.7°F
2=	Tirunelevi, India	29.3°C	84.7°F
2=	Timbuktu, Mali	29.3°C	84.7°F
1	Djibouti, Djibouti	30.0°C	86.0°F

Based on average temperatures.

NATURAL DISASTERS

SEARCHING FOR SURVIVORS
After Colombia's worst landslide, rescuers struggle to release victims from the mud and rubble.

WORST AVALANCHES AND LANDSLIDES OF THE 20TH CENTURY

(Excluding those where most deaths resulted from flooding caused by avalanches or landslides)

	Location	Incident	Date	Estimated no. killed
1	Yungay, Peru	Landslide	May 31, 1970	17,500
2	Italian Alps	Avalanche	Dec 13, 1916	10,000
3	Huarás, Peru	Avalanche	Dec 13, 1941	5,000
4	Mount Huascaran, Peru	Avalanche	Jan 10, 1962	3,500
5	Medellin, Colombia	Landslide	Sep 27, 1987	683
6	Chungar, Peru	Avalanche	Mar 19, 1971	600
7	Rio de Janeiro, Brazil	Landslide	Jan 11, 1966	550
8=	Northern Assam, India	Landslide	Feb 15, 1949	500
8=	Grand Rivière du Nord, Haiti	Landslide	Nov 13/14, 1963	500
10	Blons, Austria	Avalanche	Jan 11, 1954	411

The worst incident of all, the destruction of Yungay, Peru, in May 1970, was only part of a much larger cataclysm. The landslide, which wiped out the town and left just 2,500 survivors out of a population of 20,000, followed on the heels of an earthquake and widespread flooding that left a total of up to 70,000 dead.

WORST EARTHQUAKES IN THE WORLD

	Location	Date	Estimated no. killed
1	Near East/Mediterranean	May 20, 1202	1,100,000
2	Shenshi, China	Feb 2, 1556	820,000
3	Calcutta, India	Oct 11, 1737	300,000
4	Antioch, Syria	May 20, 526	250,000
5	Tang-shan, China	Jul 28, 1976	242,419
6	Nan-shan, China	May 22, 1927	200,000
7	Yeddo, Japan	1703 (exact date unknown)	190,000
8	Kansu, China	Dec 16, 1920	180,000
9	Messina, Italy	Dec 28, 1908	160,000
10	Tokyo/Yokohama, Japan	Sep 1, 1923	142,807

Discrepancies exist between the "official" death tolls in many of the world's worst earthquakes and the estimates of other authorities: 750,000 is sometimes given for the 1976 Tang-shan earthquake, for example, while estimates for the 1908 Messina quake range from 58,000 to 250,000. Other earthquakes in China and Turkey have also caused deaths of 100,000 or more. More recently, the Armenian earthquake of December 7, 1988 and the one in northwest Iran on June 21, 1990 caused over 55,000 (official estimate 28,854) and 50,000 deaths respectively. The 7.2 earthquake in Kobe, Japan, on January 17, 1995, was well monitored and indicates the severity of a quake in a densely populated area. It left 3,842 dead and 14,679 injured; the initial shock destroyed 54,949 buildings and damaged 31,783 more; and the fires that followed devastated an area of 162.72 acres, including a further 7,377 buildings.

WORST TSUNAMIS ("TIDAL WAVES") IN THE WORLD

	Location	Year	Estimated no. killed
1	Atlantic coast (Morocco, western Europe, West Indies)	1775	60,000
2	Sumatra, Java	1883	36,000
3=	Japan	1707	30,000
3=	Italy	1783	30,000
5	Japan	1896	27,122
6	Chile, Hawaii	1868	25,000
7	Ryukyu Islands	1771	11,941
8	Japan	1792	9,745
9=	Japan	1498	5,000
9=	Japan	1611	5,000
9=	Peru	1756	5,000
9=	Chile, Hawaii, Japan	1960	5,000
9=	Philippines	1976	5,000

THE 10

WORST VOLCANIC ERUPTIONS IN THE WORLD

	Location	Date	Estimated no. killed
1	Tambora, Indonesia	Apr 5–12, 1815	92,000

The cataclysmic eruption of Tambora killed about 10,000 islanders immediately, with a further 82,000 dying subsequently from disease and famine resulting from crops being destroyed. An estimated 1,900,000 tons of ash were hurled into the atmosphere. This blocked out the sunlight and affected the weather over large areas of the globe during the following year. One effect of this was to produce brilliantly colored sunsets, depicted strikingly in paintings from the period, especially in the works of J.M.W. Turner. It even had an influence on literary history: kept indoors by inclement weather at the Villa Diodati on Lake Geneva, Lord Byron and his companions amused themselves by writing horror stories, one of which was Mary Shelley's classic, Frankenstein.

	Location	Date	Estimated no. killed
2	Miyi-Yama, Java	1793	53,000

Miyi-Yama, the volcano dominating the island of Kiousiou, erupted during 1793, engulfing all the local villages in mudslides and killing most of the rural population.

	Location	Date	Estimated no. killed
3	Mont Pelée, Martinique	May 8, 1902	40,000

After lying dormant for centuries, Mont Pelée began to erupt in April 1902. Assured that there was no danger, the 30,000 residents of the main city, St. Pierre, stayed in their homes and were there when the volcano burst apart and showered the port with molten lava, ash, and gas, destroying all life and property. Some 50 people were killed by deadly fer-de-lance snakes, disturbed by the eruption.

	Location	Date	Estimated no. killed
4	Krakatoa, Sumatra/ Java	Aug 26–27, 1883	36,380

After a series of eruptions over several days, the uninhabited island of Krakatoa exploded with what may have been the biggest bang ever heard by humans, recorded clearly 3,000 miles/ 4,800 km away. Some sources put the deaths as high as 200,000, most of them killed by subsequent tidal waves up to 100 ft/30 m high. The events were portrayed in the 1969 film Krakatoa, East of Java, but purists should note that Krakatoa is actually west of Java.

	Location	Date	Estimated no. killed
2	Nevado del Ruiz, Colombia	Nov 13, 1985	22,940

The Andean volcano gave warning signs of erupting, but by the time authorities decided to evacuate the local inhabitants, it was too late. The hot steam, rocks, and ash ejected from mudslide engulfed the town of Armero.

	Location	Date	Estimated no. killed
6	Mount Etna, Italy	Mar 11, 1669	more than 20,000

Europe's largest volcano (10,760 ft/3,280 m) has erupted frequently, but the worst instance occurred in 1669 when the lava flow engulfed the town of Catania, killing at least 20,000.

	Location	Date	Estimated no. killed
7	Laki, Iceland	Jan–Jun 1783	20,000

Iceland is one of the most volcanically active places on Earth but, being sparsely populated, eruptions seldom result in major loss of life. The worst exception took place at the Laki volcanic ridge, culminating on June 11 with the largest-ever recorded lava flow. It engulfed many villages in a river of lava up to 50 miles/ 80 km long and 100 ft/30 m deep, releasing poisonous gases that killed those who managed to escape the lava.

	Location	Date	Estimated no. killed
8	Vesuvius, Italy	Aug 24, 79	16–20,000

When the previously dormant Vesuvius erupted suddenly, the Roman city of Herculaneum was engulfed by a mudflow while Pompeii was buried under a vast layer of pumice and volcanic ash – which ironically preserved it in a near-perfect state that was not uncovered until excavations by archaeologists in the 19th and 20th centuries.

	Location	Date	Estimated no. killed
9	Vesuvius, Italy	Dec 16–17, 1631	18,000

Although minor eruptions occurred at intervals after that of AD 79, the next major cataclysm was almost as disastrous, when lava and mudflows gushed down onto the surrounding towns, including Naples.

	Location	Date	Estimated no. killed
10	Mount Etna, Italy	1169	more than 15,000

Large numbers died in Catania cathedral where they believed they would be safe, and more were killed when a tidal wave hit the port of Messina.

CAST IN STONE
Victims in Pompeii left impressions in the deep ash that buried them, allowing plaster casts of their bodies to be made in the 19th century.

INDEX

R

S

ACKNOWLEDGMENTS

I would like to thank Caroline Ash in the UK and Luke Crampton and Dafydd Rees in the US for their indispensable assistance in compiling this book, and the following individuals and organizations who kindly supplied us with information:

John Amos, Simon Applebaum, Ken Atherton, Jim Baldassare, Helen Berry, Robert Berkebile, Peter Black, Richard Braddish, Rick Campbell, Shelly Cagner, Terry Charman, Ludo Craddock, Milly Daniel, Jim Davie, Susan DiBartolo, Paul Dickson, Tom Doyle, Christopher Forbes, Richard Halstead, Debbie Hanauer, Kim Hazelbaker, Leila Hill, Duncan Hislop, Leslie Hopkins, Gary Ink, Mary Jones, Ruth Kaplan, Robert Lamb, Barry Lazell, Dr. Benjamin Lucas, Dr. Jacqueline Mitton, Giles Moon, Ian Morrison, Theresa Napoleon, Susan Obreski, Jim Pedden, Marie Ratliffe, Sir Tim Rice, Martin Rive, Adrian Room, Tom Rubython, Michaela Sampite, Paul Sarjac, Paul Svercl, Conrad Sibkowiak, Rocky Stockman MBE, Bart Story, James Taylor, Steve van Dulken, Gordon Vince, Tony Waltham, David Way, Andrea Wiley, Stephany M. Wilken, Sharon Wray, Karen Yeager.

Academy of Motion Picture Arts and Sciences, *Advertising Age*, AEA Technology, Airport Operators Council International, American Automobile Manufacturers Association, *American Bee Journal*, American Forestry Association, American Hotel/Motel Association, American Library Association, *American Karaoke Magazine*, American Kennel Club, American Podiatry Association, American Society of Association Executives, American Veterinary Medical Association, Amtrak, Amusement and Music Operators Association, *Amusement Business*, *Animal World*, *Annual Abstract of Statistics*, Arbitron, Art Institute of Chicago, Art Sales Index, Association of American Railroads, Audit Bureau of Circulations, Ben & Jerry's, Beverage Marketing Corporation, *Billboard*, Billy Rose Theater Collection, *BioCycle*, Blackburn Marketing Services Inc., BMI, Boston Fine Arts Museum, *Boston Globe*, *Boston Herald*, Boy Scouts of America, BPA International, Breeding Bird Survey, Brewers Society, British Allergy Foundation, British Astronomical Society, British Broadcasting Corporation, British Cave Research Association, British Interplanetary Society, British Library, British Museum, Bureau of Engraving and Printing, Bureau of Federal Prisons, Bureau of Justice Statistics, Business Publications Audit, Business Travel News, Cablevision, Cadbury Schweppes Group, Cameron Mackintosh Ltd, Canadian Press, Capital Research Center, Carbon Dioxide Information Analysis Center/Greg Marland/ Tom Boden, Carson Productions, Cat Fanciers' Association of the USA, Center for the American Woman and Politics, Centers for Disease Control and Prevention, Central Intelligence Agency, *Chain Drug Review*, Chairman of the Joint Chiefs of Staff, Champagne Bureau, Championship Auto Racing Teams (CART), Channel Swimming Association, Christie's East, Christie's London, Christie's South Kensington, *Classical Music*, Coca-Cola, *Criminal Statistics England & Wales*, *Dairy Foods Magazine*, Dateline, Death Penalty Information Center, De Beers, Diamond Information Centre, *Drug Store News*, Duncan's American Radio, Inc., Entertainment Data, Inc., Environmental Protection Agency, Euromonitor, Exhibitor Relations Co., Inc., FBI, Federal Aviation Authority, Federal Highway Administration, Feste Catalogue Index Database/Alan Somerset, Food and Agriculture Organization of the United Nations, *Forbes Magazine*, *Fortune*, Generation AB, Geological Museum, Girl Scouts of the USA, Gold Fields Mineral Services Ltd., Goldmine/Neal Umphred, Governing Council of the Cat Fancy, H.J. Heinz Co Ltd., Highway Loss Data Institute, Hollywood Foreign Press Association,

Hydrographic Office, Ice Cream Association, Infoplan, Information Resources Inc., Institute of Sports Medicine, International Civil Aviation Organization, International Cocoa Organization, International Coffee Organization, International Dairy Foods Association, International Game Fishing Association, International Monetary Fund, International Tea Committee, International Union of Geological Sciences Commission on Comparative Planetology, *International Water Power and Dam Construction Handbook*, Jewish Board of Deputies, Jockey Club, Kellogg Company of Great Britain, Kennel Club, Keynote Publications, Lloyds Register of Shipping, London Theatre Record, London Transport Lost Property, Magazine Publishers of America, Major League Baseball, MARC Europe, *Marketing*, Market Power Ltd., Meat and Livestock Commission, Metropolitan Museum of Art, New York, Metropolitan Opera, New York, Metropolitan Transit Authority, MORI, Motor Vehicle Manufacturers Association of the United States, Inc., MRIB, MTV, NASA, National Association for Stock Car Auto Racing (NASCAR), National Association of America, National Association of Railroad Passengers, National Basketball Association (NBA), National Blood Transfusion Service, National Canine Defence League, National Center for Education Statistics, National Center for Health Statistics, National Climatic Data Center, National Collegiate Athletic Association (NCAA), National Environmental Technology Centre, National Football League (NFL), National Gallery, Washington, DC, National Hockey League (NHL), National Oceanic and Atmospheric Administration, National Park Service, *National Petroleum News*, National Public Radio, National Safety Council, National Solid Waste Management Association, National Sporting Goods Association, National Transportation Safety Board, NCAA, New York Drama Desk, A.C. Nielsen Co. Ltd., Nielsen Media Research, Nobel Foundation, Non-Prescription Drug Manufacturers Association, North American Breeding Bird Survey, NTL, Nuclear Engineering International, Office of Population Censuses and Surveys, UK, Organization for Economic Development and Cooperation, Overstreet Publications, Inc., Oxford University Press, Patent and Trademark Depository Library, Patent Office, UK, George Foster Peabody Awards, *Performance*, PGA Tour, Inc., *Pharmacy Times*, Phobics Society, *Playthings*, J.D. Power & Associates, Produktschap voor Gedistilleerde Dranken, Professional Golf Association, *Publishers Weekly*, Pullman Power Products Corporation, *Railway Gazette International*, Really Useful Group, Relate, *Restaurants and Institutions*, Royal Aeronautical Society, Royal College of General Practitioners, Royal Opera House, Royal Society for the Prevention of Cruelty to Animals, Dr. Scholl's, *Screen Digest*, Shakespeare Birthplace Trust, Siemens AG, Society of London Theatre, Sotheby's London, Sotheby's New York, *Spaceflight*, *Statistical Abstract of the United States*, Sugar Bureau, Taylors of Loughborough, Theatre Museum, Theatre Record, *The Times*, London, Towne Oller & Associates, *UBS Phillips & Drew Global Pharmaceutical Review*, UK Petroleum Industry Association, UNESCO, *Uniform Crime Statistics*, United Nations, United States Trotting Association (USTA), *USA Today*, US Bureau of Labor Statistics, US Bureau of the Census, US Department of Agriculture Forest Service, US Department of Commerce, International Trade Administration, US Department of Commerce, Travel and Tourism Administration, US Department of Education, US Fish and Wildlife Service, US Geological Survey, US Department of the Interior, National Register of Historic Places, US Department of Justice, US Department of Labor, US Department of Transportation, Federal Aviation Administration, US Department of

Transportation, National Highway Safety Administration, US Immigration and Naturalization Service, US Mint, US Postal Service, Postal History Department, US Social Security Administration, *Variety*, *Video Scan*, *Video Store Magazine*, *Wine Business Monthly*, World Association of Girl Guides and Girl Scouts, World Bank, World Health Organization, World Intellectual Property Organization, *World of Travel Shopping*.